P R E N T I C E

BRIEF REVIEW FOR NEW YO

Chemistry

The Physical Setting

2007 Edition

Patrick Kavanah, Retired
Monroe-Woodbury Central High School
Central Valley, New York

ORDER INFORMATION

Send orders to:

PRENTICE HALL SCHOOL DIVISION
CUSTOMER SERVICE CENTER
P. O. Box 2500
Lebanon, Indiana 46052-3009

or

CALL TOLL-FREE: 1-800-848-9500
(8:00 A.M.–6:00 P.M. EST)

or

FAX TOLL-FREE: 1-877-260-2530
(24 hours a day, 7 days a week)

• Orders processed with your call.
• Your price includes all shipping and handling.

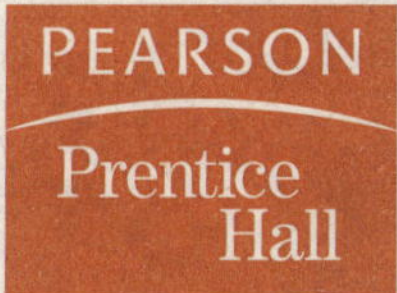

Boston, Massachusetts
Upper Saddle River, New Jersey

STAFF CREDITS

The people who made up the *Brief Review in Chemistry* team—representing editorial, editorial services, and design—are listed below.

Ken Chang, Kathy Dempsey, Terence Hegarty, Caroline Power, Kim Schmidt, Jerry Thorne

Additional Credits

Matt Walker, Frances Jenkins, Black Dot Group

Copyright © 2007 by Pearson Education, Inc., publishing as Pearson Prentice Hall, Boston, Massachusetts 02116. All rights reserved. Printed in the United States of America. This publication is protected by copyright, and permission should be obtained from the publisher prior to any prohibited reproduction, storage in a retrieval system, or transmission in any form or by any means, electronic, mechanical, photocopying, recording, or likewise. For information regarding permission(s), write to: Rights and Permissions Department, One Lake Street, Upper Saddle River, New Jersey 07458.

Pearson Prentice Hall™ is a trademark of Pearson Education, Inc.
Pearson® is a registered trademark of Pearson plc.
Prentice Hall® is a registered trademark of Pearson Education, Inc.

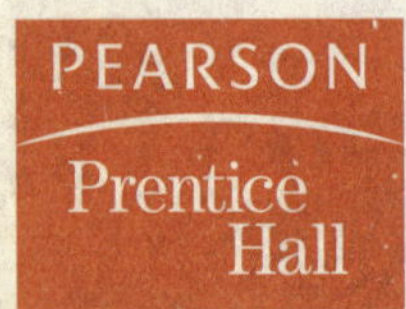

ISBN 0-13-251116-9
2 3 4 5 6 7 8 9 10 11 10 09 08 07

Brief Review in

Chemistry: The Physical Setting

About This Book

This book is designed for students planning to take the Regents Examination for The Physical Setting: Chemistry. Most students using this book will be taking or will have taken an investigative-approach chemistry course. This book is useful for studying to pass the end-of-year Regents Examination in chemistry as well as studying for topic tests during the course. Some students taking this course will need to pass the Regents Examination to meet the requirements for high school graduation, whereas other students taking this course will have already passed the Regents Examination in science needed to meet the requirements for high school graduation.

The Regents Examination will be based on the content and understandings addressed in the core curriculum for The Physical Setting: Chemistry (as covered in your chemistry course), the *Reference Tables for Physical Setting/Chemistry,* and the laboratory skills learned during the course. This book is organized to enhance your review of the concepts, skills, and application of the core curriculum that may be tested in Regents Examination for chemistry. Since the core curriculum does not provide a preferred order for the teaching of chemistry concepts, this book is organized according to a syllabus prepared by the author. For students used to a different order of topics in the classroom, note that each topic (chapter) of this book is independent of the order of presentation in this text except for the listing of vocabulary words (see below). The use of the table of contents and the index will enable you to find any topic that you need to review.

REVIEW OF CONTENT This review book focuses on the basic content that will be tested on the Regents Examination. It includes numerous illustrations to help you visualize and understand the concepts and vocabulary of chemistry. The illustrations will familiarize you with the types of drawing you will be required to interpret in Regents Examination questions. You should carefully read the illustration captions and explanations within the text.

Additional material has been added to some topics to enhance the student's understanding of chemistry. Electron configuration, the equilibrium expression, and Brønsted-Lowry acid–base theory are significant examples of added material. Such topics are identified within the text with a boxed noted stating "Additional Material." Review Questions related to the additional material are given within in the text. Note, however, that no Questions for Regents Practice relating to the additional material are provided, as these topics will not be tested on the Regents Examination.

VOCABULARY WORDS You will need to know the definitions of the vocabulary words listed at the beginning of each topic in order to answer many Regents Examination questions. These words are shown in bold type within the topic where they are first defined. Each bold word is accompanied by a simple definition in the text. These words may also appear in other topics, where they are underlined. Vocabulary words are also defined in the glossary at the back of the book.

UNDERLINED WORDS Words that are underlined in the text are either words that appear in vocabulary lists in other topics or are other words that you need to know to understand basic chemistry concepts. Although you are not likely to be tested on the specific definitions of non-vocabulary underlined words, these words may be used in Regents Examination questions. Underlined words are defined in the glossary.

SAMPLE PROBLEMS Numerous solved sample problems appear throughout this book to provide students with examples of typical problems found on the Regents Examination. The step-by-step detailed solutions guide students in the problem-solving process and help reinforce content knowledge.

MEMORY JOGGER AND DIGGING DEEPER The Memory Jogger features are designed to refresh your memory of relevant information that was covered in previous topics of this book or in previous science courses. Digging Deeper features provide specific examples of some subject matter, or describe some information that may expand core information content.

REVIEW QUESTIONS Review questions appear frequently throughout each topic to help you clarify and reinforce your understanding of the content. The questions, totaling nearly 800, are similar to the types of questions that may appear on the Regents Examination.

QUESTIONS FOR REGENTS PRACTICE These questions, totaling more than 400, appear at the end of each topic. These practice questions are written and organized in the format of the Regents Examination, with Part A, Part B, and Part C questions. In many Part B and Part C questions you will notice a number in brackets. This number indicates how many points the question is worth in a Regents Examination.

- Part A questions are entirely multiple-choice and test your knowledge of concepts from the core curriculum.
- Part B questions test skills and understandings of concepts outlined in the core curriculum and include both multiple-choice and constructed response questions.
- Part C questions often require an extended constructed response. For these questions you will often need to provide a more detailed answer, supported with applications or examples and written in complete sentences.

The back of this book contains several appendices and other items that you will find useful.

APPENDIX 1 You will need to make use of the *Reference Tables for Physical Setting/Chemistry* in most of the topics in this book. When a reference table is useful, the text will refer to the *Reference Tables for Physical Setting/Chemistry* in italic type. A list of all of the reference tables can be found in Appendix 1 on page 189.

APPENDIX 2 This appendix provides strategies for answering the types of questions typically found on the Regents Examination. It includes strategies for answering multiple-choice and constructed response questions, and for using the *Reference Tables for Physical Setting/Chemistry.*

APPENDIX 3 This appendix provides review of basic math and graphing skills. Math and graphing skills are an integral part of some Regents Examination questions.

REGENTS EXAMINATIONS Past Regents Examinations are reproduced near the end of the book to provide practice in taking a Regents Examination.

GLOSSARY All bold vocabulary words and underlined words appearing in the topics are defined in the glossary.

INDEX The index will enable you to find any topic that you need to review.

The Atom

VOCABULARY		
atom	excited state	neutron
atomic mass	ground state	nucleus
atomic mass unit	heterogeneous	orbital
atomic number	homogeneous	proton
compound	isotope	pure substance
electron	mass number	wave-mechanical model
element	mixture	

Chemistry is the study of matter, which is anything that has mass and volume. You are made up of matter, as is your desk. Even the gases that make up air are matter. Chemistry deals with the composition of matter and changes that occur in it.

Early Studies of Matter

The study of matter has roots in ancient Greece more than 2000 years ago. The Greeks proposed that matter is made up of particles, but not particles of elements, as we know them today. Instead they viewed matter as being composed of four elemental substances—fire, earth, wind, and water—as shown in Figure 1-1.

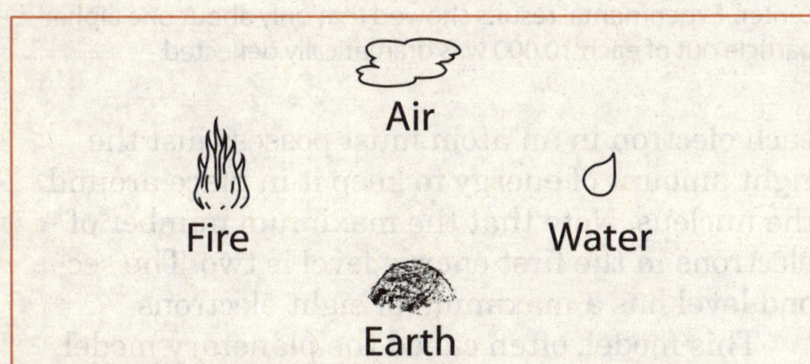

Figure 1-1. The four elements: Fire, air, earth, and water

A Change of Thought

This view of the nature of matter lasted until the 1600s when Robert Boyle identified gold and silver as themselves being elemental; that is, they are not themselves made of fire, wind, earth, or water. As Boyle's ideas were slowly accepted, additional elements were discovered, and the Greek concept of what makes up matter faded.

Dalton's Theory

The work of Boyle led John Dalton to propose his revolutionary theory in the 1700s. He theorized that the basic unit of matter is a tiny particle called an **atom.**

DALTON'S ATOMIC THEORY Dalton's theory of the atom can be summarized by the following points.

- All elements are composed of indivisible atoms.
- All atoms of a given element are identical.
- Atoms of different elements are different; that is, they have different masses.
- Compounds are formed by the combination of atoms of different elements.

Although we now know that some of Dalton's theory was not correct, it laid the important groundwork for the current concept of the atom.

Parts of the Atom

Experimental studies of the atom soon showed that it was not indivisible but was made up of even smaller parts.

ELECTRONS J. J. Thomson used a cathode ray tube to show one of these smaller units that make up an atom. Because the ray produced in the tube was deflected a certain way by an electrical or magnetic field, he concluded that the ray was formed by particles and that the particles were negatively charged. The only source available for the particles was the atoms present. Thus, Thompson theorized that an atom contains small, negatively charged particles, which he named **electrons.**

A concept of the atom developed in which these negatively charged particles were visualized as being embedded in atoms, just as we might find raisins in bread. This model was called the "plum pudding" model. In this model, the mass of the rest of the atom was evenly distributed and positively charged, taking up all of the space not occupied by the electrons.

THE NUCLEUS If electrons are present in atoms, what makes up the rest of the atom? One scientist who studied this question was Ernest Rutherford. A group of scientists that included Rutherford conducted the following experiment, with surprising results. Look at Figure 1-2A. They directed alpha particles, which are positively charged particles that are much smaller than an atom, at a thin piece of gold foil. If the plum pudding model of the atom were correct, all of the alpha particles would pass through the foil with just a few being slightly deflected.

As the scientists expected, most of the particles passed straight through the foil, and a few were slightly deflected. But to their amazement, some of the alpha particles were greatly deflected, and some even bounced back, as shown in Figure 1-2B. From this experiment, Rutherford concluded that atoms have a dense central core, called a **nucleus,** while the remainder of the atom is essentially empty space. Because alpha particles are positively charged and were repelled by the nucleus, the nucleus must also be positively charged because like charges repel each other.

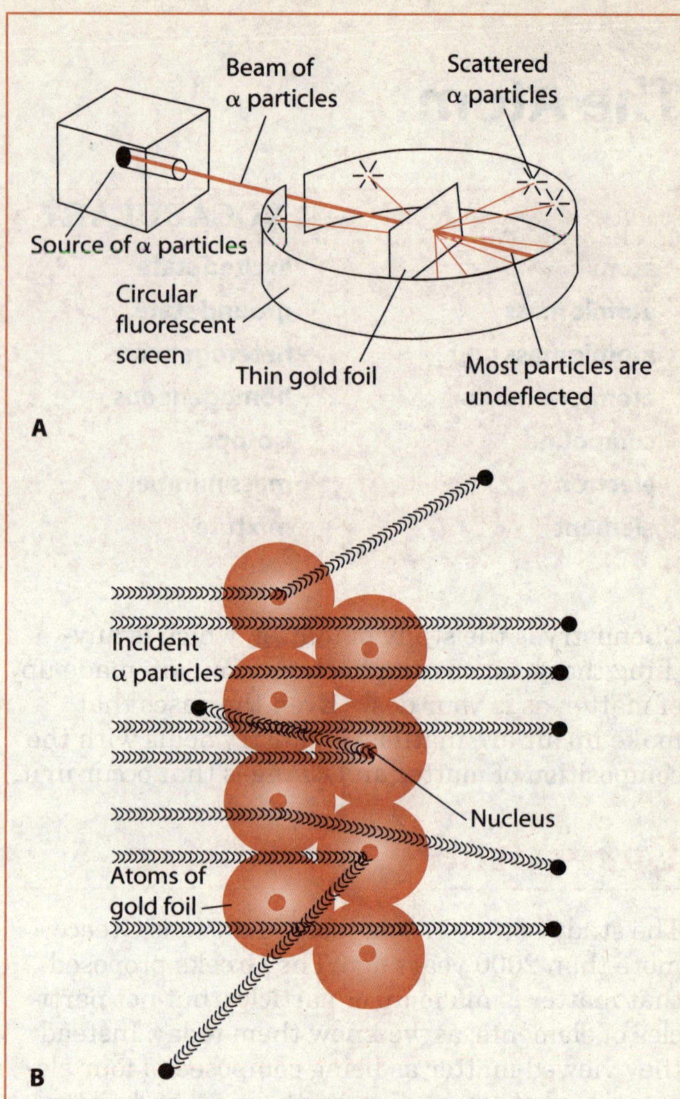

Figure 1-2. The Rutherford gold-foil experiment: **(A)** Scattering of alpha particles **(B)** The deflections of the alpha particles showed that atoms have a dense, positively charged center. Experimental results showed that only about one alpha particle out of each 10,000 was dramatically deflected.

Modern Atomic Theory

Scientists used the information derived from this and other experiments to further describe atomic structure.

THE BOHR ATOM Based on these recent developments, Neils Bohr proposed a model of the atom showing a dense nucleus with electrons found in surrounding orbits. Look at the Bohr model shown in Figure 1-3. It shows a nucleus surrounded by electrons in circular orbits. To stay in such an orbit, each electron in an atom must possess just the right amount of energy to keep it in place around the nucleus. Note that the maximum number of electrons in the first energy level is two. The second level has a maximum of eight electrons.

This model, often called the planetary model, remained the basis for the structure of the atom for some time. While this model did show the separation of the nucleus and the electrons, it had serious flaws because certain experimental evidence did not support it.

THE WAVE-MECHANICAL MODEL Advances in the study of energy aided in modifying the atomic model. Energy had been viewed as being waves,

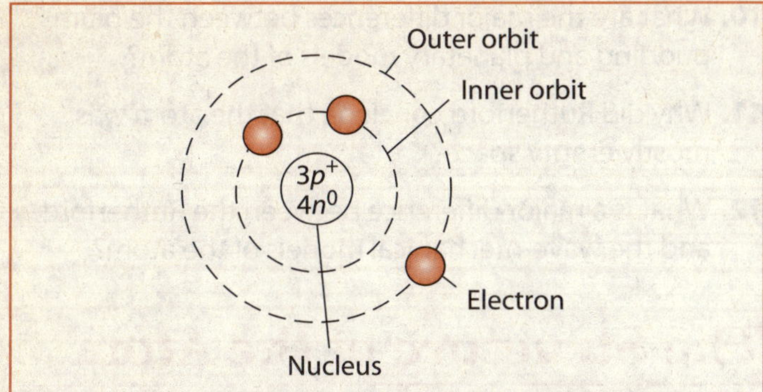

Figure 1-3. A Bohr model of the element lithium

and matter as particles. By the 1900s, energy and matter were both viewed as acting as both waves and particles. The wave aspect of nature was expanded, and it was also proposed that energy was made up of tiny packets called quanta. These energy packets acted like particles.

When it was later determined that the electron not only has properties of mass but also has wave-like properties, this concept of a dual nature was incorporated into the current model of the atom, the **wave-mechanical model.** This modern model of the atom pictures the atom as having a dense, positively charged nucleus as proposed in the planetary model. The major difference between the wave-mechanical model and the Bohr model is found in the manner in which the electrons are pictured. Instead of moving in definite, fixed orbits around the nucleus as suggested in the Bohr model, the wave-mechanical model portrays electrons with distinct amounts of energy moving in areas called orbitals. An **orbital** is described as a region in which an electron of a particular amount of energy is most likely to be located. Models of orbitals are shown in Figure 1-4.

Thus, the modern model of the atom is not the invention of a single scientist, but rather one that has evolved over a long period of time. Figure 1-5 summarizes some of the atomic models involved in the evolution of the current atomic model.

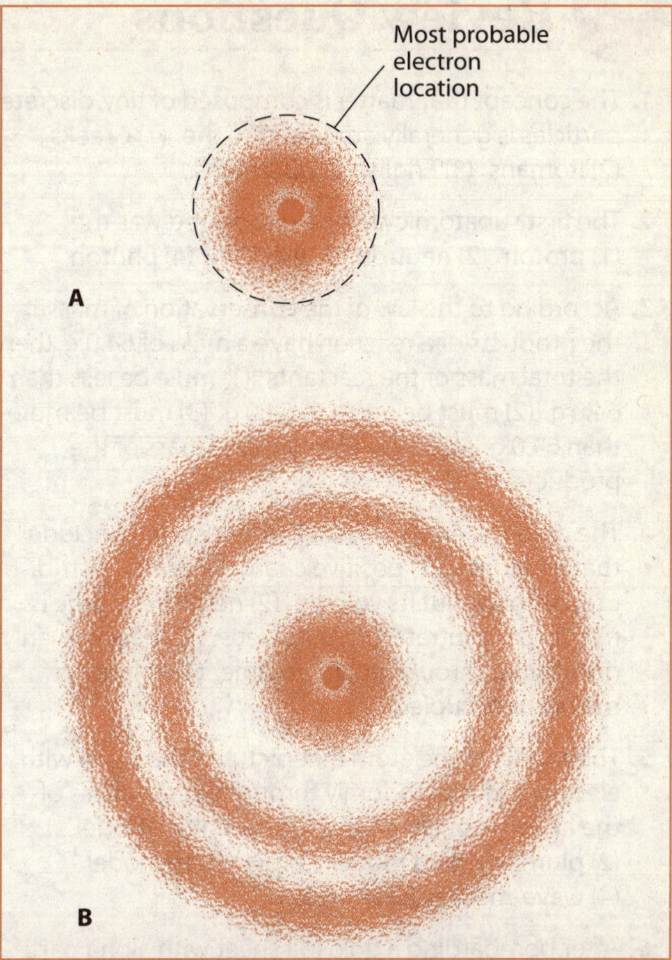

Figure 1-4. Electron cloud model of the atom: The modern model of the atom shows a dense nucleus. **(A)** In this diagram of hydrogen, each dot represents a possible location for the electron. The ring shows the most probable location of an electron. **(B)** In this model of a cross-section of a multielectron atom, the dots represent probable locations of electrons. Each of the darker circles represents an orbital.

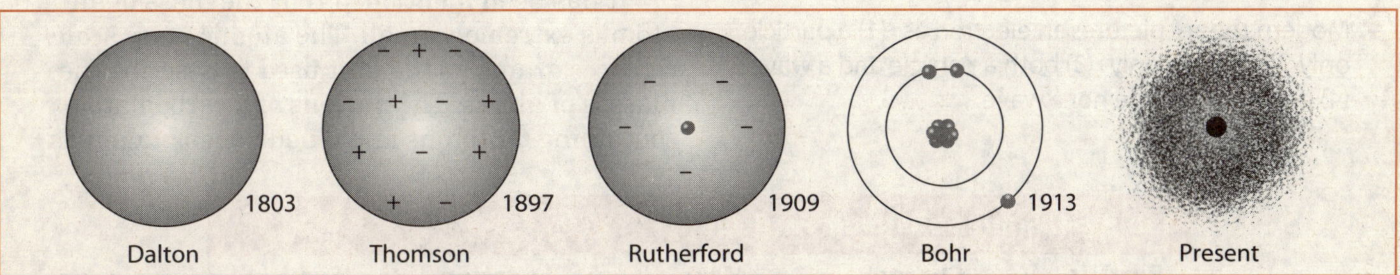

Figure 1-5. Representations of cannonball, plum pudding, nuclear, planetary, and wave-mechanical atomic models

Review Questions

1. The concept that matter is composed of tiny, discrete particles is generally attributed to the (1) Greeks (2) Romans (3) English (4) Germans
2. The first subatomic particle discovered was the (1) proton (2) neutron (3) electron (4) photon
3. According to the law of the conservation of mass, if the products of a reaction have a mass of 64.0 g, then the total mass of the reactants (1) must be less than 64.0 g (2) must be equal to 64.0 g (3) must be more than 64.0 g (4) is not related to the mass of the products
4. The gold-foil experiment led scientists to conclude that an atom's (1) positive charge is evenly distributed throughout its volume (2) negative charge is mainly concentrated in its nucleus (3) mass is evenly distributed throughout its volume (4) volume is mainly unoccupied
5. The model of the atom that pictured the atom with electrons stuck randomly throughout the mass of the atom was called the (1) cannonball model (2) plum pudding model (3) planetary model (4) wave-mechanical model
6. After bombarding a gold foil sheet with alpha particles, scientists concluded that atoms mainly consist of (1) electrons (2) empty space (3) protons (4) neutrons
7. Experimental evidence indicates that the nucleus of an atom (1) contains most of the mass of the atom (2) contains a small percentage of the mass of the atom (3) has no charge (4) has a negative charge
8. Dalton's atomic theory states that (1) all atoms of an element are positively charged (2) different elements can have the same mass (3) atoms of a given element must be identical (4) all the atoms in a compound are identical
9. Modern theory pictures an electron as (1) a particle only (2) a wave only (3) both a particle and a wave (4) neither a particle nor a wave
10. What are the major differences between the plum pudding and planetary models of the atom?
11. Why did Rutherford conclude that the atom was mostly empty space?
12. What is a major difference between the Rutherford and the wave-mechanical models of the atom?

The Structure of the Atom

You have seen that all atoms are composed of a small, dense, positively charged nucleus surrounded by a large space occupied by electrons. Research has shown that the nucleus contains two types of particles—**protons** with a positive charge, and **neutrons** with no charge.

Subatomic Particles

Protons have a mass of only 1.67×10^{-24} g. Because the mass of a proton is so small, it is more convenient to use a different scale whose units are called **atomic mass units** to represent its mass. A proton is assigned 1.0 atomic mass unit (amu). A neutron has approximately the same mass as a proton.

Each atom of a specific element must contain the same number of protons as each other atom of that element. The number of protons in the nucleus of an atom is the **atomic number** of that element. For example, chlorine has an atomic number of 17. Each chlorine atom contains 17 protons in its nucleus.

Electrons occupy the space of an atom outside the nucleus and have a charge equal to, but opposite of, a proton. Electrons are much less massive than either the proton or neutron, having a mass of only 1/1836 amu. Table 1-1 summarizes information about each of the particles that make up an atom.

It has been mentioned that the mass of an atom is extremely small. The atomic mass scale replaces grams as the unit used to describe the masses of atoms. The nucleus of a carbon atom containing 6 protons and 6 neutrons is taken as

Table 1-1. Some Subatomic Particles

Particle	Charge	Mass	Location	Symbol
Proton	+1	1 amu	nucleus	${}^{1}_{1}H$ or ${}^{1}_{1}p$
Neutron	0	1 amu	nucleus	${}^{1}_{0}n$
Electron	−1	1/1836 amu	outside	${}^{0}_{-1}e$

the standard mass, and the mass of any atom is a ratio between its mass and that of the carbon nucleus. The sum of the numbers of protons and neutrons in the nucleus is called the **mass number** of the nucleus. Thus, a nucleus with 7 protons and 7 neutrons has a mass number of 14. When determining the mass of an atom, the mass of the electrons is so small it is not considered in the calculation.

DIGGING DEEPER

The concept of protons, electrons, and neutrons as fundamental particles can be used to explain most of the chemical behavior of an atom. However, recent research has shown that protons and neutrons are themselves made of smaller particles called quarks. Each quark has a fractional charge of either $\frac{2}{3}+$ or $\frac{1}{3}-$. Each proton and neutron is composed of three quarks. Because it has a total 1+ charge, a proton must be composed of two quarks each with a charge of $\frac{2}{3}+$ and one quark with a charge of $\frac{1}{3}-$. A neutron has no charge, so it must be composed of one quark with a charge of $\frac{2}{3}+$ and two quarks each with a charge of $\frac{1}{3}-$.

ISOTOPES Although all the atoms of a given element must contain the same number of protons, the number of neutrons may vary. Most atoms of hydrogen contain only a proton. Remembering that the mass number of an atom is the sum of its protons and neutrons, this atom of hydrogen has a mass of 1 amu. In addition to this atom with a mass of 1 amu, there are some atoms of hydrogen that have a nucleus with both a proton and a neutron. While this is still an atom of hydrogen, it has a mass number of 2. There is still another type of hydrogen with a nucleus containing two neutrons in addition to a proton; this atom has a mass number of 3. These different forms of an atom are called isotopes. **Isotopes** are atoms of the same element that have different numbers of neutrons, and hence have different mass numbers. Table 1-2 describes the isotopes of the element hydrogen.

ISOTOPE SYMBOLS Isotopes can be identified by using a symbol that indicates both the element and its mass number. Thus, C-12 represents a carbon atom with a mass number of 12. The mass number represents the sum of the protons and neutrons. The difference between the atomic number of an atom and its mass number is the number of neutrons. Because the atomic number (number of protons) of C-12 is 6, the number of neutrons will also be 6. Different ways to symbolize carbon-14 isotopes are shown in Figure 1-6.

C-14	^{14}C
Carbon-14	$^{14}_{6}C$

Figure 1-6. Some symbols of isotopes: Common isotopic notations of carbon atoms that contain six protons and eight neutrons

SAMPLE PROBLEM

Find the number of neutrons in an atom of $^{79}_{34}Se$.

Solution: Identify the known and unknown values.

Known	*Unknown*
atomic number = 34	number of neutrons = ?
mass number = 79	

Write the relationship for number of neutrons, atomic number, and atomic mass.

$$\text{Neutrons} = \text{Mass number} - \text{Atomic number}$$

Substitute the known values and solve for the number of neutrons.

$$\text{Neutrons} = 79 - 34 = 45$$

Table 1-2. Isotopes of Hydrogen

Particle	Protons	Neutrons	Mass Number	Symbol
Protium	1	0	1 amu	$^{1}_{1}H$
Deuterium	1	1	2 amu	$^{2}_{1}H$
Tritium	1	2	3 amu	$^{3}_{1}H$

Atomic Masses

You have seen that the mass number of a given nucleus must be an integer because it is the sum of the numbers of protons and neutrons in the nucleus. However, when you examine the periodic table of the elements, you will notice that most of the elements have masses that are fractional values. These masses are called the **atomic masses** of the elements, and they are the average mass of all the isotopes in a sample of the element.

How can chlorine have an atomic mass of 35.454 amu? The answer is found in the relative numbers of the isotopes of chlorine. There are two major isotopes of chlorine, Cl-35 and Cl-37. The atomic mass of chlorine is the average of the two isotopes. But the average of Cl-35 and Cl-37 would seem to give chlorine an average mass of 36 amu. That would be true if Cl-35 and Cl-37 were equally abundant in nature, but such is not the case.

If you had four test grades, 90%, 90%, 90% and 80%, you would not have an average test grade of 85%. Your average would be 87.5%. In the same way, if there are many more atoms of Cl-35 than Cl-37, the average mass would be closer to 35 amu. Consult either the periodic table or a table of properties of the elements for average atomic masses.

SAMPLE PROBLEM

Atomic mass can be calculated from the mass and the abundance of naturally occurring isotopes. Carbon has two naturally occurring stable isotopes. Most carbon atoms—98.89%—are C-12, while the remaining 1.108% are C-13. What is the atomic mass of carbon?

Solution: Identify the known and unknown values.

Known	*Unknown*
98.89% C-12	atomic mass = ? amu
1.108% C-13	

Convert the percentages to decimal numbers, and multiply the mass of each isotope by its decimal abundance.

$$12 \text{ amu} \times 0.9889 = 11.87 \text{ amu}$$
$$13 \text{ amu} \times 0.01108 = 0.1440 \text{ amu}$$

Add these masses of isotopes.

$$11.87 \text{ amu} + 0.1440 \text{ amu} = 12.01 \text{ amu}$$

Location of Electrons

Remember that electrons are found in the space of the atom around the nucleus. Experiments have shown that the electrons are not found just anywhere around the nucleus; they are found in orbitals. An orbital is a region where an electron can most probably be found.

ENERGY LEVELS The orbitals in an atom form a series of energy levels in which electrons may be found. Each electron in an atom has its own distinct amount of energy that corresponds to the energy level that it occupies. Electrons can gain and lose energy and move to different energy levels, but they do so in a unique way. Instead of being able to absorb any amount of energy, an electron can only absorb a discrete, or fixed amount of energy that would allow it to move to a higher energy level. While this concept is difficult for us to understand, an analogy may help. When we climb up or down a set of stairs, we must exert enough energy to move from one step to another. We can't stop at a half a step. In a like manner, if an electron moves from one energy level to a different energy level, it must give off or absorb the energy difference between those two levels.

GROUND AND EXCITED STATES When the electrons occupy the lowest available orbitals, the atom is said to be in the **ground state.** When electrons are subjected to stimuli such as heat, light, or electricity, an electron may absorb energy and temporarily move to a higher energy level. This unstable condition is called an **excited state.** The electron quickly returns to a lower available level, emitting the same amount of energy it absorbed to go to the higher energy level. This energy may be in the form of infrared, ultraviolet, or visible light. The light given off from a fluorescent or a neon light is caused by excited electrons returning to lower energy levels. While the light appears as one color to our eyes, it is actually composed of many different wavelengths, each of which is seen as a different line when viewed through an instrument called a spectroscope.

Unlike a continuous spectrum produced by holding a prism in sunlight, the visible light produced by electrons is confined to narrow lines of color called bright line spectra. Each atom has its own distinct pattern of emission lines (or bright line spectrum), and these spectra are used to identify elements.

SAMPLE PROBLEM

What element is represented by the following line spectrum?

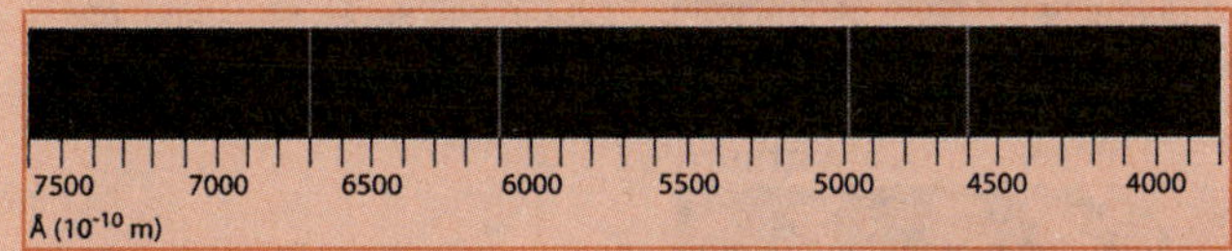

Bright-line spectrum of an element

Solution: Identify the known and unknown values.

Known	*Unknown*
Spectra of several elements	Identity of the element = ?

Compare the lines on the spectrum of the element shown above to those in Figure 1-7 on the following page.

Notice that the first line shown for the unknown element is at 4600. Two elements on the reference table have spectral lines at that frequency, Li and Sr. The second line of the unknown is at 4960. Both elements have lines approximately at this reading, but Sr has two lines between 4600 and 4960 that are not in the unknown. The unknown is Li. Check for accuracy by noting that Li has a line at 6090, while Sr does not.

Review Questions

13. The atomic mass of an element is defined as the weighted average mass of that element's (1) most abundant isotope (2) least abundant isotope (3) naturally occurring isotopes (4) radioactive isotopes

14. Element X has two isotopes. If 72.0% of the element has an isotopic mass of 84.9 amu and 28.0% has an isotopic mass of 87.0 amu, the average atomic mass of element X is numerically equal to
(1) (72.0 + 98.9) (28.0 + 87.0)
(2) (72.0 − 84.9)(28.0 − 87.0)
(3) (0.720)(84.9) + (0.280)(87.0)
(4) (72.0)(84.9) + (28.0)(87.0)

15. A neutral atom with 6 electrons and 8 neutrons is an isotope of (1) carbon (2) silicon (3) nitrogen (4) oxygen

16. The average isotopic mass of chlorine is 35.5 amu. Which mixture of isotopes (shown as percents) produces this mass? (1) 50% C-12 and 50% C-13 (2) 50% Cl-35 and 50% Cl-37 (3) 75% Cl-35 and 25% Cl-37 (4) 75% C-12 and 25% C-13

17. The major portion of an atom's mass consists of (1) electrons and protons (2) electrons and neutrons (3) neutrons and positrons (4) neutrons and protons

18. Which atoms have the same number of neutrons? (1) H-1 and He-3 (2) H-2 and He-4 (3) H-3 and He-3 (4) H-3 and He-4

19. Atoms of ^{16}O, ^{17}O and ^{18}O have the same number of
(1) neutrons but a different number of protons
(2) protons but a different number of neutrons
(3) protons but a different number of electrons
(4) electrons but a different number of protons

20. A neutron has approximately the same mass as (1) an alpha particle (2) a beta particle (3) an electron (4) a proton

21. The total number of protons and neutrons in the nuclide $^{35}_{17}Cl$ is (1) 52 (2) 35 (3) 18 (4) 17

22. The nuclides $^{14}_{6}C$ and $^{14}_{7}N$ are similar in that they both have the same (1) mass number (2) atomic number (3) number of neutrons (4) nuclear charge

23. What is the nuclear charge of an atom with a mass of 23 and an atomic number of 11? (1) 11+ (2) 12+ (3) 23+ (4) 34+

24. Compared to the charge and mass of a proton, an electron has (1) the same charge and a smaller mass (2) the same charge and the same mass (3) an opposite charge and a smaller mass (4) an opposite charge and the same mass

25. Which of the following statements is correct? (1) A proton is positively charged; a neutron is negatively charged. (2) A proton is negatively charged; a neutron is positively charged. (3) A proton is positively charged; an electron is negatively charged. (4) A proton is negatively charged; an electron is positively charged.

26. Which symbols represent atoms that are isotopes of each other? (1) ^{14}C and ^{14}N (2) ^{16}O and ^{18}O (3) ^{131}I and ^{131}I (4) ^{222}Rn and ^{222}Ra

27. When electrons in an excited state fall to lower energy levels, energy is (1) absorbed (2) released (3) neither absorbed nor released (4) both released and absorbed

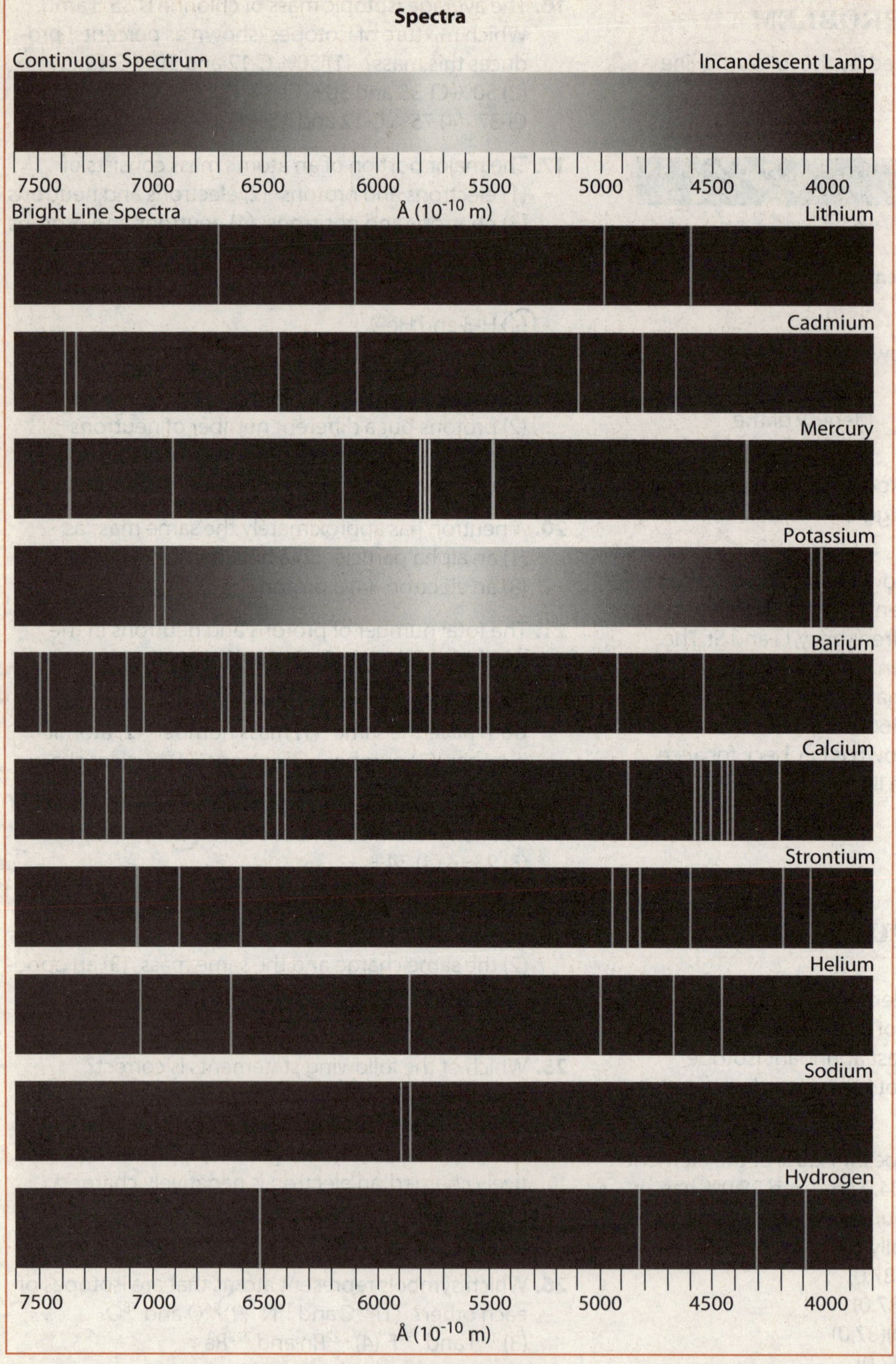

Figure 1-7. Emission spectra

28. The characteristic bright-line spectrum of an atom is produced when (1) nuclei undergo fission (2) nuclei undergo fusion (3) electrons move from higher to lower energy levels (4) electrons move from lower to higher energy levels

29. When the electrons of an excited atom fall back to lower energy levels, the emission of energy produces (1) beta particles (2) alpha particles (3) spectral lines (4) gamma radiation

30. Which nuclide contains the greatest number of neutrons? (1) Cl-37 (2) K-39 (3) Ar-40 (4) Ca-41

Use Figure 1-7 on page 8 to identify the following elements.

31.

32.

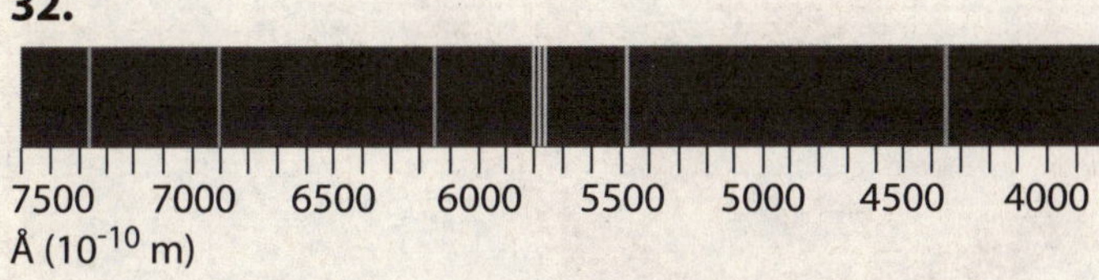

33.

7500 7000 6500 6000 5500 5000 4500 4000
Å (10^{-10} m)

34. The atomic mass of chlorine is listed as 35.454 amu on the periodic table. It has two naturally occurring isotopes, Cl-35 and Cl-37. What are the approximate percentages of each?

35. What particle or particles contribute to the mass number of an atom?

36. Compare the charge and mass of an electron and a neutron.

ADDITIONAL MATERIAL

The coverage of quantum numbers and electron configurations on pages 9–15 is not required by the Regents core curriculum in chemistry. You will not be tested on these topics in the Regents Examination for the Physical Setting/Chemistry.

Electron Arrangement

Although the electrons in an atom contribute little to the mass of an atom, their arrangement determines its chemical properties. The chemical properties of an element are based on the number of electrons in the outer energy level of its atoms. These outer electrons are called valence electrons. How can you determine how the electrons are arranged in an atom and, therefore, how many valence electrons an atom has?

Quantum Numbers

Remember that the first energy level in an atom can contain two electrons and the second can contain eight. We can't see the electron arrangement in an atom. How were these numbers determined? A theory, called the quantum theory, was developed to explain the chemical behavior of atoms.

Electrons can be described by a set of four numbers called quantum numbers. The first number describes the major energy level of the electron and is called the principal quantum number. The principal quantum number is the same as the number of the energy level that contains the electron. If an electron has a principal quantum number of 2, it is in the second energy level from the nucleus.

Each energy level has one or more sublevels associated with it. Each energy level contains as many sublevels as the number of the level. For example, energy level three has three sublevels.

The first sublevel of any energy level is designated the *s* sublevel. If a second sublevel is present, it is *p*. The third is *d*, and the fourth is *f*. Sublevels are described by using the number of the principal energy level together with the letter designation of each sublevel. For example, 3*s* describes the first sublevel of the third energy level.

The third quantum number relates to the orbitals in the sublevels and their orientations. Remember that an orbital is a location inside the atom where an electron is most likely to be found.

Electrons that are in *s* sublevels are found in orbitals with spherical shapes without sharp edges surrounding the nucleus. There is only one way a sphere can be arranged, so there is only one orbital in an *s* sublevel.

The *p* orbital is somewhat dumbbell in shape. There are three of these orbitals at each principal energy level higher than energy level one. The *p* orbitals are arranged at right angles to each other and can be designated as p_x, p_y, and p_z. Thus, each *p* sublevel contains three orbitals. Figure 1-8 on page 10 shows the shapes of *s* and *p* orbitals.

At levels three and higher, there is another type of sublevel, the *d* sublevel containing five orbitals. From principal level four and higher, *f* sublevels with seven orbitals are found. The shapes of the orbitals in both the *d* and *f* sublevels are complex, so only *s* and *p* orbitals are shown.

Figure 1-8. Shape and relative sizes of orbitals: (A) Look at the shape and relative sizes of 1*s*, 2*s*, and 3*s* orbitals. The upper diagrams are cross sections of the diagrams beneath. The dark areas show where electrons are most probably located. Notice that there are areas, called nodes, where it is unlikely to find an electron. **(B)** Shapes and orientations of *p* orbitals

Table 1-3. Orbitals and Electron Capacity				
Principal Energy Level	Type of Sublevel	Number of Orbitals in a Sublevel	Total Orbitals per Level	Maximum Number of Electrons
1	*s*	1	1	2
2	*s*	1	4	8
	p	3		
3	*s*	1	9	18
	p	3		
	d	5		
4	*s*	1	16	32
	p	3		
	d	5		
	f	7		

The fourth quantum number relates to the spin of an electron. This number indicates that each orbital can contain two electrons spinning in opposite directions.

Table 1-3 summarizes how the maximum number of electrons per energy level is determined using these four quantum numbers.

Electron Configurations

Quantum numbers describe the distribution of the electrons in an atom when you remember that electrons will occupy the lowest sublevel possible. This distribution of the electrons in an atom is called its electron configuration.

In an electron configuration, the electrons of an atom are described by identifying the energy level of each electron and its sublevel. Thus, 3*s* describes an electron at principal energy level 3 in an *s* sublevel. A superscript is added to show the number of electrons in the sublevel. The notation $4p^5$ tells the reader that there are 5 electrons in the 4*p* sublevel. Look at the example in Figure 1-9.

Principal energy level→ $3p^4$ ←Number of electrons in sublevel
↑
Type of sublevel

Figure 1-9. Orbital notation: Each part of orbital notation has a specific meaning.

The complete electron configuration of an atom is shown by writing symbols for all the occupied sublevels in sequence, starting from the orbital with the least amount of energy. For example, the electron configuration of the oxygen atom (eight electrons) is represented by $1s^22s^22p^4$.

WRITING ELECTRON CONFIGURATIONS The electron configurations of the elements can be written in order of increasing atomic number, starting with hydrogen, by adding an additional electron for each new atom. The order in which the sublevels are filled is shown in Figure 1-10, using the following rules.

- Each added electron is placed into the sublevel of lowest available energy.
- No more than two electrons can be placed in any orbital.
- A single electron must be placed into each orbital of a given sublevel before any pairing takes place. (Hund's Rule)
- The outermost principal energy level can only contain electrons in *s* and *p* orbitals.

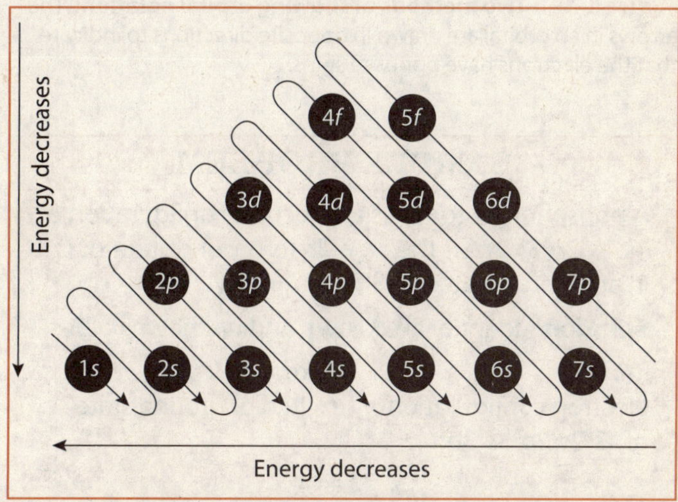

Figure 1-10. Electron configurations: To find the electron configuration of an atom, simply begin adding electrons to the 1*s* sublevel and continue adding them in the order shown.

ORDER OF ELECTRON FILL While there are many locations that electrons might fill in an atom, the most stable condition exists when they fill the lowest available energy orbitals. This simply means that the first energy level, which is less energetic than any other, is filled first. In level two, the *s* orbital, then the *p* orbitals, are filled. Next, the *s* and *p* orbitals of the third level are filled, but the 3*d* level is not filled next. Instead, the 4*s* sublevel is filled, followed by the 3*d*. Why does this change in order occur? As the number of sublevels per energy level increases, the space taken up by the sublevels increases and the energy levels begin to overlap.

ORBITAL NOTATION While electron configuration notation is useful, it does not show how electrons are distributed in each sublevel. Figure 1-11 shows two ways of illustrating the distribution of electrons in an atom. A circle or square can be used to represent an orbital. An electron is represented either by a line or an arrow. When two lines are drawn in an orbital they represent an orbital pair with opposite spins. If arrows are used to represent the electrons, two arrows pointed in opposite directions represent a pair of electrons with opposite spin.

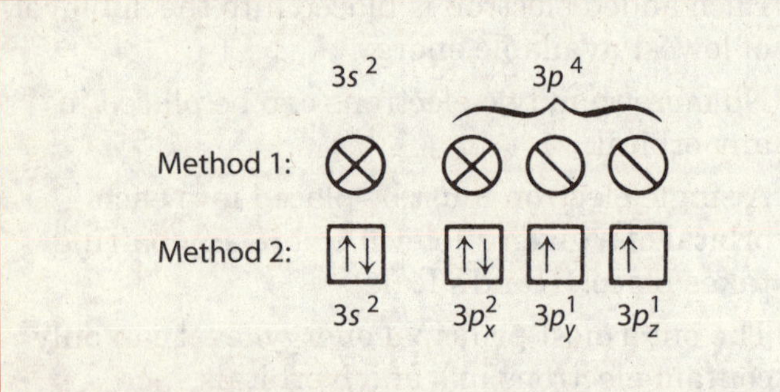

Figure 1-11. Two methods of showing orbital notation: The arrows in an orbital are drawn in opposite directions to indicate that the electrons have opposite spins.

SAMPLE PROBLEM

A phosphorus atom has an electron configuration of $1s^22s^22p^63s^13p^4$. Is the atom in its ground state, or is it in an excited state?

Solution: Identify the known and unknown values.

Known	*Unknown*
electron configuration of $1s^22s^22p^63s^13p^4$	excited or ground state

Look at Figure 1-10 for order of filling of orbitals. If the order is changed, or if a sublevel other than the last one is unfilled, the atom is probably in an excited state. The ground state configuration of a phosphorus atom would be $1s^22s^22p^63s^23p^3$. In the known configuration, one electron is in a higher sublevel than it would be in its ground state, so the atom is excited.

Review Questions

37. Which is the electron configuration of an atom in the excited state? (1) $1s^22s^22p^2$ (2) $1s^22s^22p^1$ (3) $1s^22s^22p^53s^2$ (4) $1s^22s^22p^63s^1$

38. Which atom in the ground state contains one completely filled *p* orbital? (1) Ne (2) O (3) He (4) Be

39. What is the total number of electrons in the second principal energy level of a calcium atom in the ground state? (1) 6 (2) 2 (3) 8 (4) 18

40. Which is the correct orbital notation of a lithium atom in the ground state?

(1)

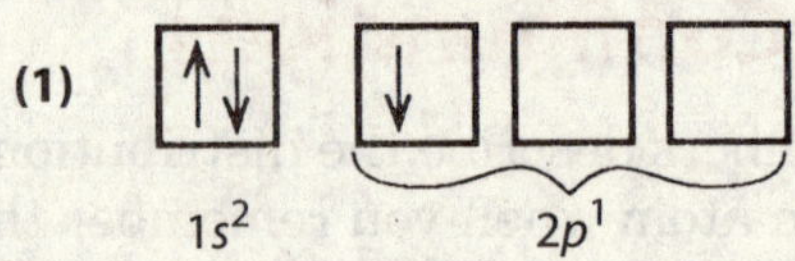

(2)

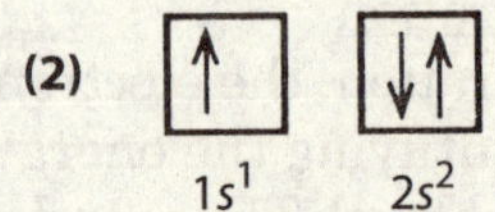

(3)

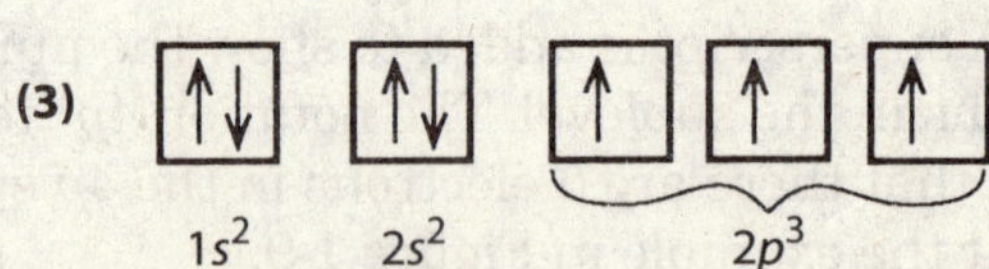

(4)

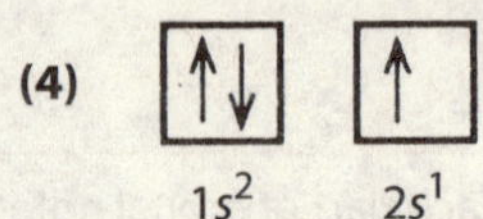

41. The atom of which element in the ground state has two unpaired electrons in the 2*p* sublevel? (1) fluorine (2) nitrogen (3) beryllium (4) carbon

42. What is the total number of occupied *s* orbitals in an atom of nickel in the ground state? (1) 1 (2) 2 (3) 3 (4) 4

43. Which atom in the ground state has only three electrons in the 3*p* sublevel? (1) phosphorus (2) potassium (3) argon (4) aluminum

44. What is the total number of occupied principal energy levels in a neutral atom of neon in the ground state? (1) 1 (2) 2 (3) 3 (4) 4

45. Which is the electron configuration of an atom in the excited state? (1) $1s^1 2s^1$ (2) $1s^2 2s^1$ (3) $1s^2 2s^2 2p^1$ (4) $1s^2 2s^2 2p^2$

46. Which orbital notation correctly represents the outermost principal energy level of a nitrogen atom in the ground state?

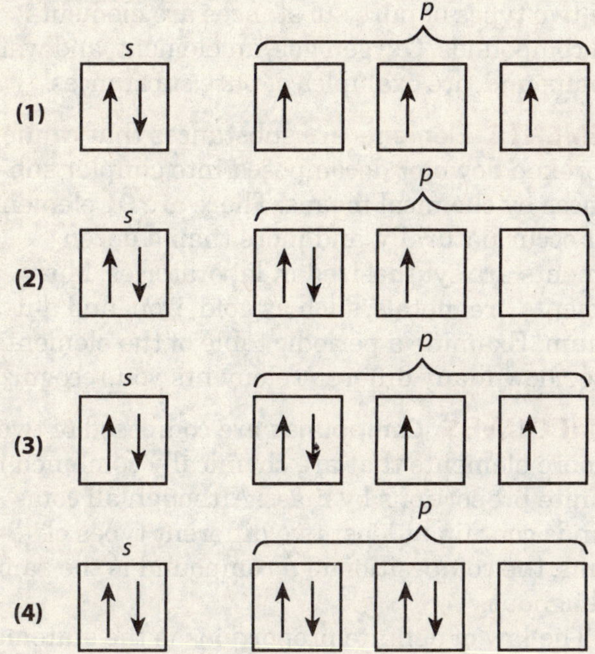

47. Which electron configuration represents a potassium atom in the excited state? (1) $1s^2 2s^2 2p^6 3s^2 3p^3$ (2) $1s^2 2s^2 2p^6 3s^1 3p^4$ (3) $1s^2 2s^2 2p^6 3s^2 3p^6 4s^1$ (4) $1s^2 2s^2 2p^6 3s^2 3p^5 4s^2$

48. In an atom of lithium in the ground state, what is the total number of orbitals that contain only one electron? (1) 1 (2) 2 (3) 3 (4) 4

49. What is the total number of completely filled principal energy levels in an atom of argon in the ground state? (1) 1 (2) 2 (3) 3 (4) 4

50. What is the total number of electrons needed to completely fill all the orbitals in an atom's second principal energy level? (1) 16 (2) 2 (3) 8 (4) 4

51. An atom in the excited state can have an electron configuration of (1) $1s^2 2s^2$ (2) $1s^2 2p^1$ (3) $1s^2 2s^2 2p^5$ (4) $1s^2 2s^2 2p^6$

52. What is the total number of sublevels in the fourth principal energy level? (1) 1 (2) 2 (3) 3 (4) 4

53. Which electron configuration represents an atom in the excited state? (1) $1s^2 2s^2 2p^6 3s^2$ (2) $1s^2 2s^2 2p^6 3s^1$ (3) $1s^2 2s^2 2p^6$ (4) $1s^2 2s^2 2p^5 3s^2$

54. Which element has atoms in the ground state with a sublevel that is only half filled? (1) helium (2) beryllium (3) nitrogen (4) neon

55. Which sublevel contains a total of five orbitals? (1) *s* (2) *p* (3) *d* (4) *f*

56. What is the maximum number of electrons that can occupy the fourth principal energy level of an atom? (1) 6 (2) 8 (3) 18 (4) 32

57. What is the total number of unpaired electrons in an atom of oxygen in the ground state? (1) 6 (2) 2 (3) 8 (4) 4

58. Which of the following sublevels has the highest energy? (1) 2*p* (2) 2*s* (3) 3*p* (4) 3*s*

59. What is the maximum number of electrons in an orbital of any atom? (1) 1 (2) 2 (3) 6 (4) 10

60. What is the electron configuration of a Mn atom in the ground state?
(1) $1s^2 2s^2 2p^6 3s^2$
(2) $1s^2 2s^2 2p^6 3s^2 3p^6 3s 3d^5 4s^2$
(3) $1s^2 2s^2 2p^6 3s^2 3p^6 3d^5 4s^1 4p^1$
(4) $1s^2 2s^2 2p^6 3s^2 3p^6 3d^7$

25

61. Which orbital notation correctly represents a noble gas in the ground state?

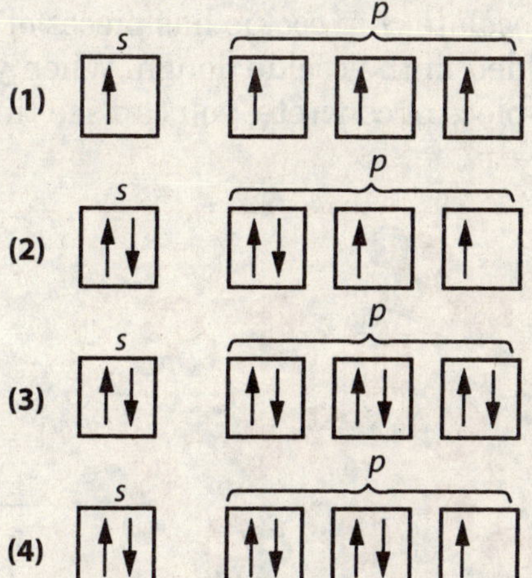

62. Which atom in the ground state has three half-filled orbitals? (1) P (2) Si (3) Al (4) Li

63. What is the total number of completely filled sublevels found in an atom of krypton in the ground state? (1) 10 (2) 2 (3) 8 (4) 4

— $1s^2 2s^2 2p^6 3s^2 3p^6$ —

64. Assuming that the orbitals of nickel fill in the order described in Figure 1-11, what is the total number of sublevels that contain electrons in the third principal energy level of a nickel atom in the ground state?
(1) 1 (2) 2 (3) 3 (4) 4

65. The third row of the periodic table (Na to Ar) follows the same pattern of electron filling as the second row (Li to Ne). Write the electron configurations and orbital structure for the elements from Na to Ar.

Types of Matter

The world is composed of millions of different materials, and they are all combinations of atoms. As we look at the world around us, two categories of matter can be distinguished.

Homogeneous and Heterogeneous Matter

Some matter looks uniform and doesn't seem to be made up of parts. A sample of pure water does not have distinguishable parts and has the same composition throughout. When a material has uniform composition throughout, the sample is said to be **homogeneous.** Homogeneous matter can contain more than one type of particle, but particles are evenly mixed. Sugar dissolved in water is an example of matter that contains both sugar and water but is homogeneous because the smallest particles that make up sugar and water are evenly mixed.

Other materials are obviously made up of parts. A chocolate chip cookie has pieces of chocolate embedded in the cookie dough. When you examine a piece of concrete, you can see tiny pebbles and pieces of sand embedded in the cement. Such materials, which have varying composition, are said to be **heterogeneous.** Heterogeneous materials are made up of parts with different chemical and physical properties. These parts are not uniformly mixed or dispersed.

Matter can be divided into the major categories of pure substances and mixtures. Pure substances are homogeneous; mixtures can be either heterogeneous or homogeneous.

Pure Substances

A sample of matter is a **pure substance** if its composition is the same throughout the sample. The two types of pure substances are elements and compounds. Oxygen gas, an element, and water, a compound, are examples of pure substances.

ELEMENTS **Elements** are substances that cannot be broken down or decomposed into simpler substances by chemical means. There are 91 elements that occur naturally, and more than a dozen elements are synthesized in laboratories. Most elements are metals, such as gold, iron, and aluminum. Examine a periodic table of the elements to see how many different elements you recognize.

COMPOUNDS **Compounds** are composed of two or more elements that are chemically combined in definite proportions by mass. Although all compounds contain at least two different types of atoms, the composition of a compound is the same throughout.

The law of definite proportions is the statement that types of atoms in a compound exist in a fixed ratio. Examine the law of definite proportions as shown in Figure 1-12. Water is a compound

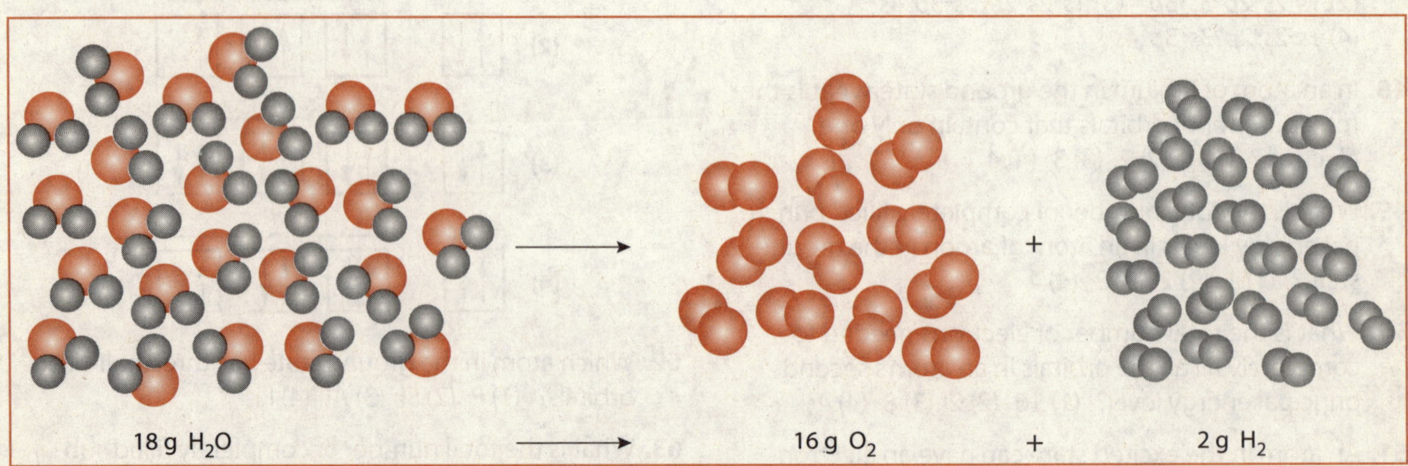

Figure 1-12. The law of definite proportions: This diagram is a model of the decomposition of water. Notice that for every 18 g of water, 16 g of oxygen and 2 g of hydrogen form.

composed of two elements—hydrogen and oxygen—that are chemically combined. Water can be decomposed into these two elements in a mass ratio of 1:8. When any sample of water is decomposed it will always yield one part by weight of hydrogen for each eight parts of oxygen. When 9 g of water are decomposed they will always produce 1 g of hydrogen and 8 g of oxygen. If 36 g of water decomposed, how many grams of oxygen would be produced? Because the proportions remain the same, 32 g of oxygen would be produced.

Pure substances have a constant composition, both within a given sample and from one sample to another. Examine another type of matter that does not have a constant composition.

Mixtures

Mixtures are combinations of two or more pure substances that can be separated by physical means. Mixtures are different from compounds because their composition is not definite or "fixed," and the parts can be separated by physical means. For example, different amounts of sugar can be dissolved in a liter of water, and each result would be a water solution of sugar. Even though the sugar seems to disappear and become part of the water, it really doesn't. If the water evaporates, the sugar is left behind; the water and sugar separate.

Some mixtures are homogeneous, and some are heterogeneous. Solutions are mixtures that are homogeneous. Most mixtures are heterogeneous. Soil and concrete are good examples of heterogeneous mixtures. The different parts of each can be easily seen.

Distinguishing Between Mixtures and Compounds

Look at Figure 1-13. Both mixtures and compounds contain two or more different elements. However, the two categories are quite different when one considers their composition and properties.

In a mixture, elements such as iron and sulfur can be present in different ratios. Each substance that makes up the mixture retains its properties. Iron is magnetic and can be separated from a mixture of iron and sulfur with a magnet. Sulfur retains its elemental yellow color in the mixture.

However, if these two elements chemically react, they combine in a mass ratio of 1.74 parts of iron to

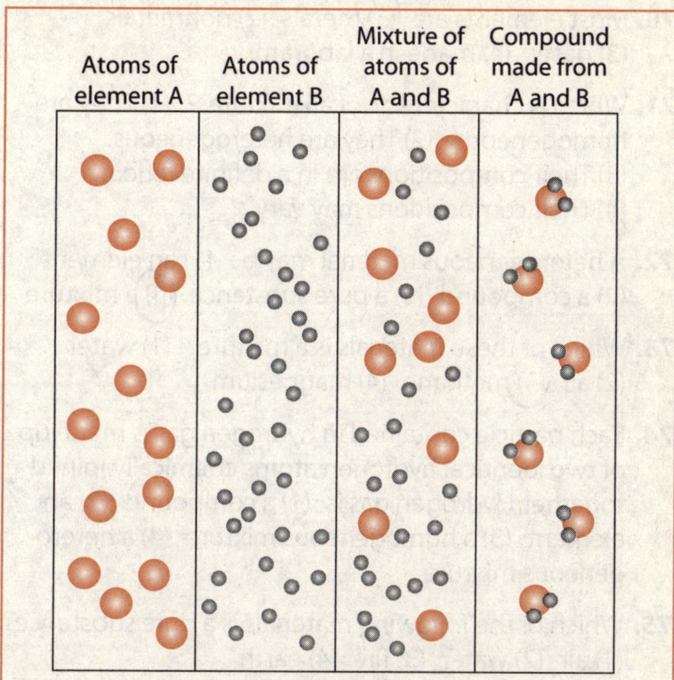

Figure 1-13. Elements, compounds and mixtures: Study the models and notice the differences among elements, compounds, and mixtures.

1.00 part of sulfur. In the compound the iron is no longer magnetic, and the sulfur loses its yellow color. The compound has its own properties. For example, iron sulfide has a different melting point than either elemental sulfur or iron.

In a later topic, you will learn about different methods that can be used to separate the parts of a mixture.

Review Questions

66. Which of the following cannot be decomposed by chemical means? (1) sodium (2) ethanol (3) sucrose (4) water

67. A compound differs from an element in that a compound (1) is homogeneous (2) has a definite composition (3) has a definite melting point (4) can be decomposed by a chemical reaction

68. A compound differs from a mixture in that a compound always has a (1) homogeneous composition (2) maximum of two elements (3) minimum of three elements (4) heterogeneous composition

69. A pure substance that is composed only of identical atoms is classified as (1) a compound (2) an element (3) a heterogeneous mixture (4) a homogeneous mixture

70. Most elements are (1) metals (2) nonmetals (3) gases (4) made in a laboratory

71. Which is characteristic of all mixtures? (1) They are homogeneous. (2) They are heterogeneous. (3) Their compositions are in a definite ratio. (4) Their compositions may vary.

72. A heterogeneous material may be (1) an element (2) a compound (3) a pure substance (4) a mixture

73. Which of these materials is a mixture? (1) water (2) air (3) methane (4) magnesium

74. Each particle contained in hydrogen gas is made up of two identical hydrogen atoms chemically joined together. Hydrogen gas is (1) a compound (2) an element (3) a homogeneous mixture (4) a heterogeneous mixture

75. Which of the following materials is a pure substance? (1) air (2) water (3) fire (4) earth

76. Which statement is an identifying characteristic of a mixture? (1) A mixture can consist of a single element. (2) A mixture can be separated by physical means. (3) A mixture must have a definite composition by weight. (4) A mixture must be homogeneous.

77. Which substance can be decomposed by a chemical change? (1) ammonia (2) aluminum (3) magnesium (4) manganese

Answer the following questions using complete sentences.

78. A sample of a material is passed through a filter paper. A white deposit remains on the paper, and a clear liquid passes through. The clear liquid is then evaporated, leaving a white residue. What can you determine about the nature of the sample?

79. A substance is found to contain only calcium and sulfur. How would you determine whether the substance is a compound or a mixture?

80. Using [hydrogen molecule symbol] to represent a hydrogen molecule and [oxygen molecule symbol] to represent an oxygen molecule, draw a picture of a mixture of hydrogen and oxygen gases.

81. What are some of the differences between a mixture of iron and oxygen and a compound composed of iron and oxygen?

82. Is a pepperoni pizza homogeneous or heterogeneous? Explain your answer.

83. Examine the contents of the four containers shown below. Use complete sentences to identify each as containing only elements, only compounds or a mixture of these. Explain each of your answers.

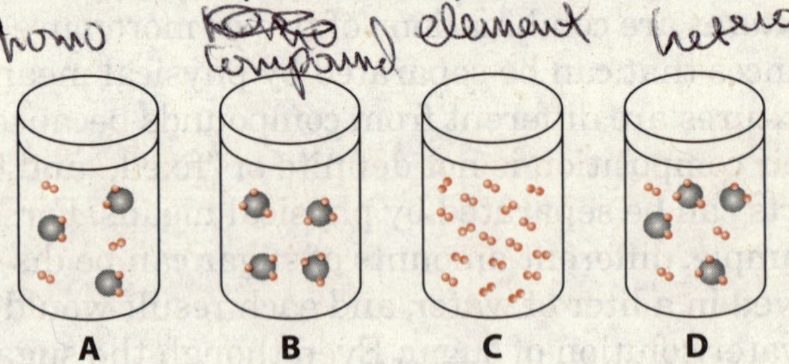

84. Are the contents of Container D in question 83 homogeneous or heterogeneous? Explain your answer.

85. A chemist receives two samples. Analysis of one sample shows it to be 88.88% oxygen by mass and 11.12% hydrogen. Analysis of the other sample shows it to be 94.12% oxygen and 5.88% hydrogen. Are these samples of the same material? Explain your answer.

Questions for Regents Practice

Part A

1. The model of the atom that pictured the atom with electrons traveling in circular orbits was called the

(1) planetary model (3) wave-mechanical model
(2) cannonball model (4) plum pudding model

2. If 14.0 g of substance X reacts completely with 16.0 g of substance Y to form the product XY, the mass of XY

(1) cannot be determined from this data
(2) will be 30.0 g
(3) will be less than 30.0 g
(4) will be more than 30.0 g

3. Compared to the entire atom, the nucleus of the atom is

(1) smaller and contains most of the atom's mass

(2) smaller and contains little of the atom's mass

(3) large and contains most of the atom's mass

(4) large and contains little of the atom's mass

4. In a famous experiment, positively charged particles were aimed at a thin sheet of gold foil. The results of this experiment were that

(1) most of the particles failed to pass through the foil

(2) most of the particles were repelled, showing that gold has a negative core

(3) a few of the particles were repelled, showing that the gold has a positive core

(4) a few of the particles were repelled, showing that the gold was neutral

5. Neutral atoms must contain equal numbers of

(1) protons and electrons

(2) protons and neutrons

(3) protons, neutrons, and electrons

(4) neutrons and electrons

6. Which of the following is true of a compound but not a mixture?

(1) A compound contains more than one element.

(2) All the nuclei in a compound contain the same number of protons.

(3) A compound may be heterogeneous.

(4) The composition of a compound does not vary.

7. Compared with an electron, a proton has

(1) more mass and the same charge

(2) more mass and an opposite charge

(3) equal mass and the same charge

(4) equal mass and an opposite charge

8. The total number of electrons in a neutral atom of any element is always equal to the atom's

(1) mass number

(2) number of neutrons

(3) number of protons

(4) number of nucleons

9. All isotopes of neutral atoms of sodium have

(1) 11 protons and 12 neutrons

(2) 12 protons and 11 neutrons

(3) 11 protons and 11 electrons

(4) 12 protons and 12 electrons

10. There are three isotopes of hydrogen, H-1, H-2, and H-3. All of these isotopes have

(1) a mass of 2 amu

(2) an atomic number of 1

(3) 1, 2, or 3 neutrons

(4) 1, 2, or 3 protons

11. An atom in the excited state contains

(1) more electrons than an atom in the ground state

(2) more protons than an atom in the ground state

(3) more potential energy than an atom in the ground state

(4) more mass than an atom in the ground state

12. As an electron moves from the excited state to the ground state, the potential energy of the electron

(1) decreases

(2) increases

(3) remains the same

(4) becomes zero

13. Which of the following particles has the smallest mass?

(1) neutron

(2) electron

(3) proton

(4) hydrogen atom

14. An element occurs as a mixture of isotopes. The atomic mass of the element is based upon

(1) the mass of the individual isotopes, only

(2) the relative abundances of the isotopes, only

(3) both the masses and the relative abundances of the individual isotopes

(4) neither the masses nor the relative abundances of the individual isotopes

Part B

15. 100. g of a clear liquid is evaporated and a few grams of white crystals remain. The original liquid was a

(1) heterogeneous compound

(2) heterogeneous mixture

(3) homogeneous compound

(4) homogeneous mixture

16. Two samples of bronze, a uniform material, are analyzed and found to contain different percentages of tin. Based on this information, bronze is likely a

(1) homogeneous compound

(2) heterogeneous compound

(3) homogeneous mixture

(4) heterogeneous mixture

17. Many companies around the world manufacture ammonia, NH_3. Which of the following is true?

(1) No matter where it is manufactured, it will have the same composition.

(2) Its composition will vary from place to place because different amounts of nitrogen and hydrogen are used.

(3) Some samples may contain more nitrogen than others.

(4) Some samples may contain more hydrogen than others.

18. There are three isotopes of oxygen: O-16, O-17, and O-18. These neutral atoms contain

(1) equal numbers of protons, neutrons, and electrons

(2) equal numbers of protons and neutrons, but different numbers of electrons

(3) equal numbers of protons and electrons, but different numbers of neutrons

(4) different numbers of protons, neutrons, and electrons

19. What is the charge on a particle that contains 9 protons, 10 neutrons, and 9 electrons?

(1) It is neutral.

(2) It has a net charge of 1+.

(3) It has a net charge of 1−.

(4) It has a net charge of 28+.

20. An element has two isotopes. 90% of the isotopes have a mass number of 20 amu, while 10% have a mass number of 22 amu. The atomic mass of the element

(1) cannot be determined without knowing the atomic number

(2) is 21 amu

(3) is closer to 20 amu than to 22 amu

(4) is closer to 22 amu than to 20 amu

21. If the atomic number of a neutral element is 35, and its nucleus contains 40 neutrons, which of the following is correct?

(1) The atom is bromine, and it has 35 electrons.

(2) The atom is bromine, and it has a mass number of 40.

(3) The atom is zirconium, and it has a mass number of 75.

(4) The atom is zirconium, and it has 40 electrons.

22. Examine the diagram of the atom. What element does it represent?

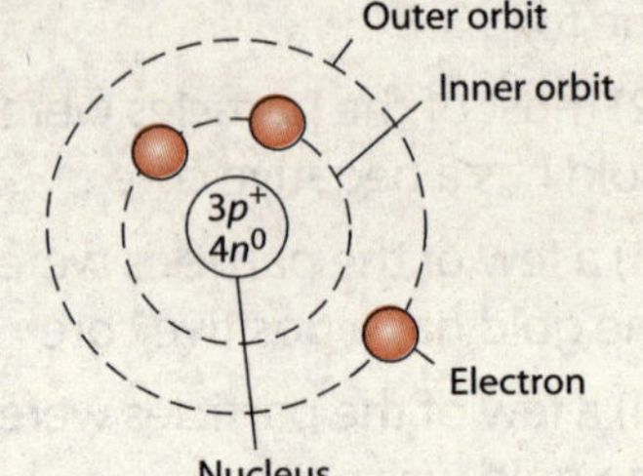

(1) hydrogen

(2) helium

(3) lithium

(4) carbon

23. An atom of Cl-35 contains

(1) 17 protons, 17 neutrons, and 18 electrons

(2) 17 protons, 18 neutrons, and 17 electrons

(3) 18 protons, 17 neutrons, and 17 electrons

(4) 18 protons, 18 neutrons, and 18 electrons

24. The electron structure of a neutral atom is $1s^22s^22p^53s^2$. This is an atom of

(1) sodium in the ground state

(2) sodium in the excited state

(3) magnesium in the ground state

(4) magnesium in the excited state

Part C

25. When electrons move from the fourth energy level to the second energy level, they emit visible light. Explain why the light emitted when an electron makes this move in a sodium atom is a different color than the light emitted by an electron moving from the fourth to the second level of a hydrogen atom. [2]

26. A chemist analyzes two samples. One sample contains 14 g of element X and 6.0 g of element Y. The second sample contains 28 g of element X and 6.0 g of element Y. Does it appear that the two samples are the same substance? Explain the reasons for your answer. [3]

27. Ernest Rutherford performed an experiment in which alpha particles (helium nuclei) were aimed at gold foil. When a few of the particles bounced back instead of passing through with little or no deflection, Rutherford is quoted as saying, "I was as surprised as if I had aimed a 14-inch artillery shell at a piece of paper and it bounced back." Why was he so surprised, and how did he modify the model of the atom to explain his results? [4]

28. Samples of two different compounds were heated in a flame, and a spectral analysis was performed on each compound. Many of the lines from the two samples matched, but others did not. Use your knowledge of chemistry to explain how this is possible. [2]

29. Complete the following: [6]

Composition of Some Neutral Atoms			
Symbol	H		U
Atomic number		19	
Mass number	3		238
Number of neutrons		20	
Number of electrons			

30. A moon sample was analyzed in a lab. The carbon in the sample was found to be 97.78% carbon-12 and 2.22% carbon-13. According to these data, what is the atomic mass of carbon? Show all of your work. [3]

Formulas and Equations

VOCABULARY		
analysis	**exothermic**	**quantitative**
chemical change	**formula**	**reactant**
coefficient	**molecular formula**	**single replacement**
decomposition	**molecule**	**subscript**
diatomic molecule	**physical change**	**symbol**
double replacement	**polyatomic ion**	**synthesis**
empirical formula	**product**	
endothermic	**qualitative**	

In this topic you will explore how chemical symbols are used to represent the names of elements. These symbols can then be combined to form the formulas of the millions of compounds that exist. Finally, you will learn how these formulas can be combined in chemical equations to show the qualitative and quantitative aspects of chemical reactions.

Chemical Symbols and Formulas

Language is the means by which people communicate with each other. Chemists have devised a universal language by which they can communicate chemical information and have the information understood by scientists around the world.

Chemical Symbols

While the names of the elements are often different in various languages of the world, it is important that a person in any country can quickly and accurately determine which element is being referred to. A system for a universal shorthand to identify the elements has been agreed upon. Each element has been assigned a unique one-, two-, or three-letter **symbol** for its identification. The first letter of a symbol is always capitalized. If there are any other letters in the symbol, they are lower case.

Some of the more common elements have a single letter symbol, such as O for oxygen and H for hydrogen. Other elements have symbols with two letters. Only recently discovered elements that don't yet have permanent names are given three-letter symbols. These elements are are given systematic names that represent their atomic number until a name can be agreed upon by the International Union of Pure and Applied Chemists (IUPAC).

Symbols are usually easy to remember, as the letters in the symbol often relate to the English name of the element, such as He for helium and Al for aluminum. Sometimes the letters of the symbol do not correspond to the common English element name but relate instead to the Latin or Greek name, such as K (Latin *kalium*) for potassium, and Na (Latin *natrium*) for sodium. Table 2-1 on the next page shows the names and symbols of elements with atomic numbers 1–20.

DIATOMIC MOLECULES When writing the symbols of uncombined elements, almost all are written as monatomic, that is, without a subscript. A **subscript** is a number to the right and slightly below a symbol that tells the number of atoms present. A subscript is not written if only one atom is present. Therefore, the symbol for iron is Fe, neon is Ne, and carbon is C.

There are, however, several important exceptions. Some elements exist in nature as two identical atoms covalently bonded into a **diatomic molecule.** Oxygen normally exists as O_2, a diatomic molecule. Other elements that exist as diatomic molecules are hydrogen (H_2), nitrogen (N_2), and the elements of Group 17 of the periodic table (F_2, Cl_2, Br_2, and I_2). Be sure that whenever you write the formulas for any of these uncombined elements, that you write them as diatomic molecules.

Table 2-1. Names and Symbols for the First 20 Elements

Atomic Number	Name	Symbol	Atomic Number	Name	Symbol
1	hydrogen	H	11	sodium	Na
2	helium	He	12	magnesium	Mg
3	lithium	Li	13	aluminum	Al
4	beryllium	Be	14	silicon	Si
5	boron	B	15	phosphorus	P
6	carbon	C	16	sulfur	S
7	nitrogen	N	17	chlorine	Cl
8	oxygen	O	18	argon	Ar
9	fluorine	F	19	potassium	K
10	neon	Ne	20	calcium	Ca

Chemical Formulas

Compounds are composed of combinations of elements chemically combined in definite proportions by weight (mass). **Formulas** use chemical symbols and numbers to show both qualitative and quantitative information about a substance. **Qualitative** information relates to things that cannot be counted or measured, such as what elements are in the compound. **Quantitative** information deals with things that can be either counted or measured, such as the number of atoms of each element present in a unit of the compound.

In a formula of a compound, the symbols for the elements supply the qualitative information. The formula CO tells the reader that the compound consists of carbon and oxygen. Notice the difference between CO and Co. The first is a combination of two elements in a compound, carbon monoxide, while the second is the symbol for an element, cobalt.

Recall that the numbers to the right and slightly below a symbol, called subscripts, supply quantitative information, telling us the number of atoms of those elements in a unit of the compound. For example, the symbols in the formula H_2SO_4 give us the qualitative information that the compound contains hydrogen, sulfur, and oxygen. The subscript 2 after the H indicates that there are two atoms of hydrogen present. No subscript is written after the S, so there is one sulfur atom. The 4 after O informs the reader that there are four atoms of oxygen present. Figure 2-1 shows the use of subscripts for the two compounds of carbon and oxygen. Table 2-2 shows some formulas for elements and compounds. Notice that the formula for a monatomic element is just its symbol.

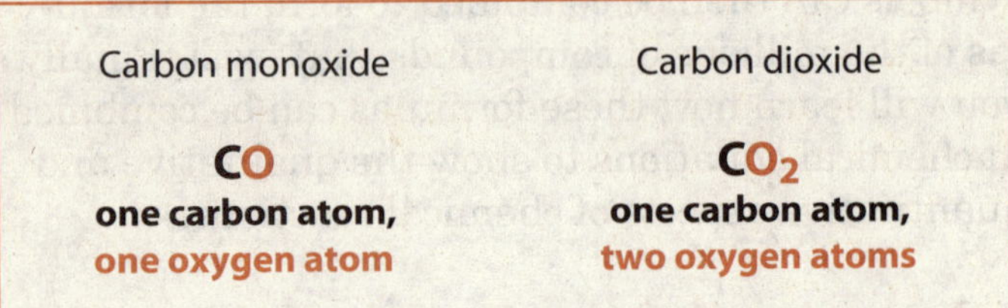

Figure 2-1. Subscripts in a formula: The use of subscripts shows the relative number of atoms of each type in a compound. No subscript is written if only one atom of an element is present.

TYPES OF FORMULAS Two basic types of formulas provide different types of information about a compound. Empirical formulas include all types of compounds. Molecular formulas are important when considering compounds formed from atoms sharing electrons.

EMPIRICAL FORMULAS An **empirical formula** represents the simplest integer ratio in which atoms combine to form a compound. Ionic substances do not form discrete units or molecules, but rather an array of ions (charged particles). Ionic formulas indicate the ratio of the ions in a compound. The formula $MgCl_2$ tells us that for every magnesium ion in the compound there are two chloride ions. Formulas of ionic substances are empirical formulas.

MOLECULAR FORMULAS Covalently bonded substances form discrete units called **molecules**. In some cases, such as H_2O, the empirical formula not

Table 2-2. Formulas for Some Elements and Compounds			
Name	**Formula**	**Name**	**Formula**
neon	Ne	calcium hydroxide	$Ca(OH)_2$
sulfuric acid	H_2SO_4	magnesium nitrate	$Mg(NO_3)_2$
glucose	$C_6H_{12}O_6$	sodium chloride	NaCl
uranium	U	gold	Au
chlorine	Cl_2	dihydrogen oxide	H_2O
ammonia	NH_3	hydrochloric acid	HCl
methane	CH_4	sodium hydroxide	NaOH
iron	Fe	benzene	C_6H_6
ammonium phosphate	$(NH_4)_3PO_4$	silver nitrate	$AgNO_3$

only represents the simplest ratio, but it also represents the actual ratio of the atoms in a molecule of water. In other cases, the **molecular formula** may be a multiple of the empirical formula. For example the molecular formula of glucose is $C_6H_{12}O_6$, which is six times the empirical formula CH_2O.

MEMORY JOGGER

A proton has a positive charge.
An electron has a negative charge.
A neutron does not have a charge.

Atoms, Compounds, and Ions

It's easy to interpret a formula for an element or a compound, but it's a bit more complicated to write the formula for a compound. How do you know what elements form the compound and in what proportion? To understand how elements form compounds, an understanding of atoms and ions is essential.

Atoms and compounds are electrically neutral; that is, they do not have a net charge. Both atoms and compounds contain positively charged protons and negatively charged electrons, but there are equal numbers of positive and negative charges, producing a neutral atom or compound.

Ions, however, are not neutral and may be either positively or negatively charged. An ion that contains more protons than electrons will be positively charged, while an ion with more electrons than protons will have a negative charge.

Positively charged ions attract negatively charged ions in a ratio that produces a neutral compound.

Ionic Charges

The charge of an ion is indicated by a superscript following the symbol of the ion. When the ion has a charge of either 1+ or 1−, the number *1* is omitted, and only the sign of the charge is shown. Thus the sodium ion with a charge of 1+ is written as Na^+, and chlorine with a charge of 1− is Cl^- The symbols of all other ions show both the size and sign of the charge. An aluminum ion is written as Al^{3+}, and an oxygen ion is shown as O^{2-}.

POLYATOMIC IONS A **polyatomic ion** is a group of atoms covalently bonded together, possessing a charge. Reference Table E in the *Reference Tables for Physical Setting/Chemistry* is a list of common polyatomic ions and their charges.

On Table 2-2 you will notice that three of the formulas contain symbols enclosed in parentheses. Parentheses are used to enclose polyatomic ions when there is more than one of the ions in a unit of a compound. The subscript written after the parentheses tells the reader how many of the ions are present in the compound. The subscript refers to each of the elements in the ion. For example, $(NH_4)_3PO_4$ tells the reader that there are three NH_4^+ ions, each containing one nitrogen atom and four hydrogen atoms, for a total of three nitrogen atoms and 12 hydrogen atoms. NH_4^+ is a polyatomic ion called the ammonium ion and has a charge of 1+. The second part of the formula, PO_4^{3-}, is the formula of one phosphate ion that contains one phosphorus atom and four oxygen atoms. Like the ammonium ion, it has a charge, but it is 3−. Figure 2-2 shows formulas, names, and models of some common polyatomic ions.

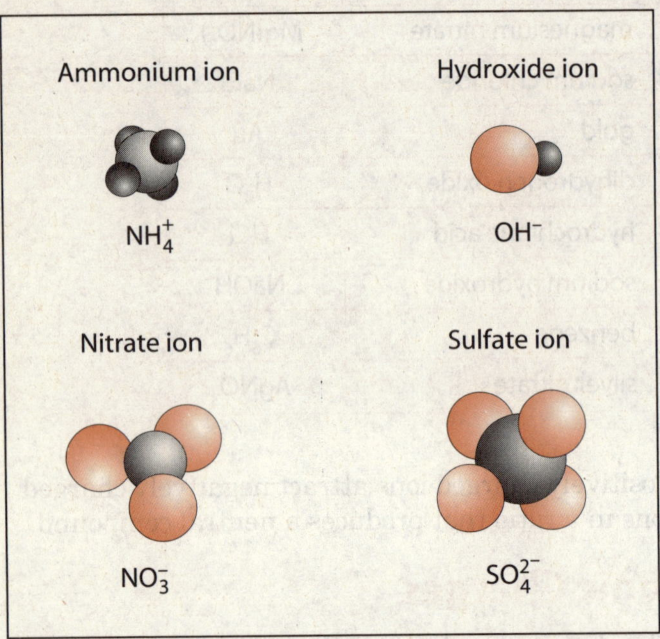

Figure 2-2. Names, formulas, and models of some polyatomic ions

FORMING A COMPOUND Compounds can form in several different ways. One way is by the attraction of oppositely charged ions. Monatomic or polyatomic ions attract each other in a ratio that produces a neutral compound. Many of the compounds listed in Table 2-2 are formed in this manner.

Coefficients

You know what information a subscript provides in a chemical formula. However, sometimes there is a number called a **coefficient** written in front of a formula. The coefficient tells how many units of the formula are present, and it applies to the entire formula. To determine the number of atoms present, consider the formula without the coefficient, and then multiply each value by the coefficient to find the total of each type of atom. For example, $2H_2O$ means that there are two molecules of water. These two molecules contain four hydrogen atoms and two oxygen atoms. The expression $4Mg(NO_3)_2$ contains four magnesium atoms, eight nitrogen atoms, and 24 oxygen atoms. As another example, consider the following, which refers to calcium nitrate ($Ca(NO_3)_2$).

Atoms in a Formula

$Ca(NO_3)_2$ contains:	1 calcium atom 2 nitrogen atoms 6 oxygen atoms
$3Ca(NO_3)_2$ contains:	3 calcium atoms 6 nitrogen atoms 18 oxygen atoms

Hydrates

When water from some ionic solutions evaporates, the solute forms a crystal lattice that binds water within the structure. Such a compound is called a hydrate. These crystals have a definite number of water molecules for each unit of the compound. Barium chloride ($BaCl_2$) traps two water molecules as shown by the formula of the hydrate, $BaCl_2 \cdot 2H_2O$. Copper sulfate ($CuSO_4$) has five water molecules and a formula of $CuSO_4 \cdot 5H_2O$. Alum ($NaAl(SO_4)_2$) has 12 water molecules attached, $NaAl(SO_4)_2 \cdot 12H_2O$. The anhydrous (not hydrated) compound can be obtained by heating the crystals to drive off the water.

In a chemical reaction, the water in a hydrate does not react. However, it adds mass to the compound. For example, 10.0 g of a truly dry crystal of copper(II) sulfate contains more $CuSO_4$ than 10.0 g of the hydrated crystal, which contains both $CuSO_4$ and H_2O. If a certain amount of a material is made from a hydrated crystal, the mass of water must be considered in determining how much of the compound must be used.

Review Questions

1. In a sample of solid $Ba(NO_3)_2$ the ratio of barium ions to nitrate ions is (1) 1:3:2 (2) 1:2 (3) 2:1 (4) 1:6

2. A chemical formula is an expression used to represent (1) mixtures only (2) elements only (3) compounds only (4) elements and compounds

3. Which formula represents a compound? (1) Ca (2) Cr (3) CO (4) Co

4. What is the total number of atoms in the formula $Ca(NO_3)_2$? (1) 7 (2) 2 (3) 3 (4) 9

5. What is the total number of sulfur atoms in the formula $(NH_4)_2SO_4$? (1) 1 (2) 2 (3) 3 (4) 4

6. What is the total number of hydrogen atoms in the formula $3Mg(C_2H_3O_2)_2$? (1) 3 (2) 6 (3) 12 (4) 18

7. An example of an empirical formula is (1) S_2H_2 (2) H_2O_2 (3) C_2Cl_2 (4) $CaCl_2$

8. Which is an empirical formula? (1) C_2H_2 (2) C_2H_4 (3) Al_2Cl_6 (4) K_2O

9. Which is an empirical formula? (1) C_2H_2 (2) H_2O (3) H_2O_2 (4) $C_6H_{12}O_6$

10. What is the empirical formula of a compound with the molecular formula $C_6H_{12}O_6$? (1) $C_4H_8O_4$ (2) $C_3H_6O_3$ (3) $C_2H_4O_2$ (4) CH_2O

11. Which compound has the same empirical and molecular formula? (1) H_2O_2 (2) NH_3 (3) C_2H_6 (4) Hg_2Cl_2

12. The empirical formula of a compound is CH_2. The molecular formula of this compound could be (1) CH_4 (2) C_2H_2 (3) C_2H_4 (4) C_3H_3

13. A hydrocarbon has the empirical formula CH_3. The most probable molecular formula for this compound is (1) CH_3 (2) C_2H_6 (3) C_3H_8 (4) C_4H_6

14. Which is an empirical formula? (1) CH (2) C_2H_2 (3) C_2H_4 (4) C_4H_8

15. Which is an empirical formula? (1) H_2O_2 (2) N_2O_4 (3) C_6H_6 (4) HCl

Answer each of the following using complete sentences.

16. What is the qualitative and quantitative information given by the formula $Ca_3(PO_4)_2$?

17. For each of the following formulas, write the name of each element and the number of atoms of that element that are in the formula. (a) K_3PO_4 (b) $Al(OH)_3$ (c) $Fe_2(SO_4)_3$

18. For each of the following formulas, write the name of each element and the number of atoms of that element that are in the formula. (a) $2K_3PO_4$ (b) $3Al(OH)_3$ (c) $5Fe_2(SO_4)_3$

19. What are the formulas and names of the polyatomic ions present in the compounds in question 18?

Writing Formulas and Naming Compounds

All compounds must be electrically neutral, that is, the sum of the charges must equal zero. Common oxidation states for each element are listed in the upper right hand corner of each element's box in the periodic table. For many elements, the oxidation state is equal to the charge on the ion. Elements from Group 1 have an oxidation number of +1 and always have a charge of 1+ in compounds. All Group 2 elements have 2+ charges in compounds. Group 3 elements usually have a 3+ charge.

Equalizing Charges

Compounds achieve neutrality by having an equal number of positive and negative charges. When a sodium ion (Na^+) and a chloride ion (Cl^-) combine, they will do so in a 1:1 ratio. The resulting formula will be NaCl, as such a ratio produces a neutral compound. Figure 2-3 shows the formulas of three compounds in which the charges of the ions are equal, but opposite.

Ion formulas:	$K^+ Cl^-$	$Mg^{2+} S^{2-}$	$Al^{3+} N^{3-}$
Compound formulas:	KCl	MgS	AlN

Figure 2-3. Examples of compounds with a 1:1 ion ratio: The three compounds shown are potassium chloride, magnesium sulfide, and aluminum nitride.

In the case of a combination of Mg^{2+} with Cl^-, a 1:1 ratio would not produce a neutral compound. To achieve neutrality there must be two Cl^- ions for each Mg^{2+}. The correct formula will be $MgCl_2$. When ions have unequal and opposite charges, a simple technique will produce the correct formula. Simply write the charge of one ion as the subscript of the other. Transfer the number only, not the sign. Notice that this procedure automatically balances the positive and negative charges, producing neutral formulas.

Polyatomic ions form compounds with oppositely charged ions in the same way as single ions. The formula for Na^+ combining with NO_3^- is simply $NaNO_3$. How would calcium (Ca^{2+}) combine with the nitrate ion (NO_3^-)? Because two nitrate ions are needed, enclose the nitrate ion in parentheses and write the subscript 2 after it, forming $Ca(NO_3)_2$.

Naming Compounds

Compounds are named according to the types of elements that form them. Ionic compounds, whether they are binary (contain only two elements) or contain polyatomic ions, are named by one method. Covalent compounds that contain only nonmetals are named by a different method.

BINARY IONIC COMPOUNDS The name of a binary ionic compound comes from the names of the elements in the compound. The positively charged particle, often a metallic ion, is placed first. The negatively charged ion will end the formula. A compound containing the sodium ion and the ion of chlorine will begin as *sodium*. The name of the negative ion is slightly changed from the element to end in *-ide*, making the negative ion of chlorine *chloride*. Hence, the compound containing the sodium and chloride ions is simply sodium chloride. Figure 2-4 summarizes naming binary compounds.

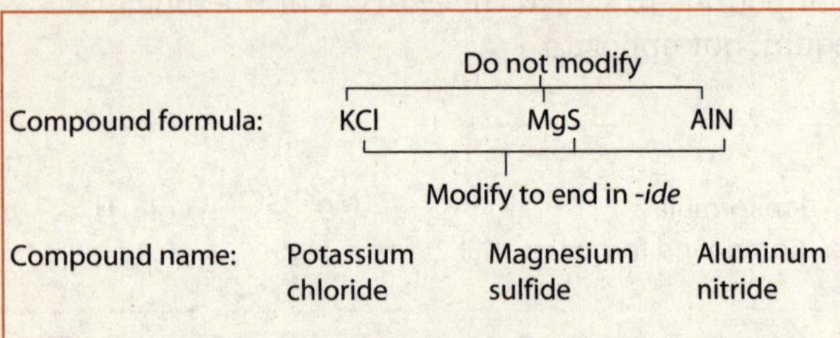

Figure 2-4. Naming binary compounds

OTHER IONIC COMPOUNDS Naming compounds containing polyatomic ions is simple. When the positive portion is a metal, use the unmodified metal name plus the name of the negative polyatomic ion. For example, the name of KNO_3 is potassium nitrate.

Most polyatomic ions are negatively charged. Ammonium (NH_4^+) is an important exception. In a compound containing the ammonium ion, if the negative ion is a nonmetal, the ending is *-ide*. If the ammonium ion is combined with another polyatomic ion, they each retain their names.

Examples:	NH_4Cl	ammonium chloride
	NH_4NO_3	ammonium nitrate

BINARY COVALENT COMPOUNDS If a binary compound contains two nonmetals rather than a metal and a nonmetal, it is a molecular substance not composed of ions. The order in which the elements are arranged in the formula can be determined by considering the electronegativity values of the elements (Table S in *Reference Tables for Physical Setting/Chemistry*). The element with the lower electronegativity value is written first. For example, consider a compound containing carbon and oxygen. Because carbon has an electronegativity value of 2.5 while oxygen has a value of 3.5, carbon is written first. As in other binary compounds, the name of the compound will end in *-ide*. Because these two elements often can form more than one compound, a prefix is used to tell the reader how many atoms of each element are present. CO is named carbon monoxide, while CO_2 is named carbon dioxide. If only one atom of the first element is present, the prefix *mono-* is not used. If the element name starts with a vowel, any final *a* or *o* in the prefix is not used. For example, NO is named nitrogen monoxide, while N_2O_4 is dinitrogen tetroxide. Table 2-3 shows common prefixes used to name these compounds.

Table 2-3. Common Prefixes

Number of Atoms	Prefix
1	mono-
2	di-
3	tri-
4	tetra-
5	penta-
6	hexa-
7	hepta-
8	octo-

THE STOCK SYSTEM Some metals have more than one common oxidation state. For example, iron can have an oxidation number of either +2 or +3, which leads to a potential difficulty in naming compounds of iron. Which oxidation number is implied in the name iron chloride, the +2 or +3? The stock system solves this problem by simply stating the oxidation number by using Roman numerals after the name of the metal. Iron(II) chloride tells the reader that the iron has an oxidation number of +2, and the formula is $FeCl_2$. In iron(III) chloride, the iron has an oxidation number of +3, and the formula is $FeCl_3$.

Review Questions

20. Pure nitrogen combines directly with an active metal to form a (1) nitrate (2) nitride (3) nitrite (4) permanganate

21. In a sample of solid $Al(NO_3)_3$, the ratio of aluminum ions to nitrate ions is (1) 1:1 (2) 1:2 (3) 1:3 (4) 1:6

22. In a sample of solid calcium phosphate ($Ca_3(PO_4)_2$), the ratio of calcium ions to phosphate ions is (1) 1:1 (2) 2:3 (3) 3:2 (4) 3:4

23. What is the total number of atoms in $(NH_4)_2SO_4$?
(1) 10 (2) 11 (3) 14 (4) 15

24. What is the total number of oxygen atoms present in one unit of $Mg(ClO_3)_2$? (1) 5 (2) 2 (3) 3 (4) 6

25. What is the total number of atoms of oxygen in the formula $Al(ClO_3)_3 \cdot 6H_2O$? (1) 6 (2) 9 (3) 10 (4) 15

26. Write the correct formulas for the following binary ionic compounds. (a) lithium fluoride (b) calcium oxide (c) aluminum nitride (d) sodium sulfide (e) magnesium bromide (f) beryllium chloride (g) potassium iodide (h) aluminum oxide (i) calcium fluoride (j) lithium oxide

27. Write the correct formulas for the following binary molecular compounds. (a) carbon monoxide (b) dinitrogen monoxide (c) phosphorus trichloride (d) boron tribromide (e) sulfur hexafluoride (f) carbon dioxide (g) carbon tetrabromide (h) nitrogen dioxide (i) sulfur dioxide (j) dichlorine monoxide

28. Write the correct formulas for the following compounds that contain polyatomic ions. (a) sodium hydroxide (b) potassium nitrate (c) potassium phosphate (d) magnesium sulfate (e) magnesium hydroxide (f) aluminum phosphate (g) aluminum nitrate (h) ammonium nitrate (i) ammonium sulfite (j) sodium carbonate

29. Name each of the following binary ionic compounds. (a) NaBr (b) MgS (c) CaO (d) AlP (e) KCl (f) $MgCl_2$ (g) AlF_3 (h) CaI_2 (i) Li_2S (j) BeO

30. Name each of the following binary molecular compounds. (a) O_2F_2 (b) SiF_4 (c) S_4N_4 (d) CF_4 (e) N_2Cl_2 (f) SF_2 (g) H_2S (h) P_4O_{10} (i) SO_3 (j) Cl_2O_7

31. Name each of the following compounds. (a) $Ca(NO_3)_2$ (b) KOH (c) $MgCO_3$ (d) $Al_2(SO_4)_3$ (e) NH_4Cl (f) Na_3PO_4 (g) $LiNO_3$ (h) $K_2Cr_2O_7$ (i) $Mg(C_2H_3O_2)_2$ (j) $(NH_4)_2SO_3$

32. Write formulas for each of the following compounds. (a) iron(II) oxide (b) tin(II) sulfide (c) copper(I) chloride (d) mercury(II) iodide (e) lead(II) nitrate (f) iron(III) oxide (g) tin(IV) oxide (h) copper(II) nitrite (i) lead(IV) oxide (j) gold(I) oxide

33. Write the names of each of the following using stock nomenclature. (a) CuCl (b) FeS (c) HgI_2 (d) $Pb(NO_3)_2$ (e) $Sn(OH)_2$ (f) $Cu(NO_3)_2$ (g) Fe_2O_3 (h) PbI_4 (i) SnO_2 (j) $FeCO_3$

34. How many metallic elements are present in the formula $NaKSO_4$?

35. When sulfur and oxygen combine to form a compound, which element should be written first? What values are considered in making this choice?

36. A student named $KClO_3$ potassium chlorine(V) oxide. Explain to her why the use of the stock system is not correct in this case, and write the correct name of the substance.

37. Vanadium has several oxidation states. Write correct formulas for vanadium(III) oxide and vanadium(V) oxide.

38. What incorrect information is given by the formula $MgOH_2$, instead of the correct formula, $Mg(OH)_2$?

Chemical Reactions and Equations

The world around us is constantly changing. Some of these changes result from substances undergoing phase changes, such as ice melting or water boiling. In these cases, the **physical changes** that have taken place have not resulted in the formation of a new substance, but rather only a change in appearance of the starting material.

Other changes are more dramatic. When a substance is burned, whether it is a piece of paper or gasoline, the substances produced are quite different from the starting materials. These changes in which the identity of the products differs from the identity of the reactants are called **chemical changes.** In this section you will learn how to use chemical symbols to form equations that represent these chemical changes. A well-defined chemical change is called a chemical reaction.

Chemical Equations

A chemical equation shows what takes place during a chemical reaction. It is similar to an algebraic equation in that what is written on one side of the equation equals what is written on the other side. An arrow is used instead of an equal sign to separate the sides of the equation. The arrow is read *produces* or *yields.*

A substance that enters into a reaction is called a **reactant** and is written to the left of the arrow. A substance that is produced by a reaction is called a **product** and is written to the right of the arrow.

The word equation for the burning of carbon is

$$\text{carbon} + \text{oxygen} \rightarrow \text{carbon dioxide}$$

The same reaction using formulas would be:

$$C(s) + O_2(g) \rightarrow CO_2(g)$$

Carbon and oxygen are reactants, and carbon dioxide is a product. Plus signs separate reactants and products. Notice that in the equation, the atoms of the reactants and products are the same, but the manner in which they are combined is different. Figure 2-5 shows how using models of the reactants and products can be used in an equation.

Endothermic and Exothermic Processes

Chemical and physical changes involve the loss or gain of energy, most often expressed as heat. It takes heat to cook an egg. Heat is released when fuel is burned. Photosynthesis requires the energy of the sun in order to occur. When sodium hydroxide dissolves in water, the water warms up. Based on whether energy is absorbed or released, you can classify these energy changes into two major groups. Because of this classification, energy is often included as either a reactant or a product in an equation.

ENDOTHERMIC PROCESSES Processes that require energy in order to occur are called **endothermic** processes. The physical change of ice melting is endothermic. Chemical changes that occur as food cooks are endothermic. The energy required is absorbed from the surroundings, thus lowering the surrounding temperature. In endothermic processes, the reactants absorb energy as they become products. Hence, the products have more potential energy than the reactants.

$$H_2O(s) + \text{energy} \rightarrow H_2O(\ell)$$

$$6CO_2 + 6H_2O + \text{energy} \rightarrow C_6H_{12}O_6 + 6O_2$$

EXOTHERMIC PROCESSES Processes that release thermal energy when they occur are **exothermic.** The burning of carbon in oxygen is an example of an exothermic reaction. Freezing of water is exothermic. The energy released from these processes is given off to the surroundings, thus raising the surrounding temperature. In exothermic reactions, the products have less potential energy than the reactants.

$$CH_4(g) + 3O_2(g) \rightarrow CO_2(g) + 2H_2O(g) + \text{energy}$$

$$C_6H_{12}O_6(s) + 6O_2(g) \rightarrow 6CO_2(g) + 6H_2O(\ell) + \text{energy}$$

Balancing Chemical Equations

You can see by examining a correctly written chemical equation that the number of each type of atom is the same on both sides of the equation. This observation confirms the law of conservation of mass, which states that matter is neither created nor destroyed in chemical reactions. In any chemical reaction, the numbers and kinds of atoms must remain unchanged in the reaction.

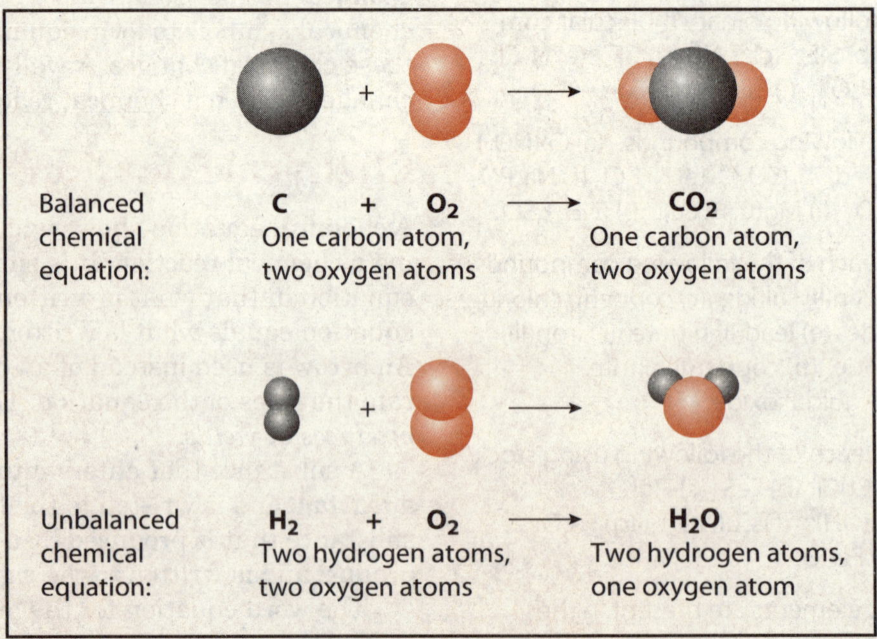

Figure 2-5. A balanced and an unbalanced equation

Look at Figure 2-5. In the first equation there is conservation of atoms. There is one carbon atom shown on both the reactant and product side and two atoms of oxygen on either side. This equation agrees with the law of conservation of mass and is called a balanced equation.

The second equation is different. While there are two atoms of hydrogen on both sides of the arrow, there are two atoms of oxygen on the reactant side but only one atom of oxygen on the product side. This equation is not balanced. As it is written, one atom of oxygen has been lost, or not conserved.

The equation must be changed so that it is balanced. How is this done? Remember that subscripts show the ratio of different types of atoms, and subscripts cannot be changed in a correctly written formula. The formula of oxygen gas is O_2 and cannot be changed. The only way to balance an equation, once correct formulas have been written, is to change the coefficients in the equation. Remember that coefficients are the numbers written before a formula.

You may want to think of balancing an equation as being similar to balancing a seesaw. In the second example the unbalanced equation is heavy with oxygen atoms on the reactant side. Because none of the reactant oxygen atoms can be removed, the only way to correct the imbalance is to add more oxygen atoms to the product side. This is done by placing a coefficient of 2 in front of the formula of water.

$$H_2(g) + O_2(g) \rightarrow \mathbf{2}H_2O(g)$$

The coefficient applies to both the hydrogen and oxygen in water. The equation is now balanced in terms of oxygen atoms, as there are two on both sides. The hydrogen atoms are now unbalanced because there are four hydrogen atoms on the product side but only two on the reactant side. This can be remedied by placing a 2 in front of the formula of hydrogen.

$$\mathbf{2}H_2(g) + O_2(g) \rightarrow 2H_2O(g)$$

Inspection of the equation shows that there now is a conservation of atoms. Four atoms of hydrogen and two atoms of oxygen are now on both sides of the equation. The equation is now balanced.

If you examine equations that involve polyatomic ions, you will notice that sometimes the ions are the same in the reactants and products, and sometimes they are not. If polyatomic ions remain the same, they can be balanced as a unit. For example, in the following unbalanced equation, the nitrate ion can be balanced as a unit because it stays a nitrate ion on the product side of the equation.

$$AgNO_3 + MgCl_2 \rightarrow Mg(NO_3)_2 + AgCl$$

However, in the following unbalanced equation, the phosphite (PO_3^{3-}) and nitrate ions are changed during the reaction. They do not appear unchanged on the product side of the equation. In such a case, each type of atom must be balanced separately, and the polyatomic ions cannot be balanced as a unit.

$$HNO_3 + H_3PO_3 \rightarrow NO + H_3PO_4 + H_2O$$

You may have noticed that some symbols have appeared in parentheses after the formulas. It is often important to indicate the physical state of the substances in an equation. The symbol (*s*) is used to show that the substance is a solid, (*ℓ*) indicates that it is a liquid, and (*g*) shows the substance to be a gas. In addition, (*aq*) means that the material is dissolved in water; that is, it is in an aqueous solution. Table 2-4 summarizes some common symbols used in equations.

Table 2-4. Common Notation Used in Equations

Symbol	Meaning
+	Separates two reactants or two products
→	Separates reactants from products; read as *yields* or *produces*
(*s*)	Identifies the substance as a solid
(*ℓ*)	Identifies the substance as a liquid
(*g*)	Identifies the substance as a gas
(*aq*)	Identifies the substance as being dissolved in aqueous (water) solution

Review Questions

39. Consider the following unbalanced equation.

$$C_3H_8(g) + O_2(g) \rightarrow H_2O(g) + CO_2(g)$$

When the equation is completely balanced using smallest whole numbers, the coefficient of O_2 is
(1) 5 (2) 2 (3) 3 (4) 7

40. When the equation $Al(s) + O_2(g) \rightarrow Al_2O_3(s)$ is correctly balanced using smallest whole numbers, the sum of the coefficients will be (1) 9 (2) 7 (3) 3 (4) 12

41. Consider the following unbalanced equation.

$$Ca(OH)_2 + (NH_4)_2SO_4 \rightarrow CaSO_4 + NH_3 + H_2O$$

What is the sum of the coefficients when the equation is completely balanced using the smallest whole-number coefficients? (1) 5 (2) 7 (3) 9 (4) 11

42. When the equation $Al_2(SO_4)_3 + ZnCl_2 \rightarrow AlCl_3 + ZnSO_4$ is correctly balanced using smallest whole numbers, the sum of the coefficients is (1) 9 (2) 8 (3) 5 (4) 4

43. Consider the following unbalanced equation.

$$C_8H_{16}(g) + O_2(g) \rightarrow H_2O(g) + CO_2(g)$$

When the equation is completely balanced using smallest whole numbers, the coefficient of CO_2 is (1) 1 (2) 8 (3) 12 (4) 16

44. Consider the following unbalanced equation.

$$FeCl_2 + Na_2CO_3 \rightarrow FeCO_3 + NaCl$$

When the equation is completely balanced using smallest whole numbers, the coefficient of NaCl is (1) 6 (2) 2 (3) 3 (4) 4

45. Consider the following unbalanced equation.

$$Ag + H_2S \rightarrow Ag_2S + H_2$$

What is the sum of the coefficients when the equation is completely balanced using the smallest whole-number coefficients? (1) 5 (2) 8 (3) 10 (4) 4

46. Consider the following unbalanced equation.

$$Li + N_2 \rightarrow Li_3N$$

When the equation is completely balanced using smallest whole numbers, the coefficient of lithium is (1) 1 (2) 2 (3) 3 (4) 6

47. Consider the following unbalanced equation.

$$N_2(g) + O_2(g) \rightarrow N_2O_5(g)$$

When the equation is completely balanced using smallest whole numbers, the coefficient of $N_2(g)$ is (1) 1 (2) 2 (3) 5 (4) 4

Types of Reactions

While it would be difficult, if not impossible, to put all chemical reactions into distinct categories, there are four major types of reactions that you should know. It is important to be able to recognize these types and write equations to represent them.

SYNTHESIS (COMBINATION) REACTIONS

When two or more reactants combine to form a single product, the reaction is a **synthesis,** or combination, reaction. The combination of hydrogen and oxygen to form water that was shown earlier is an example.

$$2H_2(g) + O_2(g) \rightarrow 2H_2O(g)$$

Many synthesis reactions are commonplace, such as the rusting of iron.

$$4Fe(s) + 3O_2(g) \rightarrow 2Fe_2O_3(s)$$

Synthesis reactions not only take place between elements, but they may also involve compounds.

$$CO_2(g) + H_2O(\ell) \rightarrow H_2CO_3(aq)$$

It is convenient to write this type of equation in a general form such as

$$A + B \rightarrow AB$$

A and B represent either elements or compounds, and AB represents a compound that is made of A and B. See Figure 2-6.

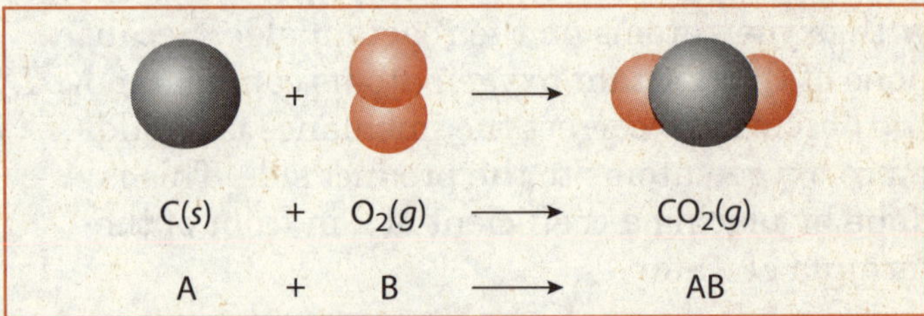

Figure 2-6. Equation of a synthesis reaction: In this example, two elements combine to form a compound.

DECOMPOSITION (ANALYSIS) REACTIONS A **decomposition,** or **analysis,** reaction is the reverse of a synthesis reaction in that a single compound is broken down (decomposed) into two or more simpler substances. All decomposition reactions begin with a single reactant.

$$H_2O(\ell) \rightarrow H_2(g) + O_2(g)$$

Although many decomposition reactions produce elements as the products, Figure 2-7 shows the breaking down of one compound into two compounds.

$$CaCO_3(s) \rightarrow CaO(s) + CO_2(g)$$

The general form of this reaction is the exact opposite of the equation for a synthesis reaction.

$$AB \rightarrow A + B$$

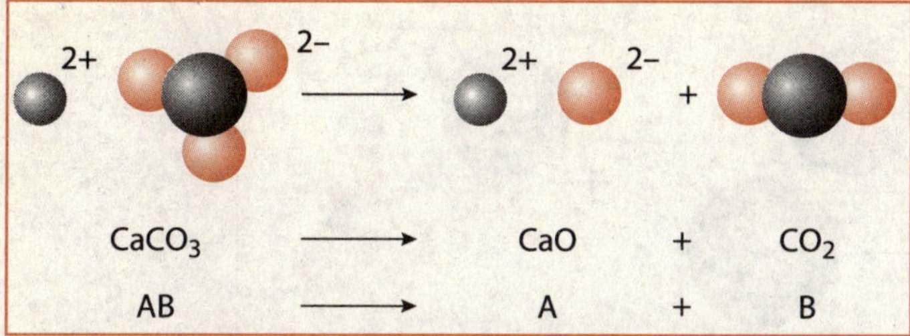

Figure 2-7. Equation of a decomposition reaction: The models for $CaCO_3$ and CaO show that the compounds are ionic and do not form molecules. They are compounds that exist as ions.

SINGLE REPLACEMENT REACTIONS When a piece of copper wire is placed into a solution of silver nitrate, a chemical reaction takes place. In a short period of time shiny crystals form on the copper wire, and the solution gradually becomes blue. Analysis of the crystals shows them to be silver metal. The blue color is caused by copper ions in solution. In this reaction the copper metal has replaced silver ions in silver nitrate, producing silver metal and copper ions.

$$Cu(s) + 2AgNO_3(aq) \rightarrow Cu(NO_3)_2(aq) + 2Ag(s)$$

This type of reaction where one element replaces another element in a compound is called a **single replacement** reaction (Figure 2-8). This type of reaction always involves an element and a compound. The general formula for this type of reaction where a metal replaces another metal in a compound is

$$A + BX \rightarrow B + AX$$

Will the reverse reaction take place, that is, will silver metal react with copper nitrate to produce copper and silver nitrate? If silver is placed into copper nitrate solution, no copper is formed. How can we predict whether or not a reaction will take place? Table J, Activity Series, of *Reference Tables for Physical Setting/Chemistry* will provide the information. The table is arranged so that a metal listed on the table will react with the compound of a metal that is below it. For example, Zn is above Cu on the table. Therefore, Zn will react with a compound of copper such as $Cu(NO_3)_2$.

$$Zn + Cu(NO_3)_2 \rightarrow Cu + Zn(NO_3)_2$$

Because Cu is below Zn, it will not react with compounds of Zn.

$$Cu + Zn(NO_3)_2 \rightarrow \text{no reaction.}$$

It is worth noting that there is one element that is not a metal in the left column of Table J, H_2. The hydrogen referred to is really the hydrogen ion in an acid (H^+). All metals above hydrogen will react with acids to release hydrogen gas and produce a salt. For example,

$$Mg + 2HCl \rightarrow H_2 + MgCl_2$$

Silver (Ag) is below hydrogen on the table, so it will not react with acids.

In the second column of Table J is a short list of nonmetals. A nonmetal will replace a less active nonmetal in a compound according to the equation

$$A + XB \rightarrow B + XA$$

Fluorine is listed as the most active nonmetal, and it will replace chlorine, bromine, and iodine from their binary compounds.

$$F_2 + 2NaCl \rightarrow Cl_2 + 2NaF$$

Because chlorine is below fluorine on the list, it will not replace fluorine in a compound.

$$Cl_2 + NaF \rightarrow \text{no reaction}$$

When given a possible reaction between an element and an ionic compound, consult Table J to determine whether or not a reaction will occur.

DOUBLE REPLACEMENT REACTIONS **Double replacement** reactions generally involve two soluble ionic compounds that react in solution to produce a precipitate, a gas, or a molecular compound such as water. Figure 2-9 on the next page shows

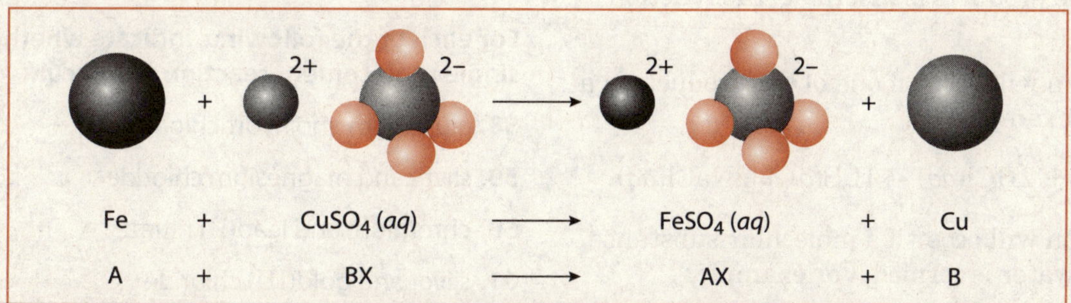

Figure 2-8. Equation of a single replacement reaction: The copper and iron ions are part of the compounds that are in solution, but the iron and copper atoms are solid metals.

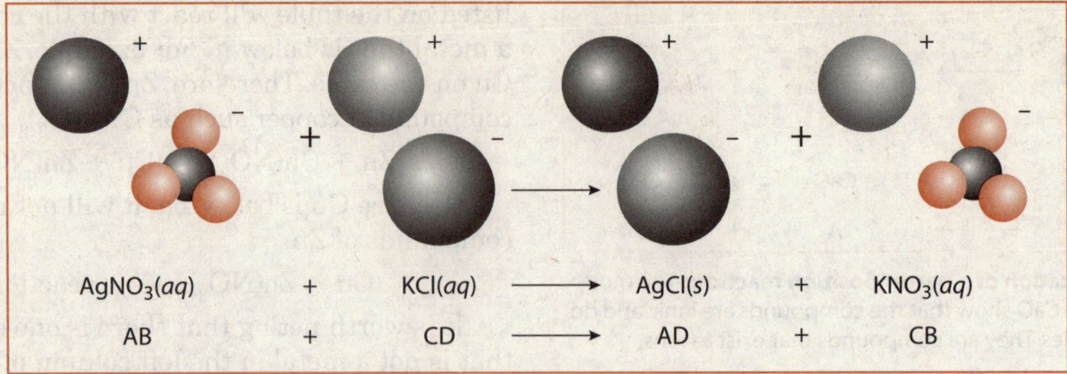

Figure 2-9. An equation for a double replacement reaction: Although all the compounds are ionic, AgCl is an ionic compound that is not soluble in water. Crystals of AgCl form a precipitate.

that when aqueous solutions of silver nitrate and sodium chloride are mixed, a white precipitate of silver chloride is produced according to the following equation.

$$AgNO_3(aq) + NaCl(aq) \rightarrow AgCl(s) + NaNO_3(aq)$$

Double replacement equations can be represented by the general equation

$$AB + CD \rightarrow AD + BC$$

Just as not all combinations of single replacement reactants will produce a reaction, so too with double replacement reactions.

How can you determine if two ionic compounds will react? There are three situations that might cause a double replacement to occur.

1. A reaction will occur if one of the products is a solid (precipitate). Consult Table F, Solubility Guidelines, *Reference Tables for Physical Setting/Chemistry*. Check the solubility of the two ionic products. For example, in

$$AgNO_3(aq) + NaCl(aq) \rightarrow AgCl(s) + NaNO_3(aq)$$

silver chloride is listed as insoluble, and sodium nitrate is listed as soluble. Because one of the products is insoluble, the reaction will occur.

2. A reaction will occur if one of the products is a gas. For example,

$$Na_2S(aq) + 2HCl(aq) \rightarrow H_2S(g) + 2NaCl(aq)$$

3. A reaction will occur if a molecular substance such as water is formed. For example,

$$NaOH(aq) + HCl(aq) \rightarrow H_2O(\ell) + NaCl(aq)$$

Review Questions

Write and balance equations for the following synthesis reactions.

48. hydrogen and bromine forming hydrogen bromide

49. fluorine and argon forming argon trifluoride

50. sulfur and oxygen forming sulfur dioxide

51. calcium and chlorine forming calcium chloride

52. nickel and oxygen forming nickel(II) oxide

Write and balance equations for the following decomposition reactions.

53. decomposition of water into hydrogen and oxygen

54. decomposition of aluminum oxide into aluminum and oxygen

55. decomposition of sodium chloride into sodium and chlorine

56. decomposition of ammonia into hydrogen and nitrogen

57. decomposition of mercury(II) oxide into mercury and oxygen

For each of the following, indicate whether or not a single replacement reaction will occur.

58. aluminum and hydrochloric acid

59. silver and magnesium chloride

60. chromium and lead(II) nitrate

61. silver and gold(III) chloride

62. chlorine and sodium iodide

For the following, write a balanced chemical equation to show how the ions would combine in a double replacement equation.

63. sodium bromide and silver nitrate form sodium nitrate and silver bromide

64. potassium carbonate and calcium nitrate form potassium nitrate and calcium carbonate

65. ammonium sulfate and barium chloride form ammonium chloride and barium sulfate

66. barium nitrate and potassium chromate form barium chromate and potassium nitrate

67. sodium hydroxide and calcium chloride form sodium chloride and calcium hydroxide

68. Identify each of the following as unbalanced equations for a synthesis (*S*), decomposition (*D*), single replacement (*SR*), or double replacement (*DR*) reactions.

(a) $Zn + HCl \rightarrow ZnCl_2 + H_2$
(b) $NaClO_3 \rightarrow NaCl + O_2$
(c) $P_4 + Cl_2 \rightarrow PCl_3$
(d) $HCl + Mg(OH)_2 \rightarrow MgCl_2 + H_2O$
(e) $BaO + SO_3 \rightarrow BaSO_4$
(f) $Pb + AgNO_3 \rightarrow Ag + Pb(NO_3)_2$
(g) $AgNO_3 + Na_2CrO_4 \rightarrow Ag_2CrO_4 + NaNO_3$
(h) $Al + Fe_3O_4 \rightarrow Al_2O_3 + Fe$
(i) $NO_2 \rightarrow 2NO + O_2$
(j) $NaN_3 \rightarrow Na + N_2$
(k) $Pb(NO_3)_2 + KI \rightarrow KNO_3 + PbI_2$
(l) $CaO + CO_2 \rightarrow CaCO_3$
(m) $MgCO_3 \rightarrow MgO + CO_2$
(n) $Na + Cl_2 \rightarrow NaCl$
(o) $HNO_3 + Mg(OH)_2 \rightarrow Mg(NO_3)_2 + H_2O$
(p) $Ca + H_2O \rightarrow Ca(OH)_2 + H_2$
(q) $Fe + O_2 \rightarrow Fe_3O_4$
(r) $Cl_2 + KI \rightarrow KCl + I_2$
(s) $Ba(NO_3)_2 + Na_2SO_4 \rightarrow BaSO_4 + NaNO_3$
(t) $Ag_2O \rightarrow Ag + O_2$

Unknown Reactants and Products

The law of conservation of mass requires that chemical reactions neither create nor destroy matter. When given a balanced equation in which either a reactant or a product is missing, you should be able to determine the formula of the missing substance. To do so, count the atoms in the formulas on both sides of the arrow. Subtract the atoms on the side with the missing formula from the side with the known substances. Any missing element must be present in the unknown.

As an example, look at the following equation.

$$2Na + 2H_2O \rightarrow X + 2NaOH$$

The reactant side is complete and contains two sodium atoms, four hydrogen atoms, and two oxygen atoms. One product is missing from the right side of the equation. There are two hydrogen atoms, two oxygen atoms, and two sodium atoms present in the other product. For the equation to balance, the missing substance must contain only two hydrogen atoms. What is the formula of a substance that contains two hydrogen atoms? H_2, hydrogen gas.

Determining Missing Mass in Equations

Just as the formula of a missing reactant or product can be determined, the mass of a missing substance can also be found. The law of conservation of mass again is the guiding principle. Matter can be neither created nor destroyed in a chemical reaction. The total mass of the reactants must equal the total mass of the products.

SAMPLE PROBLEM

If 103.0 g of potassium chlorate are decomposed to form 62.7 g of potassium chloride and oxygen gas according to the equation $2KClO_3 \rightarrow 2KCl + 3O_2$, how many grams of oxygen are formed?

Solution: Identify the known and unknown values.

Known	*Unknown*
mass of $KClO_3$ = 103.0 g	mass of O_2 = ? g
mass of KCl = 62.7 g	

Find the total mass of the reactants.

$KClO_3$ is the only reactant; it has a mass of 103.0 g.

The total mass of the reactants and products must be equal.

$$\text{mass of } KClO_3 = \text{mass of } KCl + \text{mass of } O_2$$
$$103.0\text{ g} = 62.7\text{ g} + \text{mass of } O_2$$
$$\text{mass of } O_2 = 103.0\text{ g} - 62.7\text{ g}$$
$$\text{mass of } O_2 = 40.3\text{ g}$$

Review Questions

69. Identify the missing reactant or product in each of the following equations. Include any coefficient needed to balance the equation.
(a) $2NaHCO_3 \rightarrow Na_2CO_3 + H_2O +$ ____
(b) $BaCl_2 + K_2CO_3 \rightarrow$ ____ $+ BaCO_3$
(c) $2C_6H_6 +$ ____ $\rightarrow 12CO_2 + 6H_2O$
(d) $CaCO_3 \rightarrow CaO +$ ____

70. Identify the missing reactant or product in each of the following equations. Include any coefficient needed to balance the equation.
(a) $2Al +$ ____ $\rightarrow 2AlCl_3 + 3H_2$
(b) ____ $+ H_2O \rightarrow H_2CO_3$
(c) $2NaOH +$ ____ $\rightarrow NaOCl + NaCl + H_2O$
(d) $Cr_2O_3 + 2Al \rightarrow$ ____ $+ 2Cr$

71. Identify the missing reactant or product in each of the following equations. Include any coefficient needed to balance the equation.
(a) $2HNO_3 +$ ____ $\rightarrow Mg(NO_3)_2 + 2H_2O$
(b) $2NH_4NO_3 \rightarrow$ ____ $+ 4H_2O + O_2$
(c) $H_2SO_4 + 2NaOH \rightarrow Na_2SO_4 +$ ____
(d) $3PbO +$ ____ $\rightarrow 3Pb + N_2 + 3H_2O$

72. Identify the missing reactant or product in each of the following equations. Include any coefficient needed to balance the equation.
(a) $3Cu + 8\,HNO_3 \rightarrow 3Cu(NO_3)_2 + 4H_2O +$ ____
(b) $C_6H_{11}OH \rightarrow C_6H_{10} +$ ____
(c) $4NH_3 + 5O_2 \rightarrow$ ____ $+ 6H_2O$
(d) $Ca(OH)_2 +$ ____ $\rightarrow CaCl_2 + H_2O$

73. Identify the missing reactant or product in each of the following equations. Include any coefficient needed to balance the equation.
(a) $2AgNO_3 +$ ____ $\rightarrow Ag_2S + 2NaNO_3$
(b) $H_2C_2O_4 + 2NaOH \rightarrow$ ____ $+ 2H_2O$
(c) $CCl_4 + 2HF \rightarrow CCl_2F_2 +$ ____
(d) ____ $+ CO_2 \rightarrow K_2CO_3$

74. What mass of carbon dioxide will be produced if 144 g of carbon react with 384 g of oxygen gas according to the equation $C + O_2 \rightarrow CO_2$?

75. How many grams of HCl are produced when 16.0 g of CH_4 react with 71.0 g of Cl_2 to produce 50.5 g of CH_3Cl and HCl according to the equation $CH_4 + Cl_2 \rightarrow CH_3Cl + HCl$?

76. Consider the following equation.

$$3C_2H_4O_2 + PCl_3 \rightarrow 3C_2H_3OCl + H_3PO_3$$

How many grams of products will be produced if 90 g of $C_2H_4O_2$ completely react with 68 g of PCl_3?

77. How many grams of silver nitrate are needed to react with 156.2 g of sodium sulfide to produce 595.8 g of silver sulfide and 340.0 g of sodium nitrate?

$$2AgNO_3 + Na_2S \rightarrow Ag_2S + 2NaNO_3$$

78. Given the equation $PbO_2 \rightarrow PbO + O_2$, how many grams of oxygen will be produced if 47.8 g of lead(IV) oxide decompose to form 44.6 g of lead(II) oxide and oxygen gas?

79. Consider the following equation.

$$2Al + 3CuSO_4 \rightarrow Al_2(SO_4)_3 + 3Cu$$

Copper metal is produced when aluminum metal is reacted with copper(II) sulfate. How many grams of copper metal will be produced if 10.8 g of aluminum react with 95.8 g of copper sulfate to produce copper metal and 68.5 g of aluminum sulfate?

80. How many grams of Fe are needed to react with 8.0 g of O_2 to produce 28.9 g of Fe_3O_4 according to the equation $3Fe + 2O_2 \rightarrow Fe_3O_4$?

81. How many metric tons of nitric acid are produced from the reaction of 10.8 metric tons of N_2O_5 reacting with 1.8 metric tons of water according to the equation $N_2O_5 + H_2O \rightarrow 2HNO_3$?

82. How many pounds of sulfur will be produced from the decomposition of 318.2 pounds of copper(I) sulfide to produce 254.0 pounds of copper metal and sulfur according to the equation $Cu_2S \rightarrow 2Cu + S$?

83. Given the equation $2HgO \rightarrow 2Hg + O_2$, how many grams of mercury(II) oxide are needed to produce 12.7 g of mercury and 3.2 g of oxygen?

Questions for Regents Practice

1. A chemical formula is an expression used to represent
(1) mixtures only
(2) elements only
(3) compounds only
(4) compounds and elements

2. Two molecules of hydrogen are represented by
(1) H_2
(2) $2H_2$
(3) $2H^+$
(4) 2H

3. Which of the following is a polyatomic ion?
(1) CH_3COOH
(2) $Cr_2O_7^{2-}$
(3) Na^+
(4) H_2

4. Pure oxygen reacts with metals to form
(1) oxalates (3) oxides
(2) oxalites (4) oxygenates

5. Which of the following is the formula of a compound?
(1) Fr (3) LiH
(2) Mn (4) O_3

6. A chemical formula represents
(1) qualitative information only
(2) quantitative information only
(3) both quantitative and qualitative information
(4) neither qualitative not quantitative information

7. An empirical formula represents
(1) qualitative information only
(2) only the metallic elements in the compound
(3) the lowest integer ratio of the elements in a compound
(4) a multiple of the simplest ratio of the elements in a compound

8. In an endothermic reaction
(1) energy is a product and the surrounding temperature decreases
(2) energy is a product and the surrounding temperature increases
(3) energy is a reactant and the surrounding temperature increases
(4) energy is a reactant and the surrounding temperature decreases

9. A reaction in which two substances combine to form a single product is called a
(1) decomposition
(2) synthesis
(3) single replacement
(4) double replacement

10. As an endothermic reaction occurs, the potential energy of the reactants
(1) decreases (3) remains the same
(2) increases (4) depends on the reaction

Part B

11. What is the total number of atoms of oxygen in the formula $Al(ClO_3)_3 \cdot 6H_2O$?
(1) 6 (3) 10
(2) 9 (4) 15

12. Which formula is correctly paired with its name?
(1) $MgCl_2$, magnesium chlorine
(2) K_2O, diphosphorus oxide
(3) $CuCl_2$, copper(II) chloride
(4) FeO, iron(III) oxide

13. Which of the following is an empirical formula?
(1) S_2H_2
(2) H_2O_2
(3) C_2Cl_2
(4) $CaCl_2$

14. What is the empirical formula of a compound with a molecular formula of $C_6H_{12}O_6$?
(1) $C_6H_{12}O_6$
(2) $C_3H_6O_3$
(3) $C_2H_4O_2$
(4) CH_2O

15. What is the correct formula of nickel(II) oxide?
(1) NiO
(2) Ni_2O
(3) NiO_2
(4) Ni_2O_2

16. What is the name of the compound whose formula is N_2O_5?
(1) nitrogen oxide
(2) dinitrogen pentoxide
(3) pentanitrogen dioxide
(4) dinitrogen oxide

17. Which is the correct formula of dichlorine monoxide?
(1) ClO (3) ClO_2
(2) Cl_2O (4) OCl

18. Which of the following is a synthesis reaction?
(1) $Cu + 2AgNO_3 \rightarrow Cu(NO_3)_2 + 2Ag$
(2) $2Cu + O_2 \rightarrow 2CuO$
(3) $CuCO_3 \rightarrow CuO + CO_2$
(4) $CuO + H_2 \rightarrow Cu + H_2O$

19. Which of the following reactions will *not* take place spontaneously?

(1) $Ca + AgNO_3$ (3) $Cr + Pb(NO_3)_2$

(2) $Pb + Al(NO_3)_3$ (4) $Co + HCl$

20. Consider the following unbalanced equation.

$Mg_2Si + HCl \rightarrow MgCl_2 + SiH_4$

When the equation is balanced using the smallest whole-number coefficients, the coefficient of HCl is

(1) 1 (3) 3

(2) 2 (4) 4

21. Consider the following unbalanced equation.

$Fe + H_2O \rightarrow Fe_3O_4 + H_2$

When correctly balanced using smallest whole numbers, the sum of the coefficients is

(1) 4 (3) 11

(2) 7 (4) 12

Part C

22. Write the correct formulas for iron(II) chloride and iron(III)nitrate. Why are the Roman numerals used in the names? [3]

23. What are polyatomic ions? Why do they have a charge? [2]

24. Given the formula: $Al_2(SO_4)_3$. Write the name of each element in the compound and the number of atoms of each element in the formula. [3]

25. (a) Write the formula of dinitrogen trioxide. [1]
(b) Write the name of N_2H_4 [1]

26. In which category—synthesis, decomposition, single replacement, or double replacement—does the following reaction belong? Explain your answer. [2]

$$3Cu + 2H_2O + SO_2 + O_2 \rightarrow Cu_3(OH)_4SO_4$$

27. In the equation $2CH_3OH + O_2 \rightarrow 2CO_2 + X$, the substance represented by X is _____. [2]

28. In the equation $2MnO_2 + 2H_2SO_4 \rightarrow 2MnSO_4 + 2H_2O + X$, what is the formula of X? [2]

29. Balance the following equation using the lowest integer coefficients: [2]

$$\_\_\_ CaO + \_\_\_ P_2O_5 \rightarrow \_\_\_ Ca_3(PO_4)_2$$

30. How many grams of water are produced when 80. g of NaOH react with 73 g of HCl to form 117 g of NaCl and water? Show your work. [2]

31. What is the name of a metal found on Table J that will react with hydrochloric acid? What is the name of an element that will not react with compounds of aluminum? [2]

The Mathematics of Formulas and Equations

VOCABULARY		
formula mass	**mole**	**percentage composition**
gram formula mass		

The Mathematics of Formulas

In an earlier chapter, it was noted that the mass of an atom is a relative value based on the mass of a carbon-12 atom. All atoms are compared to this standard. Thus, a magnesium atom with an atomic mass of 24 amu is twice as massive as the standard carbon atom with an atomic mass of 12. This relationship will remain the same in any system of weights or masses. As long as there is a mass ratio of 12 parts of carbon to 24 parts of magnesium, equal numbers of carbon and magnesium atoms are present. Twelve grams of carbon contains the same number of atoms as 24 grams of magnesium. These mass relationships of atoms are the basis for mass relationships in compounds.

Formula Mass

Remember that compounds are represented by formulas that show the type and number of atoms present in the compound. Because compounds are represented by formulas, the mass of the smallest unit of the compound is the **formula mass,** which is the sum of the atomic masses of all the atoms present. While the term *molecular mass* is often used to represent the mass of a unit of a compound, *formula mass* is preferred because ionic and network solids do not form discrete molecules. For example, sodium bromide (NaBr) is an ionic compound. No molecules of NaBr exist, so *molecular mass* does not apply to NaBr. However, formula mass can be calculated for a formula unit of the compound. The formula mass of NaBr is the mass of one atom of Na plus the mass of one atom of Br in amu.

SAMPLE PROBLEM

What is the formula mass of K_2CO_3?

Solution: Identify the known and unknown values.

Known	*Unknown*
formula = K_2CO_3 atomic masses from the periodic table	formula mass = ? amu

Determine the number of atoms of each element from the formula.

Element:	Number of atoms:
K	2
C	1
O	3

Consult the table of the elements for the atomic mass of each element, and multiply it by the number of atoms to determine the total mass for each element.

For K: 2 atoms × 39.1 amu/atom = 78.2 amu
For C: 1 atom × 12.0 amu/atom = 12.0 amu
For O: 3 atoms × 16.0 amu/atom = 48.0 amu

Add the total mass for each element to determine the formula mass.

formula mass = 78.2 amu + 12.0 amu + 48.0 amu
formula mass = 138.2 amu

GRAM FORMULA MASS. The **gram formula mass** of a substance is simply the formula mass expressed in grams instead of atomic mass units. Thus, the gram formula mass of K_2CO_3 is 138.2 g. Some substances, such as sucrose (table sugar), form molecules. It is common to express the gram formula masses of molecular substances as gram molecular masses.

Review Questions

1. What is the gram formula mass of $Ca(OH)_2$? (1) 29 g (2) 34 g (3) 56 g (4) 74 g

2. Which substance has the greatest molecular mass? (1) H_2O_2 (2) NO (3) CF_4 (4) I_2

3. What is the gram formula mass of $C_3H_5(OH)_3$? (1) 48 g (2) 58 g (3) 74 g (4) 92 g

4. What is the gram formula mass of Na_2CO_3? (1) 51g (2) 74 g (3) 106 g (4) 138 g

5. What is the gram formula mass of $(NH_4)_3PO_4$? (1) 113 g (2) 121 g (3) 149 g (4) 404 g

6. What is the gram formula mass of calcium nitrate ($Ca(NO_3)_2$)? (1) 70.0 g (2) 102 g (3) 150. g (4) 164 g

7. What is the gram formula mass of Li_2SO_4? (1) 54 g (2) 55 g (3) 110 g (4) 206 g

8. What is the gram formula mass of $Mg(ClO_3)_2$? (1) 107 g (2) 142 g (3) 174 g (4) 191 g

9. What is the gram molecular mass of the compound with the formula CH_3COOH? (1) 22.4 g (2) 44.0 g (3) 48.0 g (4) 60.0 g

10. Determine the formula mass and the gram formula mass of each of the following compounds.

(a) $NaHCO_3$
(b) $MgCl_2$
(c) NH_4Cl
(d) $FeCl_3$
(e) Al_2O_3
(f) $Mg(NO_3)_2$
(g) $Al_2(SO_4)_3$
(h) $(NH_4)_2SO_4$
(i) $C_5H_{10}(OH)_2$
(j) $C_{12}H_{22}O_{11}$

For each of the following, compute the answer, showing your work.

11. What is the formula mass of $Al(OH)_3$?

12. What is the formula mass of $C_6H_{12}O_6$?

13. What is the formula mass of $MgBr_2 \cdot 6H_2O$?

Percentage Composition

Formulas represent the composition of a substance. Using the subscripts and atomic masses of the elements, the percent by mass of a substance can be calculated. The **percentage composition** of a substance represents the composition as a percentage of each element compared with the total mass of the compound.

SAMPLE PROBLEM

What is the percentage of oxygen in potassium chlorate ($KClO_3$)?

Solution: Identify the known and unknown values.

Known	*Unknown*
formula = $KClO_3$	%O = ? %
atomic masses from the periodic table	

Determine the formula mass of potassium chlorate.

For K: 1 atom × 39.1 amu/atom = 39.1 amu
For Cl: 1 atom × 35.5 amu/atom = 35.5 amu
For O: 3 atoms × 16.0 amu/atom = <u>48.0 amu</u>
Formula mass = 122.6 amu

Calculate the percent of oxygen in the compound by dividing the mass of oxygen by the formula mass and multiplying by 100%.

$$\%O = \frac{48.0\ \cancel{amu}}{122.6\ \cancel{amu}} \times 100\%$$

$$\%O = 39.2\%$$

HYDRATES Ionic substances often include definite amounts of water as part of the crystal structure. The water molecules are shown as part of the formula, such as $CuSO_4 \cdot 5H_2O$. Crystals that contain attached water molecules are called <u>hydrates</u>, while substances without water are termed <u>anhydrous</u>. If it is necessary to calculate the percentage of water in such a crystal, treat the water molecule as a single unit.

SAMPLE PROBLEM

What is the percentage, by mass, of water in sodium carbonate crystals, $Na_2CO_3 \cdot 10H_2O$?

Solution: Identify the known and unknown values.

Known	*Unknown*
formula = $Na_2CO_3 \cdot 10H_2O$	$\%H_2O$ = ? %
atomic masses from the periodic table	

Determine the formula mass of the crystal. (Hint: Treat the water as a unit.)

For Na: 2 atoms × 23.0 amu/atom = 46.0 amu
For C: 1 atom × 12.0 amu/atom = 12.0 amu
For O: 3 atoms × 16.0 amu/atom = 48.0 amu
For H_2O: 10 units × 18.0 amu/unit = <u>180.0 amu</u>
Formula mass = 286.0 amu

Calculate the percent of water in the compound by dividing the mass of water by the formula mass and multiplying by 100%.

$$\%H_2O = \frac{180.0 \text{ amu}}{286.0 \text{ amu}} \times 100\%$$

$$\%H_2O = 62.9\%$$

Review Questions

14. The percent by mass of nitrogen in NH_4NO_3 is closest to (1) 15% (2) 20.% (3) 35% (4) 60%

15. What is the percent by mass of carbon in CO_2? (1) 12% (2) 27% (3) 44% (4) 73%

16. What is the percent by mass of water present in $CaSO_4 \cdot 2H_2O$? (1) 10.% (2) 12% (3) 21% (4) 79%

17. What is the percent by mass of oxygen in magnesium oxide (MgO)? (1) 20% (2) 40% (3) 50% (4) 60%

18. The percent by mass of oxygen in $H_2C_2O_4$ is equal to

(1) $\frac{90 \text{ amu}}{64 \text{ amu}} \times 100\%$ (3) $\frac{8 \text{ amu}}{4 \text{ amu}} \times 100\%$

(2) $\frac{64 \text{ amu}}{90 \text{ amu}} \times 100\%$ (4) $\frac{4 \text{ amu}}{8 \text{ amu}} \times 100\%$

19. What is the percent by mass of oxygen in Fe_2O_3? The formula mass of Fe_2O_3 = 160 amu. (1) 16% (2) 30.% (3) 56% (4) 70.%

20. What is the percent by mass of sulfur in sulfur dioxide? (1) 32 % (2) 33% (3) 50.% (4) 67%

21. The percent by mass of Ca in $CaCl_2$ is equal to

(1) $\frac{40 \text{ amu}}{111 \text{ amu}} \times 100\%$ (3) $\frac{3 \text{ amu}}{1 \text{ amu}} \times 100\%$

(2) $\frac{111 \text{ amu}}{40 \text{ amu}} \times 100\%$ (4) $\frac{1 \text{ amu}}{3 \text{ amu}} \times 100\%$

22. Which species contains the greatest percent by mass of hydrogen? (1) OH^- (2) H_2O (3) H_3O^+ (4) H_2O_2

23. The percent by mass of water in $BaCl_2 \cdot 2H_2O$ (formula mass = 243 amu) is equal to

(1) $\frac{18 \text{ amu}}{243 \text{ amu}} \times 100\%$ (3) $\frac{243 \text{ amu}}{18 \text{ amu}} \times 100\%$

(2) $\frac{36 \text{ amu}}{243 \text{ amu}} \times 100\%$ (4) $\frac{243 \text{ amu}}{36 \text{ amu}} \times 100\%$

Answer each of the following questions in complete sentences.

24. A crystalline material containing 30.0 g of barium chloride crystals was placed into an oven at 400°C and heated for two hours. It was then cooled and weighed. The new mass was less than before it was heated, containing 20.0 g of barium chloride. How is this possible?

25. Copper(II) sulfate is a hydrated crystal with the formula $CuSO_4 \cdot 5H_2O$ and a deep blue color. When it is heated the crystals crumble and turn white.
(a) Propose an explanation for this change of color.
(b) What would you do to restore the blue color?

26. A chemist needs to order $Na_2B_4O_7$. One supplier offers it in an anhydrous (without water) form, while another offers it as a hydrated crystal, $Na_2B_4O_7 \cdot 10H_2O$. If the prices from the two suppliers are the same for a 500.0-g bottle, which one would supply more of the desired $Na_2B_4O_7$? Explain your answer.

The Mole

We are quite familiar with collective nouns in our everyday life. *Dozen* is a convenient word to describe 12 of something. A gross of paper contains 144 sheets, while a ream contains 500. These units enable you to count by collective units of items instead of by individual items.

Chemists use a specific collective noun to define a particularly usable number of particles. A **mole** is defined as the number of atoms of carbon present in 12.000 grams of C-12. The number of particles in a mole of a substance is 6.022×10^{23}, which is called Avogadro's number. While it would be impossible to individually count a mole of particles, the mass of one mole of a substance can be found by determining its gram formula mass. This quantity contains 6.02×10^{23} particles of that substance. Therefore, the gram formula mass of any substance is the mass of one mole of that substance. The accepted abbreviation for mole is mol.

CONVERTING GRAMS TO MOLES One of the most important and useful conversions for the chemist is that between moles and grams of a substance.

To convert grams to moles:

$$\text{moles} = \text{number of grams} \times \frac{1 \text{ mol}}{\text{gram formula mass}}$$

SAMPLE PROBLEM

How many moles are equivalent to 4.75 g of sodium hydroxide (NaOH)?

Solution: Identify the known and unknown values.

Known	*Unknown*
mass NaOH = 4.75 g	moles NaOH = ? mol

Calculate the formula mass of sodium hydroxide.

For Na: 1 atom × 23.0 amu/atom = 23.0 amu
For O: 1 atom × 16.0 amu/atom = 16.0 amu
For H: 1 atom × 1.0 amu/atom = 1.0 amu
Formula mass NaOH = 40.0 amu

Calculate the gram formula mass of sodium hydroxide.

gram formula mass = formula mass in grams
gram formula mass of NaOH = 40.0 g

Use the gram formula mass to convert the given mass to moles.

$$\text{moles} = \text{number of grams} \times \frac{1\ \text{mol}}{\text{gram formula mass}}$$

$$\text{moles NaOH} = 4.74\ \cancel{\text{g}} \times \frac{1\ \text{mol}}{40.0\ \cancel{\text{g}}}$$

moles NaOH = 0.119 mol

CONVERTING MOLES TO GRAMS In a similar way, the number of grams in a given number of moles of a substance can by calculated using a conversion factor.

To convert moles to grams:

$$\text{grams} = \text{number of moles} \times \frac{\text{gram formula mass}}{1\ \text{mol}}$$

SAMPLE PROBLEM

How many grams are present in 40.5 mol of sulfuric acid (H_2SO_4)?

Solution: Identify the known and unknown values.

Known	*Unknown*
moles H_2SO_4 = 40.5 mol	mass H_2SO_4 = ? g

Calculate the formula mass of sulfuric acid.

For H: 2 atoms × 1.0 amu/atom = 2.0 amu
For S: 1 atom × 32.1 amu/atom = 32.1 amu
For O: 4 atoms × 16.0 amu/atom = 64.0 amu
Formula mass H_2SO_4 = 98.1 amu

Calculate the gram formula mass of sulfuric acid.

gram formula mass = formula mass in grams
gram formula mass of H_2SO_4 = 98.1 g

Use the gram formula mass to convert the given number of moles to grams.

$$\text{number of grams} = \text{moles} \times \frac{\text{gram formula mass}}{1\ \text{mol}}$$

$$\text{grams } H_2SO_4 = 40.5\ \cancel{\text{mol}} \times \frac{98.1\ \text{g}}{1\ \cancel{\text{mol}}}$$

grams H_2SO_4 = 3970 g

Review Questions

27. Which quantity is equivalent to 39 g of LiF? (1) 0.50 mol (2) 1.0 mol (3) 1.5 mol (4) 2.0 mol

28. What is the total mass of 0.75 mol of SO_2? (1) 16 g (2) 24 g (3) 32 g (4) 48 g

29. The mass in grams of 2 mol of sulfuric acid is (1) $\frac{98\text{g}}{2}$ (2) 2(98 g) (3) $\frac{196\text{g}}{2}$ (4) 2(196 g)

30. The mass of 1 mol of $NaNO_3$ is (1) 42 g (2) 53 g (3) 85 g (4) 116 g

31. The mass of a mole of nitrogen gas is (1) 7 g (2) 14 g (3) 28 g (4) 56 g

32. What is the number of moles of potassium chloride (gram formula mass = 74 g) present in 148 g of KCl? (1) 2.0 mol (2) 2.5 mol (3) 3.0 mol (4) 3.5 mol

33. How many moles are in 168 g of KOH? (gram formula mass = 56 g) (1) 0.3 mol (2) 0.5 mol (3) 1.0 mol (4) 3.0 mol

34. How many moles of oxygen atoms are in one mole of $Mg_3(PO_4)_2$? (1) 1 (2) 4 (3) 6 (4) 8

35. What is the mass of 4.5 mol of KOH? (1) 0.080 g (2) 36 g (3) 56 g (4) 252 g

36. What is the mass of 0.50 mol of $CuSO_4 \cdot 5H_2O$? (1) 47.8 g (2) 95.6 g (3) 125 g (4) 250 g

MEMORY JOGGER

In Topic 2, *Formulas and Equations,* you learned the difference between an empirical formula and a molecular formula. The empirical formula shows the simplest integer ratio of elements in a compound. C_3H_6 is the molecular formula of a substance named propene. Its empirical formula is CH_2.

Finding Molecular Formulas from Empirical Formulas

When the molecular mass of a compound and its empirical formula are known, it is possible to determine the correct molecular formula. For example, the molecular mass of propene is 42 amu. The empirical formula of propene is CH_2, and the molecular mass of CH_2 is 14 amu. Divide the mass of the compound by the mass of the empirical formula. The result will be an integer. In this case it is 3. This tells you that the molecular formula is three times the empirical formula. Simply multiply each subscript by three to find the molecular formula, C_3H_6.

SAMPLE PROBLEM

A compound has a molecular mass of 180 amu and an empirical formula of CH_2O. What is its molecular formula?

Solution: Identify the known and unknown values.

Known	*Unknown*
molecular mass = 180 amu	molecular formula = ?
empirical formula = CH_2O	

Determine the molecular mass of CH_2O:

For C: 1 atom × 12.0 amu/atom = 12.0 amu
For H: 2 atoms × 1.0 amu/atom = 2.0 amu
For O: 1 atom × 16.0 amu/atom = 16.0 amu
Molecular mass of CH_2O = 30.0 amu

Divide the molecular mass of the compound by the mass of the empirical formula.

$$\frac{180 \text{ amu}}{30 \text{ amu}} = 6$$

Multiply the subscripts in the empirical formula by 6.

$$C_{1\times6}H_{2\times6}O_{1\times6} = C_6H_{12}O_6$$

The molecular formula of the compound is $C_6H_{12}O_6$.

Review Questions

37. The empirical formula of a compound is CH_4. The molecular formula of the compound could be (1) CH_4 (2) C_2H_6 (3) C_3H_8 (4) C_4H_{10}

38. A compound with an empirical formula of CH_2 has a molecular mass of 70 amu. What is its molecular formula? (1) CH_2 (2) C_2H_4 (3) C_4H_8 (4) C_5H_{10}

39. A compound has an empirical formula of CH and a molecular mass of 78 amu. What is the molecular formula of the compound? (1) C_2H_2 (2) C_3H_3 (3) C_4H_4 (4) C_6H_6

40. A compound has an empirical formula of CH_2 and a molecular mass of 28 amu. What is its molecular formula?

41. A compound has an empirical formula of CH_2 and a molecular mass of 56 amu. What is its molecular formula?

42. Vitamin C has an empirical formula of $C_3H_4O_3$ and a molecular mass of 176 amu. What is its molecular formula?

43. A compound has a molecular mass of 30 amu and an empirical formula of CH_3. What is its molecular formula?

Mole Relations in Balanced Equations

Chemical equations include both qualitative and quantitative information about the reaction. The formulas of the compounds give qualitative information about the nature of the reactants and products, along with some quantitative information. The coefficients represent quantitative information that relates specifically to that reaction.

In problems involving chemical reactions, the relative amounts of reactants and products are represented by the coefficients. Coefficients represent both the basic unit and mole ratios in balanced equations.

Consider the equation for the combustion of ethane, C_2H_6, as shown in Figure 3-1. The coefficients tell you that 2 mol of ethane combines with

Balanced chemical equation:

$$2C_2H_6 + 7O_2 \rightarrow 4CO_2 + 6H_2O$$

Moles C_2H_6	Moles O_2	Moles CO_2	Moles H_2O
2	7	4	6
4	14	8	12
1	3.5	2	3

Figure 3-1. Mole ratios from a balanced equation: Regardless of the number of moles of any of the reactants or products, the ratio must remain 2:7:4:6 for this reaction.

7 mol of oxygen to produce 4 mol of carbon dioxide and 6 mol of water. These ratios will remain constant for any amounts of the substances involved, as shown in the figure.

SAMPLE PROBLEM

How many moles of water will be produced from the complete combustion of 3.0 mol of ethane according to the following equation?

$$2C_2H_6(g) + 7O_2(g) \rightarrow 4CO_2(g) + 6H_2O(g)$$

Solution: Identify the known and unknown values.

Known	*Unknown*
moles C_2H_6 = 3.0 mol	moles water = ? mol
balanced equation	

Use the balanced equation to determine the mole ratio between ethane and water.

moles ethane: moles water = 2:6

Set up a proportion between the known moles of ethane (3.0 mol) and the coefficient of ethane, and moles of water (x) and the coefficient of water.

$$\frac{3.0 \text{ mol } C_2H_6}{2 \text{ mol } C_2H_6} = \frac{x}{6 \text{ mol } H_2O}$$

Solve for the number of moles of H_2O (x).

$$x = \frac{(3.0 \cancel{\text{mol } C_2H_6})(6 \text{ mol } H_2O)}{2 \cancel{\text{mol } C_2H_6}}$$

$$x = 9.0 \text{ mol } H_2O$$

Review Questions

44. Given the reaction $4Al(s) + 3O_2(g) \rightarrow 2Al_2O_3(s)$, what is the minimum number of moles of oxygen gas required to produce 1.00 mol of aluminum oxide? (1) 1.0 mol (2) 1.5 mol (3) 3.0 mol (4) 6.0 mol

45. Given the reaction $4NH_3 + 5O_2 \rightarrow 4NO + 6H_2O$, what is the maximum number of moles of H_2O that can be produced when 2.0 mol of NH_3 are completely reacted? (1) 1.0 mol (2) 2.0 mol (3) 3.0 mol (4) 6.0 mol

46. Given the reaction $2KClO_3(s) \rightarrow 2KCl(s) + 3O_2(g)$, what is the total number of moles of $KClO_3$ needed to produce 6 mol of O_2? (1) 1 mol (2) 2 mol (3) 3 mol (4) 4 mol

47. Given the reaction $CH_4 + 2O_2 \rightarrow CO_2 + 2H_2O$, what amount of oxygen is needed to completely react with 1 mol of CH_4? (1) 2 mol (2) 2 atoms (3) 2 g (4) 2 molecules

48. Given the reaction $4NH_3 + 5O_2 \rightarrow 4NO + 6H_2O$, what is the total number of moles of O_2 required to produce 40 mol of NO? (1) 5 mol (2) 9 mol (3) 32 mol (4) 50 mol

49. Given the reaction $2CH_3OH(\ell) + 3O_2(g) \rightarrow 2CO_2(g) + 4H_2O(g)$, how many moles of $O_2(g)$ are needed to produce exactly 20. mol of $CO_2(g)$? (1) 10. mol (2) 20. mol (3) 30. mol (4) 40. mol

50. Given the reaction $4Na + O_2 \rightarrow 2Na_2O$, how many moles of oxygen are completely consumed in the production of 1.00 mol of Na_2O? (1) 0.50 mol (2) 1 mol (3) 2 mol (4) 4.0 mol

51. Given the reaction $Ca + 2H_2O \rightarrow Ca(OH)_2 + H_2$, what is the total number of moles of Ca needed to react completely with 4.0 mol of H_2O? (1) 0.50 mol (2) 1.0 mol (3) 2.0 mol (4) 4.0 mol

52. Consider the following equation.

$$CH_4(g) + 2O_2(g) \rightarrow CO_2(g) + 2H_2O(g)$$

How many moles of oxygen are needed for the complete combustion of 3.0 mol of $CH_4(g)$? (1) 2.0 mol (2) 3.0 mol (3) 4.0 mol (4) 6.0 mol

53. According to the reaction $2Al + 3H_2SO_4 \rightarrow 3H_2 + Al_2(SO_4)_3$, the total number of moles of H_2SO_4 needed to react completely with 5.0 mol of Al is (1) 2.5 mol (2) 5.0 mol (3) 7.5 mol (4) 9.0 mol

54. Given the equation $N_2(g) + 3H_2(g) \rightarrow 2NH_3(g)$, what is the total number of moles of NH_3 produced when 10. mol of H_2 reacts completely with N_2? (1) 2.0 mol (2) 3.0 mol (3) 6.7 mol (4) 15 mol

55. According to the equation $2K(s) + Cl_2(g) \rightarrow 2KCl(s)$, potassium reacts with chlorine to form potassium chloride. If 100 atoms of potassium react with chlorine gas, how many chlorine molecules will be needed to completely react?

56. What do coefficients represent in a balanced equation?

57. A student is given the equation $N_2 + H_2 \rightarrow NH_3$ to balance. She answers with $N_2 + 2H_2 \rightarrow 2NH_2$. Explain why her answer is not correct. Balance the equation correctly.

58. Consider the equation $H_2 + Cl_2 \rightarrow 2HCl$. A student suggests that according to the ratio shown by the coefficients, 20 g of hydrogen will react with 20 g of chlorine to form 40 g of HCl. Is the student correct? Explain.

59. The process of photosynthesis can be represented by the following equation.

$$6CO_2(g) + 6H_2O(\ell) + \text{energy} \rightarrow C_6H_{12}O_6(s) + 6O_2(g)$$

If 4 mol of $C_6H_{12}O_6$ is produced by the process, how many moles of $CO_2(g)$ and $H_2O(\ell)$ were used?

60. How many molecules of water are needed to produce 6 molecules of $C_6H_{12}O_6$ according to the equation in the previous question?

61. How many moles of oxygen gas are produced when 6 mol of CO_2 are consumed in the process of photosynthesis? (See problem 58 for the equation.)

62. Hydrogen gas and chlorine gas react to form hydrogen chloride.

$$H_2(g) + Cl_2(g) \rightarrow 2HCl(g)$$

If 2 mol of hydrogen gas are mixed with 4 mol of chlorine gas, how many moles of hydrogen chloride will be produced?

63. In the previous question, one of the reactants will not be completely used up. Which one will not be completely used, and how many moles will not react?

64. Make a drawing of 6 molecules of hydrogen gas (H_2) in a container. Using a different symbol, add the correct number of nitrogen gas (N_2) molecules to form ammonia according to the following equation.

$$N_2(g) + 3H_2(g) \rightarrow 2NH_3$$

In a second drawing, show the number and composition of ammonia molecules in the container after the reaction has been completed.

Questions for Regents Practice

Part A

1. The term *mole* is a unit used to represent
(1) density of particles
(2) kinds of particles
(3) numbers of particles
(4) reactivity of particles

2. One mole of carbon and one mole of neon both have the same
(1) mass
(2) volume
(3) number of particles
(4) number of protons

3. The mass of a mole of a substance is equal to
(1) the atomic number in grams
(2) the mass of the most common isotope in grams
(3) the gram formula mass
(4) the mass of 22.4 L of any substance

4. A hydrated crystal is one in which
(1) water molecules are part of the crystal
(2) water molecules have been removed
(3) hydrogen molecules are part of the crystal
(4) hydrogen molecules have been removed

5. To find the percent of an element in a compound
(1) divide the atomic mass of the element by its atomic number × 100%
(2) divide the total mass of an element by the total mass of the compound × 100%
(3) multiply the atomic mass of the element by the total mass of the compound × 100%
(4) multiply the atomic mass of the elements by their subscripts × 100%

6. In a balanced equation, coefficients always represent
(1) the number of atoms present
(2) the ratio of volumes of substances
(3) the mole ratios of reactants and products
(4) the volume ratios of reactants and products

Part B

7. What is the gram atomic mass of zinc?
(1) 1.33 g (3) 65 g
(2) 30. g (4) 130. g

8. The mass of a mole of $O_2(g)$ is
(1) 8.0 g
(2) 16.0 g
(3) 24.0 g
(4) 32.0 g

9. If the mass of a mole of H_2X is 34 g, then X must represent
(1) O
(2) Cl
(3) Kr
(4) S

10. The mass of a mole of $Ca(OH)_2$ is
(1) 38 g
(2) 57 g
(3) 58 g
(4) 74 g

11. Consider the following equation.
$$2C_2H_6 + O_2 \rightarrow 4CO_2 + 6H_2O$$
When 4 mol of C_2H_6 are burned the number of moles of CO_2 produced will be
(1) 2 mol
(2) 6 mol
(3) 7 mol
(4) 8 mol

12. Given the equation $Mg + 2HCl \rightarrow MgCl_2 + H_2$, how many moles of hydrochloric acid are needed to react with 0.50 mol of magnesium?
(1) 0.5 mol
(2) 1.0 mol
(3) 2.0 mol
(4) 4.0 mol

13. What is the mass in grams of 4.25 mol of $(NH_4)_2CO_3$?

14. How many grams of oxygen are present in 0.50 mol of ozone, O_3?

15. How many grams of oxygen are present in 88.0 g of CO_2?

16. Based on the equation $2SO_2 + O_2 \rightarrow 2SO_3$, how many moles of SO_3 are formed when 2 mol of oxygen gas are consumed?

17. Calculate the percentage by mass of oxygen in $Mg(OH)_2$.

18. What is the percentage by mass of water in $MgSO_4 \cdot 7H_2O$?

Part C

19. A saltshaker typically contains about 20. g of sodium chloride. How many moles of sodium chloride does this represent? [1]

20. Which contains more particles, 8.0 g of helium gas or 10. g of neon gas? Explain your answer. [2]

21. Explain the difference between an empirical and a molecular formula. [2]

22. Some years ago, pennies were made entirely of copper. These pennies have a mass of approximately 2.5 g. How many pennies are needed to make a mole of copper? [2]

23. Consider the statement: "One gram molecular mass of water contains one mole of hydrogen atoms." Is the statement true or false? If it is true, write a sentence about the amount of oxygen in one gram molecular mass of water. If it is false, rewrite the statement to make it a true statement about the amount of hydrogen in one gram molecular mass of water. [2]

24. Consider the statement: "One mole of any substance contains one mole of atoms." Using chemical formulas as examples, show why this statement is false. [2]

25. Consider the following equation.
$$Zn(s) + 2HCl(aq) \rightarrow ZnCl_2(aq) + H_2(g)$$
(a) If 2 mol of zinc reacts with hydrochloric acid, how many moles of hydrogen gas will be produced? (b) How many grams of hydrogen does this represent? [2]

26. An ordinary aspirin tablet has a mass of 0.385 g. The molecular formula of aspirin is $C_9H_8O_4$. (a) What is its empirical formula? (b) What is the mass of one mole of aspirin? (c) What is the percentage by mass of hydrogen in the compound? (d) How many aspirin tablets are needed to make a mole of aspirin? [4]

27. Benzene and ethyne both have the same empirical formula of CH. If the mass of a mole of one of the compounds is 26.0 g, what is a possible mass of a mole of the other compound? [1]

Physical Behavior of Matter

VOCABULARY		
condensation	**heat**	**liquid phase**
deposition	**heat of fusion**	**solid phase**
freezing	**heat of vaporization**	**sublimation**
fusion	**kinetic molecular theory**	**temperature**
gaseous phase		**vaporization**

In this chapter you will first examine the solid, liquid, and gaseous phases of matter. Next, you will study how to calculate the heat exchanged during heating, cooling, and phase changes. The kinetic molecular theory will then be presented to explain the behavior of gases. Finally, you'll learn about the various means of separating mixtures.

Phases of Matter

An element, compound or mixture may exist in the form of a solid, liquid, or a gas. These three forms are called the phases of matter.

The **solid phase** contains matter that is held in a rigid form. Because of this rigid form, a substance in the solid phase has a definite volume and shape. Strong attractive forces among the particles in a solid hold the particles in fixed locations. True solids have a crystalline structure.

DIGGING DEEPER

Glass is a common substance that appears to be a solid. However, careful analysis shows that glass does not have a true crystalline structure and is not a true solid. Over time, the particles making up glass are able to slowly flow past one another. Substances like glass are called supercooled liquids.

Particles in the **liquid phase** are not held together as rigidly as those in the solid phase. Liquid phase particles are able to move past one another. The mobility of the particles prevents liquids from having a definite shape. The particles, however, are held together with sufficient attractive force to give a liquid a definite volume.

Particles in the **gaseous phase** have minimal attractive forces holding them together. Due to this lack of attraction among particles, gases have neither a definite shape nor a definite volume. Gases spread out indefinitely unless they are confined in a container. In a closed container, the gaseous particles always expand to fill the volume of the container. A vapor is the gaseous phase of a substance that is a liquid or a solid at normal conditions. Figure 4-1 summarizes the three phases of matter.

DIGGING DEEPER

There is a fourth phase of matter, plasma. A plasma is a gas or vapor in which some or all of the electrons have been removed from the atoms.

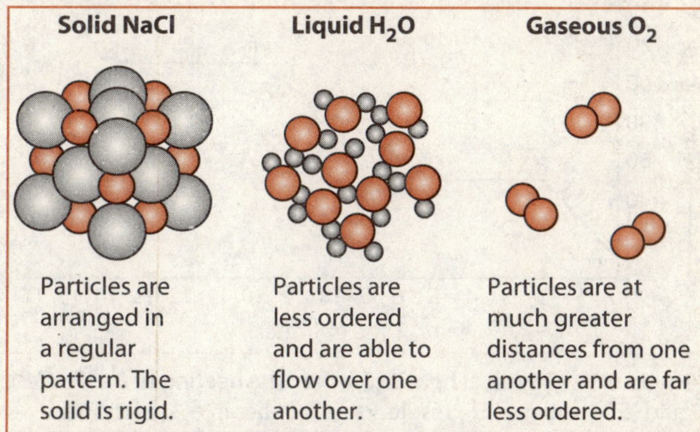

Figure 4-1. Particles of matter in three phases

Heating and Cooling Curves

Figure 4-2 shows the heating of a hypothetical substance from the solid phase to the gaseous phase. At time = 0, shown as point A on the graph, the temperature of the solid is 10°C. Heat is then added to the substance at a constant rate. From time = 0 to time = 2 minutes, the temperature rises at a constant rate until the temperature of the solid reaches its melting point (B). During this portion of the process (AB), the kinetic energy of the substance is increasing.

Eventually some of the particles in the substance possess enough kinetic energy to break the bonds holding them in the solid phase; melting, also known as **fusion,** begins (B). During the melting process (BC), the temperature remains constant even though heat is still being added at a constant rate. During this time, the heat is absorbed by the substance in the form of potential energy. Both solid and liquid phases of the substance are present during the melting process. As time goes on, the amount of liquid continually increases and the amount of solid continually decreases. Because the liquid phase of a substance has more potential energy than the solid phase, the potential energy of the substance increases during the melting process. The unchanging temperature during melting is evidence of the fact that the substance's kinetic energy remains constant during the process. The amount of heat needed to convert a solid at its melting point to a liquid is called the heat of fusion.

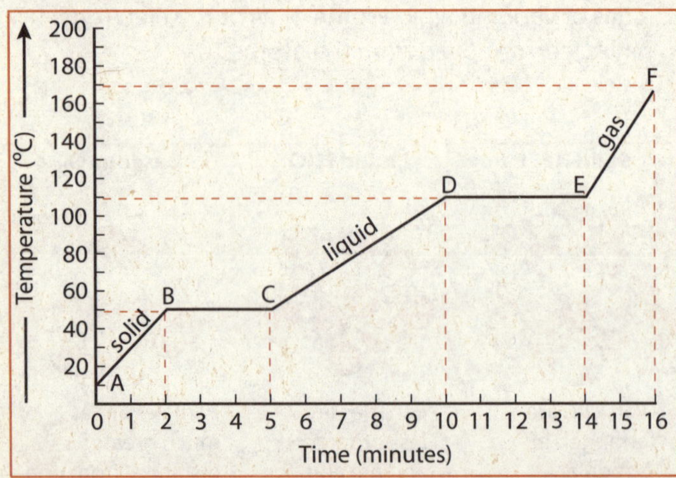

Figure 4-2. A typical heating curve: The heating of a solid (AB), liquid (CD), and gas (EF) results in an increase in the substance's temperature. Phase changes that occur during melting (BC) and boiling (DE) are not accompanied by temperature changes.

When all of the solid has melted (C) and only the liquid phase is present, the temperature once again begins to rise. This temperature rise is due to the increase in kinetic energy of the substance. The temperature continues to rise until the boiling point is reached (D). Boiling, also known as **vaporization,** begins as some of the particles in the liquid have enough kinetic energy to break free from the attractive forces holding them in the liquid phase. These particles escape the liquid and enter the gas phase. Once boiling begins, the temperature remains constant as the substance's potential energy increases. During this phase change, both the liquid and gaseous (vapor) phases are present. Because the gaseous phase of a substance has more potential energy than the liquid phase, the potential energy of the substance increases as heat is absorbed during the boiling process. If heat is added to the substance in its gas phase, the temperature of the gas begins to rise (EF).

MEMORY JOGGER

Endothermic reactions absorb heat energy (heat is a reactant). Exothermic reactions release heat energy (heat is a product).

HEATING CURVE SUMMARY All of the steps (AB, BC, CD, DE, and EF) shown in Figure 4-2 are endothermic.

AB: heating of a solid, one phase present, kinetic energy increases
BC: melting of a solid, two phases present, potential energy increases, kinetic energy remains constant
CD: heating of a liquid, one phase present, kinetic energy increases
DE: boiling of a liquid, two phases present, potential energy increases, kinetic energy remains constant
EF: heating of a gas, one phase present, kinetic energy increases

COOLING CURVE SUMMARY If a gas at high temperature is allowed to cool at a constant rate, a cooling curve results. See Figure 4-3. Note that the reverse of boiling is called **condensation**, and the reverse of melting is called **freezing.** Freezing is also called solidification. All of the steps shown in Figure 4-3 are exothermic.

AB: cooling of a gas (vapor), one phase present, kinetic energy decreases
BC: condensation of the gas (vapor) to liquid, two phases present, potential energy decreases, kinetic energy remains constant
CD: cooling of a liquid, one phase present, kinetic energy decreases
DE: solidification (freezing) of a liquid, two phases present, potential energy decreases, kinetic energy remains the same
EF: cooling of a solid, one phase present, kinetic energy decreases

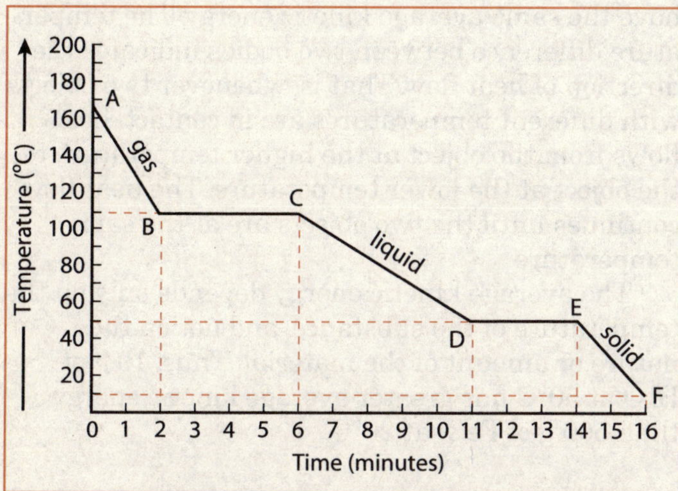

Figure 4-3. A typical cooling curve: The cooling of a gas (AB), liquid (CD), and solid (EF) results in a decrease in the substance's temperature. Phase changes occurring during condensation (BC) and freezing (DE) are not accompanied by temperature changes.

Sublimation and Deposition

Heating and cooling curves show the normal transitions between phases. Some substances, however, change directly from a solid to a gas without passing through a noticeable liquid phase. An example is solid carbon dioxide (CO_2), which changes from a solid to a gas at normal atmospheric pressure. This process, in which a solid changes directly into a gas, is called **sublimation.** A substance that undergoes sublimation is said to sublime. The reverse of the sublimation process, in which a gas changes directly into a solid, is called **deposition.**

Review Questions

1. Which substance has a definite shape and a definite volume at STP? (1) NaCl(*aq*) (2) Cl_2(*g*) (3) CCl_4(ℓ) (4) $AlCl_3$(*s*)

2. At STP, which element has a definite shape and volume? (1) Ag (2) Hg (3) Ne (4) Xe

3. Which sample is most likely to take the shape of and occupy the total volume of its container? (1) CO_2(*g*) (2) CO_2(ℓ) (3) CO_2(*aq*) (4) CO_2(*s*)

4. Which substance takes the shape of and fills the volume of any container into which it is placed? (1) H_2O(ℓ) (2) CO_2(*g*) (3) I_2(*s*) (4) Hg(ℓ)

5. As a substance changes from a liquid to a gas, the average distance between molecules (1) decreases (2) increases (3) remains the same

6. In which phase are the particles the most random? (1) solid (2) liquid (3) gas

7. Which phase change represents sublimation? (1) $H_2O(\ell) \rightarrow H_2O(s)$ (2) $H_2O(\ell) \rightarrow H_2O(g)$ (3) $I_2(s) \rightarrow I_2(g)$ (4) $I_2(s) \rightarrow I_2(\ell)$

8. Which phase change represents sublimation? (1) $NH_3(\ell) \rightarrow NH_3(g)$ (2) $CO_2(s) \rightarrow CO_2(g)$ (3) $KI(s) \rightarrow KI(\ell)$ (4) $H_2O(\ell) \rightarrow H_2O(s)$

9. A solid substance initially at a temperature below its melting point is heated at a constant rate. The heating curve for the substance is shown in the graph below.

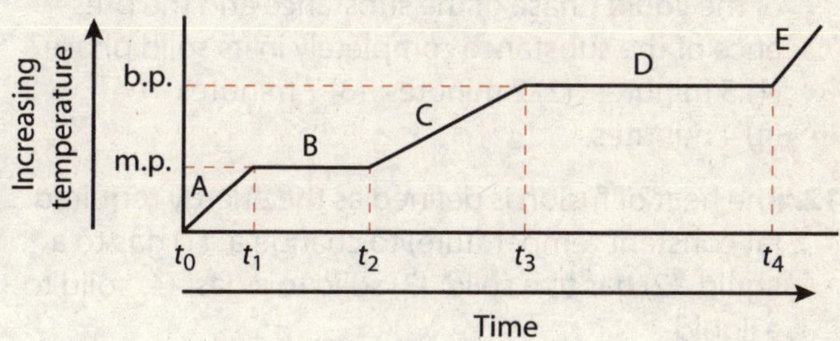

Which portions of the graph represent times when heat is absorbed and potential energy increases while kinetic energy remains constant? (1) A and B (2) B and D (3) A and C (4) C and D

10. A solid substance initially at a temperature below its melting point is heated at a constant rate. The heating curve for the substance is shown in the graph on the following page.

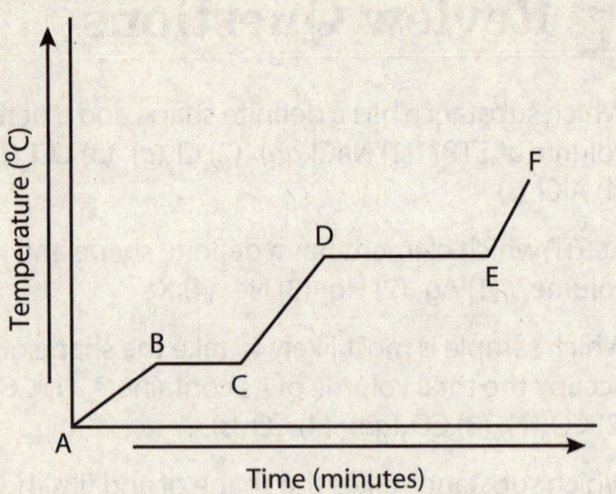

Which segment of the graph represents a time when both the solid and liquid phases are present? (1) AB (2) BC (3) DE (4) EF

11. A gaseous substance initially at a temperature above its boiling point is cooled at a constant rate. The cooling curve for the substance is shown below.

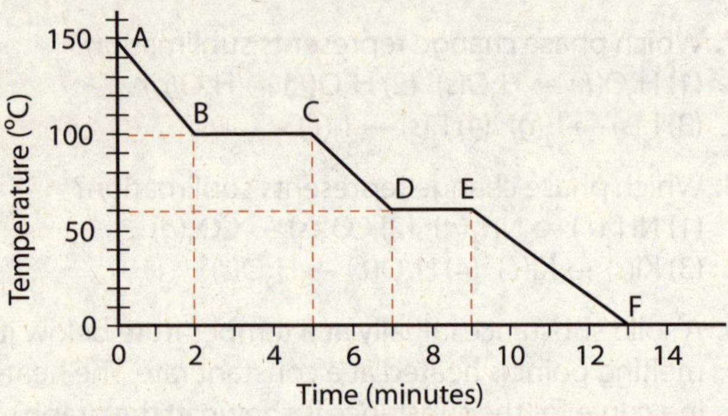

How much time passes between the first appearance of the liquid phase of the substance and the presence of the substance completely in its solid phase? (1) 5 minutes (2) 2 minutes (3) 7 minutes (4) 4 minutes

12. The heat of fusion is defined as the energy required (at constant temperature) to change a (1) gas to a liquid (2) gas to a solid (3) solid to a gas (4) solid to a liquid

13. As ice cools from 273 K to 263 K, the average kinetic energy of its molecules (1) decreases (2) increases (3) remains the same

14. Which occurs as a substance melts? (1) It changes from a solid to a liquid and heat is absorbed. (2) It changes from a solid to a liquid and heat is released. (3) It changes from a liquid to a solid and heat is absorbed. (4) It changes from a liquid to a solid and heat is released.

15. Which phase change is endothermic?
(1) gas → solid (2) gas → liquid
(3) liquid → solid (4) liquid → gas

16. Which phase change is exothermic?
(1) $H_2O(s) \rightarrow H_2O(\ell)$ (2) $H_2O(\ell) \rightarrow H_2O(s)$
(3) $H_2O(s) \rightarrow H_2O(g)$ (4) $H_2O(\ell) \rightarrow H_2O(g)$

Temperature Scales

The **temperature** of a substance is a measure of the average kinetic energy of its particles. The particles of all substances at the same temperature have the same average kinetic energy. The temperature difference between two bodies indicates the direction of heat flow. That is, whenever two objects with different temperatures are in contact, heat flows from the object at the higher temperature to the object at the lower temperature. The heat flow continues until the two objects are at the same temperature.

The average kinetic energy depends only on the temperature of the substance, and not on the nature or amount of the material. Thus, 10 g of H_2O at 50°C has greater average kinetic energy than 500 g of $Fe(s)$ at 20°C.

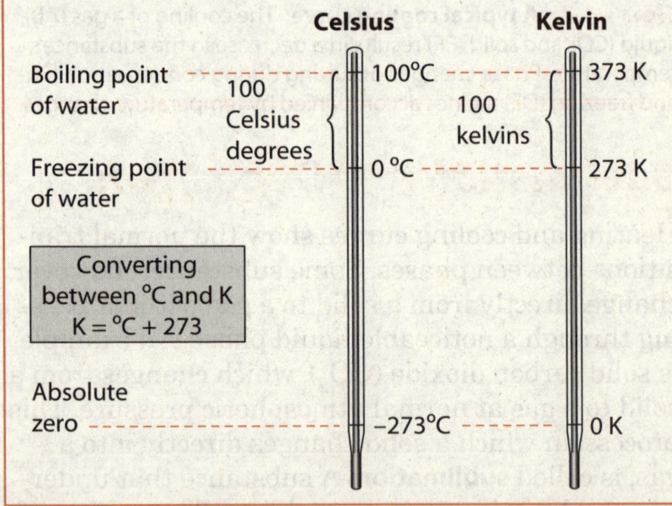

Figure 4-4. Comparison of Celsius and Kelvin temperature scales

Temperature is measured using a thermometer. Thermometers are calibrated by establishing two fixed reference points; the distance between them is then divided into the desired number of units. The fixed points on common thermometers are the freezing and boiling points of water. The freezing point of water is the ice–water (solid–liquid) equilibrium temperature at normal atmospheric pressure (101.3 kPa). The boiling point of water is the water–steam (liquid–gas) equilibrium temperature at normal atmospheric pressure. As shown in Figure 4-4, the boiling and freezing reference points are used on both the Celsius and Kelvin temperature scales. Note that there are 100 units between the two reference points on both the Celsius and Kelvin scales.

Because there are an equal number of divisions between the fixed reference points of both the Celsius and Kelvin scales, a change of one degree Celsius is equal to a change of one Kelvin. A change of 50°C represents the same temperature change as 50 Kelvins. The Celsius and Kelvin scales are related by the following equation:

$$K = °C + 273$$

Although often confused, heat and temperature are not the same. **Heat** is a measure of the amount of energy transferred from one substance to another. Heat is measured in units of calories or joules. Temperature is a measure of the average kinetic energy of a substance's particles, and is measured in degrees Celsius or in Kelvins. An example of the difference between heat and temperature involves the melting of ice. It requires more energy to melt 10 g of ice than it does to melt 1 g of ice, yet in both cases the temperature of the ice does not change.

SAMPLE PROBLEM

What Kelvin temperature is equivalent to 35°C?

Solution: Identify the known and unknown values.

Known	*Unknown*
temperature = 35°C	temperature = ? K

Substitute the known temperature into the equation relating Kelvin and Celsius, and solve.

$K = °C + 273$
$K = 35 + 273$
$K = 308$
308 K is equivalent to 35°C.

Review Questions

17. Which is not a form of energy? (1) light (2) temperature (3) electricity (4) heat

18. Which unit is used to express the amount of energy absorbed or released during a chemical reaction? (1) degree (2) torr (3) gram (4) joule

19. Which term represents a form of energy? (1) heat (2) degree (3) kilojoule (4) temperature

20. The minimum number of fixed reference points required to establish the Celsius temperature scale for a thermometer is (1) 1 (2) 2 (3) 3 (4) 4

21. What are the fixed reference points on the Celsius thermometer? (1) 32 and 100 (2) 0 and 212 (3) 32 and 212 (4) 0 and 100

22. The difference between the boiling point and the freezing point of pure water at standard pressure is (1) 32 K (2) 273 K (3) 100 K (4) 373 K

23. What is the freezing point of water on the Kelvin scale at standard pressure? (1) 0 K (2) 32 K (3) 100 K (4) 273 K

24. When the temperature of an object changes by 100°C, the same temperature change in Kelvins would be (1) 100 K (2) 173 K (3) 273 K (4) 373 K

25. Energy is added to a substance. Compared to the Celsius temperature of the substance, the Kelvin temperature (1) will always be 273 greater (2) will always be 273 lower (3) will have the same reading at 0 (4) will have the same reading at 273

26. What Kelvin temperature is equal to −73°C? (1) 100 K (2) 173 K (3) 200 K (4) 346 K

27. Which temperature is equal to 20 K? (1) −253°C (2) −293°C (3) 253°C (4) 293°C

28. Different masses of copper and iron have the same temperature. Compared to the average kinetic energy of the copper atoms, the average kinetic energy of the iron atoms is (1) less (2) greater (3) the same

29. The average kinetic energy of water molecules increases when (1) $H_2O(s)$ changes to $H_2O(\ell)$ at 0°C (2) $H_2O(\ell)$ changes to $H_2O(s)$ at 0°C (3) $H_2O(\ell)$ at 10°C changes to $H_2O(\ell)$ at 20°C (4) $H_2O(\ell)$ at 20°C changes to $H_2O(s)$ at 10°C

Measurement of Heat Energy

The amount of heat given off or absorbed in a reaction can be calculated using the following equation:

$$q = mC\Delta T$$

q = heat (in joules)
m = mass of the substance
C = specific heat capacity of substance
ΔT = (Temperature$_{initial}$ − Temperature$_{final}$)

SAMPLE PROBLEM

How many joules are absorbed when 50.0 g of water are heated from 30.2°C to 58.6°C?

Solution: Identify the known and unknown values.

Known	*Unknown*
$m = 50.0$ g	$q = ?$ J
$C_{water} = 4.18$ J/g•°C	
$\Delta T = (58.6°C - 30.2°C) = 28.4°C$	

Substitute the known values into the formula $q = mC\Delta T$ and solve for q.

$q = (50.0\ \text{g})(4.18\ \text{J/g•°C})(28.4°C)$
$q = 5936\ \text{J} = 5.94 \times 10^3\ \text{J}$

As shown in Figure 4-5, a device known as a calorimeter can be used to measure the amount of heat given off in a reaction. The reaction takes place in the reaction chamber, and the heat released by the reaction is absorbed by the surrounding water. By measuring the temperature increase of the water, the heat given off in the reaction can be calculated.

Whenever a substance undergoes a temperature change, the equation $q = mc\Delta T$ can be used to calculate the heat involved. However, this equation cannot be used to determine the amount of heat required to melt or boil a substance. Why? Temperature remains constant during a phase change, so there is no ΔT, and the equation cannot be used. Recall from Figure 4-2 that the line segment BC represents the melting of a substance. To determine the heat required for a phase change such as this, you must use an equation involving the substance's heat of fusion.

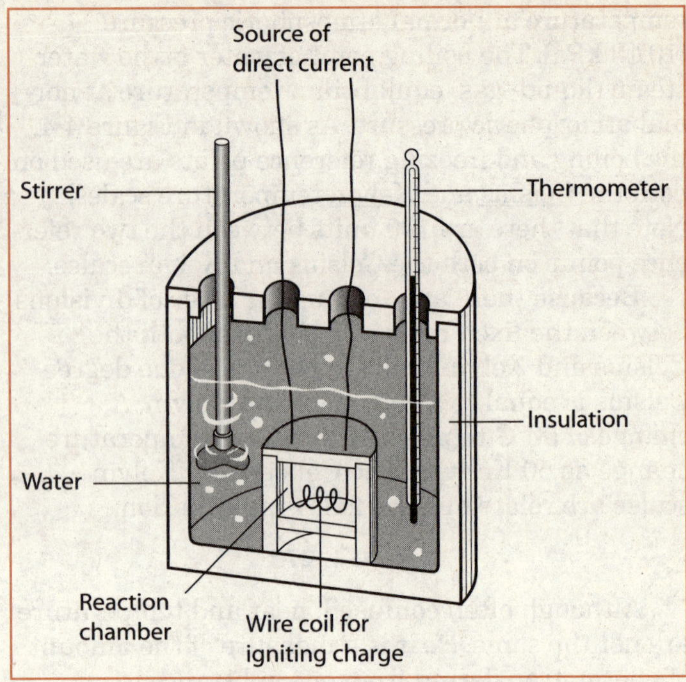

Figure 4-5. Cutaway drawing showing the components of a calorimeter

Heat of Fusion

The amount of heat needed to convert a unit mass of a substance from solid to liquid at its melting point is called the **heat of fusion.** The heat of fusion of solid water (ice) at 0°C and 1 atmosphere is 334 J/g. The heat absorbed by the substance during the melting process increases the potential energy of the substance without increasing the average kinetic energy of the substance's particles. Because there is no change in kinetic energy, there is no temperature change during the process.

SAMPLE PROBLEM

How many joules are required to melt 255 g of ice at 0°C?

Solution: Identify the known and unknown values.

Known	*Unknown*
$m = 255$ g	$q = ?$ J
heat of fusion = 334 J/g	

Multiply the heat of fusion by the total mass of ice to determine the heat required.

$q = (255\ \text{g})(334\ \text{J/g}) = 85{,}170\ \text{J} = 85.2\ \text{kJ}$

The process of melting is an endothermic process, that is, it requires heat. Therefore, the reverse process of freezing (also called solidification) must be exothermic. During the freezing process, water releases 334 J/g of heat and its potential energy decreases.

Heat of Vaporization

During the boiling process, a substance in the liquid phase is converted to the gaseous (vapor) phase. The temperature remains constant during the boiling process even though energy is constantly added. The heat energy increases the potential energy of the particles in the gaseous phase. The amount of heat needed to convert a unit mass of a substance from its liquid phase to its vapor phase at constant temperature is called its **heat of vaporization.** As heat is added, the particles absorb sufficient energy to overcome the attractive forces holding them in the liquid phase. The potential energy of the system increases as the temperature remains constant. The heat of vaporization of water at 100°C and 1 atmosphere is 2260 J/g.

SAMPLE PROBLEM

How many joules of energy are required to vaporize 423 g of water at 100°C and 1 atm?

Solution: Identify the known and unknown values.

Known	*Unknown*
$m = 423$ g	$q = ?$ J
heat of vaporization = 2260 J/g	

Multiply the heat of vaporization by the total mass of water to determine the heat required.

$q = (423 \cancel{g})(2260 \text{ J}/\cancel{g}) = 955{,}980 \text{ J} = 956 \text{ kJ}$

The condensation process is the reverse of boiling process. Therefore the heat of condensation is also 2260 J/g. Condensation is an exothermic process.

Review Questions

30. When 25.0 grams of water are cooled from 20.0°C to 10.0°C, the number of joules of heat energy released is (1) 42 (2) 105 (3) 840 (4) 1050

31. How many joules of heat energy are released when 50.0 g of water are cooled from 70.0°C to 60.0°C? (1) 41.8 J (2) 2.09×10^3 J (3) 209 J (4) 4.18×10^3 J

32. What is the total number of joules of heat energy absorbed when the temperature of 200.0 g of water is raised from 10.0°C to 40.0°C? (1) 126 J (2) 840. J (3) 2.51×10^4 J (4) 3.36×10^4 J

33. How many kilojoules of heat energy are absorbed when 100.0 g of water are heated from 20.0°C to 30.0°C? (1) 4.18 kJ (2) 41.8 kJ (3) 418 kJ (4) 0.418 kJ

34. The temperature of a sample of water in the liquid phase is raised 30.0°C by the addition of 3762 J. What is the mass of the water? (1) 0.03 g (2) 0.30 g (3) 30.0 g (4) 300.0 g

35. When 418. joules of heat energy are added to 10.0 grams of water at 20.0°C, the final temperature of the water will be (1) 10.0°C (2) 30.0°C (3) 40.0°C (4) 100.0°C

36. When 20.0 g of a substance are completely melted at its melting point, 3444 J are absorbed. What is the heat of fusion of this substance? (1) 41 J/g (2) 172 J/g (3) 16,400 J/g (4) 68,900 J/g

37. The heat of vaporization of a liquid is 1344 J/g. What is the minimum number of joules needed to change 40.0 g of the liquid to vapor at the boiling point? (1) 33.6 J (2) 1344 J (3) 13,776 J (4) 53,800 J

For each of the following problems, be sure to show your work, use the proper units, and express your answer to the correct number of significant figures.

38. A sample of water is heated from 10.0°C to 15.0°C by the addition of 125 J of heat. What is the mass of the water?

39. What is the total number of joules absorbed by 65.0 g of water when the temperature of the water is raised from 25.0°C to 40.0°C?

40. If 100.0 J are added to 20.0 g of water at 30.0°C, what will be the final temperature of the water?

41. The temperature of 50.0 g of water was raised to 50.0°C by the addition of 1.0 kJ of heat energy. What was the initial temperature of the water?

42. What would be the temperature change if 3.0 g of water absorbed 15 J of heat?

43. What is the total number of kilojoules of heat needed to change 150. g of ice to water at 0°C?

44. What is the total number of kilojoules required to completely boil 100.0 g of water at 100.0°C and 1 atmosphere?

45. How much energy is required to vaporize 10.00 g of water at its boiling point?

46. At 1 atmosphere of pressure, 25.0 g of a compound at its normal boiling point are converted to a gas by the addition of 34,400 J. What is the heat of vaporization for this compound in J/g?

Behavior of Gases

Scientists construct models to explain the behavior of substances. While the gas laws describe how gases behave, they do not explain why gases behave the way they do. The **kinetic molecular theory** (KMT) is a model or theory that is used to explain the behavior of gases. This theory describes the relationships among pressure, volume, temperature, velocity, frequency, and force of collisions.

Kinetic Molecular Theory

The major ideas of kinetic molecular theory are summarized in the following statements:

- Gases contain particles (usually molecules or atoms) that are in constant, random, straight-line motion.
- Gas particles collide with each other and with the walls of the container. These collisions may result in a transfer of energy among the particles, but there is no net loss of energy as the result of these collisions. The collisions are said to be perfectly elastic.
- Gas particles are separated by relatively great distances. Because of this, the volume occupied by the particles themselves is negligible and need not be accounted for.
- Gas particles do not attract each other.

RELATIONSHIP OF PRESSURE AND NUMBERS OF GAS PARTICLES The kinetic molecular theory easily explains why gases exert pressure. Not only do gas molecules collide with each other, but they also collide with the walls of their container. These collisions with the container wall exert a force over the surface area of the wall—the particles exert pressure on the wall. For example, if you add more air to a bicycle tire, the pressure is increased. The greater the number of air particles, the greater the pressure. Pressure and the number of gas molecules are directly proportional.

RELATIONSHIP OF PRESSURE AND VOLUME OF A GAS Picture a cylinder with a piston at one end. If the piston can be pushed in, the volume will decrease. The molecules of the gas become more concentrated and hit the walls of the container more often. The pressure increases. If the piston is moved outward so as to increase the volume, the molecules hit the walls less often, causing a decrease in pressure. Thus volume and pressure are indirectly, or inversely, related. If one of the variables (volume or pressure) increases, the other must decrease.

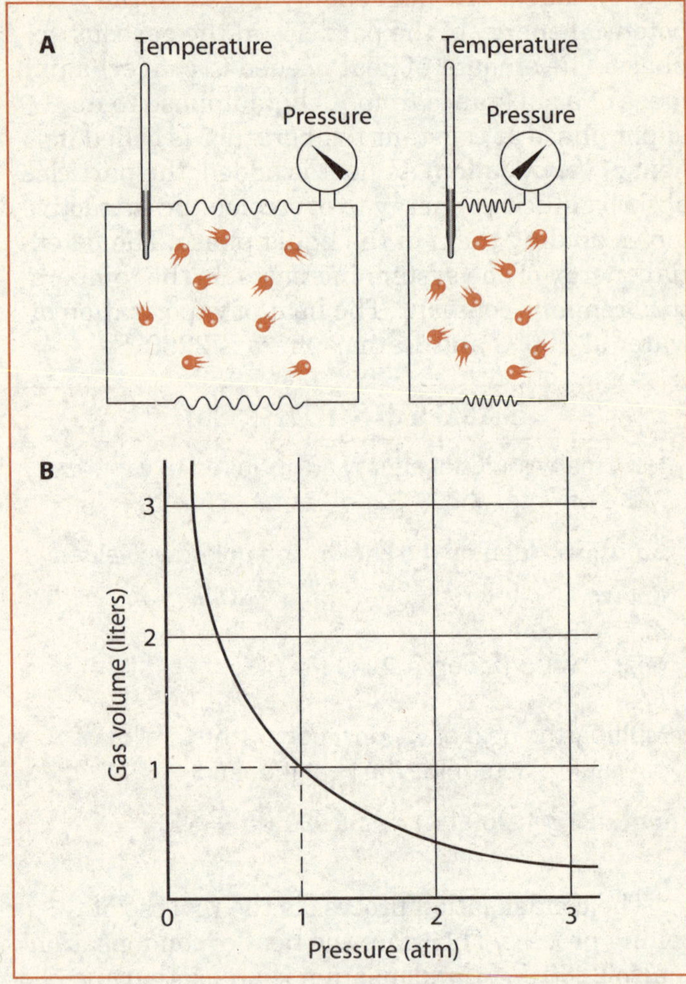

Figure 4-6. Pressure-volume relationship: (A) At constant temperature, as the volume of a gas decreases, the pressure it exerts increases. **(B)** This graph shows the variation of gas volume with changing pressure at constant temperature. PV = constant

RELATIONSHIP OF TEMPERATURE AND PRESSURE OF A GAS You may recall that the temperature of a substance is defined as a measure of the average kinetic energy of its particles. The kinetic energy (KE) is given by the formula $KE = (\frac{1}{2})mv^2$. As the temperature rises, the kinetic energy increases. This increase is due not to an increase in the mass of the particles, but rather to an increase in their velocity. As the temperature rises, the velocity of the particles increases, causing them to hit the walls of the container more often and with greater force. Thus an increase in temperature causes the pressure to increase. Pressure and temperature are directly related.

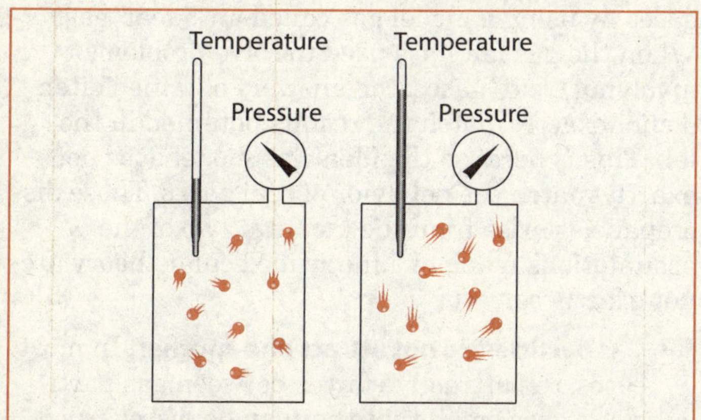

Figure 4-7. Temperature-pressure relationship: At constant volume, as the temperature of a gas increases, the pressure it exerts increases.

RELATIONSHIP OF TEMPERATURE AND VOLUME OF A GAS If the volume of a container could change while the pressure remained constant, how would volume and temperature be related? As the temperature increases, the molecules push harder on the piston of the container. When the internal pressure of the container exceeds the pressure pushing from the outside, the piston is pushed upward and the volume increases. The piston continues to move until the internal and external pressures are equal. Thus volume and temperature are directly related.

RELATIONSHIP OF TEMPERATURE AND VELOCITY You know that as the temperature of a substance increases, its kinetic energy increases. What is the cause of this increase in temperature? Obviously, the masses of the particles do not increase; therefore, it must be the velocity of the particles that increases. The higher the temperature, the greater the average velocity of the particles.

COMBINED GAS LAW EQUATION The relationships among pressure, temperature, and volume can be mathematically represented by an equation known as the combined gas law.

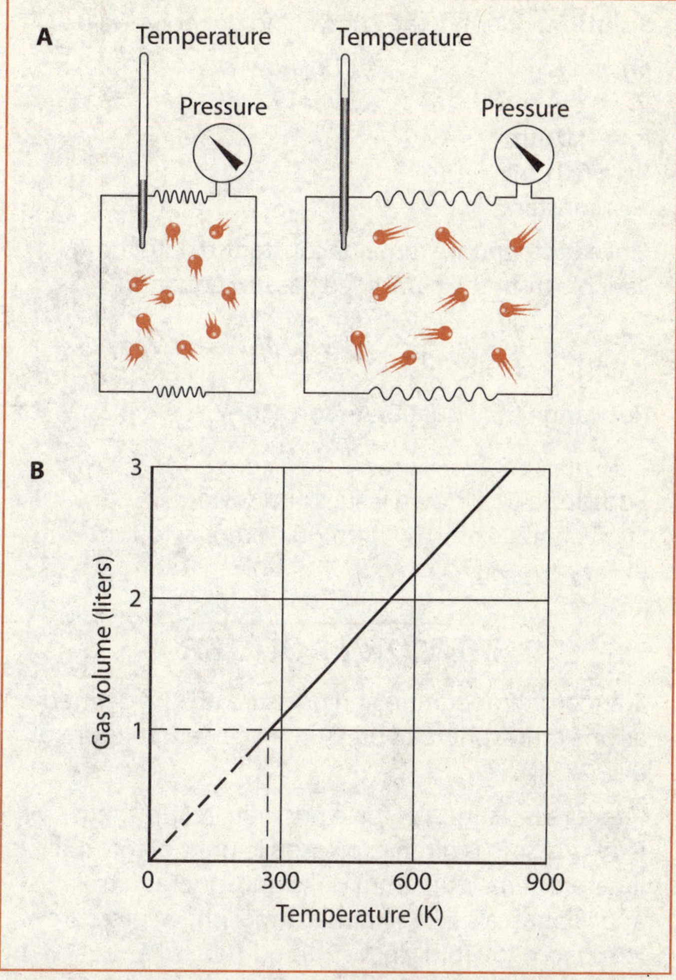

Figure 4-8. Temperature-volume relationship: **(A)** At constant pressure, as the temperature of a gas increases, the volume it occupies increases. **(B)** This graph shows the variation of gas volume with changing Kelvin temperature at constant pressure. V/T = constant

$$\frac{P_1V_1}{T_1} = \frac{P_2V_2}{T_2}$$

This law can be used to solve problems involving the gas properties of temperature (T), volume (V), and pressure (P) whenever two or more of these properties are involved. For problems in which two of the properties are involved and the third property remains constant, simply cancel out the variable representing the constant property and then solve for the remaining unknown.

SAMPLE PROBLEM

What volume will a gas occupy if the pressure on 244 cm^3 gas at 4.0 atm is increased to 6.0 atm? Assume the temperature remains constant.

Solution: Identify the known and unknown values.

Known	*Unknown*
$V_1 = 244\ cm^3$	$V_2 = ?\ cm^3$
$P_1 = 4.0$ atm	
$P_2 = 6.0$ atm	
T = constant	

Since temperature remains constant, delete the T variable from the combined gas law equation.

$$\frac{P_1V_1}{\cancel{T_1}} = \frac{P_2V_2}{\cancel{T_2}} \quad \textit{yields} \quad P_1V_1 = P_2V_2$$

Rearrange the equation to solve for V_2.

$$V_2 = (P_1V_1)/P_2$$

Substitute the known values and solve.

$$V_2 = (244\ cm^3)(4.0\ \cancel{atm})/(6.0\ \cancel{atm}) = 160\ cm^3$$

MEMORY JOGGER

Standard temperature and pressure (STP) is defined as one atmosphere of pressure and a temperature of 0°C (273 K).

Pressure is defined as force per unit area. In chemistry, pressure is often expressed in units of torr, millimeters of mercury (mm Hg), atmospheres (atm), and kilopascals (kPa). Normal atmospheric pressure is 760 torr, 760 mm Hg, 1 atm, and 101.3 kPa.

SAMPLE PROBLEM

If 75 cm^3 of a gas is at STP, what volume will the gas occupy if the temperature is raised to 75°C and the pressure is increased to 945 torr?

Solution: Identify the known and unknown values:

Known	*Unknown*
$P_1 = 760$ torr	$V_2 = ?\ cm^3$
$V_1 = 75\ cm^3$	
$T_1 = 0°C$	
$P_2 = 945$ torr	
$T_2 = 75°C$	

Convert the known temperatures into Kelvin.

$$T_1 = 0 + 273 = 273\ K$$
$$T_2 = 75 + 273 = 348\ K$$

Solve the combined gas law equation for V_2.

$$V_2 = \frac{P_1V_1T_2}{P_2T_1}$$

Substitute the known values and solve for V_2.

$$V_2 = \frac{(760\ \cancel{torr})(75\ cm^3)(348\ \cancel{K})}{(945\ \cancel{torr})(273\ \cancel{K})}$$

$$V_2 = 77\ cm^3$$

Ideal Versus Real Gases

Kinetic molecular theory explains the behavior of gases by using a model gas called an "ideal" gas. When the gas laws are used to solve problems involving "real" gases, the answers obtained often do not exactly match the results obtained in the lab. This is because the ideal gas model does not exactly match the behavior of real gases. These discrepancies arise from the fact that two of the assumptions made by kinetic molecular theory are not exactly correct.

- **Gas particles do not attract one another.** In most cases, the attractive forces between gas particles are so small that they can be disregarded. However, when conditions become extreme, these small forces become important. For example, water molecules in the atmosphere attract each other when temperatures become cold enough. The water molecules combine to form snow or rain.
- **Gas particles do not occupy volume.** Although gas particles themselves occupy a small volume of space under normal conditions, as pressure increases the volume occupied by the particles can no longer be ignored. At high pressures, the increased concentration of particles leads to more frequent collisions and far greater chances of combining.

A gas is said to be "ideal" if it behaves exactly as predicted. Although no gas is truly "ideal," hydrogen and helium are nearly ideal in behavior. In general, gases vary from ideal behavior because of two factors: increasing mass and increasing polarity. These factors become important as pressure is increased and temperature is decreased. Gases are most ideal at low pressures and high temperatures.

Review Questions

47. At constant pressure, how does the volume of 1 mole of an ideal gas vary? (1) directly with the Kelvin temperature (2) indirectly with the Kelvin temperature (3) directly with the mass of the gas (4) indirectly with the mass of the gas

48. Which graph best shows the relationship between Kelvin temperature and average kinetic energy?

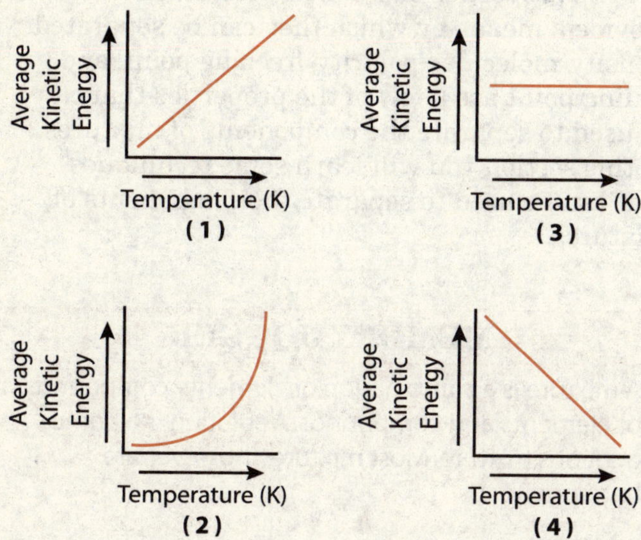

49. Under which conditions will the volume of a given sample of a gas always decrease? (1) decreased pressure and decreased temperature (2) decreased pressure and increased temperature (3) increased pressure and decreased temperature (4) increased pressure and increased temperature

50. Which graph best shows the change in the volume of 1 mole of nitrogen gas as pressure increases and temperature remains constant?

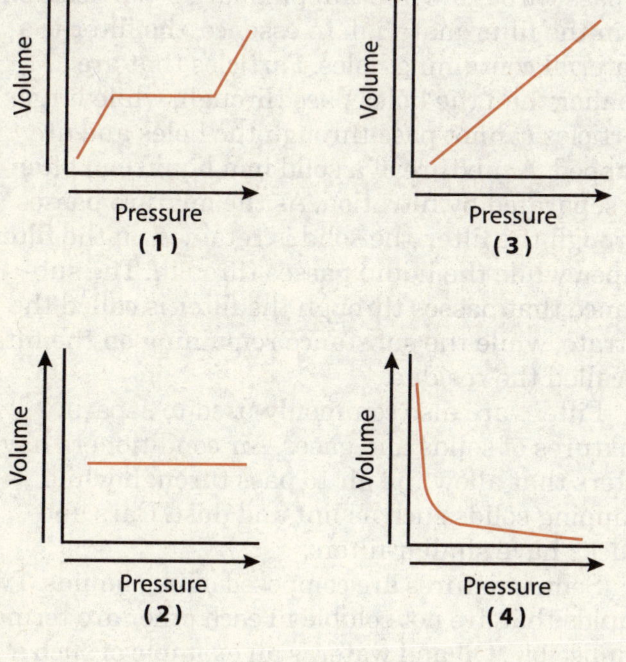

51. At constant temperature, the relationship between the volume (V) of a gas and its pressure (P) is
(1) $V = (\text{constant})P$ (2) $P = (\text{constant})V$
(3) $PV = \text{constant}$ (4) $V/P = \text{constant}$

52. Which changes in pressure and temperature occur as a given mass of gas at 380 torr and 546 K is changed to STP? (1) The pressure is doubled and the temperature is halved. (2) The pressure is doubled and the temperature is doubled. (3) The pressure is halved and the temperature is halved. (4) The pressure is halved and the temperature is doubled.

53. As the temperature of a gas is increased from 0°C to 10°C at constant pressure, the volume of the gas
(1) increases by $\frac{1}{273}$ (2) increases by $\frac{10}{273}$
(3) decreases by $\frac{1}{273}$ (4) decreases by $\frac{10}{273}$

54. The table below shows the changes in the volume of a gas as the pressure changes at constant temperature.

Pressure (atm)	Volume (mL)
0.5	1000
1.0	500
2.0	250

Which equation best expresses the relationship between pressure and volume for the gas?
(1) $\frac{P}{V} = 500$ atm•mL (2) $PV = 500$ atm•mL
(3) $\frac{V}{P} = 500$ atm•mL (4) $PV = 1/500$ atm•mL

55. A cylinder with a tightly fitted piston is shown in the diagram below. As the piston moves downward, the number of molecules of air in the cylinder
(1) decreases (2) increases (3) remains the same

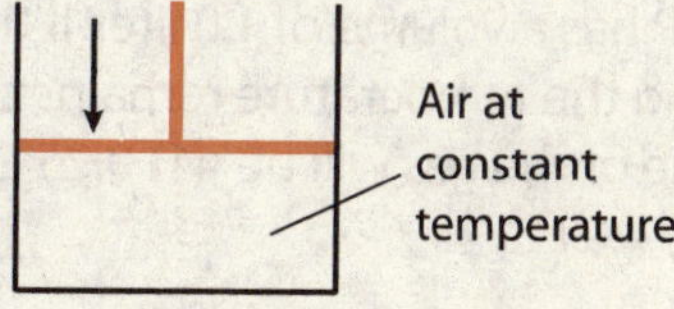

56. What volume will a 300.0 mL sample of a gas at STP occupy when the pressure is doubled at constant temperature? (1) 150.0 mL (2) 600.0 mL (3) 2000. mL (4) 4000. mL

57. A gas has a volume of 1000 mL at a temperature of 20. K and a pressure of 760 mm Hg. What will be the new volume when the temperature is changed to 40.0 K and the pressure is changed to 380 mm Hg? (1) 250 mL (2) 1000 mL (3) 4000 mL (4) 5600 mL

58. The volume of a sample of a gas at 273°C is 200.0 L. If the volume is decreased to 100.0 L at constant pressure, what will be the new temperature of the gas? (1) 0 K (2) 100 K (3) 273 K (4) 546 K

59. The graph below represents the relationship between pressure and volume of a gas at constant temperature. The product of pressure and volume is constant. According to the graph, what is the product of pressure and volume (in atm•mL)?

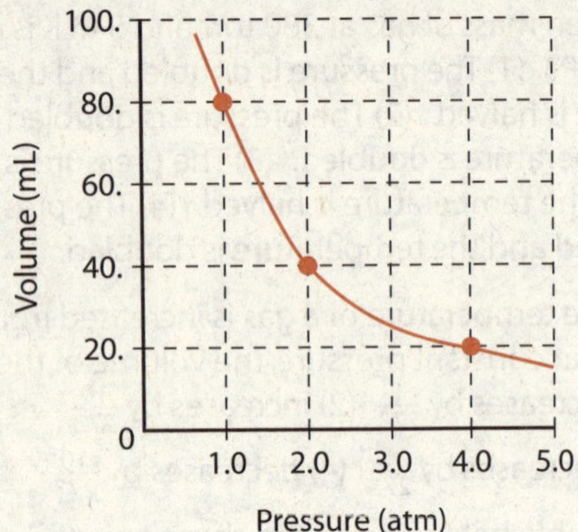

(1) 20. (2) 40. (3) 60. (4) 80.

60. A sample of gas has a volume of 12 liters at 0°C and 380 torr. What will be its volume when the pressure is changed to 760 torr at a constant temperature? (1) 24 L (2) 18 L (3) 12 L (4) 6.0 L

61. A 2.5 liter sample of gas is at STP. When the temperature is raised to 273°C and the pressure remains constant, the new volume of the gas will be (1) 1.25 L (2) 2.5 L (3) 5.0 L (4) 10.0 L

62. A gas occupies a volume of 500. mL at a pressure of 380. torr and a temperature of 298 K. At what temperature will the gas occupy a volume of 250. mL and have a pressure of 760. torr? (1) 149 K (2) 298 K (3) 447 K (4) 596 K

63. A gas at STP has a volume of 1.0 liter. If the pressure is doubled and the temperature remains constant, the new volume of the gas will be (1) 0.25 L (2) 2.0 L (3) 0.5 L (4) 4.0 L

For each of the following problems, be sure to show your work, use the proper units, and express your answer to the correct number of significant figures.

64. A gas has a volume of 2 liters at 323 K and 3 atmospheres. What will be the new volume if the temperature is changed to 273 K and the pressure is changed to 1 atmosphere?

65. What will be the new volume of 100. mL of gas if the Kelvin temperature and the pressure are both doubled?

66. The pressure exerted on 200. mL of a gas is decreased from 900. torr to 800. torr. What is the new volume of the gas if the temperature remains constant?

Separation of Mixtures

The properties of a mixture's components often provide a means by which they can be separated. Density, molecular polarity, freezing point, and boiling point are a few of the properties that can be used to separate the components of mixtures. In this section you will learn some techniques that can be used to separate the components of mixtures.

MEMORY JOGGER

A mixture is a combination of elements, compounds, or elements and compounds. A solution is a homogeneous mixture. Most mixtures, however, are heterogeneous.

Filtration

Many mixtures are made up of solids in a liquid. The solids are not dissolved in the liquid, but may be suspended. When allowed to stand undisturbed, the solids will settle to the bottom of the liquid. In some cases, you can separate the two components of the mixture by carefully pouring off the liquid without disturbing the solid. This method, though inefficient, can sometimes be used.

A filter is a material that allows small particles to pass through while trapping larger particles on or in the filter material. In essence, the filter is a material containing holes. Particles that are smaller than the holes pass through, while larger particles cannot pass through the holes and are trapped. A mixture of a solid in a liquid can often be separated by filtration. As the mixture passes through the filter, the solid is retained on the filter paper, while the liquid passes through. The substance that passes through the filter is called the filtrate, while the substance remaining on the filter is called the residue.

Filters are also commonly used to separate mixtures of solids and gases. Air conditioners have filters that allow the air to pass through while trapping solids such as lint and dust. Cars and trucks have similar filters.

Some mixtures are composed of two liquids. Two liquids that are not soluble in each other are termed immiscible. Oil and water is an example of such a mixture. Because the oil has a density less than water, the oil rises to the top when the mixture is allowed to stand. In some cases, it is possible to simply pour off the upper layer into a separate container. Figure 4-9 shows a separatory funnel that can be used to separate two liquids that do not dissolve in each other. After the two liquids have been allowed to separate, the valve is opened and the more dense liquid flows from the bottom of the funnel.

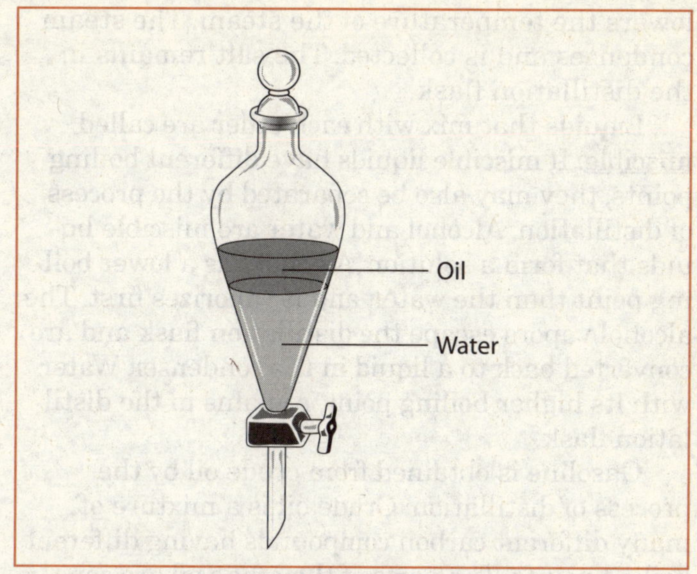

Figure 4-9. Separatory funnel: Two immiscible liquids can be separated with a separatory funnel. When the valve is opened, the denser liquid flows from the funnel.

Distillation

When solids are dissolved in liquids, making a homogeneous solution, they may be separated by distillation. Figure 4-10 shows a typical distillation apparatus. In the case of a salt and water mixture, the solution is heated and the water begins to boil. The steam passes from the distilling flask into the condensing tube. A water jacket

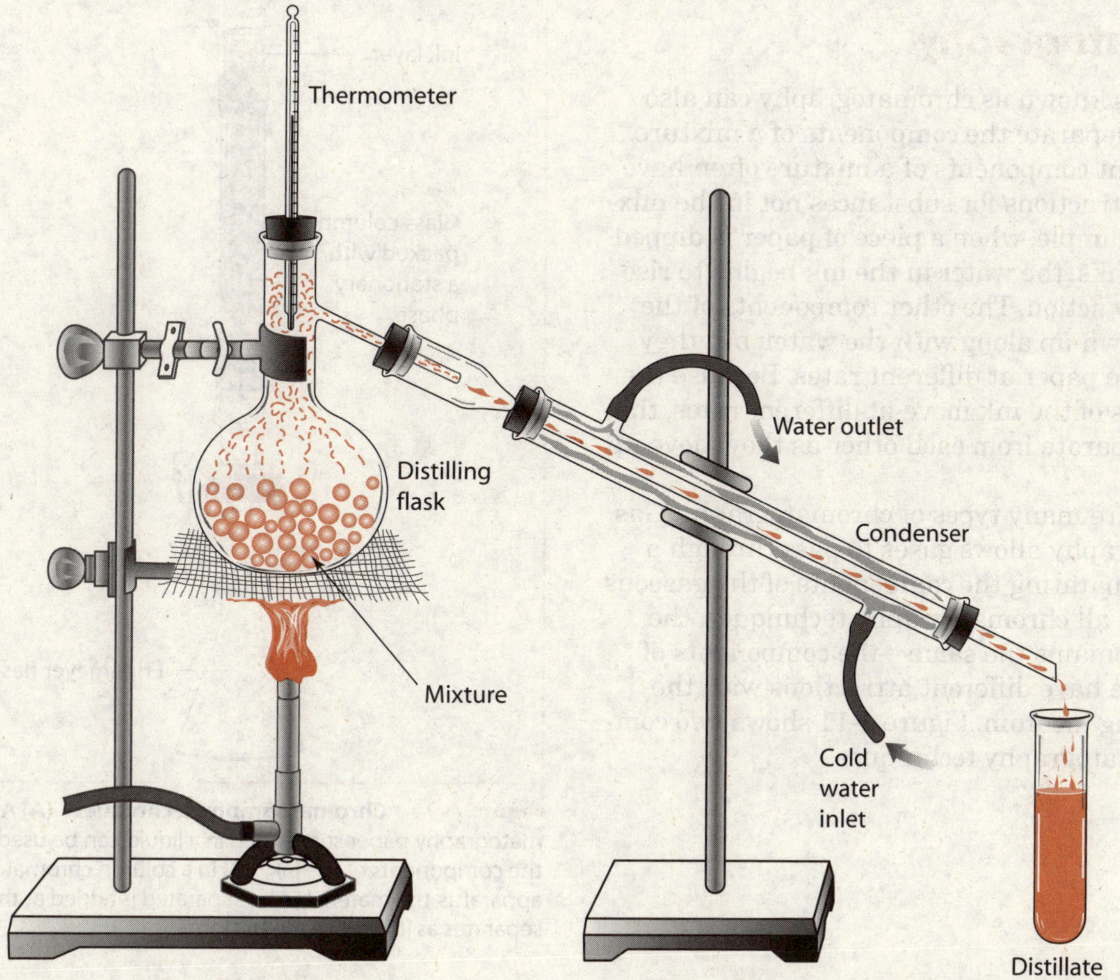

Thermometer
Distilling flask
Mixture
Water outlet
Condenser
Cold water inlet
Distillate

Figure 4-10. A simple distillation apparatus

lowers the temperature of the steam. The steam condenses and is collected. The salt remains in the distillation flask.

Liquids that mix with each other are called miscible. If miscible liquids have different boiling points, they may also be separated by the process of distillation. Alcohol and water are miscible liquids that form a solution. Alcohol has a lower boiling point than the water, and it vaporizes first. The alcohol vapors escape the distillation flask and are converted back to a liquid in the condenser. Water, with its higher boiling point, remains in the distillation flask.

Gasoline is obtained from crude oil by the process of distillation. Crude oil is a mixture of many different carbon compounds having different boiling points. The parts of the crude oil are separated into various parts, called fractions, by distillation. Gasoline is one of the lighter fractions. It has a relatively low boiling point when compared with other fractions such as diesel oil or home heating oil.

Chromatography

The process known as chromatography can also be used to separate the components of a mixture. The different components of a mixture often have different attractions for substances not in the mixture. For example, when a piece of paper is dipped into some inks, the water in the ink begins to rise by capillary action. The other components of the ink are drawn up along with the water, but they move up the paper at different rates. Because the components of the ink move at different rates, they begin to separate from each other as they move up the paper.

There are many types of chromatography. Gas chromatography allows gases to pass through a medium separating the components of the gaseous mixture. In all chromatography techniques, the principle remains the same—the components of the mixture have different attractions with the transporting medium. Figure 4-11 shows two common chromatography techniques.

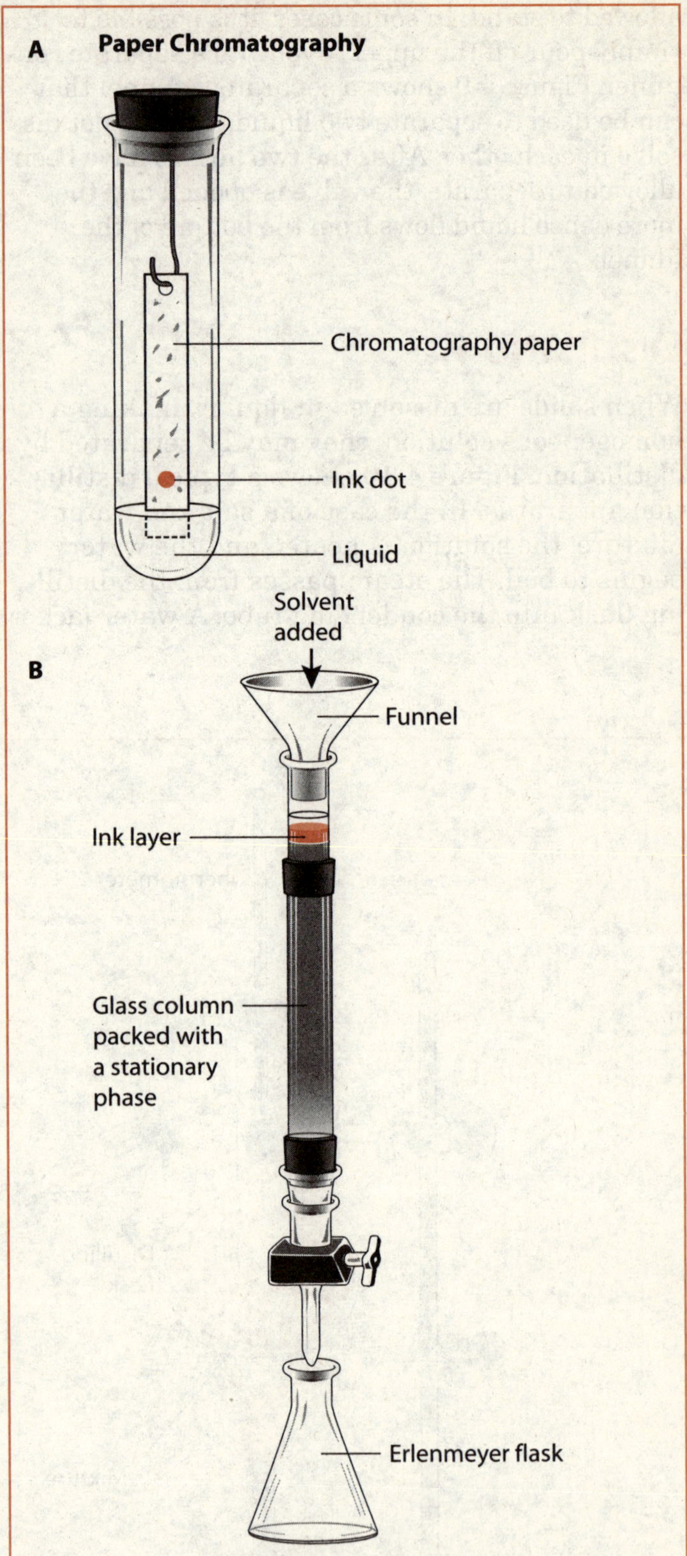

Figure 4-11. Chromatography techniques: (A) A strip of chromatography paper suspended in a liquid can be used to separate the components of the ink. **(B)** In a column chromatography apparatus, the material to be separated is added at the top and separates as it flows to the bottom.

Review Questions

67. By using a paper filter, which of the following can be separated? (1) two immiscible liquids (2) two heterogeneous solids (3) a solid in a liquid (4) two miscible liquids

68. Distillation can be used to separate (1) two solids (2) two miscible liquids with different boiling points (3) solids suspended in a gas (4) gases with different densities

69. Gasoline is separated into its components by (1) fractional distillation (2) filtration (3) paper chromatography (4) column chromatography

70. The principle that allows paper chromatography to separate mixtures depends on the different components having (1) different boiling points (2) different attractions to the paper (3) different densities (4) similar solubility in water

Questions for Regents Practice

Part A

1. Which set of properties does a substance such as $CO_2(g)$ have?

(1) definite shape and definite volume

(2) definite shape but no definite volume

(3) no definite shape but definite volume

(4) no definite shape and no definite volume

2. A liquid is poured from a volumetric flask into a beaker. Which of the following is true?

(1) It retains its original volume and shape.

(2) It retains its original volume, but its shape changes.

(3) It retains its original shape, but its volume changes.

(4) Both the volume and shape change.

3. The heat required to change 1 gram of a solid at its normal melting point to a liquid at the same temperature is called the heat of

(1) vaporization (3) reaction

(2) fusion (4) formation

4. Which statement best describes the molecules of H_2O in the solid phase?

(1) They move slowly in straight lines.

(2) They move rapidly in straight lines.

(3) They are arranged in a regular geometric pattern.

(4) They are arranged in a random pattern.

5. As the temperature of a substance rises, the average kinetic energy of the particles making up the substance

(1) increases (3) remains the same

(2) decreases

6. When a substance melts, it undergoes a process known as

(1) condensation (3) sublimation

(2) fusion (4) vaporization

7. Which phase change is accompanied by the release of heat?

(1) $H_2O(s) \rightarrow H_2O(\ell)$ (3) $H_2O(s) \rightarrow H_2O(g)$

(2) $H_2O(\ell) \rightarrow H_2O(s)$ (4) $H_2O(\ell) \rightarrow H_2O(g)$

8. Which of the following is a unit of heat?

(1) torr (3) gram

(2) degree (4) joule

9. Which of the following behave most like ideal gases?

(1) oxygen and hydrogen (3) oxygen and nitrogen

(2) helium and hydrogen (4) helium and nitrogen

Part B

10. Which is the equivalent of 750. joules?

(1) 0.750 kJ (3) 7.50 kJ

(2) 75 kJ (4) 750. kJ

11. As a solid is heated at a constant rate, its temperature increases from 10°C to 25°C, remains at 25°C for 5 minutes, and then increases to beyond 45°C. Based on this information, what conclusion can be drawn about the substance?

(1) Its melting point is 45°C.

(2) Its boiling point is 45°C.

(3) Its melting point is 25°C.

(4) Its boiling point is 25°C.

12. A liquid's freezing point is −38°C and its boiling point is 357°C. How many Kelvins are there between the boiling point and the freezing point of the liquid?

(1) 319 (3) 592

(2) 395 (4) 668

13. Which Celsius temperature is equivalent to 323 K?

(1) 50°C (3) 273°C

(2) 212°C (4) 596°C

14. When steam condenses to water, the surrounding temperature

(1) decreases (3) remains the same

(2) increases

Show all work for the following questions. Use appropriate units and follow operations with significant figures.

15. The following graph represents the relationship between temperature and time as heat was added uniformly to a substance. At the beginning, the substance was a solid below its melting point. Describe the changes in kinetic and potential energy of the substance during time periods AB and BC.

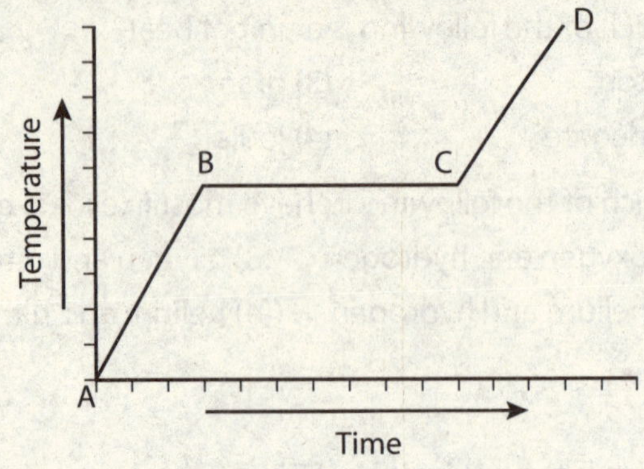

16. How many joules of energy are needed to convert 50.0 g of water at 50°C to 65°C?

17. What volume will 250. mL of gas at STP occupy if the pressure changes to 2.0 atmospheres and the temperature changes to 30°C?

18. How many joules are needed to completely boil 40.0 g of water at 100°C?

19. A substance has a specific heat capacity of 2.0 J/g•°C. How many joules are needed to raise the temperature of 30.0 g of this substance by 15°C?

20. Which graph best represents a change of phase from a gas to a solid?

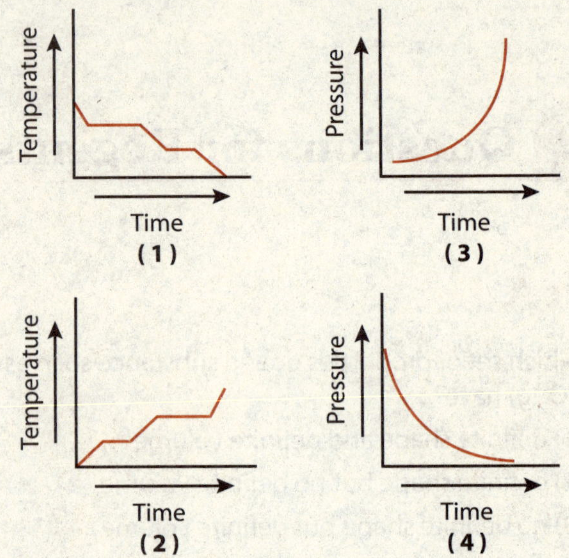

Part C

Answer question 21 in one or more complete sentences.

21. Plasmas are often described as the fourth phase of matter. Plasma particles have had some, or all, of their electrons removed. Explain how the forces between particles in a gas and particles in a plasma differ. [2]

Questions 22–24 are based on the following graphs.

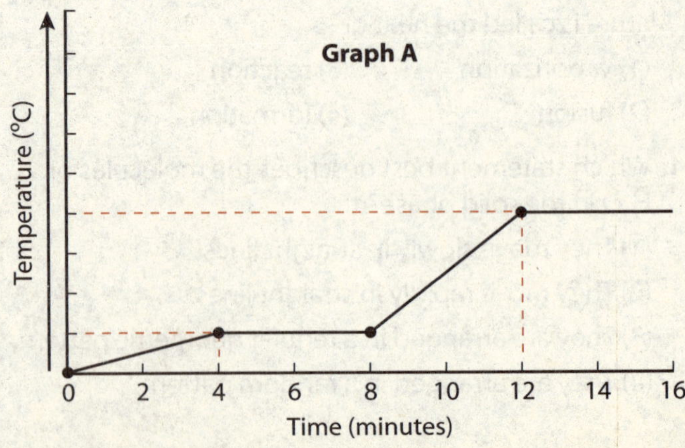

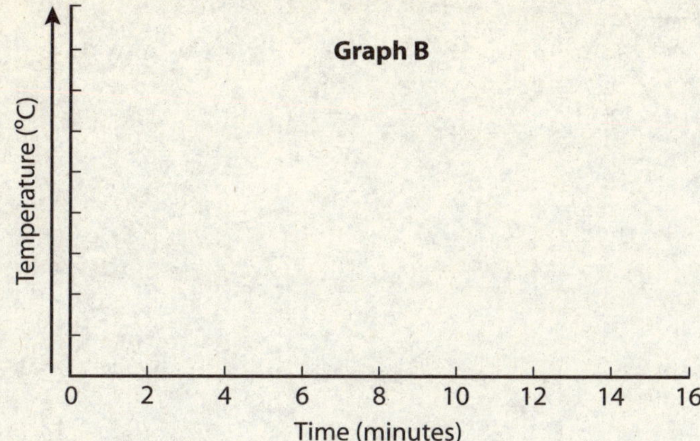

22. Graph A shows the temperature change of 10.0 g of a substance from below its melting point until after it begins boiling when heat is added at a rate of 200. J/min. Use Graph B to plot the change in temperature for the same substance when heat is added at a rate of 400. J/min. [2]

23. Based on Graph A, what is the heat of fusion of the substance? [1]

24. How do the heats of fusion in Graph A and Graph B compare? [1]

Answer questions 25–26 in one or more complete sentences.

25. A student has a flask containing two immiscible liquids. One of the liquids is a solution of a solid in water. Describe how you would separate the mixture into its three separate components. [2]

26. What data would a student need to collect in an experiment to determine the specific heat capacity of a substance? [1]

27. The following data were recorded during a lab experiment involving the heating of a substance. During the experiment, heat was added at a constant rate.

Time (minutes)	**Temperature** (°C)
0	10
1	15
2	20
3	25
4	30
5	30
6	30
7	30
8	30
9	35
10	40
11	45

What conclusion or conclusions can be drawn from the data? [2]

28. In order to solve problems involving a gas undergoing a change in temperature, the temperature must be in Kelvins. Why can't Celsius values be used? [1]

29. Consider a heating curve for 100 g of a substance when heat is applied at a constant rate. Describe the changes in the heating curve if 200 g of the substance are heated at the same rate. [2]

The Periodic Table

VOCABULARY		
atomic radius	**ionic radius**	**noble gas**
electronegativity	**ionization energy**	**nonmetal**
family	**metal**	**periodic law**
group	**metalloid**	**period**

Currently, more than 100 elements are known. Most of them occur naturally, while others are made artificially.

These elements vary greatly in their physical and chemical properties as well as in the characteristics of their compounds. It has long been recognized that if the elements could be classified, it would simplify their study. In this chapter we will present the arrangement of the periodic table. Next, we will examine different types of elements. Finally, trends of important properties will be considered.

Classifying Elements

While there were early attempts to classify and arrange the elements in some orderly fashion, it was Dmitri Mendeleev, a Russian chemist, who is given credit for first arranging elements in a usable manner. Mendeleev observed that when the elements were arranged in order of increasing atomic mass, similar chemical and physical properties appeared at regular, or periodic, intervals. Mendeleev's work in the middle of the nineteenth century laid the basis for the periodic table as we know it today.

However, in Mendeleev's periodic table, the properties of several pairs of elements, such as iodine and tellurium, seemed out of order. If they were switched on the table, the properties would match better, but they would not be in order of increasing atomic mass.

The modern periodic table is not arranged by increasing atomic mass, but rather by increasing atomic number. Henry Moseley, an English scientist, used X rays to identify the atomic number of the elements. If the elements were listed by increasing atomic number, the properties repeated periodically. Modern **periodic law** states: *The properties of the elements are periodic functions of their atomic numbers.*

Table Information about the Elements

The periodic table is an arrangement of the elements, from left to right across each descending row, in order of increasing atomic number. The periodic table used in Appendix 1, *Reference Tables for Physical Setting/Chemistry,* displays some properties of each of the elements. To fully understand some of the information the periodic table provides, refer to Figure 5-1 as the boxes on the periodic table are discussed.

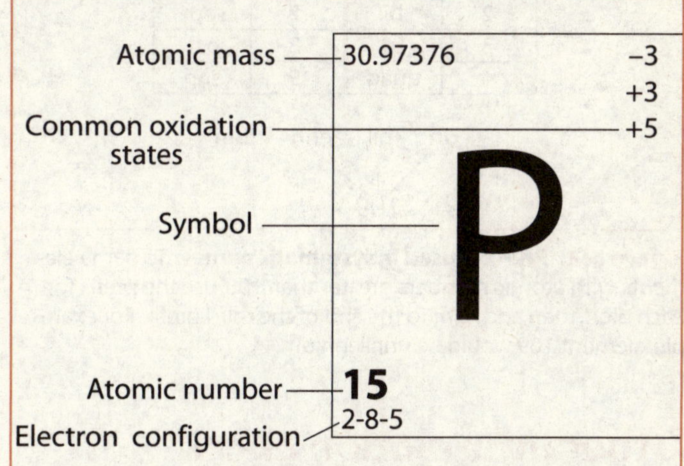

Figure 5-1. Sample information from the periodic table: Although the information about the elements can differ from one periodic table to another, some information, such as atomic mass, atomic number, and symbol, are common to almost all tables.

Chemical Symbols

The symbol of each element is usually found in the center of the box. With over 100 elements to refer to, a symbol is a short and easy way to indicate what element you're talking about, and scientists all over the world can identify an element by its symbol.

Each symbol has one, two, or three letters. The first letter is capitalized, and any other letters present are lower case.

The symbol is related to the name of the element, although sometimes the relationship is not obvious. For example, carbon has an obvious symbol of C. Sodium, however, has the symbol Na, which comes from its Latin name of *natrium*.

Symbols are assigned by an organization known as IUPAC after they agree on what the name of the element is. Agreement has been reached for the names and symbols of the first 108 elements. As shown in Figure 5-2, elements beyond 108 have not yet been assigned names and are represented by systematic names and three-letter symbols that represent their atomic numbers. Although the discovery of element 118 has been reported, subsequent attempts to duplicate it have failed. It is listed on the reference table, but its existence is doubtful at this time.

Roots Used for Naming Elements

Digit	Root	Digit	Root
0	nil	5	pent
1	un	6	hex
2	bi	7	sept
3	tri	8	oct
4	quad	9	enn

Un nil enn ium

109

Figure 5-2. Prefixes used in systematic names: To name elements with atomic numbers greater than 108, use the prefix for each digit, then add *-ium* to the end of the third prefix. For example, element 109 would be unnilennium.

Other Information about the Elements

In the boxes on the periodic table in this book, the atomic number is located below and to the left of the symbol. Below the atomic number is the electron configuration showing how the electrons are arranged according to their energy levels. The atomic mass is above the symbol and to the left. Selected oxidation states are in the upper right-hand corner of the box.

Often, a periodic table will include the name of the element and its state at room temperature. Not all tables include electron configuration and common oxidation states. The information provided by a periodic table will often depend on what information is needed. A periodic table used to determine bonding types, for example, might just include the symbols and electronegativities of the elements.

MEMORY JOGGER

The decimal atomic masses given for each element on the periodic table are the weighted average of the masses of the isotopes of that element.

Arrangement of the Periodic Table

You now know that the elements on the periodic table are listed according to increasing atomic number. But how does this arrangement allow periodic properties to be seen? As you will learn, the columns and rows of the table have special significance.

Periods

The horizontal rows of the table are called **periods.** The number at the beginning of the period indicates the principal energy level in which the valence electrons are located for the atoms of that period. Potassium (K) and bromine (Br) are members of Period 4, so they have valence electrons in the fourth principal energy level.

In each period, the number of valence electrons increases from left to right, and the properties of the elements change systematically across a period. For example, the elements on the left side of the table have common properties that are described in the next section; these elements are called **metals.** Metals comprise about 75% of all the elements. To the right of the middle of the table are elements called **metalloids,** which have some properties of both metals and nonmetals. On most periodic tables, the metalloids are located adjacent to a diagonal, stair-step line. To the right of the metalloids, each period contains one or more elements with properties also described in the next section; these elements are known as **nonmetals.** Each period of the table ends with a noble gas. The metals and metalloids are all solid with the exception of mercury, a liquid. Nonmetals include solids, a liquid (bromine), and gases. Figure 5-3 summarizes this trend on the periodic table.

Groups, or Families

The vertical columns of the periodic table are called **groups,** or **families.** With a few exceptions, each member of a given group contains the same number of valence electrons. The number of valence electrons for each element is shown as the last number in the electron configuration. Phosphorus, in Group 15, has an electron configuration of 2-8-5. Thus, phosphorus has five valence electrons. All the members of Group 15 have five valence electrons. The elements in Group 18 have eight valence electrons. Helium, in Group 18, is an exception, having only two valence electrons. Because it is the number of valence electrons that determines much of the chemical reactivity of the element, the members of a given group have similar chemical properties.

Types of Elements

You've just seen that most elements are metals, and some are metalloids or nonmetals. An element can be classified as one of these types according to where it is located on the periodic table. The properties of each type of element are quite important in determining how it can be used.

Metals

Remember that most known elements are metals. The most active metals are located in Groups 1 and 2. In any group of the periodic table, the metallic properties of the elements increase from the top to the bottom of the group.

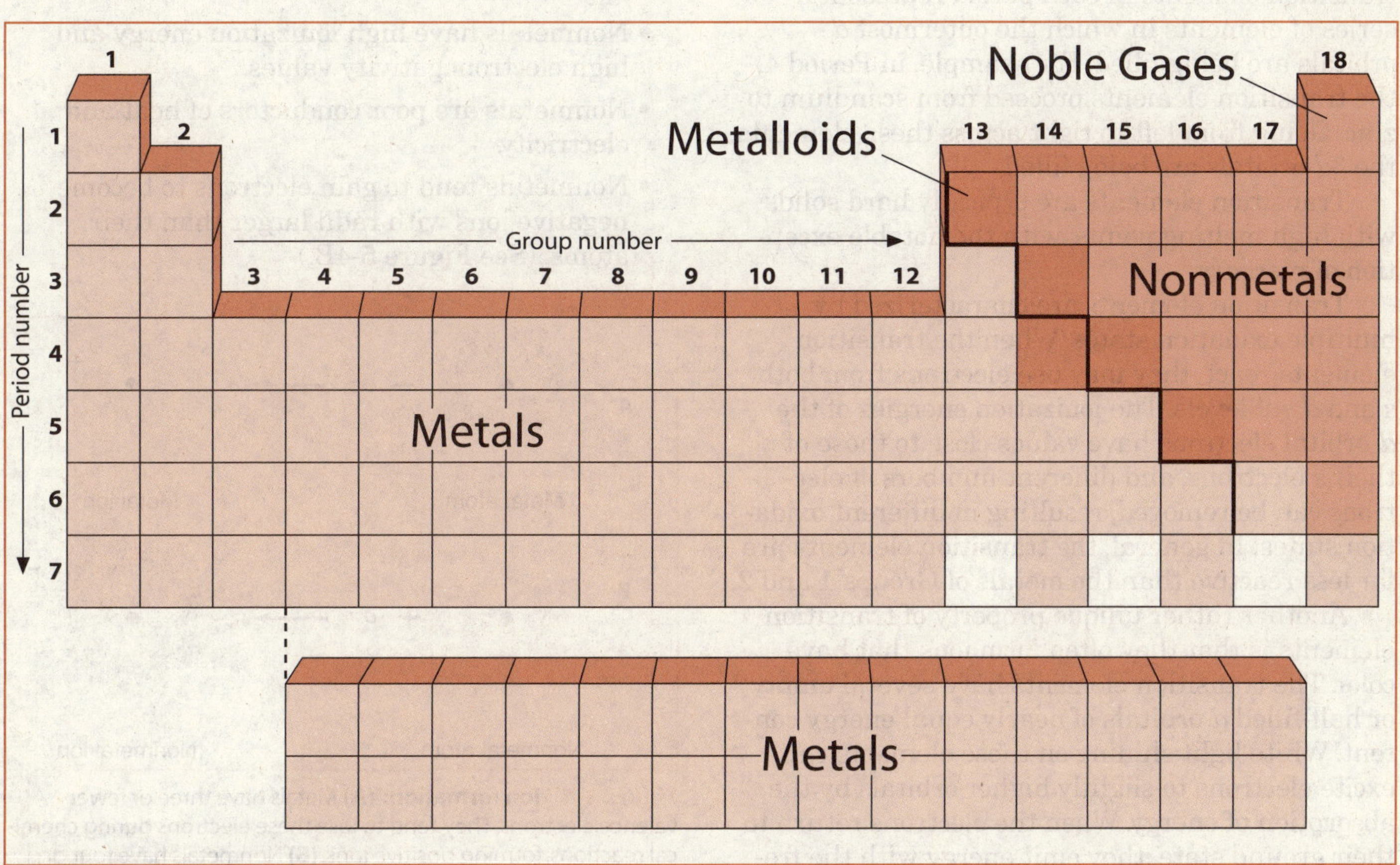

Figure 5-3. A trend from left to right across a period: Metals are found on the left of the periodic table; metalloids, on the staircase; and nonmetals, including noble gases, on the right side.

GENERAL PROPERTIES OF METALS

- Metals are solids at room temperature, with the exception of mercury, which is a liquid.
- Most of the metals have densities greater than water, but the alkali metals (Group 1) will float.
- Metals are <u>malleable</u>, which means that they can be hammered into a shape.
- Metals are <u>ductile</u>, which means that they can be drawn or pulled into a wire.
- Metals have <u>luster</u>, which means that they are shiny.
- Metals are good conductors of heat and electricity. This property stems from the mobility of their valence electrons.
- Metals have relatively low ionization energy and electronegativity values.
- Metals tend to lose electrons to form positive ions with smaller radii. (See Figure 5-4A.)

TRANSITION ELEMENTS The elements of Groups 3 through 12 are called the transition elements, or sometimes the transition metals. The transition elements in each period represent a series of elements in which the outermost *d* orbitals are being filled. For example, in Period 4, the transition elements proceed from scandium to zinc. Going from left to right across these elements, the 3*d* orbitals are being filled.

Transition elements are typically hard solids with high melting points, with the notable exception of mercury.

Transition elements are characterized by multiple oxidation states. When the transition elements react, they may use electrons from both *s* and *d* sublevels. The ionization energies of the *d*-orbital electrons have values close to those of their *s* electrons, and different numbers of electrons can be removed, resulting in different oxidation states. In general, the transition elements are far less reactive than the metals of Groups 1 and 2.

Another rather unique property of transition elements is that they often form ions that have color. The transition elements have several empty or half-filled *d* orbitals of nearly equal energy content. White light shining on these elements can excite electrons to slightly higher orbitals by the absorption of energy. When the electrons return to their ground state, they emit energy with the frequencies of visible colors.

Metalloids

The metalloids (B, Si, Ge, As, Sb, and Te), sometimes called semimetals, are sandwiched between the metals and the nonmetals. They can be found adjacent to the diagonal, stair-step line on the periodic table used in this book. Metalloids represent an intermediate type of element, displaying both metallic and nonmetallic properties.

Nonmetals

Although the properties of nonmetals vary more than those of metals, some standard properties can be observed.

GENERAL PROPERTIES OF NONMETALS

- Many nonmetals are gases or molecular or network solids at room temperature. Bromine is an exception, being a liquid at room temperature.
- Nonmetals are not malleable or ductile; they tend to be brittle in the solid phase.
- Solid nonmetals lack luster, and their surface appears dull.
- Nonmetals have high ionization energy and high electronegativity values.
- Nonmetals are poor conductors of heat and electricity.
- Nonmetals tend to gain electrons to become negative ions with radii larger than their atoms. (See Figure 5-4B.)

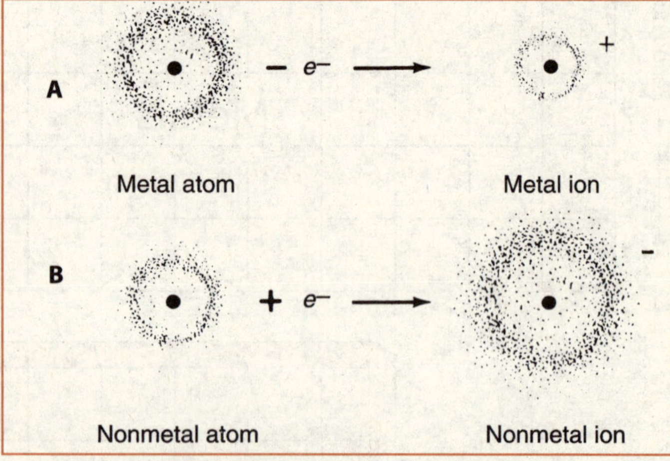

Figure 5-4. Ion formation: (A) Metals have three or fewer valence electrons. They tend to lose these electrons during chemical reactions, forming positive ions. **(B)** Nonmetals have four or more valence electrons. The more valence electrons a nonmetal has, up to seven, the more likely it is to gain electrons, forming a negative ion.

Noble Gases

The elements in Group 18 are called the **noble gases.** Noble gases don't have all the properties of nonmetals because they are generally unreactive. Only a few stable compounds containing noble gases have been formed.

Each of these elements has a completely filled outer energy level (valence level) of electrons. The valence level of helium is filled with only two electrons, whereas the rest of the noble gases have a complete octet (eight electrons), which is an extremely stable electron configuration.

ALLOTROPES Some nonmetals can exist in two or more forms in the same phase. These forms are called allotropes. Oxygen (O_2(g)) and ozone (O_3(g)) are examples of allotropes. Table 5-1 compares some physical properties of oxygen and ozone.

Table 5-1. Properties of Oxygen and Ozone

Property	Oxygen (O_2)	Ozone (O_3)
Molecular mass (amu)	32	48
Melting point (K)	54.3	80.5
Boiling point (K)	90.2	161.7
Density (g/cm^3)	1.14	1.61

The table shows that allotropes have different physical properties. They also differ chemically. Ozone is a much stronger oxidizing agent than molecular oxygen and can cause serious damage to organic molecules. In the upper layers of the atmosphere, ozone absorbs harmful ultraviolet rays preventing them from reaching ground level.

Other nonmetals also show allotropy. Carbon is found as graphite, diamond, and buckminsterfullerene, which has a formula of C_{60}. Phosphorus can be found as yellow (white), red, and black allotropes.

Review Questions

1. The observed regularities in the properties of the elements are periodic functions of their (1) atomic numbers (2) mass numbers (3) oxidation states (4) nonvalence electrons

2. Elements in Mendeleev's periodic table were arranged according to their (1) atomic number (2) atomic mass (3) relative activity (4) relative size

3. Most of the groups in the periodic table of the elements contain (1) nonmetals only (2) metals only (3) nonmetals and metals (4) metals and metalloids

4. An element is a gas at room temperature. It could be (1) a metal or a metalloid (2) a metal or a nonmetal (3) a metalloid or a nonmetal (4) a nonmetal only

5. Atoms of metals tend to (1) lose electrons and form negative ions (2) lose electrons and form positive ions (3) gain electrons and form negative ions (4) gain electrons and form positive ions

6. Which property is generally characteristic of metallic elements? (1) low electrical conductivity (2) high heat conductivity (3) existence as brittle solids (4) existence as molecular solids

7. When a metal atom combines with a nonmetal atom, the nonmetal atom will (1) lose electrons and decrease in size (2) lose electrons and increase in size (3) gain electrons and decrease in size (4) gain electrons and increase in size

8. A Mg atom differs from a Mg^{2+} ion in that the atom has a (1) smaller radius (2) larger radius (3) smaller nucleus (4) larger nucleus

9. Which of the following elements has an ionic radius smaller than its atomic radius? (1) neon (2) nitrogen (3) sodium (4) sulfur

10. When a potassium atom reacts with a bromine atom, the potassium atom will (1) lose only 1 electron (2) lose 2 electrons (3) gain only 1 electron (4) gain 2 electrons

11. At room temperature, potassium is classified as (1) a metallic solid (2) a molecular solid (3) a network solid (4) an ionic solid

12. At room temperature, which substance is the best conductor of electricity? (1) nitrogen (2) neon (3) sulfur (4) silver

13. The element arsenic has the properties of (1) metals only (2) nonmetals only (3) both metals and nonmetals (4) neither metals nor nonmetals

14. Which list of elements contains two metalloids? (1) Ga, Ge, Sn (2) Si, P, S (3) C, Si, Ge (4) B, C, N

15. Which set of elements contains a metalloid? (1) K, Mn, As, Ar (2) Li, Mg, Ca, Kr (3) Ba, Ag, Sn, Xe (4) Fr, F, O, Rn

16. On the periodic table, an element classified as a metalloid can be found in (1) Period 6, Group 5 (2) Period 2, Group 14 (3) Period 3, Group 16 (4) Period 4, Group 15

17. Which element in Period 4 is classified as an active nonmetal? (1) Ga (2) Ge (3) Br (4) Kr

18. A property of most nonmetals in the solid state is that they are (1) good conductors of heat (2) good conductors of electricity (3) brittle (4) malleable

19. Which properties are characteristic of nonmetals? (1) low thermal conductivity and low electrical conductivity (2) low thermal conductivity and high electrical conductivity (3) high thermal conductivity and low electrical conductivity (4) high thermal conductivity and high electrical conductivity

20. Which element in Period 2 of the periodic table is the most reactive nonmetal? (1) carbon (2) nitrogen (3) oxygen (4) fluorine

21. Which element is brittle in the solid phase and is a poor conductor of heat and electricity? (1) calcium (2) strontium (3) sulfur (4) copper

22. Which element in Period 4 is classified as an active metal? (1) Ca (2) V (3) Br (4) Ge

23. The presence of which ion usually produces a colored solution? (1) K^+ (2) F^- (3) Fe^{2+} (4) S^{2-}

24. Which set of properties is most characteristic of transition elements? (1) colorless ions in solution, multiple positive oxidation states (2) colorless ions in solution, multiple negative oxidation states (3) colored ions in solution, multiple positive oxidation states (4) colored ions in solution, multiple negative oxidation states

25. Which salt contains an ion that forms a colored solution? (1) $Mg(NO_3)_2$ (2) $Ca(NO_3)_2$ (3) $Ni(NO_3)_3$ (4) $Al(NO_3)_3$

26. Which group in the periodic table contains an element that can form a blue sulfate compound? (1) 1 (2) 2 (3) 11 (4) 17

27. Aqueous solutions of compounds containing element X are blue. Element X could be (1) carbon (2) copper (3) sodium (4) potassium

28. Pure silicon is chemically classified as a metalloid because silicon (1) is malleable and ductile (2) is an excellent conductor of heat and electricity (3) exhibits hydrogen bonding (4) exhibits metallic and nonmetallic properties

29. Which compound forms a colored aqueous solution? (1) $CaCl_2$ (2) $CrCl_3$ (3) NaOH (4) KBr

Properties of Elements

Some periodic properties of elements, such as metallic character, already have been discussed. However, many other properties of elements can be predicted based on the period or group the element belongs to.

Ionization Energy

The amount of energy needed to remove the most loosely bound electron from a neutral gaseous atom is called the **ionization energy** of the element.

$$X + \text{energy} \rightarrow X^+ + e^-$$

Atoms with more than one electron have more than one ionization energy, but this first ionization energy is most significant.

TRENDS IN A PERIOD Figure 5-5 illustrates the periodic function of ionization energy. Values from left to right across a period generally increase. Notice that the same pattern is seen in the two periods shown. As the atoms are considered from left to right of the table, an increase in the number of protons is revealed. As the nuclear charge increases, the electrons are more strongly attracted, and hence more energy is needed to remove them from the atom.

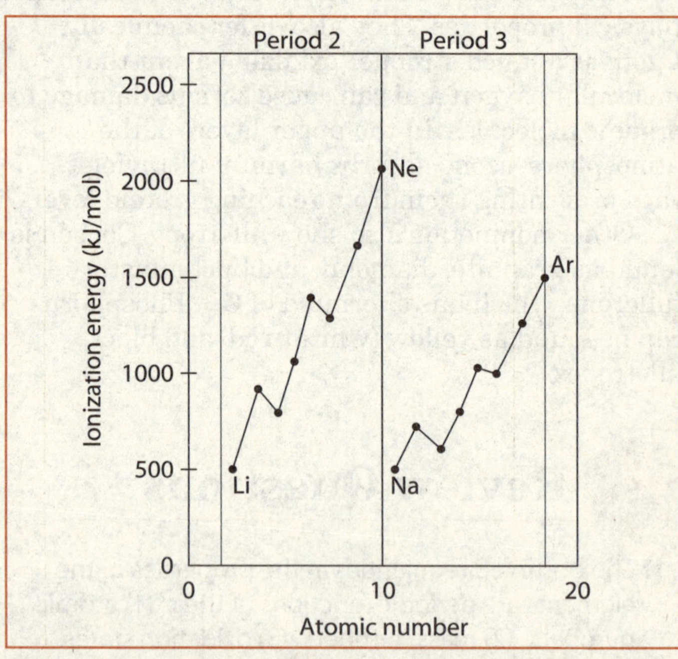

Figure 5-5. Ionization energy of Periods 2 and 3: In general, ionization energy increases from left to right across a period. The peaks in the lines result from the increased stability of filled and half-filled sublevels of electrons.

TRENDS IN A GROUP Figure 5-6 shows the ionization energy from the top to the bottom of Group 2. The ionization energy decreases because valence electrons in each successive element are at a higher energy level and, thus, farther from the nucleus. It is easier to remove them when they are farther from the positive charge of the nucleus and shielded from it by other levels of electrons.

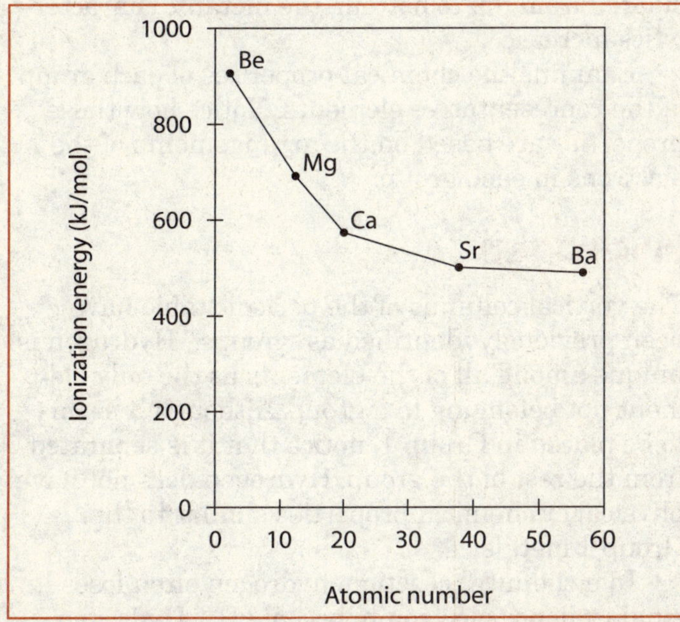

Figure 5-6. Ionization energy of Group 2: Ionization energy is less in larger atoms that have the same valence electron configuration as smaller atoms.

Atomic Radii

The radius of an atom is a good measure of the size of the atom. The **atomic radius** is defined as half the distance between two adjacent atoms in a crystal or half the distance between nuclei of identical atoms that are bonded together. Several methods can be used to determine the atomic radius of an element. No matter how the radius is measured, certain trends remain constant.

TRENDS IN A PERIOD From left to right in a period, there is a repeating pattern of decreasing atomic radii. See Figure 5.7. In each period, metals have larger radii than nonmetals. The valence electrons of all the members of a period are at the same general energy level, but the number of protons in the nucleus attracting them increases, causing the radii to decrease.

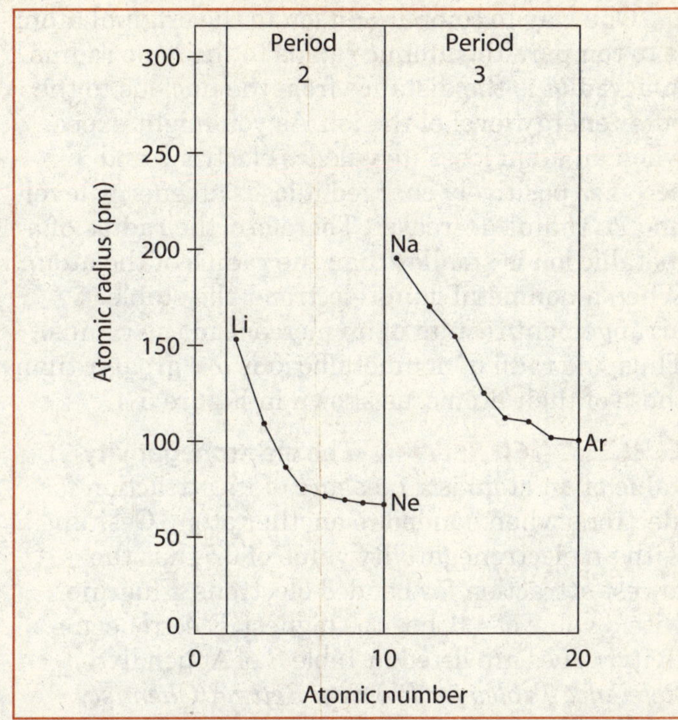

Figure 5-7. Atomic radii for Periods 2 and 3: From left to right, atomic radius decreases across a period.

TRENDS IN A GROUP In any given group, each successive member has more inner-level electrons than the preceding member. These electrons shield the valence electrons from the nucleus, reducing the attractive force of the nucleus. Additionally, the valence electrons are more energetic than those of elements higher in the group. Thus, the atomic radius increases from top to bottom of a group. The atomic radii are shown in Table S of Appendix 1, *Reference Tables for Physical Setting/Chemistry.* Atomic radii are often measured in picometers (10^{-12} m).

Other Properties and Trends

You can easily see from the properties discussed so far that properties of elements follow predictable trends. Other properties of the elements also follow patterns.

IONIC RADII Atoms gain or lose electrons to become charged particles called ions. Metals tend to lose their valence electrons in chemical reactions to become positive ions. Nonmetals tend to gain electrons in chemical reactions and become negative ions. As these atoms gain or lose electrons, they complete an octet of valence electrons.

One way to compare an ion to the original atom is to compare the atomic radius to the ionic radius. **Ionic radius** is the distance from the nucleus to the outer energy level of the ion. As you might expect, when an atom loses its valence electrons and becomes positively charged it loses an energy level and its radius decreases. Therefore, the radius of a metallic ion is smaller than the radius of the atom. When a nonmetal gains electrons, the stable arrangement results in an increase in the radius. Thus, the radii of nonmetallic ions are greater than those of their atoms, as shown in Figure 5-4.

ELECTRONEGATIVITY The **electronegativity** value of an atom is a measure of its attraction for electrons when bonded to another atom. Cesium, with an electronegativity value of 0.7, has the lowest attraction for bonded electrons. Fluorine, with a value of 4.0, has the highest. Electronegativity values are listed in Table S of Appendix 1, *Reference Tables for Physical Setting/Chemisty.*

Electronegativity values can be used to predict the type of bond that will be formed between two atoms. The noble gases are not generally assigned electronegativity values because they form very few stable chemical compounds.

There is a regular increase in the electronegativity value of each element when a period is considered from left to right. Metals tend to have low values, while the nonmetals of each period are higher.

In each group, the highest electronegativity value is found at the top. Attraction for bonded electrons is less toward the bottom of the group.

REACTIVITY OF ELEMENTS Some elements can be found uncombined in nature, that is, in the atomic state. Oxygen may be simply O_2. The noble gases are always found as free elements, as they rarely react. Other elements are so reactive that they are never found in the uncombined, or free, state. Such is the case for the elements of Groups 1, 2, and 17. Some of these elements can only be obtained by the electrolysis of their fused salts.

Properties of Groups

The elements in any group of the periodic table have related chemical properties. Inspection of a group shows that all the members have the same number of valence electrons, and it is this similarity that accounts for the similarity in chemical properties. There is a regularity that can be seen quite clearly in the manner in which the members of a group react with elements of a different group.

Although each member of a group has the same number of valence electrons, there can be a change in the type of element from top to bottom. In Group 14, the top member, carbon, is clearly a nonmetal. Silicon and germanium are metalloids, while tin and lead are metals. As each group is considered from top to bottom, the metallic characteristics increase.

Examine the chemical properties of each group of the representative elements. Notice how these properties are based on the arrangements of the electrons in each group.

Hydrogen

The vertical columns of the periodic table have been previously identified as "groups." Hydrogen is unique among all of the elements as the only element not belonging to a group. Although it seems to be placed in Group 1, notice that it is separated from the rest of the group. Hydrogen does not have physical or chemical properties similar to the Group 1 metals.

In a chemical reaction, hydrogen often loses its single valence electron to become H^+. Hydrogen also can combine with metals to form metallic hydrides, such as NaH. In these compounds the metals have a positive oxidation state, while the hydrogen is assigned 1− $(H)^-$. Hydrogen will also share electrons with another atom to gain stability. An example of hydrogen and oxygen sharing electrons can be seen in water (H_2O).

Groups 1 and 2

The elements of Group 1 (Figure 5-8), the alkali metals, and of Group 2 (Figure 5-9), the alkaline earth metals, show typical metallic characteristics. The members of both these groups easily lose their electrons and are never found in nature in their atomic state. That is, they are always found in compounds. They can be reduced to their free states by electrolysis of their compounds. All of these elements have low ionization energies and electronegativity values. They typically achieve stable octets by losing electrons to form ionic bonds.

In general, from top to bottom in both groups, reactivity increases. It should be noted that each Group 1 element is more reactive than the Group 2 element of the same period. Francium is the most reactive metal.

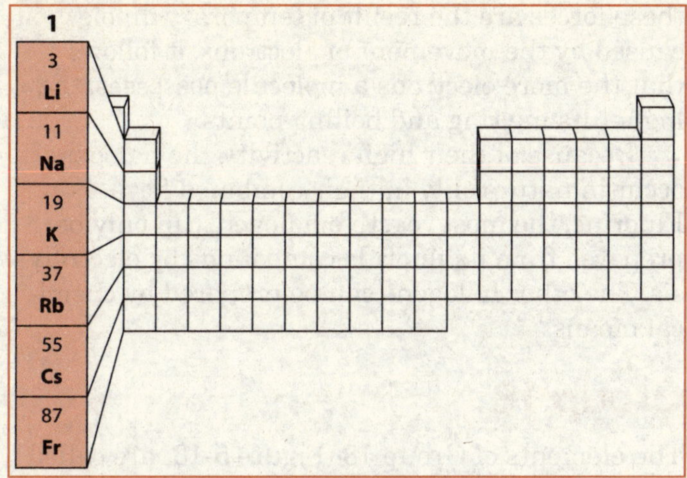

Figure 5-8. Group 1, the alkali metals

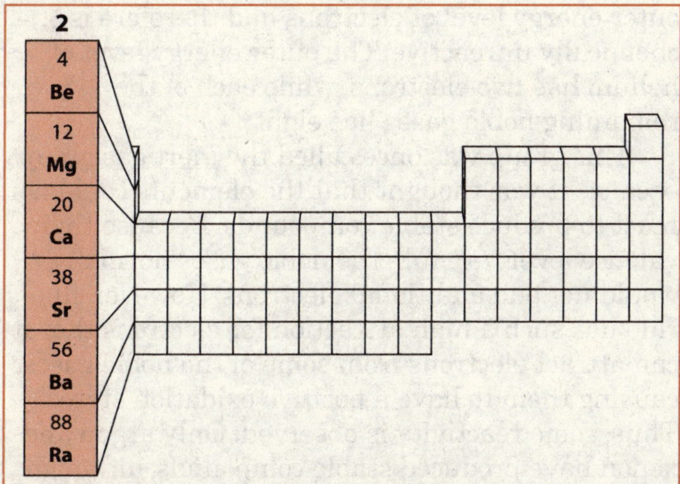

Figure 5-9. Group 2, the alkaline earth metals

Group 15

The members of Group 15 (Figure 5-10) show the change from nonmetallic to metallic properties from top to bottom of the group. Nitrogen and phosphorus are typical nonmetals and can accept three electrons to form 3− anions. Bismuth loses electrons to become a positive cation, which is typical of metals. Arsenic and antimony are generally classified as metalloids.

Nitrogen is a stable gas at room temperature, largely because it contains a triple bond between the two nitrogen atoms in N_2. Phosphorus forms P_4, which is far more reactive than N_2. Nitrogen is an essential component of protein synthesis and plant processes. Because atmospheric N_2 is so unreactive, it must be changed to a usable form. One way this is done is by nitrogen-fixing bacteria that release usable nitrogen compounds into the soil.

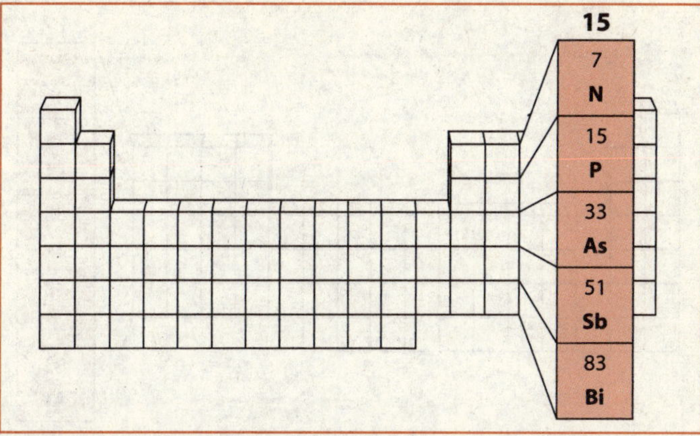

Figure 5-10. Elements in Group 15

Group 16

The elements in Group 16 (Figure 5-11) also show the expected progression from nonmetal to metal with increasing atomic number. Oxygen and sulfur are typical nonmetals, while the last member, polonium, is a metal. Selenium and tellurium are metalloids.

Oxygen may well be the most important element in the group. It is a diatomic molecule at room temperature, sharing two pairs of electrons between the two atoms. Oxygen is a reactive element, easily forming compounds with other elements. Were it not for the process of photosynthesis, all of the oxygen on Earth would be in the combined state.

In a compound, oxygen normally has an oxidation value of 2−. Its negative oxidation value results from its high electronegativity as it attracts shared electrons in a bond. Only when oxygen bonds to the only element more electronegative than itself (fluorine) does oxygen have a positive oxidation value.

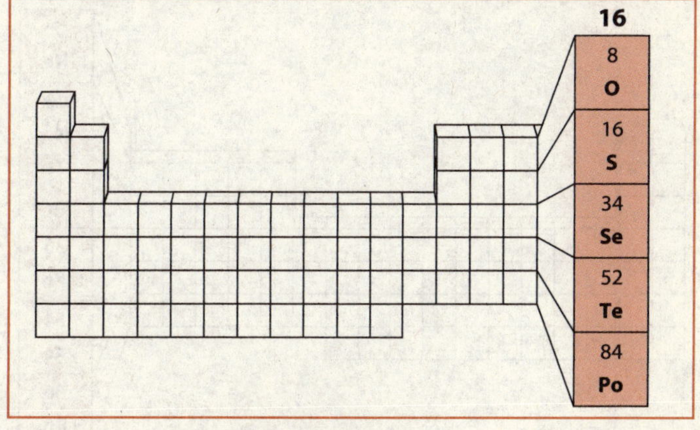

Figure 5-11. Elements in Group 16

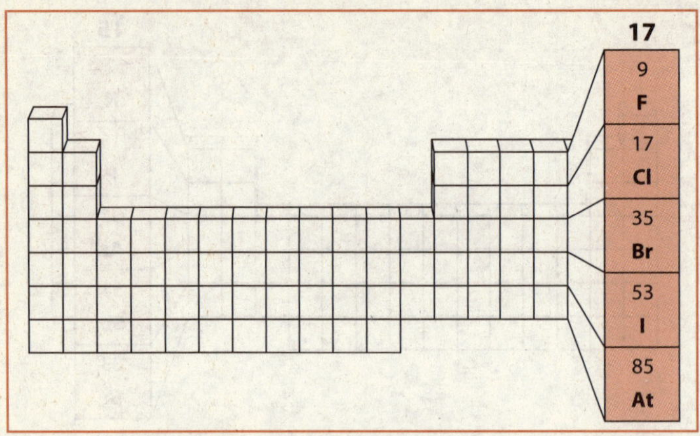

Figure 5-12. The halogens (Group 17)

Group 17

The members of Group 17 (Figure 5-12) are also known as the halogens when they are in the free state. When atoms of elements in this group gain an electron, they become an ion with a 1– charge, and the salts formed are called halides. All the members of the group are nonmetals, but the normal trend of nonmetallic to metallic characteristics is seen even in this group. Iodine, the heaviest nonradioactive member, is a solid with some luster characteristic of metals.

The halogens are the only group of the table containing all three states of matter at room conditions. Fluorine and chlorine are gases; bromine is a liquid; and iodine, a solid. Astatine is a radioactive element with no practical uses. The half-life of At-210 is only 8.3 hours. Therefore, there are no sizeable amounts of astatine in nature.

As is the case with other nonpolar molecules, the halogens are held in the solid and liquid phases by weak van der Waals forces. Because these forces are the result of temporary dipoles caused by the movement of electrons, it follows that the more electrons a molecule possesses, the higher its melting and boiling points.

Because of their high reactivity, the halogens occur in nature only in their combined form. Fluorine, the most reactive halogen, can only be prepared from its fluoride compounds by electrolysis. The other halogens can be prepared by chemical means.

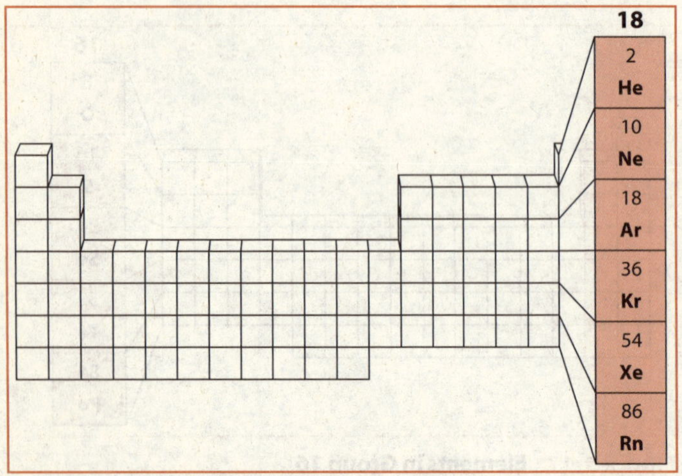

Figure 5-13. The noble gases (Group 18)

Group 18

The elements of Group 18 (Figure 5-13) are called the noble gases. They do not combine to form diatomic molecules, but rather exist as monatomic molecules. Each of these atoms has a complete outer energy level of electrons and therefore is chemically unreactive. The outer energy level of helium has two electrons, while each of the remaining noble gases has eight.

This group was once called the inert gas group because it was thought that the elements could not react to produce stable compounds. Because their valence levels are full, the noble gases normally would not add additional electrons. However, fluorine has such a high attraction for electrons that it can attract electrons from some of the noble gases, causing them to have a positive oxidation state. Thus, some reactivity is observed. Only argon and xenon have produced stable compounds, although even neon has been coaxed into reactions under severe conditions of temperature and pressure. Helium alone has not shown any reactivity at all.

Like the halogen group, the noble gases are nonpolar and are therefore held in the liquid and solid phases by van der Waals forces. As expected, helium, with the fewest electrons, has the lowest boiling point, and the boiling point increases from top to bottom in the group.

Reactions Between Groups

Consider the reactions of Group 1 (the alkali metals) with the members of Group 17 (the halogens). The members of Group 1 each have one valence electron to lose and form ions with a 1+ charge. Group 17 elements each have seven valence electrons and can accept one electron from the alkali metal, forming an ion with a 1– charge. The general formula for the combining of a Group 1 element with a Group 17 element is MX, where M represents the Group 1 element, and X represents the Group 17 element. An example is KI.

MEMORY JOGGER

In Chapter 2 you learned how to use charges to write correct formulas. Remember that all compounds must be electrically neutral. When the charges in a compound formed from two ions are the same but of opposite sign, the ions combine in a 1:1 ratio. If the charges are different, write the charge of one as the subscript of the other to obtain the correct formula.

Group 2 elements have two valence electrons and form compounds with Group 17 elements having the general formula MX_2. Examples include $BeCl_2$, $MgBr_2$, and CaF_2.

Review Questions

30. Which value represents the first ionization energy of a nonmetal? (1) 497.9 kJ (2) 577.4 kJ (3) 811.7 kJ (4) 1000. kJ

31. As the elements of Group 1 are considered in order from top to bottom, the first ionization energy of each successive element will (1) decrease (2) increase (3) remain the same (4) follow an unpredictable pattern

32. Compared to an atom of potassium, an atom of calcium has a (1) larger radius and lower reactivity (2) larger radius and higher reactivity (3) smaller radius and lower reactivity (2) smaller radius and higher reactivity

33. Which statement describes the elements in Period 3? (1) Each successive element has a greater atomic radius. (2) Each successive element has a lower electronegativity. (3) All elements have similar chemical properties. (4) All elements have valence electrons in the same principal energy level.

34. As atoms of elements in Group 16 are considered in order from top to bottom, the electronegativity of each successive element (1) decreases (2) increases (3) remains the same (4) cannot be predicted by a trend

35. A nonmetal could have an electronegativity of (1) 1.0 (2) 2.0 (3) 1.6 (4) 2.6

36. Which properties are most common in nonmetals? (1) low ionization energy and low electronegativity (2) low ionization energy and high electronegativity (3) high ionization energy and low electronegativity (4) high ionization energy and high electronegativity

37. A diatomic element with a high first ionization energy would most likely be a (1) nonmetal with a high electronegativity (2) nonmetal with a low electronegativity (3) metal with a high electronegativity (4) metal with a low electronegativity

38. Which element at room temperature is a poor conductor of electricity and has a relatively high electronegativity? (1) Cu (2) S (3) Mg (4) Fe

39. Within Period 2 of the periodic table, as the atomic number increases, the atomic radius generally (1) decreases (2) increases (3) remains the same (4) follows no pattern

40. Atoms of which element have the smallest radius? (1) Si (2) P (3) S (4) Cl

41. Which statement best compares the atomic radius of a potassium atom and the atomic radius of a calcium atom? (1) The radius of the potassium atom is smaller because of its smaller nuclear charge. (2) The radius of the potassium atom is smaller because of its larger nuclear charge. (3) The radius of the potassium atom is larger because of its smaller nuclear charge. (4) The radius of the potassium atom is larger because of its larger nuclear charge.

42. According to the reference table, which of the following elements has the smallest radius? (1) nickel (2) cobalt (3) calcium (4) potassium

43. In which area of the periodic table are the elements with the strongest nonmetallic properties located? (1) lower left (2) upper left (3) lower right (4) upper right

44. At which location in the periodic table would the most active metallic element be found? (1) in Group 1 at the top (2) in Group 1 at the bottom (3) in Group 17 at the top (4) in Group 17 at the bottom

45. In which section of the periodic table are the most active nonmetals located? (1) upper right corner (2) lower right corner (3) upper left corner (4) lower left corner

46. What is the total number of elements in Group 17 that are gases at room temperature and standard pressure? (1) 1 (2) 2 (3) 3 (4) 4

47. Which of the following groups in the periodic table contain elements so reactive that they are never found in the free state? (1) 1 and 2 (2) 1 and 11 (3) 2 and 15 (4) 11 and 15

48. Which halogen can only be prepared from its fused compounds? (1) I_2 (2) Cl_2 (3) Br_2 (4) F_2

49. As the elements in Group 15 are considered in order of increasing atomic number, which sequence in properties occurs? (1) nonmetal→metalloid→metal (2) metalloid→metal→nonmetal (3) metal→metalloid→nonmetal (4) metal→nonmetal→metalloid

50. Which elements have the most similar chemical properties? (1) K and Na (2) K and Cl (3) K and Ca (4) K and S

51. Because of its high reactivity, which element is normally obtained by the electrolysis of its fused salts? (1) sulfur (2) lithium (3) argon (4) gold

52. Which element in Group 17 is the most active nonmetal? (1) Br (2) I (3) Cl (4) F

53. Which of the following Group 15 elements has the most metallic properties? (1) Bi (2) P (3) Sb (4) N

54. The elements calcium and strontium have similar chemical properties because they both have the same (1) atomic number (2) mass number (3) number of valence electrons (4) number of completely filled subshells

55. Which Group 15 element exists as a diatomic molecule at room temperature and pressure? (1) phosphorus (2) nitrogen (3) bismuth (4) arsenic

56. Which two elements have chemical properties that are most similar? (1) Cl and Ar (2) Li and Na (3) K and Ca (4) C and N

57. In which set do the elements exhibit the most similar chemical properties? (1) N, O, and F (2) Hg, Br, and Rn (3) Li, Na, and K (4) Al, Si, and P

58. Which of these metals loses electrons most readily? (1) calcium (2) magnesium (3) potassium (4) sodium

59. If M represents an element in Group 2, the formula of its chloride would be (1) MCl (2) MCl_2 (3) M_2Cl (4) M_2Cl_2

60. Which group below contains elements with the greatest variation in chemical properties? (1) Li, Be, B (2) Li, Na, K (3) B, Al, Ga (4) Be, Mg, Ca

61. Which element in Group 15 would most likely have luster and good electrical conductivity? (1) N (2) P (3) Bi (4) As

62. Which statement best describes the Group 2 metals? (1) They have one valence electron, and they form ions with a 1+ charge. (2) They have one valence electron, and they form ions with a 1− charge. (3) They have two valence electrons, and they form ions with a 2+ charge. (4) They have two valence electrons, and they form ions with a 2− charge.

63. Which element in Group 15 has the strongest metallic character? (1) Bi (2) As (3) P (4) N

64. Which halogens are gases at room temperature and pressure? (1) chlorine and fluorine (2) chlorine and bromine (3) iodine and fluorine (4) iodine and bromine

65. In which group of elements do the atoms gain electrons most readily? (1) 1 (2) 2 (3) 16 (4) 18

66. Which element is more reactive than strontium? (1) potassium (2) calcium (3) iron (4) copper

67. The oxide of metal X has the formula XO. Which group in the periodic table contains metal X? (1) Group 1 (2) Group 2 (3) Group 13 (4) Group 17

68. As elements in a group of the periodic table are considered in order from top to bottom, the metallic character of each successive element generally (1) decreases (2) increases (3) remains the same (4) follows no pattern

69. As the elements in Period 3 are considered from left to right, they tend to (1) lose electrons more readily and increase in metallic character (2) lose electrons more readily and increase in nonmetallic character (3) gain electrons more readily and increase in metallic character (4) gain electrons more readily and increase in nonmetallic character

70. An atom of which element in the ground state has a complete outermost energy level? (1) He (2) Be (3) Hg (4) H

71. Which of the following Group 15 elements has the most metallic properties? (1) Bi (2) P (3) Sb (4) N

72. As the atoms of the elements in Group 1 of the periodic table are considered from top to bottom, the number of valence electrons in the atoms of each successive element (1) decreases (2) increases (3) remains the same (4) follows no pattern

73. Which element attains the structure of a noble gas when it becomes a 1+ ion? (1) K (2) Ca (3) F (4) Ne

74. According to the reference table, which sequence correctly places the elements in order of increasing ionization energy? (1) H→Li→Na→K (2) I→Br→Cl→F (3) O→S→Se→Te (4) H→Be→Al→Ga

Answer the following questions, using complete sentences when appropriate.

75. The ionization energy of Na is 118 kcal, while the ionization energy of Mg to form Mg^+ is 175. While this is the expected result for an adjacent element, the ionization of Na^+ to Na^{2+} is 1091 kcal, while only 345 kcal is needed to ionize Mg^+ to Mg^{2+}. Explain.

76. The Na^+ ion has a smaller radius than the Ne atom. Explain why this is so.

77. Chlorine reacts with water according to the equation:

$$Cl_2 + H_2O \rightarrow HClO + H^+ + Cl^-$$

Write an equation to show how iodine reacts with water.

78. Why is the periodic table organized by increasing atomic number rather than by increasing atomic mass, as had been suggested by Mendeleev?

79. Explain why the members of Group 1 react by losing an electron, but the members of Group 17 react by gaining an electron.

80. Let the letter M stand for a member of Group 13. What is the formula of the combination of this element with bromine? With oxygen? Explain.

81. Why is hydrogen not considered to be a member of Group 1 (the alkali metals)?

82. Consider atoms of the elements boron, carbon and aluminum. Which is the largest? The smallest? Which has the highest ionization energy? The lowest?

83. Why do elements in a given group of the periodic table show similar chemical properties?

84. Why do the elements of a given period always follow the progression of metal to metalloid to nonmetal to noble gas?

85. What change in charge takes place as a metal loses one or more electrons?

86. Using the law of octets, explain why it is unlikely for sodium to form a Na^{2+} ion.

87. What would be the general formula of a Group 2 element (represented by M) combined with chlorine of Group 17?

88. What would be the general formula of a Group 17 element (represented by X) combined with magnesium of Group 2?

89. What would be the general formula of a Group 1 element combined with an element of Group 16?

90. Mendeleev arranged the elements on the table in order of increasing atomic mass, but it was later learned that the correct order is by increasing atomic number. Study the periodic table and locate examples where the atomic number of two successive elements increases, but the atomic mass decreases.

Questions for Regents Practice

Part A

1. The elements in the modern periodic table are arranged according to their

(1) atomic number

(2) oxidation number

(3) atomic mass

(4) nuclear mass

2. Which characteristic describes most nonmetals in the solid phase?

(1) good conductors of electricity

(2) good conductors of heat

(3) malleable

(4) brittle

3. When combining with nonmetallic atoms, metallic atoms generally will
(1) lose electrons and form negative ions
(2) lose electrons and form positive ions
(3) gain electrons and form negative ions
(4) gain electrons and form positive ions

4. When metal atoms bond with nonmetal atoms, the nonmetal atoms will
(1) lose electrons and the resulting ions are smaller
(2) lose electrons and the resulting ions are larger
(3) gain electrons and the resulting ions are smaller
(4) gain electrons and the resulting ions are larger

5. Which characteristic describes most metals in the solid phase?
(1) good conductors of electricity
(2) poor conductors of heat
(3) dull
(4) brittle

6. Which element is a nonmetallic liquid at room temperature?
(1) hydrogen
(2) oxygen
(3) mercury
(4) bromine

7. Which physical characteristic of a solution may indicate the presence of a transition element?
(1) its density
(2) its color
(3) its effect on litmus
(4) its effect on phenolphthalein

8. Compared to atoms of metals, atoms of nonmetals generally
(1) have higher electronegativity values
(2) have lower first ionization energies
(3) conduct electricity more readily
(4) lose electrons more readily

9. Properties of metals include
(1) low ionization energy and high electronegativity
(2) low ionization energy and low electronegativity
(3) high ionization energy and high electronegativity
(4) high ionization energy and low electronegativity

10. Which part of the periodic table contains elements with the strongest metallic properties?
(1) upper right
(2) upper left
(3) lower right
(4) lower left

11. Which Group 17 element is a solid at room temperature and pressure?
(1) Br_2
(2) F_2
(3) Cl_2
(4) I_2

12. Which gas is monatomic at room temperature and pressure?
(1) nitrogen
(2) neon
(3) fluorine
(4) chlorine

13. Atoms of elements in a group of the periodic table have similar chemical properties. This similarity is most closely related to the atoms'
(1) number of principal energy levels
(2) number of valence electrons
(3) atomic numbers
(4) atomic masses

14. In which group are all the elements found naturally only in compounds?
(1) 18
(2) 2
(3) 11
(4) 14

Part B

15. An element is a solid at room temperature. It can be a
(1) metal only
(2) metalloid only
(3) metal or a nonmetal only
(4) metal, a metalloid, or a nonmetal

16. How does the size of a barium ion compare to the size of a barium atom?

(1) The ion is smaller because it has fewer electrons.

(2) The ion is smaller because it has more electrons.

(3) The ion is larger because it has fewer electrons.

(2) The ion is larger because it has more electrons.

17. Which element is malleable and ductile?

(1) S

(2) Si

(3) Ge

(4) Au

18. Which of the following Period 4 elements has the most metallic characteristics?

(1) Ca

(2) Ge

(3) As

(4) Br

19. Which three groups of the periodic table contain the most elements classified as metalloids?

(1) 1, 2, and 13

(2) 2, 13, and 14

(3) 14, 15, and 16

(4) 16, 17, and 18

20. An aqueous solution of XCl_2 contains colored ions. Element X could be

(1) Ba

(2) Ca

(3) Ni

(4) Bi

21. Which element has the highest first ionization energy?

(1) sodium

(2) aluminum

(3) calcium

(4) phosphorus

22. An element has a first ionization energy of 1314 kJ/mol and an electronegativity of 3.5. It is classified as a

(1) metal

(2) nonmetal

(3) metalloid

(4) halogen

23. Which sequence of elements is arranged in order of decreasing atomic radii?

(1) Al, Si, P

(2) Li, Na, K

(3) Cl, Br, I

(4) N, C, B

24. Which ion has the largest radius?

(1) Na^+

(2) Mg^{2+}

(3) K^+

(4) Ca^{2+}

25. In the ground state, atoms of the elements in Group 15 of the periodic table all have the same number of

(1) filled principal energy levels

(2) occupied principal energy levels

(3) neutrons in the nucleus

(4) electrons in the valence energy level

26. Which of the following Group 18 elements would be most likely to form a compound with fluorine?

(1) He

(2) Ne

(3) Ar

(4) Kr

27. The properties of carbon are expected to be most similar to those of

(1) boron

(2) aluminum

(3) silicon

(4) phosphorus

28. If M represents an alkali metal of Group 1, what is the formula for the compound formed by M and oxygen?

(1) MO_2

(2) M_2O

(3) M_2O_3

(4) M_3O_2

29. An atom of an element has 28 innermost electrons and 7 valence electrons. In which period of the periodic table is this element located?

(1) 2

(2) 3

(3) 4

(4) 5

Part C

30. Mendeleev arranged the periodic table in order of increasing atomic masses. Locate iodine and tellurium on the table and note that they are not arranged by increasing mass, and yet Mendeleev placed iodine in Group 17 and tellurium in Group 16. What is the likely reason that he did not arrange them by increasing mass?

31. Ions are isoelectronic when they contain the same number of electrons. Which of the following ions are isoelectronic? Mg^{2+}, Cl^-, Al^{3+}, K^+, S^{2-}, Ba^{2+}. For each of the preceding ions, name the noble gas that it is isoelectronic with.

32. If K_2O, SrO, and Al_2O_3 are correct formulas, predict the formulas of the oxides of Rb, Mg, and Ga.

33. A sample of a substance decomposes, leaving a solid that will not undergo further decomposition. It is a solid that conducts electricity and has a melting point of 2160 K and a density of 6.1 g/cm^3. Using your knowledge of chemistry and the reference tables, identify the element.

34. An element has an atomic radius of 160 pm, and an electronegativiy of 1.3. Using your reference table identify the elements that it could be. Using other properties on the table how would you test to see which of these elements it was?

35. Why does chemical reactivity increase from top to bottom of Group 1, while it decreases from top to bottom of Group 17?

36. Which of the following has the greater ionization energy, Na or Na^+? Explain your answer.

Bonding

VOCABULARY		
asymmetrical molecule	**Lewis dot diagram**	**octet**
covalent bond	**malleability**	**octet rule**
double covalent bond	**metallic bond**	**polar covalent bond**
hydrogen bond	**multiple covalent bond**	**symmetrical molecule**
ion	**nonpolar covalent bond**	**triple covalent bond**
ionic bond		

Chemical bonds provide the "glue" that holds all compounds together. There are different types of chemical bonds, and these different bond types account for the different properties of substances. In this section you will learn how the electron structure of atoms helps explain many aspects of chemical bonding. You will also use Lewis dot diagrams to aid in your understanding of electronic structure and its role in bonding.

Energy and Chemical Bonds

Chemical bonds are the forces that hold atoms together in a compound. Energy is required to overcome these attractive forces and separate the atoms in a compound. Thus, the breaking of a chemical bond is an endothermic process. If energy is required to break a bond, then the opposite process of forming a bond must release energy. The formation of a bond is an exothermic process.

MEMORY JOGGER

In exothermic reactions, heat is a product and is released; in endothermic reactions, heat is a reactant and is absorbed.

When a chemical bond is formed, the resulting compound has less potential energy than the substances from which it was formed. Why? Energy is always released when a bond is formed. The greater the energy released during the formation of a bond, the greater its stability. Consider the following two reactions.

Reaction 1 $B + C \rightarrow BC + 100$ joules
Reaction 2 $K + L \rightarrow KL + 400$ joules

The bond formed in reaction 2 is more stable than the bond formed in reaction 1. It takes 400 joules to break apart compound KL, but only 100 joules to break apart compound BC.

Review Questions

1. As energy is released during the formation of a bond, the stability of the chemical system generally (1) decreases (2) increases (3) remains the same

2. Which kind of energy is stored in a chemical bond? (1) potential energy (2) kinetic energy (3) activation energy (4) ionization energy

3. Consider the reaction below.

$$2Na(s) + Cl_2(g) \rightarrow 2NaCl(s)$$

As the reactants form products, the stability of the chemical system (1) decreases (2) increases (3) remains the same

4. When a chemical bond forms between two hydrogen atoms, the potential energy of the atoms (1) decreases (2) increases (3) remains the same

5. Energy is released when the atoms of two elements bond together to form a compound. Compared to the total potential energy of the atoms before bonding, the total potential energy of the atoms after bonding is (1) higher and the compound formed is stable (2) higher and the compound formed is unstable (3) lower and the compound formed is stable (4) lower and the compound formed is unstable

Lewis Electron Dot Structures

In the next sections you will study the two types of bonds that commonly form. These two bond types result from the transfer of electrons from one atom to another and from the sharing of valence electrons between atoms. A simple modeling technique known as a Lewis dot diagram provides an easy method for showing how electrons are transferred or shared during bond formation. Learning to draw and interpret these diagrams is an important skill.

A **Lewis dot diagram,** also called an electron dot diagram, consists of a chemical symbol surrounded by one to eight dots representing valence electrons. See Figure 6-1.

Period	Group 1	2	13	14	15	16	17	18
1	Ḣ							:He
2	L̇i	B̈e	B̈e•	:Ċ•	•N̈•	:Ö:	:F̈•	:N̈e:
3	Ṅa	M̈g	Äl•	S̈i•	•P̈•	:S̈:	:C̈l•	:Är:
4	K̇	C̈a	G̈a•	G̈e•	•Äs•	:S̈e:	:B̈r•	:K̈r:

Figure 6-1. Electron dot diagrams of elements in Periods 1 through 4

Figure 6-2 shows the Lewis dot diagram of a sodium atom. The symbol of the element (Na) represents the sodium atom's nucleus along with all of its nonvalence electrons; this portion of the diagram is called the kernel. The kernel of every atom is positively charged. The valence electrons surround the kernel and are usually represented by small dots, x's, or o's.

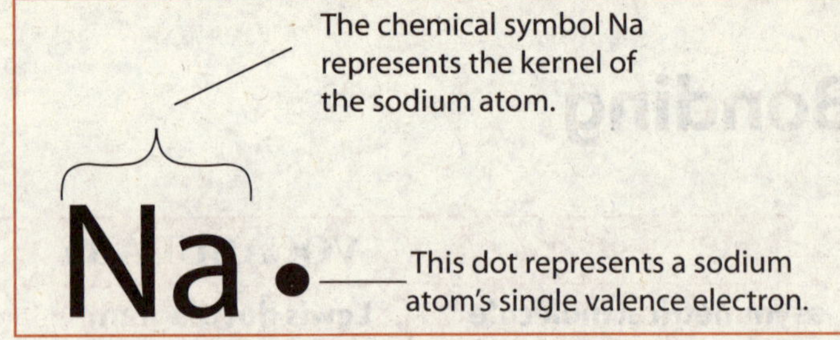

Figure 6-2. The Lewis dot diagram of a sodium atom: The kernel, represented by the symbol Na, contains 11 protons and 10 electrons; the kernel has a 1+ overall charge. The 1+ charge of the kernel is balanced by the 1− charge of the single valence electron. Overall, the sodium atom is neutral.

Figure 6-3 shows the relationship between the groups of the periodic table and the electron dot diagrams of the atoms and ions in those groups.

There are slight variations in how electrons are arranged around the kernel in an electron dot diagram. Often, the first two electrons are placed at the 12 o'clock position. As the next three electrons are added, they are placed singly at the 3, 6, and 9 o'clock positions. The last three electrons are added to make pairs in the same order, at the 3, 6, and 9 o'clock positions.

When atoms gain or lose electrons they become charged particles called **ions.** Notice in Figure 6-3 that ions are represented differently than atoms. When metals react, they do so by losing their valence electrons. Thus, there aren't any dots in the electron dot diagrams of the ions for sodium (Na^+), magnesium (Mg^{2+}), or aluminum (Al^{3+}). The square brackets around the kernel and the ionic charge written as a superscript outside the brackets indicate the diagram is that of an ion. Whereas metals lose electrons to form ions, nonmetals gain electrons to form ions. The valence electrons gained when a nonmetal ion forms are shown in its electron dot diagram. It is common to show the added valence electrons with a different symbol than that used to represent the atom's originally present valence electrons.

The number of valence electrons to use in an electron dot diagram can also be determined by consulting the periodic table. The periodic table often lists the electron configuration for the elements using a modified Bohr model. For example, the electron configuration for sodium (Na) is listed

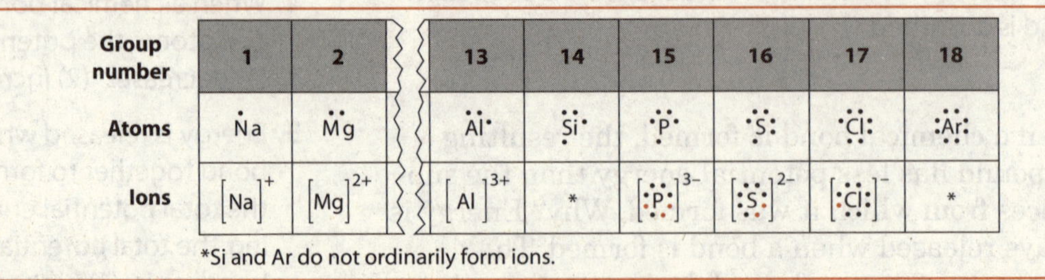

Group number	1	2	13	14	15	16	17	18
Atoms	Ṅa	M̈g	Äl•	S̈i•	•P̈•	:S̈:	:C̈l:	:Är:
Ions	$[Na]^{+}$	$[Mg]^{2+}$	$[Al]^{3+}$	*	$[:P:]^{3-}$	$[:S:]^{2-}$	$[:Cl:]^{-}$	*

*Si and Ar do not ordinarily form ions.

Figure 6-3. Electron dot diagrams of some Period 3 elements and ions

as 2-8-1. This notation indicates that there is only one outermost, or valence electron for a sodium atom. The other 10 electrons belong to the kernel of the atom. The corresponding electron dot diagram for the sodium atom would show this one valence electron as a single dot, outside the kernel.

Lewis diagrams of compounds

Lewis diagrams can also be used to show how atoms combine to form molecules. When atoms combine to form diatomic molecules, single, double, and triple covalent bonds can be shown.

The Lewis structure of a hydrogen atom is simply

H

When two hydrogen atoms combine to form the hydrogen molecule (H_2), they share the two electrons between them in a nonpolar covalent bond:

H:H

Instead of using dots to show the pair of electrons, a single dash may be used to show the covalent bond.

H — H

The members of column 17, the halogens, also form single bonds between them in their diatomic molecules. In addition to the single covalent bond, each atom has 6 additional valence electrons for a complete octet of 8.

:Cl — Cl: (each Cl with 6 nonbonding electrons)

Oxygen has 6 valence electrons with two atoms combining to form O_2. In this case, the two oxygen atoms share two pairs of electrons

:O = O: (each O with 4 nonbonding electrons)

Notice that each oxygen atom has a total of 8 valence electrons.

Nitrogen has five valence electrons and forms the diatomic N_2 molecule by forming a triple covalent bond

:N ≡ N:

When drawing Lewis diagrams for compounds, a pair of electrons forming a covalent bond is usually represented by a dashed line, while any unpaired electrons are represented by a pairs of dots.

In drawing Lewis diagrams for compounds it is helpful to remember that the octet rule calls for each atom to have 8 valence electrons. Hydrogen is an exception, having a maximum of 2 electrons. Try to follow a pattern when drawing diagrams of compounds.

The following steps are useful in determining the dot diagrams of compounds.

1. Determine the total number of valence electrons of the atoms in the compound.

   Consider the compound CH_3Cl:

1 carbon with 4 valence electrons	=	4
3 hydrogens with 1 electrons each	=	3
1 chlorine with 7 valence electrons	=	7
Total valence electrons	=	14

   The final diagram must contain 14 electrons.

2. Arrange the atoms to show bonds between them. The central atom often has the smallest electronegativity value, and generally appears once in the formula. Remember that hydrogen cannot be the central atom since it can only form one single covalent bond. If more than one atom of an element is present, they generally surround the central atom. Use a dash to show a covalent bond between the atoms. Remember that each dash represents two electrons in a covalent bond.

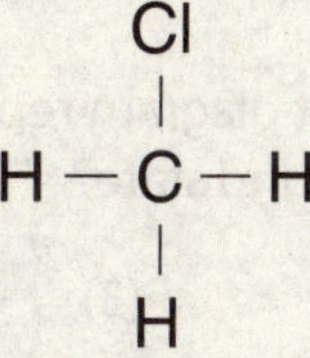

These 4 bonds account for 8 of the 14 electrons needed. The carbon atom has a complete octet of electrons. Distribute the remaining 6 electrons around the chlorine. Check to see that each atom has an octet of electrons except for hydrogen which needs only two. In this example the six remaining electrons should be distributed around the chlorine to provide it with an octet of electrons.

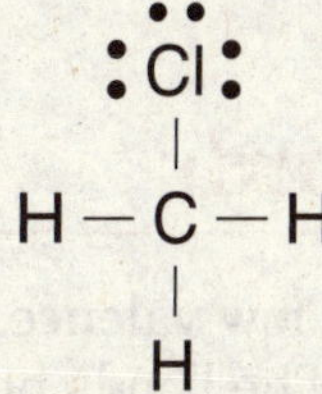

If each of the atoms does not have an octet of electrons, you will probably also have some "left over" or unassigned electrons. These can be placed as double bonds or triple bonds between atoms that do not have complete octets.

Consider the compound C_2H_2:

2 carbon atoms with
4 electrons = 8 electrons

2 hydrogen atoms with
1 electron = 2 electrons

Total = 10 electrons

Join the carbons and hydrogens with bonds:

H—C—C—H

The three bonds account for 6 of the 10 electrons. Distributing the four remaining electrons around the carbons will not produce octets of electrons, but forming a triple bond between the two carbons will.

H—C C—H

Review Questions

6. Atom X has an electron configuration of 2-8-2. Which electron dot diagram correctly represents this atom?

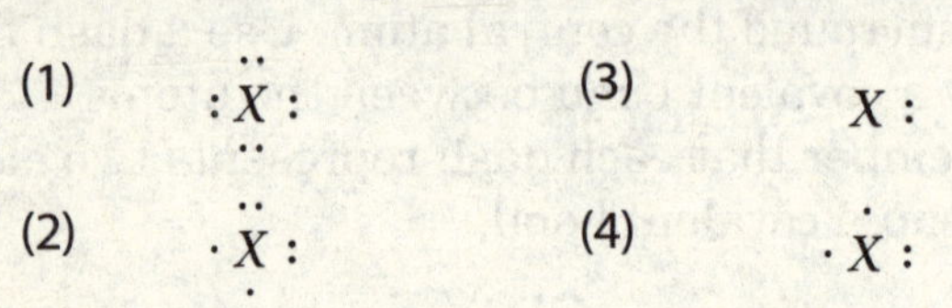

(1) :X: (eight dots) (3) X:

(2) ·X: (with two dots above and one below) (4) ·X: (with one dot above)

7. Which electron dot diagram represents an atom of chlorine in the ground state?

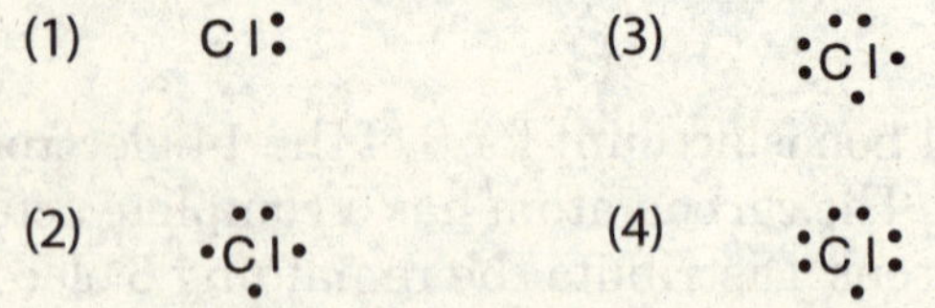

(1) Cl: (3) :Cl· (with two dots above and one below)

(2) ·Cl· (with two dots above and one below) (4) :Cl: (with two dots above and one below)

8. A) Draw a Lewis dot diagram of water
B) Draw a Lewis dot diagram of carbon dioxide

9. A) Draw an electron dot diagram of ammonia.
B) Draw an electron dot diagram of the ammonium ion

Metallic Bonds

Metallic atoms have few valence electrons and low ionization energies. The bonds holding metallic atoms together in the solid and liquid phases, however, are apparently strong, as metals have fairly high melting and boiling points. A metallic atom may be considered to have a central portion, or kernel, made up of its nucleus and its nonvalence electrons. The atom's valence electrons surround the kernel. The kernels of the metallic atoms making up a metallic solid are arranged in the fixed positions of a crystalline lattice. The valence electrons move freely throughout the crystal and do not belong to any given atom. The freely moving valence electrons give metals properties of good electrical and thermal conductivity. A **metallic bond** results from the force of attraction of the mobile valence electrons for an atom's positively charged kernel.

As shown in Figure 6-4, metals can be hammered into shapes, which is a property known as **malleability.** Although hammering forces the kernels to move to new locations, they are still surrounded by the valence electrons. The freedom of the valence electrons often leads to the use of the term "sea of mobile electrons" to describe metallic bonding.

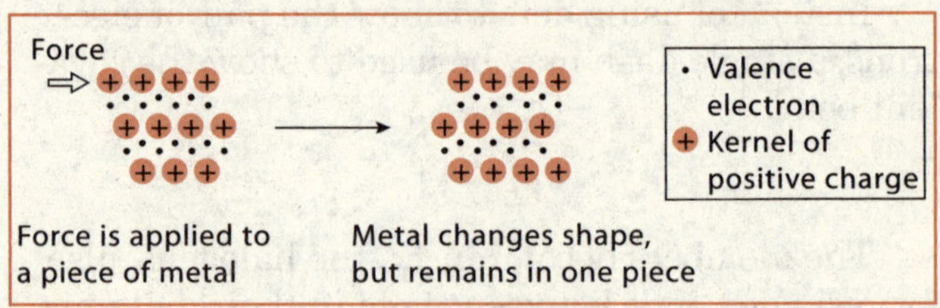

Figure 6-4. Metallic bonding: When hammered, the positively charged kernels are moved, but they are still attracted by the valence electrons.

Review Questions

10. Metallic bonding occurs between metal atoms that have (1) full valence orbitals and low ionization energies (2) full valence orbitals and high ionization energies (3) vacant valence orbitals and low ionization energies (4) vacant valence orbitals and high ionization energies

11. Which element has a crystalline lattice through which electrons flow freely? (1) bromine (2) calcium (3) carbon (4) sulfur

12. Which element has properties of good electrical conductivity and luster and exists as a liquid at STP? (1) Hg (2) Br (3) I (4) C

The Octet Rule

You may recall that the noble gases of Group 18 are extremely stable and undergo very few chemical reactions. Although there are a few stable compounds of argon and xenon combined with fluorine, these compounds are some of the rare exceptions to the noble gases' lack of reactivity. What is it about the structure of the noble gases that leads to their stability? The answer lies in their number of valence electrons. Except for helium (which only has two valence electrons) all of the noble gas atoms have eight valence electrons. The configuration of eight valence electrons is known as an **octet.** An octet represents the maximum number of valence electrons that an atom can have.

Ordinary chemical reactions result in changes to the valence electron configurations of the atoms involved. A complete octet of eight valence electrons results in an exceptionally stable electron configuration. This stable configuration is the reason why noble gases are so unreactive. Note that the noble gas helium requires only two electrons to fill its valence shell. The **octet rule** states that atoms generally react by gaining, losing, or sharing electrons in order to achieve a complete octet of eight valence electrons—the configuration of a noble gas.

DIGGING DEEPER

The composition of all substances cannot be explained by the octet rule. For example, boron hydride (BH_3) and sulfur hexafluoride (SF_6) do not obey the octet rule because their stable electron configurations do not contain eight valence electrons. Chemists use concepts such as resonance and expanded valence shells to explain some of the compounds that do not conform to the octet rule.

Covalent Bonds

When two atoms approach one another, their electrons repel each other, tending to push the atoms apart. Their positive nuclei also repel each other. An attractive force between the atoms comes from the attraction of the positively charged nucleus of one atom for the negatively charged electrons of the other atom. Chemical bonds occur when the attractive forces between atoms are greater than the repulsive forces.

A **covalent bond** is formed when two nuclei share electrons in order to achieve a stable arrangement of electrons. Covalent bonds are often formed between two nonmetal atoms of the same element. The diatomic chlorine molecule (Cl_2) is an example of a covalent bond. Atoms of different elements may also combine to form covalent bonds. Sulfur and oxygen combine covalently to form sulfur dioxide (SO_2).

NONPOLAR COVALENT BONDS When one chlorine atom forms a bond with another chlorine atom, they share a pair of electrons between them and form diatomic Cl_2. See Figure 6-5. In this way, the shared electrons of the bond are counted as part of each atom's stable octet. This bond is a **nonpolar covalent bond** because the attraction of the two chlorine nuclei for the shared electrons is equal, causing the pair of electrons to be shared equally. Nonpolar covalent bonds are formed between atoms having equal or close electronegativity values. Similar nonpolar bonds exist between each of the other Group 17 atoms in their diatomic molecules, namely F_2, Br_2, and I_2.

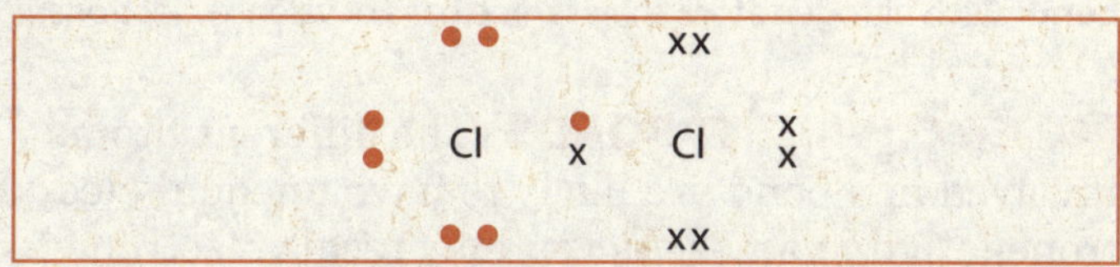

Figure 6-5. A diatomic chlorine molecule: Each chlorine atom has an octet of valence electrons.

In a similar way, two hydrogen atoms share a pair of electrons to form diatomic H_2. See Figure 6-6. In this case there is not an octet of electrons because hydrogen only needs two electrons to fill its valence level.

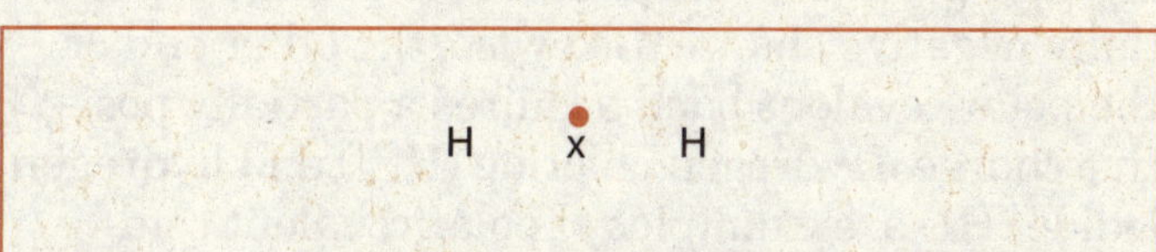

Figure 6-6. A diatomic hydrogen molecule: Each hydrogen atom has two valence electrons in its completely filled valence level.

MULTIPLE COVALENT BONDS Atoms may share more than one pair of electrons, resulting in the formation of a **multiple covalent bond.** Oxygen atoms combine with other oxygen atoms to form O_2 and achieve a stable octet configuration. In achieving this arrangement, the oxygen nuclei must share two pairs of electrons. The sharing of two pairs of valence electrons results in the type of multiple covalent bond called a **double covalent bond.** See Figure 6-7.

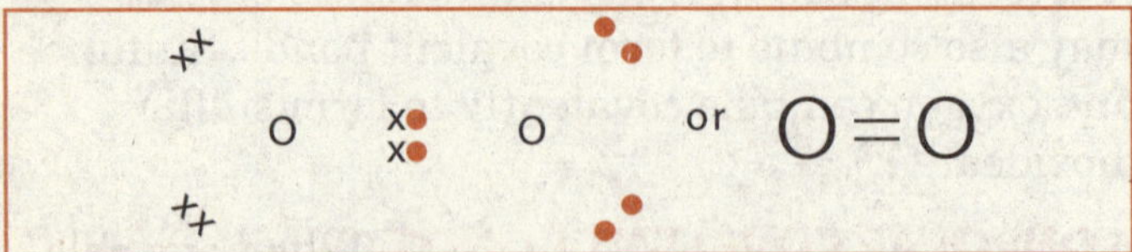

Figure 6-7. A diatomic oxygen molecule with a double covalent bond: Each oxygen atom shares two pairs of valence electrons.

Diatomic nitrogen (N_2) forms when two nitrogen atoms share three pairs of valence electrons. The sharing of three pairs of valence electrons results in a **triple covalent bond.** See Figure 6-8.

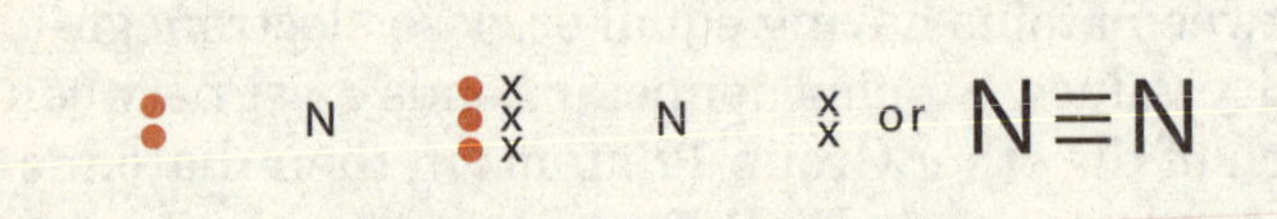

Figure 6-8. A diatomic nitrogen molecule with a triple covalent bond: Each nitrogen atom shares three pairs of valence electrons.

POLAR COVALENT BONDS The different atoms involved in a bond are likely to have unequal electronegativity values. As you may recall, electronegativity is a measure of an atom's tendency to attract bonded electrons. When the electronegativity values of the two atoms in a covalent bond are different, the sharing of electrons in the bond is unequal. The unequal sharing of electrons in a covalent bond results in a **polar covalent bond.** The element with the higher electronegativity value attracts the shared electrons more strongly, causing that portion of the molecule to acquire a partially negative charge. Likewise, the other end of the polar covalent bond acquires a partially positive charge. Hydrogen chloride (HCl) and hydrogen iodide (HI) are examples of polar covalent compounds. Look at the electron distribution for different types of bonds, as shown in Figure 6-11 on page 85.

SAMPLE PROBLEM

Which of the following bonds is the most polar in nature? (a) O_2 (b) HCl (c) NH_3 (d) HBr

Solution: Consult the *Reference Tables for Physical Setting/Chemistry* to determine the electronegativity values of each element. For each bond, determine the difference of the two electronegativity values. The bond with the smallest difference in electronegativity is the least polar, whereas the bond with the largest difference in electronegativity is the most polar.

(a) Because both oxygen atoms have the same electronegativity value (3.4), the difference is 0. This is a nonpolar covalent bond.
(b) Chlorine has an electronegativity of 3.2, and hydrogen has an electronegativity of 2.1. The electronegativity difference is 1.1, and the bond is polar covalent.
(c) Nitrogen has an electronegativity of 3.0, and hydrogen has an electronegativity of 2.1. The electronegativity difference is 0.9, and the bond is polar covalent.
(d) Bromine has an electronegativity of 3.0, and hydrogen has an electronegativity of 2.1. The electronegativity difference is 0.9, and the bond is polar covalent.

The largest electronegativity difference occurs in the bonds of HCl, hence it is the most polar in nature. The bond in diatomic oxygen is the least polar; diatomic oxygen has a nonpolar covalent bond.

Review Questions

13. The correct electron dot diagram for hydrogen chloride is

(1) $H:Cl$ (3) $H:\underset{\cdot\cdot}{\overset{\cdot\cdot}{Cl}}:$

(2) $:\underset{\cdot\cdot}{\overset{\cdot\cdot}{H}}:Cl$ (4) $:H:\overset{\cdot\cdot}{Cl}:$

14. A covalent bond forms when (1) two nuclei share electrons in order to achieve a complete octet of electrons (2) atoms form ions and then electrostatic forces of attraction bond the ions together (3) repulsive forces between atoms are greater than the attractive forces (4) a metal atom combines with a nonmetal atom

15. Which of the following bonds is the most polar in nature? (1) Cl_2 (2) HCl (3) HBr (4) HI

16. Polar covalent bonds are caused by (1) unbalanced ionic charges (2) unequal electronegativity values (3) the transfer of electrons from one atom to another (4) equally shared valence electrons

17. The bond in a diatomic nitrogen molecule (N_2) is best described as (1) polar (2) polar double covalent (3) nonpolar triple covalent (4) polar ionic

Molecular Substances

A molecule is the smallest discrete particle of an element or compound formed by covalently bonded atoms. Each atom in a molecule usually has the electron configuration of a noble gas. Molecular substances may exist as solids, liquids, or gases, depending on the strength of the forces of attraction between the molecules.

Molecules generally have properties associated with covalent bonding. Molecules are generally soft, are poor conductors of heat and electricity, and have relatively low melting and boiling points.

Water (H_2O), carbon dioxide (CO_2), and ammonia (NH_3) are examples of molecular compounds. The diatomic gases, such as oxygen (O_2) and nitrogen (N_2), are also molecular substances. Some common molecular substances are represented in Figure 6-9.

POLAR MOLECULES Although a molecule may contain polar bonds, it does not necessarily follow that the molecule itself is polar. Molecules such as hydrogen chloride and water have polar bonds and are also polar molecules. Carbon dioxide and carbon tetrachloride, however, contain polar bonds but are not polar molecules. To understand why these molecules are polar or nonpolar, you must examine their molecular shapes.

MEMORY JOGGER

Symmetrical molecules have identical parts on each side of an axis; **asymmetrical molecules** lack identical parts on each side of an axis.

Study the shapes of the molecules in Figure 6-10. The water, hydrogen chloride, and ammonia molecules are asymmetrical, whereas the carbon dioxide and carbon tetrachloride molecules are symmetrical. The symmetrical shape of the carbon dioxide and carbon tetrachloride molecules causes the pull of the various polar bonds to be offset by other bonds—the net result is a nonpolar molecule.

The charge distribution within a bond affects the nature of the bond. Figure 6-11 shows the changes in bond types with different electron distributions. The nonpolar covalent bond has an even electron distribution. As the electron distribution becomes unequal,

Name	Molecular Formula	Structural Formula	Ball-and-Stick Model	Space-Filling Model
Hydrogen	H_2	H—H		
Water	H_2O	H—O—H		
Ammonia	NH_3	H—N(—H)—H		

Figure 6-9. Models of some common molecular substances

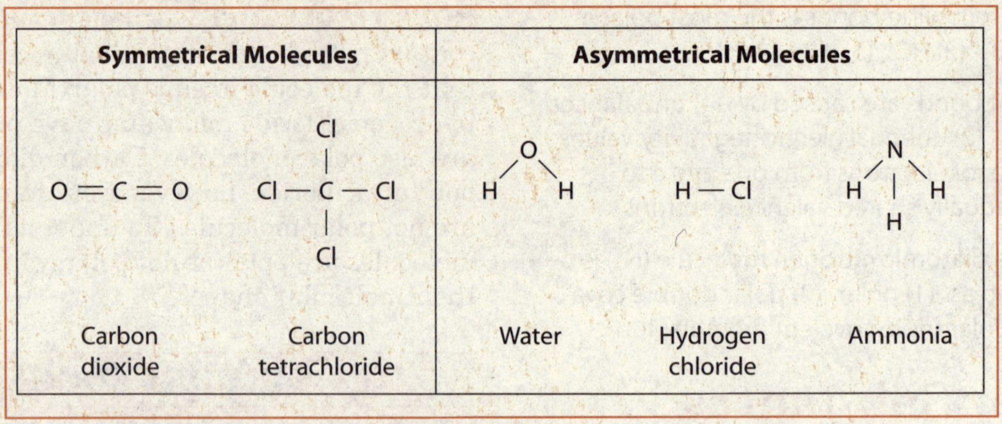

Symmetrical Molecules		Asymmetrical Molecules		
O = C = O	Cl — C(—Cl)(—Cl) — Cl	H—O—H (bent)	H — Cl	N with three H (pyramidal)
Carbon dioxide	Carbon tetrachloride	Water	Hydrogen chloride	Ammonia

Figure 6-10. Five compounds with polar bonds: The symmetrical molecules are nonpolar; the asymmetrical

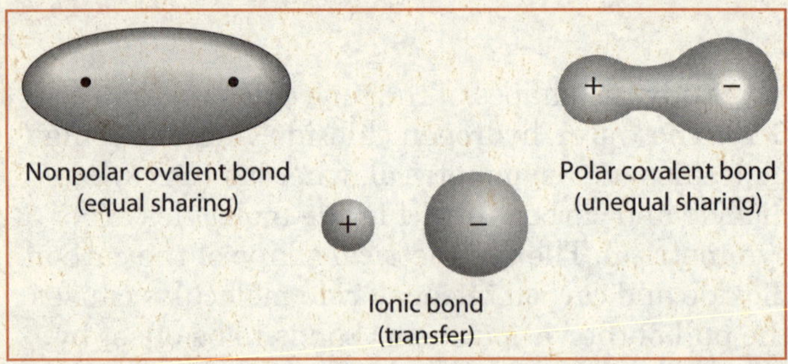

Figure 6-11. Three bond types that are dependent on electron distribution

a polar covalent bond is formed. When the electron is actually transferred, an ionic bond is formed. You will learn about ionic bonds in the next section.

Review Questions

18. Which electron dot diagram represents a polar molecule?

(1) H : H

(2) H : $\ddot{\text{Cl}}$: (with a dot pair below Cl)

(3) H : C : H, with H above and below C, bonded by dot pairs

(4) : $\ddot{\text{F}}$: $\ddot{\text{F}}$: (with dot pairs below each F)

19. Which electron dot diagram represents a polar molecule?

(1) $\ddot{\text{O}}$: : C : : $\ddot{\text{O}}$ (with dot pairs below each O)

(2) H : C : H, with H above and below C, bonded by dot pairs

(3) H : $\ddot{\text{O}}$: with a second H below O

(4) : Cl : C : Cl : with Cl above and below C; each Cl has eight dots

20. The diagram below represents a hydrogen fluoride molecule.

H : $\ddot{\text{F}}$: (with a dot pair below F)

This molecule is best described as (1) polar with polar covalent bonds (2) polar with nonpolar covalent bonds (3) nonpolar with polar covalent bonds (4) nonpolar with nonpolar covalent bonds

21. Which diagram best represents a polar molecule?

22. Which is the correct electron dot formula for a chlorine molecule?

(1) Cl • Cl

(2) • $\dot{\text{C}}$l : $\dot{\text{C}}$l • (dots above and below each Cl)

(3) : Cl • Cl : (with dot pairs above and below each Cl)

(4) : Cl : Cl : (with dot pairs above and below each Cl)

23. Which molecule contains a polar covalent bond?

(1) I : I (each I surrounded by eight electrons, shown as x's on the left I and dots on the right I)

(2) H $\times$ H (one dot and one x shared between the H atoms)

(3) H $\times$ N : H, with a second H below N; each bond is one x and one dot, and N has a dot pair above it

(4) : N $\times$ N $\times$ (triple bond shown as three dots and three x's)

24. Which electron dot diagram represents H_2?

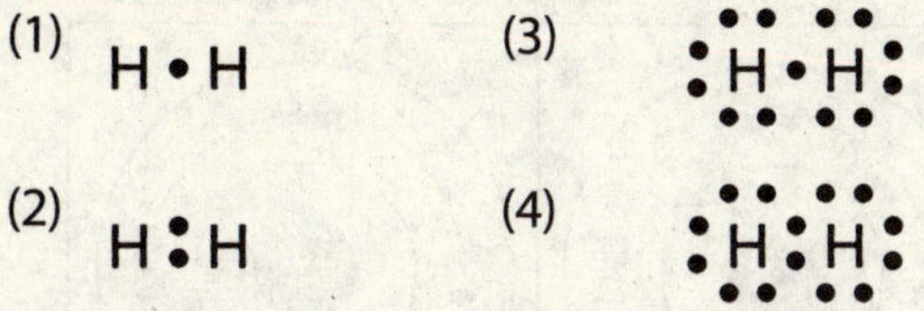

(1) H•H

(2) H:H

(3) :H•H: (with additional dots)

(4) :H:H: (with additional dots)

25. Which electron dot diagram represents the atom in Period 4 with the highest first ionization energy?

(1) X (with two dots)

(2) X (with four dots)

(3) X (with six dots)

(4) X (with eight dots)

Ionic Bonding

Recall that when atoms gain or lose electrons they become charged particles called ions. An **ionic bond** is formed when ions bond together because of the electrostatic attraction of oppositely charged ions. Figure 6-12 shows the formation of an ionic bond by the transfer of an electron.

ION FORMATION IN METALS As atoms form ions, they tend to do so in a manner that results in the formation of ions with noble gas electron configurations. Consider the metals of Group 1 with their single valence electron. When a Group 1 metallic atom reacts, it loses its electron and forms an ion with a 1+ charge. By losing its valence electron, the atom acquires the octet arrangement of a noble gas. The resulting ion is quite stable. The loss of the valence electron from the atom's outer energy level results in the ion's having a smaller radius than that atom from which it formed.

In summary, when metallic atoms react:

- they lose electrons
- they become positively charged ions
- they acquire a configuration that has a complete octet of electrons
- their radii decrease

ION FORMATION IN NONMETALS Now consider a nonmetal atom from Group 17 with its seven valence electrons. This nonmetal atom reacts by gaining a single electron to form an ion with a 1− charge. By gaining an electron, the atom has acquired the noble gas electron configuration (eight valence electrons). The resulting ion is quite stable. The addition of the valence electron to the atom's outer energy level results in the ion's having a larger radius than that atom from which it formed.

$Na^{x} + \cdot\ddot{Cl}: \longrightarrow [Na]^{+} + [{}^{x}_{\cdot}\ddot{Cl}:]^{-}$

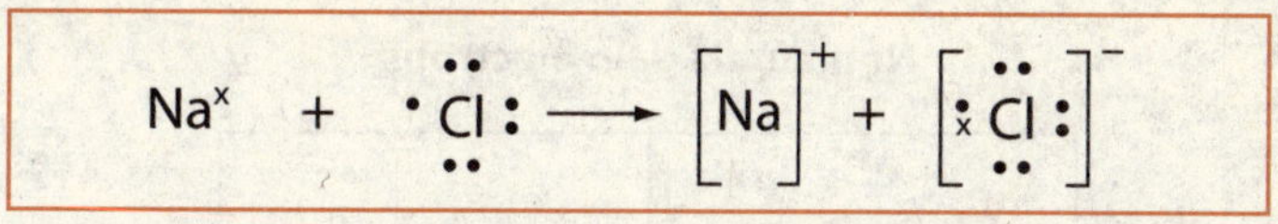

Figure 6-12. The formation of an ionic bond by the transfer of an electron

In summary, when nonmetallic atoms react:

- they gain electrons
- they become negatively charged ions
- they acquire a complete octet of electrons
- their radii increase

ION FORMATION AND THE OCTET RULE Look at Figure 6-13. Each of the atoms has a different number of electrons. When each atom reacts, it does so by losing or gaining electrons. Notice that as ions, each has an octet of valence electrons—the same number of electrons as the noble gas neon.

When metallic atoms lose electrons to form positive ions, they acquire the electron configuration of the noble gas preceding them on the periodic table. When nonmetals gain electrons, they form negative ions and acquire the electron configuration of the noble gas that follows them on the table.

ELECTRONEGATIVITY As you just learned, as the electronegativity difference between two atoms in a bond increases, the bond becomes more polar in nature. Figure 6-14 summarizes the relationship between electronegativity and bond type. As shown, as the electronegativity difference increases, the bond becomes more ionic in character. At some point the bond can no longer be considered as a sharing of electrons, but rather as a bond in which one or more electrons have actually been transferred from one atom to another. The transfer of electrons from one atom to another results in an ionic bond.

If the electronegativity difference between the bonding atoms is 1.7 or greater, the bond is generally considered to be ionic. Ionic bonds are generally formed between metals and nonmetallic atoms. Refer to Table S in the *Reference Tables for Physical Setting/Chemistry* for electronegativity values.

POLYATOMIC IONS Any compound containing a polyatomic ion must also contain an ionic bond. Consider the ionic compound ammonium carbonate $(NH_4)_2CO_3$. The ammonium ion is attracted to

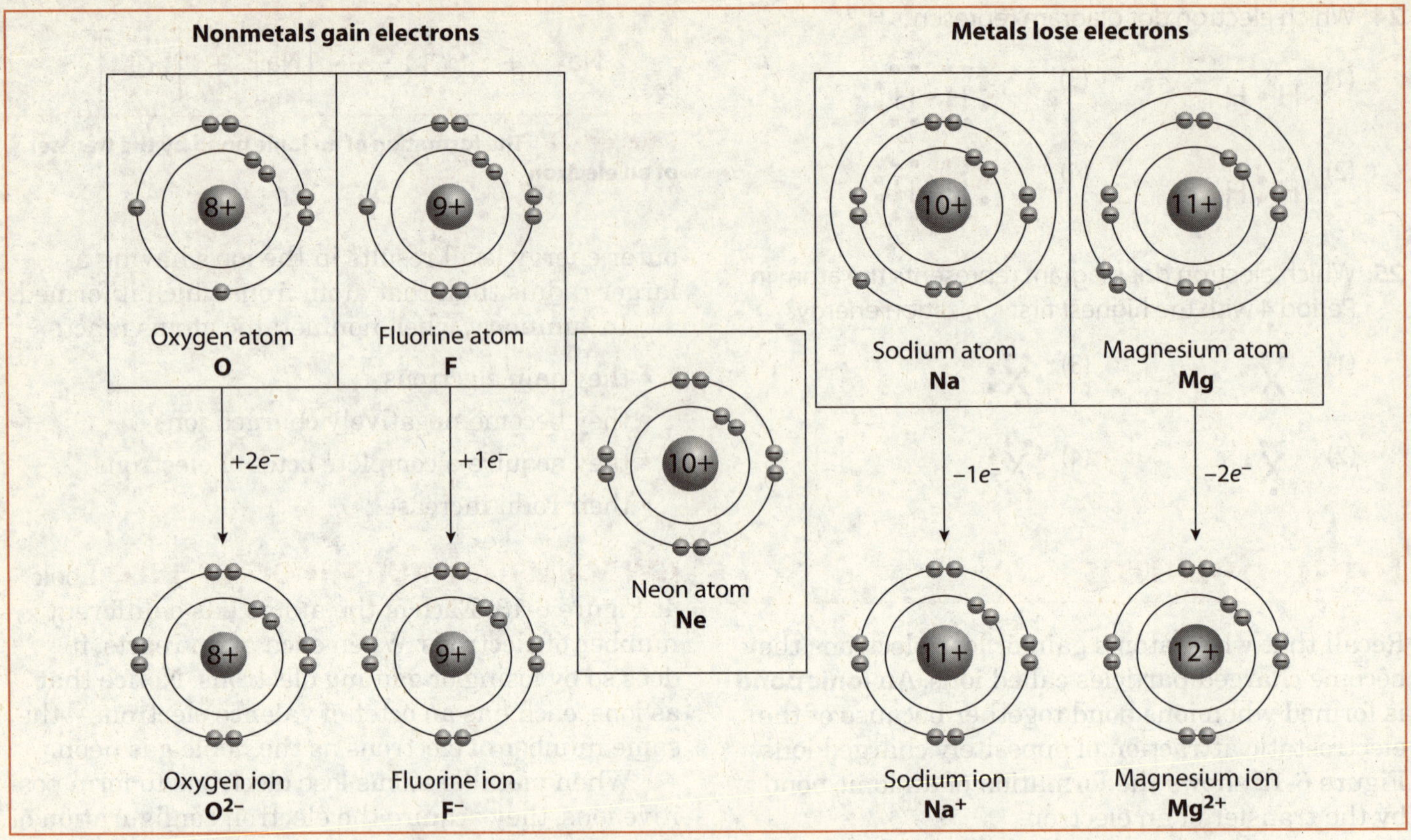

Nonmetals gain electrons

Oxygen atom
O

Fluorine atom
F

+2e⁻

+1e⁻

Neon atom
Ne

Oxygen ion
O^{2-}

Fluorine ion
F^-

Metals lose electrons

Sodium atom
Na

Magnesium atom
Mg

−1e⁻

−2e⁻

Sodium ion
Na^+

Magnesium ion
Mg^{2+}

Figure 6-13. Atoms tend to gain or lose electrons and acquire the electron configuration of the nearest noble gas

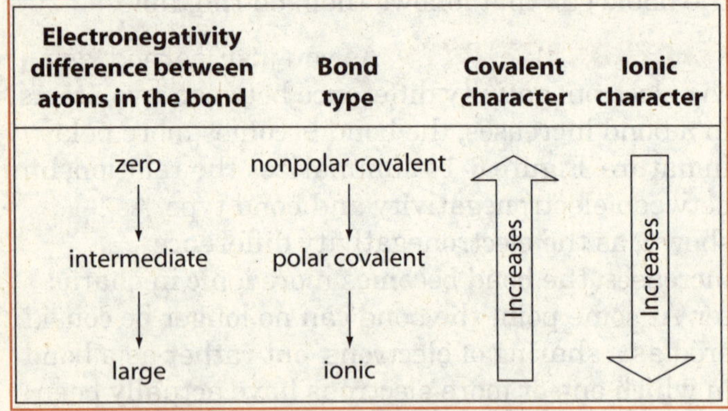

Figure 6-14. Electronegativity and bond type

the carbonate ion by an ionic bond. Within the ammonium and carbonate ions, there is a second type of bond. The nitrogen atom and hydrogen atoms of the ammonium ion and the carbon atom and oxygen atoms of the carbonate ion are held together by covalent bonds. That is, the bonds holding the atoms within the ion are themselves covalent. All compounds with polyatomic ions contain both ionic and covalent bonds.

Review Questions

26. When a calcium atom loses its valence electrons, the ion formed has an electron configuration that is the same as an atom of (1) Cl (2) Ar (3) K (4) Sc

27. The bond between which pair of elements is the least ionic in character? (1) H-F (2) H-Cl (3) H-I (4) H-O

28. Which compound has the greatest degree of ionic character? (1) NaF (2) MgF_2 (3) AlF_3 (4) SiF_4

29. Which compound contains a bond with the least ionic character? (1) CO (2) CaO (3) K_2O (4) Li_2O

30. Look at the electron dot formula shown below.

$$\begin{matrix} \mathrm{H} : \ddot{\mathrm{X}} : \\ \quad \mathrm{H} \end{matrix}$$

The attraction of X for the bonding electrons would be greatest when X represents an atom of (1) S (2) O (3) Se (4) Te

31. Which substance contains a bond with the greatest ionic character? (1) KCl (2) HCl (3) Cl_2 (4) F_2

32. Which compound contains both ionic and covalent bonds? (1) HBr (2) CBr_4 (3) NaBr (4) NaOH

33. Which element forms an ionic bond with fluorine? (1) fluorine (2) carbon (3) potassium (4) oxygen

34. Which compound is described correctly? (1) $BaCl_2$ is covalent and molecular. (2) H_2O_2 is covalent and empirical. (3) H_2O is ionic and molecular. (4) NaCl is ionic and empirical.

35. The elements Li and F combine to form an ionic compound. The electron configurations within this compound are the same as the electron configurations of atoms of Group (1) 1 (2) 14 (3) 17 (4) 18

36. An atom of which element has the same electron configuration as O^{2-}? (1) Li (2) Na (3) Ar (4) Ne

37. Which ion has the electron configuration of a noble gas? (1) Cu^{2+} (2) Fe^{2+} (3) Ca^{2+} (4) Hg^{2+}

Distinguishing Bond Types

Metallic, covalent, and ionic bonds have different properties that can be used to distinguish among them. Metals generally have high melting points. Mercury, which is a liquid at standard conditions, is an exception, as are the metals of Group 1. Ionic compounds also have high melting points, while covalently bonded molecules have relatively low melting points.

Of course, melting point alone will not accurately differentiate between bond types. Other properties must also be considered. Metallic bonds are the only type that result in good thermal and electrical conductivity. Neither ionic solids nor molecular solids are good conductors. Ionic substances become conductors when they are melted (fused) or dissolved in aqueous solutions.

Molecular substances are held together by covalent bonds. Thus, there are no charged particles to conduct an electric current. Molecular substances are poor conductors, whether they are in the solid state, in the liquid state, or in aqueous solution.

DIGGING DEEPER

Why do ionic substances conduct electricity when melted or when in aqueous solution, but not when in the solid state? In solids, electrical current is carried by electrons. In liquids, however, electrical current is carried by charged particles (ions). The ions in an ionic solid are not able to move from their fixed positions and conduct electrical current. When the ionic solid is melted or dissolved in water, the ions are free to move and conduct electrical current.

The three bond types also differ in hardness. Ionic and metallic solids are generally hard, while a majority of covalently bonded solids are soft. Table 6.1 summarizes some of the properties of the various bond types.

Review Questions

38. The electrical conductivity of KI(*aq*) is greater than the electrical conductivity of $H_2O(\ell)$ because the KI(*aq*) contains mobile (1) molecules of H_2O (2) ions from H_2O (3) molecules of KI (4) ions from KI

39. Which factor distinguishes a metallic bond from an ionic or a covalent bond? (1) the mobility of electrons (2) the mobility of protons (3) the equal sharing of electrons (4) the unequal sharing of electrons

40. Which substance has a high melting point and conducts electricity in the liquid phase? (1) Ne (2) Hg (3) NaCl (4) CO

41. Which compound in the solid state has a high melting point and conducts electricity when it is liquefied? (1) carbon dioxide (2) silicon dioxide (3) hydrogen chloride (4) potassium chloride

42. Which substance is a conductor of electricity in the liquid phase but not in the solid phase? (1) Br_2 (2) HBr (3) Na (4) NaCl

43. The water solution of which of the following substances is the best conductor of electricity? (1) KCl (2) $C_6H_{12}O_6$ (3) CO_2 (4) CO

44. Which substance is a conductor of electricity? (1) NaCl(*s*) (2) NaCl(ℓ) (3) $C_6H_{12}O_6(s)$ (4) $C_6H_{12}O_6(\ell)$

Intermolecular Forces

Just as atoms are held together by chemical bonds, molecules also have attractive forces acting on them in the solid and liquid states. It is fairly easy to understand how polar molecules are attracted to each other. Because polar molecules have positive and negative ends, polar molecules are also called <u>dipoles</u>. The positive area of one dipole molecule is

Table 6-1. Properties of Metallic, Ionic, and Covalent Bonds

Bond Type	Melting and Boiling Points	Hardness	Conductivity: Solid	Conductivity: Liquid	Conductivity: Aqueous
Metallic	High	Hard	Yes	Yes	Yes
Covalent	Low	Soft	No	No	No
Ionic	High	Hard	No	Yes	Yes

attracted to the negative portion of an adjacent dipole molecule. These attractive forces are known as dipole-dipole forces.

HYDROGEN BONDS A **hydrogen bond** is an intermolecular bond between a hydrogen atom in one molecule and a nitrogen, oxygen or fluorine atom in another molecule. See Figure 6-15. Perhaps the most important example of hydrogen bonding is found in water. Water is a polar molecule, so you might expect it to be held to other water molecules by dipole-dipole attractions. However, if only dipole-dipole forces acted to hold water molecules together, all of the water on Earth would have boiled away. The water has not boiled away because there are relatively strong hydrogen bonding forces acting on water molecules. Hydrogen bonding forces are much stronger than dipole-dipole attractions. Hydrogen bonding is responsible for the relatively high boiling point of water. Water has an abnormally high boiling point for a substance with such a small molecular mass.

Hydrogen bonding only occurs between hydrogen and the three atoms noted earlier. It is worth noting that nitrogen, oxygen, and fluorine are highly electronegative and have small radii. Ammonia (NH_3) and hydrogen fluoride (HF) are two other examples of substances with strong hydrogen bonds.

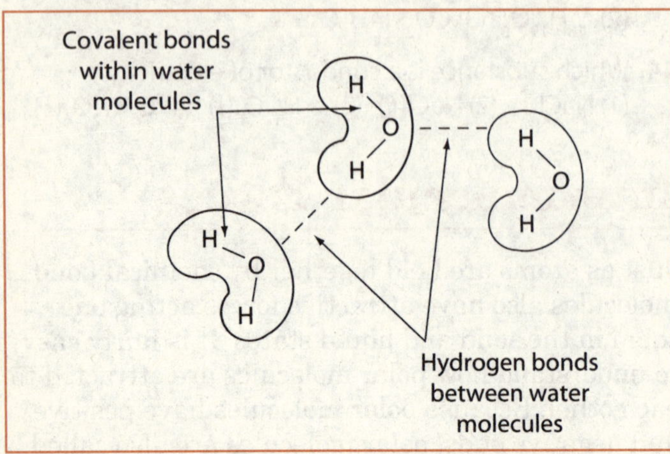

Figure 6-15. Covalent and hydrogen bonding in water

MEMORY JOGGER

You may remember the difference between *intra-* and *inter-* from your social studies class. *Intra*state traffic refers to travel within the boundaries of one state. *Inter*state refers to travel between two states. A covalent bond corresponds to the intrastate. It is a bond within a molecule. Dipole-dipole attractions and hydrogen bonds are analogous to interstate. They are found between molecules and are considerably weaker than covalent bonds.

DIGGING DEEPER

Perhaps you remember from your biology class that thymine and adenine are bonded to each other as are cytosine and quanine in the DNA molecule. The bonds that hold these parts to each other are hydrogen bonds. Hydrogen bonds are also important in holding many enzymes on to their targets.

Review Questions

45. Which molecule is a dipole?

(1) H—S (with H bonded below S)　(3) O=C=O

(2) H—C—H (with H above and below C)　(4) N≡N

46. Hydrogen bonding is strongest between molecules of (1) H_2S (2) H_2O (3) H_2Se (4) H_2Te

47. In which liquid is hydrogen bonding the most significant force of attraction? (1) HF (2) HCl (3) HBr (4) HI

48. Which atom has the least attraction for the electrons in a bond between that atom and an atom of hydrogen? (1) carbon (2) nitrogen (3) oxygen (4) fluorine

49. The unusually high boiling point of water is due to the (1) network bonds between the molecules (2) hydrogen bonds between the molecules (3) linear structure of the molecules (4) nonpolar character of the molecule

50. The strongest hydrogen bonds are formed between molecules of (1) H_2Te (2) H_2Se (3)H_2S (4) H_2O

Questions for Regents Practice

Part A

1. Which kind of energy is stored within a chemical bond?

(1) free energy

(2) activation energy

(3) kinetic energy

(4) potential energy

2. Which particles may be gained, lost, or shared by an atom when it forms a chemical bond?

(1) protons

(2) electrons

(3) neutrons

(4) nucleons

3. The forces between atoms that create chemical bonds are the result of the interactions between

(1) nuclei

(2) electrons

(3) protons and electrons

(4) protons and nuclei

4. At STP, potassium is classified as

(1) a metallic solid

(2) a molecular solid

(3) a network solid

(4) an ionic solid

5. Which element consists of positive ions immersed in a "sea" of mobile electrons?

(1) sulfur (3) calcium

(2) nitrogen (4) chlorine

6. The degree of polarity of a bond is indicated by

(1) ionization energy difference

(2) the shape of the molecule

(3) electronegativity difference

(4) the charge on the kernel

7. In a nonpolar covalent bond, electrons are

(1) located in a mobile "sea" shared by many ions

(2) transferred from one atom to another

(3) shared equally by two atoms

(4) shared unequally by two atoms

8. Which type of bond is formed when an atom of potassium transfers an electron to a bromine atom?

(1) metallic (3) nonpolar covalent

(2) ionic (4) polar covalent

9. Which type of bonding is characteristic of a substance that has a high melting point and is a good electrical conductor only when in the liquid phase?

(1) nonpolar covalent

(2) polar covalent

(3) ionic

(4) metallic

10. Which terms describe a substance that has a low melting point and poor electrical conductivity?

(1) covalent and metallic

(2) covalent and molecular

(3) ionic and molecular

(4) ionic and metallic

11. The unusually high boiling point of water is due to the presence of

(1) hydrogen bonds

(2) ionic bonds

(3) network bonds

(4) molecule-ion attractions

12. When two atoms form a chemical bond by sharing electrons, the resulting molecule will be

(1) polar only

(2) nonpolar only

(3) either polar or nonpolar

(4) neither nonpolar nor polar

13. Which type of substance is soft, has a low melting point, and is a poor conductor of electricity?
(1) covalent solid
(2) ionic solid
(3) metallic solid
(4) network solid

14. Oxygen, nitrogen, and fluorine bond with hydrogen to form molecules. These molecules are attracted to each other by
(1) ionic bonds
(2) hydrogen bonds
(3) polar covalent bonds
(4) nonpolar covalent bonds

15. Which kind of compound generally results when nonmetal atoms chemically combine with metal atoms?
(1) network
(2) molecular
(3) ionic
(4) metallic

Part B

16. Which statement is true concerning the reaction $N(g) + N(g) \rightarrow N_2(g) + \text{energy}$?
(1) A bond is broken and energy is absorbed.
(2) A bond is broken and energy is released.
(3) A bond is formed and energy is absorbed.
(4) A bond is formed and energy is released.

17. The bond between which pair of elements is the least ionic in character?
(1) H-F
(2) H-Br
(3) H-S
(4) H-O

18. Which compound has the greatest degree of ionic character?
(1) NaCl
(2) $MgCl_2$
(3) $AlCl_3$
(4) $SiCl_4$

19. Look at the electron dot diagram below.

H:F:

The electrons in the bond between hydrogen and fluorine are more strongly attracted to the atom of
(1) hydrogen, which has the higher electronegativity
(2) hydrogen, which has the lower electronegativity
(3) fluorine, which has the higher electronegativity
(4) fluorine, which has the lower electronegativity

20. Which type of bond is formed between the two chlorine atoms in a chlorine molecule?
(1) polar covalent
(2) nonpolar covalent
(3) metallic
(4) ionic

21. Which diagram best represents the structure of a water molecule?

(1) H–O–H (bent)

(3)
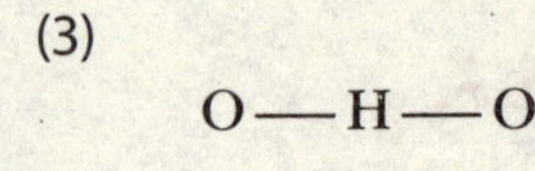

(2)
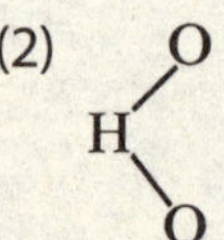

(4) H—H—O

22. Which electron dot formula represents a substance that contains a nonpolar covalent bond?

(1) $[\text{Na}]^+ [:\text{Cl}:]^-$
(3) H:Cl:
(2) :Cl:Cl:
(4)
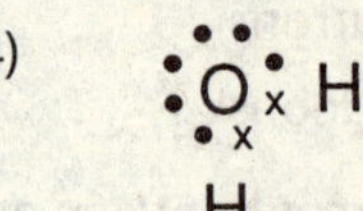

23. Which electron dot diagram represents a molecule that has a polar covalent bond?

(1) H:Cl:
(3) :Cl:Cl:
(2) $Li^+ [:\text{Cl}:]^-$
(4) $K^+ [:\text{Cl}:]^-$

24. When a sodium atom reacts with a chlorine atom to form a compound, the electron configuration of the ions forming the compound are the same as those in which noble gases?
(1) krypton and neon
(2) krypton and argon
(3) neon and helium
(4) neon and argon

25. Which atom will form an ionic bond with a Br atom?
(1) N
(2) Li
(3) O
(4) C

26. A white crystalline salt conducts electricity when it is melted and when it is dissolved in water. Which type of bond does this salt contain?

(1) ionic

(2) metallic

(3) nonpolar covalent

(4) polar covalent

27. In which molecule is hydrogen bonding the strongest?

(1) HF

(2) HCl

(3) HBr

(4) HI

28. Which statement correctly describes the bonds in the electron dot diagram shown below?

```
     H
     ••
[ H ו N ×• H ]+
     ו
     H
```

(1) One of the bonds is ionic.

(2) One of the bonds is metallic.

(3) All of the bonds are covalent.

(4) None of the bonds are covalent.

29. Which electron dot diagram best represents a compound that contains both ionic and covalent bonds?

(1) H:S: with H below (H₂S dot diagram)

(2) Ca^{2+} [:O:S:O: with O above and below]$^{2-}$

(3) K^{+}[:Br:]$^{-}$

(4) :Br:Br:

Part C

30. The boiling point of molecular substances is an indicator of the strength of the forces holding the molecules together. Using the *Reference Tables for Physical Setting/Chemistry,* arrange the following molecules in order from weakest to strongest intermolecular forces: hydrogen, iodine, nitrogen, oxygen. [1]

31. What evidence exists to show that covalent bonds are stronger than either dipole-dipole attractions or hydrogen bonds? [1]

32. Sugar reacts with oxygen in the body to produce carbon dioxide and water. Using your knowledge of chemistry, is this reaction endothermic or exothermic? State the reasons for your answer. Which is more stable, sugar or carbon dioxide? State the reasons for your answer. [4]

33. Describe the attractive and repulsive forces between an atom of oxygen and an atom of sodium. [1]

34. The Lewis dot diagram of methane is given below.

```
    H
    ו
H ×• C •× H
    ו
    H
```

What information is given by the formula? [1]

35. Draw an electron dot structure of a fluorine molecule (F_2) and an iodide ion (I^-). [2]

36. The hydrides of Group 16 are all dipoles. The graph below shows the boiling points of H_2S, H_2Se, and H_2Te.

Boiling Points of the Group 16 Hydrides

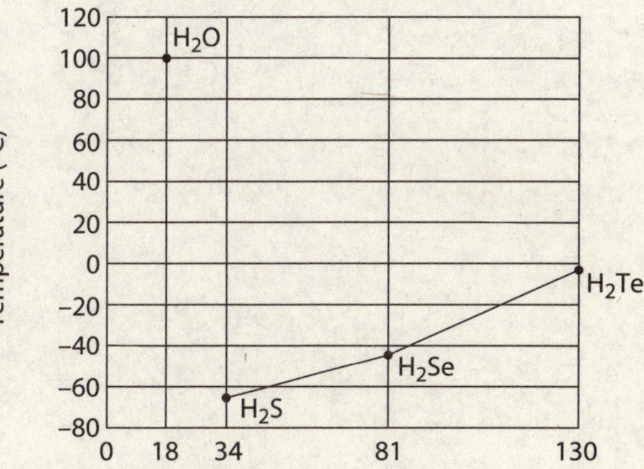

Molecular mass (g/mol)

On the basis of the trend shown by the connected points, extrapolate the data to predict the boiling point of water. What is the approximate value of the extrapolated boiling point? The actual boiling point of water is plotted on the graph at 100°C. Why is there such a difference between the extrapolated boiling point and the actual boiling point? [3]

37. The process of photosynthesis in a green plant involves the reaction between carbon dioxide and water in the presence of sunlight and chlorophyll to produce oxygen and sugar. Is the reaction endothermic or exothermic? Explain how you know. Some natural phenomena, such as volcanic eruptions, block sunlight for prolonged periods of time. How might such a phenomenon affect the levels of carbon dioxide and oxygen in the air? [3]

38. Draw a diagram that shows hydrogen bonding between ammonia molecules. Use dotted lines to show hydrogen bonds. [1]

39. Carbon atoms form four bonds with other elements or other carbon atoms. These bonds can be either single or multiple bonds. In ethane (C_2H_6), ethene (C_2H_4), and ethyne (C_2H_2), each carbon atom is bonded to the other carbon atom as well as one or more hydrogen atoms. From your knowledge of the number of bonds each atom can form, draw Lewis electron dot diagrams for each of these three compounds. [3]

40. The following table shows the percent ionic character of a bond based on the electronegativity of the elements involved.

Electronegativity difference	Percent ionic character
0.00	0
0.65	10
0.94	20
1.19	30
1.43	40
1.67	50
1.91	60
2.19	70
2.54	80
3.03	90

Using Table S in the *Reference Tables for Physical Setting/Chemistry,* list two elements that would react to produce a bond that has 40% ionic character. (Remember that a chemical bond will not form between two metals. The pair of elements must be either a metal and a nonmetal or two nonmetals.) What would be the estimated ionic character for a bond formed between nickel and oxygen? [2]

Properties of Solutions

VOCABULARY		
boiling point	**saturated**	**unsaturated**
molarity	**solute**	**vapor**
parts per million (ppm)	**solution**	**vapor pressure**
percent by volume	**solvent**	
percent mass	**supersaturated**	

Solutions

Most of the materials that you use every day are not pure substances. It is more likely that they are mixtures. This topic will explore an important type of mixture, the solution. The nature and properties of solutions are important concepts used in chemistry. One reason they are so important is that most chemical reactions take place in solutions. In this topic you will study the nature and properties of solutions and ways to express the concentration of solutions.

A **solution** is a homogeneous mixture of substances in the same physical state. Solutions contain atoms, ions, or molecules of one substance spread uniformly throughout a second substance. When salt (NaCl) is stirred into water, the individual ions of the salt separate and uniformly spread throughout the water, forming a solution.

Types of Solutions

A solid may be dissolved in another solid. Brass is a mixture of zinc and copper. When metals are mixed to form a solution, the result is called an alloy. Air is an example of a mixture of gases forming a solution.

MEMORY JOGGER

Mixtures do not have definite composition. For example, air is a mixture. The percentage of water vapor present in the air varies from day to day. Photosynthesis increases the concentration of oxygen in the air and reduces carbon dioxide. Respiration has the opposite effect, decreasing oxygen and increasing carbon dioxide.

Although solutions exist in all three states, the discussion in this topic will be limited to liquid solutions. Perhaps the most common type of solution is one in which a solid or a liquid is dissolved in a liquid.

The terms *solute* and *solvent* are commonly used to identify the parts of a solution. In general terms, the **solute** is the substance that is being dissolved, and it is the substance present in the smaller amount. When solid sodium nitrate dissolves in water, the sodium nitrate is the solute. The substance that dissolves the solute is the **solvent,** and it is present in the greater amount. Water is, perhaps, the most common solvent. Water solutions are called aqueous solutions, and the notation (*aq*) is used in equations to show that the substance is dissolved in water.

$$NaCl(s) \rightarrow Na^{+}(aq) + Cl^{-}(aq)$$

Once the salt and water are stirred and the mixture becomes homogeneous, the dissolved particles will not settle. Liquid solutions are clear, and light will pass through a solution without being dispersed, as shown in Figure 7-1 on the next page.

MEMORY JOGGER

Dissolved particles are small enough that they will pass through a filter, so filtration cannot be used to separate the parts of a solution. Distillation is one method that can be used to separate the components of a solution. If a solution consists of a solid dissolved in a liquid, distillation removes the solvent, leaving the solute behind.

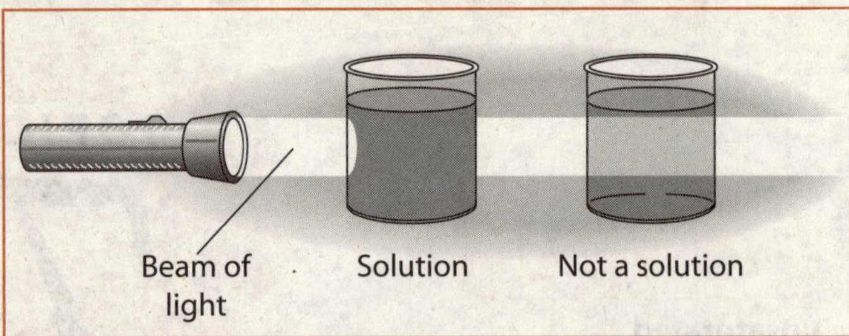

Figure 7-1. Light passing through a solution: The particles in a solution are too small to disperse light. When light passes through a liquid with larger particles, such as gelatin in water, you can see the beam because larger particles disperse light.

Solutions may or may not have color. For example, solutions of copper salts have a characteristic blue color, while a solution of sodium nitrate is colorless.

Liquid Solution Summary:

1. Solutions are homogeneous mixtures.
2. Solutions are clear and do not disperse light.
3. Solutions can have color.
4. Solutions will not settle on standing.
5. Solutions will pass through a filter.

Solubility Factors

You've noticed that some things easily dissolve in water or other solvents. When you make a cup of coffee, certain materials in the coffee grounds dissolve but other materials don't. Sugar will readily dissolve in the cup of coffee but the spoon you use to stir the solution does not dissolve. How much of a solute will dissolve in a certain amount of solvent at a certain temperature is known as solubility. Materials with a high solubility are said to be soluble; materials with a low solubility are said to be insoluble. What factors determine the solubility of a solute in a solvent?

NATURE OF SOLUTE AND SOLVENT When sodium chloride dissolves in water it does so because its positively and negatively charged ions are attracted to the oppositely charged ends of the polar water molecule. The dissolving process is shown in Figure 7-2. The positively charged sodium ions are attracted to the negative pole of the water molecules. The attractive forces between the water molecules and sodium ions are greater than the attractive forces between the sodium and chloride ions. In like manner, the negatively charged chloride ions are attracted to the positive end of the water dipole and are dissolved. Ionic and polar substances dissolve in polar solvents.

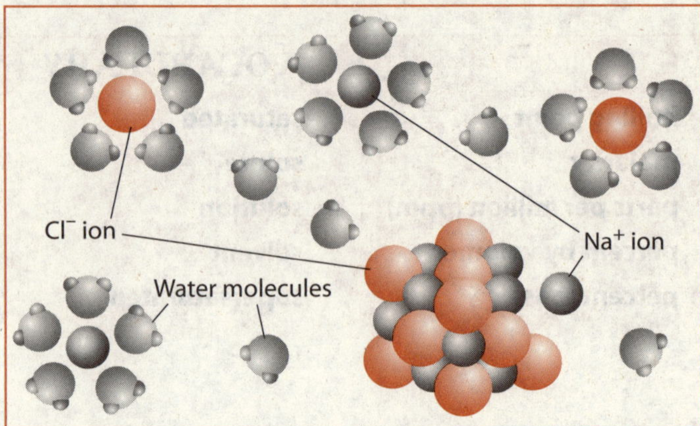

Figure 7-2. The dissolving process: Ionic and polar solutes dissolve in polar solvents because unlike charges attract each other.

Nonpolar substances, such as fats, do not dissolve in water because there aren't strong attractive forces between the fat molecules and the water molecules. Fat molecules will dissolve in nonpolar solvents. The forces that hold the nonpolar molecules to each other are quite weak, and the molecules simply mix together. The term "like dissolves like" is often used to describe what solutes will dissolve in what solvents. Table 7-1 summarizes this concept.

Table 7-1. Solubility Summary

Solute Type	Nonpolar Solvent	Polar Solvent
nonpolar	soluble	insoluble
polar	insoluble	soluble
ionic	insoluble	soluble

An interesting and important case of "like dissolves like" is found in the action of soaps. Greases, which are nonpolar, won't easily wash off our hands in water, which is polar. Soaps are long carbon chains that have one end that is polar, allowing the soap to dissolve in water. The other end of the soap is nonpolar, and grease will dissolve in it.

TEMPERATURE As temperature increases, most solids become more soluble in water. A few exceptions exist. Gases react in the opposite manner. As temperature rises, the solubility of all gases in liquids decreases.

PRESSURE Pressure has little or no effect on the solubility of solid or liquid solutes. Pressure does affect the solubility of gases in liquids. As pressure increases, the solubility of gases in liquids increases. When a can of soda is opened, the pressure decreases. The carbon dioxide is no longer as soluble at the lowered pressure, and it escapes as bubbles.

Review Questions

1. In a true solution, the dissolved particles (1) are visible to the eye (2) will settle out on standing (3) are always solids (4) cannot be removed by filtration

2. When a teaspoon of sugar is added to water and stirred, the sugar (1) melts (2) dissolves (3) condenses (4) evaporates

3. In an aqueous solution of potassium chloride, the solute is (1) Cl^- only (2) K^+ only (3) K^+Cl^- (4) H_2O

4. Which sample of matter is a mixture? (1) $H_2O(s)$ (2) $H_2O(\ell)$ (3) $NaCl(\ell)$ (4) $NaCl(aq)$

5. Most ionic substances are soluble in water because water molecules are (1) nonpolar (2) inorganic (3) ionic (4) polar

6. Nonpolar solvents will most easily dissolve solids that are (1) ionic (2) covalent (3) metallic (4) colored

7. An aqueous solution of copper sulfate is poured into a filter paper cone. What passes through the filter paper? (1) only the solvent (2) only the solute (3) both solvent and solute (4) neither the solute nor solvent

8. As the temperature rises, the solubility of all gases in water (1) decreases (2) increases (3) remains the same (4) depends on the gas

9. A decrease in pressure has the greatest effect on a solution that contains (1) a gas in a liquid (2) a solid in a solid (3) a liquid in a liquid (4) a solid in a liquid

10. Under which conditions are gases most soluble in water? (1) high temperature and high pressure (2) high temperature and low pressure (3) low temperature and high pressure (4) low temperature and low pressure

11. What happens when $NaCl(s)$ is dissolved in water? (1) Cl^- ions are attracted to the oxygen atoms of the water. (2) Cl^- ions are attracted to the hydrogen atoms of the water. (3) Na^+ ions are attracted to the hydrogen atoms of the water. (4) No attractions are involved; the crystal just falls apart.

12. Which diagram best illustrates the ion-molecule attractions that occur when the ions of $NaCl(s)$ are added to water?

(1) H>O (Na+) (Cl−) H>O

(2) O<H (Na+) (Cl−) O<H

(3) H>O (Na+) (Cl−) O<H

(4) O<H (Na+) (Cl−) H>O

Looking at Solubility

Solubility information may be presented in different ways. Table G of *Reference Tables for Physical Setting/Chemistry* presents quantitative information showing the relationship of grams of solute that may be dissolved at various temperatures. Table F provides some general guidelines about the solubility of ionic substances. You will need to be able to interpret information from both tables.

SOLUBILITY GRAPHS Table G shows the number of grams of a substance that can be dissolved in 100. g of water at temperatures between 0°C and 100°C. Each line represents the maximum amount of that substance that can be dissolved at a given temperature. All of the lines that show an increase in solubility as temperatures increase represent solids being dissolved in water. Although these lines on the graph show an increase in solubility as temperature increases, a few solids, such as cesium sulfate, become less soluble as temperature increases.

Three lines show decreasing solubility with increasing temperature. These three lines represent the gases NH_3, HCl, and SO_2. The solubility of all gases decreases with increasing temperature.

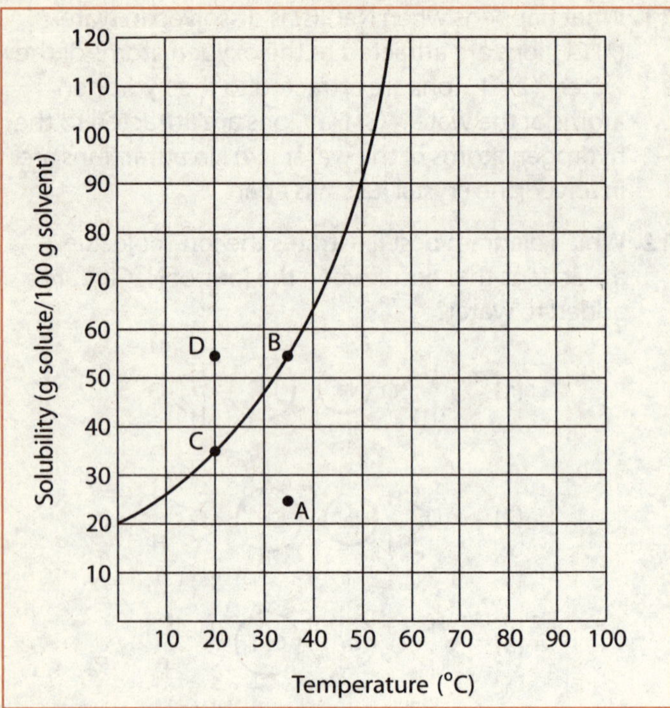

Figure 7-3. A solubility curve

Figure 7-3 shows four positions relative to a line of maximum solubility. Position A is below the maximum line of solubility. At this position, the temperature is 35°C, and 25 g of solute X dissolve. Because at this point the solution holds less solute than the maximum it can hold, the solution is said to be **unsaturated.** If there is not a temperature change, an additional 30 g can be added to bring X to position B.

Position B is on the line of maximum solubility. A solution that contains a maximum amount of solute that will dissolve at a specific temperature is **saturated.** At this position, the solution contains 55 g of X. The addition of more solid solute will not result in more being dissolved. Any additional solid that is added will simply settle to the bottom of the container.

If the temperature is reduced to 20°C, only 35 g of X can dissolve. When the temperature of the solution at B is reduced, the most likely event is that the excess 20 g of X will precipitate, and the solution will remain saturated at point C. On rather rare occasions, as the temperature decreases, crystals do not form and the substance may be at position D.

At position D, there is more solid dissolved than normal. A solution that holds more solute than is present in a saturated solution at that temperature is **supersaturated.** These solutions are quite unstable. The addition of a single solid crystal of the substance will cause additional solid to form, and the solution will return to a saturated condition. If no temperature change occurred, the solution would become saturated at point C, with 20 g of the substance precipitating. The only way to make a supersaturated solution is to cool a saturated solution in which there are no crystals or impurities, such as dust, present.

DIGGING DEEPER

There are two terms that are somewhat useful in describing concentrations of solutions. Dilute solutions contain relatively small amounts of dissolved solute in a large amount of solvent. For example, 5 g of a substance dissolved in 100. g of H_2O would be a dilute solution. Concentrated solutions contain relatively large amounts of solute. These terms should not be confused with saturated and unsaturated. Five grams of potassium chlorate dissolved in 100. g of water at 0°C would be dilute, but the solution would be saturated; 80. g of $NaNO_3$ dissolved in the same amount of water would be concentrated, but unsaturated.

MEMORY JOGGER

In Topic 2 you learned that double-replacement reactions have the general formula:

$$AB + CD \rightarrow AD + CB$$

SOLUBILITY TABLES Table F of *Reference Tables for Physical Setting/Chemistry* contains some guidelines for the solubility of common ionic compounds. The table shows that all compounds of the ammonium and the nitrate ion are soluble. All of the halide ions, such as Cl^-, form compounds that are soluble, but three exceptions are listed. Silver chloride is not soluble, nor are Pb^{2+} nor Hg_2^{2+} chlorides, and they are precipitates if they form in a double-replacement reaction. This table is useful in predicting whether or not a precipitate will form when two ionic solutions are mixed. A reaction will take place if one or both of the products is listed as insoluble.

SAMPLE PROBLEM

Silver nitrate and sodium chromate solutions are mixed together. Will a precipitate form? If so, what is the name of the precipitate?

Solution: Identify the known and unknown values.

Known	*Unknown*
Formulas of reactants	Solubility of products
Solubility table	Identity of precipitate

Write the word equation for a double-replacement reaction between silver nitrate and sodium carbonate.

silver nitrate + sodium chromate →
silver chromate + sodium nitrate

Check the solubilities of the products.

Chromates are listed as insoluble, with the exception of Group 1 ions or the ammonium ion. Nitrates are soluble.

A precipitate of silver chromate will form.

RECOGNIZING UNSATURATED, SATURATED, AND SUPERSATURATED SOLUTIONS Because solutions are clear, it is difficult to simply look at a solution and determine whether it is unsaturated, saturated, or supersaturated.

One method of recognizing the type of solution narrows the choices. If a solution contains some undissolved solute, it must be a saturated solution.

The addition of a solute crystal can also be used to determine its condition. If it dissolves, the original solution was unsaturated. If it simply falls to the bottom, the solution is saturated. If it causes additional crystals to form, the original solution was supersaturated.

Review Questions

Use the tables in *Reference Tables for Physical Setting/Chemistry* as needed in answering the following questions.

13. Which compound's solubility decreases most rapidly as the temperature changes from 10°C to 70°C? (1) NH_4Cl (2) NH_3 (3) HCl (4) KCl

14. Solubility for salt X is shown in the table below.

Temperature (°C)	Solubility $\left(\frac{\text{g salt } X}{100 \text{ g } H_2O}\right)$
10	5
20	10
30	15
40	20
50	30
60	35

Which graph most closely represents the data shown in the table?

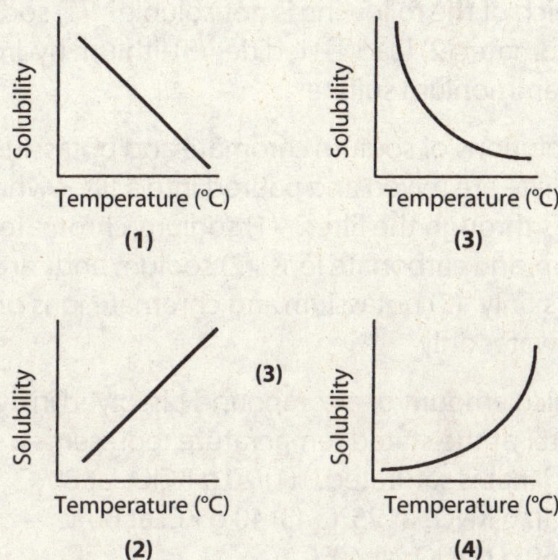

15. A solution contains 14 g of KCl in 100. g of water at 40°C. What is the minimum amount of KCl that must be added to make this a saturated solution? (1) 14 g (2) 19 g (3) 25 g (4) 44 g

16. Which salt has the greatest change in solubility between 30°C and 50°C? (1) KNO_3 (2) KCl (3) $NaNO_3$ (4) NaCl

17. Which of the following substances is least soluble in 100. g of water at 50°C? (1) NaCl (2) KCl (3) NH_4Cl (4) HCl

18. A student obtained the following data in a chemistry laboratory.

Trial	Temperature (°C)	Solubility ($g\ KNO_3/100\ g\ H_2O$)
1	25	40
2	32	50
3	43	70
4	48	60

Based on the reference tables, which of the four trials listed seems to be in error? (1) 1 (2) 2 (3) 3 (4) 4

19. How many grams of the compound potassium chloride (KCl) must be dissolved in 200. g of water to make a saturated solution at 60°C? (1) 30 g (2) 45 g (3) 56 g (4) 90 g

20. Which of the following is insoluble? (1) calcium chloride (2) ammonium phosphate (3) barium sulfate (4) potassium chromate

21. Which of the following is not soluble? (1) sodium chromate (2) lead(II) iodide (3) lithium hydroxide (4) ammonium sulfate

22. If solutions of sodium chromate and potassium carbonate are mixed and poured into a filter, what will pass through the filter? (1) sodium, chromate, potassium, and carbonate ions (2) sodium and carbonate ions only (3) potassium and chromate ions only (4) water only

23. Which amount of a compound dissolved in 100. g of water at the stated temperature represents a solution that is saturated? (1) 20 g $KClO_3$ at 80°C (2) 40 g KNO_3 at 25°C (3) 40 g KCl at 60°C (4) 60 g $NaNO_3$ at 40°C

Concentration of Solutions

Because solutions are homogeneous mixtures, their compositions can vary. Sometimes, it is adequate to refer to a solution as dilute or concentrated. However, *dilute* and *concentrated* are relative terms and are not precise regarding the amount of solute involved. In most cases it is the specific amount, or concentration, of the solute that is important. In this section you will learn several methods of expressing the specific concentration of solute in a solution.

Molarity

One of the most important methods of stating the concentration of a solution is in terms of the number of moles of solute in a given volume of solution. The **molarity** (M) of a solution is the number of moles of solute in 1 L of solution. The relationship is listed in Table T of *Reference Tables for Physical Setting/Chemistry.*

$$\textbf{molarity} = \frac{\textbf{moles of solute}}{\textbf{liters of solution}}$$

SAMPLE PROBLEM

What is the molarity of a solution that contains 4.0 mol of NaOH in 0.50 L of solution?

Solution: Identify the known and unknown values.

Known	*Unknown*
amount NaOH = 4.0 mol	molarity = ? M
volume of solution = 0.50 L	

Substitute known values into the equation for molarity, and solve for molarity.

$$M = \frac{\text{moles of solute}}{\text{liters of solution}}$$

$$M = \frac{4.0 \text{ moles NaOH}}{0.50 \text{ liter}}$$

$$M = 8.0$$

In the previous sample problem, the molarity of the solution is 8.0 M. A liter of this solution would contain 8.0 mol of the solute, NaOH. However, in many problems, the mass of solute is given instead of the number of moles. To solve this type of problem, convert grams of solute to moles of solute and solve as above.

SAMPLE PROBLEM

What is the molarity of a solution containing 82.0 g of $Ca(NO_3)_2$ in 2.0 liters of solution?

Solution: Identify the known and unknown values.

Known	*Unknown*
mass of $Ca(NO_3)_2$ = 82.0 g	molarity = ? M
volume of solution = 2.0 L	

Calculate the formula mass of $Ca(NO_3)_2$.

For Ca: 1 atom × 40. amu/atom = 40 amu
For N: 2 atoms × 14 amu/atom = 28 amu
For O: 6 atoms × 16 amu/atom = <u>96 amu</u>
Formula mass $Ca(NO_3)_2$ = 164 amu

Change the formula mass to gram formula mass.

gram formula mass = formula mass in grams
gram formula mass $Ca(NO_3)_2$ = 164 g/mol

Convert grams of $Ca(NO_3)_2$ to moles.

$$\text{moles } Ca(NO_3)_2 = \frac{\text{grams } Ca(NO_3)_2}{\text{gram formula mass } Ca(NO_3)_2}$$

$$\text{moles } Ca(NO_3)_2 = \frac{82.0\,\cancel{g}}{164\,\cancel{g}/\text{mol}} = 0.500 \text{ mol}$$

Calculate molarity.

$$M = \frac{\text{moles of solute}}{\text{liters of solution}}$$

$$M = \frac{0.500 \text{ mol NaOH}}{2.0 \text{ L solution}}$$

$$M = 0.250$$

MEMORY JOGGER

In math class you have learned how to rearrange an equation to solve for an unknown variable. For example, $a = \frac{b}{c}$ is solved for *a* but can be rearranged to solve for *b* ($b = ac$) or *c* $\left(c = \frac{b}{a}\right)$.

Recognize that the molarity equation can also be rearranged to solve for any variable included in the equation.

$$\text{molarity} = \frac{\text{moles solute}}{\text{liters of solution}}$$

$$\text{moles solute} = (\text{molarity})(\text{liters of solution})$$

$$\text{liters of solution} = \frac{\text{moles solute}}{\text{molarity}}$$

Percent by Mass

It is common to find labels that list the concentration of the ingredients by percent mass. Fertilizers often list the active ingredients as a percentage of the entire mass of the fertilizer. **Percent mass** is simply the mass of an ingredient divided by the total mass, expressed as a percent (parts per hundred). Percent mass problems are essentially the same as the percent composition problems found in Topic 3. To calculate the percent mass, use the following relationship.

$$\textbf{percent mass} = \frac{\textbf{mass of part}}{\textbf{mass of whole}} \times \textbf{100\%}$$

SAMPLE PROBLEM

What is the percent mass of sodium hydroxide if 2.50 g of NaOH are added to 50.00 g of H_2O?

Solution: Identify the known and unknown values.

Known	*Unknown*
mass of NaOH = 2.50 g	Percent mass NaOH = ? %
mass of H_2O = 50.00 g	

Substitute known values into the percent mass equation, and solve for percent mass.

$$\%\text{ mass} = \frac{\text{mass of part}}{\text{mass of whole}} \times 100\%$$

$$\%\text{ mass NaOH} = \frac{2.50\,\cancel{g}\text{ NaOH}}{(2.50 + 50.00)\,\cancel{g}\text{ solution}} \times 100\%$$

$$\%\text{ mass NaOH} = 4.76\%$$

Percent by Volume

When two liquids are mixed to form a solution, it is common to express the concentration of the solute as a percent by volume. A label on a bottle of rubbing alcohol shows a common example. Usually the label will show that the solution is 70% isopropyl alcohol by volume. The rest of the solution is water.

Percent by volume is the ratio of the volume of an ingredient divided by the total volume and expressed as a percent.

$$\textbf{percent by volume} = \frac{\textbf{volume of solute}}{\textbf{volume of solution}} \times \textbf{100\%}$$

SAMPLE PROBLEM

What is the percent by volume of alcohol if 50.0 mL of ethanol is diluted with water to form a total volume of 300. mL?

Solution: Identify the known and unknown values.

Known	*Unknown*
volume of ethanol = 50.0 mL	percent by volume
total volume = 300. mL	ethanol = ? %

Substitute known values into the percent by volume equation, and solve for percent by volume.

$$\%\text{ by volume} = \frac{\text{volume of solute}}{\text{volume of solution}} \times 100\%$$

$$\%\text{ by volume ethanol} = \frac{50.0\,\cancel{mL}\text{ ethanol}}{300.\,\cancel{mL}\text{ solution}} \times 100\%$$

$$\%\text{ by volume ethanol} = 16.7\%$$

Parts per Million

Parts per million is similar to percent composition because it compares masses. **Parts per million (ppm)** is a ratio between the mass of a solute and the total mass of the solution. This method of reporting concentrations is useful for extremely dilute solutions when molarity and percent mass would be difficult to interpret. For example, chlorine is used as a disinfectant in swimming pools. Only about 2 g of chlorine per 1,000,000 g of swimming pool water is necessary to keep the pool sanitized. Finding molarity and percent mass would result in numbers too small to be useful. Parts per million is often used to report a measured amount of air or water pollutants.

Percent composition uses the amount present per hundred parts because it is a percent. The only difference in finding ppm is that you multiply by 1,000,000 ppm instead of 100 percent.

$$\text{ppm} = \frac{\text{grams of solute}}{\text{grams of solution}} \times 1{,}000{,}000 \text{ ppm}$$

SAMPLE PROBLEM

Approximately 0.0043 g of oxygen can be dissolved in 100. mL of water at 20°C. Express this in terms of parts per million.

Solution: Identify the known and unknown values.

Known	*Unknown*
mass of O_2 = 0.0043 g	ppm O_2 = ?
volume of H_2O = 100. mL	

Substitute known values into the ppm equation, and solve for ppm O_2.

$$\text{ppm} = \frac{\text{grams of solute}}{\text{grams of solution}} \times 1{,}000{,}000 \text{ ppm}$$

$$\text{ppm } O_2 = \frac{0.0043 \cancel{g}}{100.0043 \cancel{g}} \times 1{,}000{,}000 \text{ ppm}$$

$$\text{ppm } O_2 = 43 \text{ ppm}$$

Preparation of a Solution of Known Concentration

It is important to be able to calculate the amount of solute to be added to a known volume of solvent to make a solution of specified concentration. The following sample problem shows you how to determine the amount of solute needed to prepare a solution of known molarity.

SAMPLE PROBLEM

What mass of sodium carbonate is required to prepare 2.00 L of a 0.250 M sodium carbonate solution?

Solution: Identify the known and unknown values.

Known	*Unknown*
concentration of solution = 0.250 M	mass of Na_2CO_3 = ? g
volume of solution = 2.00 L	

Determine the number of moles of solute needed by using molarity and volume.

$$\text{moles} = MV = \text{molarity} \times \text{liters of solution}$$

$$\text{moles } Na_2CO_3 = \frac{0.250 \text{ mol}}{1 \cancel{L}} \times 2.00 \cancel{L} = 0.500 \text{ mol}$$

The following steps are used to convert moles Na_2CO_3 to grams Na_2CO_3:

Determine the formula mass of Na_2CO_3.

For Na: 2 atoms × 23.0 amu/atom = 46.0 amu
For C: 1 atom × 12.0 amu/atom = 12.0 amu
For O: 3 atoms × 16.0 amu/atom = 48.0 amu
formula mass Na_2CO_3 = 106.0 amu

Change the formula mass to gram formula mass.

gram formula mass = formula mass in grams
gram formula mass Na_2CO_3 = 106.0 g/mol

Convert moles of Na_2CO_3 into grams of Na_2CO_3.

$$\text{mass} = \text{moles} \times \text{gram formula mass}$$

$$\text{mass } Na_2CO_3 = 0.500 \cancel{\text{mol}} \times 106.0 \text{ g}/\cancel{\text{mol}}$$

$$\text{mass } Na_2CO_3 = 53.0 \text{ g}$$

You now know how much solute and solvent you need to actually prepare the solution in the sample problem, but the procedure used in preparation is also essential. The steps outlined below are specific for the solution used in the sample problem, but they apply to the preparation of any solution of known concentration.

First, add 53.0 g of sodium carbonate to a 2.00-L volumetric flask. Then, add some distilled water and swirl until the solute is dissolved and thoroughly mixed. Finally, fill with distilled water to the mark on the neck of the flask, and again stir to make sure the solution is homogeneous. The reason the water is added in two steps is that it is easier to dissolve the solute if the flask is not full and there is room for the water to be adequately stirred or shaken.

Review Questions

24. What is the molarity of a KF(*aq*) solution containing 116 g of KF in 1.00 L of solution? (1) 1.00 M (2) 2.00 M (3) 3.00 M (4) 4.00 M

25. What is the molarity of an H_2SO_4 solution if 0.25 L of the solution contains 0.75 mol of H_2SO_4? (1) 0.33 M (2) 0.75 M (3) 3.0 M (4) 6.0 M

26. What is the total number of moles of the solute H_2SO_4 needed to prepare 5.0 L of a 2.0 M solution of H_2SO_4? (1) 2.5 mol (2) 5.0 mol (3) 10. mol (4) 20. mol

27. What volume of a 2.0 M solution is needed to provide 0.50 mol of NaOH? (1) 0.25 L (2) 0.50 L (3) 1.0 L (4) 2.0 L

28. What is the molarity of a solution that contains 40. g of NaOH in 0.50 L of solution? (1) 1.0 M (2) 2.0 M (3) 0.50 M (4) 0.25 M

29. If 100. mL of a 1.0 M solution is evaporated to a volume of 25 mL, what will be the concentration of the resulting solution? (1) 0.25 M (2) 0.50 M (3) 2.0 M (4) 4.0 M

30. What is the percent by mass of a solution in which 60. g of NaOH are dissolved in sufficient water to make 100 g of solution? (1) 16% (2) 40% (3) 60% (4) 160%

31. What is the percent by mass of a solution if 60. g of acetic acid are added to 90. g of water? (1) 20% (2) 30% (3) 40% (4) 67%

32. Carbon dioxide gas has a solubility of 0.0972 g/100 g H_2O at 40°C. Expressed in parts per million, this concentration is closest to (1) 0.972 ppm (2) 9.72 ppm (3) 97.2 ppm (4) 972 ppm

33. A substance has a solubility of 350 ppm. How many grams of the substance are present in 1.0 L of a saturated solution? (1) 0.0350 g (2) 0.350 g (3) 3.50 g (4) 35.0 g

Use the reference tables and your knowledge of chemistry to answer each of the following questions. Be sure to show all work if calculations are needed.

34. What is the percent mass of a saturated solution of $KClO_3$ at 20°C?

35. A saturated solution of ammonium chloride in 100. g H_2O at 85°C is cooled to 20°C and filtered. What was the mass of the solution at 85°C? What is the mass of the liquid that passes through the filter?

36. Barium sulfate is listed as insoluble on solubility tables. It does, however, dissolve to a small extent. Its solubility at 50°C is 0.00034 g in 100. g of water. Express this solubility in parts per million.

37. The table below gives the solubility of $Ca(OH)_2(s)$ in 100. g of H_2O at various temperatures. What is unusual about the behavior of the solubility of this salt?

Temperature (°C)	**Solubility** (g $Ca(OH)_2$/100. g H_2O)
0	0.189
20	0.173
40	0.141
60	0.121
80	0.094

Colligative Properties

The freezing and boiling points of water change when nonvolatile solutes are added. When any salt is added to water, the freezing point of the water decreases. This helps explain why salt is applied to roads and sidewalks when they are covered with snow and ice. The added salt lowers the freezing point and helps to melt the snow or ice. The amount of the lowering of the freezing point is not dependent on the nature of the added particle. One mole of any particles will have the same effect on the freezing point. One mole of particles lowers the freezing point of 1000 g of water by 1.86°C.

Molecular Versus Ionic

When one mole of sugar, a molecular substance, is dissolved in water, one mole of particles is produced in solution.

$$\underset{1\text{ mol}}{C_{12}H_{22}O_{11}(s)} \rightarrow \underset{1\text{ mol}}{C_{12}H_{22}O_{11}(aq)}$$

When one mole of an ionic substance is dissolved in water, the results are different. The ionic substance separates into individual ions.

$$NaCl(s) \rightarrow Na^+(aq) + Cl^-(aq)$$
$$1\text{ mol NaCl} \rightarrow 1\text{ mol Na}^+ + 1\text{ mol Cl}^-$$

Thus, one mole of sodium chloride produces two moles of particles and will depress the freezing point of water twice as much as the mole of sugar. The greater the number of ions, the greater the effect on the freezing point. $CaCl_2$ contains three ions, and one mole of this salt will depress the freezing point three times as much as a mole of sugar.

The situation is similar with the boiling point. One mole of particles will elevate the boiling point of 1000. g of water by 0.52°C. One mole of dissolved sugar will elevate the boiling point of 1000. g of water by 0.52°C, while one mole of dissolved sodium chloride will elevate the temperature of the same amount of water by 1.04°C.

Review Questions

38. Why is salt (NaCl) put on icy roads and sidewalks in the winter? (1) It is ionic and lowers the freezing point of water. (2) It is ionic and raises the freezing point of water. (3) It is covalent and lowers the freezing point of water. (4) It is covalent and raises the freezing point of water.

39. What occurs as a salt dissolves in water? (1) The number of ions in the solution decreases, and the freezing point decreases. (2) The number of ions in the solution decreases, and the freezing point increases. (3) The number of ions in the solution increases, and the freezing point decreases. (4) The number of ions in the solution increases, and the freezing point increases.

40. Assume equal aqueous concentrations of each of the following substances. Which has the lowest freezing point? (1) $C_2H_{12}O_6$ (2) CH_3OH (3) $C_{12}H_{22}O_{11}$ (4) NaOH

41. What occurs when sugar is added to water? (1) The freezing point of the water will decrease, and the boiling point will decrease. (2) The freezing point of the water will decrease, and the boiling point will increase. (3) The freezing point of the water will increase, and the boiling point will decrease. (4) The freezing point of the water will increase, and the boiling point will increase.

42. Which solution has the highest boiling point? (1) 1.0 M KNO_3 (2) 2.0 M KNO_3 (3) 1.0 M $Ca(NO_3)_2$ (4) 2.0 M $Ca(NO_3)_2$

43. Which property of a distilled water solution will *not* be affected by adding 50 mL of CH_3OH to 100. mL of the water solution at 25°C? (1) conductivity (2) mass (3) freezing point (4) boiling point

Vapor Pressure

The molecules in a liquid are held together by rather weak forces. Polar molecules called dipoles are held in the liquid phase by dipole-dipole forces. In molecules containing hydrogen and one of oxygen, nitrogen, or fluorine, the force of attraction holding them in the liquid phase are hydrogen bonds.

MEMORY JOGGER

Hydrogen bonds are formed when a hydrogen atom in one molecule is attracted to an oxygen, nitrogen, or fluorine atom in another molecule. Because hydrogen bonding is stronger than dipole-dipole attraction, substances with hydrogen bonding have abnormally high boiling points.

In any sample of a liquid, some of the particles at the surface have sufficient energy to escape from their neighboring molecules and enter the gas phase. When a substance that is normally a solid or a liquid at room temperature enters the gas phase it is called a **vapor.** Thus, you will often hear about water vapor or gasoline vapor, as water and gasoline are normally liquids at room temperature.

As the temperature of a liquid increases, the particles have more energy, and more particles escape from the surface. These vapor particles are gaseous particles and exert pressure in the gaseous phase. The pressure that a vapor exerts is called **vapor pressure.** Table H of *Reference Tables for Physical Setting/Chemistry* is a graph showing the vapor pressure of four substances measured in pressure units of kilopascals (kPa).

Of the substances shown on the graph, propanone exerts the most pressure, about 93 kPa at a temperature of 50°C. It can be inferred that propanone has the weakest intermolecular forces holding it in the liquid phase, while ethanoic acid has the greatest, exerting only about 8 kPa of pressure.

Boiling Point

As the temperature of a liquid rises, vapor pressure increases. Finally the vapor pressure becomes equal to atmospheric pressure. At this point the gas may vaporize, not only on the surface but at any point in the container. A bubble of vapor below the surface has enough pressure that it does not collapse from the atmospheric pressure pushing against it. When a bubble can occur at any point in the liquid, the process is called boiling. The normal **boiling point** of a liquid is the temperature at which the vapor pressure of the liquid is 101.3 kPa, standard atmospheric pressure. Equivalent pressures are 1 atm, 760 mm Hg, and 760 torr.

The heat required to change 1 mol of a substance from a liquid at its boiling point to 1 mol of a vapor is termed the heat of vaporization.

The normal boiling point of water is 100.°C. At this temperature, the vapor pressure of water is 101.3 kPa. The line representing 101.3 kPa on Table H shows the normal boiling point of ethanol to be 78°C. When the pressure is less than 101.3 kPa, the boiling point will be less than the normal value. Water will boil at about 70°C when the pressure is about 30 kPa. If the pressure is greater than normal, liquids will boil at temperatures above their normal boiling points. When atmospheric pressure is about 145 kPa, water boils at 110.°C.

Review Questions

Use the tables in *Reference Tables for Physical Setting/Chemistry* as needed in answering the following questions.

44. What is the vapor pressure of water at 105°C? (1) 100 kPa (2) 101.3 kPa (3) 110 kPa (4) 120 kPa

45. As the pressure on a liquid is changed from 100. kPa to 120. kPa, the temperature at which the liquid will boil (1) decreases (2) increases (3) remains the same (4) depends on the liquid

46. In a closed system at 40°C, a liquid has a vapor pressure of 50 kPa. The liquid's normal boiling point could be (1) 10°C (2) 30°C (3) 40°C (4) 60°C

47. If the pressure on the surface of water in the liquid state is 30 kPa, the water will boil at (1) 0°C (2) 30°C (3) 70°C (4) 100°C

48. A sample of ethanoic acid at 100°C has a vapor pressure of (1) 53 kPa (2) 100 kPa (3) 101.3 kPa (4) 125 kPa

49. Which substance has the greatest intermolecular forces of attraction between molecules? (1) propanone (2) ethanol (3) water (4) ethanoic acid

50. The vapor pressure of ethanol at its normal boiling point would be (1) 80 kPa (2) 101.3 kPa (3) 273 kPa (4) 373 kPa

Questions for Regents Practice

Use the tables in *Reference Tables for Physical Setting/Chemistry* as needed in answering the following questions.

Part A

1. When a teaspoon of sugar is added to water in a beaker, the sugar dissolves. The resulting mixture is

(1) a compound
(2) a homogeneous solution
(3) a heterogeneous solution
(4) an emulsion

2. A small quantity of a salt is stirred into a liter of water until it dissolves. In the resulting mixture, the water is

(1) the solvent
(2) the solute
(3) dispersed material
(4) a precipitate

3. A solution

(1) will separate on standing
(2) may have color
(3) can be cloudy
(4) can be heterogeneous

4. Nonpolar solvents will most easily dissolve solids that are

(1) ionic
(2) covalent
(3) metallic
(4) heterogeneous

5. What happens when a crystal of a salt is dropped into an unsaturated solution of the same salt?

(1) Excess solute crystals form.
(2) The crystal dissolves.
(3) The crystal drops to the bottom, unchanged.
(4) The solution becomes colorless.

6. The depression of the freezing point is dependent on
(1) the nature of the solute
(2) the formula mass of the solute
(3) the concentration of dissolved particles
(4) hydrogen bonding

7. The process of recovering a salt from a solution by evaporating the solvent is known as
(1) crystallization
(2) filtration
(3) reduction
(4) decomposition

8. What happens when a crystal of solute is dropped into a supersaturated solution of the salt?
(1) The crystal dissolves.
(2) Excess solute crystals form.
(3) The crystal drops to the bottom, unchanged.
(4) The solution begins to boil.

9. Under which conditions are gases most soluble in water?
(1) high temperature and high pressure
(2) high temperature and low pressure
(3) low temperature and high pressure
(4) low temperature and low pressure

10. As the temperature of a liquid decreases, the amount of a gas that can be dissolved
(1) decreases
(2) increases
(3) remains the same
(4) depends on the identity of the gas

11. As the temperature of liquid water decreases, its vapor pressure
(1) decreases
(2) increases
(3) remains the same
(4) disappears

12. The heat energy required to change one mole of a liquid into a vapor at the boiling point is called the
(1) heat of vaporization
(2) heat of formation
(3) heat of solution
(4) heat of fusion

Part B

13. Which substance increases in solubility as the temperature decreases?
(1) $KClO_3$
(2) NH_3
(3) KNO_3
(4) NaCl

14. The diagrams below represent an ionic crystal being dissolved in water.

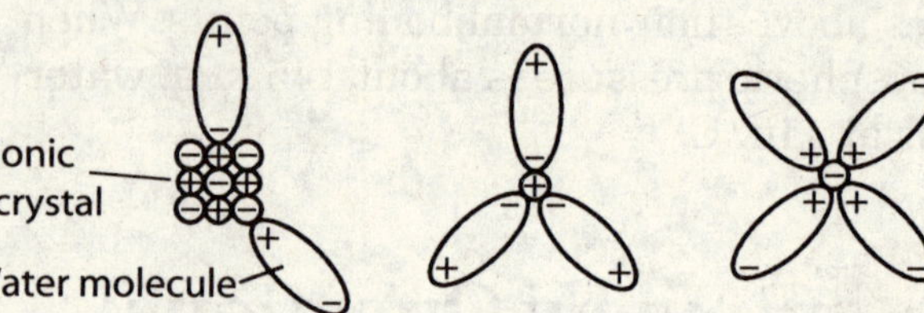

According to the diagrams, the dissolving process takes place by
(1) hydrogen bond formation
(2) metallic bonding
(3) dipole-dipole attractions
(4) molecule-ion attractions

15. If solutions of barium nitrate and sodium sulfate are mixed and then poured into a filter, the solid remaining on the filter will be
(1) barium nitrate
(2) sodium nitrate
(3) barium sulfate
(4) sodium sulfate

16. A student tested the solubility of a salt at different temperatures and then used the *Reference Tables for Physical Setting/Chemistry* to identify the salt. The student's data appears below.

Temperature (°C)	Solubility Data (g of salt per 10 g of water)
30	1.2
50	2.2
62	3.0
76	4.0

What is the identity of the salt?
(1) potassium nitrate
(2) sodium chloride
(3) potassium chlorate
(4) ammonium chloride

17. If 100. g of water at 80°C contains 45 g of KCl and 45 g of $NaNO_3$, the solution is

(1) saturated with respect to both KCl and $NaNO_3$

(2) saturated with respect to KCl and unsaturated with respect to $NaNO_3$

(3) unsaturated with respect to both KCl and $NaNO_3$

(4) supersaturated with respect to both KCl and $NaNO_3$

18. What happens when KI(*s*) is dissolved in water?

(1) I^- ions are attracted to the oxygen atoms of the water.

(2) K^+ ions are attracted to the oxygen atoms of the water.

(3) K^+ ions are attracted to the hydrogen atoms of the water.

(4) No attractions are involved; the crystal just falls apart.

19. A student drops a crystal of NaCl into a beaker of NaCl(*aq*) and the crystal dissolves. The original solution must have been

(1) supersaturated

(2) saturated

(3) unsaturated

(4) heterogeneous

20. Which two compounds contain only polar molecules?

(1) CCl_4 and CH_4

(2) HCl and Cl_2

(3) HCl and NH_3

(4) CO and CO_2

21. A saturated solution of potassium chloride at 10°C is heated to 30°C. As the solution is heated in a closed container, the total mass of the solution

(1) decreases

(2) increases

(3) remains the same

(4) depends on the pressure

22. Water boils at 90°C when the pressure exerted on the liquid equals

(1) 82 kPa

(2) 90 kPa

(3) 101.3 kPa

(4) 120 kPa

23. Consider the following data for NaCl:

Temperature (°C)	0	20	50	100
Solubility (g/100 g H_2O)	35.7	36.0	37.0	39.2

When the salt is added to water, the temperature of the solution decreases. Which of the following statements is correct?

(1) The process is endothermic, and solubility and temperature are directly related.

(2) The process is endothermic, and solubility and temperature are indirectly related.

(3) The process is exothermic, and solubility and temperature are directly related.

(4) The process is exothermic, and solubility and temperature are indirectly related.

24. Which sample of ethanol will have the highest vapor pressure?

(1) 10. mL at 62°C

(2) 20.0 mL at 52°C

(3) 30. mL at 42°C

(4) 40 mL at 32°C

25. The vapor pressure of water is 50 kPa. The temperature of this sample of water is

(1) 37°C

(2) 62°C

(3) 82°C

(4) 92°C

Show all work for problems 26–30.

26. What is the percent mass of NaOH if 12.5 g is dissolved in 100. g of water?

27. What volume of 3.0 M HCl contains 0.20 mol of HCl?

28. A swimming pool reading reports that chlorine is present at 30 ppm. How many grams of chlorine are present per liter of pool water?

29. What is the molarity of a solution that contains 24 g of $NaNO_3$ in 200 mL of solution?

30. How many grams of KNO_3 are present in 250 mL of 2.0 M potassium nitrate solution?

Part C

31. Describe two methods by which you could remove gases that are dissolved in water. [2]

32. Consider the following data for Na_2SO_4.

Temperature (°C)	0	20	50	100
Solubility (g/100 g H_2O)	4.76	62	50.	41

What is the relationship between the temperature and the amount of dissolved material? Given that sodium sulfate is a solid, what is unusual about the data given above? [2]

33. One mole of ethanol (C_2H_5OH) will depress the freezing point of 1000. g of water by 1.86°C. How many grams of ethanol would be needed to depress the freezing point of 1000. g of H_2O by 3.72°C? [1]

34. Describe how to prepare 500. mL of 4.0 M NaOH(*aq*). Show any calculations. [2]

Use the following figure to answer questions 35 and 36.

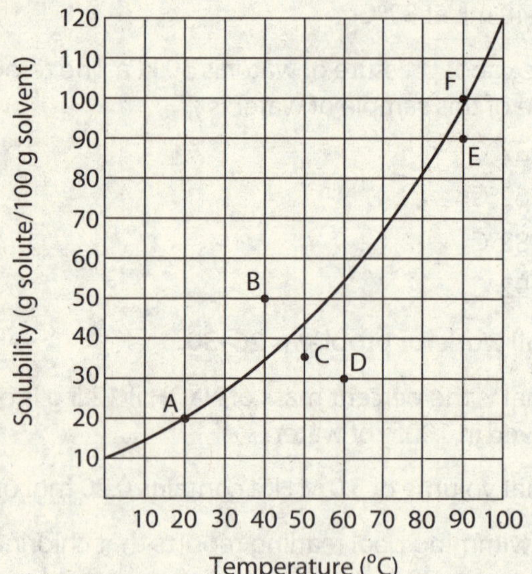

35. The figure represents the line showing the solubility of substance X. A solution of substance X is represented by point D. What are two ways that this solution can be made saturated? [2]

36. Point B represents a supersaturated solution. Consider the equation:

$$X(aq) \rightarrow X(s) + \text{heat}$$

When a crystal is placed into the supersaturated solution, additional crystals form and fall to the bottom of the beaker, and the solution returns to a saturated condition. Which of the two positions shown on the line of saturation would best represent the solution when the crystals first settled to the bottom? Explain the reason for your answer. [2]

37. Substance X is a molecular substance that is soluble in water. It costs \$.90/ton. Substance Y is an ionic substance that costs \$1.00/ton. Both have the same environmental impacts, are easy to handle, and are nontoxic. Using your knowledge of chemistry, which would be a better choice to use to melt snow on walks or driveways? Justify your answer. [2]

38. If 0.169 g of carbon dioxide can be dissolved in 100. g of H_2O at 20°C, what is the concentration in parts per million? [1]

Kinetics and Equilibrium

VOCABULARY		
activated complex	entropy	potential energy diagram
activation energy	equilibrium	stress
catalyst	Le Châtelier's principle	

Kinetics

Kinetics is the branch of chemistry that is concerned with the rates of chemical reactions. Several different factors affect how quickly chemical reactions occur. One of the basic concepts of kinetics is that in order for a reaction to occur, reactant particles must collide. This is called the collision theory. Collisions between particles can produce a reaction if both the spatial orientation and energy of the colliding particles are conducive to a reaction.

Factors Affecting Rate of Reaction

The rate of a chemical reaction is dependent on factors such as the nature of the reactants, concentration, surface area, the presence of a catalyst, and temperature. All these factors affect rate of reaction by changing the number of effective collisions that take place between particles. Pressure can also be a factor that affects rate of reaction.

NATURE OF THE REACTANTS Reactions involve the breaking of existing bonds and the formation of new ones. In general, covalently bonded substances are slower to react than ionic substances due to the greater number of bonds that must be broken before a reaction can occur. Breaking more bonds requires that the particles must have more energy when they collide.

CONCENTRATION Most chemical reactions will proceed at a faster rate if the concentration of one or more reactants is increased. An obvious example is the rate of combustion of paper in air, which is 20% oxygen, compared with the much faster rate in pure oxygen. The kinetic molecular theory would predict that because there are more collisions between the paper and oxygen in pure oxygen than in air, the rate in pure oxygen would be faster. Indeed, this is the case.

SURFACE AREA When more surface area of a substance is exposed, there are more chances for reactant particles to collide, thus increasing the reaction rate. A finely divided powder will react more rapidly than a single lump of the same mass.

PRESSURE While pressure has little or no effect on the rate of reactions between solids or liquids, it has a pronounced effect on gases. An increase in pressure has the effect of increasing the concentration of gaseous particles. Therefore, it increases the rate of a reaction that involves only gases.

THE PRESENCE OF A CATALYST **Catalysts** are substances that increase the rate of a reaction by providing a different and easier pathway for a reaction. Catalysts take part in a reaction, but they are unchanged when the reaction is complete.

TEMPERATURE By definition, temperature implies that the greater the temperature of a substance, the faster the molecules will move. The kinetic molecular theory states that collisions must occur in order for a reaction to take place. When these two concepts are put together you can see that if the particles are moving faster, there will be more collisions, thus increasing the likelihood that a reaction will occur. At a higher temperature, not only will there be more collisions, but the reacting particles will have more energy, making it more likely that the collisions will be effective.

Table 8-1. Factors that Affect Rate of Reaction	
Factor	**Increases Rate**
Nature of reactants	ionic more than covalent
Concentration	increased concentration
Pressure	increased pressure for gases
Temperature	increased temperature
Surface area	increased surface area
Catalyst	presence of a catalyst

Review Questions

1. As the number of effective collisions between reacting particles increases, the rate of the reaction (1) decreases (2) increases (3) remains the same (4) depends on the reactants

2. Which of the following pairs of reactants will react most quickly? (1) sodium chloride and silver nitrate (2) water and hydrogen chloride (3) hydrogen and propene (4) oxygen and methane (CH_4)

3. In the reaction $2Mg(s) + O_2(g) \rightarrow 2MgO(s)$, as the surface area of Mg(*s*) increases, the rate of the reaction (1) decreases (2) increases (3) remains the same (4) depends on the amount of oxygen present

4. The reaction $A(g) + B(g) \rightarrow C(g)$ is occurring in the apparatus shown below.

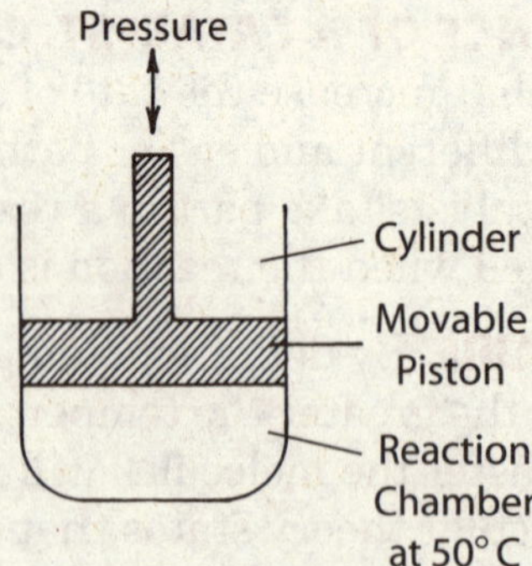

The rate of the reaction can be decreased by increasing the (1) pressure on the reactants (2) temperature of the reactants (3) concentration of reactant A(*g*) (4) volume of the reaction chamber

5. Consider the following equation.

$$Mg(s) + 2H_2O(\ell) \rightarrow Mg(OH)_2(s) + H_2(g)$$

For the reaction to occur at the fastest rate, 1 g of Mg(*s*) should be added in the form of (1) large chunks (2) small chunks (3) a ribbon (4) a powder

6. If the pressure on gaseous reactants is increased, the rate of reaction is increased because there is an increase in the (1) temperature (2) volume (3) concentration (4) heat of reaction

7. Raising the temperature speeds up the rate of chemical reaction by increasing (1) the effectiveness of the collisions only (2) the frequency of the collisions only (3) both the effectiveness and frequency of the collisions (4) neither the effectiveness nor frequency of the collisions

8. Consider the following equation.

$$Fe(s) + CuSO_4(aq) \rightarrow Cu(s) + FeSO_4(aq)$$

The Fe reacts more rapidly when it is powdered because the increased surface due to powdering permits (1) increased reactant contact (2) decreased reactant contact (3) pressure to affect reaction rate (4) warmer solution to be used

9. Consider the following equation.

$$A(g) + B(g) \rightarrow C(g)$$

As the concentration of A(*g*) increases, the frequency of collisions of A(*g*) with B(*g*) (1) decreases (2) increases (3) remains the same (4) increases only if temperature increases

10. Consider the following equation.

$$Zn(s) + 2HCl(aq) \rightarrow ZnCl_2(aq) + H_2(g)$$

The reaction occurs more slowly when a single piece of zinc is used than when the same mass of powdered zinc is used. Why does this happen? (1) The powdered zinc is more concentrated. (2) The powdered zinc has a greater surface area. (3) The powdered zinc requires less activation energy. (4) The powdered zinc generates more heat energy.

Potential Energy Diagram

As was mentioned when discussing the nature of the reactants, chemical bonds contain energy. Specifically, they contain potential chemical energy. A diagram, called a **potential energy diagram,** illustrates the potential energy change that occur during a chemical reaction. The vertical axis of this diagram represents the change in potential energy. The horizontal axis is called the reaction coordinate, which represents the progress of the reaction.

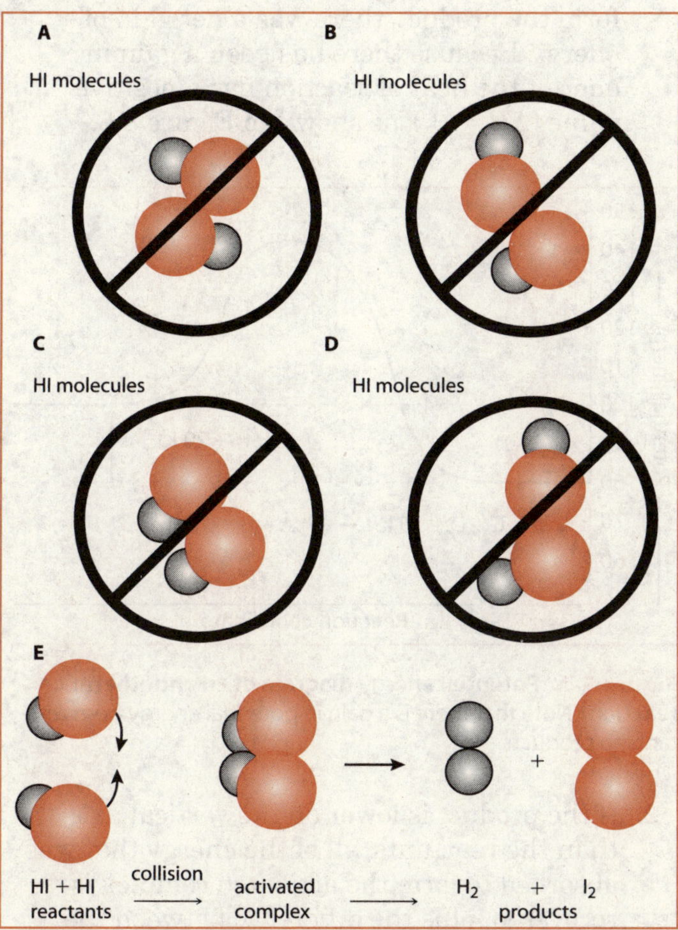

Figure 8-1. Collisions of molecules: If HI molecules collide in any arrangement other than the one shown in part E, the collision is not effective and no products form.

In order for a reaction to occur, the reactants must have sufficient energy to collide effectively. As the reactant particles approach each other, kinetic energy is converted into potential energy.

Not only must the particles collide in order for a reaction to occur, they must be properly positioned. Look at Figure 8-1. If the particles collide in the proper orientation, an activated complex is formed. This **activated complex** is a temporary, intermediate product that may either break apart and reform the reactants or rearrange the atoms and form new products.

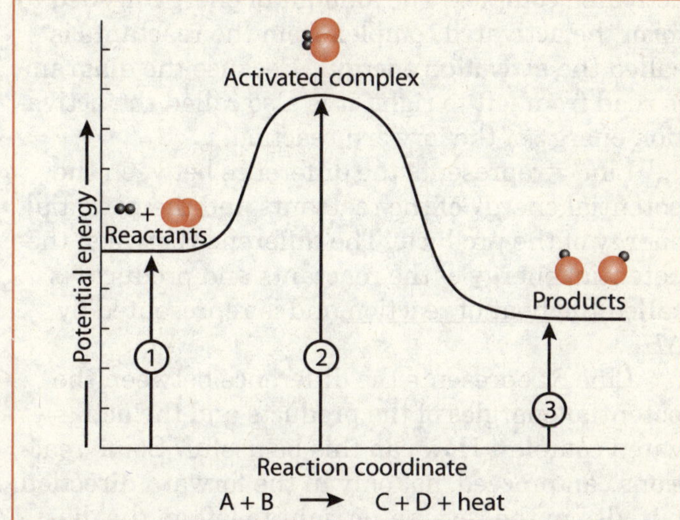

Figure 8-2. Potential energy diagram: This figure shows the potential energy of the reactants, the activated complex, and the products of the reaction.

Figure 8-2 shows a potential energy diagram for the following reaction.

$$A + B \rightarrow C + D + \text{heat}$$

Line 1 extends from the origin of the *y*-axis to the reactants and represents the amount of potential energy of the reactants. Line 2 extends from the origin of the *y*-axis to the activated complex and represents the potential energy of the complex. Line 3 represents the potential energy of the products. Any line that begins at the origin of the *y*-axis of such a graph is a measure of potential energy.

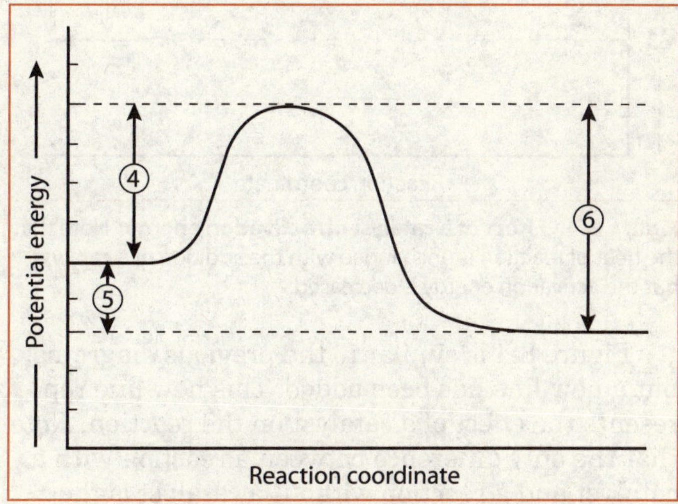

Figure 8-3. Activation energies and heat of reaction

Figure 8-3 on the previous page shows the same potential energy diagram, but the lines represent the differences between the potential energies of different substances. Line 4 represents the difference in potential energy between the reactants and the activated complex. The amount of energy needed to form the activated complex from the reactants is called the **activation energy.** Because the diagram is read from left to right, it is also called the activation energy of the forward reaction.

Line 5 represents the difference between the potential energy of the reactants and the potential energy of the products. The difference between the potential energy of the reactants and products is called the heat of reaction and is represented by ΔH.

Line 6 represents the difference between the potential energies of the products and the activated complex. How can this be useful? Some reactions can proceed, not only in the forward direction, but also in the reverse, or right to left on the diagram. In this case, the line represents the activation energy of the reverse reaction.

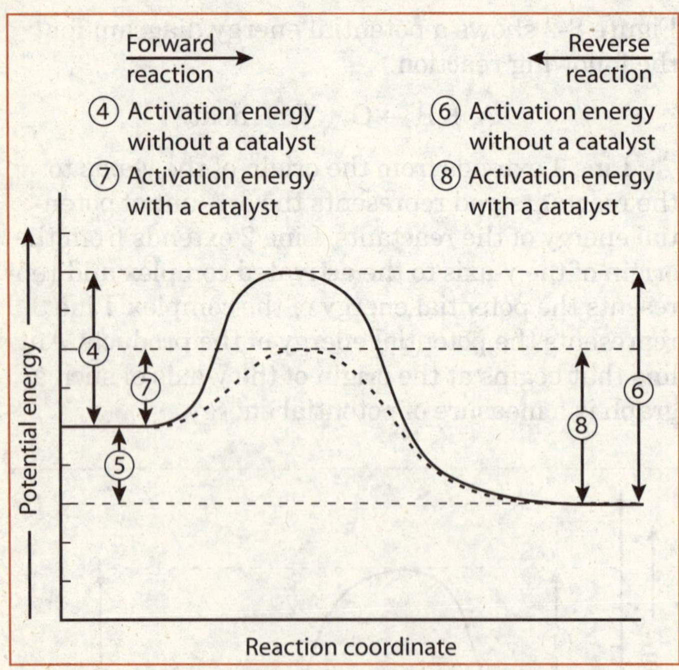

Figure 8-4. Effect of a catalyst on activation energy: Note that the heat of reaction is unchanged with the addition of a catalyst, but the activation energy is decreased.

Figure 8-4 is similar to the previous diagrams, but a new line has been added. This new line represents the effect of a catalyst on the reaction. Note that the only difference between a reaction with a catalyst and a reaction without a catalyst is the activation energy. Most catalysts speed up a reaction by providing a new pathway with a lower activation energy. The activation energy of the reverse reaction is also lowered. Note that ΔH remains unchanged.

As the reaction proceeds toward the product side, two outcomes are possible.

1. As the activated complex changes to become the product, it will lose energy. If the product is has more potential energy than the reactants, the reaction will be endothermic. Because more energy was absorbed to form the activated complex than was released to form the product, there was a net gain of energy. Because there has been a gain in energy, the heat of reaction has a positive value ($\Delta H = +$), as shown in Figure 8-5.

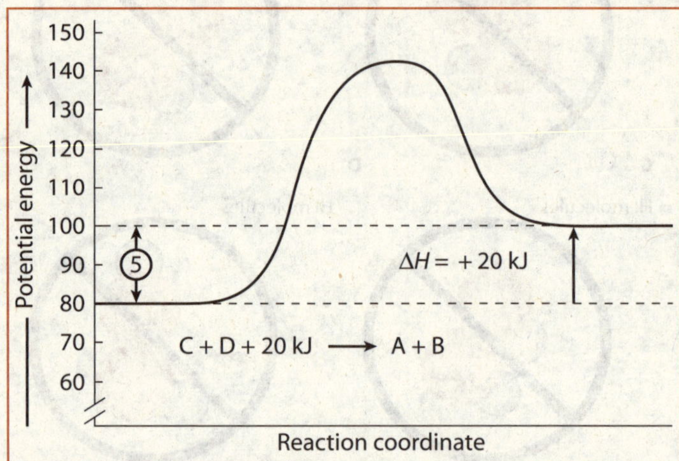

Figure 8-5. Potential energy diagram of an endothermic reaction: Note that there is a gain in potential energy from reactants to products.

2. If the product is lower on the vertical axis than the reactants, all of the energy that was absorbed to form the activated complex is recovered, plus the difference between the potential energy of the reactants and products. This represents a loss of potential energy compared to the reactants, indicating a release of energy and an exothermic reaction. In this case the heat of reaction has a negative value ($\Delta H = -$), as shown in Figure 8-6.

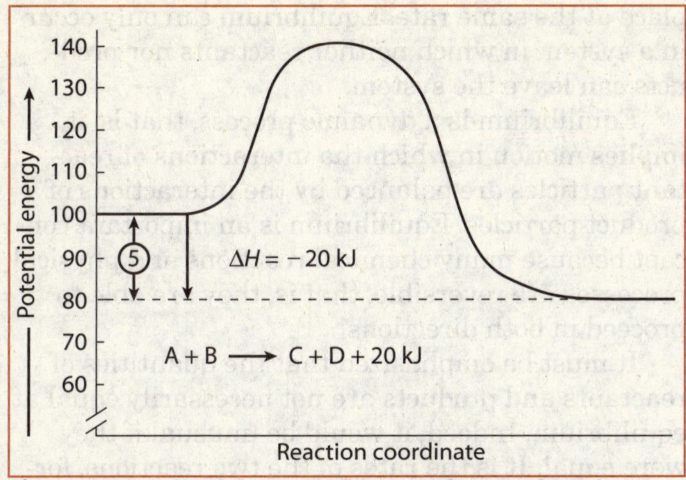

Figure 8-6. Potential energy diagram of an exothermic reaction: Note that there is a loss of potential energy from reactants to products.

Review Questions

Base your answers to Questions 11 and 12 on the diagram below, which represents the reaction:

$$A + B \rightarrow C + \text{energy}$$

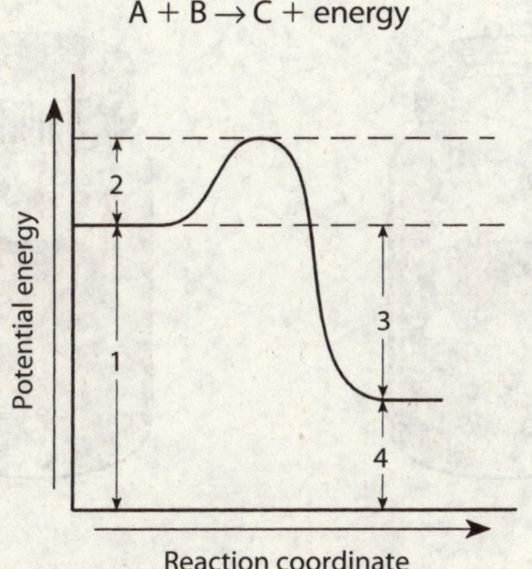

11. Which statement correctly describes this reaction? (1) It is endothermic and energy is absorbed. (2) It is endothermic and energy is released. (3) It is exothermic and energy is absorbed. (4) It is exothermic and energy is released.

12. Which numbered interval will change with the addition of a catalyst to the system? (1) 1 (2) 2 (3) 3 (4) 4

13. A potential energy diagram of a chemical system is shown below.

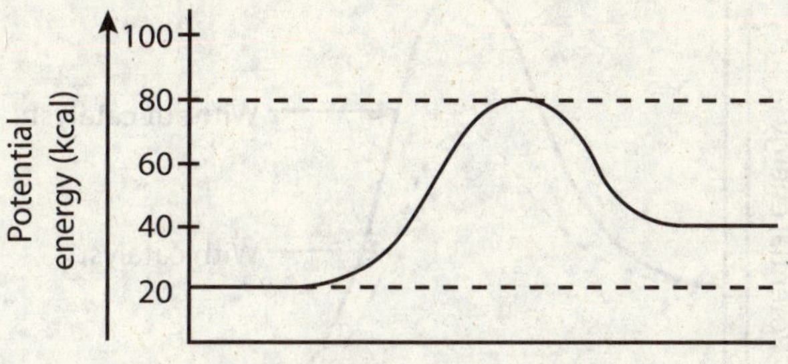

What is the difference between the potential energy of the reactants and the potential energy of the products? (1) 20. kcal (2) 40. kcal (3) 60. kcal (4) 80. kcal

14. Consider the reaction for which $\Delta H = +33$ kJ/mol.

$$N_2(g) + 2O_2(g) \rightleftarrows 2NO_2(g)$$

The potential energy diagram of the reaction is shown below.

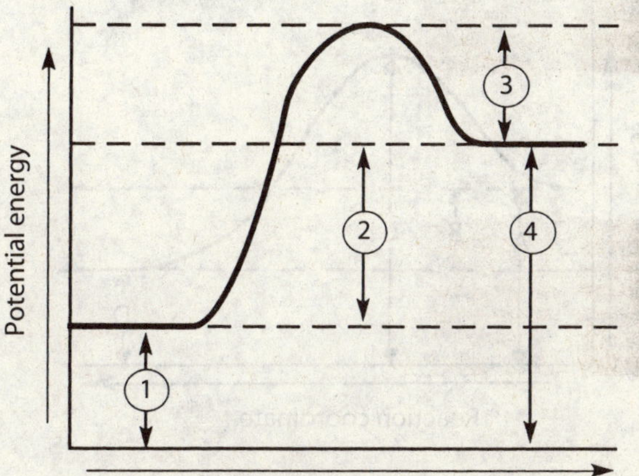

Which arrow represents the heat of reaction for the reverse reaction? (1) 1 (2) 2 (3) 3 (4) 4

15. The potential energy diagram of a chemical reaction is shown below.

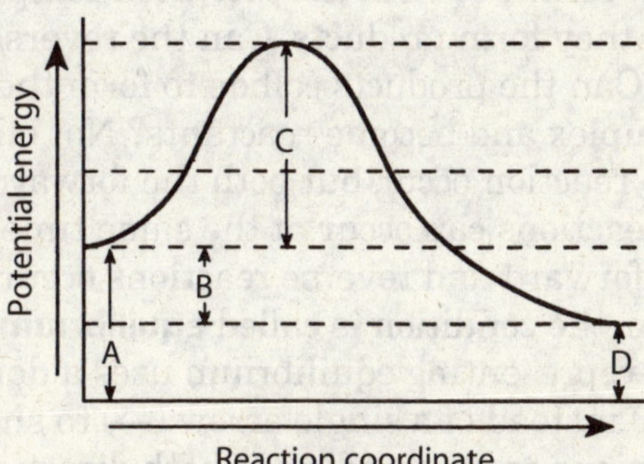

Which letter in the diagram represents the heat of reaction? (1) A (2) B (3) C (4) D

16. A potential energy diagram is shown below.

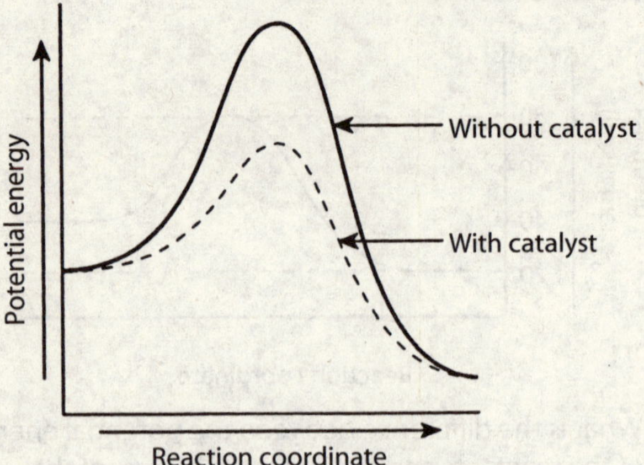

Which reaction would have the lowest activation energy? (1) the forward catalyzed reaction (2) the forward uncatalyzed reaction (3) the reverse catalyzed reaction (4) the reverse uncatalyzed reaction

17. In the potential energy diagram below, which arrow represents the potential energy of the activated complex? (1) A (2) B (3) C (4) D

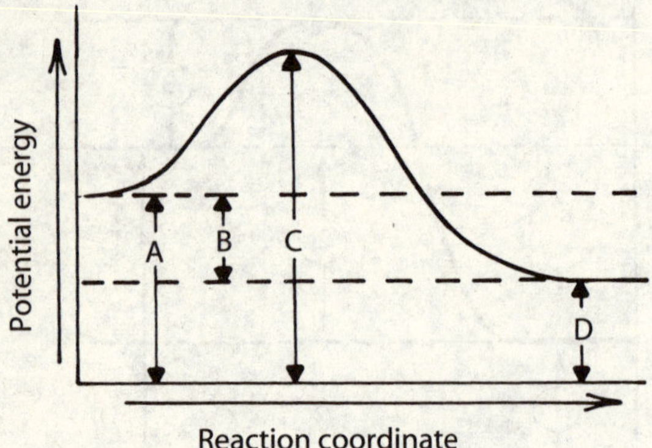

Equilibrium

Each of the potential energy diagrams shown depicts a reaction that is proceeding from left to right, that is, in the forward direction. The reactants first collide to form the activated complex, and then they form products. Can the reverse ever happen? Can the products collide to form the activated complex and become reactants? Not only can a reverse reaction occur, but both the forward and reverse reactions can occur at the same time. When both the forward and reverse reactions occur at the same rate, the condition is called **equilibrium.** An equation representing equilibrium uses a double arrow ($\rightleftarrows$) instead of a single arrow ($\rightarrow$) to show that reactions are proceeding in both directions.

Equilibrium is a state of balance between the rates of two opposite processes that are taking place at the same rate. Equilibrium can only occur in a system in which neither reactants nor products can leave the system.

Equilibrium is a dynamic process, that is, it implies motion in which the interactions of reactant particles are balanced by the interactions of product particles. Equilibrium is an important concept because many chemical reactions and physical processes are reversible, that is, they are able to proceed in both directions.

It must be emphasized that the quantities of reactants and products are not necessarily equal at equilibrium. Indeed, it would be unusual if they were equal. It is the rates of the two reactions, forward and reverse, that are equal. As shown in Figure 8-7, in a closed container half-filled with water, there is equilibrium between the evaporating liquid water and the condensing water vapor. Obviously there is far more liquid water than water vapor. At equilibrium, it is the rate of evaporation and condensation that are equal.

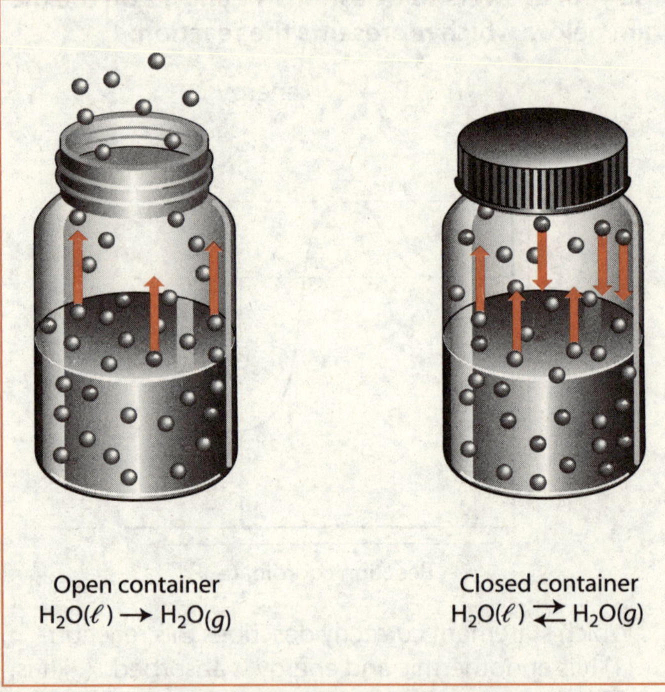

Figure 8-7. Equilibrium in a closed container: In the open container, the liquid evaporates at a constant rate until it is all evaporated. In the closed container, evaporation continues, but it is balanced by condensation.

Physical Equilibrium

Although many examples of equilibrium involve chemical reactions, equilibrium also occurs during physical processes such as change of state (phase) or dissolving.

PHASE EQUILIBRIUM Phase equilibrium can exist between the solid and liquid phases of a substance. We define this condition as the melting point of the solid phase or the freezing point of the liquid phase. At 0°C in a closed container, both water and ice exist at the same time. Some of the ice is melting, and some of the water is freezing. An equation can be written to show that both the forward and reverse processes are taking place. The double-pointed arrow shows that both reactions are taking place at the same rate.

$$H_2O(s) \rightleftarrows H_2O(\ell)$$

There may not be the same amounts of solid and liquid present, but the rate of melting will be equal to the rate of freezing.

A similar relationship can exist in a closed container for liquid-gas equilibrium, where the rate of evaporation is equal to the rate of condensation.

$$H_2O(\ell) \rightleftarrows H_2O(g)$$

SOLUTION EQUILIBRIUM Solids in liquids exist in equilibrium in a saturated solution. When solid sugar is first placed into water, the sugar dissolves, but no sugar is recrystallizing. When all of the sugar dissolves that can be dissolved at that temperature, the solution is saturated. If additional solid sugar is placed into the saturated solution, the process of dissolving will continue, but it is exactly balanced by the process of recrystallization. When the rate of dissolving and recrystallizing are equal, equilibrium exists, and the solution is saturated.

$$C_{12}H_{22}O_{11}(s) \rightleftarrows C_{12}H_{22}O_{11}(aq)$$

Equilibrium may also be attained in a closed system between a gas dissolved in a liquid and the undissolved gas. In a closed bottle or can of soda there is equilibrium between the gaseous and dissolved state of carbon dioxide.

$$CO_2(g) \rightleftarrows CO_2(aq)$$

In both of these cases, the equilibrium can be disturbed by a change in temperature. If the temperature is raised, a solid generally becomes more soluble in a liquid. For a short time the rate of dissolving exceeds the rate of recrystallization. As more solid is placed into solution, the rate of recrystallization increases until a new equilibrium is reached.

The opposite is true when the temperature of a solution of a gas in a liquid is raised. As the temperature increases, the rate of the gas escaping from the liquid increases, while the rate at which gas particles dissolve decreases. This decreases the solubility of the gas in the liquid. As the temperature rises, the solubility of all gases decreases in a liquid.

Chemical Equilibrium

When reactants are first mixed and no products are present, only the forward reaction can occur. Examine what happens in the chemical reaction between water vapor and methane.

$$CH_4(g) + H_2O(g) \rightarrow 3H_2(g) + CO(g)$$

As time progresses, the concentrations of $CH_4(g)$ and $H_2O(g)$ decrease, causing the forward reaction to slow, while the concentrations of $H_2(g)$ and $CO(g)$ increase, causing the rate of the reverse reaction to increase.

This slowing of the forward reaction and speeding up of the reverse reaction continues until the rates of the two reactions become the same. At this point, chemical equilibrium exists. Figure 8-8 summarizes this process.

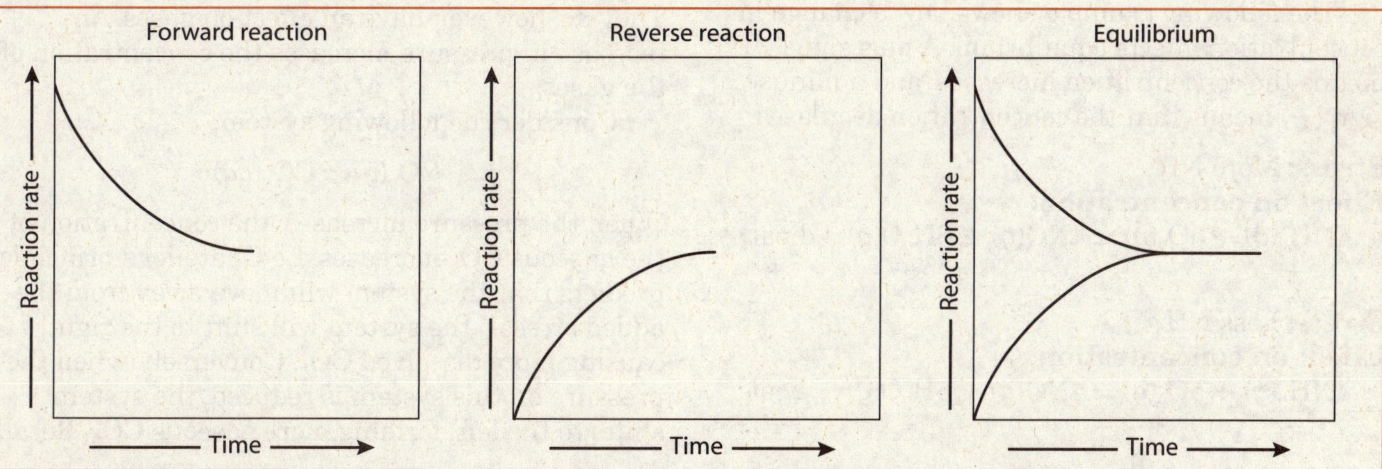

Figure 8-8. Chemical equilibrium: Equilibrium occurs when opposite reactions occur at the same rate.

As with physical equilibrium, it is important to remember that no reactant or product can leave the system. If a precipitate is formed or a gas is formed in a system that is not closed, equilibrium will not be reached. The effect of any change in equilibrium is explained by Le Châtelier's principle.

Le Châtelier's Principle

Any change in temperature, concentration or pressure on an equilibrium system is called a **stress. Le Châtelier's principle** explains how a system at equilibrium responds to relieve any stress on the system. Examined below are several types of stress and how equilibrium shifts to relieve them.

CONCENTRATION CHANGES Again consider the reaction represented by the following equation.

$$CH_4(g) + H_2O(g) \rightleftarrows 3H_2(g) + CO(g)$$

If the stress is the addition of more methane (CH_4), the rate of the forward reaction will increase and more products will form. If the concentration of one substance is increased, the reaction that reduces the amount of the added substance is favored. In this example, the system is said to shift to the right as more product is formed. As more product forms, the rate of the reverse reaction also increases until once again the rates of the forward and reverse reactions are equal.

If the concentration of methane is reduced, the rate of the forward reaction decreases. When the concentration of a substance decreases, the reaction that produces that substance is favored. Initially the reverse reaction will take place faster than the forward reaction, and the system is said to be shifting to the left, or toward the reactant side.

The following example shows how a change in concentration affects equilibrium. A plus sign (+) means the concentration increases, and a minus sign (−) means that the concentration decreases.

Stress: More NH_3
Effect on concentration:

$$\underset{+}{4NH_3(g)} + \underset{-}{5O_2(g)} \rightleftarrows \underset{+}{4NO(g)} + \underset{+}{6H_2O(g)} + \underset{+}{\text{heat}}$$

Stress: Less NH_3
Effect on concentration:

$$\underset{-}{4NH_3(g)} + \underset{+}{5O_2(g)} \rightleftarrows \underset{-}{4NO(g)} + \underset{-}{6H_2O(g)} + \underset{-}{\text{heat}}$$

TEMPERATURE CHANGES Consider the production of ammonia:

$$N_2(g) + 3H_2(g) \rightleftarrows 2NH_3(g) + \text{heat}$$

Le Châtelier's principle states that a system will undergo changes to reduce a stress. For this reaction, heat can be considered as a product. If the temperature is raised, the rates of both the forward and reverse reactions are increased, but not equally. The reverse reaction is endothermic and will absorb some of the applied heat. The endothermic reverse reaction is favored over the exothermic forward reaction. In other words, more reactants will form when temperature is increased in this reaction. A decrease in temperature will favor the exothermic reaction and, for this reaction, more products will form.

In the following representation of how a temperature change affects equilibrium, note that the results are seen in a change of concentration of reactants and products, even though the stress is actually a change of energy. Because heat is a product of the reaction, a change in temperature is essentially a change in the concentration of that product.

Stress: More heat
Effect on concentration:

$$\underset{+}{4NH_3(g)} + \underset{+}{5O_2(g)} \rightleftarrows \underset{-}{4NO(g)} + \underset{-}{6H_2O(g)} + \underset{+}{\text{heat}}$$

Stress: Less heat
Effect on concentration:

$$\underset{-}{4NH_3(g)} + \underset{-}{5O_2(g)} \rightleftarrows \underset{+}{4NO(g)} + \underset{+}{6H_2O(g)} + \underset{-}{\text{heat}}$$

PRESSURE CHANGES Remember that pressure changes do not have an effect on the rate of reaction when only solids and liquids are involved. They do, however, have an effect on gases. An increase in pressure increases the concentration of the gases.

Consider the following system.

$$CO_2(g) \rightleftarrows CO_2(aq)$$

When the pressure increases, the concentration of the gaseous CO_2 increases. Le Châtelier's principle predicts that the system will move away from the added stress—the system will shift to the right, causing more dissolved CO_2. Conversely, when the pressure on this system is reduced, the system shifts to the left, forming more gaseous CO_2. Recall what happens when a soda bottle is opened. The pressure is reduced, and the dissolved gas becomes bubbles of gaseous CO_2.

In the $CO_2(g) \rightleftarrows CO_2(aq)$ reaction, only one side of the equation contains a gaseous molecule. How will a system react when there are gaseous molecules on both sides? An increase in pressure will increase the concentration of gaseous molecules on both reactant and product sides of the equation, but the effects will be unequal. An increase in pressure will favor the reaction toward the side with fewer gas molecules. In the system:

$$N_2(g) + 3H_2(g) \rightleftarrows 2NH_3(g)$$

there are four gaseous molecules on the reactant side and only two on the product side. An increase in pressure will favor the reaction toward the product side, increasing the amount of NH_3 formed.

A decrease in pressure has the opposite effect. A decrease in pressure favors the reaction toward the side with the greater number of gas molecules. Thus, when the pressure is reduced the reaction shifts to the left, forming more $N_2(g)$ and $H_2(g)$ and decreasing the amount of $NH_3(g)$.

One more case remains. What happens if there are the same number of gaseous molecules on both sides? In the equation, $H_2(g) + Cl_2(g) \rightleftarrows 2HCl(g)$, the reactant and product sides each have two gaseous molecules. Where there are the same number of gaseous reactant and product molecules, pressure changes have no effect on the system.

EFFECT OF A CATALYST The addition of a catalyst changes the rates of both the forward and reverse reactions equally. A catalyst may cause equilibrium to be established more quickly but does not change any of the equilibrium concentrations.

Review Questions

18. Which factors must be equal when a reversible chemical process reaches equilibrium? (1) mass of the reactants and mass of the products (2) rate of the forward reaction and rate of the reverse reaction (3) concentration of the reactants and concentration of the products (4) activation energy of the forward reaction and activation energy of the reverse reaction

19. A solute is added to water and a portion of the solute remains undissolved. When equilibrium between the dissolved and undissolved solute is reached, the solution must be (1) dilute (2) saturated (3) unsaturated (4) supersaturated

20. Which description applies to a system in a sealed flask that is half full of water? (1) Only evaporation occurs, but it eventually stops. (2) Only condensation occurs, but it eventually stops. (3) Neither evaporation nor condensation occurs. (4) Both evaporation and condensation occur.

21. Solution equilibrium always exists in a solution that is (1) unsaturated (2) saturated (3) dilute (4) concentrated

22. Given the reaction at equilibrium:

$$A(g) + B(g) \rightleftarrows C(g) + D(g)$$

The addition of a catalyst will (1) shift the equilibrium to the right (2) shift the equilibrium to the left (3) increase the rate of forward and reverse reactions equally (4) have no effect on the forward or reverse reactions

23. If a catalyst is added to a system at equilibrium and the temperature and pressure remain constant, there will be no effect on the (1) rate of the forward reaction (2) rate of the reverse reaction (3) activation energy of the reaction (4) heat of reaction

24. Consider the equation for the following reaction at equilibrium.

$$X + Y \rightleftarrows 2Z + \text{heat}$$

The concentration of the product could be increased by (1) adding a catalyst (2) adding more heat to the system (3) increasing the concentration of Y (4) decreasing the concentration of X

25. In a reversible reaction, chemical equilibrium is attained when the (1) rate of the forward reaction is greater than the rate of the reverse reaction (2) rate of the reverse reaction is greater than the rate of the forward reaction (3) concentration of the reactants reaches zero (4) concentration of the products remains constant

26. Consider the following equation.

$$N_2(g) + 3H_2(g) \rightleftarrows 2NH_3(g) + \text{heat}$$

What stress would cause the equilibrium to shift to the left? (1) increasing the temperature (2) increasing the pressure (3) adding $N_2(g)$ to the system (4) adding $H_2(g)$ to the system

27. Consider the equation for the following reaction at equilibrium.

$$CaSO_4(s) \rightleftarrows Ca^{2+}(aq) + SO_4^{2-}(aq)$$

When Na_2SO_4 is added to the system, how will the equilibrium shift? (1) The amount of $CaSO_4$ will decrease, and the concentration of $Ca^{2+}(aq)$ will decrease. (2) The amount of $CaSO_4$ will decrease, and the concentration of $Ca^{2+}(aq)$ will increase. (3) The amount of $CaSO_4$ will increase, and the concentration of $Ca^{2+}(aq)$ will decrease. (4) The amount of $CaSO_4$ will increase, and the concentration of $Ca^{2+}(aq)$ will increase.

28. Consider the following equation.

$$Zn(s) + HCl(aq) \rightarrow ZnCl_2(aq) + H_2(g)$$

As the concentration of the HCl(*aq*) decreases at constant temperature, the rate of the forward reaction (1) decreases (2) increases (3) remains the same (4) equals the rate of the reverse reaction

29. Consider the following equation.

$$H_2(g) + F_2(g) \rightleftarrows 2HF(g) + \text{heat}$$

Which change will not shift the point of equilibrium? (1) changing the pressure (2) changing the temperature (3) changing the concentration of $H_2(g)$ (4) changing the concentration of HF(*g*)

30. Consider the following equation.

$$H_2(g) + Cl_2(g) \rightleftarrows 2HCl(g)$$

As the pressure increases at constant temperature, the mass of $H_2(g)$ (1) decreases (2) increases (3) remains the same (4) depends on the mass of HCl

31. Consider a reaction at STP and at equilibrium.

$$H_2(g) + Cl_2(g) \rightleftarrows 2HCl(g)$$

Which change will result in an increase in the concentration of $Cl_2(g)$? (1) decreasing the pressure on the system (2) decreasing the concentration of HCl (3) increasing the concentration of $H_2(g)$ (4) increasing the concentration of HCl

32. Consider the following equation.

$$N_2(g) + O_2(g) \rightleftarrows 2NO(g)$$

As the concentration of $N_2(g)$ increases, the concentration of $O_2(g)$ will (1) decrease (2) increase (3) remain the same (4) vary directly

33. Consider the following equation.

$$2SO_2(g) + O_2(g) \rightleftarrows 2SO_3(g) + \text{heat}$$

Which change will shift the equilibrium to the right? (1) decreasing the concentration of SO_2 (2) decreasing the pressure (3) increasing the concentration of O_2 (4) increasing the temperature

34. The addition of a catalyst to a system at equilibrium will increase the rate of (1) the forward reaction only (2) the reverse reaction only (3) both the forward and reverse reactions (4) neither the forward nor the reverse reaction

35. A system is said to be in a state of dynamic equilibrium when the (1) concentration of products is greater than the concentration of reactants (2) concentration of products is less than the concentration of reactants (3) rate at which products are formed is greater than the rate at which reactants are formed (4) rate at which products are formed is the same as the rate at which reactants are formed

Entropy And Enthalpy

What are the factors that cause chemical and physical changes to occur? There are two fundamental tendencies in nature that help determine whether or not these changes will occur.

Enthalpy

There is a tendency in nature to change to a state of lower energy (enthalpy). Exothermic reactions move toward a lower energy state because some of the energy contained in the reactants is released. The products have less potential energy than do the reactants.

A study of potential energy diagrams for reversible chemical reactions shows that the activation energy for the exothermic direction is less than that for the endothermic direction. Therefore, at any given temperature, the particles in a system are more likely to collide with enough energy to react in the exothermic direction than in the endothermic direction. On the basis of energy change alone, we expect reactions to go in the exothermic direction. This drive toward lower energy is also called a drive toward lower enthalpy.

Entropy

There is a tendency in nature to change to a state of greater randomness or disorder, which refers to the lack of regularity in a system. **Entropy** is a measure of the disorder or randomness of a system. The greater the disorder, the higher the entropy. Figure 8-9 illustrates the concept of increasing entropy as an originally ordered state becomes "messy" or more random.

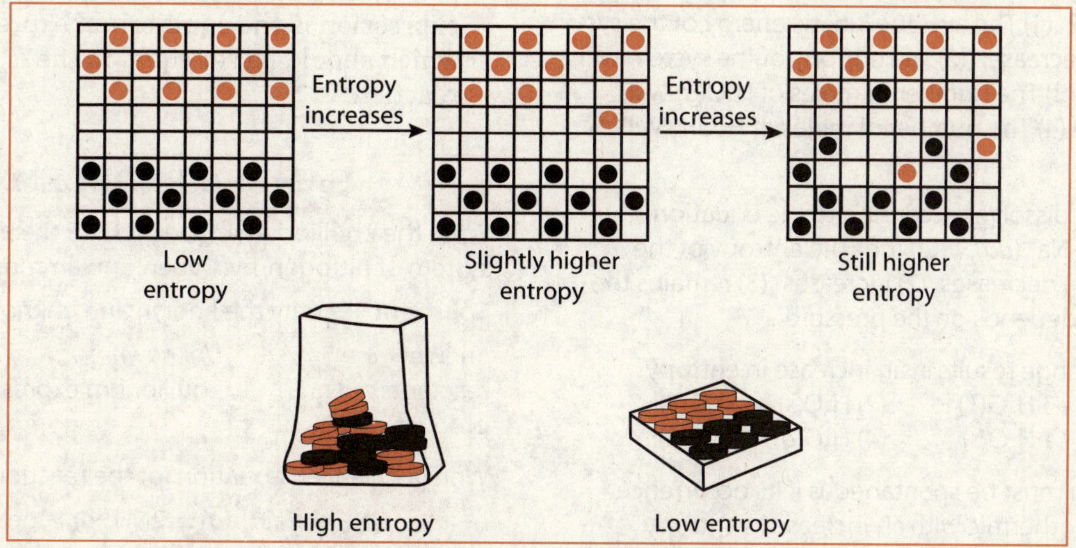

Figure 8-9. Entropy: Entropy is a measure of disorder or randomness.

It is usually necessary for particles to collide in a special way in order to form a more highly organized or regular arrangement. On the other hand, there are many ways in which they can collide to produce more disorder. Therefore, it is to be expected that systems will often go from conditions of greater order (lower entropy) to conditions of greater disorder (higher entropy). On the basis of entropy change alone, we expect reactions to go in the direction of greater entropy.

Examples of entropy change are physical changes from the solid, crystalline phase (great order, low entropy), to the liquid phase (more randomness, higher entropy), to the gaseous phase (maximum randomness, highest entropy). For chemical changes, compounds represent a state of greater order and lower entropy than the free elements of which they are composed.

Review Questions

36. Which change in a sample of water is accompanied by the greatest increase in entropy?
(1) $H_2O(\ell)$ at 100°C is changed to $H_2O(g)$ at 200°C
(2) $H_2O(g)$ at 100°C is changed to $H_2O(g)$ at 200°C
(3) $H_2O(s)$ at −100°C is changed to $H_2O(s)$ at 0°C
(4) $H_2O(\ell)$ at −100°C is changed to $H_2O(\ell)$ at 0°C

37. What occurs when a sample of $CO_2(s)$ changes to $CO_2(g)$? (1) The gas has greater entropy and less order. (2) The gas has greater entropy and more order. (3) The gas has less entropy and less order. (4) The gas has less entropy and more order.

38. The diagram below shows a system of gases with the valve closed.

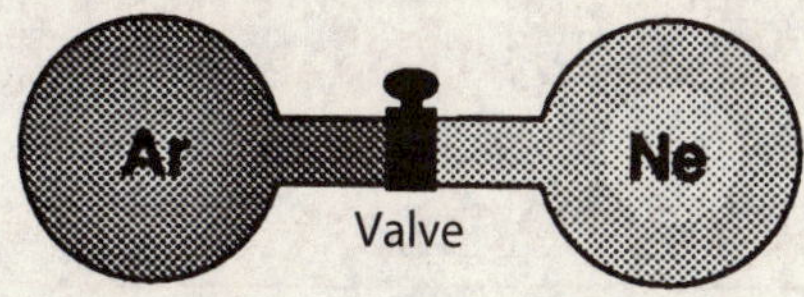

As the valve is opened, the entropy of the gaseous system (1) decreases (2) increases (3) remains the same (4) depends on the temperature

39. Which series of physical changes represents an entropy increase during each change?
(1) gas → liquid → solid
(2) liquid → gas → solid
(3) solid → gas → solid
(4) solid → liquid → gas

40. Which tendencies favor a spontaneous reaction? (1) lower energy and decreasing entropy (2)) lower energy and increasing entropy (3) higher energy and decreasing entropy (4) higher energy and increasing entropy

41. Consider the following equation.

$$H_2O(\ell) + \text{heat} \rightleftarrows H_2O(g)$$

Which will occur if the temperature of the system is increased? (1) The average kinetic energy of the system will decrease. (2) The entropy of the system will increase. (3) The number of moles of $H_2O(g)$ will decrease. (4) The number of moles of $H_2O(\ell)$ will increase.

42. As NaCl(*s*) dissolves according to the equation $NaCl(s) \rightarrow Na^+(aq) + Cl^-(aq)$, the entropy of the system (1) decreases (2) increases (3) remains the same (4) depends on the pressure

43. Which change results in an increase in entropy?
(1) $H_2O(g) \rightarrow H_2O(\ell)$ (2) $H_2O(s) \rightarrow H_2O(\ell)$
(3) $H_2O(\ell) \rightarrow H_2O(s)$ (4) $H_2O(g) \rightarrow H_2O(s)$

44. A reaction must be spontaneous if its occurrence is (1) endothermic with an increase in entropy (2) endothermic with a decrease in entropy (3) exothermic with an increase in entropy (4) exothermic with a decrease in entropy

ADDITIONAL MATERIAL

The coverage of equilibrium expressions on page 120 is not required by the Regents core curriculum in chemistry. You will not be tested on this topic in the Regents Examination for the Physical Setting/Chemistry.

The Equilibrium Expression

The mathematical expression that shows the relationship of reactants and products in a system at equilibrium is called the equilibrium expression. It is a fraction with the concentrations of reactants and products expressed in moles per liter. Each concentration is then raised to the power of its coefficient in a balanced equation. This expression equals a value called the equilibrium constant (K_{eq}), which remains the same for a particular reaction at a specified temperature.

To write an equilibrium expression, follow these steps.

1. Write a balanced equation for the system.
2. Place the products as factors in the numerator of a fraction and the reactants as factors in the denominator.
3. Place a square bracket around each formula. The square bracket means *molar concentration*.
4. Write the coefficient of each substance as the power of its concentration. The resulting expression is the equilibrium expression, which should be set equal to the K_{eq} for that reaction.

SAMPLE PROBLEM

Write the equilibrium expression for the equilibrium system of nitrogen, hydrogen, and ammonia.

Solution: Identify the known and unknown values.

Known	*Unknown*
reactants = N_2, H_2	equilibrium expression = K_{eq}
product = NH_3	

Write a balanced equation for the reaction.

$$N_2(g) + 3H_2(g) \rightleftarrows 2NH_3(g) + \text{heat}$$

Place the products as factors in the numerator of a fraction and the reactants as factors in the denominator.

$$\frac{NH_3}{H_2 \times N_2}$$

Place a square bracket around each formula to show the concentration of each.

$$\frac{[NH_3]}{[H_2][N_2]}$$

Write the coefficient of each substance as the power of its concentration. This is the equilibrium expression, labeled K_{eq}.

$$K_{eq} = \frac{[NH_3]^2}{[H_2]^3[N_2]}$$

The equilibrium constant is a specific numerical value for a given system at a specified temperature. Changes in concentrations will not cause a change in the value of K_{eq}, nor will the addition of a catalyst. Only a change in temperature will affect the value of K_{eq}.

When the value of K_{eq} is large, the numerator is larger than the denominator, indicating that the products are present in larger concentration than the reactants. Chemists would simply say that the products are favored. If the value is small, the opposite is true, and the reactants are favored.

Questions for Regents Practice

Part A

1. In order for a chemical reaction to occur, there must always be
(1) an effective collision between reacting particles
(2) a bond that breaks in a reactant particle
(3) reacting particles with a high charge
(4) reacting particles with high kinetic energy

2. As the number of effective collisions between reacting particles increases, the rate of reaction
(1) decreases
(2) increases
(3) remains the same
(4) changes the orientation of the particles

3. Activation energy is required to initiate
(1) exothermic reactions only
(2) endothermic reactions only
(3) both endothermic and exothermic reactions
(4) neither endothermic nor exothermic reactions

4. In a chemical reaction, as the concentrations of the reacting particles increase, the rate of reactions generally
(1) decreases
(2) increases
(3) remains the same
(4) reaches equilibrium

5. Which conditions will increase the rate of a chemical reaction?
(1) decreased temperature and decreased concentration of reactants
(2) decreased temperature and increased concentration of reactants
(3) increased temperature and decreased concentration of reactants
(4) increased temperature and increased concentration of reactants

6. What will change when a catalyst is added to a chemical reaction?
(1) activation energy
(2) heat of reaction
(3) potential energy of the reactants
(4) potential energy of the products

7. The energy needed to start a chemical reaction is called
(1) potential energy
(2) kinetic energy
(3) activation energy
(4) ionization energy

Use the potential energy diagram of a chemical reaction shown below to answer questions 8 and 9.

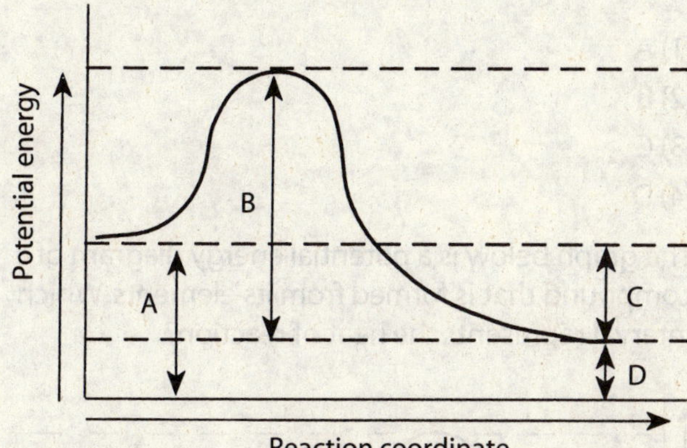

8. Which arrow represents the part of the reaction most likely to be changed by the addition of a catalyst?
(1) A
(2) B
(3) C
(4) D

9. Which letter represents the activation energy for the reverse reaction?
(1) A
(2) B
(3) C
(4) D

10. Adding a catalyst to a chemical reaction will
(1) lower the activation energy needed
(2) lower the potential energy of the reactants
(3) increase the activation energy
(4) increase the potential energy of the reactants

11. Given the potential energy diagram below, which lettered interval represents the potential energy of the activated complex?

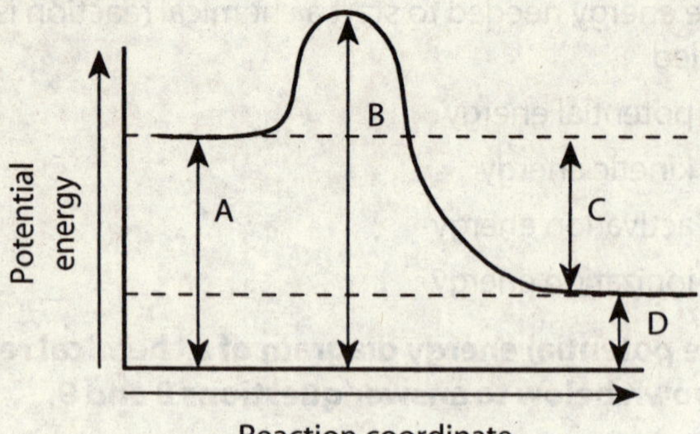

(1) A

(2) B

(3) C

(4) D

12. The graph below is a potential energy diagram of a compound that is formed from its elements. Which interval represents the heat of reaction?

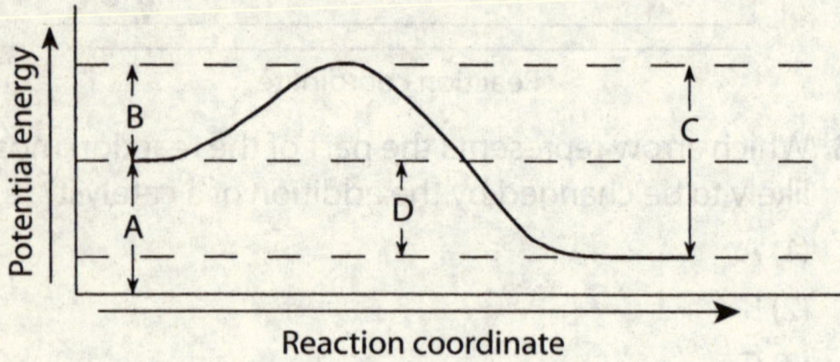

(1) A

(2) B

(3) C

(4) D

13. For any chemical reaction at equilibrium, the rate of the forward reaction is

(1) less than the rate of the reverse

(2) greater than the rate of the reverse

(3) equal to the rate of the reverse

(4) unrelated to the rate of the reverse

14. As the temperature of a system increases, the entropy of the system

(1) decreases

(2) increases

(3) remains the same

(4) depends on the enthalpy

15. Which potential energy diagram represents the reaction A + B $\rightarrow$ C + energy?

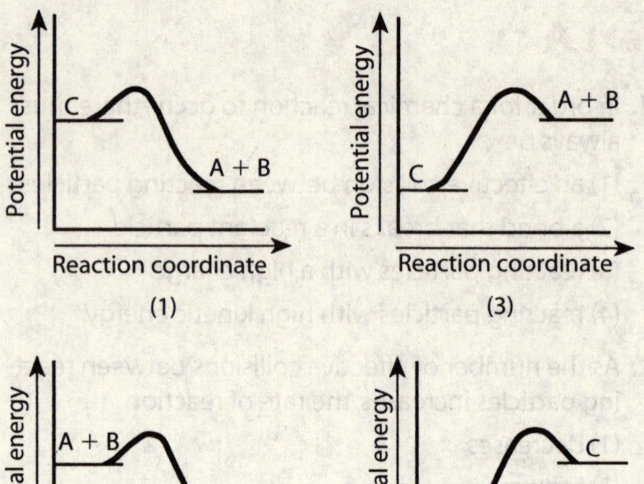

16. Given the potential energy diagram below, what does interval B represent?

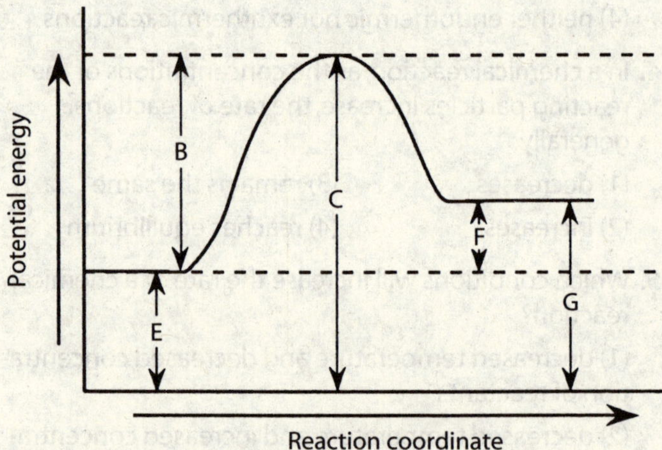

(1) potential energy of the reactants

(2) potential energy of the products

(3) activation energy

(4) activated complex

17. Solution equilibrium most likely exists in which type of solution?

(1) supersaturated

(2) unsaturated

(3) saturated

(4) dilute

Part B

18. A student adds two 50-milligram pieces of Ca(*s*) to water. A reaction takes place according to the following equation.

$$Ca(s) + 2H_2O(\ell) \rightarrow Ca(OH)_2(aq) + H_2(g)$$

Which change could the student have made that would most likely have increased the rate of the reaction?

(1) used 10 10-mg pieces of Ca(*s*)

(2) used one 100-mg piece of Ca(*s*)

(3) decreased the amount of water

(4) decreased the temperature of the water

19. Under which conditions will the forward rate of a chemical reaction most often decrease?

(1) The concentration of the reactants decreases, and the temperature decreases.

(2) The concentration of the reactants decreases, and the temperature increases.

(3) The concentration of the reactants increases, and the temperature decreases.

(4) The concentration of the reactants increases, and the temperature increases.

20. The diagram below shows a bottle containing $NH_3(g)$ dissolved in water. How can the equilibrium $NH_3(g) \rightleftarrows NH_3(aq)$ be reached?

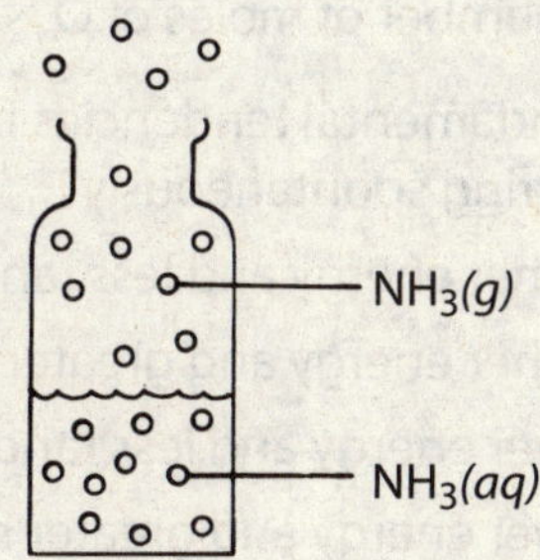

(1) Add more water.
(2) Add more NH_3.
(3) Cool the contents.
(4) Stopper the bottle.

21. A 1-cm³ cube of sodium reacts more rapidly in water at 25°C than does a 1-cm³ cube of calcium at 25°C. This difference in rate of reaction is most closely associated with the different

(1) surface area of the metal cubes

(2) nature of the metals

(3) density of the metals

(4) concentration of the metals

22. At room temperature, which reaction would be expected to have the fastest reaction rate?

(1) $Pb^{2+}(aq) + S^{2-}(aq) \rightarrow PbS(s)$

(2) $2H_2(g) + O_2(g) \rightarrow 2H_2O(\ell)$

(3) $N_2(g) + 2O_2(g) \rightarrow 2NO_2(g)$

(4) $2KClO_3(s) \rightarrow 2KCl(s) + 3O_2(g)$

23. Consider the following equation.

$$A(s) + B(aq) \rightarrow C(aq) + D(s)$$

Which change would most likely increase the rate of this reaction?

(1) a decrease in pressure

(2) an increase in pressure

(3) a decrease in temperature

(4) an increase in temperature

24. The potential energy diagram shown below represents the reaction A + B → AB.

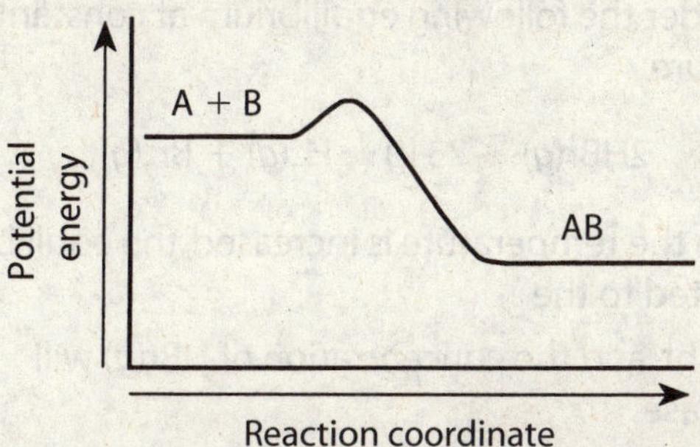

Which statement correctly describes this reaction?

(1) It is endothermic and energy is absorbed.

(2) It is endothermic and energy is released.

(3) It is exothermic and energy is absorbed.

(4) It is exothermic and energy is released.

25. Consider the following equation.

$$AgBr(s) \rightleftarrows Ag^+(aq) + Br^-(aq)$$

Which change occurs when KBr(*s*) is dissolved in the reaction mixture?

(1) The amount of AgBr(*s*) decreases.

(2) The amount of AgBr(*s*) remains the same.

(3) The concentration of $Ag^+(aq)$ decreases.

(4) The concentration of $Ag^+(aq)$ remains the same.

26. Consider the following equation.

$$C(s) + O_2(g) \rightleftarrows CO_2(g) + \text{heat}$$

Which stress on the system will increase the concentration of $CO_2(g)$?

(1) increasing the temperature of the reaction

(2) increasing the concentration of $O_2(g)$

(3) decreasing the pressure on the reaction

(4) decreasing the amount of C(*s*)

27. Consider the following equation.

$$2SO_2(g) + O_2(g) \rightleftarrows 2SO_3(g) + \text{heat}$$

The concentration of $SO_3(g)$ will be increased by

(1) decreasing the concentration of $SO_2(g)$

(2) decreasing the concentration of $O_2(g)$

(3) increasing the pressure

(4) increasing the temperature

28. Consider the following equilibrium at constant pressure.

$$2HBr(g) + 73\text{ kJ} \rightleftarrows H_2(g) + Br_2(g)$$

When the temperature is increased, the equilibrium is shifted to the

(1) right, and the concentration of HBr(*g*) will decrease

(2) right, and the concentration of HBr(*g*) will increase

(3) left, and the concentration of HBr(*g*) will decrease

(4) left, and the concentration of HBr(*g*) will increase

29. Consider the following change of phase.

$$CO_2(g) \rightarrow CO_2(s)$$

As $CO_2(g)$ changes to $CO_2(s)$, the entropy of the system

(1) decreases

(2) increases

(3) remains the same

(4) depends on the enthalpy

30. Which reaction system tends to become less random as reactants form products?

(1) $C(s) + O_2(g) \rightarrow CO_2(g)$

(2) $S(s) + O_2(g) \rightarrow SO_2(g)$

(3) $I_2(s) + Cl_2(g) \rightarrow 2ICl(g)$

(4) $2Mg(s) + O_2(g) \rightarrow 2MgO(s)$

31. In which reaction will the point of equilibrium shift to the left when the pressure on the system is increased?

(1) $C(s) + O_2(g) \rightleftarrows CO_2(g)$

(2) $CaCO_3(s) \rightleftarrows CaO(s) + CO_2(g)$

(3) $2Mg(s) + O_2(g) \rightleftarrows 2MgO(s)$

(4) $2H_2(g) + O_2(g) \rightleftarrows 2H_2O(g)$

32. Consider the following equation.

$$A(g) + B(g) \rightleftarrows C(g) + D(g)$$

Which relationship is an indication that this reaction has reached equilibrium?

(1) The concentration of A equals the concentration of B.

(2) The concentration of C equals the concentration of D.

(3) The concentrations of A, B, C, and D are constant.

(4) The concentrations of A, B, C, and D are equal.

33. Consider the following equation.

$$N_2(g) + O_2(g) \rightleftarrows 2NO(g)$$

If the temperature remains constant and the pressure increases, the number of moles of NO(*g*) will

(1) decrease

(2) increase

(3) remain the same

(4) equal the number of moles of O_2

34. Which two fundamental tendencies favor a chemical reaction occurring spontaneously?

(1) toward higher energy and less randomness

(2) toward higher energy and greater randomness

(3) toward lower energy and less randomness

(4) toward lower energy and greater randomness

Part C

35. Explain why the addition of $SO_2(g)$ to the following system will cause the rate of the forward reaction to increase.

$$2SO_2(g) + O_2(g) \rightleftarrows 2SO_3(g) + \text{heat}$$

What effect will this have on the rate of the reverse reaction? [2]

36. Consider the following equation.

$$X_2(g) + 2Y_2(g) \rightleftarrows 2XY_2(g) + \text{heat}$$

What are two changes that could cause the reaction to shift to the left? [2]

37. Prepare a potential energy diagram to represent the following reaction: $B(s) + C(aq) \rightarrow D(aq) + 30$ kJ. The heat of activation is 20 kJ. [2]

38. A potential energy diagram is shown below. For each of the measures of energy described in parts a–e below, draw an arrow on the diagram. Label each arrow with the correct letter. Then answer question f.

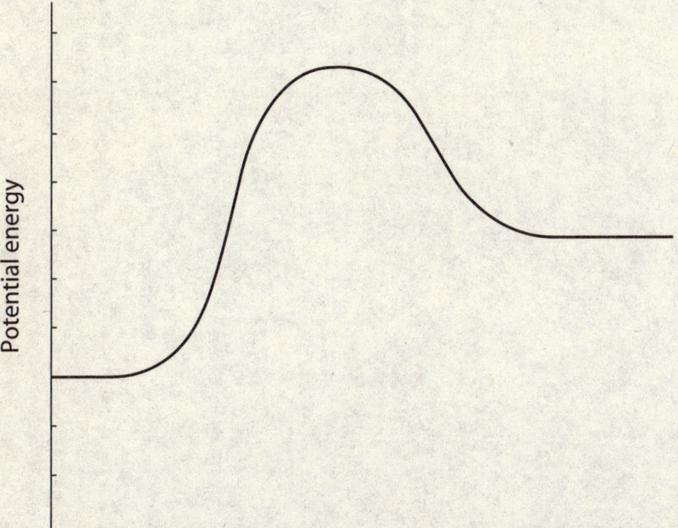

a. activation energy for the forward reaction [1]

b. potential energy of the reactants [1]

c. potential energy of the products [1]

d. activation energy for the reverse reaction [1]

e. heat of reaction [1]

f. Is the reaction endothermic or exothermic? [2] Explain your answer.

39. Study the potential energy diagrams in Figures 8-5 and 8-6. Propose a reason why ΔH has a negative value for an exothermic reaction and a positive value for an endothermic reaction. [2]

40. Consider the following equation.

$$N_2(g) + 3H_2(g) \rightleftarrows 2NH_3(g) + \text{heat}$$

Propose changes in concentration, pressure and temperature that would increase the production of NH_3. [3]

41. Give an example in your home of something that is highly organized. Explain why you think it has low entropy. Give a second example of something in your home that is not well organized. Explain why you think it has high entropy. [4]

Oxidation-Reduction

VOCABULARY		
anode	**electrolytic cell**	**redox**
cathode	**half-reaction**	**reduction**
electrochemical cell	**oxidation**	**salt bridge**
electrode	**oxidation number (state)**	**voltaic cell**
electrolysis		

Oxidation and reduction are important chemical reactions. They work both for our benefit, in forms such as batteries, and against us, in ways such as the corrosion of important metals. Originally, the term *oxidation* meant the combination of a substance with oxygen. *Reduction* was the opposite, the loss of oxygen. Today, both terms have a wider interpretation. They are also recognized as interdependent—one cannot occur without the other.

Oxidation and Reduction

When magnesium is burned in oxygen, the octet rule allows us to understand the transfer of electrons. Each magnesium atom loses two electrons as each oxygen atom gains two electrons. Both atoms acquire a stable octet, as shown in Figure 9-1.

$$\text{Mg:} + \cdot\ddot{\text{O}}\text{:} \longrightarrow \text{Mg}^{2+} + [\text{:}\ddot{\text{O}}\text{:}]^{2-}$$

$$\text{Mg} + \tfrac{1}{2}\text{O}_2 \longrightarrow \text{MgO}$$

Figure 9-1. Chemical reaction between magnesium and oxygen: In the reaction between magnesium and oxygen, a magnesium atom transfers two electrons to an oxygen atom.

The same electron transfer occurs as magnesium reacts with chlorine, as shown in Figure 9-2. Again the magnesium atom loses two electrons, while the two chlorine atoms each accept an electron, acquiring a stable octet.

In both of the equations, while the magnesium atom was losing electrons, other atoms were gaining them. **Oxidation** is defined as the loss of electrons by an atom or ion. **Reduction** is the gain of electrons by an atom or ion.

$$\text{Mg:} + 2\,\cdot\ddot{\text{Cl}}\text{:} \longrightarrow \text{Mg}^{2+} + 2[\text{:}\ddot{\text{Cl}}\text{:}]^{-}$$

$$\text{Mg} + \text{Cl}_2 \longrightarrow \text{MgCl}_2$$

Figure 9-2. Chemical reaction between magnesium and chlorine: In the reaction between magnesium and chlorine, a magnesium atom transfers one electron to each of two chlorine atoms.

REDOX Whenever one atom loses an electron, there must be another atom available to gain the electron. Neither reduction nor oxidation can ever occur alone. Whenever one occurs, the other must occur at the same time. Because these reactions must accompany each other, the two terms are often combined, and reactions in which both reduction and oxidation occur are called **redox** reactions.

Oxidation Numbers

It is not always possible to simply read an equation and determine whether atoms have exchanged electrons. However, chemists have devised a system that makes it easy to keep track of the number of electrons lost or gained by an atom in a reaction. Positive, negative, or neutral values known as **oxidation numbers (states)** can be assigned to atoms. These oxidation states identify how many electrons are either gained or lost by an atom or ion. The use of these oxidation numbers also provides a more complete way to define oxidation and reduction.

Oxidation is defined as the loss of electrons and a gain in oxidation number. Reduction is defined as the gain of electrons and a loss in oxidation number.

Oxidation numbers are used to identify the path of electrons in redox reactions. A simple device may help in remembering the definitions.

LEO says **GER**
LEO = **L**oss of **E**lectrons is **O**xidation
GER = **G**ain of **E**lectrons is **R**eduction

Oxidation numbers are written differently than ionic charges. The charge on the magnesium ion is 2+, while the oxidation number is written as +2. The periodic table in the *Reference Tables for Physical Setting/Chemistry* supplies some common oxidation numbers for elements in compounds.

It is important to learn the rules for assigning oxidation states to atoms in an equation. These numbers are used to identify what has been oxidized and what has been reduced. Here are some rules for assigning oxidation numbers.

1. Each uncombined element has an oxidation number of zero. In the chemical equation $2Na + Cl_2 \rightarrow 2NaCl$, both the uncombined Na and Cl_2 have oxidation numbers of 0.
2. Monatomic ions have an oxidation number equal to the ionic charge. In the equation $2Na + Cl_2 \rightarrow 2NaCl$, the sodium in the product NaCl has a charge of 1+ and an oxidation number of +1. The chlorine in NaCl has a charge of 1− and an oxidation number of −1.
3. The metals of Group 1 always have an oxidation number of +1 in compounds, and the metals of Group 2 always have an oxidation number of +2 in compounds.
4. Fluorine is always −1 in compounds. The other halogens are also −1 when they are the most electronegative element in the compound.
5. Hydrogen is +1 in compounds unless it is combined with a metal, in which case it is −1. Hydrogen is +1 in HCl but −1 in LiH.
6. Oxygen is usually −2 in compounds. When it is combined with fluorine, which is more electronegative, it is +2. Oxygen is −2 in H_2O, and +2 in OF_2. In the peroxide ion (O_2^{2-}), oxygen is −1.

These six rules can be used to assign oxidation numbers to many atoms in equations. They can be used with the following two additional rules to calculate oxidation numbers for other elements in compounds or polyatomic ions.

7. The sum of the oxidation numbers in all compounds must be zero.

SAMPLE PROBLEM

What are the oxidation numbers of the atoms in HNO_3?

Solution: Identify the known and unknown values.

Known	*Unknown*
formula HNO_3	oxidation number of H = ?
	oxidation number of N = ?
	oxidation number of O = ?

Use as many of the first six rules as possible.

Hydrogen has an oxidation number of +1 (Rule 5). Each oxygen atom has an oxidation number of −2 (Rule 6), making the total for three oxygen atoms −6.

The sum of all oxidation numbers is zero.

oxidation number of N + (+1) + (−6) = 0

oxidation number of N = +5

The oxidation number for H is +1; for N, +5; and for O, −2.

8. The sum of the oxidation numbers in polyatomic ions must be equal to the charge on the ion.

SAMPLE PROBLEM

What is the oxidation number of chromium in the dichromate ion ($Cr_2O_7^{2-}$)?

Solution: Identify the known and unknown values.

Known	*Unknown*
formula $Cr_2O_7^{2-}$	oxidation number of Cr = ?

Use as many of the first six rules as possible. O has an oxidation number of −2, producing a total of −14 for the seven O atoms.

The sum of the atoms in a polyatomic ion must equal the charge on the ion.

2(oxidation number of Cr) + (−14) = −2

$$\text{oxidation number of Cr} = \frac{+12}{2}$$

oxidation number of Cr = +6

Review Questions

1. What is the sum of the oxidation numbers in the compound CO_2? (1) 0 (2) -2 (3) -4 (4) $+4$

2. The oxidation number of nitrogen in N_2 is (1) $+1$ (2) 0 (3) $+3$ (4) -3

3. What is the oxidation number of Pt in K_2PtCl_6? (1) -2 (2) $+2$ (3) -4 (4) $+4$

4. In which substance does phosphorus have a $+3$ oxidation state? (1) P_4O_{10} (2) PCl_5 (3) $Ca_3(PO_4)_4$ (4) KH_2PO_3

5. What is the oxidation number of sulfur in H_2SO_4? (1) 0 (2) -2 (3) $+6$ (4) $+4$

6. In which substance does sulfur have a negative oxidation number? (1) Na_2S (2) $CaSO_4$ (3) S (4) SO_2

7. In which compound is the oxidation number of oxygen -1? (1) CO (2) CO_2 (3) H_2O (4) H_2O_2

8. Oxygen has an oxidation number of -2 in (1) O_2 (2) NO_2 (3) Na_2O_2 (3) OF_2

9. Oxygen will have a positive oxidation number when combined with (1) fluorine (2) chlorine (3) bromine (4) iodine

10. In which compound does hydrogen have an oxidation number of -1? (1) NH_3 (2) KH (3) HCl (4) H_2O

Examining Redox Reactions

Sometimes it's important to know whether a reaction is redox or not. Once it has been determined that a reaction is redox, it is important to know what is oxidized, what is reduced, and what brings about oxidation and reduction.

Recognizing Redox Reactions

Not all reactions are redox reactions. To determine whether or not a reaction is redox, assign oxidation numbers to each atom, both on the reactant and product side. If there is a change in oxidation number for a particular type of atom, the reaction is redox.

Sometimes it is easy to spot a redox reaction. If an uncombined element appears on one side of an equation and is in a compound on the other side, the reaction must be a redox reaction. If you recognize a reaction as a double replacement reaction, it is not redox.

Identifying Oxidation and Reduction

Once oxidation numbers are assigned, the atom that has shown an increase can be identified as the one that has undergone oxidation. The atom that has a decrease in oxidation number has undergone reduction.

Consider the following reaction.

$$MnO_2 + 4HCl \rightarrow MnCl_2 + Cl_2 + 2H_2O$$

In the equation, chlorine has an oxidation number of -1 as a reactant in HCl. On the product side, some chlorine ions are still -1, but others have an oxidation state of 0 in Cl_2. Because the chloride ion (Cl^-) changes from a lower oxidation number to a higher one, it has been oxidized. Manganese changes from $+4$ as a reactant to $+2$ as a product. Because it changed from a higher oxidation number to a lower one, Mn^{4+} has undergone reduction.

Oxidizing Agents and Reducing Agents

In the previous reaction, Mn^{+4} underwent reduction, having received electrons from the Cl^-. The Cl^- caused the reduction of the Mn^{+4} and is called the reducing agent. By accepting electrons from Cl^-, the Mn^{+4} caused the Cl^- to be oxidized. The Mn^{+4} is the oxidizing agent. In summary, the substance oxidized is the reducing agent, and the substance reduced is the oxidizing agent.

Review Questions

11. Which equation represents an oxidation-reduction reaction?
(1) $HCl + KOH \rightarrow KCl + H_2O$
(2) $4HCl + MnO_2 \rightarrow MnCl_2 + 2H_2O + Cl_2$
(3) $2HCl + CaCO_3 \rightarrow CaCl_2 + H_2O + CO_2$
(4) $2HCl + FeS \rightarrow FeCl_2 + H_2S$

12. Which equation represents an oxidation-reduction reaction?
(1) $Zn + 2HCl \rightarrow ZnCl_2 + H_2$
(2) $Zn(OH)_2 + 2HCl \rightarrow ZnCl_2 + 2H_2O$
(3) $H_2O + NH_3 \rightarrow NH^{4+} + OH^-$
(4) $H_2O + H_2O \rightarrow H_3O^+ + OH^-$

13. Which equation represents an oxidation-reduction reaction?
(1) $HCl + KOH \rightarrow KCl + H_2O$
(2) $4HCl + MnO_2 \rightarrow MnCl_2 + 2H_2O + Cl_2$
(3) $2HCl + CaCO_3 \rightarrow CaCl_2 + H_2O + CO_2$
(4) $2HCl + FeS \rightarrow FeCl_2 + H_2S$

14. Oxidation-reduction reactions occur because of the competition between particles for (1) neutrons (2) electrons (3) protons (4) positrons

15. Which statement correctly describes a redox reaction? (1) Oxidation and reduction occur simultaneously. (2) Oxidation occurs before reduction. (3) Oxidation occurs after reduction. (4) Oxidation occurs, but reduction does not.

16. A redox reaction is a reaction in which (1) only reduction occurs (2) only oxidation occurs (3) reduction and oxidation occur at the same time (4) reduction occurs first and then oxidation occurs

17. All redox reaction involve (1) the gain of electrons only (2) the loss of electrons only (3) both the gain and the loss of electrons (4) neither the gain nor the loss of electrons

18. Consider the following equation.

$$Zn(s) + Cu^{2+}(aq) \rightarrow Zn^{2+}(aq) + Cu(s)$$

Which particles must be transferred from one reactant to the other reactant? (1) ions (2) neutrons (3) protons (4) electrons

19. What occurs during the reaction below?

$$4HCl + MnO_2 \rightarrow MnCl_2 + 2H_2O + Cl_2$$

(1) The manganese is reduced and its oxidation number changes from +4 to +2. (2) The manganese is oxidized and its oxidation number changes from +4 to +2. (3) The manganese is reduced and its oxidation number changes from +2 to +4. (4) The manganese is oxidized and its oxidation number changes from +2 to +4.

20. What occurs when an atom is oxidized in a chemical reaction? (1) a loss of electrons and a decrease in oxidation number (2) a loss of electrons and an increase in oxidation number (3) a gain of electrons and a decrease in oxidation number (4) a gain of electrons and an increase in oxidation number

21. When a substance is oxidized, it (1) loses protons (2) gains protons (3) acts as an oxidizing agent (4) acts as a reducing agent

22. Consider the following redox reaction.

$$Co(s) + PbCl_2(aq) \rightarrow CoCl_2(aq) + Pb(s)$$

Which statement correctly describes the oxidation and reduction that occur? (1) Co(s) is oxidized and $Cl^-(aq)$ is reduced. (2) Co(s) is oxidized and $Pb^{2+}(aq)$ is reduced. (3) Co(s) is reduced and $Cl^-(aq)$ is oxidized. (4) Co(s) is oxidized and $Pb^{2+}(aq)$ is oxidized.

23. Consider the following equation.

$$MnO_2(s) + 4H^+(aq) + 2Fe^{2+}(aq) \rightarrow Mn^{2+}(aq) + 2Fe^{3+}(aq) + 2H_2O(\ell)$$

Which species is oxidized? (1) $H^+(aq)$ (2) $H_2O(\ell)$ (3) $Fe^{2+}(aq)$ (4) $MnO_2(s)$

24. Consider the following equation.

$$Zn(s) + 2HCl(aq) \rightarrow ZnCl_2(aq) + H_2(g)$$

Which substance is oxidized? (1) Zn(s) (2) HCl(aq) (3) $Cl^-(aq)$ (4) $H^+(aq)$

25. Consider the following redox reaction.

$$Ni + Sn^{4+} \rightarrow Ni^{2+} + Sn^{2+}$$

Which species has been reduced? (1) Ni (2) Sn^{4+} (3) Ni^{2+} (4) Sn^{2+}

26. Consider the following equation.

$$2Fe^{3+} + Sn^{2+} \rightarrow 2Fe^{2+} + Sn^{4+}$$

Which species is the oxidizing agent? (1) Fe^{3+} (2) Sn^{2+} (3) Fe^{2+} (4) Sn^{4+}

27. Consider the following equation.

$$Pb^0(s) + Cu^{2+}(aq) \rightarrow Pb^{2+}(aq) + Cu^0(s)$$

What is the reducing agent? (1) $Pb^{2+}(aq)$ (2) $Cu^{2+}(aq)$ (3) $Pb^0(s)$ (4) $Cu^0(s)$

28. Consider the following equation.

$$Mg(s) + CuSO_4(aq) \rightarrow MgSO_4(aq) + Cu(s)$$

Which species acts as the oxidizing agent? (1) Cu(s) (2) $Cu^{2+}(aq)$ (3) Mg(s) (4) $Mg^{2+}(aq)$

29. In the reaction $2H_2S + 3O_2 \rightarrow 2SO_2 + 2H_2O$, the oxidizing agent is (1) oxygen (2) water (3) sulfur dioxide (4) hydrogen sulfide

30. In the reaction $Cu + 2Ag^+ \rightarrow Cu^{2+} + 2Ag$, the oxidizing agent is (1) Cu (2) Cu^{2+} (3) Ag^+ (4) Ag

31. In a redox reaction, the reducing agent will (1) lose electrons and be reduced (2) lose electrons and be oxidized (3) gain electrons and be reduced (4) gain electrons and be oxidized

Half-Reactions

Chemical equations show the formulas of reactants and products, but they do not show the exchange of electrons. A **half-reaction** shows either the oxidation or reduction portion of a redox reaction, including the electrons gained or lost.

A reduction half-reaction shows an atom or ion gaining one or more electrons while its oxidation number decreases.

$$Fe^{3+}(aq) + 3e^- \rightarrow Fe(s)$$

An oxidation half-reaction shows an atom or an ion losing one or more electrons while its oxidation number increases.

$$Fe(s) \rightarrow Fe^{3+}(aq) + 3e^-$$

Like other chemical equations, half-reactions follow the law of conservation of matter; that is, there must be the same number of atoms on both sides of the arrow. Generally, in a half reaction there will only be one type of atom or ion shown on both reactant and product side of the equation.

In addition to conservation of mass, there must also be a conservation of charge. In molecular equations, because no charges are shown, the net charge will be zero on both reactant and product side. In half-reactions, the net charge must be the same on both sides of the equation, but it does not necessarily equal zero.

$Fe^{3+}(aq) + 3e^- \rightarrow Fe(s)$	Net charge/side = 0
$Fe(s) \rightarrow Fe^{3+}(aq) + 3e^-$	Net charge/side = 0
$Sn^{4+}(aq) + 2e^- \rightarrow Sn^{2+}(aq)$	Net charge/side = 2+
$Sn^{2+}(aq) \rightarrow Sn^{4+}(aq) + 2e^-$	Net charge/side = 2+

To write a half-reaction from an equation such as

$$Cu + AgNO_3 \rightarrow Cu(NO_3)_2 + Ag$$

first assign an oxidation number to each element, then write a partial half-reaction to show the change in oxidation state.

Oxidation: $Cu \rightarrow Cu^{2+}$
Reduction: $Ag^+ \rightarrow Ag$

Then show the number of electrons needed to explain how the oxidation number changed, and to achieve a conservation of charge. Check to see that the net charge is the same on both sides of these equations.

Oxidation: $Cu \rightarrow Cu^{2+} + 2e^-$	Net charge/side = 0
Reduction: $Ag^+ + e^- \rightarrow Ag$	Net charge/side = 0

DIGGING DEEPER

In all redox reactions, there must be a balance between the number of electrons lost and gained. In the previous example,

Oxidation: $Cu \rightarrow Cu^{2+} + 2e^-$
Reduction: $Ag^+ + e^- \rightarrow Ag$

balance can be achieved by multiplying the reduction equation by two. Thus, there are two electrons lost and two electrons gained. Redox equations can be balanced by first balancing the number of electrons lost and gained. After balancing the redox portion of the equation, the remainder can be balanced by inspection.

Review Questions

32. Which half-reaction correctly represents reduction?

(1) $Fe^{2+} + 2e^- \rightarrow Fe$
(2) $Fe^{2+} + e^- \rightarrow Fe^{3+}$
(3) $Fe + 2e^- \rightarrow Fe^{2+}$
(4) $Fe + e^- \rightarrow Fe^{3+}$

33. Consider the following oxidation reduction equation.

$$Hg^{2+} + 2I^- \rightarrow Hg + I_2$$

Which equation correctly represents the half-reaction for the oxidation that occurs?

(1) $Hg^{2+} \rightarrow Hg + 2e^-$
(2) $Hg^{2+} + 2e^- \rightarrow Hg$
(3) $2I^- \rightarrow I_2 + 2e^-$
(4) $2I^- + 2e^- \rightarrow I_2$

34. Which statement describes what occurs in the following redox reaction?

$$Cu(s) + 2Ag^+(aq) \rightarrow Cu^{2+}(aq) + 2Ag(s)$$

(1) Only mass is conserved. (2) Only charge is conserved. (3) Both mass and charge are conserved. (4) Neither mass nor charge is conserved.

35. Which equation is correctly balanced?

(1) $Fe^{3+} + 2Ni \rightarrow Fe^{2+} + 2Ni^{2+}$
(2) $2Fe^{3+} + Ni \rightarrow 2Fe^{2+} + Ni^{2+}$
(3) $Fe^{3+} + Ni \rightarrow Fe^{2+} + Ni^{2+}$
(4) $2Fe^{2+} + 2Ni \rightarrow 2Fe^{2+} + 2Ni^{2+}$

36. Which equation is correctly balanced?

(1) $Cr^{3+} + Mg \rightarrow Cr + Mg^{2+}$

(2) $Al^{3+} + K \rightarrow Al + K^{+}$

(3) $Sn^{4+} + H_2 \rightarrow Sn + 2H^{+}$

(4) $Br_2 + Hg \rightarrow Hg^{2+} + 2Br^{-}$

Electrochemical Cells

In redox reactions there is a chemical reaction and an exchange of electrons between the particles being oxidized and reduced. One practical use of such a reaction is in an electrochemical cell. An **electrochemical cell** involves a chemical reaction and a flow of electrons.

There are two common types of electrochemical cells. A **voltaic cell** is an electrochemical cell in which a spontaneous chemical reaction produces a flow of electrons. An **electrolytic cell** requires an electric current to force a nonspontaneous chemical reaction to occur.

Electrochemical cells have two surfaces called electrodes that can conduct electricity. An **electrode** is the site at which oxidation or reduction occurs. The electrode at which oxidation occurs is called the **anode.** The electrode at which reduction occurs is called the **cathode.**

MEMORY JOGGER

In Topic 2, the use of Table J in *Reference Tables for Physical Setting/Chemistry* was presented. A metal will react with the compound of another metal found below it on the table. For example, zinc metal will react with lead nitrate, but not with aluminum nitrate.

$$Zn + Pb(NO_3)_2 \rightarrow Pb + Zn(NO_3)_2$$
$$Zn + Al(NO_3)_3 \rightarrow \text{no reaction}$$

Spontaneous Reactions—Voltaic Cells

If a strip of zinc is placed into a solution of lead nitrate, the zinc will be oxidized and the lead ions will be reduced according to the following equation.

$$Zn(s) + Pb^{2+}(aq) \rightarrow Pb(s) + Zn^{2+}(aq)$$

The exchange of electrons takes place on the surface of the zinc, as shown by equations for the two half-reactions.

$$Zn(s) \rightarrow Zn^{2+}(aq) + 2e^{-}$$
$$Pb^{2+}(aq) + 2e^{-} \rightarrow Pb(s)$$

It is also possible to have these materials separated into two containers, so the electrons travel through a wire connecting them. In a voltaic cell, a **salt bridge** connects the two containers and provides a path for a flow of ions between the two beakers. This makes a complete circuit and allows the reaction to proceed. The diagram in Figure 9-3 shows a voltaic cell. In a voltaic cell, chemical energy is spontaneously converted to electrical energy.

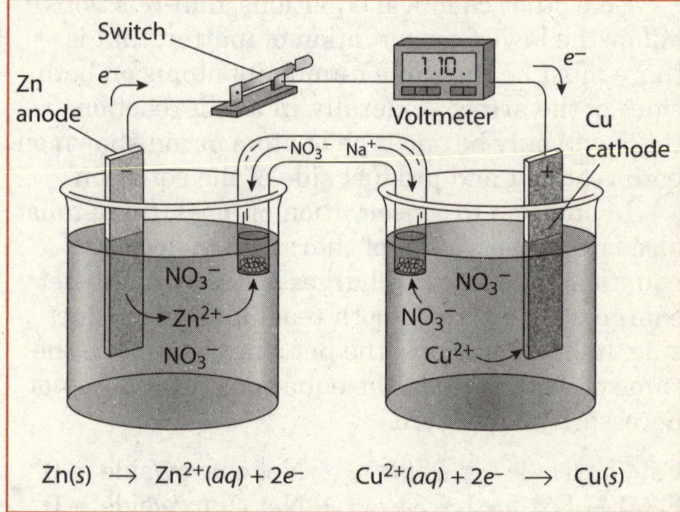

Figure 9-3. A typical voltaic cell

In such a voltaic cell, when a strip of zinc metal is located in one beaker and copper ions are in solution in another beaker, the reaction can occur as if the solutions were in the same beaker. An electrical current is produced by separating the solutions into two beakers and forcing electrons to flow through the wire to complete the circuit.

When electrons are lost during oxidation at the anode, they travel through the wire to the cathode. At this electrode, the material being reduced gains electrons. As with all redox reactions, the substance being oxidized loses electrons, and the substance being reduced gains them. The number of electrons lost must be equal to the number of electrons gained.

Table J in *Reference Tables for Physical Setting/Chemistry* can be used to identify the anode and cathode in a voltaic cell. Identify the two metals shown in the cell, and locate them on the table. The metal that is higher on the chart will be oxidized, and is thus the anode. The lower metal is the site of reduction and will be the cathode. Notice that the cathode itself is not reduced; it is the place where the reduction occurs. Ions in solution are reduced. To help you identify the anode and cathode, remember **RED CAT** and **AN OX.**

REDuction occurs at the **CAT**hode.
ANode is the site of **OX**idation.

SAMPLE PROBLEM

Consider the following equation.

$Zn^0(s) + Pb^{2+}(aq) \rightarrow Zn^{2+}(aq) + Pb^0(s)$

Identify the anode and the cathode, and give the direction of electron flow.

Solution: Identify the known and unknown values.

Known	*Unknown*
reaction equation	anode = ?
Data in Table J	cathode = ?
	direction of electron flow

Locate zinc and lead on Table J. Zinc is higher on the table. Thus, it is more reactive. Zinc will undergo oxidation and is the anode. The Pb^{2+} ions are not the cathode, but they will be reduced at the cathode. If the cell has a strip of lead metal in the beaker with the Pb^{2+} ions, the lead metal will be the cathode.

The zinc is oxidized and is losing electrons. The electrons will flow from the zinc to the lead, which is from anode to cathode.

ADDITIONAL MATERIAL

The following coverage of voltaic cells is not required by the Regents core curriculum in chemistry. You will not be tested on this topic in the Regents examination for the Physical Setting/Chemistry.

When a voltaic cell begins to react, the electrons flow from the anode to the cathode. A voltmeter placed in the circuit measures the electric potential between the metals in the electrodes in units of volts. Table 9-1 shows a series of reduction pairs as ions are reduced to the atomic state. The voltage for each pair is the voltage obtained when the given pair is compared to the standard hydrogen cell, which is assigned a value of 0.00 V.

The reductions at the top of the table are the least likely to occur. The more positive the E^0 value, the more likely the reduction. Thus, when Zn^{2+}/Zn and Cu^{2+}/Cu are in a voltaic cell, the reduction of Cu^{2+} to Cu will occur, while the oxidation of Zn to Zn^{2+} will supply the electrons. The voltage between the two can be calculated using the following relationship.

$$\begin{aligned} E^0_{cell} &= E^0_{reduction} - E^0_{oxidation} \\ &= E^0_{Cu^{2+}} - E^0_{Zn^{2+}} \\ &= +0.34V - (-0.76V) \\ &= +1.10V \end{aligned}$$

Table 9-1. Reduction Potentials

Ion/Metal	E^0 (Volts)
Li^+/Li	−3.04
Rb^+/Rb	−2.98
K^+/K	−2.93
Cs^+/Cs	−2.92
Ba^{2+}/Ba	−2.91
Sr^{2+}/Sr	−2.89
Ca^{2+}/Ca	−2.87
Na^+/Na	−2.71
Mg^{2+}/Mg	−2.37
Al^{3+}/Al	−1.66
Mn^{2+}/Mn	−1.19
Zn^{2+}/Zn	−0.76
Cr^{3+}/Cr	−0.74
Co^{2+}/Co	−0.28
Ni^{2+}/Ni	−0.26
Pb^{2+}/Pb	−0.13
H^+/H_2	0.00
Cu^{2+}/Cu	+0.34
Ag^+/Ag	+0.80
Au^{3+}/Au	+1.50

Nonspontaneous Reactions—Electrolytic Cells

In a voltaic cell, the electrons flow spontaneously from the anode to the cathode. In the example given, electrons from the oxidation of zinc travel through the wire to reduce lead ions. Can the reverse take place? Can the electrons travel from the lead to the zinc causing the lead metal to be oxidized and the zinc ions to be reduced?

The answer is yes, but the reaction cannot occur spontaneously. There must be some electrical generator placed into the circuit to force the electrons to flow from the cathode to the anode. When electricity is used to force a chemical reaction to occur, the process is called **electrolysis.** In an automobile, both spontaneous and nonspontaneous redox reactions occur. When the car is started, a spontaneous chemical reaction occurs in the battery, providing electricity to start the car. Once the car has been started, the alternator, in a nonspontaneous reaction, recharges the battery.

Electrolysis can be used to obtain active elements such as sodium and chlorine by the electrolysis of fused (molten) salts.

$$2NaCl(\ell) \rightarrow 2Na(s) + Cl_2(g)$$

Electrolysis can also be used to electroplate metals onto a surface. The material to be plated with a metal is the cathode. The anode is made of the metal used for the plating. The electrolyte contains ions of the desired metal. Figure 9-4 shows the diagram of an apparatus used to plate silver. The anode is itself a piece of silver. As silver ions are produced by oxidation, they travel through the solution to the cathode. At the cathode, they are reduced back to silver atoms and adhere to the metal being plated.

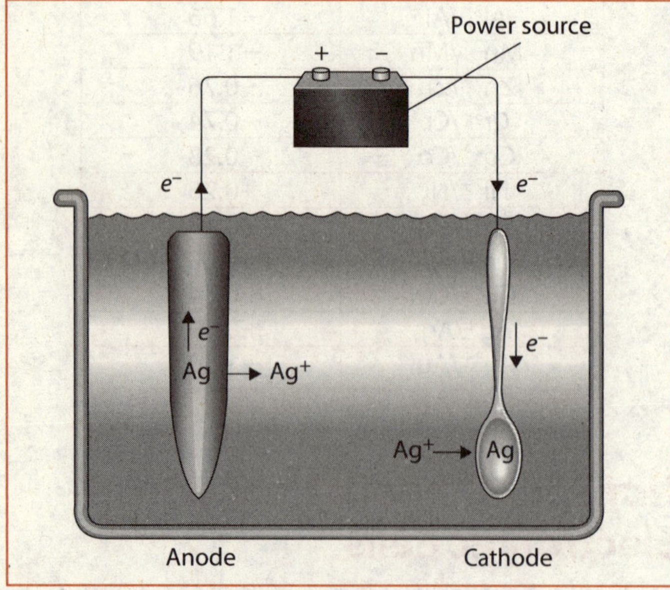

Figure 9-4. An electroplating apparatus

Notice that the positive silver ions migrate away from the anode. Because like charges repel, the anode is positive in an electrolytic cell. The positive silver ions migrate through the solution toward the cathode, which must have a negative charge. The external power source forces the electrons in the wire to travel from the anode to the cathode.

Although there are distinct differences in voltaic and electrolytic cells, they also have several things in common.

- Both use redox reactions.
- The anode is the site of oxidation.
- The cathode is the site of reduction.
- The electrons flow through the wire from anode to cathode.

Differences between voltaic and electrolytic cells include the following.

- The redox reaction in a voltaic cell is spontaneous, but it is nonspontaneous in an electrolytic cell.
- In a voltaic cell the anode is negative and the cathode is positive. In an electrolytic cell, the anode is positive and the cathode is negative.

Review Questions

37. The type of reaction in a voltaic cell is best described as (1) spontaneous oxidation reaction only (2) nonspontaneous oxidation reaction only (3) spontaneous oxidation-reduction reaction (4) nonspontaneous oxidation-reduction reaction

38. An electrochemical cell is made up of two half-cells connected by a salt bridge and an external conductor. What is the function of the salt bridge? (1) to permit the migration of ions (2) to prevent the migration of ions (3) to permit the mixing of solutions (4) to prevent the flow of electrons

39. Compared to the total mass and total charge at the beginning of a redox reaction, the total mass and total charge upon completion of the reaction is (1) less (2) greater (3) the same (4) dependent on what the reaction is

40. The diagram below shows an electrochemical cell.

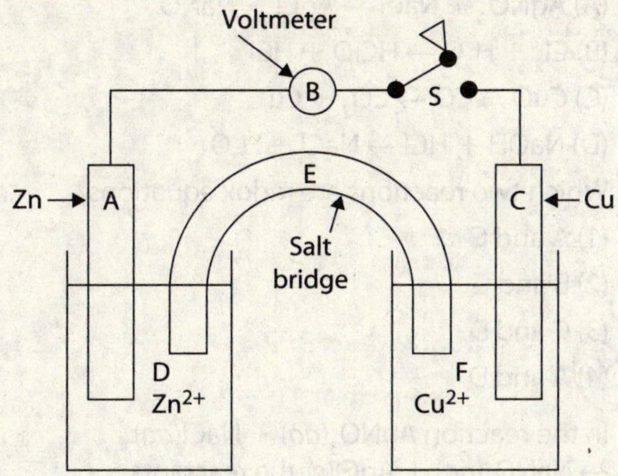

When the switch is closed, which series of letters shows the path and direction of electron flow?
(1) ABC (2) CBA (3) DEF (4) FED

41. Consider the following equation.

$$2H_2O + \text{electricity} \rightarrow 2H_2 + O_2$$

In which type of cell would this reaction most likely occur? (1) a voltaic cell, because it releases energy
(2) an electrolytic cell, because it releases energy
(3) a voltaic cell, because it absorbs energy
(4) an electrolytic cell, because it absorbs energy

Questions for Regents Review

Part A

1. The oxidation number of an uncombined Group 2 metal is
(1) +1
(2) +2
(3) −2
(4) 0

2. In all oxidation-reduction reactions there is conservation of
(1) charge, but not mass
(2) mass, but not charge
(3) neither mass nor charge
(4) both mass and charge

3. During a reduction reaction there is a
(1) loss of electrons and a loss of oxidation number
(2) loss of electrons and a gain of oxidation number
(3) gain of electrons and a loss of oxidation number
(4) gain of electrons and a gain of oxidation number

4. As an atom is oxidized, the number of protons in the nucleus
(1) decreases
(2) increases
(3) remains the same
(4) depends on the atom

5. In a redox reaction, the species reduced
(1) gains electrons
(2) gains oxidation number
(3) loses electrons and is the oxidizing agent
(4) loses electrons and is the reducing agent

6. A redox reaction always involves
(1) a change in oxidation number
(2) a change of phase
(3) a transfer of protons
(4) the formation of ions

7. The function of a salt bridge in a voltaic cell is to
(1) allow the flow of electrons
(2) allow the flow of protons
(3) allow the flow of ions
(4) provide a site for electron transfer

8. Which of the following occurs in an electrolytic cell?
(1) A chemical reaction produces an electric current.
(2) An electric current produces a chemical reaction.
(3) An oxidation reaction takes place at the cathode.
(4) A reduction reaction takes place at the anode.

9. Hydrogen has an oxidation number of
(1) 0 only
(2) +1 only
(3) −1 only
(4) 0, +1, or −1

10. Voltaic cells differ from electrolytic cells because in a voltaic cell
(1) the cathode is positively charged
(2) the anode is positively charged
(3) electrons flow from anode to cathode
(4) electrons flow from cathode to anode

11. In a half-reaction
(1) mass only is conserved
(2) charge only is conserved
(3) both mass and charge are conserved
(4) neither mass nor charge is conserved

12. Which reaction occurs at the anode in voltaic and electrolytic cells?
(1) reduction only
(2) oxidation only
(3) both reduction and oxidation
(4) neither reduction nor oxidation

Part B

13. What is the oxidation number of carbon in $NaHCO_3$?
(1) −2
(2) +2
(3) −4
(4) +4

14. Chlorine has an oxidation state of +3 in the compound
(1) HClO
(2) $HClO_2$
(3) $HClO_3$
(4) $HClO_4$

15. What are the two oxidation states of nitrogen in the compound NH_4NO_3?
(1) −3 and +5
(2) −3 and −5
(3) +3 and +5
(4) +3 and −5

16. Which equation represents a redox reaction?
(1) $NaCl + AgNO_3 \rightarrow AgCl + NaNO_3$
(2) $HCl + KOH \rightarrow H_2O + KCl$
(3) $2KClO_3 \rightarrow 2KCl + 3O_2$
(4) $H_2CO_3 \rightarrow H_2O + CO_2$

17. Consider the equations A, B, C, and D.
(A) $AgNO_3 + NaCl \rightarrow AgCl + NaNO_3$
(B) $Cl_2 + H_2O \rightarrow HClO + HCl$
(C) $CuO + CO \rightarrow CO_2 + Cu$
(D) $NaOH + HCl \rightarrow NaCl + H_2O$
Which two reactions are redox equations?
(1) A and C
(2) B and C
(3) C and D
(4) A and D

18. In the reaction $AgNO_3(aq) + NaCl(aq) \rightarrow NaNO_3(aq) + AgCl(s)$, the reactants
(1) gain electrons only
(2) lose electrons only
(3) both gain and lose electrons
(4) neither gain nor lose electrons

19. In the reaction $Cl_2 + H_2O \rightarrow HClO + HCl$, hydrogen is
(1) oxidized only
(2) reduced only
(3) both oxidized and reduced
(4) neither oxidized nor reduced

20. In the reaction $2KCl(\ell) \rightarrow 2K(s) + Cl_2(g)$, the K^+ ions are
(1) reduced by losing electrons
(2) reduced by gaining electrons
(3) oxidized by losing electrons
(4) oxidized by gaining electrons

21. Which equation correctly represents a reduction half-reaction?
(1) $Sn^0 + 2e^- \rightarrow Sn^{2+}$
(2) $Na^0 + e^- \rightarrow Na^+$
(3) $Li^0 + e^- \rightarrow Li^+$
(4) $Br_2{}^0 + 2e^- \rightarrow 2Br^-$

22. In the reaction $Mg + Cl_2 \rightarrow MgCl_2$, the correct half-reaction for the oxidation that occurs is
(1) $Mg + 2e^- \rightarrow Mg^{2+}$
(2) $Cl_2 + 2e^- \rightarrow 2Cl^-$
(3) $Mg \rightarrow Mg^{2+} + 2e^-$
(4) $Cl_2 \rightarrow 2Cl^- + 2e^-$

23. In an electrolytic cell, which ion would migrate through the solution to the positive electrode?

(1) a hydrogen ion (3) an ammonium ion

(2) a chloride ion (4) a hydronium ion

24. The diagram below represents a voltaic cell.

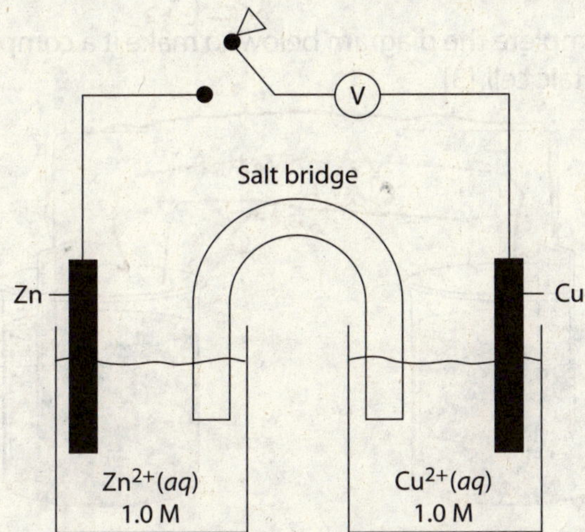

What occurs when the switch is closed?

(1) Zn is reduced. (3) Electrons flow from Cu to Zn.

(2) Cu is oxidized. (4) Electrons flow from Zn to Cu.

25. The diagram below shows a spoon that will be electroplated with nickel metal. What will occur when switch S is closed?

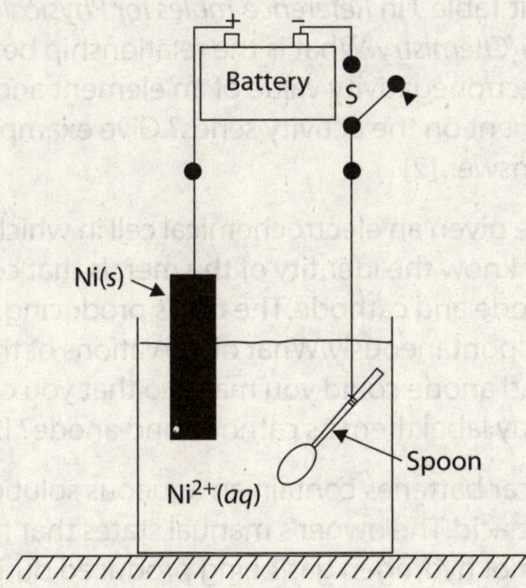

(1) The spoon will lose mass, and the Ni(*s*) will be reduced.

(2) The spoon will lose mass, and the Ni(*s*) will be oxidized.

(3) The spoon will gain mass, and the Ni(*s*) will be reduced.

(4) The spoon will gain mass, and the Ni(*s*) will be oxidized.

26. The diagram below represents a chemical cell.

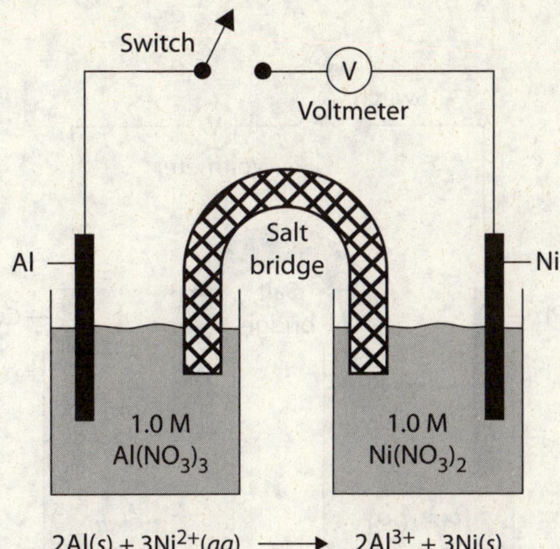

$$2Al(s) + 3Ni^{2+}(aq) \longrightarrow 2Al^{3+} + 3Ni(s)$$

When the switch is closed, electrons flow from

(1) $Al(s)$ to $Ni(s)$ (3) $Al^{3+}(aq)$ to $Ni^{2+}(aq)$

(2) $Ni(s)$ to $Al(s)$ (4) $Ni^{2+}(aq)$ to $Al^{3+}(aq)$

27. The diagram below represents a voltaic cell.

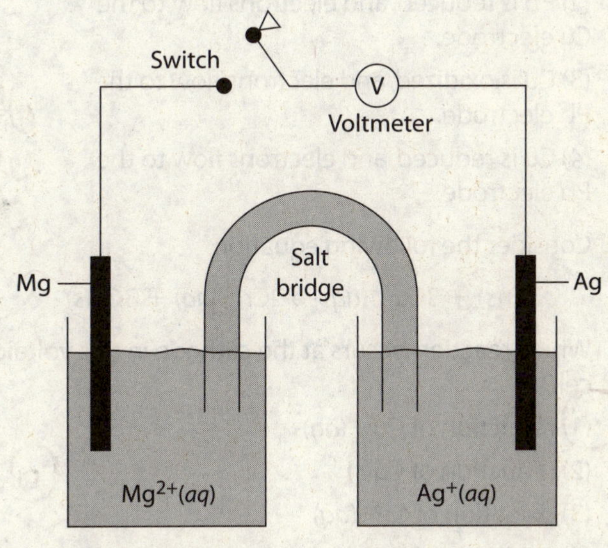

$$Mg(s) + 2Ag^{+}(aq) \longrightarrow Mg^{2+}(aq) + 2Ag(s)$$

Which species is oxidized when the switch is closed?

(1) $Mg(s)$ (3) $Ag(s)$

(2) $Mg^{2+}(aq)$ (4) $Ag^{+}(aq)$

28. The overall reaction in an electrochemical cell is $Zn(s) + Cu^{2+}(aq) \rightarrow Cu(s) + Zn^{2+}$. As the reaction in this cell takes place,

(1) oxidation occurs at the cathode

(2) the Cu^{2+} is oxidized

(3) the concentration of Zn^{2+} increases

(4) the concentration of Cu^{2+} increases

29. The diagram below represents an electrochemical cell.

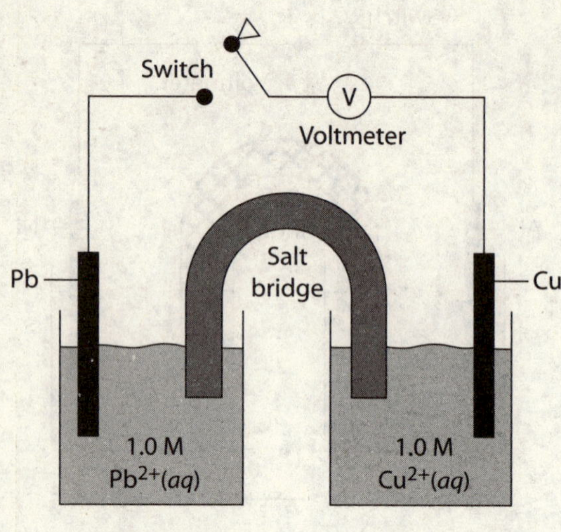

$$Pb(s) + Cu^{2+}(aq) \longrightarrow Pb^{2+}(aq) + Cu(s)$$

Which change occurs when the switch is closed?

(1) Pb is oxidized, and electrons flow to the Cu electrode.

(2) Pb is reduced, and electrons flow to the Cu electrode.

(3) Cu is oxidized, and electrons flow to the Pb electrode.

(4) Cu is reduced, and electrons flow to the Pb electrode.

30. Consider the following equation.

$$2Cr(s) + 3Cu^{2+}(aq) \rightarrow 2Cr^{3+}(aq) + 3Cu(s)$$

Which reaction occurs at the cathode in this voltaic cell?

(1) reduction of $Cu^{2+}(aq)$

(2) reduction of $Cu(s)$

(3) oxidation of $Cr^{3+}(aq)$

(4) oxidation of $Cr(s)$

Part C

31. Write the oxidation number of the element underlined in each of the following. [3]

(a) $K_2\underline{Cr}O_4$

(b) $\underline{S}O_2$

(c) $Ca(\underline{O}H)_2$

32. Complete the equation $Al(s) \rightarrow Al^{3+}(aq) +$ ____. [1]

33. Write the complete half-reaction for the reduction of Fe^{3+} to Fe^0. [1]

34. Complete the equation: $Mn^{7+} + X \rightarrow Mn^{2+}$. [1]

35. Complete the equation: $2Cl^- \rightarrow X + 2e^-$. [1]

36. Complete the diagram below to make it a complete voltaic cell. [3]

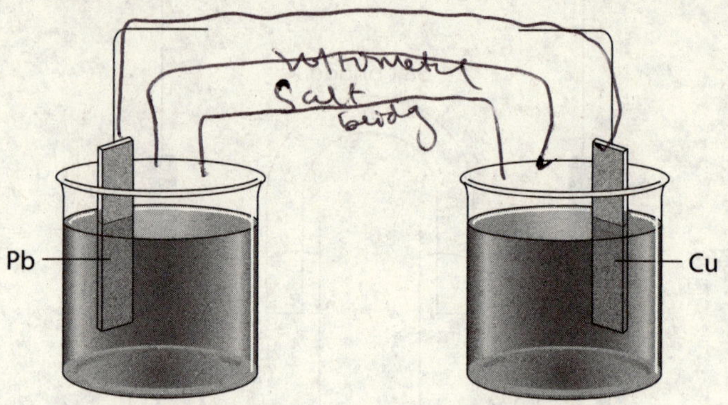

37. Consult Table J in *Reference Tables for Physical Setting/Chemistry.*

(a) Cite an example of a combination of a metal and another metallic ion that will produce a spontaneous reaction. [1]

(b) Cite an example of a combination that will not react spontaneously. [1]

38. Consult Table J in *Reference Tables for Physical Setting/Chemistry.* What is the relationship between the electronegativity value of an element and its placement on the activity series? Give examples with your answer. [2]

39. You are given an electrochemical cell in which you do not know the identity of the metals that comprise the anode and cathode. The cell is producing electricity spontaneously. What observations of the cathode and anode could you make so that you could correctly label them as cathode and anode? [2]

40. Many car batteries contain an aqueous solution of sulfuric acid. The owner's manual states that there is a danger of hydrogen gas being produced during the charging process. What would be the source of the hydrogen? If hydrogen is produced, would another gas be produced at the same time? If so, what gas would it be? [3]

Acids, Bases, and Salts

VOCABULARY		
acidity	electrolyte	neutralization
alkalinity	hydrogen ion	pH scale
Arrhenius acid	hydronium ion	salt
Arrhenius base	indicator	titration

Tables K and L in the *Reference Tables for Physical Setting/Chemistry* list a few of the most common acids and bases. But what exactly are acids and bases? Acids and bases are classes of compounds that can be recognized by their easily observed properties. In this chapter you will learn about these properties, the definitions that are used to explain these properties, and the important reactions that occur between acids and bases.

Properties of Acids and Bases

Certain observable properties can be used to identify both acids and bases. Although these properties can indicate whether or not a substance is an acid or a base, they do not explain why acids and bases behave the way they do.

Characterisitic Properties of Acids

- *Dilute solutions of acids have a sour taste.* It would be foolish to taste a substance to see if it is an acid. However, there are acids in many of the foods that we eat. You have probably noticed the sour taste of lemons; the sour taste is due to the presence of citric acid. Vinegar contains acetic acid, and carbonated drinks have carbonic acid as one of the ingredients.
- *Aqueous solutions of acids conduct an electric current.* Substances that conduct an electric current are called **electrolytes**. The ability of a solution to conduct an electric current is dependent on the concentration (number) of ions in solution. That is, the greater the number of ions in solution, the greater the electrical conductivity. If a solution of an acid is a good conductor of electricity, it is called a strong acid. If such a solution is a poor conductor, it is termed a weak acid.
- *Acids react with bases to form water and a salt.* This type of reaction is called a **neutralization** reaction. Neutralization reactions are in fact a type of double replacement reaction. The **salt** that is formed as a product of a neutralization reaction is an ionic substance composed of a positively charged metallic or polyatomic ion and a negative ion other than the hydroxide ion.
- *Acids react with certain metals to produce hydrogen gas.* The metals listed in Table J of the *Reference Tables for Physical Setting/Chemistry* that are above hydrogen (H_2) will react with acids to produce hydrogen gas and a salt. Thus, magnesium will react with hydrochloric acid, whereas copper will not.
- *Acids cause acid-base indicators to change color.* Indicators are substances that have different colors when mixed in acidic and basic solutions. Table M of the *Reference Tables for Physical Setting/Chemistry* lists several common indicators and the color changes that they undergo.

Characterisitic Properties of Bases

- *Bases have a bitter taste.*
- *Bases have a slippery or soapy feeling.*
- *Bases conduct an electric current.* Note that the terminology used to describe the strength of a

base is the same as that used for acids. Thus, a solution of a base with a high concentration of ions that conducts electricity is called a strong base. Weak bases are poor conductors of electricity and are not highly ionized.

- *Bases react with acids to produce water and a salt.*
- *Bases cause acid-base indicators to change color.*

Arrhenius Theory

There have been several attempts to develop explanations for the observable properties of acids and bases. Svante Arrhenius, a Swedish chemist, proposed a commonality of all acids to explain their similar properties. An **Arrhenius acid** is defined as a substance whose water solution contains the hydrogen ion as the only positive ion. For example, hydrochloric acid ionizes in water to form hydrogen and chloride ions.

$$HCl \rightarrow H^+ + Cl^-$$

Not all substances that contain hydrogen are acids. Methane (CH_4) is an organic compound containing hydrogen, yet it is not an acid. The hydrogen atoms in methane are bonded to the carbon by covalent bonds. These hydrogen atoms do not ionize in solution: rather, they remain attached to the molecule. Because the hydrogen atoms do not form ions, methane is neither an electrolyte nor an acid.

The Nature of the Hydrogen Ion

A hydrogen atom consists of a single electron orbiting a nucleus that contains a single proton. As shown in Figure 10-1, when the hydrogen atom becomes a positive ion, the electron is lost, leaving behind the proton. Thus, a positive **hydrogen ion** is a proton.

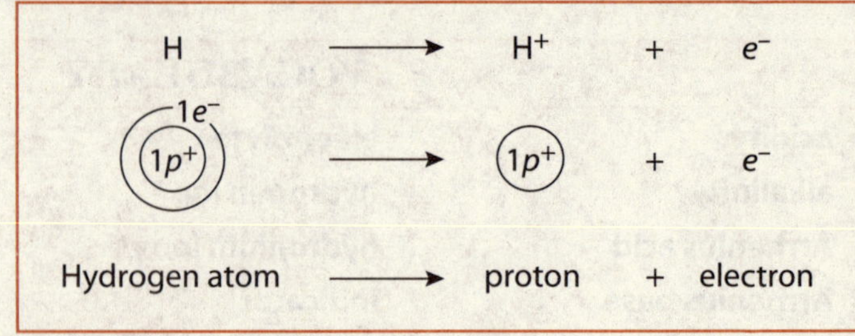

Figure 10-1. An H^+ ion is a proton.

Chemists believe that this proton cannot exist in a water solution as an isolated proton. The positively charged proton is attracted to an unshared pair of electrons in the water molecule. See Figure 10-2. The proton covalently bonds with the water forming H_3O^+, the **hydronium ion.** Acids dissolve in water and react to produce hydronium and negative ions.

$$HCl + H_2O \rightarrow H_3O^+ + Cl^-$$
$$H^+ + H_2O \rightarrow H_3O^+$$

According to the Arrhenius theory, the properties of acids are properties of the hydrogen (hydronium) ion.

As shown in the first equation above, each molecule of hydrochloric acid (HCl) that ionizes in water produces a single hydrogen ion. Hydrochloric acid and other acids that produce a single hydrogen ion are called monoprotic acids. Sulfuric acid (H_2SO_4), however, ionizes in two steps.

$$H_2SO_4 \rightarrow H^+ + HSO_4^-$$
$$HSO_4^- \rightarrow H^+ + SO_4^{2-}$$

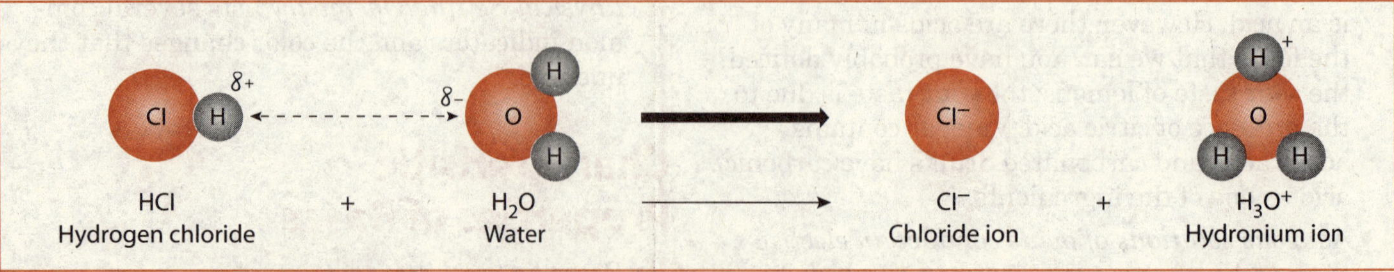

Figure 10-2. Acids react with water to produce the hydronium ion.

Each molecule of H_2SO_4 that ionizes produces two hydrogen ions. Sulfuric acid and other acids that produce two hydrogen ions are called diprotic acids. Similarly, an H_3PO_4 molecule ionizes to yield three hydrogen ions and is called a triprotic acid.

DIGGING DEEPER

Some organic compounds that are acids have chemical formulas that are somewhat misleading. These compounds contain a carboxyl group (–COOH) that gives them the appearance of a base. However, the hydrogen atom in the carboxyl group does ionize in water, thus defining these compounds as acids.

$$CH_3COOH \rightarrow H^+ + CH_3COO^-$$

The Nature of the Hydroxide Ion

In a parallel manner to acids, the properties of bases are explained as properties of the hydroxide ion (OH^-) in solution. Each **Arrhenius base** produces hydroxide ions when dissolved in water. The presence of the hydroxide ion makes the base an electrolyte. It is also the presence of the hydroxide ion that produces the slippery feel and bitter taste common to Arrhenius bases.

Ammonia (NH_3) and organic compounds called amines are bases, though at first glance their chemical formulas do not show the presence of hydroxide ions. However, ammonia reacts with water to form the ammonium and hydroxide ions.

$$NH_3 + H_2O \rightarrow NH_4{}^+ + OH^-$$

Amines are compounds containing carbon and nitrogen that are related to ammonia. Amines also react with water to produce hydroxide ions.

$$CH_3NH_2 + H_2O \rightarrow CH_3NH_3{}^+ + OH^-$$

There are also other compounds whose formulas do contain an –OH group but which are not bases. The hydroxyl group is composed of an oxygen atom and a hydrogen atom covalently bonded to a carbon chain. This group of organic compounds, called alcohols, are not bases as they do not ionize in water. Thus, they are nonelectrolytes and do not have the characteristics of bases. CH_3OH and CH_3CH_2OH are examples of alcohols, and they do not ionize to produce the hydroxide ion.

MEMORY JOGGER

Electrolytes are substances whose water solutions conduct an electric current. When there are many ions in solution, the substance is termed a strong electrolyte and is a good conductor. Weak electrolytes have relatively few ions in solution, and are poor conductors or nonconductors.

Strength of Acids and Bases

Hydrochloric acid is a dangerous acid that can cause severe injury to your skin. Citric acid is present in citrus and other fruits that we commonly eat. Even more surprising, boric acid is used as an eye-washing solution. How can we explain that these substances are all acids, yet have such different effects? The answer involves the strength of each acid.

When one hundred molecules of hydrochloric acid dissolve in water, all one hundred molecules dissociate and form ions. When an acid completely ionizes, it is called a strong acid. Other acids ionize to a much smaller degree. Perhaps only one molecule out of one hundred ionizes. Acids that ionize only slightly are called weak acids.

The degree of ionization is a function of the number of ions that are produced. Highly ionized (strong) acids and bases produce large numbers of ions. These strong acids and bases are strong electrolytes, and hence good conductors of electricity.

Naming Acids and Base

Binary acids are composed of hydrogen and one other element. Hydrogen chloride (HCl) is a molecular gas, but becomes an Arrhenius acid when it reacts with water to produce hydrogen ions. The names of binary acids begin with *hydro-* followed by the name of the other element modified to end with *–ic*. Thus, hydrogen chloride gas becomes hydrochloric acid when dissolved in water. Other binary acids are named in the same fashion.

Ternary acids are also molecular substances that produce hydrogen ions when dissolved in water. They consist of an oxygen-containing polyatomic anion such as nitrate ($NO_3{}^-$) or sulfate ($SO_4{}^{2-}$). To name a ternary acid, the anion suffixes *–ate* and *–ite* usually are replaced by the suffixes *–ic* and *–ous* respectively. For example,

HNO_3 is nitric acid. Sometimes the names are modified slightly, as in H_2SO_4, sul<u>furic</u> acid. Table 10-1 lists the names of several common acids.

Table 10-1. Names of Several Acids and Their Ions

Acid Name	Formula of Acid	Anion Name
Hydrochloric	HCl	chloride
Sulfuric	H_2SO_4	sulfate
Sulfurous	H_2SO_3	sulfite
Nitric	HNO_3	nitrate
Nitrous	HNO_2	nitrite

Bases are quite simple to name. The name of the positive ion is not modified, and the name of the base ends with hydroxide. For example, $Ca(OH)_2$ is named calcium hydroxide.

Review Questions

1. According to the Arrhenius theory, when an acidic substance is dissolved in water it will produce a solution containing only one kind of positive ion. To which ion does the theory refer? (1) acetate (2) hydrogen (3) chloride (4) sodium

2. When an Arrhenius base is dissolved in H_2O, the only negative ion present in the solution is (1) OH^- (2) H_3O^- (3) H^- (4) O^{2-}

3. According to the Arrhenius theory of acids, citric acid in oranges and acetic acid in vinegar are classified as acids because their aqueous solutions contain (1) hydrogen ions (2) hydrogen atoms (3) hydroxide ions (4) hydroxide atoms

4. In an aqueous solution, which substance yields hydrogen ions as the only positive ion? (1) C_2H_5OH (2) CH_3COOH (3) KH (4) KOH

5. Which compound is an electrolyte? (1) $C_6H_{12}O_6$ (2) $C_{12}H_{22}O_{11}$ (3) CH_3CH_2OH (4) CH_3COOH

6. If 1 mol of each of the following substances were dissolved in 1 L of water, which solution would contain the highest concentration of OH^- ions? (1) H_2SO_4 (2) NH_4Cl (3) KNO_3 (4) $NaOH$

7. If 1 mol of each of the following substances were dissolved in 1 L of water, which solution would contain the highest concentration of H_3O^+ ions? (1) CH_3COOH (2) $NaCl$ (3) KBr (4) $Ba(OH)_2$

8. When substance X is dissolved in water, the only positive ions in the solution are hydrogen ions. Substance X could be (1) $NaOH$ (2) NaH (3) H_2S (4) NH_3

9. Which species is classified as an Arrhenius base? (1) CH_3OH (2) $LiOH$ (3) PO_4^{3-} (4) CO_3^{2-}

10. As 1 g of sodium hydroxide dissolves in 100 g of water, the conductivity of the water (1) decreases (2) increases (3) remains the same

11. A solution of a base differs from a solution of an acid in that the solution of a base (1) is able to conduct electricity (2) is able to cause an indicator color change (3) has a greater $[H_3O^+]$ (4) has a greater $[OH^-]$

12. A solution of hydrochloric acid is a stronger acid than a solution of acetic acid of the same concentration because (1) it has more hydrogen ions in solution (2) it has more hydroxide ions in solution (3) it has fewer hydrogen ions in solution (4) it has fewer hydroxide ions in solution.

13. When an Arrhenius acid is dissolved in water, it produces (1) H^+ as the only positive ion in solution (2) NH_3^+ as the only positive ion in solution (3) OH^- as the only negative ion in solution (4) HCO_3^- as the only negative ion in solution

14. What would be the name of ClO_3^- if the name of $HClO_3$ is chloric acid?

15. Name the following acids and bases.
    (a) H_2S
    (b) HBr
    (c) $LiOH$
    (d) $Mg(OH)_2$

16. A student tests the conductivity of an unknown substance and determines it to be a good conductor of electricity. Based on this he decides that it is an acid. Criticize the student's conclusion. Is there enough evidence to warrant the conclusion? What additional test or tests could be performed to confirm the conclusion? For each test, indicate the result that would verify the substance to be an acid.

Reactions Involving Acids and Bases

Chemical reactions involving acids and bases are common in industrial and consumer applications, natural processes, and in classroom experiments.

Acids and bases undergo many reactions because they are able to react with each other as well as with other compounds and elements.

Reactions of Acids with Metals

You may recall from Topic 2 that any element in Table J of the *Reference Tables for Physical Setting/Chemistry* will react with the ion of any element below it. Note that hydrogen (H_2) is found near the bottom of the table. Thus, any metal above hydrogen in the table will react with a hydrogen-containing acid to produce H_2 and a salt. The reaction between zinc and hydrochloric acid is an example.

$$Zn(s) + 2HCl(aq) \rightarrow H_2(g) + ZnCl_2(aq)$$

Copper, which is below hydrogen in the table, will not react with a hydrogen-containing acid to produce hydrogen gas.

> **MEMORY JOGGER**
>
> Single-replacement reactions have the general formula:
>
> $$A + BC \rightarrow AC + B$$

Neutralization Reactions

In a neutralization reaction, an Arrhenius acid reacts with an Arrhenius base to produce water and a salt. There are several ways that these reactions can be expressed. For example, consider the neutralization reaction between hydrochloric acid (HCl) and sodium hydroxide (NaOH).

This reaction can be expressed as a word equation:

Hydrochloric acid + Sodium hydroxide → Water + Sodium chloride

Substituting the chemical formulas for words yields the formula equation:

$$HCl(aq) + NaOH(aq) \rightarrow H_2O(\ell) + NaCl(aq)$$

Writing the equation to take the ions in solution into account yields the ionic equation:

$$H^+(aq) + Cl^-(aq) + Na^+(aq) + OH^-(aq) \rightarrow H_2O(\ell) + Na^+(aq) + Cl^-(aq)$$

Note that the sodium and chloride ions are present on both sides of the reaction arrow. Because they have not taken part in the reaction, they are called spectator ions and can be omitted.

$$H^+(aq) + \cancel{Cl^-(aq)} + \cancel{Na^+(aq)} + OH^-(aq) \rightarrow H_2O(\ell) + \cancel{Na^+(aq)} + \cancel{Cl^-(aq)}$$

Omitting the spectator ions yields the net ionic equation:

$$H^+(aq) + OH^-(aq) \rightarrow H_2O(\ell)$$

Because hydrogen ions exist in solution as hydronium ions (H_3O^+), this equation can also be written as the reaction between hydronium and hydroxide ions.

$$H_3O^+(aq) + OH^-(aq) \rightarrow 2H_2O(\ell)$$

All neutralization reactions have the same net equation. The Arrhenius definition is able to explain the process of neutralization as a reaction between hydrogen (hydronium) ions and hydroxide ions to form water and a salt.

> **MEMORY JOGGER**
>
> When writing equations, first write correct formulas using charges and subscripts. Then, balance the equation using coefficients.

WRITING NEUTRALIZATION REACTIONS

Writing neutralization reactions is not a difficult task, as shown in the following Sample Problem.

> **SAMPLE PROBLEM**
>
> Write the equation for the neutralization reaction between dilute nitric acid and potassium hydroxide.
>
> **Solution:** Identify the known and unknown values.
>
> *Known*
> reactant 1 = nitric acid (HNO_3)
> reactant 2 = potassium hydroxide (KOH)
>
> *Unknown*
> neutralization equation = ?
>
> Write a simple word equation for the neutralization reaction.
>
> acid + base → water + salt
>
> Substitute the known compounds into the general word equation.
>
> HNO_3 + KOH → water + salt
>
> Picture a box enclosing the hydroxide (OH^-) of the base and the hydrogen (H^+) of the acid. These particles combine to form water (H_2O).
>
> HNO_3 + KOH → H_2O + salt

The remaining K^+ and NO_3^- ions combine to form the salt KNO_3.

$$HNO_3 + KOH \rightarrow H_2O + KNO_3$$

Now check to see that the equation is balanced. Because the hydroxide and hydrogen ions combine in a 1:1 ratio to form water molecules, they must be present in equal numbers. If needed, the coefficients of the acid and the base are adjusted to balance these ions. In this example, there is one hydroxide ion and one hydrogen ion, so the coefficients are both 1. A coefficient of 1 is not written; the above equation is balanced. Note that the spectator ions form the salt.

MEMORY JOGGER

When writing the formula of the salt in a neutralization reaction, check the charge on both ions. If the ionic charges are not equal and opposite, write the charge of one ion as the subscript of the other.

When a diprotic acid reacts with a dihydroxy base, there are two hydrogen ions and two hydroxide ions. These will combine to form two molecules of water. The remaining ions will form the salt.

$$Ca(OH)_2 + H_2SO_4 \rightarrow 2H_2O + CaSO_4$$

Combinations of acids and bases that do not have an equal number of hydroxide and hydrogen ions are also easy to balance. Consider the following unbalanced equation:

$$Mg(OH)_2 + HCl \rightarrow H_2O + MgCl_2$$

Note that there are two hydroxide ions but only one hydrogen ion. Placing a 2 in front of the HCl balances the hydroxide and hydrogen ions that form two molecules of water. The 2 coefficient also supplies the two chloride ions needed to form the salt. The equation is now balanced:

$$Mg(OH)_2 + 2HCl \rightarrow 2H_2O + MgCl_2$$

Salts

As you learned earlier, when a metal reacts with an acid, hydrogen gas and a salt are formed. In a neutralization reaction, an acid and a base react to form water and a salt. The salts in these reactions are ionic substances composed of positively charged metallic or polyatomic ions, and negative ions other than hydroxide ions. Sodium chloride (NaCl) and ammonium phosphate ($(NH_4)_3PO_4$) are examples of salts. Salts are named by using the name of the positive ion of the base, and the negative ion of the acid.

DIGGING DEEPER

Because salts are produced by neutralization, it would seem logical that a salt would be neutral, that is, neither acidic nor basic. There are, however, acidic, basic, and neutral salts. Salts that were formed from a strong acid and a strong base are neutral salts. If the salt was formed by the reaction of a strong acid and a weak base, it will be acidic. If the opposite is the case, that is, a salt formed from a strong base and a weak acid, the salt will be basic. The acidity or basicity of a salt formed from a weak acid and a weak base must be evaluated on a case-by-case basis.

Review Questions

17. According to the *Reference Tables for Physical Setting/Chemistry*, which metal would react spontaneously with hydrochloric acid? (1) gold (2) silver (3) copper (4) zinc

18. According to the *Reference Tables for Physical Setting/Chemistry*, which of the following metals will react most readily with HCl to release hydrogen gas? (1) aluminum (2) copper (3) silver (4) gold

19. Which metal will release $H_2(g)$ when it reacts with HCl? (1) Au(*s*) (2) Zn(*s*) (3) Hg(*ℓ*) (4) Ag(*s*)

20. The reaction between one mole of hydrogen ions and one mole of hydroxide ions is called (1) oxidation (2) reduction (3) hydrolysis (4) neutralization

21. Which type of reaction occurs when equal volumes of 0.1M HCl and 0.1M NaOH are mixed? (1) neutralization (2) ionization (3) electrolysis (4) hydrolysis

22. Which type of reaction occurs when 50-mL quantities of 1 M $Ba(OH)_2(aq)$ and $H_2SO_4(aq)$ are combined? (1) hydrolysis (2) ionization (3) hydrogenation (4) neutralization

23. Which compound reacts with an acid to produce water and a salt? (1) CH_3Cl (2) CH_3COOH (3) KCl (4) KOH

24. How much water is formed when 1.0 mol of HCl reacts completely with 1.0 mol of NaOH?
(1) 1.0 mol (2) 2.0 mol (3) 0.50 mol (4) 0.25 mol

25. A water solution contains 0.50 mol of HCl. How much NaOH should be added to the HCl solution to exactly neutralize it? (1) 1.0 mol (2) 2.0 mol (3) 0.25 mol (4) 0.50 mol

26. Which is the net ionic equation for a neutralization?
(1) $H^+ + H_2O \rightarrow H_3O^+$ (2) $H^+ + NH_3 \rightarrow NH_4^+$
(3) $2H^+ + 2O^{2-} \rightarrow 2OH^-$ (4) $H^+ + OH^- \rightarrow H_2O$

27. Which substance is always produced by a neutralization reaction? (1) water (2) acid (3) ester (4) base

28. Which products are formed when an acid reacts with a base? (1) an alcohol and carbon dioxide (2) an ester and water (3) a soap and glycerin (4) a salt and water

29. Which compound is a salt? (1) Na_3PO_4 (2) H_3PO_4 (3) CH_3COOH (4) $Ca(OH)_2$

30. Which compound is classified as a salt?
(1) CH_3COOH (2) C_2H_5OH (3) NaOH (4) $NaC_2H_3O_2$

31. Which formula represents a salt? (1) KOH (2) KCl (3) CH_3OH (4) CH_3COOH

32. The diagram below shows an acid being added to a base.

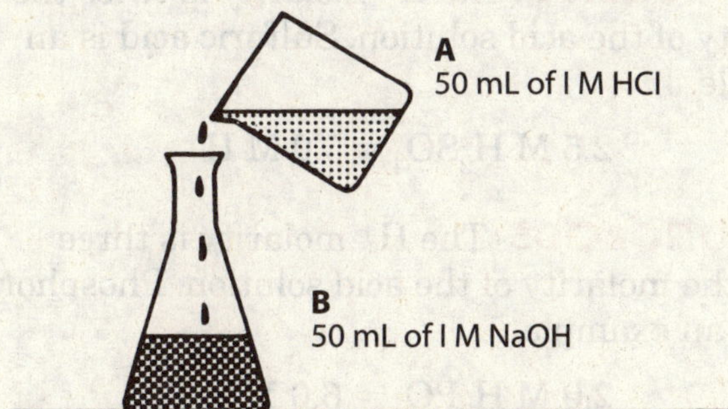

As the acid in beaker A is added to the base in flask B, the number of OH^- ions in flask B

(1) decreases and the number of Na^+ ions decreases

(2) increases and the number of Na^+ ions decreases

(3) decreases and the number of Na^+ ions remains the same

(4) increases and the number of Na^+ ions remains the same

33. The diagram below illustrates an apparatus used to test the conductivity of various solutions.

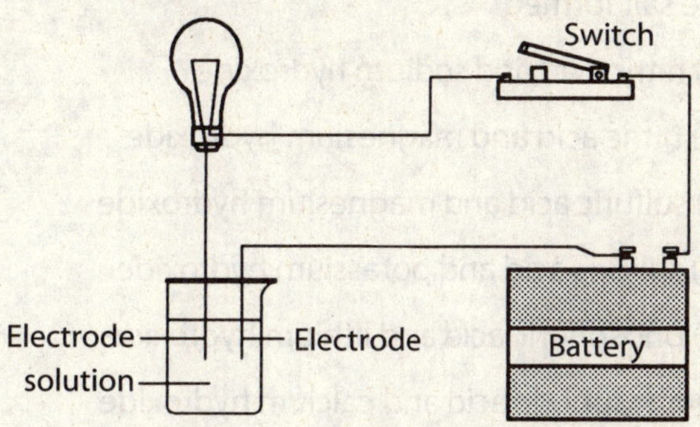

When the switch is closed, which of the following 1-molar solutions would cause the bulb to glow most brightly?

(1) ammonia (3) carbonic acid

(2) acetic acid (4) sulfuric acid

34. Which salt is formed when hydrochloric acid is neutralized by a potassium hydroxide solution?

(1) potassium chloride (3) potassium chlorite

(2) potassium chlorate (4) potassium perchlorate

35. In the neutralization reaction between hydrochloric acid and sodium hydroxide, the spectator ions are (1) H^+ and OH^- (2) Cl^- and OH^- (3) Na^+ and H^+ (4) Na^+ and Cl^-

36. When NaOH(*aq*) reacts completely with HCl(*aq*) and the resulting solution is evaporated to dryness, the solid remaining is (1) an ester (2) an alcohol (3) a salt (4) a metal

37. Name each of the following.

(a) HF

(b) H_2Se

(c) HI

38. Consult Table J in the *Reference Tables for Physical Setting/Chemistry* to determine if the following reactions actually occur. If a reaction does occur, write the correctly balanced equation. If the reaction does not occur, write "No reaction."

(a) calcium and hydrochloric acid

(b) zinc and dilute nitric acid

(c) lead and carbonic acid

(d) aluminum and acetic acid

(e) copper and phosphoric acid

39. Write the balanced equation for each of the following neutralization reactions, and write the name of the salt formed.

(a) nitric acid and sodium hydroxide

(b) nitric acid and magnesium hydroxide

(c) sulfuric acid and magnesium hydroxide

(d) sulfuric acid and potassium hydroxide

(e) phosphoric acid and lithium hydroxide

(f) phosphoric acid and calcium hydroxide

Acid–Base Titration

Titration is the process of adding measured volumes of an acid or a base of known concentration to an acid or a base of unknown concentration until neutralization occurs. The solution of known concentration is called the standard solution. Knowing the volumes of acid and base used in the titration, together with the known concentration of the standard solution, it is possible to calculate the concentration of the unknown solution.

In all neutralization reactions there must be a 1:1 ratio between the moles of hydrogen ions (H^+) and the moles of hydroxide ions (OH^-). The equation for concentration shows the relationship among number of moles, volume in liters, and molarity.

$$\text{molarity} = \frac{\text{moles}}{\text{volume}}$$

or

$$\text{moles} = \text{molarity} \times \text{volume}$$

In a neutralization reaction, the number of moles of H^+ ions must equal the number of moles of OH^- ions. Thus, equating mol H^+ and mol OH^- yields the following equation.

$$\text{molarity } H^+ \times \text{volume}_{\text{acid}} = \text{molarity } OH^- \times \text{volume}_{\text{base}}$$

or

$$M_A \times V_A = M_B \times V_B$$

In the above equation, M_A = molarity of H^+, V_A = volume of acid in milliliters, M_B = molarity of OH^-, and V_B = volume of base in milliliters.

To solve any titration problem, the molarity of the acid and base must be expressed as the molarity of the hydrogen ion (H^+) and the molarity of the hydroxide ion (OH^-), respectively. In the case of monoprotic acids such as HCl, the molarity of the H^+ is the same as the molarity of the acid. Thus, a 2.0 M HCl solution has a 2.0 M H^+ concentration. The same applies to monohydroxy bases. That is, a 2.5 M NaOH solution has a 2.5 M OH^- concentration.

The case is different for diprotic and triprotic acids. Consider the complete ionization of a 1.0 M solution of sulfuric acid (H_2SO_4).

$$H_2SO_4(aq) \rightarrow 2H^+(aq) + SO_4^{2-}(aq)$$

One liter of 1.0 M solution of H_2SO_4 yields 2 mol of H^+ ions. The molarity of the H^+ ions will be twice the molarity of the acid solution. Similarly, a triprotic acid produces an H^+ ion molarity three times that of the molarity of the acid solution.

The following examples summarize the relationships between the concentration of an acid or base and the resulting concentration of hydrogen ions (H^+) or hydroxide ions (OH^-) in solution for mono-, di-, and triprotic acids and mono- and dihydroxy bases.

MONOPROTIC ACIDS The H^+ molarity equals the molarity of the acid solution. Hydrochloric acid is an example.

$$2.5 \text{ M HCl} = 2.5 \text{ M } H^+$$

DIPROTIC ACIDS The H^+ molarity is twice the molarity of the acid solution. Sulfuric acid is an example.

$$2.5 \text{ M } H_2SO_4 = 5.0 \text{ M } H^+$$

TRIPROTIC ACIDS The H^+ molarity is three times the molarity of the acid solution. Phosphoric acid is an example.

$$2.0 \text{ M } H_3PO_4 = 6.0 \text{ M } H^+$$

MONOHYDROXY BASES The OH^- molarity equals the molarity of the base solution. Sodium hydroxide is an example.

$$3.0 \text{ M NaOH} = 3.0 \text{ M } OH^-$$

DIHYDROXY BASES The OH^- molarity is twice the molarity of the base solution. Barium hydroxide is an example.

$$0.5 \text{ M Ba(OH)}_2 = 1.0 \text{ M } OH^-$$

MEMORY JOGGER

Square brackets [ ] are used to indicate concentration of a particle in units of moles per liter, molarity (M). For example, $[OH^-]$ stands for the concentration of OH^- ions in units of moles of OH^- per liter of solution.

SAMPLE PROBLEM

What is the concentration of a hydrochloric acid solution if 50.0 mL of a 0.250 M KOH are needed to neutralize 20.0 mL of the HCl solution of unknown concentration?

Solution: Identify the known and unknown values.

Known	*Unknown*
molarity of KOH = 0.250 M	M_A = molarity of HCl = ? M
V_B = volume of KOH = 50.0 mL	
V_A = volume of HCl = 20.0 mL	

Write the balanced equation for the neutralization reaction.

$$KOH + HCl \rightarrow H_2O + KCl$$

Determine the molarity of the hydroxide ion. Because KOH is a monohydroxy base, the molarity of the hydroxide ion is the same as the molarity of the base solution.

$$M_B = \text{molarity KOH} = 0.250\text{ M}$$

Solve the neutralization reaction equation for M_A, substitute the known values, and solve.

$$M_A \times V_A = M_B \times V_B$$
$$M_A = (M_B \times V_B)/V_A$$
$$M_A = \frac{(0.250\text{ M})(50.0\text{ mL})}{20.0\text{ mL}}$$
$$M_A = 0.625\text{ M}$$

The molarity of the hydrogen ion is 0.625 M. Because HCl is a monprotic acid, the molarity of the acid is also 0.625 M.

SAMPLE PROBLEM

What is the concentration of a sulfuric acid solution if 50. mL of a 0.25 M KOH are needed to neutralize 20. mL of the H_2SO_4 solution of unknown concentration?

Solution: Identify the known and unknown values.

Known	*Unknown*
molarity of KOH = 0.25 M	M_A = molarity of H_2SO_4 = ? M
V_B = volume of KOH = 50. mL	
V_A = volume of H_2SO_4 = 20. mL	

Write the balanced equation for the neutralization reaction.

$$2KOH + H_2SO_4 \rightarrow 2H_2O + K_2SO_4$$

Determine the molarity of the hydroxide ion. Because KOH is a monohydroxy base, the molarity of the hydroxide ion is the same as the molarity of base solution.

$$M_B = \text{molarity KOH} = 0.25\text{ M}$$

Solve the neutralization reaction equation for M_A, substitute the known values, and solve.

$$M_A \times V_A = M_B \times V_B$$
$$M_A = (M_B \times V_B)/V_A$$
$$M_A = \frac{(0.250\text{ M})(50.0\text{ mL})}{20.0\text{ mL}}$$
$$M_A = 0.625\text{ M}$$

To determine the molarity of the H_2SO_4, adjust for the fact that the acid is diprotic. That is, the molarity of the acid is only half that of the hydrogen ion.

$$\text{molarity } H_2SO_4 = \frac{[H^+]}{2} = \frac{0.625\text{ M}}{2} = 0.31\text{ M}$$

Review Questions

40. Which compound reacts with an acid to form a salt and water? (1) CH_3F (2) C_2H_5COOH (3) LiCl (4) LiOH

41. To neutralize 1 mol of sulfuric acid, 2 mol of sodium hydroxide are required. How many liters of 1 M NaOH are needed to exactly neutralize 1 L of 1 M H_2SO_4? (1) 1 (2) 2 (3) 0.5 (4) 4

42. How many moles of sodium hydroxide (NaOH) are required to completely neutralize 2 mol of nitric acid (HNO_3)? (1) 1 (2) 2 (3) 40 (4) 63

43. During an acid-base neutralization, how many moles of hydroxide ions will react with one mole of hydrogen ions? (1) 1.0 mol (2) 0.5 mol (3) 17.0 mol (4) 22.4 mol

44. How many moles of KOH are needed to exactly neutralize 500. mL of 1.0 M HCl? (1) 1.0 mol (2) 2.0 mol (3) 0.25 mol (4) 0.50 mol

45. One liter of 1 M NaOH will completely neutralize one liter of (1) 1 M H_2SO_4 (2) 0.5 M H_2SO_4 (3) 2 M H_2SO_4 (4) 1.5 M H_2SO_4

For questions 46–54, show all of your work.

46. Consider the following reaction.

$$KOH + HCl \rightarrow H_2O + HOH$$

How many milliliters of 2.0 M KOH are necessary to neutralize 50. mL of 1.0 M HCl?

47. How many milliliters of 0.20 M H_2SO_4 are required to completely neutralize 40. mL of 0.10 M $Ca(OH)_2$?

48. How many milliliters of 2.5 M HCl are required to exactly neutralize 1.5 L of 5.0 M NaOH?

49. How many milliliters of 0.200 M NaOH are needed to neutralize 100. mL of 0.100 M HCl?

50. A 2.0-mL sample of NaOH solution is exactly neutralized by 4.0 mL of 3.0 M HCl solution. What is the concentration of the NaOH solution?

51. A 10.-mL sample of hydrochloric acid neutralizes 15 mL of a 0.40 M solution of NaOH. What is the molarity of the hydrochloric acid?

52. How many mL of 0.20 M hydrochloric acid is required to neutralize 100. mL of 0.80 M potassium hydroxide?

53. A 3.0-mL sample of HNO_3 solution is exactly neutralized by 6.0 mL of 0.50 M KOH. What is the molarity of the HNO_3 solution?

54. What is the molarity of hydrogen ions in a 2.7 M solution of the strong acid HCl?

55. Write the electron dot diagram of a hydrogen chloride molecule.

56. Write the electron dot diagram for the hydronium ion (H_3O^+).

57. Write the electron dot diagram for the hydroxide ion (OH^-).

58. Write the word equation form of the net ionic equation for all neutralization equations.

59. Write the electron dot diagram for the net ionic equation for a neutralization reaction. Be sure to include the charge on any ionic substance.

60. Phosphoric acid is neutralized by a solution of sodium hydroxide. What is the name of the salt formed from the neutralization?

Acidity and Alkalinity of Solutions

Although water is a covalently bonded substance, it does ionize to a very small extent as shown by the equation below.

$$HOH \leftrightarrow H^+ + OH^-$$

It can be seen that in pure water $[H^+] = [OH^-]$. Le Châtelier's principle tells us that if one of these factors increases, the other decreases. When HCl is added to pure water, the concentration of the hydrogen ion increases, and the concentration of the hydroxide ion decreases. When $[H^+] > [OH^-]$, the solution is acidic. If the reverse is true, and the concentration of OH^- is greater than the concentration of the H^+, the solution is alkaline, or basic. The terms **acidity** and **alkalinity** (or basicity) refer to the relative strength of the acid or base in terms of their H^+ and OH^- concentrations.

pH Scale

A scale, called the **pH scale,** has been developed to express $[H^+]$ as a number from 0 to 14. A pH of 0 is strongly acidic, a pH of 7 is neutral, and a pH of 14 is strongly basic. The pH scale is logarithmic. Each change of a single pH unit signifies a tenfold change in the concentration of the hydrogen ion. Thus the $[H^+]$ is ten times greater in a solution with a pH of 5 as in a solution with a pH of 6.

Because $[H^+]$ and $[OH^-]$ are directly related, a pH change of one unit represents a tenfold increase or decrease of both the hydrogen ion and hydroxide ion concentration. As the concentration of the hydrogen ion increases, the concentration of the hydroxide ion decreases.

Acid-Base Indicators

An **indicator** is a substance that changes its color when it gains or loses a proton. Phenolphthalein is a common indicator that is colorless when it is protonated, that is, when it contains a hydrogen atom. When a base is gradually added to an acid containing phenolphthalein, the solution is initially colorless. Once the acid has been neutralized by the addition of the base, the base then reacts with the hydrogen atom of the indicator. As the phenolphthalein loses its hydrogen (proton), it turns pink. This color change is why phenolphthalein is an indicator; the color change in the phenolphthalein shows (indicates) when a titration has reached an end point.

Other indicators react in a similar way to phenolphthalein, but each has a unique color change that occurs over a specific pH range. Table M of the *Reference Tables for Physical Setting/Chemistry* lists several common indicators, the color changes they undergo, and the pH range over which the color change occurs.

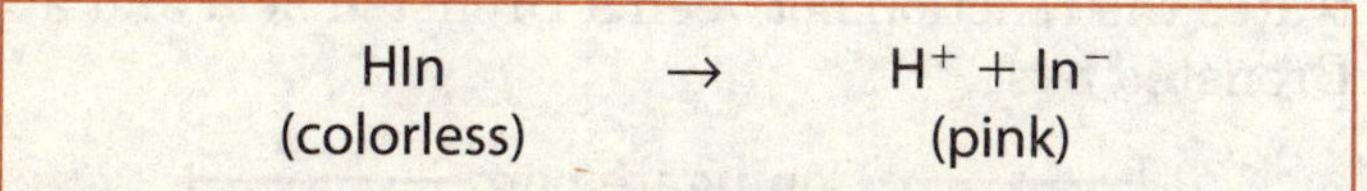

Figure 10-3. Color change in phenolphthalein: Indicators are weak acids that have different colors depending on the presence or absence of hydrogen. In the diagram above, HIn represents the indicator phenolphthalein.

Another example of an indicator is methyl orange. An acid solution with a pH of 2.0 containing methyl orange is red in color. As a base is added to the acid solution, the pH slowly increases. Between pH 3.2 and 4.4, the solution contains both the red and the yellow forms of the indicator, resulting in an orange color. When a pH of 4.4 is achieved, there is no longer an appreciable number of red molecules present, and the solution appears yellow. This same process occurs in other indicators as well. That is, indicators tend to have a distinct color at each end of their useful pH range and pass through an intermediate color region that is a mixture of these two colors.

Review Questions

61. Which pH value indicates the most basic solution? (1) 7 (2) 8 (3) 3 (4) 11

62. Which pH value represents a solution with the lowest OH^- ion concentration? (1) 1 (2) 7 (3) 10 (4) 14

63. When tested, a solution turns red litmus to blue. This indicates that the solution contains more (1) H^+ ions than OH^- ions (2) H_3O^+ ions than OH^- ions (3) OH^- ions than H_3O^+ ions (4) H^+ and OH^- ions than H_2O molecules

64. Pure water at 25°C has a pH of (1) 1 (2) 5 (3) 7 (4) 14

65. If an aqueous solution turns blue litmus red, which relationship exists between the hydronium ion and hydroxide ion?
(1) $[H_3O^+] < [OH^-]$ (3) $[H_3O^+] > [OH^-]$
(2) $[H_3O^+] = [OH^-]$ (4) neither ion is present

66. The pH of a 0.1 M CH_3COOH solution is (1) less than 1 (2) greater than 1, but less than 7 (3) equal to 7 (4) greater than 7 but less than 14

67. As 0.1 M HCl is added to 0.1 M KOH, the pH of the basic solution (1) decreases and the basicity decreases (2) decreases and the acidity decreases (3) increases and the basicity decreases (4) increases and the acidity decreases

68. As an acidic solution is added to a basic solution, the pH of the basic solution (1) decreases (2) increases (3) remains the same

69. As the H_3O^+ ion concentration of a solution increases, the pH of the solution (1) decreases (2) increases (3) remains the same

70. As a strong acid is added to a beaker containing NaOH, the number of OH^- ions in the beaker (1) decreases and the number of Na^+ ions decreases (2) decreases and the number of Na^+ ions remains the same (3) increases and the number of Na^+ ions decreases (4) increases and the number of Na^+ ions remains the same

71. An indicator was used to test a water solution with a pH of 12. Which indicator color would be observed? (1) colorless phenolphthalein (2) red litmus (3) colorless litmus (4) pink phenolphthalein

Answer questions 72–75 using complete sentences.

72. A blue solution containing an acid-base indicator was tested with a pH meter and found to have a pH of 5.5. Which of the indicators on Table M of the *Reference Tables for Physical Setting/Chemistry* could be this indicator?

73. A solution was yellow in bromthymol blue and blue in bromcresol green. According to Table M of the *Reference Tables for Physical Setting/Chemistry*, what could be the pH of the solution?

74. A solution was tested with a pH meter and found to have a pH of 7.8. What color would the solution have if the following indicators were added?

(a) bromthymol blue

(b) thymol blue

75. Acid was added to a solution containing an indicator until the solution turned from blue to yellow. Which of the following would be most acidic?

(a) a yellow solution containing bromthymol blue

(b) a yellow solution containing bromcresol green

(c) a yellow solution containing thymol blue

ADDITIONAL MATERIAL

The coverage of Brønsted-Lowry theory and conjugate acid-base pairs on page 150 is not required by the Regents core curriculum in chemistry. You will not be tested on these topics in the Regents Examination for The Physical Setting/Chemistry.

Brønsted-Lowry Acids and Bases

There are other acid-base definitions that expand upon the Arrhenius definition of acids and bases. One of these, the Brønsted-Lowry theory, defines an acid as any substance that donates a hydrogen ion (H^+). As you know, a hydrogen ion is a hydrogen atom without an electron, that is, it is simply a proton. Thus, a Brønsted-Lowry acid is defined as a proton donor. All Arrhenius acids are also Brønsted-Lowry acids. Brønsted-Lowry theory expands upon the Arrhenius concept by including proton donors that are not in aqueous solution.

The Brønsted-Lowry theory defines a base as any substance that accepts a proton (H^+). Like the Arrhenius definition, the Brønsted-Lowry definition treats the hydroxide ion (OH^-) as a base. Compared with the Arrhenius definition, however, the Brønsted-Lowry definition greatly expands the number of substances that are considered bases.

CONJUGATE ACID-BASE PAIRS When an acid loses a proton, the remaining portion of the acid has an unshared pair of electrons that can act as a base. Consider the following reaction.

$$HCl \rightarrow H^+ + Cl^-$$

HCl is an acid because it donates a proton. The chloride ion is a base because it is capable of accepting a proton to form HCl. Note that HCl and Cl^- differ only by a hydrogen ion (H^+). A pair of chemical formulas that differ only by the presence of a hydrogen ion are known as a conjugate acid-base pair. HCl cannot donate a proton unless there is a proton acceptor (base) available to accept the proton.

The reaction between HNO_3 and water illustrates the reaction between a Brønsted acid and a Brønsted base.

Conjugate pair (HNO_3 / NO_3^-)

Conjugate pair (H_2O / H_3O^+)

$$\underset{\text{acid}}{HNO_3} + \underset{\text{base}}{H_2O} \rightarrow \underset{\text{acid}}{H_3O^+} + \underset{\text{base}}{NO_3^-}$$

The HNO_3 acts as an acid, donating its proton to the water (which acts as a base) producing the hydronium and nitrate ions. If the reaction is reversed, the hydronium ion acts as an acid, donating its proton to the nitrate ion (which acts as a base) to produce nitric acid and water. Note that HNO_3 and NO_3^- are a conjugate acid-base pair because they differ by a hydrogen ion. Likewise, H_2O and H_3O^+ are also a conjugate acid-base pair.

LEWIS ACIDS AND BASES In still a further expansion of the definition of acids and bases, the great American chemist Gilbert Lewis defined acids as electron acceptors and bases as electron donors. Each of the acid-base definitions has advantages for certain situations. In terms of the concepts needed to answer acid-base questions on the Regents Examination in Chemistry, understanding the Arrhenius acid-base definitions are adequate.

Questions for Regents Practice

Part A

1. According to the Arrhenius theory, the only negative ions in an aqueous solution of a base are

(1) OH^- ions

(2) HS^- ions

(3) H^- ions

(4) HCO_3^- ions

2. Which statement best describes the solution produced when an Arrhenius acid is dissolved in water?

(1) The only negative ion in solution is OH^-.

(2) The only negative ion in solution is HCO_3^-.

(3) The only positive ion in solution is H^+.

(4) The only positive ion in solution is NH_4^+.

3. Which substance can act as an Arrhenius acid in aqueous solution?

(1) NaI

(2) HI

(3) LiH

(4) NH_3

4. Unlike an acid, an aqueous solution of a base

(1) causes some indicators to change color

(2) conducts electricity

(3) contains more H^+ than OH^-

(4) contains more OH^- than H^+

5. According to the Arrhenius theory, when a base is dissolved in water it will produce a solution containing only one kind of negative ion. To which ion does the theory refer?

(1) hydride

(2) hydroxide

(3) hydrogen

(4) hydronium

6. Acidic solutions are those that contain an excess of

(1) H_2 molecules

(2) H_2O molecules

(3) H^+ ions

(4) OH^- ions

7. What are the relative ion concentrations in an acid solution?

(1) more H^+ ions than OH^- ions

(2) fewer H^+ ions than OH^- ions

(3) an equal number of H^+ ions and OH^- ions

(4) H^+ ions, but no OH^- ions

8. What color is phenolphthalein in a basic solution?

(1) blue (3) yellow

(2) pink (4) colorless

9. Which substance is always produced by a neutralization reaction?

(1) water (3) ester

(2) acid (4) base

10. The reaction between one mole of hydrogen ions and one mole of hydroxide ions is called

(1) oxidation

(2) reduction

(3) hydrolysis

(4) neutralization

11. Pure water has a pH of

(1) 1 (3) 10

(2) 7 (4) 4

Part B

12. Which substance is classified as a salt?

(1) $Ca(OH)_2$

(2) C_2H_4OH

(3) CCl_4

(4) $CaCl_2$

13. Consider this neutralization reaction.

$$H_2SO_4 + 2KOH \rightarrow K_2SO_4 + 2HOH$$

Which compound is a salt?

(1) KOH

(2) H_2SO_4

(3) K_2SO_4

(4) HOH

14. An aqueous solution turns litmus red. The pH of the solution could be

(1) 14

(2) 11

(3) 8

(4) 4

15. If equal volumes of 0.1 M NaOH and 0.1 M HCl are mixed, the resulting solution will contain a salt and

(1) HCl

(2) NaOH

(3) H_2O

(4) NaCl

16. If equal volumes of 0.1 M NaOH and 0.1 M H_2SO_4 are mixed, the resulting solution will contain water,

(1) H_2SO_4 and Na_2SO_4

(2) H_2SO_4 and NaOH

(3) NaOH and Na_2SO_4

(4) and Na_2SO_4

17. A sample of a solution with a pH of 10 is tested separately with phenolphthalein and litmus. The colors of the indicators are as follows:

(1) litmus is blue; phenolphthalein is pink

(2) litmus is red; phenolphthalein is pink

(3) litmus is blue; phenolphthalein is colorless

(4) litmus is red; phenolphthalein is colorless

18. A student observes that an unknown solution conducts electricity and turns blue litmus red. The student should be able to conclude that the unknown solution is most likely

(1) an acid

(2) a base

(3) an ester

(4) an alcohol

19. An aqueous solution of an ionic compound turns red litmus blue, conducts electricity, and reacts with an acid to form a salt and water. This compound could be

(1) HCl

(2) NaI

(3) KNO_3

(4) LiOH

20. What will be the concentration of 150. mL of a 2.4 M NaOH solution if it is diluted to form 200. mL of solution? (1) 1.6 M (2) 1.8 M (3) 2.0 M (4) 3.2 M

21. Both HNO_3 and CH_3COOH can be classified as

(1) Arrhenius acids that turn blue litmus red

(2) Arrhenius bases that turn blue litmus red

(3) Arrhenius acids that turn red litmus blue

(4) Arrhenius bases that turn red litmus blue

22. A substance is added to a water solution containing phenolphthalein, causing the solution to turn pink. Which substance would produce this result?

(1) $HC_2H_3O_2$

(2) H_2CO_3

(3) KOH

(4) CH_3OH

23. A student accidentally spills an unknown chemical on her hand. She quickly washes it off, and notices that her skin feels slippery. She has a electrical conductivity tester at her lab station and tests the conductivity of the solution. It is a good conductor of electricity. She then places a strip of litmus paper in a sample of the liquid and it turns blue. She can conclude that the liquid is

(1) a strong base

(2) a weak base

(3) a strong acid

(4) a weak acid

24. What ions are present in a 1.0 M solution of HCl?

25. What is the molarity of the hydrogen (hydronium) ion in a 2.0 M solution of sulfuric acid, assuming 100% ionization?

26. What are the formulas of the two products formed when nitric acid dissolves in water?

27. What is the name of the acid formed when hydrogen sulfide is dissolved in water?

28. Write the balanced equation for the reaction of aluminum metal with hydrochloric acid.

29. Write the balanced equation for the reaction of sulfuric acid with lithium hydroxide.

30. What is known about the pH of a solution if an aqueous solution of the substance is pink after phenolphthalein is added?

31. What is the name of the salt formed when phosphoric acid is neutralized with potassium hydroxide?

32. Describe the differences in composition of a basic (alkaline) solution and an acidic solution.

33. A solution with a pH of 10 is to be titrated to achieve a pH of 7. Which indicator is the best choice for this titration? How would you know when a pH of 7 is reached?

Part C

34. A certain solution makes methyl orange turn yellow and bromthymol blue turn yellow. What are the upper and lower pH limits of the solution? [1]

35. Alizarin yellow is an indicator that changes from yellow to red as the pH changes from 10.0 to 12.0. Explain why alizarin yellow is not a suitable indicator to use during the neutralization titration of hydrochloric acid and potassium hydroxide. Select a more suitable indicator from Table M of the *Reference Tables for Physical Setting/Chemistry* and explain why your selection would be better. [2]

36. Write the balanced equation for the reaction of hydrogen ions and water. Draw the Lewis dot diagram of the product. [2]

37. How many moles of hydroxide ion are there in 500 mL of 2.0M NaOH solution? [2]

38. A student dilutes 49.0 g H_2SO_4 with water to make a total of 1000 mL of solution.

    (a) What is the molarity of the solution? [1]

    (b) Assuming complete ionization, what is the concentration of hydrogen ions? [1]

    (c) How many milliliters of 2.0M NaOH are be needed to completely neutralize 1000 mL of the solution? [1]

39. Dilute solutions of acetic acid and ammonia are both poor conductors of electricity. When the two undergo a neutralization reaction, the resulting solution is a good conductor. Use your knowledge of chemistry to explain why this is so. [2]

40. Liquid HCl is a nonconductor, but aqueous HCl is a good conductor. Use your knowledge of chemistry to explain why this is so. [2]

41. A student obtained the following data from a titration lab.

    Standard solution: 2.50M HCl
    Unknown solution: NaOH of unknown concentration

    Four titrations were performed. In each case 20.0 mL of acid were used. The results of each trial are shown below. For each trial, the volume of NaOH used is given, along with the student's comments.

Trial	NaOH Added	Comments
1	26.4 mL	phenolphthalein turned a dark pink
2	22.0 mL	phenolphthalein turned a light pink
3	21.8 mL	phenolphthalein turned a light pink
4	22.0 mL	phenolphthalein turned a light pink

The student discarded the results from Trial 1 and calculated the average molarity of the sodium hydroxide.

(a) Give a reason why the student was justified in not using the results from Trial 1. [1]

(b) Calculate the average molarity of the sodium hydroxide. Exclude the data from Trial 1. [3]

Organic Chemistry

VOCABULARY		
addition reaction	**esterification**	**organic halide**
alcohol	**ester**	**polymer**
aldehyde	**ether**	**polymerization**
alkane	**fermentation**	**saponification**
alkene	**functional group**	**saturated**
alkyne	**hydrocarbon**	**substitution reaction**
amide	**isomer**	**unsaturated**
amine	**ketone**	
amino acid	**organic acid**	

Organic chemistry is the study of carbon and most carbon compounds. The name *organic* is a remnant of a time when it was thought that carbon compounds could only be made by living things; hence the term *organic*. Today it is widely recognized that organic chemistry contains far more compounds than only those made by living things. The number of organic compounds is enormous. Tens of thousands of new organic compounds are discovered every year, and there seems to be no end in sight to future discoveries.

The number of carbon compounds far exceeds the number of inorganic compounds. Why can carbon form so many compounds? The answer lies in the ability of carbon atoms to bond with other carbon atoms to form chains, rings, and networks. In this topic you will be introduced to the wide variety of organic compounds and the types of reactions that they undergo.

Bonding of Carbon Atoms

The ability of carbon to form many different compounds is based, to a large extent, on the tendency of carbon atoms to covalently bond with other carbon atoms and form chains. This process can be continued indefinitely, leading to chains of thousands of carbon atoms. Figure 11.1 shows electron dot diagrams of the ground state and the bonded state of a carbon atom and a three-dimensional representation of a tetrahedron with a carbon atom at its center. Note that when carbon bonds, the formerly paired electrons occupy separate orbitals, enabling carbon atoms to form four covalent bonds.

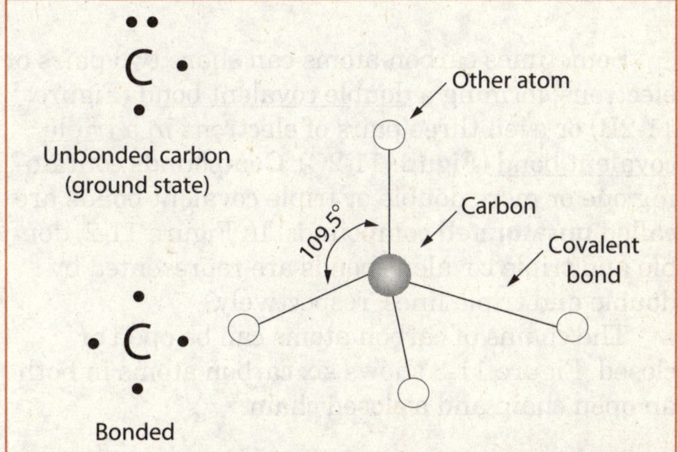

Figure 11-1. Lewis diagrams of carbon and bonded carbon: Carbon forms four equivalent covalent bonds. The tetrahedral molecular shape allows for equal spacing between these bonds.

MEMORY JOGGER
Substances that are covalently bonded form molecules. They generally have low melting and boiling points, and are poor conductors of heat and electricity. They are generally nonpolar and tend to dissolve in nonpolar solvents. Covalently bonded substances tend to react more slowly than ionic compounds.

Study the diagram of carbon in Figure 11.1. Note that when carbon is in the bonded state it has four potential sites for covalent bonds. Although the angle between adjacent electrons appears to be 90°, the atom is actually three dimensional, and the electrons are located at the corners of a tetrahedron with an angle of 109.5° between each pair of electrons.

Figure 11-2 shows carbon atoms sharing electrons to form a chain. In such diagrams, a single line is often used to represent the pair of shared electrons (C–C). When one pair of electrons is shared between two carbon atoms, the bond is called a single covalent bond (Figure 11-2A). Organic compounds containing only single bonds are said to be **saturated.**

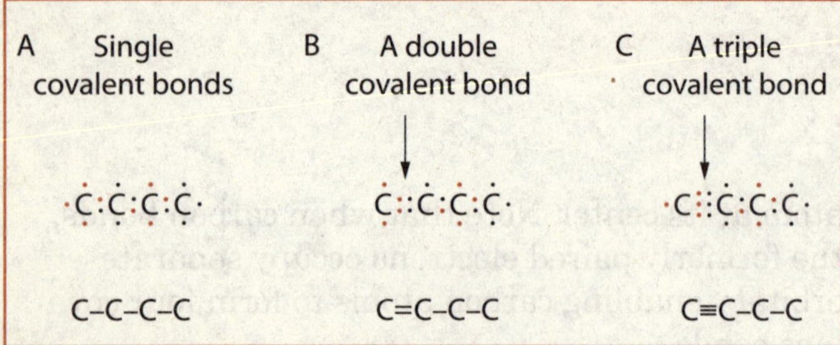

Figure 11-2. Carbon atoms share electrons in covalent bonds to form chains

Sometimes carbon atoms can share two pairs of electrons, forming a double covalent bond (Figure 11-2B) or even three pairs of electrons in a triple covalent bond (Figure 11-2C). Compounds containing one or more double or triple covalent bonds are called **unsaturated** compounds. In Figure 11-2, double and triple covalent bonds are represented by double and triple lines, respectively.

The chains of carbon atoms can be open or closed. Figure 11-3 shows six carbon atoms in both an open chain and a closed chain.

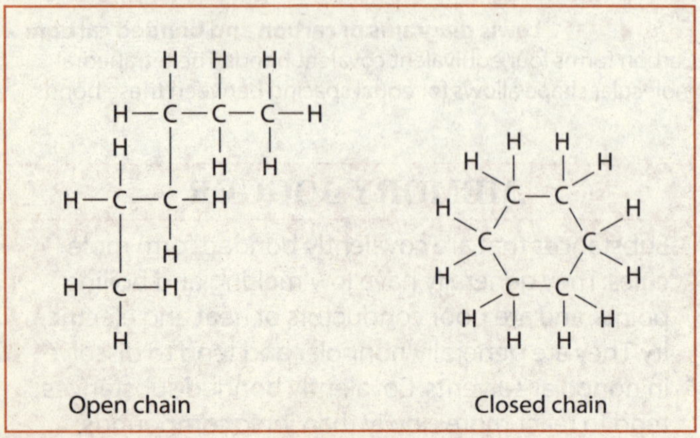

Open chain

Closed chain

Figure 11-3: Open and closed carbon chains

Carbon atoms can also bond with other carbon atoms forming three-dimensional networks. Diamonds are made of networks of carbon atoms in which each carbon atom is bonded to four other carbon atoms in a characteristic network structure. As recent discoveries have shown, carbon atoms can be arranged in large networks in which each carbon atom is bonded with a single bond to two other carbon atoms and with a double bond to one other carbon atom. The most common of these forms is buckminsterfullerene, also called a buckyball, which contains 60 carbons atoms forming a pattern similar to that on a soccer ball. The carbon atoms form a framework, and the inside of the network is empty space.

STRUCTURAL FORMULAS The molecular formula shows the kind and number of atoms in a compound. For example, the molecular formula C_3H_8 tells the reader that the compound contains three carbon atoms and eight hydrogen atoms. Structural formulas attempt to show not only the kinds and numbers of atoms but also the bonding patterns and approximate shapes of molecules. Figure 11-4 shows the molecular formulas and structural formulas for two organic compounds. It is important to remember that these structural formulas are two-dimensional representations of three-dimensional molecules. Each carbon atom can be pictured as the center of a tetrahedron, and a short line can represent each of its covalent bonds.

Hydrocarbons

Although there exists an extremely large number of organic compounds, the study of these compounds is simplified because they can be classified into groups called homologous series, the members of which have related structures and properties. A homologous series of compounds is a group of related compounds in which each member differs from the one before it by the same additional unit.

Hydrocarbons are organic compounds that contain only atoms of hydrogen and carbon. These compounds are the parent compounds from which many other organic compounds derive. Alkanes, alkenes, and alkynes are three important homologous series of hydrocarbons. By studying these series you will more easily understand other organic series closely related to them.

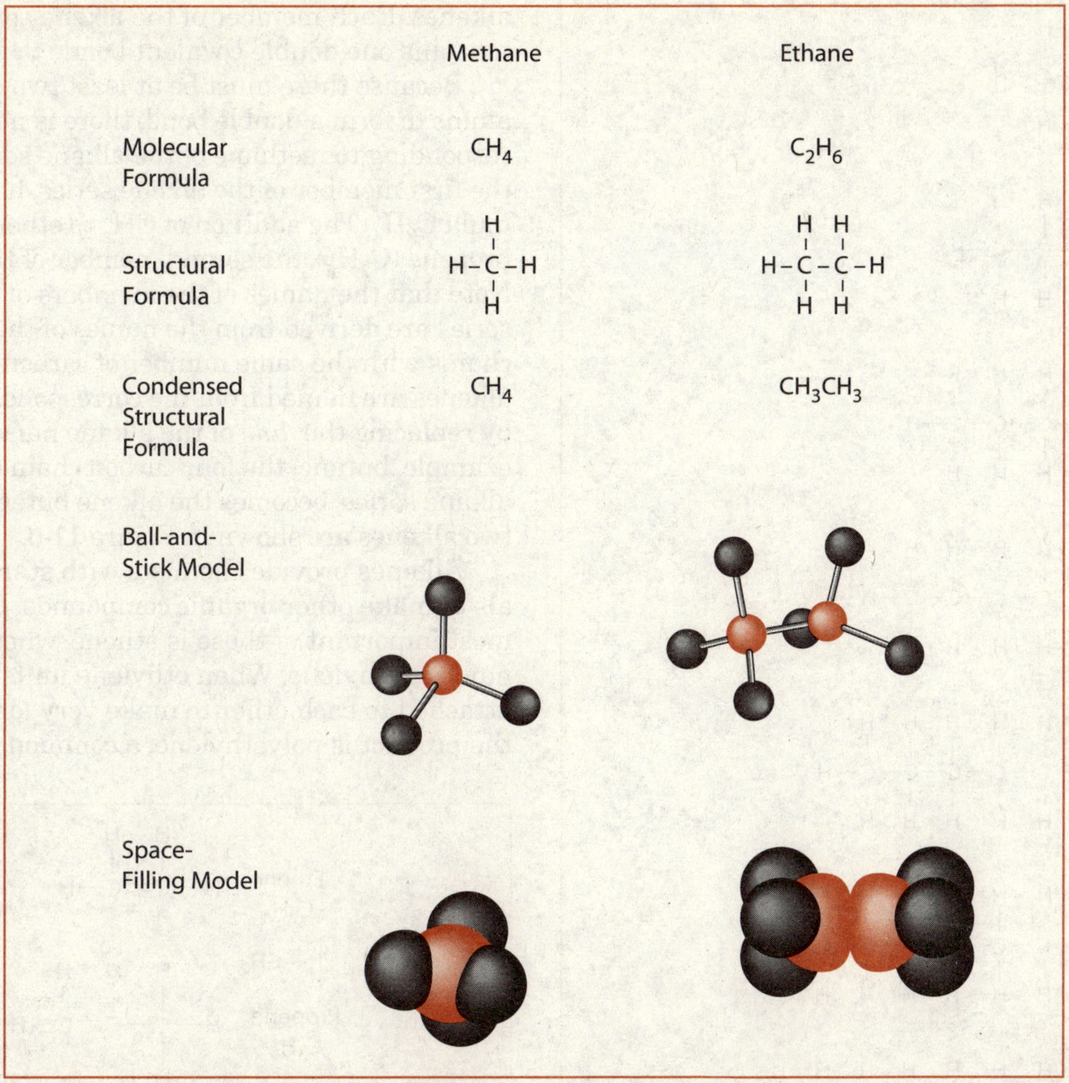

	Methane	Ethane
Molecular Formula	CH_4	C_2H_6
Structural Formula	H | H–C–H | H	H H | | H–C–C–H | | H H
Condensed Structural Formula	CH_4	CH_3CH_3
Ball-and-Stick Model		
Space-Filling Model		

Figure 11-4. Various formulas and models of two organic compounds

Alkanes

The **alkanes** are a homologous series of saturated hydrocarbons that release energy when burned. Methane (CH_4), the first member of the series, comprises about 90% of natural gas, which is used to heat many homes. The second member, ethane (C_2H_6), accounts for most of the rest of natural gas. Propane (C_3H_8) is familiar as a home heating fuel and is also used for outdoor grills and camping equipment. The fourth alkane, butane (C_4H_{10}), is found in disposable lighters.

As the number of carbons increases in the alkane series, the boiling point increases. Chains of five to 12 carbon atoms are found in gasoline. Home heating oils contain 10 to 16 carbon atoms in chains. Paraffin wax, common in candles, contains 20 or more carbon atoms per chain, while road tar (asphalt) may contain 40 carbons in a chain. The names and molecular and structural formulas of the first ten members of this series are found in Figure 11-5 on the next page.

Study the formulas for the members of the alkane series shown in Figure 11-5. Notice that there is a constant relationship between each succeeding member. Ethane has one more carbon atom and two more hydrogen atoms than the preceding member, methane. The same relationship exists between propane and ethane, and butane and propane. This relationship, in which each member differs by one carbon atom and two hydrogen atoms (CH_2), defines the nature of a homologous series.

Alkenes

The same relationship between successive members can be found in the homologous series of

```
             H
             |
Methane  H—C—H
CH4          |
             H

          H  H
          |  |
Ethane  H—C—C—H
C2H6      |  |
          H  H

           H  H  H
           |  |  |
Propane  H—C—C—C—H
C3H8       |  |  |
           H  H  H

          H  H  H  H
          |  |  |  |
Butane  H—C—C—C—C—H
C4H10     |  |  |  |
          H  H  H  H

           H  H  H  H  H
           |  |  |  |  |
Pentane  H—C—C—C—C—C—H
C5H12      |  |  |  |  |
           H  H  H  H  H

          H  H  H  H  H  H
          |  |  |  |  |  |
Hexane  H—C—C—C—C—C—C—H
C6H14     |  |  |  |  |  |
          H  H  H  H  H  H

           H  H  H  H  H  H  H
           |  |  |  |  |  |  |
Heptane  H—C—C—C—C—C—C—C—H
C7H16      |  |  |  |  |  |  |
           H  H  H  H  H  H  H

          H  H  H  H  H  H  H  H
          |  |  |  |  |  |  |  |
Octane  H—C—C—C—C—C—C—C—C—H
C8H18     |  |  |  |  |  |  |  |
          H  H  H  H  H  H  H  H

          H  H  H  H  H  H  H  H  H
          |  |  |  |  |  |  |  |  |
Nonane  H—C—C—C—C—C—C—C—C—C—H
C9H20     |  |  |  |  |  |  |  |  |
          H  H  H  H  H  H  H  H  H

          H  H  H  H  H  H  H  H  H  H
          |  |  |  |  |  |  |  |  |  |
Decane  H—C—C—C—C—C—C—C—C—C—C—H
C10H22    |  |  |  |  |  |  |  |  |  |
          H  H  H  H  H  H  H  H  H  H
```

Figure 11-5. The first ten members of the alkane family

alkenes. Each member of the **alkene** series contains one double covalent bond.

Because there must be at least two carbon atoms to form a double bond, there is no alkene corresponding to methane of the alkane series. Ethene, the first member of the alkene series, has the formula C_2H_4. The addition of CH_2 to ethene produces propene (C_3H_6), the second member of the series. Note that the names of the members of the alkene series are derived from the names of the alkane chains with the same number of carbon atoms. The alkenes are named from the corresponding alkane by replacing the *-ane* of the alkane name to *-ene*. For example, butane, the four-carbon chain of the alkane series, becomes the alkene butene. The first two alkenes are shown in Figure 11-6.

Alkenes provide chemists with starting materials to make other organic compounds. Probably the most important of these is ethene, whose common name is ethylene. When ethylene units are attached to each other to make very long chains, the product is polyethylene, a common plastic.

```
           H  H
           |  |
Ethene   H—C=C—H
C2H4
  | + CH2
  ↓        H  H  H
           |  |  |
Propene  H—C—C=C—H
C3H6       |
           H

Ethyne   H—C≡C—H
C2H2
  | + CH2
  ↓        H
           |
Propyne  H—C—C≡C—H
C3H4       |
           H
```

Figure 11-6. Some members of the alkene and alkyne families

Alkynes

The **alkynes** are a homologous series of unsaturated hydrocarbons that contain one triple bond. The naming of the alkyne series repeats the pattern observed in the alkenes. To find the alkyne name, use the corresponding name from the alkane series, and change the *-ane* ending to *-yne*. Thus the first member of the series is ethyne (C_2H_2), as shown in Figure 11-6.

The alkynes, like the alkenes, provide chemists with starting materials to make other organic compounds. The first member of the series, ethyne, is commonly known as acetylene, used as a fuel in welding torches.

General Formulas

In every homologous series there is a definite relationship between the number of carbon and hydrogen atoms. Note that in the alkene series, there are always twice as many hydrogen atoms as carbon atoms. Hence it is possible to show this by writing C_nH_{2n}, the general formula of alkenes. If it is known that a certain alkene contains 10 carbon atoms, then it will contain 20 hydrogen atoms.

Each corresponding member of the alkane series has two more hydrogen atoms than found in the alkenes. C_4H_8 is the formula of butene, but C_4H_{10} is the formula of butane. The general formula of the alkanes shows this change by adding two hydrogen atoms to the general formula, C_nH_{2n+2}. Ethyne (C_2H_2) has two fewer hydrogens than are present in ethene (C_2H_4). In a similar way, all alkynes have two fewer hydrogen atoms than the corresponding alkenes. This is shown in the general formula of the alkynes, C_nH_{2n-2}.

Review Questions

1. All organic compounds must contain the element (1) hydrogen (2) nitrogen (3) carbon (4) oxygen
2. Which element is composed of atoms that can form more than one covalent bond with one another? (1) hydrogen (2) helium (3) carbon (4) calcium
3. What is the total number of valence electrons in a carbon atom in the ground state? (1) 12 (2) 2 (3) 6 (4) 4
4. Which property is generally characteristic of an organic compound? (1) low melting point (2) high melting point (3) soluble in polar solvents (4) insoluble in nonpolar solvents
5. In general, which property do organic compounds share? (1) high melting point (2) high electrical conductivity (3) readily soluble in water (4) slow reaction rate
6. A hydrocarbon molecule containing one triple covalent bond is classified as an (1) alkene (2) alkane (3) alkyne (4) alkadiene
7. What is the total number of hydrogen atoms in a molecule of butene? (1) 10 (2) 6 (3) 8 (4) 4
8. By how many carbon atoms does each member of a homologous series differ from the previous member? (1) 1 (2) 2 (3) 3 (4) 4
9. Which of the following is a saturated hydrocarbon? (1) ethene (2) ethyne (3) propene (4) propane
10. What is the total number of pairs of electrons shared between the two adjacent carbon atoms in an ethyne molecule? (1) 1 (2) 2 (3) 3 (4) 4
11. Which compound is a member of the same homologous series as C_3H_6? (1) C_2H_4 (2) C_2H_6 (3) C_3H_4 (4) C_3H_8
12. Which hydrocarbon is a member of the series with the general formula C_nH_{2n-2}? (1) ethyne (2) ethene (3) butane (4) benzene
13. Which compound belongs to the alkene series? (1) C_2H_2 (2) C_2H_4 (3) C_6H_6 (4) C_6H_{14}
14. Which type of bond occurs in a saturated hydrocarbon molecule? (1) single covalent (2) double covalent (3) triple covalent (4) ionic
15. Which type of bonds and solids are characteristic of organic compounds? (1) ionic bonds and ionic solids (2) ionic bonds and molecular solids (3) covalent bonds and ionic solids (4) covalent bonds and molecular solids
16. The four single bonds of a carbon atom are directed in space toward the corners of a (1) regular tetrahedron (2) regular octahedron (3) square plane (4) trigonal bipyramid
17. In which group could the hydrocarbons all belong to the same homologous series?
    (1) C_2H_2, C_2H_4, C_2H_6
    (2) C_2H_4, C_3H_4, C_4H_8
    (3) C_2H_4, C_2H_6, C_3H_6
    (4) C_2H_4, C_3H_6, C_4H_8 alkene
18. Which formula represents butane? C_4H_{10}
    (1) CH_3CH_3
    (2) $CH_3CH_2CH_3$
    (3) $CH_3CH_2CH_2CH_3$
    (4) $CH_3CH_2CH_2CH_2CH_3$

Isomers

Each of the alkanes listed on Figure 11-5 is composed of a continuous chain of carbon atoms. However, beginning with butane there is more than one way of combining the carbon and hydrogen atoms. In Figure 11-7, structural formulas show two different ways in which four carbon atoms and 10 hydrogen atoms can be combined. Not only can the carbon atoms be attached to each other in a continuous chain of four atoms, but they can also be arranged in a chain of three carbon atoms, with the fourth attached to the middle carbon. When a molecular formula can be represented by more than one structural arrangement, the compounds are called **isomers**. Isomers, while having the same molecular formula, have different chemical and physical properties. The boiling point of *n*-butane is 0.5°C, while its isomer boils at −10°C.

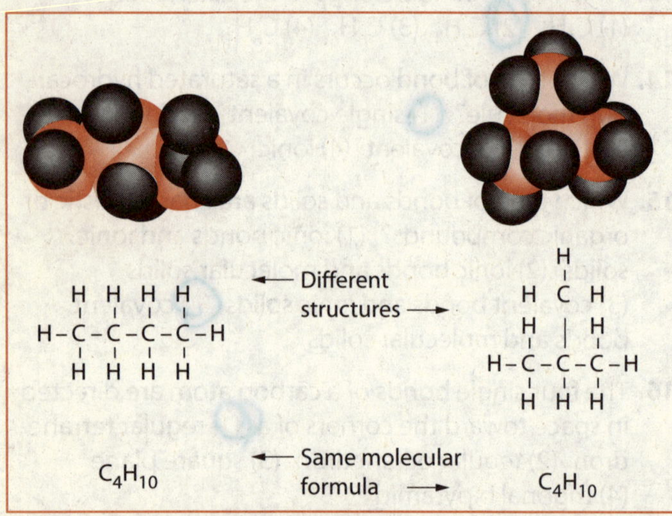

Figure 11-7. Isomers of butane

As the number of carbon atoms increases, so does the number of possible isomers. While butane has two isomers, octane (C_8H_{18}) has 18, and decane ($C_{10}H_{22}$) has 75. It is this ability to form isomers that is largely responsible for the large number of organic compounds.

Naming Organic Compounds

When carbon atoms are attached to each other in one continuous chain, the compounds are called straight-chain hydrocarbons. This arrangement is called the normal form, and the letter *n*- precedes the name (*n*-butane). Compounds with branched chains must be given names that are different from the straight-chain name because they have different chemical and physical properties. The rules for naming organic compounds are governed by the International Union of Pure and Applied Chemistry (IUPAC). The following rules will produce names of branched compounds that are approved by the IUPAC.

1. Each compound is named by finding the longest continuous chain of carbon atoms. In the structure on the left in Figure 11-8, the longest chain consists of three carbon atoms, and, hence the compound is named as a derivative of propane, the third alkane. In the second example, the longest continuous chain consists of six carbon atoms, and the compound will be named as a hexane. Note that the chain does not have to appear as a straight chain, but it must be continuous.

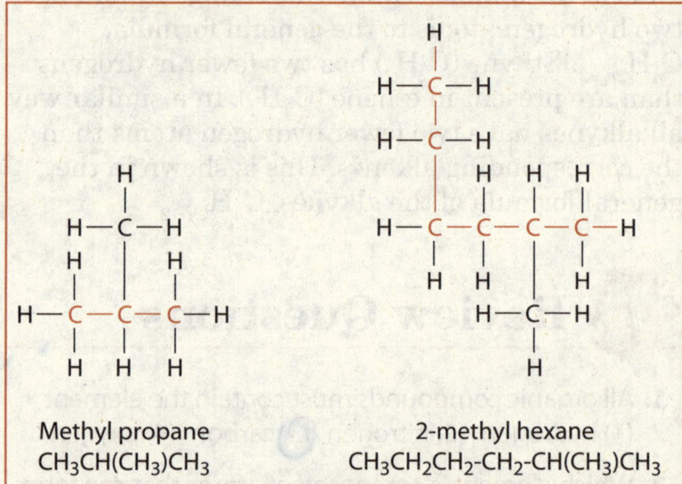

Figure 11-8. Naming organic compounds

2. While the name for the longest chain in the first example is propane, there is a CH_3 group attached to the chain. How should it be named? A group that contains one less hydrogen atom than an alkane with the same number of carbon atoms is classified as one of the alkyl groups, with a group name derived from the name of its corresponding alkane. Thus, the CH_3 that is attached to the propane belongs to the methyl group, so called because, like methane, it has one carbon atom. Table 11-1 shows the relationship between the alkanes and the common alkyl groups. The compound in the first example is called methyl propane. There is no need to identify the location of the methyl group because it can only be attached to the central carbon.

3. If necessary, the location of the alkyl group is shown by assigning numbers to the carbon atoms in the longest chain. The carbon chain must be numbered from the end that will give the lowest number for the attached group. In the second example, the compound should be named 2-methyl hexane rather than 4-methyl hexane.

4. There may be more than one of the same type of group attached to the parent chain. A prefix is used to indicate the number of attached groups of each type that are present. If two methyl groups are attached, the prefix *di-* will be used. *Tri-* will indicate three, and *tetra-*, four. In addition, commas are used to indicate the specific carbon to which each group is attached. For example, if two methyl groups are attached to the second carbon atom in a five-carbon chain, and another methyl group is attached to the third carbon atom, the compound would be 2,2,3-trimethyl pentane. When more than one group is attached to the parent chain, the chain must be numbered in such a way to produce the smaller total value of the attached chains.

Table 11-1. Relationship of Alkanes and Alkyl Groups

Alkane		Alkyl Group	
Name	**Formula**	**Name**	**Formula**
methane	CH_4	methyl	CH_3
ethane	C_2H_6	ethyl	C_2H_5
n-propane	C_3H_8	*n*-propyl	C_3H_7

Review Questions

19. Which compound is an isomer of C_4H_9OH?
(1) $C_3H_7CH_3$
(2) $C_2H_5OC_2H_5$
(3) $C_2H_5COOC_2H_5$
(4) CH_3COOH

20. Which compound is an isomer of CH_3CH_2OH?
(1) CH_3COOH
(2) $CH_3CH_2CH_3$
(3) CH_3OCH_3
(4) CH_3COCH_3

21. Which formula represents an isomer of the compound propanoic acid (CH_3CH_2COOH)?
(1) $CH_3CH_2CH_2OH$
(2) $CH_3CH_2CH_2COOH$
(3) $CH_3CH(OH)CH_2OH$
(4) CH_3COOCH_3

22. Given the compound:

```
    H   H   H
    |   |   |
H — C — C — C — Cl
    |   |   |
    H   H   Cl
```

Which structural formula represents an isomer?

(1)
```
    H   H   H   H
    |   |   |   |
H — C — C — C — C — Cl
    |   |   |   |
    H   H   H   Cl
```

(2)
```
     H   H   H
     |   |   |
Cl — C — C — C — H
     |   |   |
     H   Cl  H
```

(3)
```
    H   H   H
    |   |   |
H — C — C — C — Cl
    |   |   |
    H   H   H
```

(4)
```
     H   H   H   H
     |   |   |   |
Cl — C — C — C — C — Cl
     |   |   |   |
     H   H   H   Cl
```

23. Which compounds are isomers?
(1) CH_3Br and CH_2Br_2
(2) CH_3OH and CH_3CH_2OH
(3) CH_3OH and CH_3CHO
(4) CH_3OCH_3 and CH_3CH_2OH

24. An $-ol$ suffix indicates that an $-OH$ group has been added to a hydrocarbon. Which formula represents 1,2-ethanediol? (1) $C_2H_4(OH)_2$ (2) $C_3H_5(OH)_3$ (3) $Ca(OH)_2$ (4) $Co(OH)_3$

25. Which structural formula represents 1,1-dibromopropane?

(1)
```
    H   H
    |   |
H — C — C — H
    |   |
    Br  Br
```

(2)
```
    Br  H
    |   |
H — C — C — H
    |   |
    Br  H
```

(3)
```
    H   H   H
    |   |   |
H — C — C — C — H
    |   |   |
    Br  Br  H
```

(4)
```
    Br  H   H
    |   |   |
H — C — C — C — H
    |   |   |
    Br  H   H
```

26. Which is an isomer of H–C–C–OH?

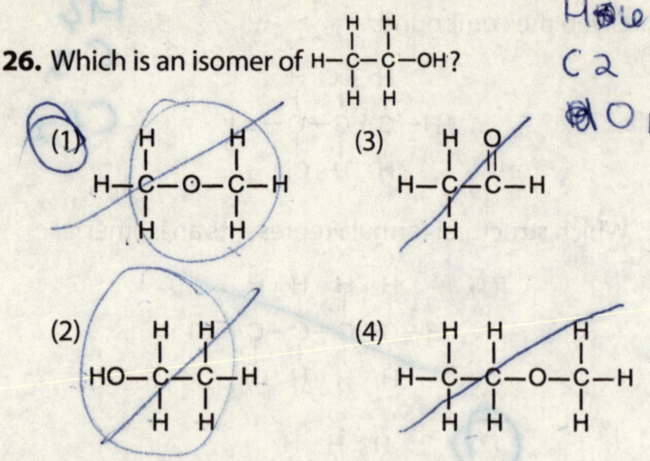

27. Which structural formula represents 2,2-dimethyl propane?

(1)

(2)

(3)

(4)

28. Which is the correct IUPAC name for the hydrocarbon with the structural formula shown below?

(1) 1-methyl-2-ethylenethane (2) 1-propylethane (3) *n*-propane (4) *n*-pentane

29. Which compound has the molecular formula C_5H_{12}?
(1) butane (2) pentane (3) 2,2-dimethyl butane (4) 2,2-dimethyl pentane

30. Write the structural formula for 3-methyl pentane.

31. Write the structural formula for 2, 2-dimethyl hexane.

32. Write the structural formula for 2-methyl, 3-ethyl hexane.

33. Write the structural formula for 2,2,3-trimethyl heptane.

34. Write the structural formula for 3,3-dimethyl, 4-ethyl octane.

Functional Groups

Although hydrocarbons are the most basic organic compounds, many other organic compounds form when other atoms replace one or more hydrogen atoms in a hydrocarbon. These atoms or groups of atoms, called **functional groups**, replace hydrogen atoms in a hydrocarbon and give the compound distinctive physical and chemical properties. The naming of these compounds is made easy because they derive their names from the hydrocarbon with the corresponding number of carbon atoms.

Halides

When any of the halogens (F,Cl, Br, or I) replaces a hydrogen atom in an alkane, the compound is called an **organic halide**, or halocarbon. The functional group of an organic halide is the halogen that is attached to the chain. Organic halides are often used as organic solvents and are found in some pesticides. They are named by citing the location of the halogen attached to the chain. Figure 11-9 shows some examples of halocarbons and shows how the chain is numbered when necessary to show the location of the halogen.

```
    H
    |
H — C — Cl
    |
    H
```

Chloromethane
CH_3Cl

```
    H   F   H
    |   |   |
H — C — C — C — H
    |   |   |
    H   H   H
```

2-fluoropropane
CH_3CHFCH_3

```
    H   Cl  Cl  H
    |   |   |   |
H — C — C — C — C — H
    |   |   |   |
    H   Cl  H   H
```

2,2,3-trichlorobutane
$CH_3\text{-}CCl_2CHClCH_3$

Figure 11-9. Some typical organic halides

Alcohols

Alcohols are organic compounds in which one or more hydrogen atoms of a hydrocarbon are replaced by an −OH group. The −OH group is called a hydroxyl group and is the functional group that gives alcohols their specific chemical and physical properties. Although the −OH group resembles the hydroxide ion of inorganic bases, it does not form an ion in water. Hence, alcohols are nonelectrolytes and do not turn indicators characteristic acid or basic colors. While these hydroxyl groups do not form ions in solution, they are quite polar. This polarity allows alcohols to be soluble in water, which is also polar.

There are several different types of alcohols. The type is dependent on the number of hydroxyl groups in the compound and on the position of each hydroxyl group on the main carbon chain.

CLASSIFICATION OF ALCOHOLS Alcohols are classified as primary, secondary or tertiary based on whether the hydroxyl group is attached to a primary, secondary, or tertiary carbon atom. Primary carbon atoms are attached directly to only one other carbon atom and are located at the end of a chain or branch. Secondary carbon atoms are directly attached to two other carbon atoms. Tertiary carbon atoms are attached directly to three other carbon atoms.

Alcohols are classified according to the carbon atom to which the hydroxyl group is attached. A primary alcohol has a hydroxyl group attached to a primary carbon atom at the end of the chain. Primary alcohols are represented by R–OH or RCH_2OH, where the R represents a hydrocarbon chain in which a hydrogen atom is replaced by the functional group shown.

A secondary alcohol has a hydroxyl group attached to a secondary carbon atom. Secondary alcohols can be represented by R–CH(OH)–R', where R and R' represent two hydrocarbon chains.

A tertiary alcohol has a hydroxyl group attached to a tertiary carbon atom. A tertiary alcohol can be represented by $R_1R_2R_3COH$.

DIHYDROXY AND TRIHYDROXY ALCOHOLS Alcohols can also be classified by the number of hydroxyl groups that are attached to the carbon chain. In addition to alcohols that have one hydroxyl group (monohydroxy), there are families of alcohols with two or more attached groups. Ethylene glycol, also known as antifreeze, is the common name for a dihydroxy (two hydroxyl groups) alcohol. Its proper name is 1,2-ethanediol. 1,2,3-propanetriol is another common substance, glycerol, which is used as a moistening agent in cosmetics. Figure 11-10 on the next page shows examples of the various types of alcohols.

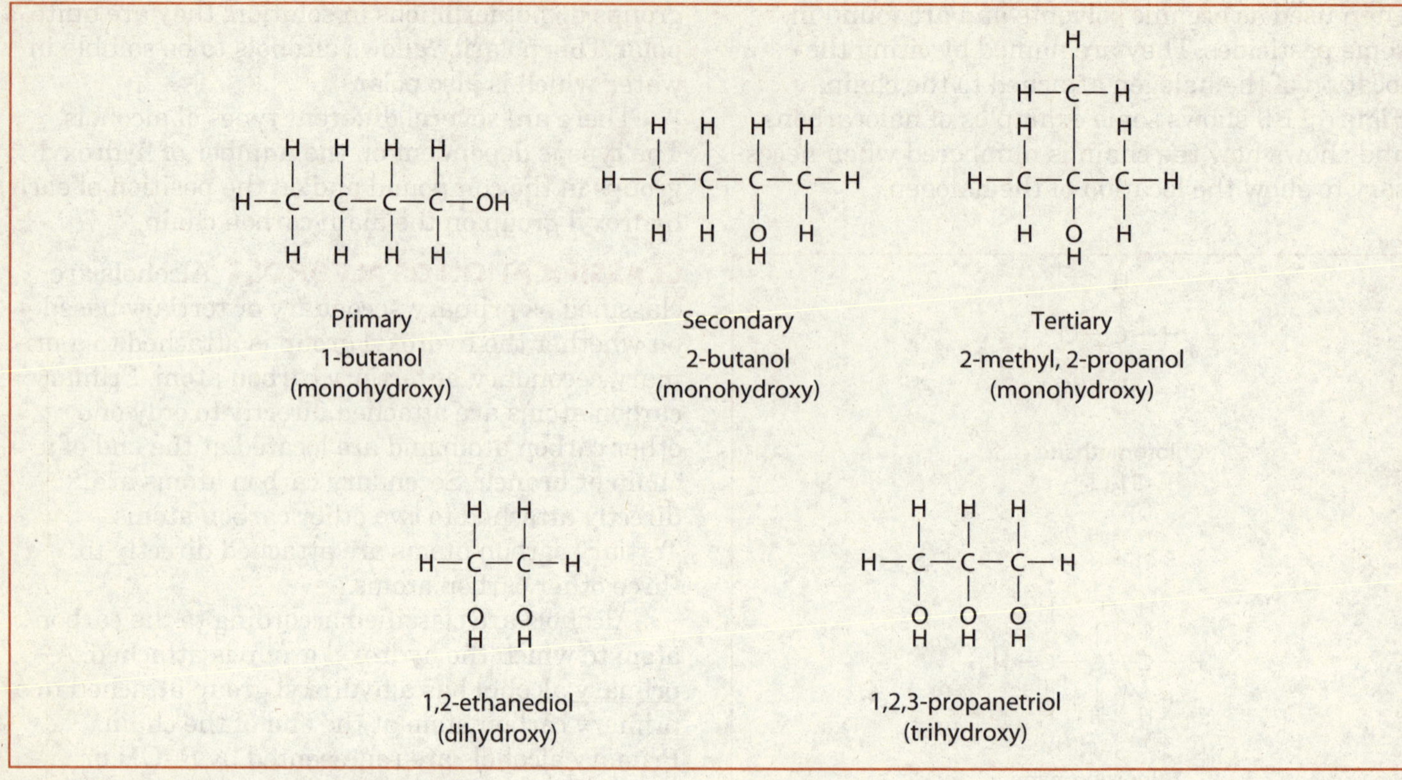

Figure 11-10. Some representative alcohols

Other Substituted Hydrocarbons

ALDEHYDES When an oxygen atom is attached to a carbon chain by a double covalent bond, it is called a carbonyl group (–C=O). **Aldehydes** are organic compounds in which the carbonyl group is found on the end carbon (a primary carbon), as shown in Figure 11-11. Aldehydes are named by substituting –*al* in place of the final –*e* of the corresponding alkane name. The first member of the series has the IUPAC name methanal. Its common name is formaldehyde, and it is used as a preservative. An aldehyde can be recognized from its structural formula by the presence of a double bonded oxygen atom together with a hydrogen atom attached to an end carbon.

Propan**al**, an aldehyde

Propan**one**, a ketone

Figure 11-11. An aldehyde and a ketone: Both aldehydes and ketones contain the carbonyl group.

KETONES A **ketone** is formed when the carbonyl group (–C=O) is found on an interior carbon atom that is attached to two other carbon atoms, as shown in Figure 11-11. Ketones are named by replacing the final –*e* from the corresponding alkane name with –*one*. The first ketone is a formed by a carbonyl group attached to the central carbon atom of a chain of three carbon atoms. Its IUPAC name is propanone. The common name of propanone is acetone. Ketones are often used as solvents. The carbonyl group is quite polar, allowing the ketone to dissolve in water. The remainder of the molecule causes the ketone to be soluble in other organic compounds.

ETHERS **Ethers** are a series of organic compounds in which two carbon chains are joined together by an oxygen atom bonded between two carbon atoms. The general formula is written *R*–O–*R′* to show the oxygen bridge between the two carbon chains. Structures and common and IUPAC names for some ethers are shown in Figure 11-12.

ORGANIC ACIDS **Organic acids** are a homologous series of organic compounds whose functional group is a carboxyl group (–COOH). Organic acids derive their names from the corresponding hydro-

```
    H       H
    |       |
H — C — O — C — H
    |       |
    H       H
```

Common name: dimethyl ether
IUPAC name: methoxymethane

```
    H       H   H
    |       |   |
H — C — O — C — C — H
    |       |   |
    H       H   H
```

Common name: ethylmethyl ether
IUPAC name: methoxyethane

```
    H   H       H   H
    |   |       |   |
H — C — C — O — C — C — H
    |   |       |   |
    H   H       H   H
```

Common name: diethyl ether
IUPAC name: ethoxyethane

Figure 11-12. Some common ethers

carbons by replacing the *–e* with *–oic acid*. Thus the two-carbon hydrocarbon is ethane, while the corresponding acid is ethanoic acid. Ethanoic acid is commonly known as acetic acid, which is found in vinegar. Although most organic compounds are nonelectrolytes, organic acids are generally weak electrolytes.

ESTERS **Esters** are organic compounds whose type formula is $R{-}CO{-}OR'$. The $R{-}CO{-}O{-}$ part of the formula comes from an organic acid, and the R' part of the formula comes from an alcohol. Esters have strong, fragrant aromas and are responsible for the odors of many foods and flavorings, such as pineapples, bananas, wintergreen, and oranges.

AMINES Perhaps the easiest way to understand amines is as a derivative of ammonia. An **amine** is formed when one or more of the hydrogen atoms of ammonia are replaced by an alkyl group. To name an amine, the *−e* ending of the alkane name is changed to end in *−amine*, and the alkane chain is numbered to show the location of the amine group. Figure 11-13 shows the relation of amines to ammonia. Amines are important biological chemicals present in the B vitamins, hormones, and anesthetics. They are also used commercially in the preparation of dyes.

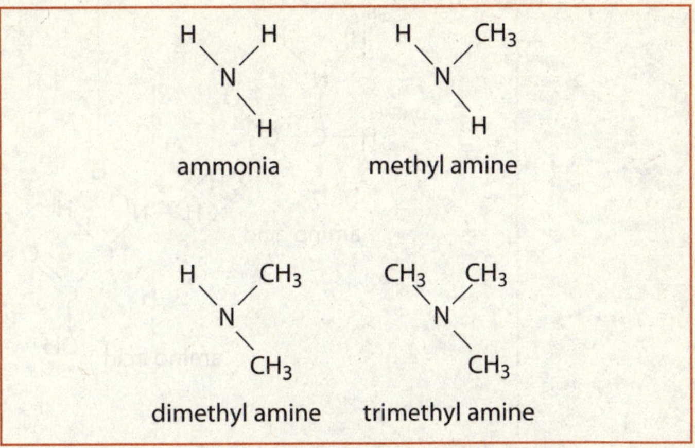

Figure 11-13. The relation of amines and ammonia

AMINO ACIDS Like all organic acids, **amino acids** contain the carboxylic group (–COOH) but also contain an amine group. The amine group is attached to the carbon atom that is adjacent to the acid group (Figure 11-14). The remainder of the molecule is represented by *R*, which indicates the side chain. There are ten essential amino acids that the body must obtain through diet because it cannot synthesize them. The remaining amino acids can be synthesized. Amino acids are the building blocks of protein.

```
        H   H
         \ /
    H     N
    |     |     O
H — C  —  C — C//
    |     |     \
    H     H      OH
```

alanine

Figure 11-14. An amino acid: Amino acids have both an acid group and an amine group.

AMIDES When one of the hydrogen atoms of the amino group reacts with the –OH of an organic acid, a condensation reaction occurs. This reaction produces water and an **amide**, which is a compound formed by the combination of the two amino acids. Look at Figure 11-15 on the following page. Peptide bonding holds amino acid molecules together, forming long protein chains. While organic chemists call this linkage an amide, biologists refer to it as a peptide link. Additional condensation reactions occur, first producing a polypeptide. Eventually the chain is long enough to be a protein.

```
   H   H
    \ /
     N
     |      O
     |    //
 H — C — C              +
     |    \             H
     H     OH          /
               H — N       H
                    \     /
                      C        O               H   H
                    /   \    //                 \ /
                   H      C          ——>  H2O +  N
                          |                      |      O
                          OH                     |    //
                                            H — C — C       H
                                                 |    \     /
                                                 H      N
                                                         \     H
                                                           \  /
                                                            C      O
                                                          /   \  //
                                                         H      C
                                                                |
                                                                OH
```
amino acid   amino acid

Figure 11-15. Formation of an amide: Two amino acids combine to form an amide (peptide).

DIGGING DEEPER

Proteins are extremely long chains of amino acids. They have molecular masses well over 100 000 grams/mol. These proteins are different sequences of 20 different amino acids, providing an almost infinite variety of combinations. Proteins compose the tendons and contractile myosin of our muscles, the hemoglobin in our blood, and many essential enzymes and hormones.

Review Questions

35. When the name of an alcohol is derived from the corresponding alkane, the final *-e* of the name of the alkane should be replaced by the suffix (1) *-al* (2) *-ol* (3) *-one* (4) *-ole*

36. In a secondary alcohol, the carbon bonded to the —OH group must also be bonded to (1) one carbon atom (2) two carbon atoms (3) three carbon atoms (4) four carbon atoms.

37. Which class of compounds has the general formula *R*–O–*R′*? (1) esters (2) alcohols (3) ethers (4) aldehydes

38. The formula $C_5H_{11}OH$ represents an (1) acid (2) ester (3) ether (4) alcohol

39. The general formula *R*–COOH represents a class of compounds called (1) alkanes (2) alkenes (3) acids (4) alcohols

40. Which structural formula represents a secondary alcohol?

(1)
```
     H   H
     |   |
 H — C — C — OH
     |   |
     H   H
```

(2)
```
              H
              |
     H    H — C — H    H
     |        |        |
 H — C ———————C——————— C — H
     |        |        |
     H        OH       H
```

(3)
```
     H   H   H
     |   |   |
 H — C — C — C — H
     |   |   |
     H   OH  H
```

(4)
```
     H
     |
 H — C — C — OH
     |   ||
     H   O
```

41. Which is the general formula for an aldehyde?

(1)
```
      O
      ||
 R —  C — H
```

(2)
```
 R — OH
```

(3)
```
      O
      ||
 R —  C — O — H
```

(4)
```
      O
      ||
 R —  C — R′
```

42. Which structural formula represents a tertiary alcohol?

(1)
```
    H   H   H
    |   |   |
H — C — C — C — OH
    |   |   |
    H   H   H
```
(2)
```
    H   OH  H
    |   |   |
H — C — C — C — H
    |   |   |
    H   H   H
```
(3)
```
    H   O   H
    |   ||  |
H — C — C — C — H
    |       |
    H       H
```
(4)
```
    H   OH  H
    |   |   |
H — C — C — C — H
    |   |   |
    H   |   H
    H — C — H
        |
        H
```

43. Which structural formula represents a tertiary alcohol?

(1)
```
    H   H   H   H
    |   |   |   |
H — C — C — C — C — OH
    |   |   |   |
    H   H   H   H
```
(2)
```
    H   H   H   H
    |   |   |   |
H — C — C — C — C — OH
    |   |   |   |
    OH  H   H   H
```
(3)
```
            H
            |
    H   H — C — H   H
    |       |       |
H — C ————— C ————— C — H
    |       |       |
    H       OH      H
```
(4)
```
            H
            |
    H   H — C — H   H
    |       |       |
H — C ————— C ————— C — OH
    |       |       |
    H       H       H
```

44. Which functional group is found in all organic acids?

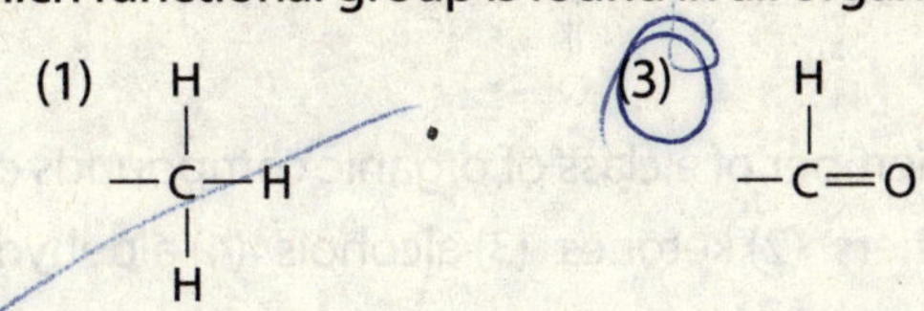

45. Which general formula represents a ketone?

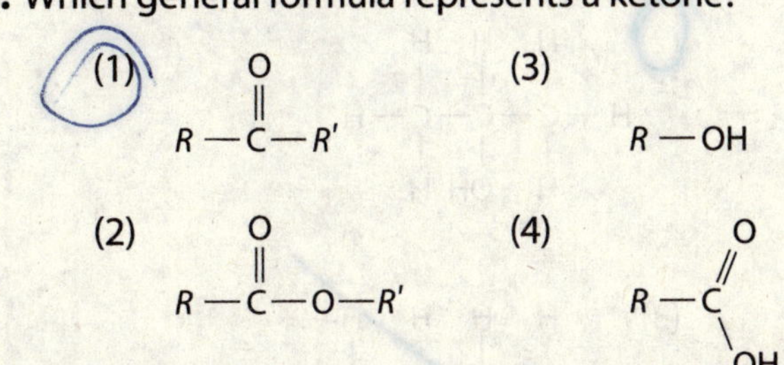

46. Which structural formula represents a monohydroxy alcohol?

(1)
```
    H   O   H
    |   ||  |
H — C — C — C — H
    |       |
    H       H
```
(2)
```
    H   OH  OH
    |   |   |
H — C — C — C — H
    |   |   |
    H   H   H
```
(3)
```
    H   OH  H
    |   |   |
H — C — C — C — H
    |   |   |
    H   H   H
```
(4)
```
    H   H       H
    |   |       |
H — C — C — O — C — H
    |   |       |
    H   H       H
```

47. The molecule $CH_3-C(=O)-CH_3$ is a member of a class of organic compounds called

(1) ethers (2) ketones (3) alcohols (4) aldehydes

48. Which is the structural formula for 2-propanol?

(1) $H-C(H)(H)-C(H)(H)-C(H)(H)-OH$

(2) $H-C(H)(H)-C(H)(OH)-C(H)(H)-H$

(3) $H-C(H)(H)-C(H)(H)-C(H)(H)-C(H)(H)-OH$

(4) $H-C(H)(H)-C(H)(H)-C(H)(OH)-C(H)(H)-H$

49. Which is the general formula for organic acids?

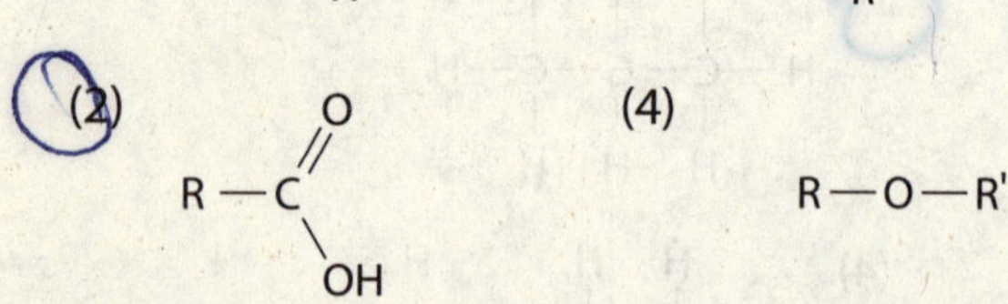

(1) $R-C(=O)-H$

(2) $R-C(=O)-OH$

(3) $R-C(=O)-R'$

(4) $R-O-R'$

Organic Reactions

Organic reactions generally occur more slowly than inorganic reactions. When covalently bonded substances react, they must first break relatively strong existing bonds before making new bonds.

Combustion

Perhaps the most common type of organic reaction is combustion. Almost all organic compounds will burn. When sufficient oxygen is present, hydrocarbons will burn to produce water and carbon dioxide. Propane, commonly used in outdoor grills, burns according to the following equation.

$$C_3H_8(g) + 5O_2(g) \rightarrow 3CO_2(g) + 4H_2O(g)$$

When the supply of oxygen is limited, carbon monoxide may be produced instead of carbon dioxide.

$$2C_3H_8(g) + 7O_2(g) \rightarrow 6CO(g) + 8H_2O(g)$$

When carbon dioxide is produced the reaction is called complete combustion, while incomplete combustion describes the production of carbon monoxide and water.

Substitution

A **substitution reaction** involves the replacement of one or more of the hydrogen atoms in a saturated hydrocarbon with another atom or group. For example, halogen atoms can replace hydrogen atoms in saturated hydrocarbons. When ethane reacts with chlorine in a substitution reaction, the products of the reaction are chloroethane and hydrogen chloride.

$$C_2H_6 + Cl_2 \rightarrow C_2H_5Cl + HCl$$

Because all of the bonding sites on a saturated hydrocarbon are filled, chlorine must first remove a hydrogen atom from the hydrocarbon chain, forming hydrogen chloride. The removal of a hydrogen atom from the chain provides an open bond site where a chlorine atom can then attach itself.

Addition

Addition reactions involve adding one or more atoms at a double or triple bond. When ethene and chlorine react, the double bond of the ethene is opened and a chlorine atom is added to each carbon atom.

$$C_2H_4 + Cl_2 \rightarrow C_2H_4Cl_2$$

Unsaturated hydrocarbons can also react with hydrogen by addition reactions. In this case, the final product is a saturated hydrocarbon.

$$C_2H_4 + H_2 \rightarrow C_2H_6$$

Esterification

Esterification is the reaction between an organic acid and an alcohol to produce an ester plus water. An example of an esterification reaction between acetic acid and ethanol to produce the ester ethyl ethanoate is shown in Figure 11-16. Sulfuric acid is used as a dehydrating agent. It removes two hydrogen atoms and an oxygen atom to form water, with the remaining fragments combining to form the ester. Esters are named by using the alkyl name of the alcohol followed by the acid group modified to end in *−oate*. The ester produced by the reaction of methanol with ethanoic acid is methyl ethanoate.

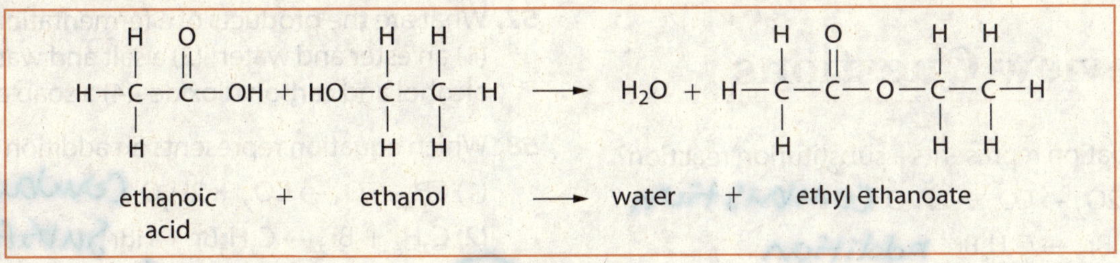

ethanoic acid + ethanol ⟶ water + ethyl ethanoate

Figure 11-16. Esterification: An acid and an alcohol react to produce water and an ester.

Saponification

When an ester reacts with an inorganic base to produce an alcohol and a soap, the reaction is called a **saponification** reaction (Figure 11-17).

One of the most common saponification reactions involves the reaction of a fat with a strong base such as sodium hydroxide. The products of this reaction are soap and glycerol.

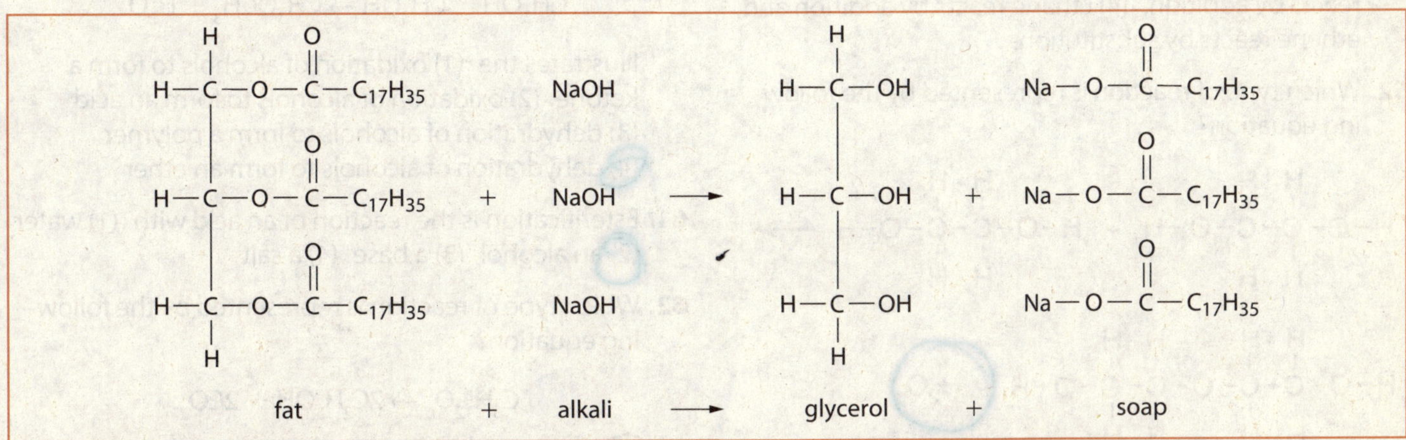

Figure 11-17. Saponification: A fat and an alkali react to produce glycerol and a soap, which is a salt of a fatty acid.

Fermentation

Fermentation is a chemical process in which yeast cells secrete the enzyme zymase and break the six-carbon chain of sugars into carbon dioxide and two-carbon fragments of alcohol. The following equation shows what happens during fermentation.

$$C_6H_{12}O_6 \rightarrow 2C_2H_5OH + 2CO_2$$

Polymerization

Polymers are organic compounds made up of chains of smaller units covalently bonded together. The formation of these large polymer molecules is called **polymerization,** and each individual unit of a polymer is called a monomer. Synthetic plastics such as nylon, rayon, and polyethylene, are the best-known polymers. There are also many naturally occurring polymers, such as proteins, starches, and cellulose.

ADDITION POLYMERIZATION Addition polymerization reactions involve the joining of monomers of unsaturated compounds. When the double bond between the carbon atoms of ethane breaks, the resulting bond site is called a free radical because of the two unbonded electrons. These electrons can bond with similar open bonds of adjacent molecules to form long chains. A typical addition polymerization reaction can be shown as follows.

$$nC_2H_2 \rightarrow (C_2H_2)_n$$

CONDENSATION POLYMERIZATION

Condensation polymerization reactions result from the bonding of monomers by removing water from hydroxyl groups and joining the monomers by an ether or ester linkage.

Review Questions

50. Which equation represents a substitution reaction?
(1) $CH_4 + 2O_2 \rightarrow CO_2 + 2H_2O$
(2) $C_2H_4 + Br_2 \rightarrow C_2H_4Br_2$
(3) $C_3H_6 + H_2 \rightarrow C_3H_8$
(4) $C_4H_{10} + Cl_2 \rightarrow C_4H_9Cl + HCl$

51. Which type of reaction do ethane molecules and ethene molecules undergo when they react with chlorine? (1) Ethane and ethene both react by addition. (2) Ethane and ethene both react by substitution. (3) Ethane reacts by substitution and ethene reacts by addition. (4) Ethane reacts by addition and ethene reacts by substitution.

52. Which type of reaction is represented by the following equation?

$$\begin{array}{c} \text{H}\ \ \text{H} \\ |\ \ \ | \\ \text{H–O–C–C–O–H} \\ |\ \ \ | \\ \text{H}\ \ \text{H} \end{array} + \begin{array}{c} \text{H}\ \ \text{H} \\ |\ \ \ | \\ \text{H–O–C–C–O–H} \\ |\ \ \ | \\ \text{H}\ \ \text{H} \end{array} \longrightarrow$$

$$\begin{array}{c} \text{H}\ \ \text{H}\ \ \ \ \ \text{H}\ \ \text{H} \\ |\ \ \ |\ \ \ \ \ \ |\ \ \ | \\ \text{H–O–C–C–O–C–C–O–H} \\ |\ \ \ |\ \ \ \ \ \ |\ \ \ | \\ \text{H}\ \ \text{H}\ \ \ \ \ \text{H}\ \ \text{H} \end{array} + H_2O$$

(1) condensation polymerization (2) addition polymerization (3) esterification (4) saponification

53. Which substance is made up of monomers joined together in long chains? (1) ketone (2) protein (3) ester (4) acid

54. When C_3H_8 burns completely in an excess of oxygen, the products formed are (1) CO and H_2O (2) CO_2 and H_2O (3) CO and H_2 (4) CO_2 and H_2

55. Molecules of propene combine in a chemical reaction to produce a single molecule. The reaction is called (1) substitution (2) saponification (3) polymerization (4) esterification

56. The reaction represented by

$$CH_3CHCH_2 + Br_2 \rightarrow CH_3CHBrCH_2Br$$

is an example of (1) fermentation (2) addition (3) substitution (4) saponification

57. What are the products of a fermentation reaction? (1) an ester and water (2) a salt and water (3) an alcohol and carbon dioxide (4) a soap and glycerol

58. Which equation represents an addition reaction?
(1) $CH_4 + O_2 \rightarrow CO_2 + 2H_2O$
(2) $C_2H_6 + Br_2 \rightarrow C_2H_5Br + HBr$
(3) $C_3H_6 + Cl_2 \rightarrow C_3H_6Cl_2$
(4) $C_4H_{10} + Cl_2 \rightarrow C_4H_9Cl + HCl$

59. Which hydrocarbon will undergo a substitution reaction with chlorine? (1) methane (2) ethyne (3) propene (4) butene

60. The equation

$$CH_3OH + CH_3OH \rightarrow CH_3OCH_3 + H_2O$$

illustrates the (1) oxidation of alcohols to form a ketone (2) oxidation of alcohols to form an acid (3) dehydration of alcohols to form a polymer (4) dehydration of alcohols to form an ether

61. Esterification is the reaction of an acid with (1) water (2) an alcohol (3) a base (4) a salt

62. Which type of reaction is represented by the following equation?

$$C_6H_{12}O_6 \rightarrow 2C_2H_5OH + 2CO_2$$

(1) saponification (2) polymerization (3) esterification (4) fermentation

63. Which process usually produces water as one of the products? (1) cracking (2) hydrolysis (3) addition polymerization (4) condensation polymerization

64. (a) Write the structure of two different amino acids. (b) Show how these two acids would combine to become an amide (show a peptide linkage).

65. Write a word equation for a saponification reaction.

66. Explain the difference between a substitution reaction and a replacement reaction.

For each substance in questions 67-71, write the number of the organic reaction, chosen from the list below, that will produce this substance.

Organic Reactions

(1) esterification
(2) saponification
(3) polymerization
(4) fermentation
(5) substitution
(6) halogen addition

67. ethanol

68. glycerol

69. methyl acetate

70. polyethylene

71. dichloromethane

Questions for Regents Practice

Part A

1. In the alkane series, each molecule contains
(1) only one double bond
(2) two double bonds
(3) one triple bond
(4) all single bonds

2. Which kind of bond is most common in organic compounds?
(1) covalent
(2) ionic
(3) hydrogen
(4) metallic

3. A carbon atom in an alkane has a total of
(1) two covalent bonds
(2) two ionic bonds
(3) four covalent bonds
(4) four ionic bonds

4. What is the maximum number of covalent bonds that a carbon atom can form?
(1) 1 (3) 3
(2) 2 (4) 4

5. A hydrocarbon molecule is saturated if the molecule contains
(1) single covalent bonds only
(2) only one double covalent bond
(3) a triple covalent bond
(4) single and double covalent bonds

6. Which statement explains why the element carbon forms so many compounds?
(1) Carbon atoms combine readily with oxygen.
(2) Carbon atoms have a high electronegativity value.
(3) Carbon atoms readily form ionic bonds with other carbon atoms.
(4) Carbon atoms readily form covalent bonds with other carbon atoms.

7. In the alkane family, each member differs from the preceding member by one carbon atom and two hydrogen atoms. Such a series of hydrocarbons is called
(1) a homologous series
(2) a periodic series
(3) an actinide series
(4) a lanthanide series

8. A molecule of ethane and a molecule of ethene both have the same
(1) empirical formula
(2) molecular formula
(3) number of carbon atoms
(4) number of hydrogen atoms

9. The products of condensation polymerization are a polymer and
(1) carbon dioxide (3) ethanol
(2) water (4) glycerol

10. Which type of compound is represented by the structural formula shown below?

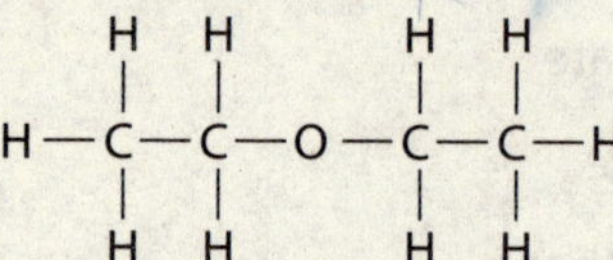

(1) a ketone
(2) an aldehyde
(3) an ester
(4) an ether

11. If a hydrocarbon molecule contains a triple bond, its IUPAC name ends in

(1) *-ane*
(2) *-ene*
(3) *-one*
(4) *-yne*

12. Which compound is an organic acid?

(1) CH_3OH
(2) CH_3OCH_3
(3) CH_3COOH
(4) CH_3COOCH_3

13. Which is the structural formula of an aldehyde?

(1)

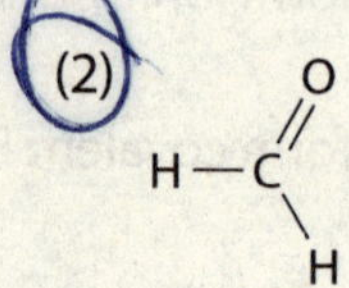

(2)

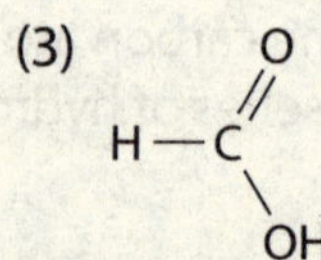

(3)

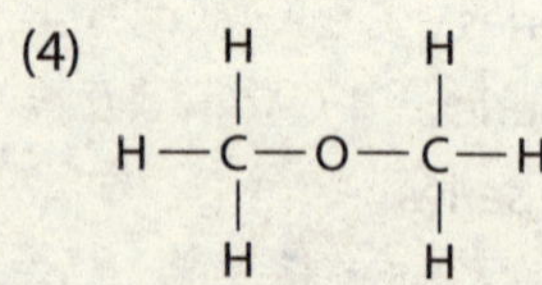

(4)

14. Which general formula represents an ether?

(1) *R*–OH
(2) *R*–CHO
(3) *R*–O–*R′*
(4) *R*–COOH

15. What are the products of a fermentation reaction?

(1) an alcohol and carbon monoxide
(2) an alcohol and carbon dioxide
(3) a salt and water
(4) a salt and an acid

Part B

16. Which compounds are isomers?

(1) 1-propanol and 2-propanol
(2) methanoic acid and ethanoic acid
(3) methanol and methanal
(4) ethane and ethanol

17. Which is the correct structural formula for 2, 2-dimethylpropane?

(1)

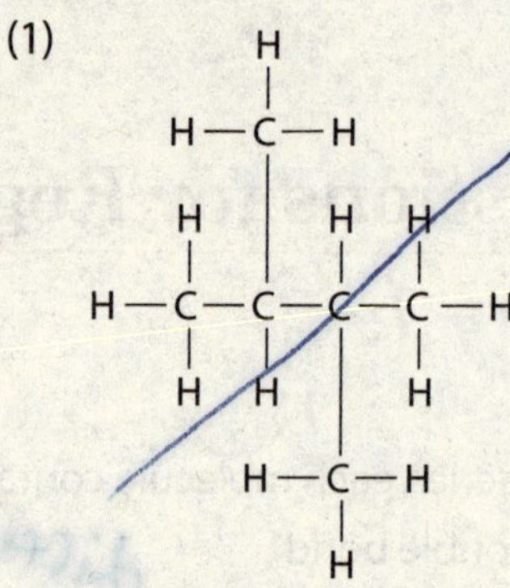

(2)

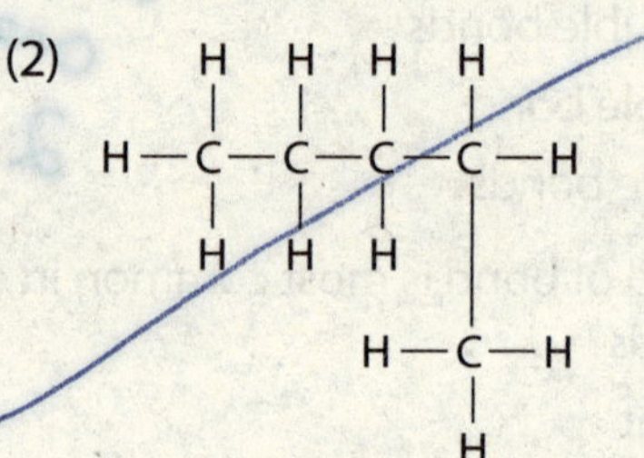

(3)

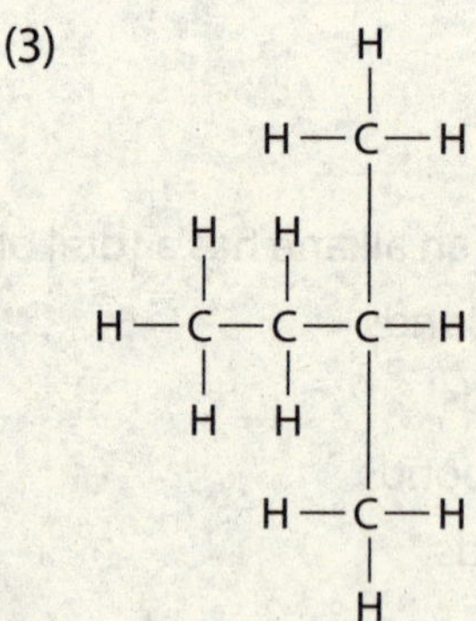

(4)

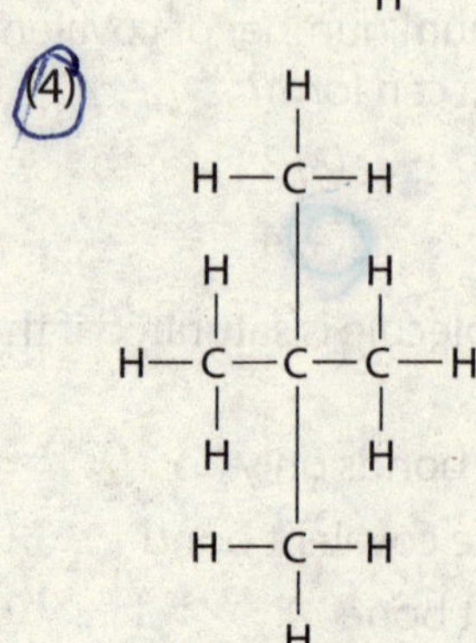

18. What is the chemical process illustrated by the following equation?

$$C_6H_{12}O_6 \rightarrow 2C_2H_5OH + 2CO_2$$

(1) fermentation (3) esterification
(2) saponification (4) polymerization

19. Which reaction is used to produce polyethylene $(C_2H_4)_n$ from ethylene?

(1) addition polymerization
(2) substitution
(3) condensation polymerization
(4) reduction

20. Which structural formula represents the product formed from the reaction of Cl_2 and C_2H_4?

(1) 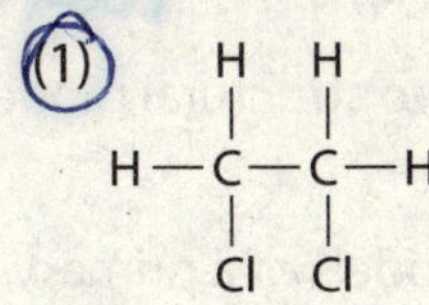

(2)
```
  Cl  Cl
  |   |
H—C═C—H
```

(3) H—C≡C—Cl

(4)
```
  H   H
  |   |
H—C—C—Cl
  |   |
  H   H
```

21. Methanol is classified as a

(1) monohydroxy alcohol
(2) secondary alcohol
(3) tertiary alcohol
(4) dihydroxy alcohol

22. What is the total number of pairs of electrons that one carbon atom shares with the other carbon atom in the molecule C_2H_4?

(1) 1
(2) 2
(3) 3
(4) 4

23. To be classified as a tertiary alcohol, the functional −OH group is bonded to a carbon atom that must be bonded to how many other carbon atoms?

(1) 1
(2) 2
(3) 3
(4) 4

24. A student investigated four different substances in the solid phase. The table below is a record of the characteristics (marked with an *X*) exhibited by each substance. Which substance has characteristics most like those of an organic compound?

(1) A (3) C
(2) B (4) D

Characteristic Tested	Substance A	Substance B	Substance C	Substance D
High melting point	*X*		*X*	
Low melting point		*X*		*X*
Soluble in water	*X*			*X*
Insoluble in water		*X*	*X*	
Decomposed under high heat		*X*		
Stable under high heat	*X*		*X*	*X*
Electrolyte	*X*			*X*
Nonelectrolyte		*X*	*X*	

25. Which hydrocarbon is a member of the alkene family?

(1) C_2H_2 (3) C_4H_{10}
(2) C_3H_6 (4) C_5H_{12}

26. Which structural formula represents a dihydroxy alcohol?

```
(1)    H  H              (3)    H  H  H
       |  |                     |  |  |
    H—C—C—H                 H—C—C—C—H
       |  |                     |  |  |
       H  OH                    OH OH OH

(2)    H  H              (4)    H  H    O
       |  |                     |  |   //
    H—C—C—H                 H—C—C—C
       |  |                     |  |   \
       OH OH                    H  H    H
```

27. Which organic compound will dissolve in water to produce a solution that will turn blue litmus red?

```
(1)    H  H
       |  |
    H—C—C—H
       |  |
       H  H

(2)    H     H
       |     |
    H—C—O—C—H
       |     |
       H     H

(3)    H  O
       |  ||
    H—C—C—O—H
       |
       H

(4)    H  O  H
       |  ||  |
    H—C—C—C—H
       |     |
       H     H
```

28. The compound 1,2-ethanediol is a

(1) monohydroxy alcohol
(2) dihydroxy alcohol
(3) primary alcohol
(4) secondary alcohol

29. Which formula represents a ketone?

(1) CH_3COOH (3) CH_3COCH_3
(2) C_2H_5OH (4) CH_3COOCH_3

30. Which condensed structural formula represents a saturated hydrocarbon?

(1) $CH_3CH_2CH_2OH$
(2) $CH_3CHOHCH_3$
(3) $CH_3CH_2CH_3$
(4) CH_2CHCH_3

Part C

31. What is the formula of the alcohol that reacts with C_2H_5COOH to produce the ester $C_2H_5COOC_2H_5$? [1]

32. What are the products of condensation polymerization? [1]

33. Why are organic reactions generally slower than reactions between ions? [1]

34. Draw and name two structural models of isomers of hexane. [2]

35. Draw structural models of a primary, secondary, and a tertiary five-carbon alcohol. [3]

36. (a) Draw the structural formula for an organic acid.

(b) Draw the structural formula for a primary alcohol.

(c) Draw the structure of the ester formed when the alcohol and acid combine in an esterification reaction. [3]

For each type of reaction in questions 37 through 41, write the number preceding the equation, chosen from the list below, that best represents that type of reaction.

(1) $C_2H_6 + Cl_2 \rightarrow C_2H_5Cl + HCl$
(2) $C_6H_{12}O_6 \rightarrow 2C_2H_5OH + 2CO_2$
(3) $CH_3COOH + CH_3OH \rightarrow CH_3COOCH_3 + H_2O$
(4) $nC_2H_4 \rightarrow (C_2H_4)n$
(5) $C_3H_5(C_{17}H_{35}COO)_3 + 3NaOH \rightarrow C_3H_5(OH)_3 + 3C_{17}H_{35}COONa$
(6) $C_2H_2 + 2Br_2 \rightarrow C_2H_2Br_4$

37. halogen substitution [1]

38. halogen addition [1]

39. esterification [1]

40. fermentation [1]

41. polymerization [1]

Nuclear Chemistry

VOCABULARY		
alpha particle	**fusion**	**tracer**
artificial transmutation	**gamma ray**	**transmutation**
beta particle	**half-life**	
fission	**radioisotope**	

Most chemical reactions involve either the exchange or sharing of electrons between atoms. Nuclear chemistry is quite different in nature because it involves changes in the nucleus. When the atomic nucleus of one element is changed into the nucleus of a different element, the reaction is called a **transmutation**. In this topic you will study various types of transmutations and learn about properties of radioactive substances.

Stability of Nuclei

Nuclei are composed of combinations of protons and neutrons. Hydrogen, with one proton, is the only element that does not contain one or more neutrons. Most nuclei are stable; that is, they are found within the "belt of stability" shown in Figure 12-1. It is the ratio of neutrons to protons that determines the stability of a given nucleus. The ratio in all nuclei with atomic numbers greater than 83 makes those nuclei unstable.

Because of this instability, all nuclei with atomic numbers greater than 83 are also radioactive, as explained in the next paragraph. For any element, an isotope that is unstable and thus radioactive is called a **radioisotope.**

An unstable nucleus spontaneously decays, forming products that are more stable. When an unstable nucleus decays, it emits radiation in the form of alpha particles, beta particles, positrons, and/or gamma radiation. An **alpha particle** is a helium nucleus composed of two protons and two neutrons. It is represented by the symbol $^{4}_{2}He$ or the symbol α, which is the Greek letter alpha. A **beta particle** (β) is an electron whose source is an atomic nucleus, while a positron is identical to an

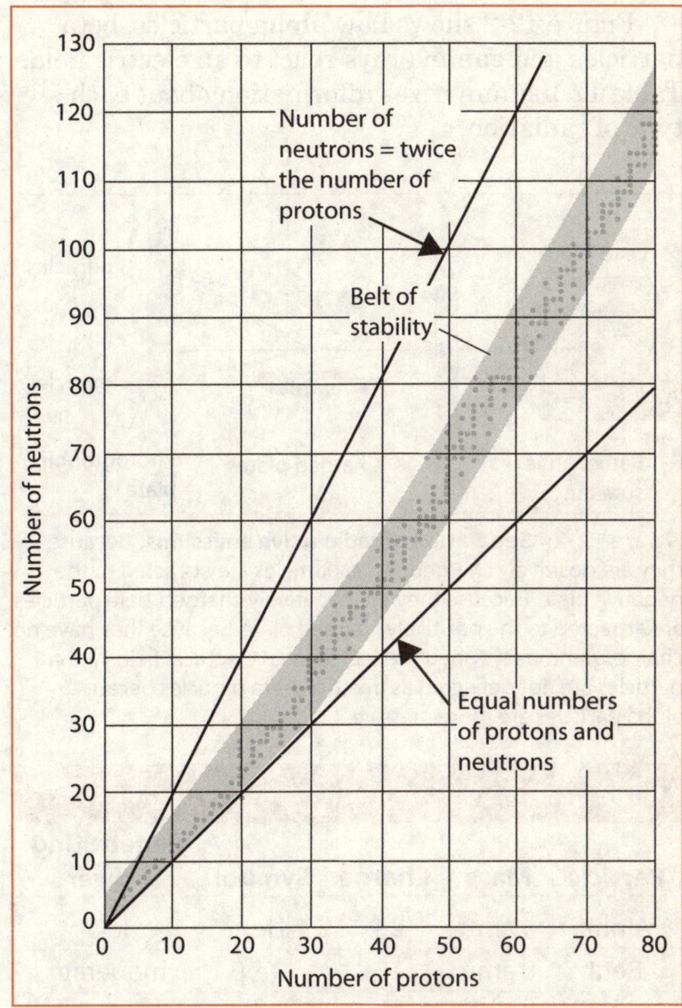

Figure 12-1. Composition of stable nuclei

electron except that it has a positive charge. Almost all nuclear decay also releases some energy in the form of **gamma rays** (γ), which are similar to X rays but have greater energy.

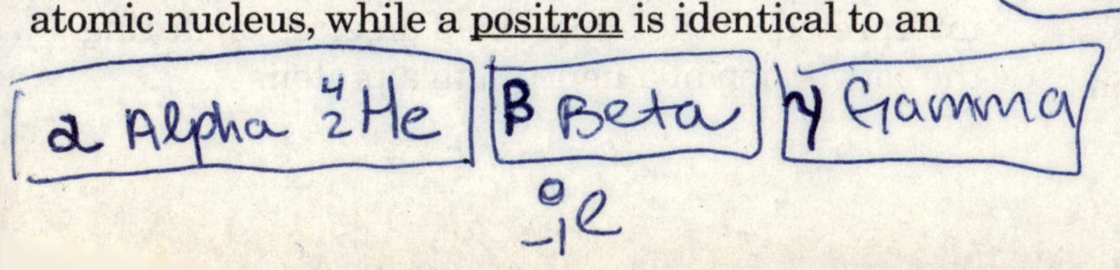

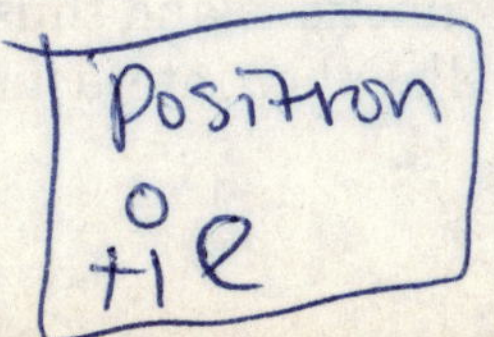

MEMORY JOGGER

A notation frequently used to show the makeup of a nucleus or subatomic particle uses a superscript before the symbol of the element to show the mass, in amu, of the particle. It also uses a subscript beneath the superscript to show the charge on the particle. For example, $^{35}_{17}Cl$ represents the nucleus of a chlorine atom. It has a mass of 35 amu and a charge of 17+. Note that for an element, the charge equals the atomic number. For a particle such as a beta particle, the symbol $^{0}_{-1}e$ shows that the particle has no appreciable mass and a charge of 1−.

Figure 12-2 shows how alpha particles, beta particles and gamma rays react to an electric field. Table 12.1 summarizes information about each type of radiation.

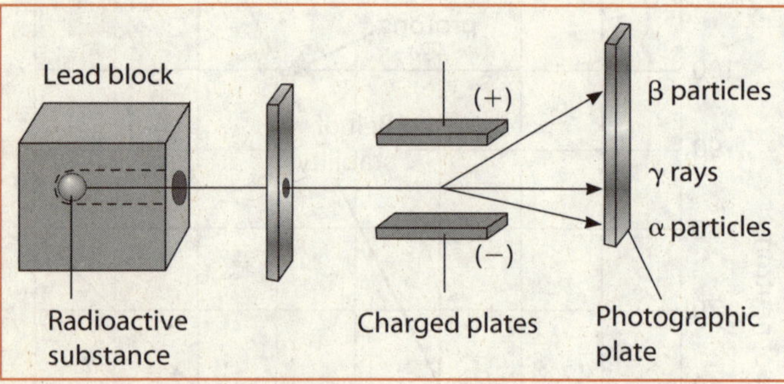

Figure 12-2. Separation of radioactive emissions: Because they are positively charged, alpha particles are attracted to the negative plate. Because they are negatively charged, beta particles are attracted to the positively charged plate. Because they have no charge, gamma rays are undeflected in an electrical field. Alpha particles are not deflected as much as beta particles because alpha particles are more massive.

Table 12-1. Some Common Forms of Radiation

Particle	Mass	Charge	Symbol	Penetrating Power
Alpha	4 amu	2+	$^{4}_{2}He$, α	low
Beta	0 amu	1−	$^{0}_{-1}e$, β	moderate
Positron	0 amu	1+	$^{0}_{+1}e$	moderate
Gamma	0 amu	none	γ	high

Radiation can be harmful when it interacts with living things. Serious damage occurs when radioactivity causes ionization of normal tissue. When molecules in a cell are ionized, they may no longer carry on their normal functions and thus may cause the death of the cell. Other interactions of radioactivity with the DNA of a cell may cause mutations to occur. When these mutations occur in sperm or egg cells, they can cause mutations to be transmitted from generation to generation.

Alpha Decay

When an unstable nucleus emits an alpha particle, the nucleus is called an alpha emitter. Alpha emission is characteristic of heavy nuclei, especially of atoms with atomic numbers greater than 82. As a nucleus emits an alpha particle, its atomic number decreases by two (the two protons of the alpha particle), and its mass number decreases by four (the two protons and two neutrons of the alpha particle). For example, when radium-226 emits an alpha particle, its atomic number decreases by two, from 88 to 86. It is then no longer an atom of radium; it has become an atom of radon (atomic number 86). During the process, the nucleus has lost a total of 4 amu, and the new radon nucleus has a total mass of 222. The alpha decay of radium-226 is shown in Figure 12-3. The process is a transmutation because the atom undergoes a change in its atomic number and becomes a different element.

Alpha decay can be summarized as follows.

- atomic number decreases by two
- number of protons decreases by two
- number of neutrons decreases by two
- mass number decreases by four

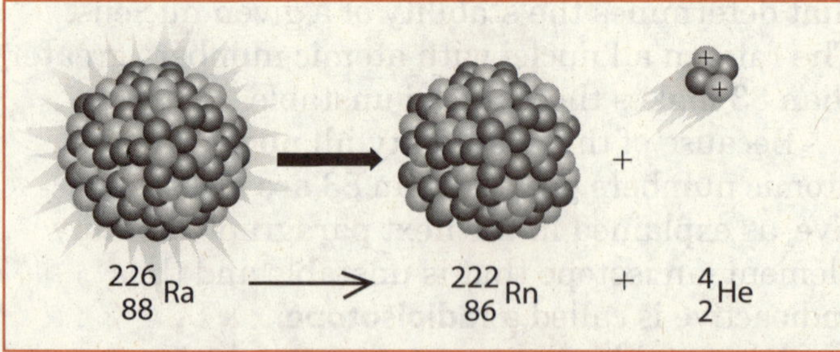

Figure 12-3. Alpha decay: In alpha decay, a nucleus ejects an alpha particle and becomes a smaller nucleus with less positive charge.

Beta Decay

A nucleus that emits a beta particle as a result of nuclear disintegration is said to undergo beta decay and is called a beta emitter. Beta decay is interpreted as the emission of an electron during the conversion of a neutron to a proton.

$$^{1}_{0}n \rightarrow ^{1}_{1}p + ^{0}_{-1}e$$

When a nucleus emits a beta particle, which has a charge of 1−, the charge on the nucleus increases by one, which also means that the atomic number increases by one. The beta decay of lead-214 to bismuth-214 is shown in Figure 12-4.

Beta decay can be summarized as follows.

- atomic number increases by one
- number of protons increases by one
- number of neutrons decreases by one
- mass number remains the same

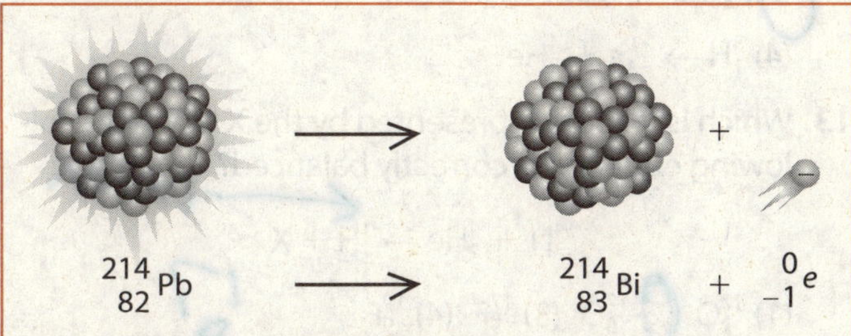

Figure 12-4. Beta decay: Beta decay has the effect of turning a neutron in the nucleus into a proton and an electron.

Positron Emission

Positron emission is interpreted as the production of a positron during the conversion of a proton to a neutron.

$$^{1}_{1}p \rightarrow ^{1}_{0}n + ^{0}_{+1}e$$

When a nucleus emits a positron, which has a charge of 1+, the charge on the nucleus decreases by one, and thus the atomic number decreases by one. For example the positron emission of potassium-37 to argon-37 is represented by the following equation.

$$^{37}_{19}\text{K} \rightarrow ^{37}_{18}\text{Ar} + ^{0}_{+1}e$$

DIGGING DEEPER

Although positron emission is a natural type of transmutation, there is another reaction that will produce the same result. When a radioactive nucleus captures one of its least energetic electrons, the result is the same as a positron emission.

$$^{37}_{19}\text{K} + ^{0}_{-1}e \rightarrow ^{37}_{18}\text{Ar}$$

This capture of a low-energy electron is called a K-capture.

Positron emission can be summarized as follows.

- atomic number decreases by one
- number of protons decreases by one
- number of neutron increases by one
- mass number remains the same

Nuclear Equations

As you have seen in this section, nuclear reactions can be represented by equations. As in chemical equations, mass and charge must balance on both sides of the equation.

For example, the following equation is balanced because the sum of charges and the sum of mass numbers are the same on both sides of the equation. For this equation, the sum of the charges of reactants equals 9 and so does the sum of the charges of the products. The sum of the mass numbers of the reactants is 18, which balances the sum of the mass numbers of the products.

$$^{14}_{7}\text{N} + ^{4}_{2}\text{He} \rightarrow ^{17}_{8}\text{O} + ^{1}_{1}\text{H}$$

By using the concept of the conservation of charge and mass number, you can identify a missing particle in an equation.

SAMPLE PROBLEM

What particle is represented by X in the following equation?

$$^{27}_{13}\text{Al} + ^{1}_{0}n \rightarrow ^{24}_{11}\text{Na} + \text{X}$$

Solution: Identify the known and unknown values.

Known	*Unknown*
charge and mass numbers for Al, neutron, and Na	identity of X = ?

Balance charge on both sides of the equation:

The sum of the charges on the left is 13. Therefore, the sum on the right must also be 13. Na accounts for 11, so X must have a charge of 2.

Balance mass numbers on both sides of the equation:

The sum of the mass numbers on the left is 28, so the sum on the right must also be 28. Na accounts for 24, so X must have mass number of 4.

The particle with an atomic number of 2 and a mass number of 4 is the alpha particle ($^{4}_{2}$He). X is an alpha particle.

Review Questions

1. Which particle has the greatest mass? (1) an alpha particle (2) a beta particle (3) an electron (4) a neutron

2. In the following equation, which particle is represented by the letter X?

$$^{14}_{6}C \rightarrow ^{14}_{7}N + X$$

(1) an alpha particle (2) a beta particle (3) a neutron (4) a proton

3. Which radioactive emanations have a charge of 2+? (1) alpha particles (2) beta particles (3) gamma rays (4) neutrons

4. Which species has a negative charge? (1) a lithium ion (2) an alpha particle (3) an aluminum ion (4) a beta particle

5. According to Reference Table N in the *Reference Tables for Physical Setting/Chemistry*, a product of the radioactive decay of Ra-226 is (1) $^{4}_{2}He$ (2) $^{226}_{89}U$ (3) $^{0}_{-1}e$ (4) $^{230}_{90}U$

6. Which equation represents nuclear disintegration resulting in release of a beta particle?

(1) $^{220}_{87}Fr + ^{4}_{2}He \rightarrow ^{224}_{89}Ac$

(2) $^{239}_{94}Pu \rightarrow ^{235}_{92}U + ^{4}_{2}He$

(3) $^{32}_{15}P + ^{0}_{-1}e \rightarrow ^{32}_{14}Si$

(4) $^{198}_{79}Au \rightarrow ^{198}_{80}Hg + ^{0}_{-1}e$

7. In the nuclear equation $^{232}_{90}Th \rightarrow ^{228}_{88}Ra + X$, The letter X represents (1) an alpha particle (2) a beta particle (3) a gamma ray (4) a neutron

8. In the reaction $^{238}_{92}U \rightarrow X + ^{4}_{2}He$, the particle represented by X is (1) $^{234}_{90}Th$ (2) $^{234}_{92}U$ (3) $^{238}_{93}Np$ (4) $^{242}_{94}Pu$

9. Which nuclear equation represents beta decay?

(1) $^{27}_{13}Al + ^{4}_{2}He \rightarrow ^{30}_{15}P + ^{1}_{0}n$

(2) $^{238}_{92}U \rightarrow ^{234}_{90}Th + ^{4}_{2}He$

(3) $^{14}_{6}C \rightarrow ^{14}_{7}N + ^{0}_{-1}e$

(4) $^{37}_{18}Ar + ^{0}_{-1}e \rightarrow ^{37}_{17}Cl$

10. In which reaction does the letter X represent an alpha particle?

(1) $^{226}_{88}Ra \rightarrow ^{222}_{86}Rn + X$ (3) $^{230}_{90}Th \rightarrow ^{230}_{88}Ra + X$

(2) $^{234}_{90}Th \rightarrow ^{235}_{91}Pa + X$ (4) $^{234}_{92}U \rightarrow ^{234}_{90}Th + X$

11. What does the X represent in the following reaction?

$$^{2}_{1}H + ^{3}_{1}H \rightarrow ^{4}_{2}He + ^{1}_{0}n + X$$

(1) a released electron (2) another neutron (3) energy converted from mass (4) mass converted from energy

12. Which of the following nuclear reactions is classified as alpha decay?

(1) $^{14}_{6}C \rightarrow ^{14}_{7}N + ^{0}_{+1}e$

(2) $^{42}_{19}K \rightarrow ^{42}_{20}Ca + ^{0}_{-1}e$

(3) $^{226}_{88}Ra \rightarrow ^{222}_{86}Rn + ^{4}_{2}He$

(4) $^{3}_{1}H \rightarrow ^{0}_{-1}e + ^{4}_{2}He$

13. Which isotope is represented by the X when the following equation is correctly balanced?

$$^{14}_{7}N + ^{4}_{2}He \rightarrow ^{1}_{1}H + X$$

(1) $^{17}_{2}O$ (2) $^{17}_{8}O$ (3) $^{17}_{9}F$ (4) $^{19}_{9}F$

14. Which element has no stable isotopes? (1) $_{27}Co$ (2) $_{51}Sb$ (3) $_{90}Th$ (4) $_{82}Pb$

15. Write balanced nuclear equations for each of the following:

(a) beta decay of Pb-210

(b) beta decay of Cs-137

(c) alpha decay of Rn-222

(d) alpha decay of Au-185

(e) positron emission of Fe-53

(f) positron emission of Ca-37

Transmutations

Nuclear reactions can be either naturally occurring or artificial. Alpha decay, beta decay, and positron emission occur in nature as a result of unstable neutron-to-proton ratios. When bombarding the nucleus with high-energy particles brings about the change, the process is given the name of **artificial transmutation**. Scientists in research and commercial settings perform artificial transmutations.

TYPES OF TRANSMUTATIONS There are two types of artificial transmutations. The first type involves the collision of a charged particle with a target nucleus. If charged particles such as protons or alpha particles are to react with atomic nuclei, they must have sufficient energy to overcome the repulsive forces that exist between positively charged objects. Scientists can supply this energy by accelerating charged particles in devices called cyclotrons and synchrotrons, which use magnetic or electrostatic fields to speed up protons and other charged particles.

A second type of artificial transmutation occurs when a neutron collides with a target nucleus. Neutrons can be obtained as by-products of nuclear reactors similar to those used to generate electricity. Because the neutron does not possess a charge, it is not repelled by the target nucleus and can be captured by the "strong" force that holds protons and neutrons in the nucleus. These reactions are used to prepare radioactive nuclei from stable nuclei. Listed below are a few examples.

$$^{238}_{92}U + ^{1}_{0}n \rightarrow ^{239}_{92}U$$

$$^{59}_{27}Co + ^{1}_{0}n \rightarrow ^{60}_{27}Co$$

$$^{32}_{16}S + ^{1}_{0}n \rightarrow ^{32}_{15}P + ^{1}_{1}H$$

It is easy to tell the difference between natural and artificial transmutation. Natural transmutation consists of a single nucleus undergoing decay. Artificial transmutation will have two reactants, a fast-moving particle and a target material.

Review Questions

16. The nuclear reaction

$$^{4}_{2}He + ^{27}_{13}Al \rightarrow ^{30}_{15}P + ^{1}_{0}n$$

is an example of (1) nuclear fusion (2) nuclear fission (3) natural transmutation (4) artificial transmutation

17. Which particle is represented by X in the following transmutation?

$$^{234}_{90}Th \rightarrow ^{234}_{91}Pa + X$$

(1) $^{0}_{-1}e$ (2) $^{4}_{2}He$ (3) $^{1}_{1}H$ (4) $^{0}_{+1}e$

18. Which equation represents a nuclear reaction that is an example of an artificial transmutation?

(1) $^{43}_{21}Sc \rightarrow ^{43}_{20}Ca + ^{0}_{+1}e$

(2) $^{14}_{7}N + ^{4}_{2}He \rightarrow ^{17}_{8}O + ^{1}_{1}H$

(3) $^{10}_{4}Be \rightarrow ^{10}_{5}B + ^{0}_{-1}e$

(4) $^{14}_{6}C \rightarrow ^{14}_{7}N + ^{0}_{-1}e$

19. Which particle is represented by X in the following transmutation?

$$^{131}_{53}I \rightarrow ^{131}_{54}Xe + X$$

(1) alpha (2) beta (3) neutron (4) proton

20. What is the charge of the element represented by X in the following transmutation?

$$^{1}_{0}n + ^{235}_{92}U \rightarrow ^{141}_{56}Ba + X + 3^{1}_{0}n$$

(1) 36 (2) 89 (3) 92 (4) 93

21. Which species is represented by X in the following transmutation?

$$^{9}_{4}Be + ^{1}_{1}H \rightarrow ^{4}_{2}He + X$$

(1) $^{8}_{3}Li$ (2) $^{6}_{3}Li$ (3) $^{8}_{5}B$ (4) $^{10}_{5}B$

22. Which species is represented by X in the following transmutation?

$$^{7}_{3}Li + X \rightarrow ^{8}_{4}Be$$

(1) $^{1}_{1}H$ (2) $^{2}_{1}H$ (3) $^{3}_{2}He$ (4) $^{4}_{2}He$

23. What is the identity of particle X in the following transmutation?

$$^{9}_{4}Be + X \rightarrow ^{6}_{3}Li + ^{4}_{2}He$$

(1) $^{1}_{1}H$ (2) $^{2}_{1}H$ (3) $^{0}_{-1}e$ (4) $^{1}_{0}n$

Fission and Fusion

A **fission** reaction involves the splitting of a heavy nucleus to produce lighter nuclei. A **fusion** reaction involves the combining of light nuclei to produce a heavier nucleus. In both types of reactions, the total mass of the products is less than the total nuclear mass of the reactants.

Conversion of Matter to Energy

At first glance this loss of mass seems to contradict our concept that matter (mass) can neither be created nor destroyed. Properly expressed, the law states that the total amount of matter and energy cannot be destroyed. The loss of mass in these nuclear reactions represents a conversion of some matter into energy. The relationship was expressed by Albert Einstein in his famous equation

$$E = mc^2$$

where E is energy, m is mass, and c is the speed of light, which is 3.00×10^8 m/s. Because the speed of light is such a large number, you can see that the conversion of a minute amount of matter produces an extremely large amount of energy.

The energy produced by nuclear reactions is far greater than that of ordinary chemical reactions. The conversion of 1.00 g of matter into energy yields 9.00×10^{13} J. When 1.00 g of methane is burned in an ordinary chemical reaction, there is a release of 5.56×10^4 J of energy. Gram for gram, the nuclear reaction gives off over a billion times as much energy.

This conversion of matter into energy occurs when protons and neutrons are combined into nuclei. The total mass of the nucleus is less than the sum of the masses of the individual protons and neutrons. The matter that has been converted into energy is called the mass defect.

Fission Reactions

A fission reaction begins with the capture of a neutron by the nucleus of a heavy element such as uranium-235 or plutonium-239. The nucleus produced by the capture is unstable. It immediately splits, undergoing the process of fission. The products of fission are two middle-weight nuclei, one or more neutrons, and a large amount of energy. A small amount of matter from the original atom of uranium or plutonium is converted into energy.

$$^{1}_{0}n + ^{235}_{92}\text{U} \rightarrow ^{142}_{56}\text{Ba} + ^{91}_{36}\text{Kr} + 3^{1}_{0}n + \text{energy}$$

The products shown in this equation are only two of more than 200 different radioactive products that may be produced by the fission process. Some other possible products are shown in Figure 12-5.

Fusion Reactions

Fusion reactions involve the combining of light nuclei to form heavier ones. The most common example of fusion occurs in the sun where hydrogen nuclei react in a series to produce helium nuclei. These fusion reactions produce the huge amounts of energy released by the sun. One of the possible series of reactions involving the fusion of hydrogen nuclei to form helium and release energy is given by the following sequence.

$$^{1}_{1}\text{H} + ^{1}_{1}\text{H} \rightarrow ^{2}_{1}\text{H} + ^{0}_{+1}e$$

$$^{1}_{1}\text{H} + ^{2}_{1}\text{H} \rightarrow ^{3}_{2}\text{He}$$

$$^{3}_{2}\text{He} + ^{3}_{2}\text{He} \rightarrow ^{4}_{2}\text{He} + 2^{1}_{1}\text{H}$$

$$^{3}_{2}\text{He} + ^{1}_{1}\text{H} \rightarrow ^{4}_{2}\text{He} + ^{0}_{+1}e$$

While these reactions produce the energy from the sun, they are not yet available to produce energy here on Earth. Extremely high temperatures and pressures are needed to allow the positively charged hydrogen nuclei to fuse into helium. When methods are developed that will contain a reaction such as these and make it practical, an important new energy source will have been developed. One major advantage of fusion as an energy source is that the products are not highly radioactive, like the products of fission reactions.

Review Questions

24. High energy is a requirement for fusion reactions to occur because the nuclei involved (1) attract each other because they have like charges (2) attract each other because they have unlike charges (3) repel each other because they have like charges (4) repel each other because they have unlike charges

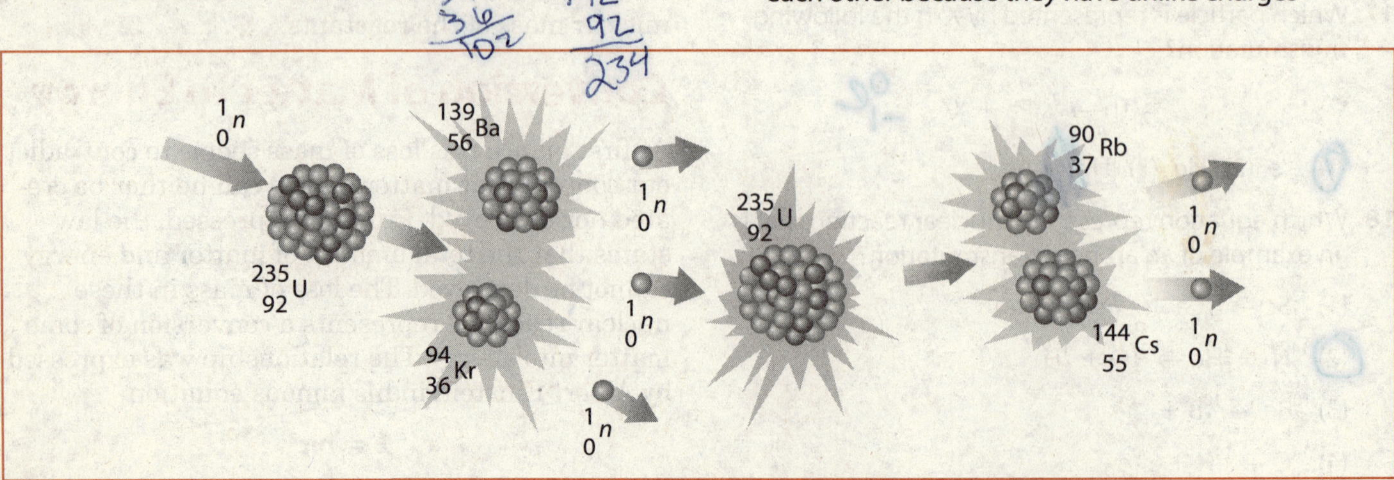

Figure 12-5. Fission: Fission involves the splitting of a large nucleus into middle-weight nuclei and neutrons.

25. When a uranium nucleus breaks up into fragments, which type of nuclear reaction occurs? (1) fusion (2) fission (3) replacement (4) redox

26. Which pair of nuclei can undergo a fusion reaction? (1) potassium-40 and cadmium-113 (2) zinc-64 and calcium-44 (3) uranium-238 and lead-208 (4) hydrogen-2 and hydrogen-3

27. What process is represented by the following reaction?

$$^{2}_{1}H + ^{2}_{1}H \rightarrow ^{4}_{2}He + \text{energy}$$

(1) fission (2) fusion (3) artificial transmutation (4) alpha decay

28. During a fission reaction, which type of particle is captured by a nucleus? (1) deuteron (2) electron (3) neutron (4) proton

29. What is the primary result of a fission reaction? (1) conversion of mass to energy (2) conversion of energy to mass (3) binding together of two heavy nuclei (3) binding together of two light nuclei

30. Compared to an ordinary chemical reaction, a fission reaction will (1) release smaller amounts of energy (2) release larger amounts of energy (3) absorb small amounts of energy (4) absorb larger amounts of energy

31. Which type of reaction produces energy and intensely radioactive waste products? (1) fusion of tritium and deuterium (2) fission of uranium (3) burning of heating oil (4) burning of wood

32. Which process occurs in a controlled fusion reaction? (1) Light nuclei collide to produce heavier nuclei. (2) Heavy nuclei collide to produce lighter nuclei. (3) Neutron bombardment splits light nuclei. (4) Neutron bombardment splits heavy nuclei.

33. Consider this reaction.

$$^{235}_{92}U + ^{1}_{0}n \rightarrow ^{138}_{56}Ba + ^{95}_{36}Kr + 3^{1}_{0}n + \text{energy}$$

This equation can best be described as (1) fission (2) fusion (3) natural decay (4) endothermic

Half-Life

Radioactive substances decay at a constant rate that is not dependent on factors such as temperature, pressure or concentration. It is also a random event. That is, it is impossible to predict when a given unstable nucleus will decay. However, the number of unstable nuclei that will decay in a given time in a sample of the element can be predicted. The time it takes for half of the atoms in a given sample of an element to decay is called the **half-life** of the element. Each isotope has its own half-life. The shorter the half-life of an isotope, the less stable it is. Table N in *Reference Tables for Physical Setting/Chemistry* lists various isotopes together with their half-lives and the mode by which they decay. Figure 12-6 shows the decay of carbon-14.

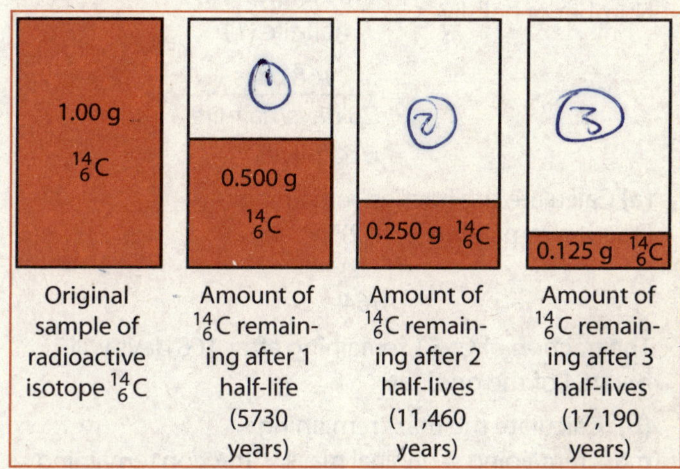

Figure 12-6. The half-life of C-14

If radioactive substance X has a half-life of 5 s, each five seconds will result in the amount of X present at the beginning of the time being reduced by half. If 20 g of X begins to decay, after 5 s only 10 g will remain. Five seconds later, only 5 g of the original 20 g will remain. ($1/2 \times 1/2 = 1/4$). The fraction remaining after a given number of half-lives is calculated using the relationship

$$\text{fraction remaining} = (1/2)^n$$

where n is equal to the number of half-lives. The number of half-lives is calculated by dividing the total time that the substance has decayed by the half-life of the isotope.

SAMPLE PROBLEM

Most chromium atoms are stable, but Cr-51 is an unstable isotope with a half-life of 28 days.

(a) What fraction of a sample of Cr-51 will remain after 168 days?

(b) If a sample of Cr-51 has an original mass of 52.0 g, what mass will remain after 168 days?

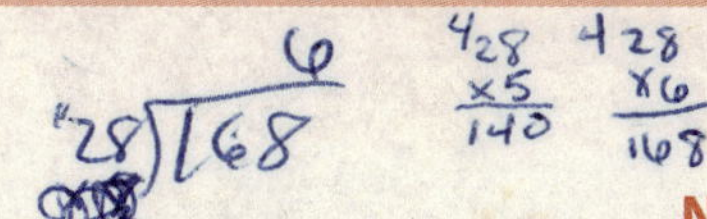

Solution: Identify the known and unknown values.

Known	*Unknown*
half-life of Cr-51 = 28 days	fraction of Cr-51 remaining after 168 days = ?
time = 168 days	mass of Cr-51 remaining after 168 days = ? g
original mass = 52.0 g	

Determine how many half-lives elapse during 168 days.

$$\text{Number of half-lives} = \frac{\text{time elapsed } (t)}{\text{half-life } (T)}$$

$$= \frac{168 \text{ days}}{28 \text{ days/half-life}}$$

$$= 6 \text{ half-lives}$$

(a) Calculate the fraction remaining.

$$\text{Fraction remaining} = (1/2)^{t/T}$$
$$= (1/2)^{6}$$
$$= 1/64$$

The fraction of Cr-51 remaining after 168 days will be 1/64 of the original.

(b) Calculate the mass remaining.

$$\text{mass remaining} = \text{original mass} \times \text{fraction remaining}$$
$$= 52.0 \text{ g} \times 1/64 = 0.813 \text{ g}$$

Mass remaining can also be calculated by dividing the current mass by 2 at the end of each half-life.

After 1 half-life, mass = 52.0 g/2 = 26.0 g
After 2 half-lives, mass = 26.0 g/2 = 13.0 g
After 3 half-lives, mass = 13.0 g/2 = 6.50 g
After 4 half-lives, mass = 6.50 g/2 = 3.25 g
After 5 half-lives, mass = 3.25 g/2 = 1.63 g
After 6 half-lives, mass = 1.63 g/2 = 0.815 g

The initial amount of a substance can be determined from the half-life, the amount remaining, and the time passed. When determining an original amount, each half-life represents a doubling of the amount present.

SAMPLE PROBLEM

How much was present originally in a sample of Cr-51 if 0.75 mg remains after 168 days?

Solution: Identify the known and unknown values.

Known	*Unknown*
half-life of Cr-51 = 28 days	original mass = ? g
time = 168 days	
final mass = 0.75 mg	

From the previous sample problem, 168 days represents 6 half-life periods for Cr-51. The sample will double for each half-life period. Multiply the remaining amount by a factor of 2 for each half-life.

$$\text{original mass} = \text{final mass} \times 2^{n}$$
$$= 0.75 \text{ mg} \times 2^{6}$$
$$= 48 \text{ mg}$$

GRAPHING HALF-LIFE DATA As a radioactive substance decays, a Geiger counter can be used to record the individual decay events. When this data is graphed, it provides a way to measure the half-life of an isotope. Figure 12-7 is a graph of the data of the decay of a hypothetical radioisotope. To determine the half-life, select a convenient count on the y-axis (1). Draw a vertical line to a value of half of the original (2). In this case the line extends from 6000 counts to 3000 counts. The half-life is represented by the time segment on the x-axis (2 to 3), or 15 minutes. It does not matter where you begin, the half-life will still be the same. Simply draw a line to reduce the count by half, and then read the half-life.

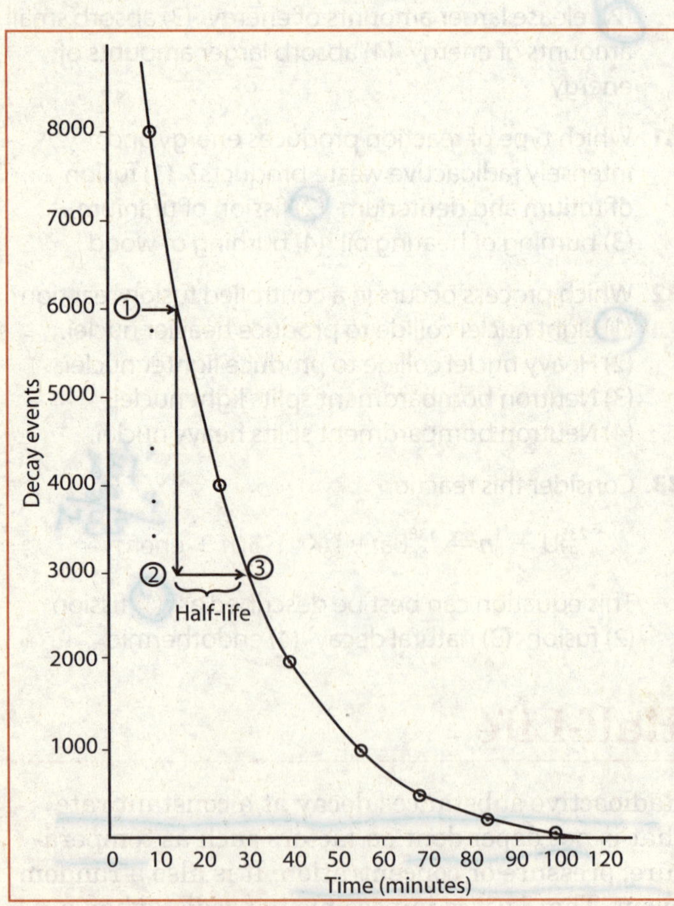

Figure 12-7. A hypothetical half-life

Review Questions

Refer to Table N in *Reference Tables for Physical Setting/Chemistry* for half-life values as needed.

34. After 62.0 hours, 1.0 g remains unchanged from a sample of ^{42}K. How much ^{42}K was in the original sample? (1) 8.0 g (2) 16 g (3) 32 g (4) 64 g

35. If 80 mg of a radioactive element decays to 10 mg in 30 min, what is the element's half-life in minutes? (1) 10 (2) 20 (3) 30 (4) 40

36. In 6.20 h, a 100.-g sample of Ag-112 decays to 25.0 g. What is the half-life of Ag-112? (1) 1.60 h (2) 3.10 h (3) 6.20 h (4) 12.4 h

37. Which of the following 10-g samples of a radioisotope will decay to the greatest extent in 28 days? (1) P-32 (2) Kr-85 (3) Fr-220 (4) I-131

38. How many hours are required for potassium-42 to undergo three half-life periods? (1) 6.2 h (2) 12.4 h (3) 24.8 h (4) 37.2 h

39. What is the mass of K-42 remaining in a 16-g sample of K-42 after 37.2 h? (1) 1.0 g (2) 2.0 g (3) 8.0 g (4) 4.0 g

40. If 3.0 g of Sr-90 in a rock sample remained in 1999, approximately how many grams of Sr-90 were present in the original rock sample in 1943? (1) 9.0 g (2) 6.0 g (3) 3.0 g (4) 12 g

41. A sample of I-131 decays to 1.0 g in 40 days. What was the mass of the original sample? (1) 8.0 g (2) 16 g (3) 32 g (4) 4.0 g

42. What is the total mass of Rn-222 remaining in an original 160-mg sample of Rn-222 after 19.1 days? (1) 2.5 mg (2) 5.0 mg (3) 10. mg (4) 20. mg

43. Which radioactive sample would contain the greatest remaining mass of the radioactive isotope after 10 years? (1) 2.0 grams of Au-198 (2) 2.0 grams of K-42 (3) 4.0 grams of P-32 (4) 4.0 grams of Co-60

44. A radioactive element has a half-life of 2 days. Which fraction represents the amount of an original sample of this element remaining after 6 days? (1) $\frac{1}{8}$ (2) $\frac{1}{2}$ (3) $\frac{1}{3}$ (4) $\frac{1}{4}$

45. Which of the following radioisotopes has the shortest half-life? (1) ^{14}C (2) ^{3}H (3) ^{37}K (4) ^{32}P

46. As the temperature of a sample of a radioactive element decreases, the half-life of the element (1) decreases (2) increases (3) remains the same (4) varies with the pressure

47. If one-eighth of the mass of the original sample of a radioisotope remains unchanged after 4800 years, the isotope could be (1) H-3 (2) K-42 (3) Sr-90 (4) Ra-226

Uses and Dangers of Radioisotopes

Radioisotopes have many practical applications in industry, medicine, and research. They also have potential dangers because of harm that could be done by the radiation released.

Uses of Radioisotopes

The following applications represent just a few of the many uses of radioisotopes. Although they must be used with proper precautions, certain radioisotopes provide information that could not be determined from isotopes that are not radioactive.

DATING Carbon-14 is perhaps best known for its use in dating previously living materials. There is an extremely small amount of C-14 in the atmosphere. When an organism is alive, it uses this radioactive carbon in the same way as it uses stable C-12. When the organism dies, it no longer takes in any carbon.

Each gram of carbon in a living organism emits about 15 disintegrations per minute (dpm). After the organism dies and time passes, the radioactive C-14 continues to decay, but it is not replaced. Therefore the dpm decreases with time. Because the half-life of C-14 is 5730 years, after that time period there will only be about 7 dpm for each gram of carbon in the organism. Therefore, a reading of 7 dpm/g carbon indicates the remains are about 5700 years old, while a reading of 3.5 dpm would show a material to be about twice as old, about 11,000 years. After about four half-lives, C-14 becomes ineffective as a method for dating materials because too little C-14 remains to be accurately measured.

U-238 is a radioactive material that spontaneously decays through a series of steps until it forms stable Pb-206. As time passes, the amount of lead in the sample will increase as the amount of uranium decreases. Scientists can use the ratio of U-238/Pb-206 to date rocks and other geological formations.

CHEMICAL TRACERS The ability to detect radioactive materials and their decay products makes it possible to determine their presence or absence in a substance. Any radioisotope used to follow the path of a material in a system is called a **tracer.** If radioactive P-31 is present in fertilizer administered to a plant, the uptake of the phosphorus can be traced by detectors. Scientists can then determine the proper amounts and timing of fertilizer applications. C-14 is another tracer used to map the path of carbon in metabolic processes.

INDUSTRIAL APPLICATIONS Radioactive isotopes and gamma rays are absorbed in varying amounts by different materials. The thicker the material, the more radiation that will be absorbed. Thus, radiation products can be used to measure the thickness of materials such as a plastic wrap or aluminum foil or to test the strength of a weld.

MEDICAL APPLICATIONS Certain radioisotopes that are quickly eliminated from the body and have short half-lives are important as tracers in medical diagnosis. Many are also used in treatment of various disorders and diseases. Others might be used to make materials free from bacteria or other disease-causing organisms.

I-131 has uses both in the detection and treatment of thyroid conditions. Because iodine accumulates in the thyroid gland, small amounts of I-131 can be administered to a patient and a radiogram made of the thyroid to diagnose a disorder. When a person has an overactive thyroid (hyperthyroidism), I-131 can be given in large enough doses to destroy some of the thyroid and reduce its production of thyroxin.

Cobalt-60 emits large amounts of gamma radiation as it decays. These rays can be aimed at cancerous tumors. The rapidly growing cells of the tumor are more likely to be killed than normal cells by the gamma rays.

Intense beams of gamma radiation can be used to irradiate foods to kill bacteria. Certain types of foods, such as spices, are irradiated on a regular basis. Irradiation of produce and meats has also been approved in many locations. By killing the bacteria present, the food lasts longer without spoiling and causes fewer bacterial infections in those who consume it. Other destruction of bacteria by radiation is also important. Co-60 and Cs-137 are two of the sources of gamma radiation currently being used to destroy anthrax bacilli.

Technetium, atomic number 43, is a radioactive element that is rapidly absorbed by cancerous cells. When Tc-99 is given to patients with cancerous tumors, it accumulates in the tumor and can easily be detected by a scan. When radioisotopes are used for diagnostic purposes, it is advantageous if they have a short half-life and are quickly eliminated by the body so that they do not damage healthy tissue.

Radiation Risks

The uses of radiation are not without risks. While radioisotopes can be used to kill cancerous cells, they also have the potential of damaging normal tissue. High doses of radiation can cause serious illness and death. Radiation can cause mutations that could potentially be passed from generation to generation.

Nuclear power plants are a particular problem. After the fuel rods no longer have enough uranium to make them useful in the reactor, they contain many decay products, many with long half-lives. It is difficult to store and dispose of these waste products.

Of major concern to many people is the overall safety issue of nuclear power plants themselves. While the plants are designed to protect the public, there is still a danger of a nuclear accident that might release radioactivity into the air or water. The 1986 accident at Chernobyl in Ukraine destroyed farmland that will probably be unusable for generations.

Review Questions

48. Which radioisotope is used for diagnosing thyroid disorders? (1) cobalt-60 (2) uranium-238 (3) lead-206 (4) iodine-131

49. Which procedure is based on the half-life of a radioisotope? (1) accelerating to increase kinetic energy (2) radiation to kill cancer cells (3) counting to determine a level of radioactivity (4) dating to determine age

50. Radiated food can be safely stored for a longer time because radiation (1) prevents air oxidation (2) prevents air reduction (3) kills bacteria (4) causes bacteria to mutate

51. Which two characteristics do radioisotopes have that are useful in medical diagnosis? (1) long half-lives and slow elimination from the body (2) long half-lives and quick elimination from the body (3) short half-lives and slow elimination from the body (4) short half-lives and quick elimination from the body

52. A radioactive-dating procedure to determine the age of a mineral compares the mineral's remaining amounts of U-238 and the isotope (1) Pb-206 (2) Bi-206 (3) Pb-214 (4) Bi-214

53. Which isotopic ratio needs to be determined when the age of ancient wooden objects is investigated? (1) U-235 to U-238 (2) H-2 to H-3 (3) N-16 to N-14 (4) C-14 to C-12

54. A radioisotope is called a tracer when it is used to (1) kill bacteria (2) kill cancerous tissue (3) determine the age of animal skeletal remains (4) determine the path of an element in an organism

55. Which radioactive isotope is used in geological dating? (1) U-238 (2) I-131 (3) Co-60 (4) Tc-99

56. Which isotope can be used as a tracer to study the age of organic material? (1) C-12 (2) C-14 (3) Sr-88 (4) Sr-90

57. Brain tumors can be located by using an isotope of (1) C-14 (2) I-131 (3) Tc-99 (4) U-238

Questions for Regents Practice

Part A

1. Samples of elements that are radioactive must contain atoms
(1) with stable nuclei
(2) with unstable nuclei
(3) in the excited state
(4) in the ground state

2. Organic molecules react to form a product. These reactions can be studied using
(1) Sr-90
(2) Co-60
(3) N-16
(4) C-14

3. Radiation used in the processing of food is intended to
(1) increase the rate of nutrient decomposition
(2) kill microorganisms that are found in food
(3) convert ordinary nutrients to more stable forms
(4) replace chemical energy with nuclear energy

4. The age of certain minerals can be determined if they contain the nuclide
(1) P-32
(2) Co-60
(3) U-238
(4) Au-198

5. The course of a chemical reaction can be traced by using a
(1) polar molecule
(2) diatomic molecule
(3) stable isotope
(4) radioisotope

6. Bombarding a nucleus with high-energy particles that change it from one element into another is called
(1) a half-reaction
(2) a breeder reaction
(3) artificial transmutation
(4) natural transmutation

7. An alpha decay results in the formation of a new element with the atomic number
(1) increased by two
(2) increased by four
(3) decreased by two
(4) decreased by four

8. When a radioactive nucleus emits a beta particle, the atom's
(1) mass number is increased by 1
(2) mass number is decreased by 1
(3) atomic number is increased by 1
(4) atomic number is decreased by 1

9. As the temperature increases, pressure remaining constant, the half-life of a radioactive element

(1) decreases (3) remains the same
(2) increases (4) depends on the mass

10. Which of the following is not deflected by an electric field?

(1) alpha (3) positron
(2) beta (4) gamma ray

Part B

11. Which statement explains why fusion reactions are difficult to initiate?

(1) Positive nuclei attract each other.

(2) Positive nuclei repel each other.

(3) Neutrons prevent nuclei from getting close enough to fuse.

(4) Electrons prevent nuclei from getting close enough to fuse.

12. Which particle has the greatest chance of overcoming the electrostatic forces surrounding the nucleus of an atom?

(1) an alpha particle (3) a proton
(2) a beta particle (4) a neutron

13. The diagram below shows a nuclear reaction in which a neutron is captured by a heavy nucleus. Which type of reaction is illustrated by the diagram?

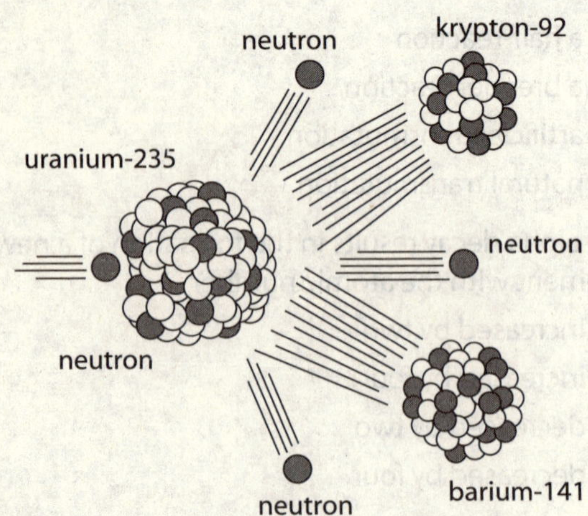

(1) an endothermic fission reaction

(2) an exothermic fission reaction

(3) an endothermic fusion reaction

(4) an exothermic fusion reaction

14. Which equation represents a fusion reaction?

(1) ${}^{3}_{1}H + {}^{1}_{1}H \rightarrow {}^{2}_{4}He$

(2) ${}^{40}_{18}Ar + {}^{1}_{1}H \rightarrow {}^{40}_{19}K + {}^{1}_{0}n$

(3) ${}^{234}_{91}Pa \rightarrow {}^{234}_{92}U + {}^{0}_{-1}e$

(4) ${}^{226}_{88}Ra \rightarrow {}^{222}_{86}Rn + {}^{2}_{4}He$

15. Consider this reaction.

$${}^{27}_{13}Al + {}^{4}_{2}He \rightarrow {}^{30}_{15}P + {}^{1}_{0}n$$

This reaction can best be described as

(1) beta decay

(2) artificial transmutation

(3) fission

(4) fusion

16. When I-131 undergoes radioactive decay, which element is formed?

(1) Te-132

(2) Xe-131

(3) I-130

(4) Sb-127

17. Which is a gaseous radioactive waste product that is released into the atmosphere after it has decayed to a safe radiation level?

(1) radon-222

(2) radium-226

(3) cesium-137

(4) cobalt-60

18. In which list can all particles be accelerated by an electric field?

(1) alpha particles, beta particles, and neutrons

(2) alpha particles, beta particles, and protons

(3) alpha particles, protons, and neutrons

(4) beta particles, protons, and neutrons

19. Which particle is represented by X in the following correctly balanced nuclear equation?

$${}^{12}_{6}C + {}^{249}_{98}Cf \rightarrow {}^{257}_{104}Unq + 4X$$

(1) ${}^{14}_{7}H$

(2) ${}^{1}_{0}n$

(3) ${}^{4}_{2}He$

(4) ${}^{0}_{-1}e$

20. The diagram below shows a nuclear reaction in which a neutron is captured by a heavy nucleus.

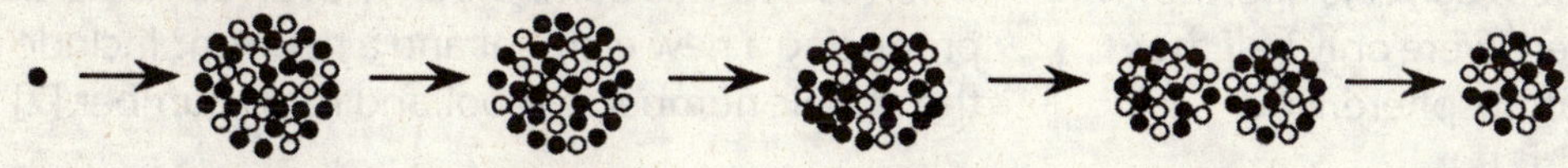

Which type of reaction is illustrated by the diagram?

(1) an endothermic fission reaction

(2) an exothermic fission reaction

(3) an endothermic fusion reaction

(4) an exothermic fusion reaction

21. In which process is mass converted to energy by the process of fission?

(1) ${}^{14}_{7}N + {}^{1}_{0}n \rightarrow {}^{14}_{6}C + {}^{1}_{1}H$

(2) ${}^{235}_{92}U + {}^{1}_{0}n \rightarrow {}^{87}_{35}Br + {}^{146}_{57}La + 3{}^{1}_{0}n$

(3) ${}^{226}_{88}Ra \rightarrow {}^{222}_{86}Rn + {}^{4}_{2}He$

(4) ${}^{2}_{1}H + {}^{2}_{1}H \rightarrow {}^{4}_{2}He$

22. Write a balanced nuclear equation for the positron emission of Al-24.

23. Write a balanced nuclear equation for the beta decay of Si-35.

24. Write a balanced nuclear equation for the alpha decay of Ra-226.

25. How many grams of a 20-g sample of C-14 would remain after 17,190 years?

26. Complete the equation:

$${}^{1}_{0}n + {}^{235}_{92}U \rightarrow {}^{72}_{30}Zn + X + 4{}^{1}_{0}n$$

Part C

27. Write an equation for the alpha decay of ${}^{214}_{84}Po$, followed by a beta decay of the product. [2]

28. Using Figure 12-1 as a guide, indicate whether each of the following nuclei is stable or unstable. [3]

(a) ${}^{110}_{40}X$ (c) ${}^{110}_{60}X$

(b) ${}^{90}_{60}X$

29. Explain why it is more difficult to cause an artificial transmutation with an alpha particle than with a neutron. [2]

30. Plot the following data and determine the half-life of the isotope. [3]

Time (min)	**Counts** (per min)
0	12 000
2	7 000
4	4 000
8	1 400
10	800
12	450

31. Points X and Y lie outside the zone of stability on the graph shown below. Write a beta decay equation for X and a positron emission equation for Y. Plot the positions of the products of the decay of X and Y on the graph. [4]

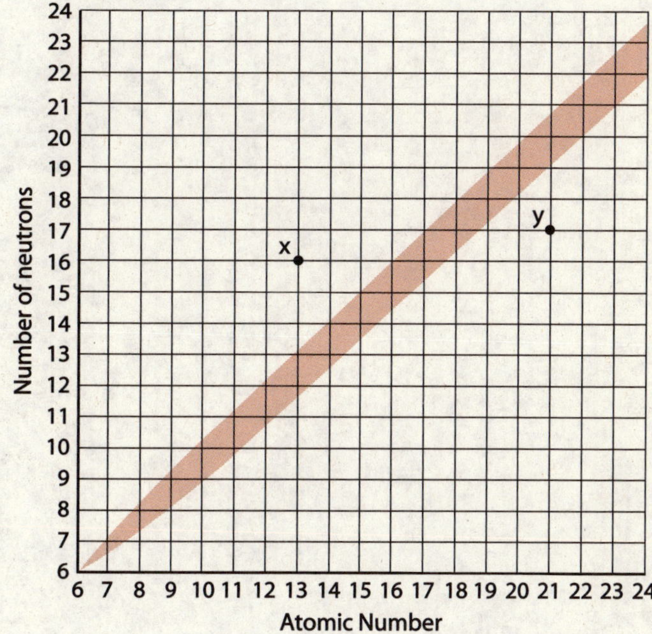

32. Carbon dating presumes that the amount of C-14 has been constant in the atmosphere over many thousands of years. Suppose that 5700 years ago, the amount of C-14 in the atmosphere were only half the amount that is currently in the atmosphere. How would this affect carbon dating? [1]

33. The elements with atomic numbers greater than 92 are all human-made. What element was produced when Es-253 was bombarded with an alpha particle, producing a new element and a neutron? Include the atomic number, symbol, and mass number. [2]

Appendix 1: Reference Tables for Physical Setting/Chemistry

2003 Edition • Reference Tables for Physical Setting/Chemistry

Table A
Standard Temperature and Pressure

Name	Value	Unit
Standard Pressure	101.3 kPa 1 atm	kilopascal atmosphere
Standard Temperature	273 K 0°C	kelvin degree Celsius

Table B
Physical Constants for Water

Heat of Fusion	334 J/g
Heat of Vaporization	2260 J/g
Specific Heat Capacity of H_2O (ℓ)	4.18 J/g•K

Table C
Selected Prefixes

Factor	Prefix	Symbol
10^3	kilo-	k
10^{-1}	deci-	d
10^{-2}	centi-	c
10^{-3}	milli-	m
10^{-6}	micro-	μ
10^{-9}	nano-	n
10^{-12}	pico-	p

Table D
Selected Units

Symbol	Name	Quantity
m	meter	length
kg	kilogram	mass
Pa	pascal	pressure
K	kelvin	temperature
mol	mole	amount of substance
J	joule	energy, work, quantity of heat
s	second	time
L	liter	volume
ppm	part per million	concentration
M	molarity	solution concentration

Table E
Selected Polyatomic Ions

H_3O^+	hydronium	CrO_4^{2-}	chromate
Hg_2^{2+}	dimercury (I)	$Cr_2O_7^{2-}$	dichromate
NH_4^+	ammonium	MnO_4^-	permanganate
$C_2H_3O_2^-$ CH_3COO^-	acetate	NO_2^-	nitrite
		NO_3^-	nitrate
CN^-	cyanide	O_2^{2-}	peroxide
CO_3^{2-}	carbonate	OH^-	hydroxide
HCO_3^-	hydrogen carbonate	PO_4^{3-}	phosphate
$C_2O_4^{2-}$	oxalate	SCN^-	thiocyanate
ClO^-	hypochlorite	SO_3^{2-}	sulfite
ClO_2^-	chlorite	SO_4^{2-}	sulfate
ClO_3^-	chlorate	HSO_4^-	hydrogen sulfate
ClO_4^-	perchlorate	$S_2O_3^{2-}$	thiosulfate

Table F
Solubility Guidelines

Ions That Form *Soluble* Compounds	Exceptions
Group 1 ions (Li^+, Na^+, etc.)	
ammonium (NH_4^+)	
nitrate (NO_3^-)	
acetate ($C_2H_3O_2^-$ or CH_3COO^-)	
hydrogen carbonate (HCO_3^-)	
chlorate (ClO_3^-)	
perchlorate (ClO_4^-)	
halides (Cl^-, Br^-, I^-)	when combined with Ag^+, Pb^{2+}, and Hg_2^{2+}
sulfates (SO_4^{2-})	when combined with Ag^+, Ca^{2+}, Sr^{2+}, Ba^{2+}, and Pb^{2+}

Ions That Form *Insoluble* Compounds	Exceptions
carbonate (CO_3^{2-})	when combined with Group 1 ions or ammonium (NH_4^+)
chromate (CrO_4^{2-})	when combined with Group 1 ions or ammonium (NH_4^+)
phosphate (PO_4^{3-})	when combined with Group 1 ions or ammonium (NH_4^+)
sulfide (S^{2-})	when combined with Group 1 ions or ammonium (NH_4^+)
hydroxide (OH^-)	when combined with Group 1 ions, Ca^{2+}, Ba^{2+}, or Sr^{2+}

Table G Solubility Curves

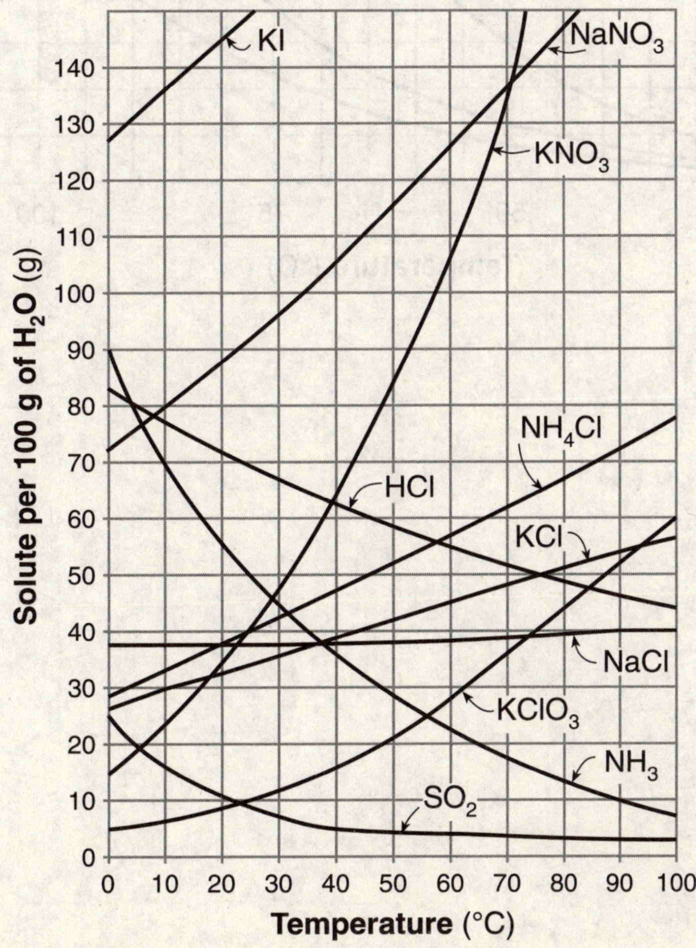

Table H
Vapor Pressure of Four Liquids

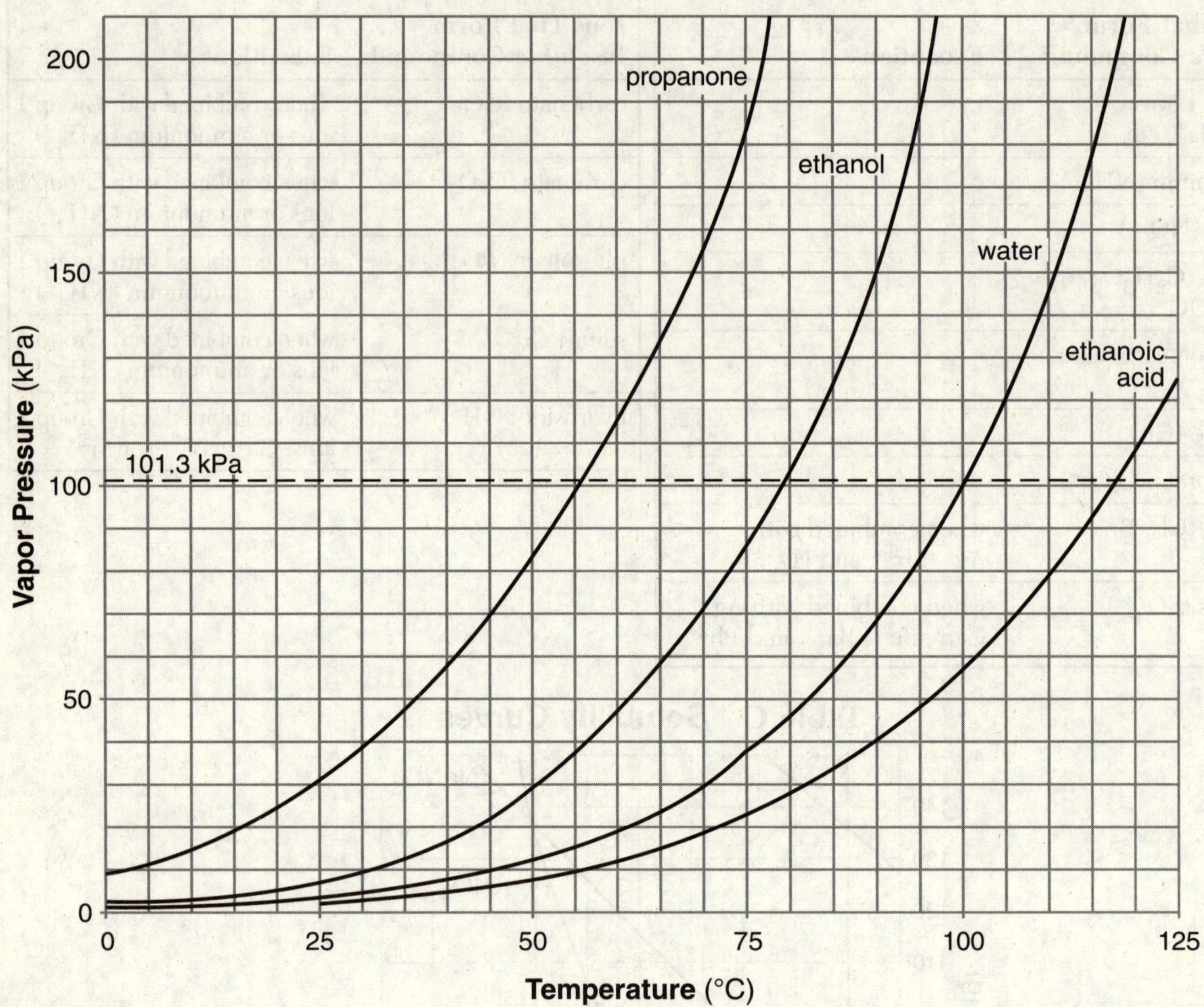

Table I
Heats of Reaction at 101.3 kPa and 298 K

Reaction	ΔH (kJ)*
$CH_4(g) + 2O_2(g) \longrightarrow CO_2(g) + 2H_2O(\ell)$	–890.4
$C_3H_8(g) + 5O_2(g) \longrightarrow 3CO_2(g) + 4H_2O(\ell)$	–2219.2
$2C_8H_{18}(\ell) + 25O_2(g) \longrightarrow 16CO_2(g) + 18H_2O(\ell)$	–10943
$2CH_3OH(\ell) + 3O_2(g) \longrightarrow 2CO_2(g) + 4H_2O(\ell)$	–1452
$C_2H_5OH(\ell) + 3O_2(g) \longrightarrow 2CO_2(g) + 3H_2O(\ell)$	–1367
$C_6H_{12}O_6(s) + 6O_2(g) \longrightarrow 6CO_2(g) + 6H_2O(\ell)$	–2804
$2CO(g) + O_2(g) \longrightarrow 2CO_2(g)$	–566.0
$C(s) + O_2(g) \longrightarrow CO_2(g)$	–393.5
$4Al(s) + 3O_2(g) \longrightarrow 2Al_2O_3(s)$	–3351
$N_2(g) + O_2(g) \longrightarrow 2NO(g)$	+182.6
$N_2(g) + 2O_2(g) \longrightarrow 2NO_2(g)$	+66.4
$2H_2(g) + O_2(g) \longrightarrow 2H_2O(g)$	–483.6
$2H_2(g) + O_2(g) \longrightarrow 2H_2O(\ell)$	–571.6
$N_2(g) + 3H_2(g) \longrightarrow 2NH_3(g)$	–91.8
$2C(s) + 3H_2(g) \longrightarrow C_2H_6(g)$	–84.0
$2C(s) + 2H_2(g) \longrightarrow C_2H_4(g)$	+52.4
$2C(s) + H_2(g) \longrightarrow C_2H_2(g)$	+227.4
$H_2(g) + I_2(g) \longrightarrow 2HI(g)$	+53.0
$KNO_3(s) \xrightarrow{H_2O} K^+(aq) + NO_3^-(aq)$	+34.89
$NaOH(s) \xrightarrow{H_2O} Na^+(aq) + OH^-(aq)$	–44.51
$NH_4Cl(s) \xrightarrow{H_2O} NH_4^+(aq) + Cl^-(aq)$	+14.78
$NH_4NO_3(s) \xrightarrow{H_2O} NH_4^+(aq) + NO_3^-(aq)$	+25.69
$NaCl(s) \xrightarrow{H_2O} Na^+(aq) + Cl^-(aq)$	+3.88
$LiBr(s) \xrightarrow{H_2O} Li^+(aq) + Br^-(aq)$	–48.83
$H^+(aq) + OH^-(aq) \longrightarrow H_2O(\ell)$	–55.8

*Minus sign indicates an exothermic reaction.

Table J
Activity Series**

Most ↓ Least	Metals	Nonmetals	Most ↓ Least
Most	Li	F_2	Most
	Rb	Cl_2	
	K	Br_2	
	Cs	I_2	
	Ba		
	Sr		
	Ca		
	Na		
	Mg		
	Al		
	Ti		
	Mn		
	Zn		
	Cr		
	Fe		
	Co		
	Ni		
	Sn		
	Pb		
	**H_2		
	Cu		
	Ag		
Least	Au		Least

**Activity Series based on hydrogen standard

Table K
Common Acids

Formula	Name
$HCl(aq)$	hydrochloric acid
$HNO_3(aq)$	nitric acid
$H_2SO_4(aq)$	sulfuric acid
$H_3PO_4(aq)$	phosphoric acid
$H_2CO_3(aq)$ or $CO_2(aq)$	carbonic acid
$CH_3COOH(aq)$ or $HC_2H_3O_2(aq)$	ethanoic acid (acetic acid)

Table L
Common Bases

Formula	Name
$NaOH(aq)$	sodium hydroxide
$KOH(aq)$	potassium hydroxide
$Ca(OH)_2(aq)$	calcium hydroxide
$NH_3(aq)$	aqueous ammonia

Table M
Common Acid–Base Indicators

Indicator	Approximate pH Range for Color Change	Color Change
methyl orange	3.2–4.4	red to yellow
bromthymol blue	6.0–7.6	yellow to blue
phenolphthalein	8.2–10	colorless to pink
litmus	5.5–8.2	red to blue
bromcresol green	3.8–5.4	yellow to blue
thymol blue	8.0–9.6	yellow to blue

Table N
Selected Radioisotopes

Nuclide	Half-Life	Decay Mode	Nuclide Name
^{198}Au	2.69 d	β^-	gold-198
^{14}C	5730 y	β^-	carbon-14
^{37}Ca	175 ms	β^+	calcium-37
^{60}Co	5.26 y	β^-	cobalt-60
^{137}Cs	30.23 y	β^-	cesium-137
^{53}Fe	8.51 min	β^+	iron-53
^{220}Fr	27.5 s	α	francium-220
^{3}H	12.26 y	β^-	hydrogen-3
^{131}I	8.07 d	β^-	iodine-131
^{37}K	1.23 s	β^+	potassium-37
^{42}K	12.4 h	β^-	potassium-42
^{85}Kr	10.76 y	β^-	krypton-85
^{16}N	7.2 s	β^-	nitrogen-16
^{19}Ne	17.2 s	β^+	neon-19
^{32}P	14.3 d	β^-	phosphorus-32
^{239}Pu	2.44×10^4 y	α	plutonium-239
^{226}Ra	1600 y	α	radium-226
^{222}Rn	3.82 d	α	radon-222
^{90}Sr	28.1 y	β^-	strontium-90
^{99}Tc	2.13×10^5 y	β^-	technetium-99
^{232}Th	1.4×10^{10} y	α	thorium-232
^{233}U	1.62×10^5 y	α	uranium-233
^{235}U	7.1×10^8 y	α	uranium-235
^{238}U	4.51×10^9 y	α	uranium-238

ms = milliseconds; s = seconds; min = minutes;
h = hours; d = days; y = years

Table O
Symbols Used in Nuclear Chemistry

Name	Notation	Symbol
alpha particle	${}^{4}_{2}\text{He}$ or ${}^{4}_{2}\alpha$	α
beta particle (electron)	${}^{0}_{-1}\text{e}$ or ${}^{0}_{-1}\beta$	β^-
gamma radiation	${}^{0}_{0}\gamma$	γ
neutron	${}^{1}_{0}\text{n}$	n
proton	${}^{1}_{1}\text{H}$ or ${}^{1}_{1}\text{p}$	p
positron	${}^{0}_{+1}\text{e}$ or ${}^{0}_{+1}\beta$	β^+

Table P
Organic Prefixes

Prefix	Number of Carbon Atoms
meth-	1
eth-	2
prop-	3
but-	4
pent-	5
hex-	6
hept-	7
oct-	8
non-	9
dec-	10

Table Q
Homologous Series of Hydrocarbons

Name	General Formula	Examples	
		Name	Structural Formula
alkanes	C_nH_{2n+2}	ethane	H H | | H—C—C—H | | H H
alkenes	C_nH_{2n}	ethene	H H \ / C=C / \ H H
alkynes	C_nH_{2n-2}	ethyne	H—C≡C—H

n = number of carbon atoms

Table R
Organic Functional Groups

Class of Compound	Functional Group	General Formula	Example
halide (halocarbon)	$-F$ (fluoro-) $-Cl$ (chloro-) $-Br$ (bromo-) $-I$ (iodo-)	$R-X$ (X represents any halogen)	$CH_3CHClCH_3$ 2-chloropropane
alcohol	$-OH$	$R-OH$	$CH_3CH_2CH_2OH$ 1-propanol
ether	$-O-$	$R-O-R'$	$CH_3OCH_2CH_3$ methyl ethyl ether
aldehyde	$-\overset{O}{\overset{\parallel}{C}}-H$	$R-\overset{O}{\overset{\parallel}{C}}-H$	$CH_3CH_2\overset{O}{\overset{\parallel}{C}}-H$ propanal
ketone	$-\overset{O}{\overset{\parallel}{C}}-$	$R-\overset{O}{\overset{\parallel}{C}}-R'$	$CH_3\overset{O}{\overset{\parallel}{C}}CH_2CH_2CH_3$ 2-pentanone
organic acid	$-\overset{O}{\overset{\parallel}{C}}-OH$	$R-\overset{O}{\overset{\parallel}{C}}-OH$	$CH_3CH_2\overset{O}{\overset{\parallel}{C}}-OH$ propanoic acid
ester	$-\overset{O}{\overset{\parallel}{C}}-O-$	$R-\overset{O}{\overset{\parallel}{C}}-O-R'$	$CH_3CH_2\overset{O}{\overset{\parallel}{C}}OCH_3$ methyl propanoate
amine	$-\overset{\mid}{N}-$	$R-\overset{R'}{\overset{\mid}{N}}-R''$	$CH_3CH_2CH_2NH_2$ 1-propanamine
amide	$-\overset{O}{\overset{\parallel}{C}}-\overset{\mid}{N}H$	$R-\overset{O}{\overset{\parallel}{C}}-\overset{R'}{\overset{\mid}{N}}H$	$CH_3CH_2\overset{O}{\overset{\parallel}{C}}-NH_2$ propanamide

R represents a bonded atom or group of atoms.

Periodic Table of the Elements

KEY

Atomic Mass →	12.0111	−4 +2 +4 ← Selected Oxidation States
Symbol →	**C**	
Atomic Number →	6	
Electron Configuration →	2-4	

Relative atomic masses are based on ^{12}C = 12.000

Note: Mass numbers in parentheses are mass numbers of the most stable or common isotope.

Period	Group 1	2	3	4	5	6	7	8	9	10	11	12	13	14	15	16	17	18
1	1.00794 +1 −1 **H** 1 1																	4.00260 0 **He** 2 2
2	6.941 +1 **Li** 3 2-1	9.01218 +2 **Be** 4 2-2											10.81 +3 **B** 5 2-3	12.0111 −4 +2 +4 **C** 6 2-4	14.0067 −3 −2 −1 +1 +2 +3 +4 +5 **N** 7 2-5	15.9994 −2 **O** 8 2-6	18.998403 −1 **F** 9 2-7	20.179 0 **Ne** 10 2-8
3	22.98977 +1 **Na** 11 2-8-1	24.305 +2 **Mg** 12 2-8-2											26.98154 +3 **Al** 13 2-8-3	28.0855 −4 +2 +4 **Si** 14 2-8-4	30.97376 −3 +3 +5 **P** 15 2-8-5	32.06 −2 +4 +6 **S** 16 2-8-6	35.453 −1 +1 +3 +5 +7 **Cl** 17 2-8-7	39.948 0 **Ar** 18 2-8-8
4	39.0983 +1 **K** 19 2-8-8-1	40.08 +2 **Ca** 20 2-8-8-2	44.9559 +3 **Sc** 21 2-8-9-2	47.88 +2 +3 +4 **Ti** 22 2-8-10-2	50.9415 +2 +3 +4 +5 **V** 23 2-8-11-2	51.996 +2 +3 +6 **Cr** 24 2-8-13-1	54.9380 +2 +3 +4 +7 **Mn** 25 2-8-13-2	55.847 +2 +3 **Fe** 26 2-8-14-2	58.9332 +2 +3 **Co** 27 2-8-15-2	58.69 +2 +3 **Ni** 28 2-8-16-2	63.546 +1 +2 **Cu** 29 2-8-18-1	65.39 +2 **Zn** 30 2-8-18-2	69.72 +3 **Ga** 31 2-8-18-3	72.59 −4 +2 +4 **Ge** 32 2-8-18-4	74.9216 −3 +3 +5 **As** 33 2-8-18-5	78.96 −2 +4 +6 **Se** 34 2-8-18-6	79.904 −1 +1 +5 **Br** 35 2-8-18-7	83.80 0 +2 **Kr** 36 2-8-18-8
5	85.4678 +1 **Rb** 37 2-8-18-8-1	87.62 +2 **Sr** 38 2-8-18-8-2	88.9059 +3 **Y** 39 2-8-18-9-2	91.224 +4 **Zr** 40 2-8-18-10-2	92.9064 +3 +5 **Nb** 41 2-8-18-12-1	95.94 +3 +6 **Mo** 42 2-8-18-13-1	(98) +4 +6 +7 **Tc** 43 2-8-18-14-1	101.07 +3 **Ru** 44 2-8-18-15-1	102.906 +3 **Rh** 45 2-8-18-16-1	106.42 +2 +4 **Pd** 46 2-8-18-18	107.868 +1 **Ag** 47 2-8-18-18-1	112.41 +2 **Cd** 48 2-8-18-18-2	114.82 +3 **In** 49 2-8-18-18-3	118.71 +2 +4 **Sn** 50 2-8-18-18-4	121.75 −3 +3 +5 **Sb** 51 2-8-18-18-5	127.60 −2 +4 +6 **Te** 52 2-8-18-18-6	126.905 −1 +1 +5 +7 **I** 53 2-8-18-18-7	131.29 0 +2 +4 +6 **Xe** 54 2-8-18-18-8
6	132.905 +1 **Cs** 55 2-8-18-18-8-1	137.33 +2 **Ba** 56 2-8-18-18-8-2	138.906 +3 **La** 57 2-8-18-18-9-2	178.49 +4 **Hf** 72 **18-32-10-2	180.948 +5 **Ta** 73 -18-32-11-2	183.85 +6 **W** 74 -18-32-12-2	186.207 +4 +6 +7 **Re** 75 -18-32-13-2	190.2 +3 +4 **Os** 76 -18-32-14-2	192.22 +3 +4 **Ir** 77 -18-32-15-2	195.08 +2 +4 **Pt** 78 -18-32-17-1	196.967 +1 +3 **Au** 79 -18-32-18-1	200.59 +1 +2 **Hg** 80 -18-32-18-2	204.383 +1 +3 **Tl** 81 -18-32-18-3	207.2 +2 +4 **Pb** 82 -18-32-18-4	208.980 +3 +5 **Bi** 83 -18-32-18-5	(209) +2 +4 **Po** 84 -18-32-18-6	(210) **At** 85 -18-32-18-7	(222) 0 **Rn** 86 -18-32-18-8
7	(223) +1 **Fr** 87 -18-32-18-8-1	226.025 +2 **Ra** 88 -18-32-18-8-2	227.028 +3 **Ac** 89 -18-32-18-9-2	(261) **Rf** 104	(262) **Db** 105	(263) **Sg** 106	(264) **Bh** 107	(265) **Hs** 108	(268) **Mt** 109	(269) **Uun*** 110	(272) **Uuu** 111	(277) **Uub** 112		(285) **Uuq** 114				

140.12 +3 +4 **Ce** 58	140.908 +3 **Pr** 59	144.24 +3 **Nd** 60	(145) +3 **Pm** 61	150.36 +2 +3 **Sm** 62	151.96 +2 +3 **Eu** 63	157.25 +3 **Gd** 64	158.925 +3 **Tb** 65	162.50 +3 **Dy** 66	164.930 +3 **Ho** 67	167.26 +3 **Er** 68	168.934 +3 **Tm** 69	173.04 +2 +3 **Yb** 70	174.967 +3 **Lu** 71
232.038 +4 **Th** 90	231.036 +4 +5 **Pa** 91	238.029 +3 +4 +5 +6 **U** 92	237.048 +3 +4 +5 +6 **Np** 93	(244) +3 +4 +5 +6 **Pu** 94	(243) +3 +4 +5 +6 **Am** 95	(247) +3 **Cm** 96	(247) +3 +4 **Bk** 97	(251) +3 **Cf** 98	(252) **Es** 99	(257) **Fm** 100	(258) **Md** 101	(259) **No** 102	(260) **Lr** 103

**Denotes the presence of (2-8-) for elements 72 and above

*The systematic names and symbols for elements of atomic numbers above 109 will be used until the approval of trivial names by IUPAC.

Table S
Properties of Selected Elements

Atomic Number	Symbol	Name	Ionization Energy (kJ/mol)	Electro-negativity	Melting Point (K)	Boiling Point (K)	Density** (g/cm^3)	Atomic Radius (pm)
1	H	hydrogen	1312	2.1	14	20	0.00009	37
2	He	helium	2372	—	1	4	0.000179	32
3	Li	lithium	520	1.0	454	1620	0.534	155
4	Be	beryllium	900	1.6	1551	3243	1.8477	112
5	B	boron	801	2.0	2573	3931	2.340	98
6	C	carbon	1086	2.6	3820	5100	3.513	91
7	N	nitrogen	1402	3.0	63	77	0.00125	92
8	O	oxygen	1314	3.4	55	90	0.001429	65
9	F	fluorine	1681	4.0	54	85	0.001696	57
10	Ne	neon	2081	—	24	27	0.0009	51
11	Na	sodium	496	0.9	371	1156	0.971	190
12	Mg	magnesium	736	1.3	922	1363	1.738	160
13	Al	aluminum	578	1.6	934	2740	2.698	143
14	Si	silicon	787	1.9	1683	2628	2.329	132
15	P	phosphorus	1012	2.2	44	553	1.820	128
16	S	sulfur	1000	2.6	386	718	2.070	127
17	Cl	chlorine	1251	3.2	172	239	0.003214	97
18	Ar	argon	1521	—	84	87	0.001783	88
19	K	potassium	419	0.8	337	1047	0.862	235
20	Ca	calcium	590	1.0	1112	1757	1.550	197
21	Sc	scandium	633	1.4	1814	3104	2.989	162
22	Ti	titanium	659	1.5	1933	3580	4.540	145
23	V	vanadium	651	1.6	2160	3650	6.100	134
24	Cr	chromium	653	1.7	2130	2945	7.190	130
25	Mn	manganese	717	1.6	1517	2235	7.440	135
26	Fe	iron	762	1.8	1808	3023	7.874	126
27	Co	cobalt	760	1.9	1768	3143	8.900	125
28	Ni	nickel	737	1.9	1726	3005	8.902	124
29	Cu	copper	745	1.9	1357	2840	8.960	128
30	Zn	zinc	906	1.7	693	1180	7.133	138
31	Ga	gallium	579	1.8	303	2676	5.907	141
32	Ge	germanium	762	2.0	1211	3103	5.323	137
33	As	arsenic	944	2.2	1090	889	5.780	139
34	Se	selenium	941	2.6	490	958	4.790	140
35	Br	bromine	1140	3.0	266	332	3.122	112
36	Kr	krypton	1351	—	117	121	0.00375	103
37	Rb	rubidium	403	0.8	312	961	1.532	248
38	Sr	strontium	549	1.0	1042	1657	2.540	215
39	Y	yttrium	600	1.2	1795	3611	4.469	178
40	Zr	zirconium	640	1.3	2125	4650	6.506	160

Table S
Properties of Selected Elements (cont.)

Atomic Number	Symbol	Name	Ionization Energy (kJ/mol)	Electro-negativity	Melting Point (K)	Boiling Point (K)	Density** (g/cm^3)	Atomic Radius (pm)
41	Nb	niobium	652	1.6	2741	5015	8.570	146
42	Mo	molybdenum	684	2.2	2890	4885	10.220	139
43	Tc	technetium	702	1.9	2445	5150	11.500	136
44	Ru	ruthenium	710	2.2	2583	4173	12.370	134
45	Rh	rhodium	720	2.3	2239	4000	12.410	134
46	Pd	palladium	804	2.2	1825	3413	12.020	137
47	Ag	silver	731	1.9	1235	2485	10.500	144
48	Cd	cadmium	868	1.7	594	1038	8.650	171
49	In	indium	558	1.8	429	2353	7.310	166
50	Sn	tin	709	2.0	505	2543	7.310	162
51	Sb	antimony	831	2.1	904	1908	6.691	159
52	Te	tellurium	869	2.1	723	1263	6.240	142
53	I	iodine	1008	2.7	387	458	4.930	132
54	Xe	xenon	1170	2.6	161	166	0.0059	124
55	Cs	cesium	376	0.8	302	952	1.873	267
56	Ba	barium	503	0.9	1002	1910	3.594	222
57	La	lanthanum	538	1.1	1194	3730	6.145	138
Elements 58–71 have been omitted.								
72	Hf	hafnium	659	1.3	2503	5470	13.310	167
73	Ta	tantalum	728	1.5	3269	5698	16.654	149
74	W	tungsten	759	2.4	3680	5930	19.300	141
75	Re	rhenium	756	1.9	3453	5900	21.020	137
76	Os	osmium	814	2.2	3327	5300	22.590	135
77	Ir	iridium	865	2.2	2683	4403	22.560	136
78	Pt	platinum	864	2.3	2045	4100	21.450	139
79	Au	gold	890	2.5	1338	3080	19.320	146
80	Hg	mercury	1007	2.0	234	630	13.546	160
81	Tl	thallium	589	2.0	577	1730	11.850	171
82	Pb	lead	716	2.3	601	2013	11.350	175
83	Bi	bismuth	703	2.0	545	1833	9.747	170
84	Po	polonium	812	2.0	527	1235	9.320	167
85	At	astatine	—	2.2	575	610	—	145
86	Rn	radon	1037	—	202	211	0.00973	134
87	Fr	francium	393	0.7	300	950	—	270
88	Ra	radium	—	0.9	973	1413	5.000	233
89	Ac	actinium	499	1.1	1320	3470	10.060	—
Elements 90 and above have been omitted.								

*Boiling point at standard pressure

**Density at STP

Table T
Important Formulas and Equations

Density	$d = \frac{m}{V}$	d = density m = mass V = volume
Mole Calculations	number of moles = $\frac{\text{given mass (g)}}{\text{gram-formula mass}}$	
Percent Error	% error = $\frac{\text{measured value} - \text{accepted value}}{\text{accepted value}} \times 100$	
Percent Composition	% composition by mass = $\frac{\text{mass of part}}{\text{mass of whole}} \times 100$	
Concentration	parts per million = $\frac{\text{grams of solute}}{\text{grams of solution}} \times 1\,000\,000$	
	molarity = $\frac{\text{moles of solute}}{\text{liters of solution}}$	
Combined Gas Law	$\frac{P_1V_1}{T_1} = \frac{P_2V_2}{T_2}$	P = pressure V = volume T = temperature (K)
Titration	$M_AV_A = M_BV_B$	M_A = molarity of H^+ M_B = molarity of OH^- V_A = volume of acid V_B = volume of base
Heat	$q = mC\Delta T$ $q = mH_f$ $q = mH_v$	q = heat H_f = heat of fusion m = mass H_v = heat of vaporization C = specific heat capacity ΔT = change in temperature
Temperature	K = °C + 273	K = kelvin °C = degrees Celsius
Radioactive Decay	fraction remaining = $\left(\frac{1}{2}\right)^{\frac{t}{T}}$ number of half-life periods = $\frac{t}{T}$	t = total time elapsed T = half-life

Appendix 2: Strategies for Answering Test Questions

This appendix provides strategies to help you answer various types of questions on the Regents Examination for The Physical Setting/Chemistry. Strategies are provided for answering multiple-choice and constructed-response questions as well as for questions based on diagrams, data tables, and graphs and questions that use the *Reference Tables for Physical Setting/Chemistry.*

Strategies for Multiple-Choice Questions

Multiple-choice questions will likely account for more than 50% of the Regents Examination for The Physical Setting/Chemistry. Part A is comprised totally of multiple-choice questions, whereas Part B contains some, but not all, multiple-choice questions. Therefore, it is important to be good at deciphering multiple-choice questions. Here are a few helpful strategies. For any one question, not all strategies will need to be used. The numbers are provided for reference, not to specify an order (except for Strategies 1 and 2).

1. Always read the entire question, but wait to read the choices. (See Strategy 4).
2. Carefully examine any data tables, diagrams, photographs or relevant part(s) of the *Reference Tables for Physical Setting/Chemistry* associated with the question.
3. Underline key words and phrases in the question that signal what you should be looking for in the answer. This will make you read the question more carefully. This strategy applies mostly to questions with a long introduction.
4. Try to think of an answer to the question before looking at the choices given. If you think you know the answer, write it on a separate piece of paper before reading the choices. Next, read all of the choices and compare them to your answer before making a decision. Do not select the first answer that seems correct. If your answer matches one of the choices, and you are quite sure of your response, you are probably correct. Even if your answer matches one of the choices, carefully consider all of the answers because the obvious choice is not always the correct one. If there are no exact matches, re-read the question and look for the choice that is most similar to your answer.
5. Eliminate any choices that you know are incorrect. Lightly cross out the numbers for those choices on the exam paper. Each choice you can eliminate increases your chances of selecting the correct answer.
6. If the question makes no sense after reading through it several times, leave it for later. After completing the rest of the exam, return to the question. Something you read on the other parts of the exam may give you some ideas about how to answer this question. If you are still unsure, go with your best guess. There is no penalty for guessing, but answers left blank will be counted as wrong. If you employ your best test-taking strategies, you just may select the correct answer.

Strategies for Constructed-Response Questions

Some questions in Part B and all questions in Part C of the Regents Examination for Physical Setting/Chemistry require a constructed response. Some of these questions may require you to write one or two sentences, while others may require a paragraph. No matter which type of answer is requested, the following strategies will help you write constructed responses.

1. Always read through the entire question.
2. Underline key words and phrases in the question that signal what you should be looking for in the answer. This will make you read the question more carefully.
3. Look over the *Reference Tables for Physical Setting/Chemistry* for any helpful information related to the question.
4. Write a brief outline, or at least a few notes to yourself, about what should be included in the answer.
5. Pay attention to key words that indicate how to answer the question and what you need to say in your answer. Several of these words are very common. For example, you might be asked to discuss, describe, explain, define, compare, contrast, or design. The table below lists key words and directions for your answers.
6. When you write your answer, don't be so general that you are not really saying anything. Be very specific. You should use the correct terms and clearly explain the processes and relationships. Be sure to provide details, such as the names of processes, names of structures, and, if it is appropriate, how they are related. If only one example or term is required, do not give two or more. If one is correct and the other is wrong, your answer will be marked wrong.
7. If a question has two or three parts, answer each part in a separate sentence or paragraph. This will make it easy for the person scoring your paper to find all of the information. When writing your answer, don't shortchange one part of the question by spending too much time on another part.
8. If sentences are called for in the answer, be sure that you write sentences. A sentence should always have a subject and a verb, and it should not start with the word *because.* Note that you will not lose points for incorrect grammar, spelling, punctuation, or poor penmanship. However, such errors and poor penmanship could impair your ability to make your answer clear to the person scoring your paper. If that person cannot understand what you are trying to say, you will not receive the maximum number of points.

Using Key Words to Direct Your Answers

Key Word	What Direction Your Answer Should Take
Analyze	• Break the idea, concept, or situation into parts, and explain how they relate. • Carefully explain relationships, such as cause and effect.
Discuss	• Make observations about the topic or situation using facts. • Thoroughly write about various aspects of the topic or situation.
Describe	• Illustrate the subject using words. • Provide a thorough account of the topic. • Give complete answers.
Explain	• Clarify the topic of the question by spelling it out completely. • Make the topic understandable. • Provide reasons for the outcome.
Define	• State the exact meaning of topic or word. • Explain what something is or what it means.
Compare	• Relate two or more topics with an emphasis on how they are alike. • State the similarities between two or more examples.
Contrast	• Relate two or more topics with an emphasis on how they are different. • State the differences between two or more examples.
Design	• Plan an experiment or component of an experiment. Map out your proposal being sure to provide information about all of the required parts.
State	• Express or tell in words. • Explain or describe using at least one fact, term, or relationship.

9. When the question calls for you to write the answer in paragraphs, do not write a "standard" essay such as you would write for social studies. Do not spend time writing an introduction, several short paragraphs, and a conclusion. Write your outline, and then answer the question directly.

Strategies for Questions Based on Diagrams

Both multiple-choice and extended-response question frequently include diagrams or pictures. Usually the diagrams provide information needed to answer the question. The diagrams may be realistic, or they may be schematic. Schematic drawings show the relationships among parts and sometimes the sequence in a system. Follow these strategies:

1. First study the diagram and think about what the diagram shows you. Be sure to read any information, such as titles or labels, that go with the diagram.
2. Read the question. Follow the strategies for either multiple-choice or constructed-response questions listed previously.

Strategies for Questions Based on Data Tables

Most data tables contain information that summarizes a topic. A table uses rows and columns to condense information and to present it in an organized way. Rows are the horizontal divisions going from left to right across the table, while columns are vertical divisions going from top to bottom. Column headings name the type of information included in a table. Sometimes different categories of information are listed down the left-hand column of the table. When answering a question with a data table, use the following strategies.

1. Find the title of the table. It is usually located across the top.
2. Determine the number of columns in the table and their purpose.
3. Determine the number of rows and their purpose.
4. Read across the rows and down the columns to determine what the relationships are.
5. Now you are ready to read the question with the data table. Answer the question by using the suggested strategies for multiple-choice or constructed-response questions listed previously.

Strategies for Questions Based on Graphs

Graphs represent relationships in a visual form that is easy to read. Three different types of graphs commonly used on science Regents Examinations are line graphs, bar graphs, and circle graphs. Line graphs are the most common, and they show the relationship between two changing quantities, or variables. When a question is based on any of the three types of graphs, the information you need to correctly answer the question can usually be found on the graph.

When answering a question that includes a graph, first ask yourself these questions:

- What information does the graph provide?
- What are the variables?
- What seems to happen to one variable as the other changes?

After a careful analysis of the graph, use the appropriate strategies for multiple-choice or constructed-response questions.

Strategies for Questions Based on Readings

Some questions in Part C of the Regents Examination will require the reading of a chemistry-related passage. The answers to the questions will be based upon the article's content and your knowledge of chemistry. The key to doing well on these questions is a thorough reading and comprehension of the article and a strong overall knowledge of chemistry. To help prepare for this portion of the Regents Examination, read the following sample reading passages and answer the related questions.

Smoke Detectors

Each year over than 3000 people are killed in home fires, a majority of which occur between 11 P.M. and 6 A.M. It is estimated that over 2000 lives a year could be saved if more home had properly installed and working smoke detectors. There are two basic types of smoke detectors commonly purchased for home use, photoelectric and ionization. Both types are able to detect fire and both must pass the same tests in order to be certified for home use.

A photoelectric smoke detector operates by sending a beam of light through a tube. A photosensitive (light) detector is located along the inside wall of the tube. If smoke from a fire enters the tube, it causes the light beam to scatter, scattering some of the light onto the detector. The detector then sounds an alarm to warn of the fire.

An ionization detector contains a small amount (0.0002 g) of the radioisotope Am-241. The radioisotope, present in the detector as americium(IV) oxide, is manufactured by the beta decay of plutonium-241. The half-life of this decay reaction is 432 years. The Am-241 in the detector decays by alpha particle emission. The alpha particles ionize oxygen and nitrogen atoms in the air, resulting in the release of electrons. These ions and electrons are attracted to charged electrical plates they pass between, generating the flow of a small electric current. When smoke particles from a fire enter the detector, they combine with the ionized particles, neutralizing their charge. This results in a decreased electric current flow and sets off the alarm. Ionization detectors are usually more sensitive than the photoelectric detectors, but they are also easily set off by the normal products of cooking.

Base your answers to the following questions on the article and on your knowledge of chemistry.

1. Why aren't the alpha particles emitted by the Am-241 a danger to the occupants of the house?
2. Write a nuclear equation showing the production of Am-241 by the beta decay of Pu-241.
3. Write a nuclear equation showing the decay of Am-241
4. The batteries in an ionization detector must be replaced regularly. Why is it not necessary to replace the Am-241 even though it emits millions of alpha particles per second?
5. Write an equation showing the ionization of an oxygen atom.
6. What is the chemical formula of americium(IV) oxide?
7. The plates of an ionization smoke detector are positively and negatively charged. Draw a diagram showing the attractions of oxygen ions and electrons for the charged plates.
8. Assuming that both detectors are about the same cost, which detector would you pick for your house? Explain your answer.

Halogen Lights

You are probably already familiar with the ordinary light bulb, also known as an incandescent bulb. Inside the glass shell of the bulb is a thin metallic tungsten wire known as the filament. When an electric current flows through the wire, the temperature of the wire begins to increase. The temperature of the tungsten increases until it becomes white hot, a temperature at which it emits energy in the visible range by a process called incandescence. Not all of the electrical energy supplied to the bulb is converted into light. In fact, most of the energy is given off in the form of heat. The heat given off from the bulb is considered wasted energy, as the purpose of the bulb is give off light, not heat.

The space between the filament and the glass in an incandescent bulb is usually filled with a mixture of argon and nitrogen gases. While the bulb is lit, the tungsten filament is constantly evaporating. The evaporated tungsten atoms from the filament collide with the argon and nitrogen atoms, allowing them to cool and return to the filament. However, some of the tungsten atoms do not collide with the gas molecules and reach the glass shell of the bulb, causing it to darken. Eventually, the evaporating filament develops thin spots. The temperature of the filament increases at the location of the thin spot, finally reaching the melting point of tungsten. The tungsten melts and the filament breaks.

Halogen lamps, a relatively new development, are really incandescent bulbs with tungsten filaments, a noble gas, and one of the halogens, usually iodine. The iodine solid sublimes as it is heated, and makes up about 1% of the gas in the bulb. Some of the tungsten atoms that evaporate from the hot filament do not collide with the inert noble gas. As the tungsten atoms approach the glass shell of the bulb where the temperature is only about 800°C, they react with the gaseous iodine atoms to produce gaseous tungsten iodide. These molecules migrate back toward the filament where intense heat causes them to decompose. The decomposition of the tungsten iodide regenerates the reactants (tungsten and iodine). The tungsten atoms redeposit on the filament and the iodine atoms are ready to repeat the cycle.

Base your answers to the following questions on the article and on your knowledge of chemistry.

1. Why is a noble gas used rather than oxygen to fill the interior of the bulb?
2. The iodine sublimes as the halogen bulb gets hot. What is the process of sublimation? Write an equation to show the process.
3. Write an equation for the vaporization of tungsten. Include heat in your equation.
4. Write an equation to show the formation of tungsten(VI) iodide
5. Is the decomposition of tungsten(VI) iodide endothermic or exothermic? Explain your reasoning.
6. What would be the effect of using krypton or xenon in place of argon? Krypton and xenon do not conduct heat as well as argon.
7. The higher the temperature, the whiter the color of the light produced by the bulb. Adding more gas to the bulb would retain more heat, and increase the brightness. What is the maximum temperature that can be reached inside the light bulb and still have the filament remain intact?
8. Two equilibrium systems are operating in the bulb when it is lit. Describe one of them

Hydrogen: Fuel of the Future?

Today, hydrocarbons form the chief energy source on our planet. We use these fuels to heat our homes, produce electricity, and power our vehicles. Hydrocarbon fuels have two important shortcomings. First, they are in limited supply. Although new sources are still being discovered, there is a finite amount of hydrocarbon-based fuel available on Earth. Secondly, air pollution produced by the combustion of these fuels contributes to the greenhouse effect. Because of these shortcomings, scientists are researching for alternatives to fossil fuels.

One of the more promising alternatives is hydrogen. Hydrogen is a reactive gas, perhaps best known for the fire and explosion of the German airship the Hindenburg in 1937. When hydrogen and oxygen are mixed in a device called a fuel cell, they combine to form water during an exothermic reaction that produces electricity. This electricity could be used to power electric motors. The only product of this reaction is water, a nonpolluting substance.

At normal pressure and room temperature, it takes 238,000 liters of hydrogen to provide the equivalent amount of energy contained in just 80 liters (20 gallons) of gasoline. Even when hydrogen is stored at 200 atmospheres of pressure, too much space is required to make it a practical fuel for use in an automobile.

Metal hydrides, such as magnesium hydride, have been proposed as a safe and efficient storage method for hydrogen. The metal lattice of the magnesium acts as a sponge and absorbs the hydrogen into the spaces between the metallic atoms. This reaction can be represented by the following equation.

$$Mg(s) + H_2(g) \rightleftarrows MgH_2(s) + \text{heat}$$

As the temperature rises, the hydrogen is released into the fuel cell.

Today there are a few hydrogen-fuel buses in operation. Only testing and time will show if hydrogen fuel cells are a practical solution to some of our energy problems.

Base your answers to the following questions on the article and on your knowledge of chemistry.

1. What factors would make it difficult to store hydrogen as a liquid for use as a fuel in a car?
2. What is the major pollutant from the combustion of fossil fuels?
3. What is the oxidation number of hydrogen in magnesium hydride?
4. Write a balanced equation showing the reaction of hydrogen and oxygen.
5. What volume would 238,000 L of hydrogen at standard temperature and pressure occupy if the pressure were increased to 200. atm while the temperature remained constant?

6. Consider the reaction between magnesium and hydrogen.

$$Mg(s) + H_2(g) \rightleftarrows MgH_2(s) + \text{heat}$$

Why does raising the temperature shift the system to the left?

Use of *Reference Tables for Physical Setting/Chemistry* to Help Answer Questions

In recent Regents Examinations between 20% and 35% of the questions have involved the use of the *Reference Tables for Physical Setting/Chemistry.* You should become thoroughly familiar with all details of these tables. Sometimes the questions will specifically refer you to the reference tables, but most often you will be expected to know what information is included within the reference tables.

Listed below are some of the ways these reference tables are used in Regents Examination questions.

- to find a specific fact, such as the value of an electronvolt expressed in joules
- using an equation on the reference tables to solve a problem, such as determining the potential energy of a moving object
- graphing or recognizing the correct graph of data on the reference tables, such as the absolute indices of refraction
- decoding a graphic symbol in a question, such as quark or lepton
- performing a procedure using part of the reference tables, such as approximating the wavelength of red light from the frequency data given in the electromagnetic spectrum
- interpretation of data on the reference tables, such as the ionization energies for mercury

Appendix 3: Graphing and Math Skills

This appendix provides a review of basic graphing skills that will be helpful in answering various types of questions on the Regents Examination for Physical Setting/Chemistry.

Graphing

A graph of data collected during an experiment provides a single cohesive picture of many separate pieces of data. Graphs often allow you to see patterns and relationships in the data that are not otherwise obvious.

VARIABLES Each of a graph's axes represents a variable. In a typical science experiment, the scientist changes one variable in order to see how a second variable changes in response. The variable that the scientist controls and changes is called the *independent variable.* Normally the independent variable is plotted on the horizontal or x-axis. The variable that responds to changes in the independent variable is called the *dependent variable.* The dependent variable is usually plotted on the vertical or y-axis.

DATA TABLES As data is collected during an experiment it is often organized and displayed in the form of a data table. The data table should have a title that briefly describes the experiment or data. This data table title may be the same title used for the graph of the data. Data tables typically have at least two columns, one for the dependent variable and one for the independent variable. The independent variable is placed in the first column, and the dependent variable is placed in the second column. Label each column with the name of the variable being measured.

PREPARING A GRAPH In order to prepare the graph, first look at the data table. Take note of the range of values of each of the variables in the data table. Determine if the origin of the graph will have a value of zero. Although origins with zero values are common, they are not mandatory.

Considering the range of data values, divide each axis into convenient units based on the graph paper's grid. If you are drawing your own axes on blank paper, choose divisions that are convenient for clearly displaying the data. Be sure that each box represents the same increment. Axis scales should be chosen to spread the data over as much space as possible. Label each axis with the name of the variable being plotted and the units being used.

Now that the blank graph is prepared, the x-y data point pairs are plotted. Once the points have been plotted, a best-fit line is drawn to show the trend indicated by the data. The best-fit line does not have to pass through every point. In fact, the chance of that happening is quite small. When a best-fit line is properly drawn, there are often as many points above the line as there are below the line. Remember that the data represents measurements, and that all measurements have some amount of uncertainty. You may want to think of the line as an average relationship between the variables.

SAMPLE PROBLEM

During a lab period each team was assigned to determine the relationship between the volume and mass of an unknown liquid. Each team was assigned two volumes. They carefully filled graduated cylinders to the assigned volumes and then massed the cylinders and their contents. Knowing the masses of the empty graduated cylinders, they calculated the mass of the liquid. The following data were collected and posted on the blackboard. Prepare a data table to display the data in an organized way, and then graph the data.

Team A
volume 10 mL mass 9.5 g
volume 15 mL mass 13.0 g

Team D
volume 40 mL mass 34.4 g
volume 45 mL mass 37.8 g

Team B
volume 20 mL mass 17.0 g
volume 25 mL mass 21.5 g

Team C
volume 30 mL mass 25.5 g
volume 35 mL mass 30.1 g

Solution:

Independent and Dependent Variables:

In this case, each team was assigned two specific volumes. Thus, volume is the variable being changed during the experiment; volume is the independent variable. The teams observed how mass changed in response to the change in volume. Thus, mass is the dependent variable.

Preparing the Data Table:

Prepare the data table by placing the volume data in the first column and the mass data in the second column. Order the volume data from the lowest value to highest value. Give the table a title that reflects the type of data it contains.

Relationship Between Volume and Mass of an Unknown Liquid

Volume (mL)	Mass (g)
10.0	9.5
15.0	13.0
20.0	17.0
25.0	21.5
30.0	25.5
35.0	30.1
40.0	34.4
45.0	37.8

Note that with the data organized as shown in the data table, there is a clear relationship between the variables. As the volume of the liquid increases, the mass of the liquid also increases.

Preparing the Graph:

Because the volume is the independent variable, it is plotted on the *x*-axis. The *x*-label is Volume (mL). Because the *x*-axis data ranges from 10.0 mL to 45.0 mL, a range of 0.0 mL to 50.0 mL is chosen for the *x*-axis. Each box along the axis has a value of 2.0 mL.

Mass is the dependent variable and is plotted on the *y*-axis. The *y*-axis label is Mass (g). Because the *y*-axis data ranges from 9.5 g to 37.8 g, a range of 0.0 g to 40.0 g is chosen for the *y*-axis. Each box along the axis has a value of 2.0 g.

Plotting the Data:

Now that the blank graph is prepared, the x-y data point pairs are plotted. For this example, the points are plotted as a solid dot. See Figure A.

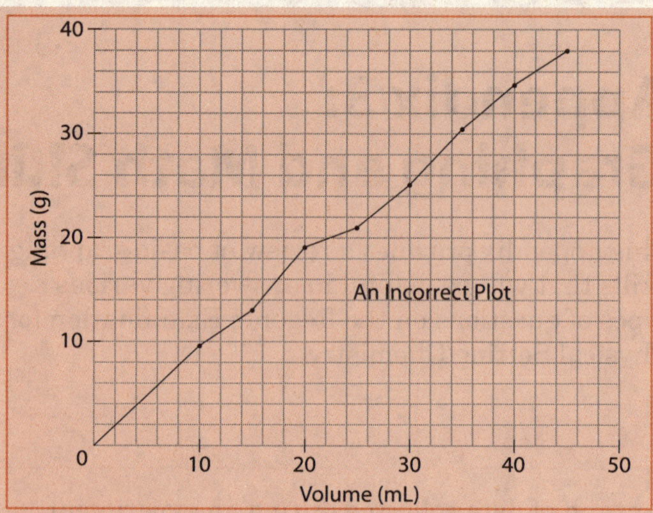

Figure A. Graph of volume versus mass for an unknown liquid

The graph above shows the plotted data and the data points connected by straight lines. The line on the graph indicates that the relationship between the volume of liquid and the mass of the liquid is not uniform. This is unlikely. Figure B shows why the use of a best-fit line is appropriate in this case. The best-fit straight line can be described by the equation $y = mx + b$. In this case, b (the *y*-intercept) occurs at the origin, so b has a value of zero. This is logical, for if there is no volume, the mass must be zero.

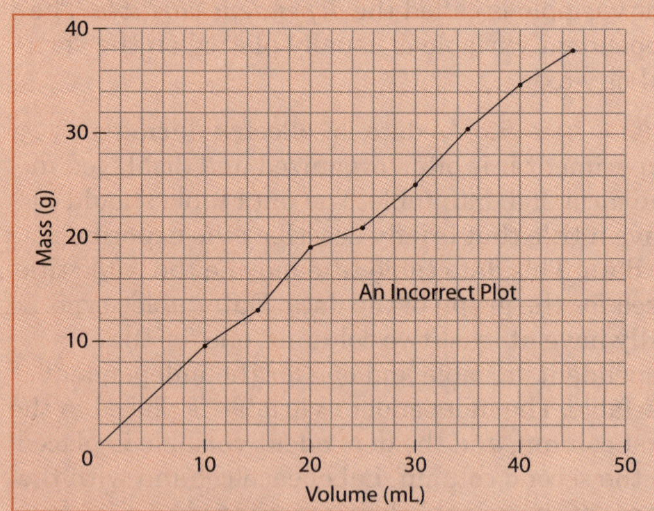

Figure B. Best-fit line drawn of the graph of volume versus mass for an unknown liquid

The slope of the line can be calculated by dividing the rise by the run. The rise over run is equal to $\Delta y/\Delta x$. (Note that the Δ symbol means "change in.") The units of $\Delta y/\Delta x$ are g/mL, which are the units commonly used for the density of a liquid. Thus the slope of the best-fit line represents the density of the unknown liquid. The density of a liquid should be a constant value.

If each student had used their own data points to calculate the slope, there would be four different density calculations. Substituting each team's data in the equation

$$\text{density} = \frac{\text{mass}}{\text{volume}} = \frac{\Delta y}{\Delta x}$$

yields the following results:

Team A

$$\text{density} = \frac{(13.0\text{ g} - 9.5\text{ g})}{(15.0\text{ mL} - 10.0\text{ mL})} = \frac{0.70\text{ g}}{\text{mL}}$$

Team B

$$\text{density} = \frac{(21.5\text{ g} - 17.0\text{ g})}{(25.0\text{ mL} - 20.0\text{ mL})} = \frac{0.90\text{ g}}{\text{mL}}$$

Team C

$$\text{density} = \frac{(30.1\text{ g} - 25.5\text{ g})}{(35.0\text{ mL} - 30.0\text{ mL})} = \frac{0.92\text{ g}}{\text{mL}}$$

Team D

$$\text{density} = \frac{(37.8\text{ g} - 34.4\text{ g})}{(45.0\text{ mL} - 40.0\text{ mL})} = \frac{0.68\text{ g}}{\text{mL}}$$

Constructing the slope using the best-fit line simply involves picking two convenient points on the line and making a calculation using these values. Figure C shows the density to be 0.88 g/mL.

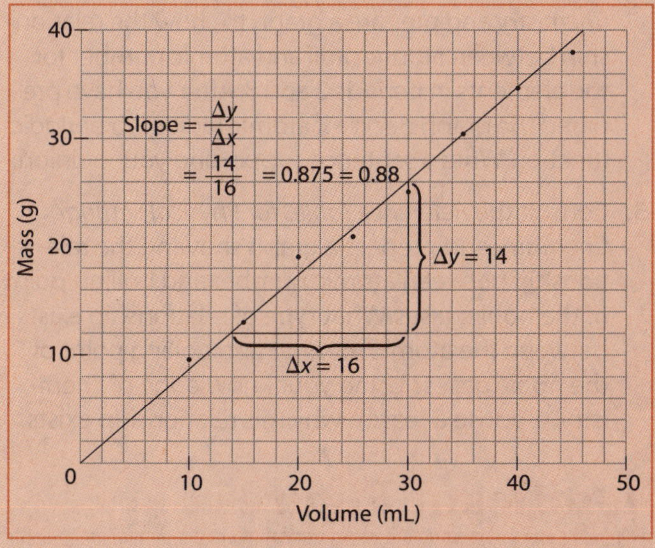

Figure C. Calculation of slope using data points from the best-fit line

INTERPOLATION AND EXTRAPOLATION A graph is also useful because it allows you to estimate values that are not part of the data table. When a value is read from the graph's curve that falls within data table's values, the process in called *interpolation.* Interpolating from the graph in Figure B shows that a volume of 37 mL of the unknown liquid has a mass of approximately 32 g.

When the curve or line on a graph is extended beyond the known plotted values and used to make predictions, the process is called extrapolation. Extrapolating from the graph in Figure B shows that a volume of 8.0 mL of the unknown liquid should have a mass of approximately 7 g.

GRAPH SHAPES AND RELATIONSHIPS Figure D shows several typical graph shapes. If one variable increases as the other variable increases, the relationship is said to be direct. If one variable increases as the other decreases, the relationship is said to be indirect or inverse.

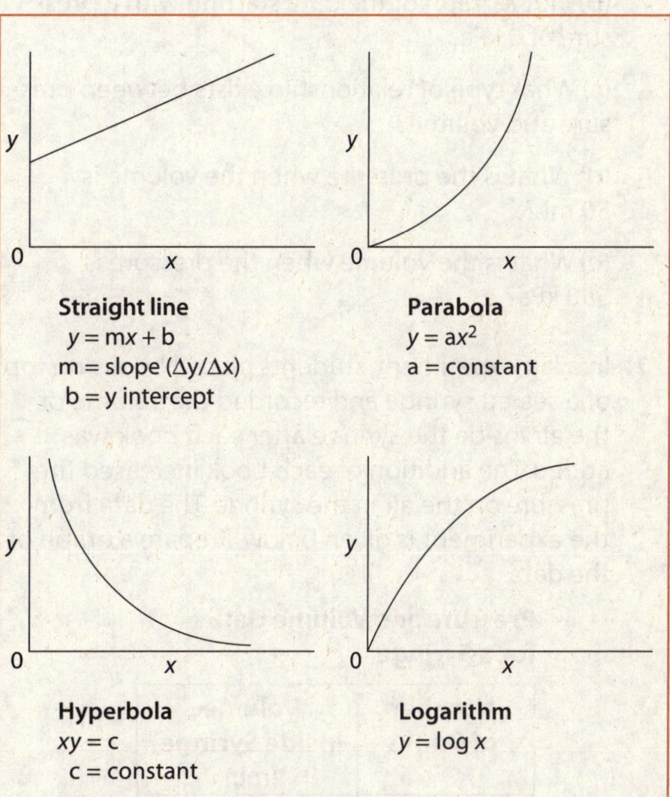

Figure D. Typical graph shapes

Practice Problems

1. In a laboratory experiment, the pressure on a confined gas was increased and the resulting changes in volume were recorded. The temperature of the gas was kept constant during the experiment.

Pressure and Volume Data for a Confined Gas

Pressure (kPa)	Volume (mL)
100	93.0
200	46.5
300	31.0
400	23.2
500	18.6
600	15.5

(a) What are the independent and dependent variables?

(b) Plot a graph of the data starting with a pressure of 0 kPa.

(c) What type of relationship exists between pressure and volume?

(d) What is the pressure when the volume is 50 mL?

(e) What is the volume when the pressure is 550 kPa?

2. In a lab experiment, students placed books on top of a sealed syringe and recorded the volume of the air inside the syringe after each book was added. The addition of each book increased the pressure on the air in the syringe. The data from the experiment is given below. Prepare a graph of the data.

Pressure and Volume Data for a Syringe

Number of Books	Volume Inside Syringe (mL)
0	64
1	61
2	53
3	48
4	43
5	39
6	36
7	32

3. In a laboratory exercise, the volume of a gas is measured at various temperatures while the pressure is held constant. Data from the experiment is given in the data table below.

Trial	Temperature (°C)	Volume (cm^3)
A	0	100
B	50	120
C	100	135
D	150	155
E	200	173

(a) Graph the data. In preparing the graph, extend the temperature axis out to 300°C. Based on the trend in the behavior of the gas, extend the volume axis so you can extrapolate the volume at a temperature of 300°C. When preparing your graph decide if the axis used for the volume of the gas should begin at 0 cm^3 or 100 cm^3.

(b) What type of relationship exists between temperature and volume?

(c) Identify the independent and dependent variables.

(d) Extrapolate to determine the volume at 300°C.

4. Consult the *Reference Tables for Physical Setting/Chemistry* and prepare a graph to show the relationship between atomic radii and atomic number for the elements in periods 2 and 3. After you have prepared the graph decide if atomic radius is a periodic function. Write a sentence supporting your opinion.

5. Consult the *Reference Tables for Physical Setting/Chemistry* and prepare a graph showing the relationship between atomic number and boiling point of the noble gases. What type of relationship exists between the atomic number and boiling point of the noble gases? Using your knowledge of chemistry, propose a reason why this relationship exists.

Significant Figures

You may find some of the rules for determining the number of significant figures in a number a bit confusing. If so, a simple memory aid known as the Atlantic and Pacific rule may help you.

THE ATLANTIC AND PACIFIC RULE Imagine a map of the United States, with the Pacific Ocean on the left and the Atlantic Ocean on the right.

- When a decimal is **P**resent in a measurement, start on the **P**acific side (left side of the number) with the first nonzero digit. All the following digits are significant.
- When a decimal is **A**bsent in a measurement, start on the **A**tlantic side (right side of the number) with the first nonzero digit. All the preceding digits are significant.

Practice Problems

1. Which milligram quantity contains a total of four significant figures? (1) 0.30310 mg (2) 3010 mg (3) 3100. mg (4) 30,001 mg
2. Which measurement contains three significant figures? (1) 0.05 g (2) 0.050 g (3) 0.056 g (4) 0.0563 g
3. Which volume measurement is expressed with four significant figures? (1) 5.50 mL (2) 550. mL (3) 5500 mL (4) 5500. mL
4. Which measurement contains a total of three significant figures? (1) 0.012 g (2) 0.125 g (3) 1205 g (4) 12,050 g
5. Which measurement has the greatest number of significant figures? (1) 6.060 mg (2) 60.6 mg (3) 606 mg (4) 60,600 mg
6. Which mass measurement contains a total of three significant figures? (1) 22.0 g (2) 22.00 g (3) 220 g (4) 2200 g
7. Which measurement contains a total of three significant figures? (1) 0.12 g (2) 120 g (3) 120. g (4) 012 g
8. Expressed to the correct number of significant figures, what is the correct sum of (3.04 g + 4.134 g + 6.1 g)? (1) 13 g (2) 13.3 g (3) 13.27 g (4) 13.274 g
9. Which quantity expresses the sum (2.1 g + 33.566 g + 12.22 g) to the proper degree of precision? (1) 47.886 g (2) 47.89 g (3) 47.9 g (4) 48.0 g
10. When 1.255 g of X reacts completely with 3.2 g of Y, Z is the only product of the reaction. What is the total mass of Z, expressed to the proper number of significant figures? (1) 4.455 g (2) 4.46 g (3) 4.5 g (4) 5 g
11. What is the sum of 0.0421 g + 5.263 g + 2.13 g to the correct number of significant figures? (1) 7 g (2) 7.4 g (3) 7.44 g (4)7.435 g
12. What is the sum of 6.6412 g + 12.85 g + 0.046 g + 3.48 g expressed to the correct number of significant figures? (1) 23 g (2) 23.0 g (3) 23.017 g (4) 23.02 g
13. Which quantity expresses the sum of 22.1 g + 375.66 g + 5400.132 g to the correct number of significant figures? (1) 5800 g (2) 5798 g (3) 5797.9 g (4) 5797.892 g
14. The mass of a solid is 3.60 g and its volume is 1.8 cm^3. What is the density of the solid, expressed to the correct number of significant figures? (1) 12 g/cm^3 (2) 2.0 g/cm^3 (3) 0.5 g/cm^3 (4) 0.50 g/cm^3
15. A cubic object has sides with lengths of 6.0 cm, 3.0 cm, and 2.0 cm. The mass of the cube is 162.2 g. What is its density to the correct number of significant figures? (1) 0.22 g/cm^3 (2) 0.2219 g/cm^3 (3) 4.5 g/cm^3 (4) 4.505 g/cm^3
16. The volume of a gas sample is 22 L at STP. The density of the gas is 1.35 g/L. What is the mass of the gas sample, expressed to the correct number of significant figures? (1) 16.7 g (2) 17 g (3) 30. g (4) 30.0 g
17. What is the quotient of 8.01 g divided by 3.127 g, expressed to the correct number of significant figures? (1) 2.6 (2) 2.56 (3) 2.5562 (4) 2.5616
18. What is the product of 2.324 cm × 1.11 cm expressed to the correct number of significant figures? (1) 2.58 cm^2 (2) 2.5780 cm^2 (3) 2.5796 cm^2 (4) 2.57964 cm^2
19. A solution contains 12.55 grams of a solid dissolved in 50.0 milliliters of water. What is the number of grams of solid dissolved per milliliter of water, rounded to the correct number of significant figures? (1) 0.25 g/mL (2) 0.251 g/mL (3) 0.3 g/mL (4) 0.2510 g/mL

20. A cube has a volume of 8.0 cm^3 and a mass of 21.6 g. The density of the cube, in grams per cubic centimeter, is best expressed as (1) 2.7 (2) 2.70 (3) 0.37 (4) 0.370

21. Add the following using the rules for significant figures.

(a) 35.7 g + 432.33 g + 5142.312 g

(b) 0.027 g + 0.0023 g

22. For each of the following, express the answer to the correct number of significant figures.

(a) Determine the density of a substance that has a mass of 21.6 g and a volume of 8.00 cm^3.

(b) Determine the mass of an object that has a density of 4.0 g/mL and a volume of 2.55 mL.

Regents Examinations

The following New York Regents Examinations are provided so that you can practice a Regents Examination for The Physical Setting/Chemistry.

The examinations starting with June, 2002 follow the current New York State Core Curriculum. Earlier tests are included to help you practice.

The January, 2002 exam follows the new core curriculum, but has a different format than later exams.

The Sample test was not given to students as an actual exam. It follows the new core, but has a slightly different format.

Exams earlier than January 2002 have a different format than the current tests and include some additional concepts not in the new core. They are still valuable practice in preparing for the current exam.

The best way to use these examinations is to take an entire test after you have reviewed the course content. Use the tests to determine if you have reviewed enough to do well on the Regents Examination and to determine where further review will be helpful.

Do not look up any information or answers while you take the examination. Answer each question just as you would during a real test. As you take the examination, use the margin of the paper to note any question where you are just guessing. Leave the more difficult questions for last, but be sure to answer each question. Every point counts, so do not skip over a long question that is only worth a point or two. A long question could be easier than it looks and may make the difference between an A and a B, or between passing and failing.

When you finish, have your teacher score your examination and help you determine the areas where you need the most work. Also review the "guesses" you noted in the margin to find out what you need to study to ensure that you will be able to answer similar questions on the next test. Once you have determined your weaknesses, you can focus your review on those topics in this book.

Reviewing the areas where you know the least will give you the best chance of improving your final score. Spending time on areas where you are doing quite well will not produce much improvement in your total score, but is still important if time permits.

Physical Setting Chemistry Sample

Part A

Answer all questions in this part.

Directions (1–35): For *each* statement or question, write on the separate answer sheet the *number* of the word or expression that, of those given, best completes the statement or answers the question. Some questions may require the use of the *Reference Tables for Physical Setting/Chemistry*.

1 Compared to an atom of hydrogen in the ground state, an atom of hydrogen in the excited state has

(1) absorbed energy, only
(2) released energy, only
(3) neither released nor absorbed energy
(4) both released and absorbed energy

2 What is the total number of electrons in the outermost shell of a phosphorus atom in the ground state?

(1) 1
(2) 2
(3) 3
(4) 5

3 Based on Reference Table *S*, which of the following atoms requires the *least* energy for the removal of the most loosely bound electron?

(1) Sn
(2) Sr
(3) Be
(4) Br

4 What is the mass number of ${}^{19}_{9}F$?

(1) 9
(2) 10
(3) 19
(4) 28

5 All atoms of a given element *must* contain the same number of

(1) protons
(2) neutrons
(3) electrons plus neutrons
(4) protons plus neutrons

6 Which element is a brittle, nonconducting solid at 25°C?

(1) Br
(2) S
(3) Al
(4) Bi

7 An atom of helium-4 differs from an atom of lithium-7 in that the atom of helium-4 has

(1) one more proton
(2) one more neutron
(3) two less protons
(4) two less neutrons

8 Antimony is classified as a

(1) metal
(2) nonmetal
(3) metalloid
(4) noble gas

9 Given the reaction:

$$2\ C_2H_6 + 7\ O_2 \rightarrow 4\ CO_2 + 6\ H_2O$$

What is the ratio of moles of CO_2 produced to moles of C_2H_6 consumed?

(1) 1 to 1
(2) 2 to 1
(3) 3 to 2
(4) 7 to 2

10 Which equation shows conservation of charge?

(1) $Fe \rightarrow Fe^{2+} + e^-$

(2) $Fe + 2e^- \rightarrow Fe^{2+}$

(3) $Fe \rightarrow Fe^{2+} + 2e^-$

(4) $Fe + 2e^- \rightarrow Fe^{3+}$

11 What is the formula of nitrogen (II) oxide?

(1) NO
(2) NO_2
(3) N_2O
(4) N_2O_4

12 Which formula represents an ionic compound?

(1) H_2O
(2) KCl
(3) NH_3
(4) CH_4

13 An oxide ion (O^{2-}) formed from an oxygen-18 atom contains exactly

(1) 8 protons, 8 neutrons, 10 electrons
(2) 8 protons, 10 neutrons, 8 electrons
(3) 8 protons, 10 neutrons, 10 electrons
(4) 10 protons, 8 neutrons, 8 electrons

14 Which bond is *least* polar?

(1) As–Cl
(2) Bi–Cl
(3) P–Cl
(4) N–Cl

15 Which pair of characteristics describes the molecule illustrated below?

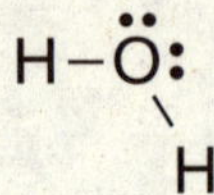

(1) symmetrical and polar
(2) symmetrical and nonpolar
(3) asymmetrical and polar
(4) asymmetrical and nonpolar

16 A sample of unknown composition was tested in a laboratory. The sample could *not* be decomposed by physical or chemical means. On the basis of these results, the laboratory reported that the unknown sample was most likely

(1) a compound
(2) an element
(3) a mixture
(4) a solution

17 Which intermolecular force of attraction accounts for the relatively high boiling point of water?

(1) hydrogen bonding
(2) covalent bonding
(3) metallic bonding
(4) ionic bonding

18 Based on Reference Table *H*, which substance has the weakest intermolecular forces?

(1) ethanoic acid
(2) ethanol
(3) propanone
(4) water

19 At 1 atmosphere and 298 K, 1 mole of H_2O (ℓ) molecules and 1 mole of C_2H_5OH (ℓ) molecules both have the same

(1) vapor pressure
(2) average kinetic energy
(3) mass
(4) density

20 Given the reaction at equilibrium:

$$C_2(g) + D_2(g) \rightleftharpoons 2\ CD(g) + \text{energy}$$

Which change will cause the equilibrium to shift?

(1) increase in pressure
(2) increase in volume
(3) addition of heat
(4) addition of a catalyst

21 Given the equilibrium at 101.3 kPa:

$$H_2O\ (s) \rightleftharpoons H_2O(\ell)$$

At what temperature does this equilibrium occur?

(1) 100 K
(2) 273 K
(3) 298 K
(4) 373 K

22 Given the diagram below that shows carbon dioxide in an equilibrium system at a temperature of 298 K and a pressure of 1 atm:

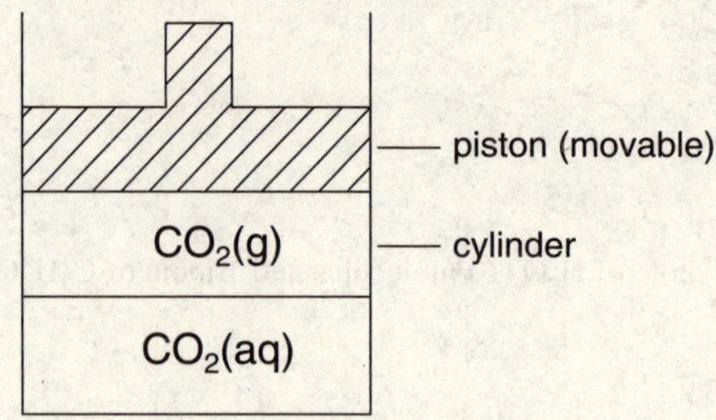

Which changes *must* increase the solubility of the carbon dioxide?

(1) increase pressure and decrease temperature
(2) increase pressure and increase temperature
(3) decrease pressure and decrease temperature
(4) decrease pressure and increase temperature

23 Which formula represents a molecule of a saturated hydrocarbon?

(1) C_2H_2
(2) C_4H_{10}
(3) C_5H_8
(4) C_6H_6

24 Molecules of 2-methyl butane and 2,2-dimethyl propane have different

(1) structural formulas
(2) molecular formulas
(3) numbers of carbon atoms
(4) numbers of covalent bonds

25 The molecule below belongs to which class of compounds?

```
     O   H   H
     ‖   |   |
 HO— C — C — N—H
         |
     H — C — H
         |
         H
```

(1) alcohol
(2) ester
(3) aldehyde
(4) amino acid

26 The transfer of which particle is required for a redox reaction to occur?

(1) electron
(2) ion
(3) neutron
(4) proton

27 What is the oxidation number of chromium in $K_2Cr_2O_7$?

(1) +6
(2) +2
(3) +7
(4) +12

28 Given the reaction:

$$Mg + CuSO_4 \rightarrow MgSO_4 + Cu$$

Which equation represents the oxidation that takes place?

(1) $Mg^{2+} + 2e^- \rightarrow Mg$
(2) $Mg \rightarrow Mg^{2+} + 2e^-$
(3) $Cu^{2+} + 2e^- \rightarrow Cu$
(4) $Cu \rightarrow Cu^{2+} + 2e^-$

29 Which substance is an Arrhenius acid?

(1) NH_3
(2) KOH
(3) $HC_2H_3O_2$
(4) CH_3OH

30 Which of the following pH values indicates the highest concentration of hydronium ions in a solution?

(1) pH = 1
(2) pH = 2
(3) pH = 3
(4) pH = 4

31 Which substance yields hydroxide ion as the only negative ion in aqueous solution?

(1) $Mg(OH)_2$
(2) $C_2H_4(OH)_2$
(3) $MgCl_2$
(4) CH_3Cl

32 Which type of radiation is identical in mass and charge to a helium nucleus?

(1) alpha
(2) beta
(3) positron
(4) proton

33 Which isotope is radioactive?

(1) C–12
(2) Ne–20
(3) Tc–99
(4) Pb–206

34 Which equation represents nuclear fusion?

(1) ${}^{14}_{6}C \rightarrow {}^{14}_{7}N + {}^{0}_{-1}e$
(2) ${}^{27}_{13}Al + {}^{4}_{2}He \rightarrow {}^{30}_{15}P + {}^{1}_{0}n$
(3) ${}^{235}_{92}U + {}^{1}_{0}n \rightarrow {}^{139}_{56}Ba + {}^{94}_{36}Kr + 3{}^{1}_{0}n$
(4) ${}^{2}_{1}H + {}^{3}_{1}H \rightarrow {}^{4}_{2}He + {}^{1}_{0}n$

Note that question 35 has only three choices.

35 In a gaseous system at equilibrium with its surroundings, as molecules of *A*(g) collide with molecules of *B*(g) without reacting, the total energy of the gaseous system

(1) decreases
(2) increases
(3) remains the same

Part B

Answer all questions in this part.

Directions (36–50): For *each* statement or question, write on the separate answer sheet the *number* of the word or expression that, of those given, best completes the statement or answers the question. Some questions may require the use of the *Reference Tables for Physical Setting/Chemistry*.

36 The temperature of a 2.0-liter sample of helium gas at STP is increased to 27°C and the pressure is decreased to 80. kPa What is the new volume of the helium sample?

(1) 1.4 L
(2) 2.0 L
(3) 2.8 L
(4) 4.0 L

37 Given the reaction:

$$2\ C_2H_6 + 7\ O_2 \rightarrow 4\ CO_2 + 6\ H_2O$$

What is the total number of moles of CO_2 produced by the complete combustion of 5.0 moles of C_2H_6 ?

(1) 1.0 mole
(2) 2.0 moles
(3) 5.0 moles
(4) 10. moles

38 Approximately what fraction of an original Co–60 sample remains after 21 years?

(1) $\frac{1}{2}$
(2) $\frac{1}{4}$
(3) $\frac{1}{8}$
(4) $\frac{1}{16}$

39 Which graph best shows the relationship between the pressure of a gas and its average kinetic energy at constant volume?

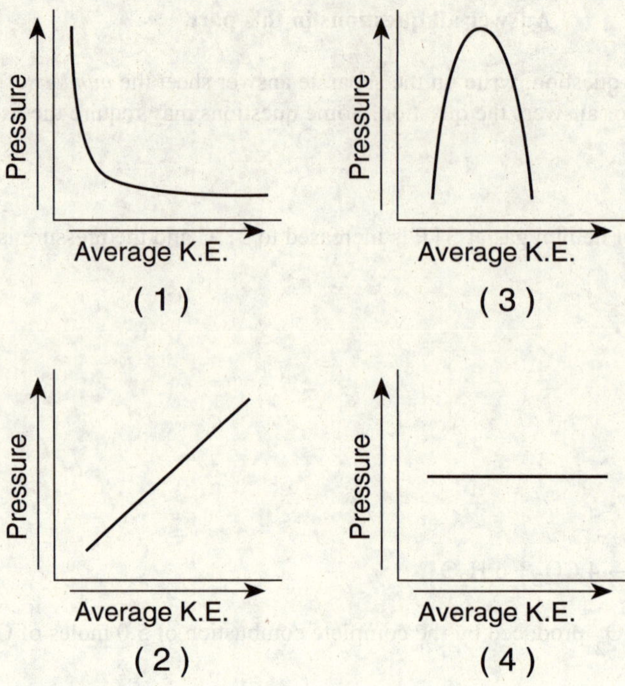

40 Which two solutions, when mixed together, will undergo a double replacement reaction and form a white, solid substance?

(1) NaCl(aq) and $LiNO_3$(aq)
(2) KCl(aq) and $AgNO_3$(aq)
(3) KCl(aq) and LiCl(aq)
(4) $NaNO_3$(aq) and $AgNO_3$(aq)

41 An unknown substance, liquid *X*, is tested in the laboratory. The chemical and physical test results are listed below.

- Nonconductor of electricity
- Insoluble in water
- Soluble in hexane
- Low melting point as a solid
- Combustion produces only CO_2 and H_2O

Based on these results, a student should conclude that liquid *X* is

(1) ionic and organic
(2) ionic and inorganic
(3) covalent and organic
(4) covalent and inorganic

42 How many milliliters of 12.0 M HCl(aq) must be diluted with water to make exactly 500. mL of 3.00 M hydrochloric acid?

(1) 100. mL
(2) 125. mL
(3) 200. mL
(4) 250. mL

43 Based on Reference Table *G*, what is the maximum number of grams of KCl(s) that will dissolve in 200 grams of water at 50°C to produce a saturated solution?

(1) 38 g
(2) 42 g
(3) 58 g
(4) 84 g

44 What is the molarity of an HCl solution if 20. milliliters of this acid is needed to neutralize 10. milliliters of a 0.50 M NaOH solution?

(1) 1.0 M
(2) 0.75 M
(3) 0.50 M
(4) 0.25 M

45 During a laboratory experiment, a sample of aluminum is found to have a mass of 12.50 grams and a volume of 4.6 milliliters. What is the density of this sample, expressed to the correct number of significant figures?

(1) 2.717 g/mL
(2) 2.72 g/mL
(3) 3 g/mL
(4) 2.7 g/mL

46 Given the incomplete reaction:

$$CH_3CH_2CH_2\overset{\overset{\displaystyle O}{\|}}{C}{-}OH + x \rightarrow CH_3CH_2CH_2\overset{\overset{\displaystyle O}{\|}}{C}{-}OCH_2CH_3 + H_2O$$

Which compound is represented by *x*?

(1) CH_3CH_2OH

(2) $CH_3\overset{\overset{\displaystyle O}{\|}}{C}{-}H$

(3) $CH_3OCH_2CH_3$

(4) $CH_3\overset{\overset{\displaystyle O}{\|}}{C}CH_3$

47 A hydrate is a compound with water molecules incorporated into its crystal structure. In an experiment to find the percent by mass of water in a hydrated compound, the following data were recorded:

Mass of crucible + hydrated crystals before heating	7.50 grams
Mass of crucible	6.90 grams
Mass of crucible + anhydrous crystals after heating	7.20 grams

What is the percent by mass of water in the hydrate?

(1) 8.0 %
(2) 50. %
(3) 72. %
(4) 96. %

48 When a spark is applied to a mixture of hydrogen and oxygen, the gases react explosively. Which potential energy diagram best represents the reaction?

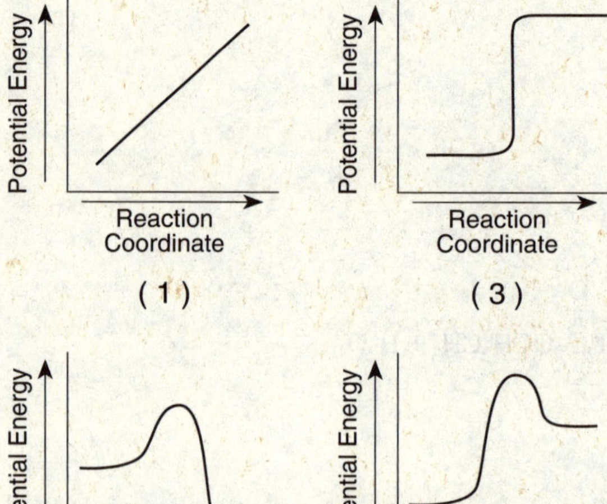

49 Which equation shows an increase in entropy?

(1) $CO_2(g) \rightarrow CO_2(s)$
(2) $CO_2(\ell) \rightarrow CO_2(g)$
(3) $CH_3OH(\ell) \rightarrow CH_3OH(s)$
(4) $CH_3OH(g) \rightarrow CH_3OH(\ell)$

50 The laboratory process of distillation does *not* involve

(1) changing a liquid to vapor
(2) changing a vapor to liquid
(3) liquids with different boiling points
(4) liquids with the same boiling points

Directions (51–55): Record your answers in the spaces provided in your answer booklet. Some questions may require the use of the *Reference Tables for Physical Setting/Chemistry*.

51 In a laboratory experiment, a student determined the mass of the product, NaCl(s), to be 1.84 grams.

a Calculate the gram formula mass of NaCl(s). Round atomic masses from the Periodic Table to the nearest tenth. Show all work. [1]

Indicate the correct answer, including an appropriate unit. [1]

b Calculate the number of moles of NaCl(s) produced. Show all work. [1]

Indicate the correct answer. [1]

52 Draw a correct Lewis electron-dot structure for each of the following in the boxes provided *in your answer booklet*.

a An atom of hydrogen [1]

b An atom of nitrogen [1]

c A molecule of ammonia (NH_3) [1]

53 Given the equation:

$$CaCO_3(s) \rightarrow CaO(s) + CO_2(g)$$

a Name the type of reaction this equation represents. [1]

b Explain, in terms of particle behavior, why entropy is increasing during this reaction. [1]

54 Base your answers to question 54 on the information below:

○○ represents one molecule of nitrogen

a In the space provided *in your answer booklet*, draw a particle model that shows at least six molecules of nitrogen gas. [1]

b In the space provided *in your answer booklet*, draw a particle model that shows at least six molecules of liquid nitrogen. [1]

c Describe, in terms of particle arrangement, the difference between nitrogen gas and liquid nitrogen. [1]

d Good models should reflect the true nature of the concept being represented. What is a limitation of two-dimensional models? [1]

55 Given the graph below that represents the uniform cooling of a sample of lauric acid starting as a liquid above freezing point.

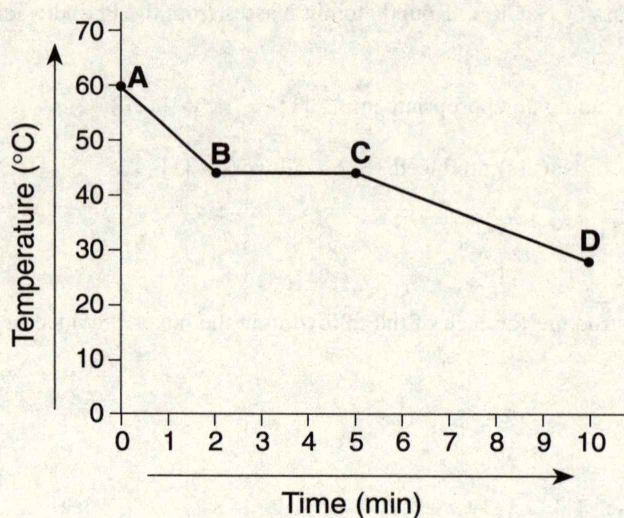

a Which line segment represents a phase change, only? [1]

b What is the melting point of lauric acid? [1]

c At which point do the particles of lauric acid have the highest average kinetic energy? [1]

d Name the phase change that takes place during this 10-minute cooling time. [1]

Part C

Answer all questions in this part.

Directions (56–60): Record your answers in the spaces provided in your answer booklet. Some questions may require the use of the *Reference Tables for Physical Setting/Chemistry*.

56 Skiers, snowmobilers, and others involved in outdoor winter recreation use disposable heat packs. These heat packs are porous paper pouches containing sawdust, powdered carbon, sodium chloride, powdered iron, and Zeolite™. During production, this mixture is moistened slightly with water and then sealed in an airtight plastic pack. The reaction starts when the pack is opened and the mixture is exposed to air.

Given the unbalanced equation:

$$\_\_\_\_ Fe(s) + \_\_\_\_ O_2(g) \rightarrow \_\_\_\_ Fe_2O_3(s)$$

a *In your answer booklet*, balance the equation, using smallest whole number coefficients. [1]

b If the word "energy" was added to the equation to correctly indicate the energy change in this heat pack reaction, would the word "energy" be placed on the "reactant side" or on the "product side" of the equation? [1]

57 Given the data table below showing the solubility of salt *X*:

Temperature (°C)	Mass of Solute per 100 g of H_2O (g)
10	22
25	40.
30	48
60	107
70	135

a Which salt on Table G is most likely to be salt *X*? [1]

b On the graph provided *in your answer booklet,* scale and label the *y*-axis including appropriate units. [1]

c Plot the data from the data table. Surround each point with a small circle and draw a best-fit curve for the solubility of salt *X*. [1]

d Using your graph, predict the solubility of salt *X* at 50°C. [1]

e If the pressure on the salt solution was increased, what effect would this pressure change have on the solubility of the salt? [1]

58 In the early 1900s, evidence was discovered that atoms were not "hard spheres." It was shown that atoms themselves had an internal structure. One experiment involved gold metal foil.

a *In your answer booklet,* complete the simple model for an atom of gold-197 by placing the correct numbers in the two blanks. [1]

b In the gold-foil experiment, alpha particles were directed toward the foil. Most of the alpha particles passed directly through the foil with no effect. This result did not agree with the "hard spheres model" for the atom. What conclusion about the internal structure of the atom did this evidence show? [1]

c In the same experiment, some of the alpha particles returned toward the source. What does this evidence indicate about the charge of the atom's nucleus? [1]

59 A student wishes to determine how the rate of reaction of magnesium strips with hydrochloric acid, HCl(aq), varies as a function of temperature of the HCl(aq). Give *two* additional factors, other than the temperature, that could affect the rate of reaction and must be held constant during the experiment. [2]

Base your answers to question 60 on the article below and on your knowledge of chemistry.

The Decaffeinating Tradition

For coffee beans to be labeled "decaffeinated," at least 97% of the caffeine must be removed. There are three primary methods for decaffeination: chemical extraction, the Swiss water process, and supercritical fluid extraction.

Although all methods of decaffeinating coffee involve the use of "chemicals," one process has been traditionally referred to as "chemical extraction," probably because it uses organic solvents that are not typically part of our normal environment. The traditional method offers two slightly varied options using dichloromethane (CH_2Cl_2) or ethyl acetate ($CH_3COOC_2H_5$) as solvents. With both solvents, the beans are first soaked in water to soften them and speed the decaffeinating process. The beans are then soaked in one of the two solvents, which dissolves the caffeine in the bean. Once the solvent has removed the caffeine, the coffee beans are treated with steam. This evaporates the organic solvent along with the caffeine.

The process is identical for both solvents, but many coffee companies prefer to use ethyl acetate to decaffeinate their coffee. This allows them to label the beans "naturally decaffeinated," because ethyl acetate occurs naturally in orange rinds and many other fruits. Although consumers may prefer this label, it is misleading. The ethyl acetate used is actually synthesized; it is not extracted from fruits because it would be too costly.

Both of these commercial methods have a growing number of detractors, prompting many coffee companies to turn toward other methods. Opposition arises because the solvents used can never be completely removed from the coffee beans. The traces left behind, however, are below the amounts required for the "decaffeinated" label. Because of the recognized potential hazards associated with the use of dichloromethane and ethyl acetate, the United States Food and Drug Administration and the United States Department of Agriculture continue to investigate and evaluate any possible dangers that might be associated with the use of these chemicals.

60 *a* In the space provided *in your answer booklet*, draw the structural formula for ethyl acetate. (The correct IUPAC name is ethyl ethanoate.) [1]

b To what class of organic compounds does ethyl acetate belong? [1]

c In the space provided *in your answer booklet*, draw a correct structural formula for dichloromethane. [1]

d To what class of organic compounds does dichloromethane belong? [1]

e Which do you think is better, ethyl acetate or dichloromethane, as a decaffeinating agent for coffee? Explain your choice in terms of the information found in the article. [1]

f Indicate whether you think the caffeine molecule is polar or nonpolar; then explain your answer in terms of the solubility of the caffeine molecule. [1]

Sample Answer Paper

Part B

51 *a*

b

52 *a*

hydrogen

b

nitrogen

c

ammonia

Sample Answer Paper

Part B

53 *a*

b

54 *a*

b

c

d

55 *a*

b

c

d

Sample Answer Paper

Part C

56 *a* ______ $Fe(s)$ + ______ $O_2(g)$ → ______ $Fe_2O_3(s)$

b ______________________________

57 *a* ______________________________

b-c

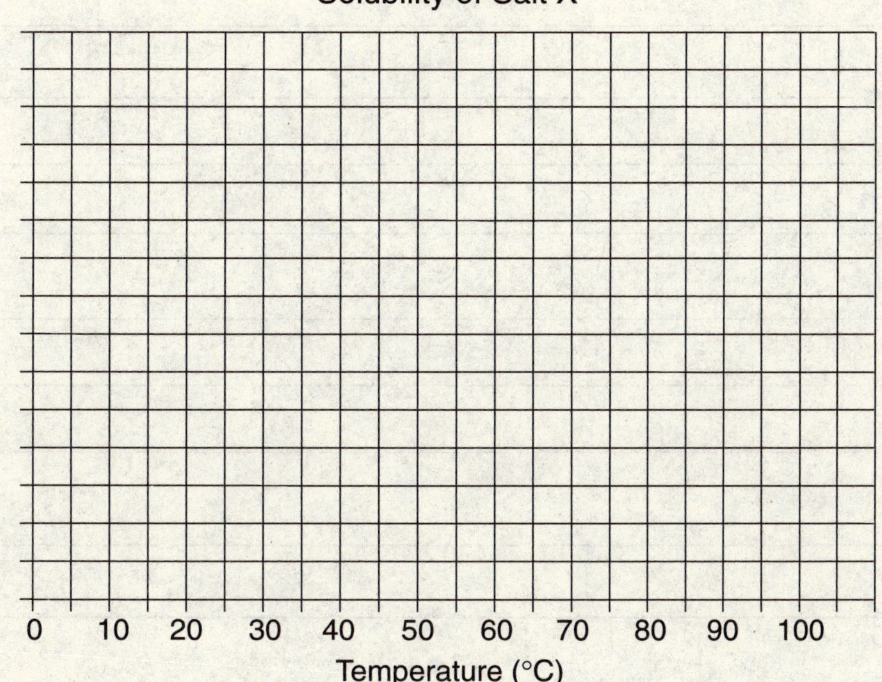

d ______________________________

e ______________________________

Sample Answer Paper

Part C

58 *a*

79 protons

___ neutrons

___ electrons

b ______________________________

____

____

____

c ______________________________

____

____

59 (1) ______________________________

____

(2) ______________________________

____

Sample Answer Paper

Part C

60 *a*

b ______________________

c

d ______________________

e ______________________

____

____

f ______________________

____

____

Physical Setting Chemistry June, 2006

Part A

Answer all questions in this part.

Directions (1–30): For *each* statement or question, write on the separate answer sheet the *number* of the word or expression that, of those given, best completes the statement or answers the question. Some questions may require the use of the *Reference Tables for Physical Setting/Chemistry*.

1 Which notation represents an atom of sodium with an atomic number of 11 and a mass number of 24?

(1) $^{24}_{11}Na$ (3) $^{13}_{11}Na$
(2) $^{11}_{24}Na$ (4) $^{35}_{11}Na$

2 Which element has chemical properties that are most similar to those of calcium?

(1) Co (3) N
(2) K (4) Sr

3 Which element is malleable and can conduct electricity in the solid phase?

(1) iodine (3) sulfur
(2) phosphorus (4) tin

4 Atoms of different isotopes of the same element differ in their total number of

(1) electrons (3) protons
(2) neutrons (4) valence electrons

5 Which statement correctly describes two forms of oxygen, O_2 and O_3?

(1) They have identical molecular structures and identical properties.
(2) They have identical molecular structures and different properties.
(3) They have different molecular structures and identical properties.
(4) They have different molecular structures and different properties.

6 What is the IUPAC name for the compound FeS?

(1) iron(II) sulfate (3) iron(II) sulfide
(2) iron(III) sulfate (4) iron(III) sulfide

7 Given the balanced equation representing a reaction:

$$F_2(g) + H_2(g) \rightarrow 2HF(g)$$

What is the mole ratio of $H_2(g)$ to HF(g) in this reaction?

(1) 1:1 (3) 2:1
(2) 1:2 (4) 2:3

8 Which list includes three types of chemical reactions?

(1) condensation, double replacement, and sublimation
(2) condensation, solidification, and synthesis
(3) decomposition, double replacement, and synthesis
(4) decomposition, solidification, and sublimation

9 Which type of bond results when one or more valence electrons are transferred from one atom to another?

(1) a hydrogen bond
(2) an ionic bond
(3) a nonpolar covalent bond
(4) a polar covalent bond

10 What is the total number of electrons shared in the bonds between the two carbon atoms in a molecule of H—C≡C—H?

(1) 6 (3) 3
(2) 2 (4) 8

11 Which formula represents a nonpolar molecule?

(1) CH_4 (3) H_2O
(2) HCl (4) NH_3

12 Which changes occur as a cadmium atom, Cd, becomes a cadmium ion, Cd^{2+}?

(1) The Cd atom gains two electrons and its radius decreases.
(2) The Cd atom gains two electrons and its radius increases.
(3) The Cd atom loses two electrons and its radius decreases.
(4) The Cd atom loses two electrons and its radius increases.

13 Which element has atoms with the greatest attraction for electrons in a chemical bond?

(1) beryllium
(2) fluorine
(3) lithium
(4) oxygen

14 Two substances, *A* and *Z*, are to be identified. Substance *A* can *not* be broken down by a chemical change. Substance *Z* can be broken down by a chemical change. What can be concluded about these substances?

(1) Both substances are elements.
(2) Both substances are compounds.
(3) Substance *A* is an element and substance *Z* is a compound.
(4) Substance *A* is a compound and substance *Z* is an element.

15 Which ion, when combined with chloride ions, Cl^-, forms an insoluble substance in water?

(1) Fe^{2+}
(2) Mg^{2+}
(3) Pb^{2+}
(4) Zn^{2+}

16 Molarity is defined as the

(1) moles of solute per kilogram of solvent
(2) moles of solute per liter of solution
(3) mass of a solution
(4) volume of a solvent

17 Which formula represents a hydrocarbon?

(1) $CH_3CH_2CH_2CHO$
(2) $CH_3CH_2CH_2CH_3$
(3) $CH_3CH_2CH_2COOH$
(4) $CH_3CH_2COOCH_3$

18 Which expression represents the ΔH for a chemical reaction in terms of the potential energy, *PE*, of its products and reactants?

(1) *PE* of products + *PE* of reactants
(2) *PE* of products – *PE* of reactants
(3) *PE* of products × *PE* of reactants
(4) *PE* of products ÷ *PE* of reactants

19 Which balanced equation represents an endothermic reaction?

(1) $C(s) + O_2(g) \rightarrow CO_2(g)$
(2) $CH_4(g) + 2O_2(g) \rightarrow CO_2(g) + 2H_2O(\ell)$
(3) $N_2(g) + 3H_2(g) \rightarrow 2NH_3(g)$
(4) $N_2(g) + O_2(g) \rightarrow 2NO(g)$

20 Which formula represents propyne?

(1) C_3H_4
(2) C_3H_6
(3) C_5H_8
(4) C_5H_{10}

21 Which factors must be equal in a reversible chemical reaction at equilibrium?

(1) the activation energies of the forward and reverse reactions
(2) the rates of the forward and reverse reactions
(3) the concentrations of the reactants and products
(4) the potential energies of the reactants and products

22 The compounds CH_3OCH_3 and CH_3CH_2OH are isomers of each other. These two compounds must have the same

(1) density
(2) reactivity
(3) melting point
(4) molecular formula

23 Which balanced equation represents a redox reaction?

(1) $AgNO_3 + NaCl \rightarrow AgCl + NaNO_3$
(2) $BaCl_2 + K_2CO_3 \rightarrow BaCO_3 + 2KCl$
(3) $CuO + CO \rightarrow Cu + CO_2$
(4) $HCl + KOH \rightarrow KCl + H_2O$

24 Which process occurs at the anode in an electrochemical cell?

(1) the loss of protons
(2) the loss of electrons
(3) the gain of protons
(4) the gain of electrons

25 Which substance is an electrolyte?

(1) CH_3OH
(2) $C_6H_{12}O_6$
(3) H_2O
(4) KOH

26 Which ion is the only negative ion present in an aqueous solution of an Arrhenius base?

(1) hydride ion
(2) hydrogen ion
(3) hydronium ion
(4) hydroxide ion

27 According to Reference Table *N*, which pair of isotopes spontaneously decays?

(1) C-12 and N-14
(2) C-12 and N-16
(3) C-14 and N-14
(4) C-14 and N-16

28 Which equation represents the radioactive decay of $^{226}_{88}Ra$?

(1) $^{226}_{88}Ra \rightarrow ^{222}_{86}Rn + ^{4}_{2}He$
(2) $^{226}_{88}Ra \rightarrow ^{226}_{89}Ac + ^{0}_{-1}e$
(3) $^{226}_{88}Ra \rightarrow ^{226}_{87}Fr + ^{0}_{+1}e$
(4) $^{226}_{88}Ra \rightarrow ^{225}_{88}Ra + ^{1}_{0}n$

29 Which type of reaction converts one element to another element?

(1) neutralization
(2) polymerization
(3) substitution
(4) transmutation

30 Which nuclear emission has the greatest mass?

(1) α
(2) γ
(3) β^-
(4) β^+

Part B–1

Answer all questions in this part.

Directions (31–50): For *each* statement or question, write on the separate answer sheet the *number* of the word or expression that, of those given, best completes the statement or answers the question. Some questions may require the use of the *Reference Tables for Physical Setting/Chemistry*.

31 Which trends are observed as each of the elements within Group 15 on the Periodic Table is considered in order from top to bottom?

(1) Their metallic properties decrease and their atomic radii decrease.
(2) Their metallic properties decrease and their atomic radii increase.
(3) Their metallic properties increase and their atomic radii decrease.
(4) Their metallic properties increase and their atomic radii increase.

32 What is the total number of electrons in a S^{2-} ion?

(1) 10 (3) 16
(2) 14 (4) 18

33 A substance has an empirical formula of CH_2 and a molar mass of 56 grams per mole. The molecular formula for this compound is

(1) CH_2 (3) C_4H_8
(2) C_4H_6 (4) C_8H_4

34 Compared to an atom of phosphorus-31, an atom of sulfur-32 contains

(1) one less neutron (3) one more neutron
(2) one less proton (4) one more proton

35 In which compound is the percent composition by mass of chlorine equal to 42%?

(1) HClO (gram-formula mass = 52 g/mol)
(2) $HClO_2$ (gram-formula mass = 68 g/mol)
(3) $HClO_3$ (gram-formula mass = 84 g/mol)
(4) $HClO_4$ (gram-formula mass = 100. g/mol)

36 A metal, *M*, forms an oxide compound with the general formula M_2O. In which group on the Periodic Table could metal *M* be found?

(1) Group 1 (3) Group 16
(2) Group 2 (4) Group 17

37 Given the key:

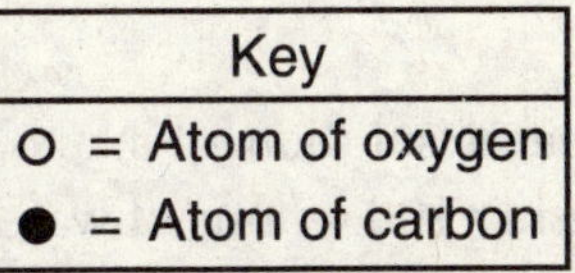

Which particle diagram represents a sample containing the compound CO(g)?

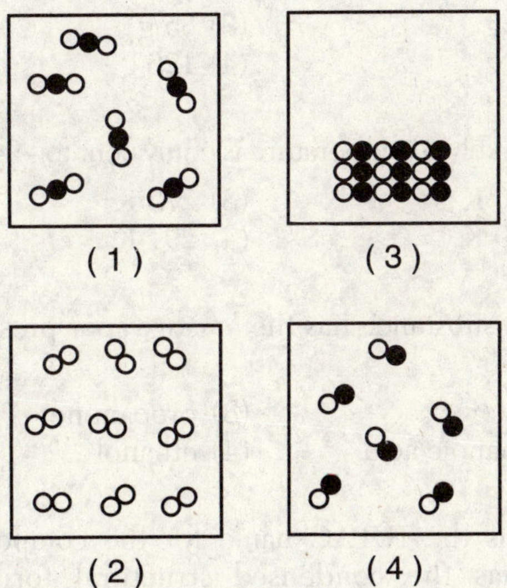

38 At standard pressure, which element has a melting point higher than standard temperature?

(1) F_2 (3) Fe
(2) Br_2 (4) Hg

39 Which Lewis electron-dot diagram represents chloroethene?

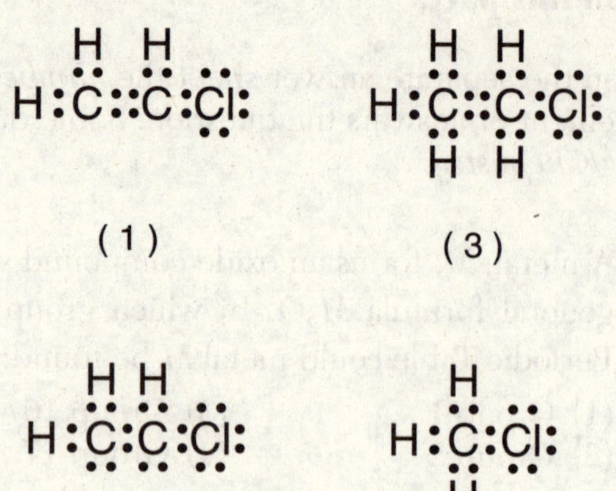

40 A saturated solution of $NaNO_3$ is prepared at 60.°C using 100. grams of water. As this solution is cooled to 10.°C, $NaNO_3$ precipitates (settles) out of the solution. The resulting solution is saturated. Approximately how many grams of $NaNO_3$ settled out of the original solution?

(1) 46 g	(3) 85 g
(2) 61 g	(4) 126 g

41 Which kelvin temperature is equivalent to –24°C?

(1) 226 K	(3) 273 K
(2) 249 K	(4) 297 K

42 Which substance has the *lowest* vapor pressure at 75°C?

(1) water	(3) propanone
(2) ethanoic acid	(4) ethanol

43 What is the IUPAC name for the compound that has the condensed structural formula $CH_3CH_2CH_2CHO$?

(1) butanal	(3) propanal
(2) butanol	(4) propanol

44 What volume of 0.500 M HNO_3(aq) must completely react to neutralize 100.0 milliliters of 0.100 M KOH(aq)?

(1) 10.0 mL	(3) 50.0 mL
(2) 20.0 mL	(4) 500. mL

45 Given the formula:

```
    H   H   H   O
    |   |   |   ‖    H
H — C — C — C — C — N
    |   |   |        H
    H   H   H
```

This compound is classified as

(1) an aldehyde	(3) an amine
(2) an amide	(4) a ketone

46 Given the balanced equation with an unknown compound represented by *X*:

$$C_6H_{12}O_6(aq) \xrightarrow{\text{enzyme}} 2X + 2CO_2(g)$$

Which compound is represented by *X*?

(1) $CH_3OH(aq)$
(2) $CH_2(OH)_4(aq)$
(3) $CH_3CH_2OH(aq)$
(4) $CH_2OHCH_2OH(aq)$

47 Which reactants form the salt $CaSO_4(s)$ in a neutralization reaction?

(1) $H_2S(g)$ and $Ca(ClO_4)_2(s)$
(2) $H_2SO_3(aq)$ and $Ca(NO_3)_2(aq)$
(3) $H_2SO_4(aq)$ and $Ca(OH)_2(aq)$
(4) $SO_2(g)$ and $CaO(s)$

48 A student tested a 0.1 M aqueous solution and made the following observations:

- conducts electricity
- turns blue litmus to red
- reacts with Zn(s) to produce gas bubbles

Which compound could be the solute in this solution?

(1) CH_3OH	(3) HBr
(2) LiBr	(4) LiOH

49 What is the half-life of sodium-25 if 1.00 gram of a 16.00-gram sample of sodium-25 remains unchanged after 237 seconds?

(1) 47.4 s	(3) 79.0 s
(2) 59.3 s	(4) 118 s

50 Given the table below that shows students' examples of proposed models of the atom:

Proposed Models of the Atom

Model	Location of Protons	Location of Electrons
A	in the nucleus	specific shells
B	in the nucleus	regions of most probable location
C	dispersed throughout the atom	specific shells
D	dispersed throughout the atom	regions of most probable location

Which model correctly describes the locations of protons and electrons in the wave-mechanical model of the atom?

(1) *A*
(2) *B*
(3) *C*
(4) *D*

Part B–2

Answer all questions in this part.

Directions (51–66): Record your answers in the spaces provided in your answer booklet. Some questions may require the use of the *Reference Tables for Physical Setting/Chemistry.*

Base your answers to questions 51 and 52 on the balanced equation below.

$$Fe(s) + 2HNO_3(aq) \rightarrow Fe(NO_3)_2(aq) + H_2(g)$$

51 What is the total number of oxygen atoms represented in the formula of the iron compound produced? [1]

52 Explain, using information from Reference Table *J*, why this reaction is spontaneous. [1]

Base your answers to questions 53 and 54 on the information below.

An atom has an atomic number of 9, a mass number of 19, and an electron configuration of 2–6–1.

53 What is the total number of neutrons in this atom? [1]

54 Explain why the number of electrons in the second and third shells shows that this atom is in an excited state. [1]

55 To which homologous series does $CH_3CH_2CH_2CH_3$ belong? [1]

56 What is the mass of 4.76 moles of Na_3PO_4 (gram-formula mass = 164 grams/mole)? [1]

Base your answers to questions 57 and 58 on the information below.

Given the balanced equation for dissolving $NH_4Cl(s)$ in water:

$$NH_4Cl(s) \xrightarrow{H_2O} NH_4^+(aq) + Cl^-(aq)$$

57 A student is holding a test tube containing 5.0 milliliters of water. When a sample of $NH_4Cl(s)$ is placed in the test tube, the test tube feels colder to the student's hand. Describe the direction of heat flow between the test tube and the hand. [1]

58 Using the key *in your answer booklet,* draw *at least two* water molecules in the box, showing the correct orientation of each water molecule when it is near the Cl^- ion in the aqueous solution. [1]

Base your answers to questions 59 and 60 on the information below.

Given the reaction at equilibrium:

$$2NO_2(g) \rightleftharpoons N_2O_4(g) + 55.3 \text{ kJ}$$

59 Explain, in terms of energy, why the forward reaction is exothermic. [1]

60 Explain, in terms of Le Chatelier's principle, why the equilibrium shifts to the right to relieve the stress when the pressure on the system is increased at constant temperature. [1]

Base your answers to questions 61 through 63 on the information below.

Given the balanced equation for an organic reaction between butane and chlorine that takes place at 300.°C and 101.3 kilopascals:

$$C_4H_{10} + Cl_2 \rightarrow C_4H_9Cl + HCl$$

61 Identify the type of organic reaction shown. [1]

62 In the space *in your answer booklet,* draw a structural formula for the organic product. [1]

63 Explain, in terms of collision theory, why the rate of the reaction would *decrease* if the temperature of the reaction mixture was lowered to 200.°C with pressure remaining unchanged. [1]

Base your answers to questions 64 through 66 on the information below.

Ethanol, C_2H_5OH, is a volatile and flammable liquid with a distinct odor at room temperature. Ethanol is soluble in water. The boiling point of ethanol is 78.2°C at 1 atmosphere. Ethanol can be used as a fuel to produce heat energy, as shown by the balanced equation below.

$$C_2H_5OH(\ell) + 3O_2(g) \rightarrow 2CO_2(g) + 3H_2O(\ell) + 1367 \text{ kJ}$$

64 At 1 atmosphere, compare the boiling point of pure ethanol to the boiling point of a solution in which a nonvolatile substance is dissolved in ethanol. [1]

65 Determine the total amount of heat produced by the complete combustion of 2.00 moles of ethanol. [1]

66 Identify *one* physical property of ethanol, stated in the passage, that can be explained in terms of chemical bonds and intermolecular forces. [1]

Part C

Answer all questions in this part.

Directions (67–84): Record your answers in the spaces provided in your answer booklet. Some questions may require the use of the *Reference Tables for Physical Setting/Chemistry.*

Base your answers to questions 67 and 68 on the information below.

The graph shows the relationship between the solubility of a sequence of primary alcohols in water and the total number of carbon atoms in a molecule of the corresponding alcohol at the same temperature and pressure. A primary alcohol has the —OH group located on an end carbon of the hydrocarbon chain.

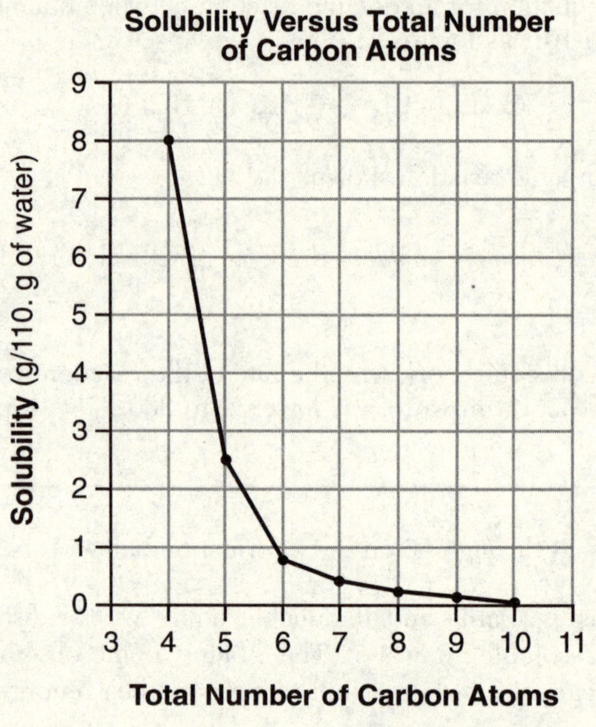

Adapted from *Chemistry*, Collins Educational Publishing, pp. 227-231

67 Describe the relationship between the solubility of a primary alcohol in water and the total number of carbon atoms in the primary alcohol. [1]

68 Determine the total mass of 1-pentanol that will dissolve in 110. grams of water to produce a saturated solution. [1]

Base your answers to questions 69 and 70 on the information below.

Air bags are an important safety feature in modern automobiles. An air bag is inflated in milliseconds by the explosive decomposition of $NaN_3(s)$. The decomposition reaction produces $N_2(g)$, as well as Na(s), according to the unbalanced equation below.

$$NaN_3(s) \rightarrow Na(s) + N_2(g)$$

69 Balance the equation *in your answer booklet* for the decomposition of NaN_3, using the smallest whole-number coefficients. [1]

70 When the air bag inflates, the nitrogen gas is at a pressure of 1.30 atmospheres, a temperature of 301 K, and has a volume of 40.0 liters. In the space *in your answer booklet,* calculate the volume of the nitrogen gas at STP. Your response must include *both* a correct numerical setup and the calculated volume. [2]

Base your answers to questions 71 and 72 on the information below.

A thiol is very similar to an alcohol, but a thiol has a sulfur atom instead of an oxygen atom in the functional group. One of the compounds in a skunk's spray is 2-butene-1-thiol. The formula of this compound is shown below.

```
    H  H     H
    |  |     |
 H—C—C=C—C—H
    |     |  |
    SH    H  H
```

71 Explain, in terms of composition, why this compound is a thiol. [1]

72 Explain, in terms of electron configuration, why oxygen atoms and sulfur atoms form compounds with similar molecular structures. [1]

Base your answers to questions 73 through 75 on the graph below. The graph shows the relationship between pH value and hydronium ion concentration for common aqueous solutions and mixtures.

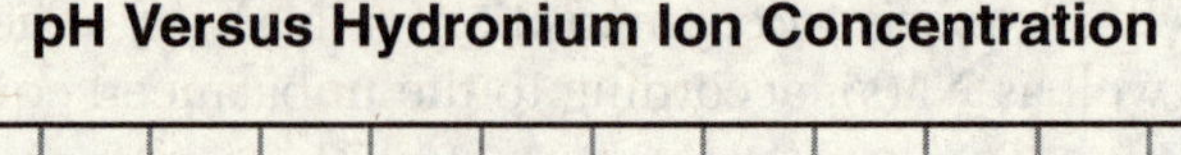

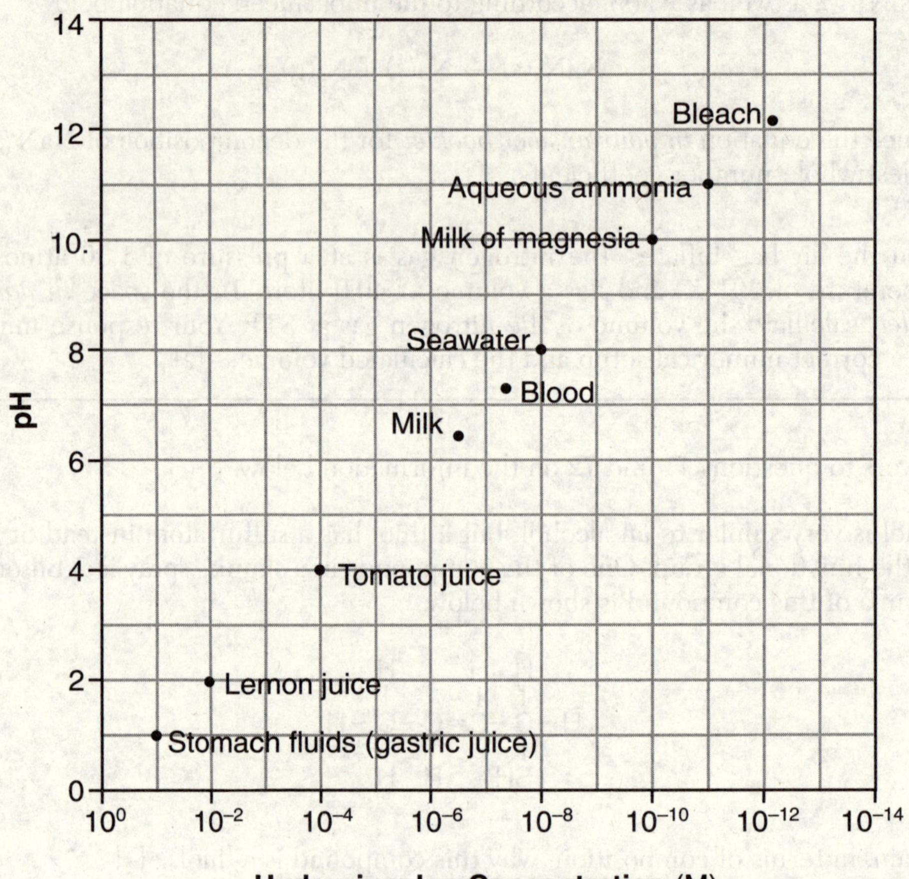

73 What is the hydronium ion concentration of tomato juice? [1]

74 What color is thymol blue when added to milk of magnesia? [1]

75 According to this graph, which mixture is approximately 100 times more acidic than milk of magnesia? [1]

Base your answers to questions 76 and 77 on the information below.

Archimedes (287–212 BC), a Greek inventor and mathematician, made several discoveries important to science today. According to a legend, Hiero, the king of Syracuse, commanded Archimedes to find out if the royal crown was made of gold, only. The king suspected that the crown consisted of a mixture of gold, tin, and copper.

Archimedes measured the mass of the crown and the total amount of water displaced by the crown when it was completely submerged. He repeated the procedure using individual samples, one of gold, one of tin, and one of copper. Archimedes was able to determine that the crown was not made entirely of gold without damaging it.

76 Identify *one* physical property that Archimedes used in his comparison of the metal samples. [1]

77 Determine the volume of a 75-gram sample of gold at STP. [1]

Base your answers to questions 78 through 81 on the information below.

Aluminum is one of the most abundant metals in Earth's crust. The aluminum compound found in bauxite ore is Al_2O_3. Over one hundred years ago, it was difficult and expensive to isolate aluminum from bauxite ore. In 1886, a brother and sister team, Charles and Julia Hall, found that molten (melted) cryolite, Na_3AlF_6, would dissolve bauxite ore. Electrolysis of the resulting mixture caused the aluminum ions in the Al_2O_3 to be reduced to molten aluminum metal. This less expensive process is known as the Hall process.

78 Write the oxidation state for *each* of the elements in cryolite. [1]

79 Write the balanced half-reaction equation for the reduction of Al^{3+} to Al. [1]

80 Explain, in terms of ions, why molten cryolite conducts electricity. [1]

81 Explain, in terms of electrical energy, how the operation of a voltaic cell differs from the operation of an electrolytic cell used in the Hall process. Include *both* the voltaic cell and the electrolytic cell in your answer. [1]

Base your answers to questions 82 through 84 on the information below.

A glass tube is filled with hydrogen gas at low pressure. An electric current is passed through the gas, causing it to emit light. This light is passed through a prism to separate the light into the bright, colored lines of hydrogen's visible spectrum. Each colored line corresponds to a particular wavelength of light. One of hydrogen's spectral lines is red light with a wavelength of 656 nanometers.

Tubes filled with other gases produce different bright-line spectra that are characteristic of each kind of gas. These spectra have been observed and recorded.

82 Explain, in terms of electron energy states and energy changes, how hydrogen's bright-line spectrum is produced. [1]

83 Explain how the elements present on the surface of a star can be identified using bright-line spectra. [1]

84 A student measured the wavelength of hydrogen's visible red spectral line to be 647 nanometers. In the space *in your answer booklet,* show a correct numerical setup for calculating the student's percent error. [1]

The University of the State of New York

REGENTS HIGH SCHOOL EXAMINATION

PHYSICAL SETTING CHEMISTRY

Wednesday, June 21, 2006 — 1:15 to 4:15 p.m., only

ANSWER BOOKLET

Student . . . . Sex: ☐ Male ☐ Female

Teacher. . . . .

School . . . . Grade . . . .

Answer all questions in Part B–2 and Part C. Record your answers in this booklet.

Part	Maximum Score	Student's Score
A	30	
B–1	20	
B–2	16	
C	19	

Total Written Test Score (Maximum Raw Score: 85) ☐

Final Score (from conversion chart) ☐

Raters' Initials:

Rater 1 . . . . **Rater 2** . . . .

Part B–2

For Raters Only

51 ______________ | 51 ☐

52 ____

____ | 52 ☐

____

53 ______________ | 53 ☐

54 ____

____ | 54 ☐

____

For Raters Only

55 ______________________________ 55

56 __________________ g 56

57 ____ 57

____

58

Key
● = Hydrogen atom
○ = Oxygen atom
= Water molecule

Cl^-

58

59 ____

____ 59

____

60 ____

____ 60

____

[2]

61 ________________________

62

63 ____

____

____

64 ____

____

65 ________________ kJ

66 ________________________

For Raters Only

61 ☐

62 ☐

63 ☐

64 ☐

65 ☐

66 ☐

Total Score for Part B–2

Part C

For Raters Only

67 ____

____ 67 [ ]

68 ______________ g 68 [ ]

69 ____ $NaN_3(s) \rightarrow$ ____ $Na(s)$ + ____ $N_2(g)$ 69 [ ]

70

70 [ ]

______________ L

71 ____

____ 71 [ ]

____

72 ____

____ 72 [ ]

____

For Raters Only

73 ____________ M | 73 [ ]

74 ________________________ | 74 [ ]

75 ________________________ | 75 [ ]

76 ________________________ | 76 [ ]

77 ____________ cm^3 | 77 [ ]

78 Na_3AlF_6 Na: __________

Al: __________ | 78 [ ]

F: __________

79 ________________________ | 79 [ ]

80 ____

____ | 80 [ ]

____

81 ____

____ | 81 [ ]

____

For Raters Only

82

82

83

83

84

84

Total Score for Part C

Physical Setting Chemistry January, 2006

Part A

Answer all questions in this part.

Directions (1–30): For *each* statement or question, write on the separate answer sheet the *number* of the word or expression that, of those given, best completes the statement or answers the question. Some questions may require the use of the *Reference Tables for Physical Setting/Chemistry*.

1 Which two nuclides are isotopes of the same element?

(1) $^{20}_{11}Na$ and $^{20}_{10}Ne$
(2) $^{39}_{19}K$ and $^{40}_{20}Ca$
(3) $^{39}_{19}K$ and $^{42}_{19}K$
(4) $^{14}_{6}C$ and $^{14}_{7}N$

2 An atom of oxygen is in an excited state. When an electron in this atom moves from the third shell to the second shell, energy is

(1) emitted by the nucleus
(2) emitted by the electron
(3) absorbed by the nucleus
(4) absorbed by the electron

3 The charge of a beryllium-9 nucleus is

(1) +13
(2) +9
(3) +5
(4) +4

4 Which sequence represents a correct order of historical developments leading to the modern model of the atom?

(1) the atom is a hard sphere → most of the atom is empty space → electrons exist in orbitals outside the nucleus
(2) the atom is a hard sphere → electrons exist in orbitals outside the nucleus → most of the atom is empty space
(3) most of the atom is empty space → electrons exist in orbitals outside the nucleus → the atom is a hard sphere
(4) most of the atom is empty space → the atom is a hard sphere → electrons exist in orbitals outside the nucleus

5 Which statement describes a chemical property of oxygen?

(1) Oxygen has a melting point of 55 K.
(2) Oxygen can combine with a metal to produce a compound.
(3) Oxygen gas is slightly soluble in water.
(4) Oxygen gas can be compressed.

6 The element in Group 14, Period 3 on the Periodic Table is classified as a

(1) metal
(2) noble gas
(3) metalloid
(4) nonmetal

7 Which trends are observed when the elements in Period 3 on the Periodic Table are considered in order of increasing atomic number?

(1) The atomic radius decreases, and the first ionization energy generally increases.
(2) The atomic radius decreases, and the first ionization energy generally decreases.
(3) The atomic radius increases, and the first ionization energy generally increases.
(4) The atomic radius increases, and the first ionization energy generally decreases.

8 What is the chemical formula for sodium sulfate?

(1) Na_2SO_3
(2) Na_2SO_4
(3) $NaSO_3$
(4) $NaSO_4$

9 Given the structural formula:

```
    H   H   H   H
    |   |   |   |
HO—C—C—C—C—OH
    |   |   |   |
    H   H   H   H
```

What is the empirical formula of this compound?

(1) CH_3O
(2) C_2H_5O
(3) $C_4H_{10}O_2$
(4) $C_8H_{20}O_4$

10 Which chemical equation is correctly balanced?

(1) $H_2(g) + O_2(g) \rightarrow H_2O(g)$
(2) $N_2(g) + H_2(g) \rightarrow NH_3(g)$
(3) $2NaCl(s) \rightarrow Na(s) + Cl_2(g)$
(4) $2KCl(s) \rightarrow 2K(s) + Cl_2(g)$

11 Compared to a calcium atom, the calcium ion Ca^{2+} has

(1) more protons (3) more electrons
(2) fewer protons (4) fewer electrons

12 Which type of bond is found in sodium bromide?

(1) covalent (3) ionic
(2) hydrogen (4) metallic

13 Which substance can *not* be decomposed by ordinary chemical means?

(1) methane (3) ethanol
(2) mercury (4) ammonia

14 A mixture of crystals of salt and sugar is added to water and stirred until all solids have dissolved. Which statement best describes the resulting mixture?

(1) The mixture is homogeneous and can be separated by filtration.
(2) The mixture is homogeneous and cannot be separated by filtration.
(3) The mixture is heterogeneous and can be separated by filtration.
(4) The mixture is heterogeneous and cannot be separated by filtration.

15 Under which conditions of temperature and pressure would a sample of $H_2(g)$ behave most like an ideal gas?

(1) 0°C and 100 kPa
(2) 0°C and 300 kPa
(3) 150°C and 100 kPa
(4) 150°C and 300 kPa

16 In a chemical reaction, the difference between the potential energy of the products and the potential energy of the reactants is defined as the

(1) activation energy
(2) ionization energy
(3) heat of reaction
(4) heat of vaporization

17 Which substance is an Arrhenius base?

(1) KCl (3) KOH
(2) CH_3Cl (4) CH_3OH

18 Given the balanced equation:

$$I_2(s) + \text{energy} \rightarrow I_2(g)$$

As a sample of $I_2(s)$ sublimes to $I_2(g)$, the entropy of the sample

(1) increases because the particles are less randomly arranged
(2) increases because the particles are more randomly arranged
(3) decreases because the particles are less randomly arranged
(4) decreases because the particles are more randomly arranged

19 The multiple covalent bond in a molecule of 1-butene is a

(1) double covalent bond that has 6 shared electrons
(2) double covalent bond that has 4 shared electrons
(3) triple covalent bond that has 6 shared electrons
(4) triple covalent bond that has 4 shared electrons

20 In an oxidation-reduction reaction, reduction is defined as the

(1) loss of protons (3) loss of electrons
(2) gain of protons (4) gain of electrons

21 What is the oxidation number assigned to manganese in $KMnO_4$?

(1) +7 (3) +3
(2) +2 (4) +4

22 Which of the following aqueous solutions is the best conductor of electricity?

(1) 0.10 M CH_3OH (3) 0.10 M NaOH
(2) 1.0 M CH_3OH (4) 1.0 M NaOH

23 One acid-base theory states that an acid is

(1) an H^- donor (3) an H^+ donor
(2) an H^- acceptor (4) an H^+ acceptor

24 Positrons are spontaneously emitted from the nuclei of

(1) potassium-37 (3) nitrogen-16
(2) radium-226 (4) thorium-232

25 The amount of energy released from a fission reaction is much greater than the energy released from a chemical reaction because in a fission reaction

(1) mass is converted into energy
(2) energy is converted into mass
(3) ionic bonds are broken
(4) covalent bonds are broken

26 Which Lewis electron-dot diagram is correct for CO_2?

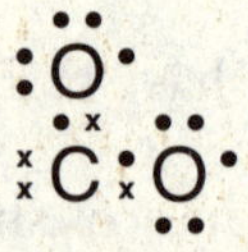

(1) 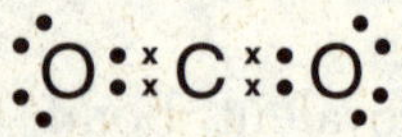 (3)

(2) 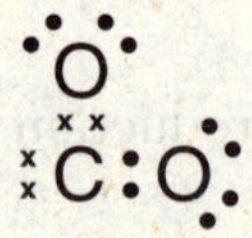 (4)

27 Types of nuclear reactions include fission, fusion, and

(1) single replacement
(2) neutralization
(3) oxidation-reduction
(4) transmutation

28 Which structural formula is correct for 2-methyl-3-pentanol?

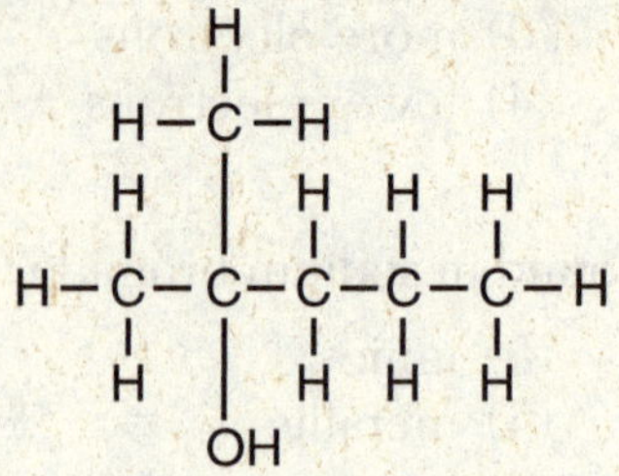

(1) 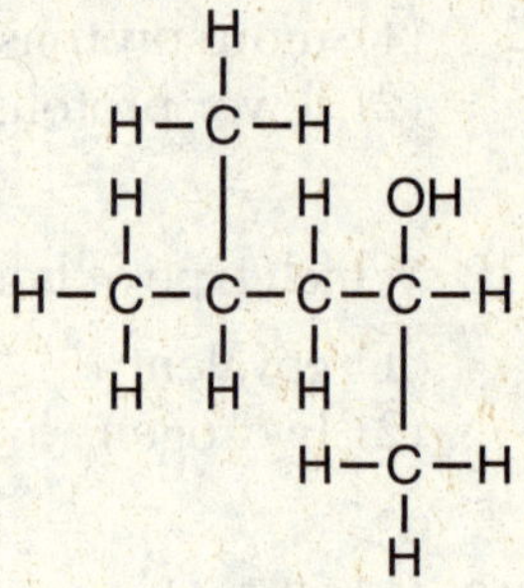 (3)

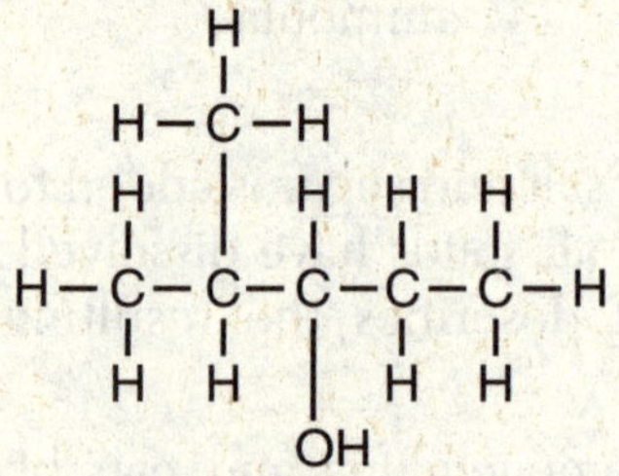

(2) 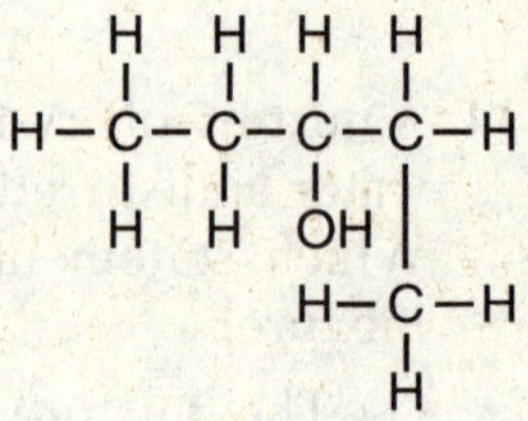 (4)

Note that questions 29 and 30 have only three choices.

29 When an atom becomes a positive ion, the radius of the atom

(1) decreases
(2) increases
(3) remains the same

30 Compared to the freezing point of 1.0 M KCl(aq) at standard pressure, the freezing point of 1.0 M $CaCl_2$(aq) at standard pressure is

(1) lower
(2) higher
(3) the same

Part B–1

Answer all questions in this part.

Directions (31–50): For *each* statement or question, write on the separate answer sheet the *number* of the word or expression that, of those given, best completes the statement or answers the question. Some questions may require the use of the *Reference Tables for Physical Setting/Chemistry*.

31 Which electron configuration represents the electrons in an atom of chlorine in an excited state?

(1) 2-7-7
(2) 2-7-8
(3) 2-8-7
(4) 2-8-8

32 Given the particle diagram representing four molecules of a substance:

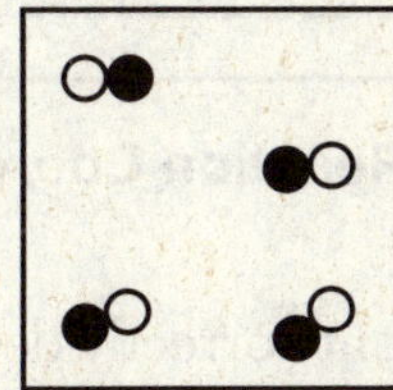

Which particle diagram best represents this same substance after a physical change has taken place?

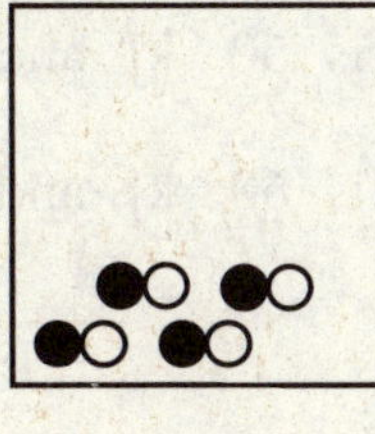

(1)

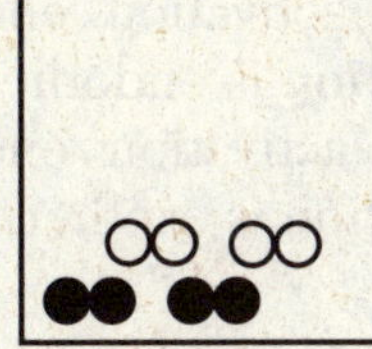

(3)

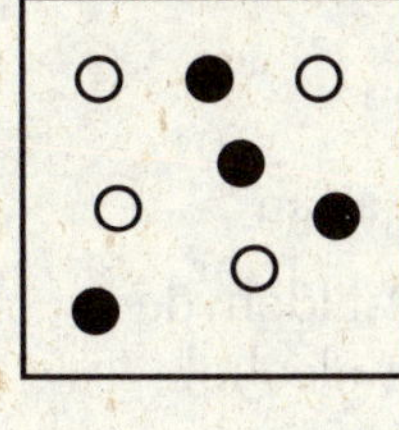

(2)

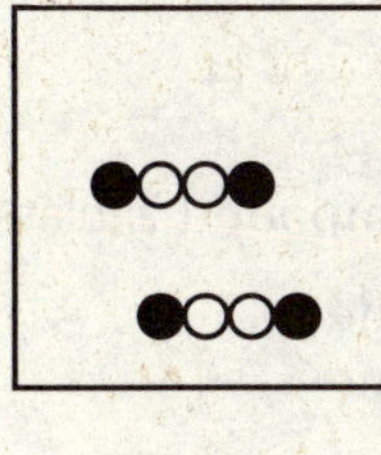

(4)

33 What is the percent composition by mass of nitrogen in NH_4NO_3 (gram-formula mass = 80.0 grams/mole)?

(1) 17.5%
(2) 35.0%
(3) 52.5%
(4) 60.0%

34 The atomic mass of element *A* is 63.6 atomic mass units. The only naturally occurring isotopes of element *A* are *A*-63 and *A*-65. The percent abundances in a naturally occurring sample of element *A* are closest to

(1) 31% A-63 and 69% A-65
(2) 50% A-63 and 50% A-65
(3) 69% A-63 and 31% A-65
(4) 100% A-63 and 0% A-65

35 Elements *Q*, *X*, and *Z* are in the same group on the Periodic Table and are listed in order of increasing atomic number. The melting point of element *Q* is –219°C and the melting point of element Z is –7°C. Which temperature is closest to the melting point of element *X*?

(1) –7°C
(2) –101°C
(3) –219°C
(4) –226°C

36 Given the balanced equation:

$$2C + 3H_2 \rightarrow C_2H_6$$

What is the total number of moles of C that must completely react to produce 2.0 moles of C_2H_6?

(1) 1.0 mol
(2) 2.0 mol
(3) 3.0 mol
(4) 4.0 mol

37 Given the balanced equation:

$$2KClO_3 \rightarrow 2KCl + 3O_2$$

Which type of reaction is represented by this equation?

(1) synthesis
(2) decomposition
(3) single replacement
(4) double replacement

38 A solid substance was tested in the laboratory. The test results are listed below.

- dissolves in water
- is an electrolyte
- melts at a high temperature

Based on these results, the solid substance could be

(1) Cu (3) C
(2) $CuBr_2$ (4) $C_6H_{12}O_6$

39 If 0.025 gram of $Pb(NO_3)_2$ is dissolved in 100. grams of H_2O, what is the concentration of the resulting solution, in parts per million?

(1) 2.5×10^{-4} ppm (3) 250 ppm
(2) 2.5 ppm (4) 4.0×10^{3} ppm

40 Given the balanced equation:

$$4Fe(s) + 3O_2(g) \rightarrow 2Fe_2O_3(s) + 1640 \text{ kJ}$$

Which phrase best describes this reaction?

(1) endothermic with $\Delta H = +1640$ kJ
(2) endothermic with $\Delta H = -1640$ kJ
(3) exothermic with $\Delta H = +1640$ kJ
(4) exothermic with $\Delta H = -1640$ kJ

41 A student adds solid KCl to water in a flask. The flask is sealed with a stopper and thoroughly shaken until no more solid KCl dissolves. Some solid KCl is still visible in the flask. The solution in the flask is

(1) saturated and is at equilibrium with the solid KCl
(2) saturated and is not at equilibrium with the solid KCl
(3) unsaturated and is at equilibrium with the solid KCl
(4) unsaturated and is not at equilibrium with the solid KCl

42 Given the incomplete equation for the combustion of ethane:

$$2C_2H_6 + 7O_2 \rightarrow 4CO_2 + 6 \_\_\_\_$$

What is the formula of the missing product?

(1) CH_3OH (3) H_2O
(2) HCOOH (4) H_2O_2

43 Given the potential energy diagram for a chemical reaction:

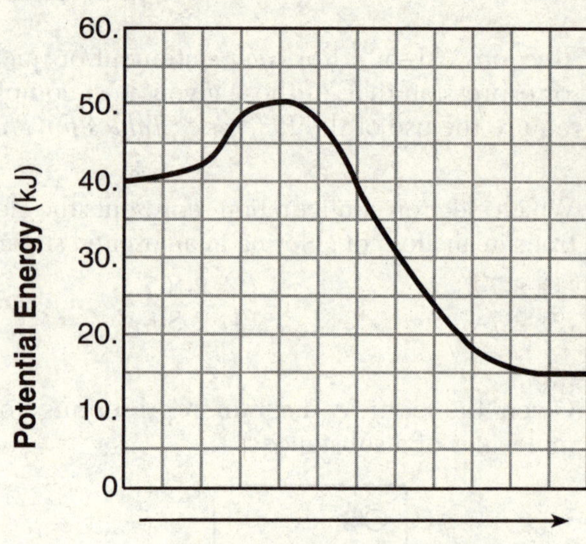

Which statement correctly describes the energy changes that occur in the forward reaction?

(1) The activation energy is 10. kJ and the reaction is endothermic.
(2) The activation energy is 10. kJ and the reaction is exothermic.
(3) The activation energy is 50. kJ and the reaction is endothermic.
(4) The activation energy is 50. kJ and the reaction is exothermic.

44 Given the structural formula:

```
   H  O     H
   |  ||   /
H—C—C—N
   |       \
   H        H
```

This compound is classified as an

(1) amide (3) aldehyde
(2) amine (4) alcohol

45 Which formula represents an unsaturated hydrocarbon?

(1) CH_2CHCl (3) $CH_3CH_2CH_3$
(2) CH_3CH_2Cl (4) CH_3CHCH_2

46 Given the balanced equation for an organic reaction:

$$C_2H_2 + 2Cl_2 \rightarrow C_2H_2Cl_4$$

This reaction is best classified as

(1) addition
(2) esterification
(3) fermentation
(4) substitution

47 Which indicator is yellow in a solution with a pH of 9.8?

(1) methyl orange
(2) bromthymol blue
(3) bromcresol green
(4) thymol blue

48 How many milliliters of 0.100 M NaOH(aq) would be needed to completely neutralize 50.0 milliliters of 0.300 M HCl(aq)?

(1) 16.7 mL
(2) 50.0 mL
(3) 150. mL
(4) 300. mL

49 Given the nuclear equation:

$$^{1}_{1}H + X \rightarrow ^{6}_{3}Li + ^{4}_{2}He$$

The particle represented by *X* is

(1) $^{9}_{4}Li$
(2) $^{9}_{4}Be$
(3) $^{10}_{5}Be$
(4) $^{10}_{6}C$

50 The decay of which radioisotope can be used to estimate the age of the fossilized remains of an insect?

(1) Rn-222
(2) I-131
(3) Co-60
(4) C-14

Part B–2

Answer all questions in this part.

Directions (51–67): Record your answers in the spaces provided in your answer booklet. Some questions may require the use of the *Reference Tables for Physical Setting/Chemistry.*

51 What is the total number of neutrons in an atom of aluminum-27? [1]

52 Explain, in terms of atomic structure, why the atomic radius of iodine is greater than the atomic radius of fluorine. [1]

53 In the space *in your answer booklet,* draw a Lewis electron-dot diagram of a selenium atom in the ground state. [1]

54 Explain, in terms of atomic structure, why liquid mercury is a good electrical conductor. [1]

55 Given the structural formula of pentane:

```
   H  H  H  H  H
   |  |  |  |  |
H—C—C—C—C—C—H
   |  |  |  |  |
   H  H  H  H  H
```

In the space *in your answer booklet,* draw a structural formula for an isomer of pentane. [1]

56 Based on Reference Table *N*, what is the fraction of a sample of potassium-42 that will remain unchanged after 62.0 hours? [1]

57 What is the total number of moles in 80.0 grams of C_2H_5Cl (gram-formula mass = 64.5 grams/mole)? [1]

58 What is the total amount of heat energy, in joules, absorbed by 25.0 grams of water when the temperature of the water increases from 24.0°C to 36.0°C? [1]

Base your answers to questions 59 and 60 on the information and balanced equation below.

Given the equation for a reaction at equilibrium:

$$2SO_2(g) + O_2(g) \rightleftharpoons 2SO_3(g) + \text{energy}$$

59 Explain, in terms of LeChatelier's principle, why the concentration of $SO_2(g)$ increases when the temperature is increased. [1]

60 Explain, in terms of collisions between molecules, why increasing the concentration of $O_2(g)$ produces a *decrease* in the concentration of $SO_2(g)$. [1]

Base your answers to questions 61 through 65 on the table below.

Physical Properties of Four Gases

Name of Gas	hydrogen	hydrogen chloride	hydrogen bromide	hydrogen iodide
Molecular Structure	H–H	H–Cl	H–Br	H–I
Boiling Point (K) at 1 Atm	20.	188	207	237
Density (g/L) at STP	0.0899	1.64	?	5.66

61 The volume of 1.00 mole of hydrogen bromide at STP is 22.4 liters. The gram-formula mass of hydrogen bromide is 80.9 grams per mole. What is the density of hydrogen bromide at STP? [1]

62 The density of hydrogen at STP is 0.0899 gram per liter. Express this density to *two significant figures.* [1]

63 Explain, in terms of electronegativity difference, why the bond in H–Cl is more polar than the bond in H–I. [1]

64 Explain, in terms of intermolecular forces, why hydrogen has a *lower* boiling point than hydrogen bromide. [1]

65 Explain, in terms of molecular polarity, why hydrogen chloride is more soluble than hydrogen in water under the same conditions of temperature and pressure. [1]

Base your answers to questions 66 and 67 on the graph below, which represents the cooling of a substance starting at a temperature above its boiling point.

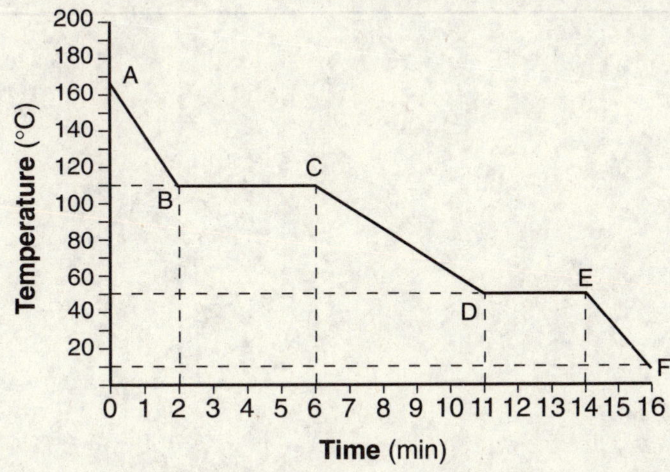

66 What is the melting point of this substance? [1]

67 Which segment of the graph represents the gas phase, only? [1]

Part C

Answer all questions in this part.

Directions (68–85): Record your answers in the spaces provided in your answer booklet. Some questions may require the use of the *Reference Tables for Physical Setting/Chemistry*.

Base your answers to questions 68 through 70 on the information and table below.

A student conducts an experiment to determine how the temperature of water affects the rate at which an antacid tablet dissolves in the water. The student has three antacid tablets of the same size and composition. The student drops one tablet into each of three beakers containing 200. milliliters of water at different temperatures and measures the time it takes for each tablet to completely dissolve. The results are shown in the table below.

Dissolving Data for Three Antacid Tablets

Beaker	Original Temperature of Water (°C)	Time for Tablet to Dissolve (s)
1	20.	40.
2	30.	25
3	40.	10.

68 Describe the effect of water temperature on the rate of dissolving. [1]

69 Explain, in terms of collision theory, how water temperature influences the rate of dissolving. [1]

70 What change, other than temperature, would affect the rate of dissolving? [1]

Base your answers to questions 71 through 74 on the passage below.

Acid rain lowers the pH in ponds and lakes and over time can cause the death of some aquatic life. Acid rain is caused in large part by the burning of fossil fuels in power plants and by gasoline-powered vehicles. The acids commonly associated with acid rain are sulfurous acid, sulfuric acid, and nitric acid.

In general, fish can tolerate a pH range between 5 and 9. However, even small changes in pH can significantly affect the solubility and toxicity of common pollutants. Increased concentrations of these pollutants can adversely affect the behavior and normal life processes of fish and cause deformity, lower egg production, and less egg hatching.

71 Acid rain caused the pH of a body of water to decrease. Explain this pH decrease in terms of the change in concentration of hydronium ions. [1]

72 Write the chemical formula of a *negative* polyatomic ion present in an aqueous nitric acid solution. [1]

73 Using information in the passage, describe *one* effect of acid rain on future generations of fish species in ponds and lakes. [1]

74 Sulfur dioxide, SO_2, is one of the gases that reacts with water to produce acid rain. According to Reference Table *G*, describe how the solubility of sulfur dioxide in water is affected by an increase in water temperature. [1]

Base your answers to questions 75 through 77 on the information below.

A student is instructed to make 0.250 liter of a 0.200 M aqueous solution of $Ca(NO_3)_2$.

75 What is the gram-formula mass of $Ca(NO_3)_2$? [1]

76 In the space *in your answer booklet,* show a correct numerical setup for calculating the total number of moles of $Ca(NO_3)_2$ needed to make 0.250 liter of the 0.200 M calcium nitrate solution. [1]

77 In order to prepare the described solution in the laboratory, two quantities must be measured accurately. One of these quantities is the volume of the solution. What other quantity must be measured to prepare this solution? [1]

Base your answers to questions 78 through 80 on the data in Reference Table *S*.

78 On the data table *in your answer booklet,* record the boiling points for He, Ne, Ar, Kr, and Xe. [1]

79 On the grid *in your answer booklet,* plot the boiling point versus the atomic number for He, Ne, Ar, Kr, and Xe. Circle and connect the points. [1]

Example:

80 Based on your graph, describe the trend in the boiling points of these elements as the atomic number increases. [1]

Base your answers to questions 81 and 82 on the information below.

A lightbulb contains argon gas at a temperature of 295 K and at a pressure of 75 kilopascals. The lightbulb is switched on, and after 30 minutes its temperature is 418 K.

81 In the space *in your answer booklet,* show a correct numerical setup for calculating the pressure of the gas inside the lightbulb at 418 K. Assume the volume of the lightbulb remains constant. [1]

82 What Celsius temperature is equal to 418 K? [1]

---

83 Because tap water is slightly acidic, water pipes made of iron corrode over time, as shown by the balanced ionic equation below:

$$2Fe + 6H^+ \rightarrow 2Fe^{3+} + 3H_2$$

Explain, in terms of chemical reactivity, why copper pipes are *less* likely to corrode than iron pipes. [1]

Base your answers to questions 84 and 85 on the information and diagram below.

The apparatus shown in the diagram consists of two inert platinum electrodes immersed in water. A small amount of an electrolyte, H_2SO_4, must be added to the water for the reaction to take place. The electrodes are connected to a source that supplies electricity.

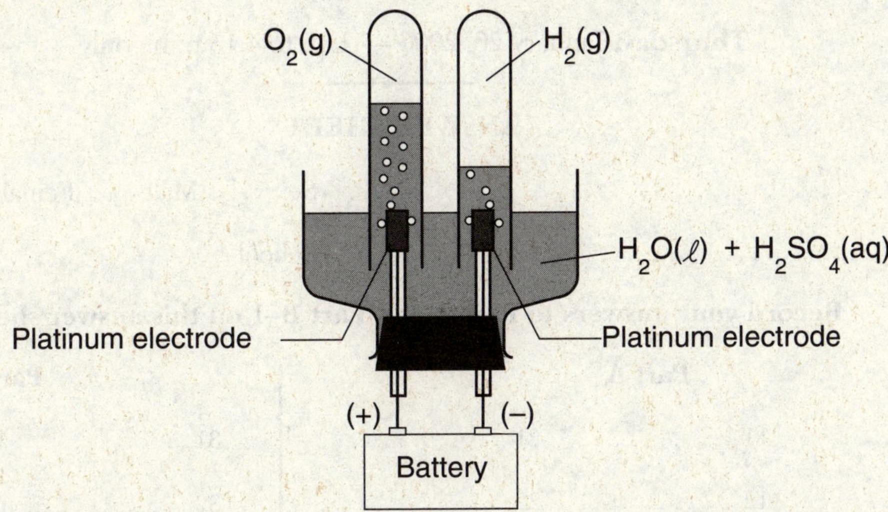

84 What type of electrochemical cell is shown? [1]

85 What particles are provided by the electrolyte that allow an electric current to flow? [1]

Tear Here

The University of the State of New York

REGENTS HIGH SCHOOL EXAMINATION

PHYSICAL SETTING CHEMISTRY

Thursday, January 26, 2006 — 1:15 to 4:15 p.m., only

ANSWER SHEET

Student .... Sex: ☐ Male ☐ Female Grade ....

Teacher .... School ....

Record your answers to Part A and Part B–1 on this answer sheet.

Part A

1	11	21 ....
2	12	22 ....
3	13	23 ....
4	14	24 ....
5	15	25 ....
6	16	26 ....
7	17	27 ....
8	18	28 ....
9	19	29 ....
10	20	30 ....

Part A Score

☐

Part B–1

31	41 ....
32	42 ....
33	43 ....
34	44 ....
35	45 ....
36	46 ....
37	47 ....
38	48 ....
39	49 ....
40	50 ....

Part B–1 Score

☐

Write your answers to Part B–2 and Part C in your answer booklet.

The declaration below should be signed when you have completed the examination.

I do hereby affirm, at the close of this examination, that I had no unlawful knowledge of the questions or answers prior to the examination and that I have neither given nor received assistance in answering any of the questions during the examination.

Tear Here

____
Signature

The University of the State of New York

REGENTS HIGH SCHOOL EXAMINATION

PHYSICAL SETTING CHEMISTRY

Thursday, January 26, 2006 — 1:15 to 4:15 p.m., only

ANSWER BOOKLET

Student . . . . Sex: ☐ Male ☐ Female

Teacher . . . .

School . . . . Grade . . . .

Answer all questions in Part B–2 and Part C. Record your answers in this booklet.

Part	Maximum Score	Student's Score
A	30	
B–1	20	
B–2	17	
C	18	

Total Written Test Score (Maximum Raw Score: 85) ☐

Final Score (from conversion chart) ☐

Raters' Initials:

Rater 1 . . . . **Rater 2** . . . .

Part B–2

For Raters Only

51 ____________________ **51** ☐

52 ____ **52** ☐

____

____

53 **53** ☐

For Raters Only

54 ____________________ 54

55 ____________________ 55

56 __________ 56

57 __________ mol 57

58 __________ J 58

59 ____________________ 59

60 ____________________ 60

[2]

For Raters Only

61 ____________________ g/L | 61 [ ]

62 ____________________ g/L | 62 [ ]

63 ____

____ | 63 [ ]

____

64 ____

____ | 64 [ ]

____

65 ____

____ | 65 [ ]

____

66 ____________________ °C | 66 [ ]

67 ________________________________ | 67 [ ]

[ ]

Total Score for Part B–2

Part C

68 ____

____

69 ____

____

____

70 ____

____

71 ____

____

____

72 ______________________

73 ____

____

74 ____

____

For Raters Only

68
69
70
71
72
73
74

For Raters Only

75 ______________________ g/mol | 75 [ ]

76 | 76 [ ]

77 ________________________________ | 77 [ ]

GO RIGHT ON TO THE NEXT PAGE ⇨

For Raters Only

78

Data Table

Symbol	Atomic Number	Boiling Point (K)
He	2	
Ne	10	
Ar	18	
Kr	36	
Xe	54	

78

79

Boiling Point Versus Atomic Number for He, Ne, Ar, Kr, and Xe

Boiling Point (K): 0, 50., 100., 150., 200.

Atomic Number: 0, 20, 40, 60

79

80 ______________________________

____

80

For Raters Only

81

81

82 ______________ °C

82

83 ____

____

____

83

84 ______________________________

84

85 ______________________________

85

Total Score for Part C

[7]

Physical Setting Chemistry August, 2005

Part A

Answer all questions in this part.

Directions (1–30): For *each* statement or question, write on the separate answer sheet the *number* of the word or expression that, of those given, best completes the statement or answers the question. Some questions may require the use of the *Reference Tables for Physical Setting/Chemistry*.

1 Which subatomic particle has a negative charge?

(1) proton
(2) electron
(3) neutron
(4) positron

2 Which statement best describes the nucleus of an aluminum atom?

(1) It has a charge of +13 and is surrounded by a total of 10 electrons.
(2) It has a charge of +13 and is surrounded by a total of 13 electrons.
(3) It has a charge of –13 and is surrounded by a total of 10 electrons.
(4) It has a charge of –13 and is surrounded by a total of 13 electrons.

3 The atomic mass of an element is the weighted average of the

(1) number of protons in the isotopes of that element
(2) number of neutrons in the isotopes of that element
(3) atomic numbers of the naturally occurring isotopes of that element
(4) atomic masses of the naturally occurring isotopes of that element

4 In which pair do the particles have approximately the same mass?

(1) proton and electron
(2) proton and neutron
(3) neutron and electron
(4) neutron and beta particle

5 Two different samples decompose when heated. Only one of the samples is soluble in water. Based on this information, these two samples are

(1) both the same element
(2) two different elements
(3) both the same compound
(4) two different compounds

6 The elements located in the lower left corner of the Periodic Table are classified as

(1) metals
(2) nonmetals
(3) metalloids
(4) noble gases

7 Which of these elements has the *lowest* melting point?

(1) Li
(2) Na
(3) K
(4) Rb

8 Which list consists of elements that have the most similar chemical properties?

(1) Mg, Al, and Si
(2) Mg, Ca, and Ba
(3) K, Al, and Ni
(4) K, Ca, and Ga

9 The correct chemical formula for iron(II) sulfide is

(1) FeS
(2) Fe_2S_3
(3) $FeSO_4$
(4) $Fe_2(SO_4)_3$

10 Which list consists of types of chemical formulas?

(1) atoms, ions, molecules
(2) metals, nonmetals, metalloids
(3) empirical, molecular, structural
(4) synthesis, decomposition, neutralization

11 Which type of bonding is found in all molecular substances?

(1) covalent bonding
(2) hydrogen bonding
(3) ionic bonding
(4) metallic bonding

12 An aqueous solution of sodium chloride is best classified as a

(1) homogeneous compound
(2) homogeneous mixture
(3) heterogeneous compound
(4) heterogeneous mixture

13 What is the total number of electrons shared in a double covalent bond between two atoms?

(1) 1 (3) 8
(2) 2 (4) 4

14 Which formula represents a nonpolar molecule?

(1) H_2S (3) CH_4
(2) HCl (4) NH_3

15 What occurs when an atom loses an electron?

(1) The atom's radius decreases and the atom becomes a negative ion.
(2) The atom's radius decreases and the atom becomes a positive ion.
(3) The atom's radius increases and the atom becomes a negative ion.
(4) The atom's radius increases and the atom becomes a positive ion.

16 Two samples of gold that have different temperatures are placed in contact with one another. Heat will flow spontaneously from a sample of gold at 60°C to a sample of gold that has a temperature of

(1) 50°C (3) 70°C
(2) 60°C (4) 80°C

17 Under which conditions of temperature and pressure would helium behave most like an ideal gas?

(1) 50 K and 20 kPa (3) 750 K and 20 kPa
(2) 50 K and 600 kPa (4) 750 K and 600 kPa

18 A sample of oxygen gas is sealed in container *X*. A sample of hydrogen gas is sealed in container Z. Both samples have the same volume, temperature, and pressure. Which statement is true?

(1) Container *X* contains more gas molecules than container Z.
(2) Container *X* contains fewer gas molecules than container Z.
(3) Containers *X* and Z both contain the same number of gas molecules.
(4) Containers *X* and Z both contain the same mass of gas.

19 Which formula represents an unsaturated hydrocarbon?

```
   H H              H O
   | |              | ‖
 H-C-C-H          H-C-C-H
   | |              |
   H H              H
   (1)              (3)

 H     H            H H
  \   /             | |
   C=C            H-C-C-Cl
  /   \             | |
 H     H            H H
   (2)              (4)
```

20 Given the formula:

```
   H H     H H
   | |     | |
 H-C-C=C-C-C-H
   |   | | |
   H   H H H
```

What is the IUPAC name of this compound?

(1) 2-pentene (3) 2-butene
(2) 2-pentyne (4) 2-butyne

21 Given the reaction system in a closed container at equilibrium and at a temperature of 298 K:

$$N_2O_4(g) \rightleftharpoons 2NO_2(g)$$

The measurable quantities of the gases at equilibrium must be

(1) decreasing (3) equal
(2) increasing (4) constant

22 Atoms of which element can bond with each other to form ring and chain structures in compounds?

(1) C (3) H
(2) Ca (4) Na

23 In a voltaic cell, chemical energy is converted to

(1) electrical energy, spontaneously
(2) electrical energy, nonspontaneously
(3) nuclear energy, spontaneously
(4) nuclear energy, nonspontaneously

24 In each of the four beakers shown below, a 2.0-centimeter strip of magnesium ribbon reacts with 100 milliliters of HCl(aq) under the conditions shown.

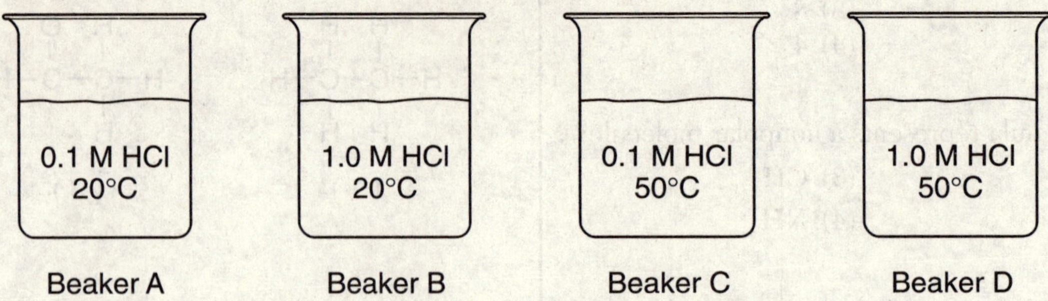

In which beaker will the reaction occur at the fastest rate?

(1) *A*
(2) *B*
(3) *C*
(4) *D*

---

25 Which aqueous solution is the best conductor of an electrical current?

(1) 0.01 M CH_3OH
(2) 0.01 M KOH
(3) 0.1 M CH_3OH
(4) 0.1 M KOH

26 A hydrogen ion, H^+, in aqueous solution may also be written as

(1) H_2O
(2) H_2O_2
(3) H_3O^+
(4) OH^-

27 One acid-base theory states that an acid is

(1) an electron donor
(2) a neutron donor
(3) an H^+ donor
(4) an OH^- donor

28 Which isotope will spontaneously decay and emit particles with a charge of +2?

(1) ^{53}Fe
(2) ^{137}Cs
(3) ^{198}Au
(4) ^{220}Fr

29 Radioactive cobalt-60 is used in radiation therapy treatment. Cobalt-60 undergoes beta decay. This type of nuclear reaction is called

(1) natural transmutation
(2) artificial transmutation
(3) nuclear fusion
(4) nuclear fission

Note that question 30 has only three choices.

30 Given the balanced ionic equation:

$$2Al(s) + 3Cu^{2+}(aq) \rightarrow 2Al^{3+}(aq) + 3Cu(s)$$

Compared to the total charge of the reactants, the total charge of the products is

(1) less
(2) greater
(3) the same

Part B–1

Answer all questions in this part.

Directions (31–50): For *each* statement or question, write on the separate answer sheet the *number* of the word or expression that, of those given, best completes the statement or answers the question. Some questions may require the use of the *Reference Tables for Physical Setting/Chemistry*.

31 The percentage by mass of Br in the compound $AlBr_3$ is closest to

(1) 10.% (3) 75%
(2) 25% (4) 90.%

32 Which symbol represents a particle with a total of 10 electrons?

(1) N (3) Al
(2) N^{3+} (4) Al^{3+}

33 Which electron configuration represents an atom of aluminum in an excited state?

(1) 2-7-4 (3) 2-8-3
(2) 2-7-7 (4) 2-8-6

34 At STP, an element that is a brittle solid and a poor conductor of heat and electricity could have an atomic number of

(1) 12 (3) 16
(2) 13 (4) 17

35 Based on Reference Table *S*, atoms of which of these elements have the strongest attraction for the electrons in a chemical bond?

(1) Al (3) P
(2) Si (4) S

36 A sample of a compound contains 65.4 grams of zinc, 12.0 grams of carbon, and 48.0 grams of oxygen. What is the mole ratio of zinc to carbon to oxygen in this compound?

(1) 1:1:2 (3) 1:4:6
(2) 1:1:3 (4) 5:1:4

37 Which process would most effectively separate two liquids with different molecular polarities?

(1) filtration (3) distillation
(2) fermentation (4) conductivity

38 Given the balanced equation:

$$AgNO_3(aq) + NaCl(aq) \rightarrow NaNO_3(aq) + AgCl(s)$$

This reaction is classified as

(1) synthesis
(2) decomposition
(3) single replacement
(4) double replacement

39 A solution contains 35 grams of KNO_3 dissolved in 100 grams of water at 40°C. How much *more* KNO_3 would have to be added to make it a saturated solution?

(1) 29 g (3) 12 g
(2) 24 g (4) 4 g

40 Which diagram best represents a gas in a closed container?

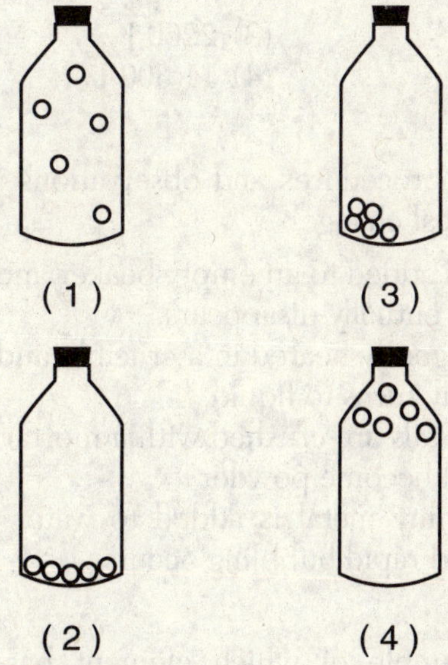

41 What is the total number of moles of NaCl(s) needed to make 3.0 liters of a 2.0 M NaCl solution?

(1) 1.0 mol (3) 6.0 mol
(2) 0.70 mol (4) 8.0 mol

42 Which Lewis electron-dot diagram is correct for a S^{2-} ion?

(1) $\left[\cdot\overset{\cdot\cdot}{S}\cdot\right]^{2-}$ (3) $\left[:\overset{\cdot\cdot}{S}\cdot\right]^{2-}$

(2) $\left[\overset{\cdot\cdot}{S}\right]^{2-}$ (4) $\left[:\overset{\cdot\cdot}{\underset{\cdot\cdot}{S}}:\right]^{2-}$

43 A student wants to prepare a 1.0-liter solution of a specific molarity. The student determines that the mass of the solute needs to be 30. grams. What is the proper procedure to follow?

(1) Add 30. g of solute to 1.0 L of solvent.
(2) Add 30. g of solute to 970. mL of solvent to make 1.0 L of solution.
(3) Add 1000. g of solvent to 30. g of solute.
(4) Add enough solvent to 30. g of solute to make 1.0 L of solution.

44 What is the total number of joules released when a 5.00-gram sample of water changes from liquid to solid at 0°C?

(1) 334 J (3) 2260 J
(2) 1670 J (4) 11 300 J

45 Which set of procedures and observations indicates a chemical change?

(1) Ethanol is added to an empty beaker and the ethanol eventually disappears.
(2) A solid is gently heated in a crucible and the solid slowly turns to liquid.
(3) Large crystals are crushed with a mortar and pestle and become powder.
(4) A cool, shiny metal is added to water in a beaker and rapid bubbling occurs.

46 At STP, a sample of which element has the highest entropy?

(1) Na(s) (3) $Br_2(\ell)$
(2) $Hg(\ell)$ (4) $F_2(g)$

47 Given the incomplete equation representing an organic addition reaction:

$$X(g) + Cl_2(g) \rightarrow XCl_2(g)$$

Which compound could be represented by *X*?

(1) CH_4 (3) C_3H_8
(2) C_2H_4 (4) C_4H_{10}

48 Given the incomplete equation:

$$4Fe + 3O_2 \rightarrow 2X$$

Which compound is represented by *X*?

(1) FeO (3) Fe_3O_2
(2) Fe_2O_3 (4) Fe_3O_4

49 How are $HNO_3(aq)$ and $CH_3COOH(aq)$ similar?

(1) They are Arrhenius acids and they turn blue litmus red.
(2) They are Arrhenius acids and they turn red litmus blue.
(3) They are Arrhenius bases and they turn blue litmus red.
(4) They are Arrhenius bases and they turn red litmus blue.

50 The chart below shows the spontaneous nuclear decay of U-238 to Th-234 to Pa-234 to U-234.

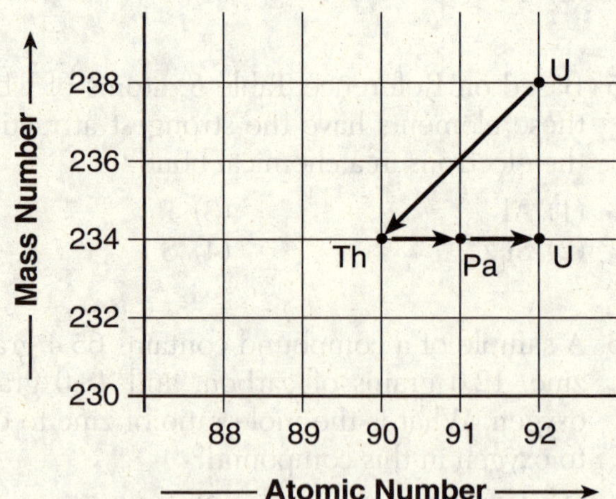

What is the correct order of nuclear decay modes for the change from U-238 to U-234?

(1) β^- decay, γ decay, β^- decay
(2) β^- decay, β^- decay, α decay
(3) α decay, α decay, β^- decay
(4) α decay, β^- decay, β^- decay

Part B–2

Answer all questions in this part.

Directions (51–67): Record your answers in the spaces provided in your answer booklet. Some questions may require the use of the *Reference Tables for Physical Setting/Chemistry.*

51 In the space *in your answer booklet,* show a correct numerical setup for calculating the formula mass of glucose, $C_6H_{12}O_6$. [1]

52 Write the empirical formula for the compound $C_6H_{12}O_6$. [1]

Base your answers to questions 53 through 55 on the potential energy diagram below.

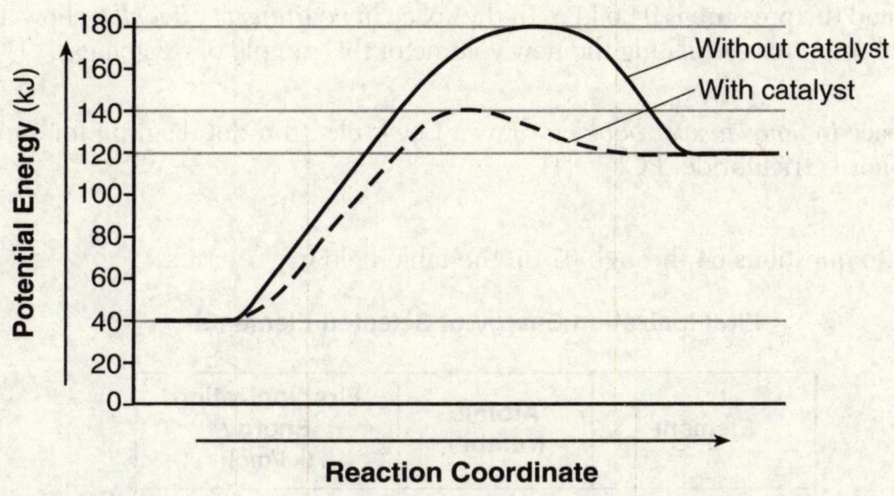

53 What is the heat of reaction for the forward reaction? [1]

54 What is the activation energy for the forward reaction with the catalyst? [1]

55 Explain, in terms of the function of a catalyst, why the curves on the potential energy diagram for the catalyzed and uncatalyzed reactions are different. [1]

Base your answers to questions 56 through 58 on the properties of propanone.

56 In the space *in your answer booklet,* draw the structural formula for propanone. [1]

57 Explain, in terms of molecular energy, why the vapor pressure of propanone increases when its temperature increases. [1]

58 A liquid's boiling point is the temperature at which its vapor pressure is equal to the atmospheric pressure. Using Reference Table *H*, what is the boiling point of propanone at an atmospheric pressure of 70 kPa? [1]

Base your answers to questions 59 through 61 on the information below.

Two isotopes of potassium are K-37 and K-42.

59 What is the total number of neutrons in the nucleus of a K-37 atom? [1]

60 How many valence electrons are in an atom of K-42 in the ground state? [1]

61 Explain, in terms of subatomic particles, why K-37 and K-42 are isotopes of potassium. [1]

---

62 A sample of oxygen gas in one container has a volume of 20.0 milliliters at 297 K and 101.3 kPa. The entire sample is transferred to another container where the temperature is 283 K and the pressure is 94.6 kPa. In the space *in your answer booklet,* show a correct numerical setup for calculating the new volume of this sample of oxygen gas. [1]

63 In the space *in your answer booklet,* draw a Lewis electron-dot diagram for a molecule of phosphorus trichloride, PCl_3. [1]

Base your answers to questions 64 through 67 on the table below.

First Ionization Energy of Selected Elements

Element	Atomic Number	First Ionization Energy (kJ/mol)
lithium	3	520
sodium	11	496
potassium	19	419
rubidium	37	403
cesium	55	376

64 On the grid *in your answer booklet,* mark an appropriate scale on the axis labeled "First Ionization Energy (kJ/mol)." An appropriate scale is one that allows a trend to be seen. [1]

65 On the same grid, plot the data from the table. Circle and connect the points. [1]

Example:

66 State the trend in first ionization energy for the elements in the table as the atomic number increases. [1]

67 Explain, in terms of atomic structure, why cesium has a *lower* first ionization energy than rubidium. [1]

Part C

Answer all questions in this part.

Directions (68–85): Record your answers in the spaces provided in your answer booklet. Some questions may require the use of the *Reference Tables for Physical Setting/Chemistry.*

Base your answers to questions 68 through 70 on the information below.

The decomposition of sodium azide, $NaN_3(s)$, is used to inflate airbags. On impact, the $NaN_3(s)$ is ignited by an electrical spark, producing $N_2(g)$ and Na(s). The $N_2(g)$ inflates the airbag.

68 Balance the equation *in your answer booklet,* using the smallest whole-number coefficients. [1]

69 What is the total number of moles present in a 52.0-gram sample of $NaN_3(s)$ (gram-formula mass = 65.0 gram/mole)? [1]

70 An inflated airbag has a volume of 5.00×10^4 cm^3 at STP. The density of $N_2(g)$ at STP is 0.00125 g/cm^3. What is the total number of grams of $N_2(g)$ in the airbag? [1]

Base your answers to questions 71 through 73 on the information below.

Element *X* is a solid metal that reacts with chlorine to form a water-soluble binary compound.

71 State *one* physical property of element *X* that makes it a good material for making pots and pans. [1]

72 Explain, in terms of particles, why an aqueous solution of the binary compound conducts an electric current. [1]

73 The binary compound consists of element *X* and chlorine in a 1:2 molar ratio. What is the oxidation number of element *X* in this compound? [1]

Base your answers to questions 74 through 76 on the diagram and balanced equation below, which represent the electrolysis of molten NaCl.

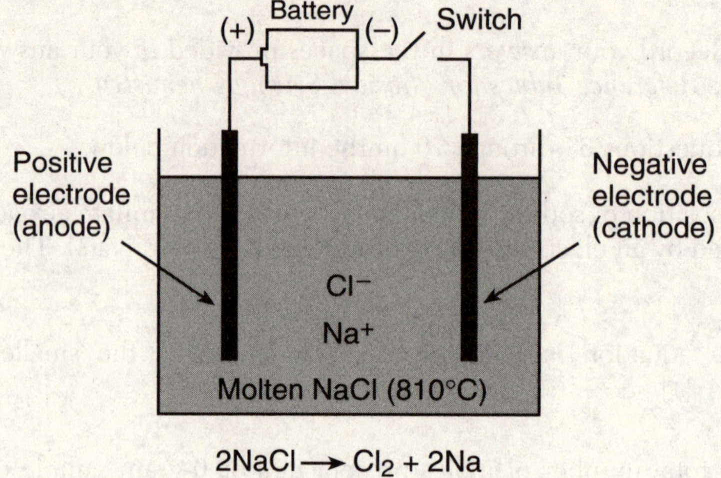

$$2NaCl \rightarrow Cl_2 + 2Na$$

74 When the switch is closed, which electrode will attract the sodium ions? [1]

75 What is the purpose of the battery in this electrolytic cell? [1]

76 Write the balanced half-reaction for the reduction that occurs in this electrolytic cell. [1]

Base your answers to questions 77 through 79 on the information below.

In a titration, 3.00 M NaOH(aq) was added to an Erlenmeyer flask containing 25.00 milliliters of HCl(aq) and three drops of phenolphthalein until one drop of the NaOH(aq) turned the solution a light-pink color. The following data were collected by a student performing this titration.

Initial NaOH(aq) buret reading: 14.45 milliliters

Final NaOH(aq) buret reading: 32.66 milliliters

77 What is the total volume of NaOH(aq) that was used in this titration? [1]

78 In the space *in your answer booklet,* show a correct numerical setup for calculating the molarity of the HCl(aq). [1]

79 Based on the data given, what is the correct number of significant figures that should be shown in the molarity of the HCl(aq)? [1]

Base your answers to questions 80 through 82 on the information below.

A student was studying the pH differences in samples from two Adirondack streams. The student measured a pH of 4 in stream *A* and a pH of 6 in stream *B*.

80 Compare the hydronium ion concentration in stream *A* to the hydronium ion concentration in stream *B*. [1]

81 What is the color of bromthymol blue in the sample from stream *A*? [1]

82 Identify *one* compound that could be used to neutralize the sample from stream *A*. [1]

Base your answers to questions 83 through 85 on the information below.

The radioisotopes carbon-14 and nitrogen-16 are present in a living organism. Carbon-14 is commonly used to date a once-living organism.

83 Complete the nuclear equation *in your answer booklet* for the decay of C-14. Include *both* the atomic number and the mass number of the missing particle. [1]

84 Explain why N-16 is a poor choice for radioactive dating of a bone. [1]

85 A sample of wood is found to contain $\frac{1}{8}$ as much C-14 as is present in the wood of a living tree. What is the approximate age, in years, of this sample of wood? [1]

The University of the State of New York

REGENTS HIGH SCHOOL EXAMINATION

PHYSICAL SETTING CHEMISTRY

Tuesday, August 16, 2005 — 12:30 to 3:30 p.m., only

ANSWER BOOKLET

Part	Maximum Score	Student's Score
A	30	
B–1	20	
B–2	17	
C	18	

Total Written Test Score (Maximum Raw Score: 85) ☐

Final Score (from conversion chart) ☐

Raters' Initials:

Rater 1 .... Rater 2 ....

Student .... Sex: ☐ Male ☐ Female

Teacher ....

School .... Grade ....

Answer all questions in Part B–2 and Part C. Record your answers in this booklet.

For Raters Only

Part B–2

51   51 ☐

52 ______________________   52 ☐

53 ____________ kJ   53 ☐

54 ____________ kJ   54 ☐

55 ____

____   55 ☐

____

For Raters Only

56

56

57

57

58 °C

58

59

59

60

60

61

61

62

63

For Raters Only

62

63

For Raters Only

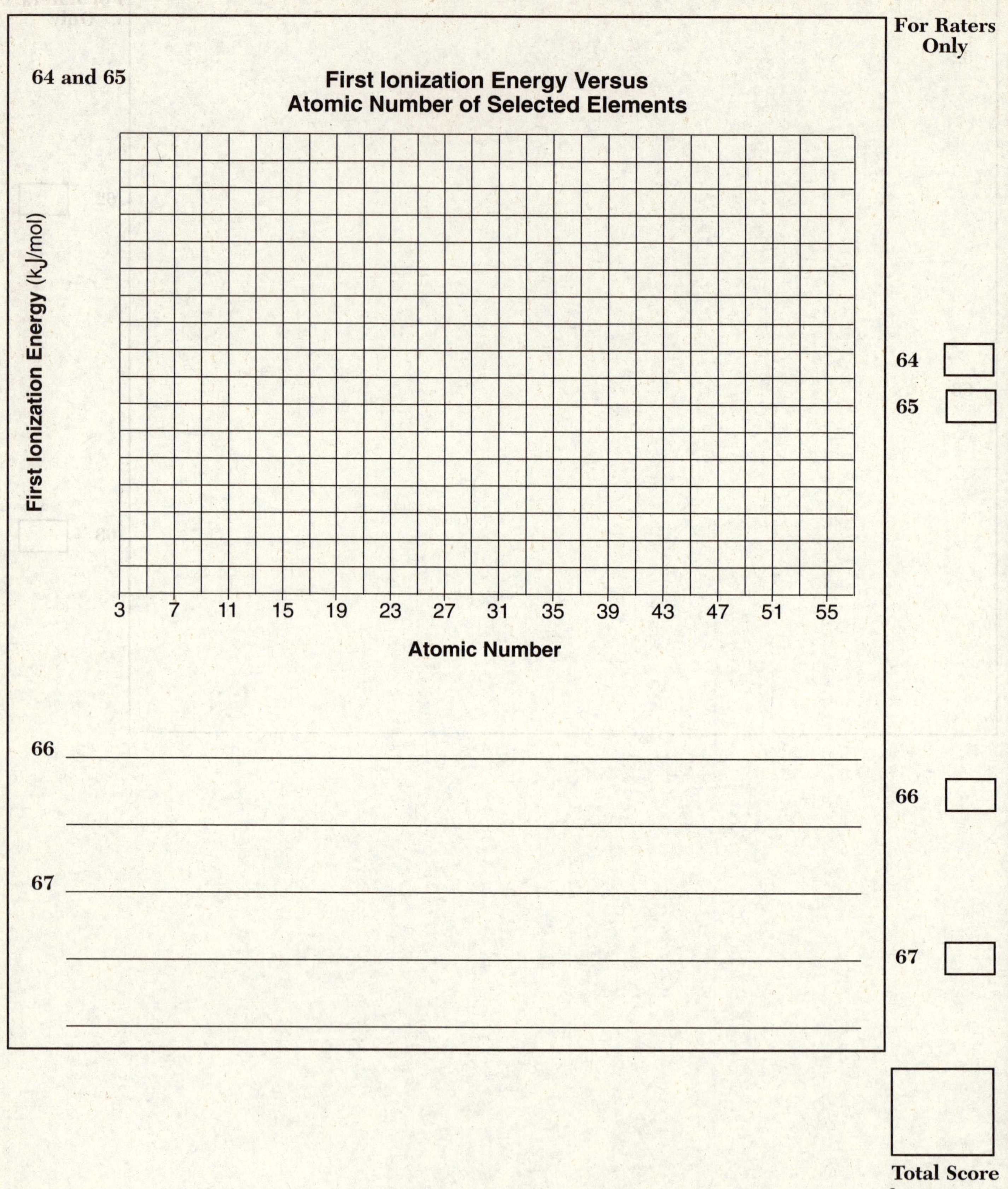

64

65

66

67

Total Score for Part B–2

Part C

68 ______ $NaN_3(s) \rightarrow$ ______ $Na(s)$ + ______ $N_2(g)$

69 ____________________ **mol**

70 ____________________ **g**

71 ____

72 ____

____

____

73 ____________________

74 ____________________

75 ____

____

76 ____________________

For Raters Only

68	
69	
70	
71	
72	
73	
74	
75	
76	

For Raters Only

77 ____________ mL | 77 [ ]

78 | 78 [ ]

79 ____________ | 79 [ ]

80 ______________________________________

______________________________________ | 80 [ ]

81 ____________ | 81 [ ]

82 ____________ | 82 [ ]

83 ${}^{14}_{6}C \rightarrow$ ______ $+ {}^{0}_{-1}e$ | 83 [ ]

84 ______________________________________

____

______________________________________ | 84 [ ]

85 ____________ y | 85 [ ]

Total Score for Part C

Physical Setting Chemistry June, 2005

Part A

Answer all questions in this part.

Directions (1–33): For *each* statement or question, write on the separate answer sheet the *number* of the word or expression that, of those given, best completes the statement or answers the question. Some questions may require the use of the *Reference Tables for Physical Setting/Chemistry*.

1 In the modern wave-mechanical model of the atom, the orbitals are regions of the most probable location of

(1) protons
(2) neutrons
(3) electrons
(4) positrons

2 Compared to a proton, an electron has

(1) a greater quantity of charge and the same sign
(2) a greater quantity of charge and the opposite sign
(3) the same quantity of charge and the same sign
(4) the same quantity of charge and the opposite sign

3 Which two notations represent atoms that are isotopes of the same element?

(1) $^{121}_{50}Sn$ and $^{119}_{50}Sn$
(2) $^{121}_{50}Sn$ and $^{121}_{50}Sn$
(3) $^{19}_{8}O$ and $^{19}_{9}F$
(4) $^{39}_{17}Cl$ and $^{39}_{19}K$

4 The elements in Period 5 on the Periodic Table are arranged from left to right in order of

(1) decreasing atomic mass
(2) decreasing atomic number
(3) increasing atomic mass
(4) increasing atomic number

5 Which list of elements contains a metal, a metalloid, and a nonmetal?

(1) Zn, Ga, Ge
(2) Si, Ge, Sn
(3) Cd, Sb, I
(4) F, Cl, Br

6 An example of a physical property of an element is the element's ability to

(1) react with an acid
(2) react with oxygen
(3) form a compound with chlorine
(4) form an aqueous solution

7 Which element is malleable and conducts electricity?

(1) iron
(2) iodine
(3) sulfur
(4) phosphorus

8 At STP, solid carbon can exist as graphite or as diamond. These two forms of carbon have

(1) the same properties and the same crystal structures
(2) the same properties and different crystal structures
(3) different properties and the same crystal structures
(4) different properties and different crystal structures

9 What is the formula of titanium(II) oxide?

(1) TiO
(2) TiO_2
(3) Ti_2O
(4) Ti_2O_3

10 Which substance can be decomposed by a chemical change?

(1) calcium
(2) potassium
(3) copper
(4) ammonia

11 As a chlorine atom becomes a negative ion, the atom

(1) gains an electron and its radius increases
(2) gains an electron and its radius decreases
(3) loses an electron and its radius increases
(4) loses an electron and its radius decreases

12 Based on Reference Table S, the atoms of which of these elements have the strongest attraction for electrons in a chemical bond?

(1) N
(2) Na
(3) P
(4) Pt

13 Which terms are used to identify pure substances?

(1) an element and a mixture
(2) an element and a compound
(3) a solution and a mixture
(4) a solution and a compound

14 The solubility of $KClO_3(s)$ in water increases as the

(1) temperature of the solution increases
(2) temperature of the solution decreases
(3) pressure on the solution increases
(4) pressure on the solution decreases

15 Compared to a 0.1 M aqueous solution of NaCl, a 0.8 M aqueous solution of NaCl has a

(1) higher boiling point and a higher freezing point
(2) higher boiling point and a lower freezing point
(3) lower boiling point and a higher freezing point
(4) lower boiling point and a lower freezing point

16 The kinetic molecular theory assumes that the particles of an ideal gas

(1) are in random, constant, straight-line motion
(2) are arranged in a regular geometric pattern
(3) have strong attractive forces between them
(4) have collisions that result in the system losing energy

17 In which process does a solid change directly into a vapor?

(1) condensation (3) deposition
(2) sublimation (4) solidification

18 Which statement must be true about a chemical system at equilibrium?

(1) The forward and reverse reactions stop.
(2) The concentration of reactants and products are equal.
(3) The rate of the forward reaction is equal to the rate of the reverse reaction.
(4) The number of moles of reactants is equal to the number of moles of product.

19 Adding a catalyst to a chemical reaction results in

(1) a decrease in activation energy and a decrease in the reaction rate
(2) a decrease in activation energy and an increase in the reaction rate
(3) an increase in activation energy and a decrease in the reaction rate
(4) an increase in activation energy and an increase in the reaction rate

20 Systems in nature tend to undergo changes toward

(1) lower energy and lower entropy
(2) lower energy and higher entropy
(3) higher energy and lower entropy
(4) higher energy and higher entropy

21 Which element has atoms that can bond with each other to form long chains or rings?

(1) carbon (3) oxygen
(2) nitrogen (4) fluorine

22 Which formula represents an unsaturated hydrocarbon?

(1) C_2H_6 (3) C_5H_8
(2) C_3H_8 (4) C_6H_{14}

23 Given the structural formula:

```
H       H
 \     /
  C = C      H
 /     \    /
H        C
        / \
       H   H
```

What is the IUPAC name of this compound?

(1) propane (3) propanone
(2) propene (4) propanal

24 What is the oxidation state of nitrogen in $NaNO_2$?

(1) +1 (3) +3
(2) +2 (4) +4

25 The three isomers of pentane have different

(1) formula masses
(2) molecular formulas
(3) empirical formulas
(4) structural formulas

26 Where does oxidation occur in an electrochemical cell?

(1) at the cathode in both an electrolytic cell and a voltaic cell
(2) at the cathode in an electrolytic cell and at the anode in a voltaic cell
(3) at the anode in both an electrolytic cell and a voltaic cell
(4) at the anode in an electrolytic cell and at the cathode in a voltaic cell

27 Which formula represents an electrolyte?

(1) CH_3OCH_3 (3) CH_3COOH
(2) CH_3OH (4) C_2H_5CHO

28 When an Arrhenius acid dissolves in water, the only positive ion in the solution is

(1) H^+ (3) Na^+
(2) Li^+ (4) K^+

29 What is the half-life and decay mode of Rn-222?

(1) 1.91 days and alpha decay
(2) 1.91 days and beta decay
(3) 3.82 days and alpha decay
(4) 3.82 days and beta decay

30 Which equation represents a transmutation reaction?

(1) $^{239}_{92}U \rightarrow ^{239}_{92}U + ^{0}_{0}\gamma$
(2) $^{14}_{6}C \rightarrow ^{14}_{7}N + ^{0}_{-1}e$
(3) $C_3H_8 + 5O_2 \rightarrow 3CO_2 + 4H_2O$
(4) $nC_2H_4 \xrightarrow{\text{catalyst}} (\text{–}C_2H_4\text{–})_n$

31 Which equation represents positron decay?

(1) $^{87}_{37}Rb \rightarrow ^{0}_{-1}e + ^{87}_{38}Sr$
(2) $^{227}_{92}U \rightarrow ^{223}_{90}Th + ^{4}_{2}He$
(3) $^{27}_{13}Al + ^{4}_{2}He \rightarrow ^{30}_{15}P + ^{1}_{0}n$
(4) $^{11}_{6}C \rightarrow ^{0}_{+1}e + ^{11}_{5}B$

32 Which equation represents a fusion reaction?

(1) $H_2O(g) \rightarrow H_2O(\ell)$
(2) $C(s) + O_2(g) \rightarrow CO_2(g)$
(3) $^{2}_{1}H + ^{3}_{1}H \rightarrow ^{4}_{2}He + ^{1}_{0}n$
(4) $^{235}_{92}U + ^{1}_{0}n \rightarrow ^{142}_{56}Ba + ^{91}_{36}Kr + 3^{1}_{0}n$

Note that question 33 has only three choices.

33 An electron in an atom moves from the ground state to an excited state when the energy of the electron

(1) decreases
(2) increases
(3) remains the same

Part B–1

Answer all questions in this part.

Directions (34–50): For *each* statement or question, write on the separate answer sheet the *number* of the word or expression that, of those given, best completes the statement or answers the question. Some questions may require the use of the *Reference Tables for Physical Setting/Chemistry*.

34 Which symbol represents a particle that has the same total number of electrons as S^{2-}?

(1) O^{2-} (3) Se^{2-}
(2) Si (4) Ar

35 The data table below shows elements *Xx*, *Yy*, and *Zz* from the same group on the Periodic Table.

Element	Atomic Mass (atomic mass unit)	Atomic Radius (pm)
Xx	69.7	141
Yy	114.8	?
Zz	204.4	171

What is the most likely atomic radius of element *Yy*?

(1) 103 pm (3) 166 pm
(2) 127 pm (4) 185 pm

36 Which substance has a chemical formula with the same ratio of metal ions to nonmetal ions as in potassium sulfide?

(1) sodium oxide
(2) sodium chloride
(3) magnesium oxide
(4) magnesium chloride

37 The molecular formula of glucose is $C_6H_{12}O_6$. What is the empirical formula of glucose?

(1) CHO (3) $C_6H_{12}O_6$
(2) CH_2O (4) $C_{12}H_{24}O_{12}$

38 According to Reference Table *F*, which of these compounds is the *least* soluble in water?

(1) K_2CO_3 (3) $Ca_3(PO_4)_2$
(2) $KC_2H_3O_2$ (4) $Ca(NO_3)_2$

39 A sample of a substance containing only magnesium and chlorine was tested in the laboratory and was found to be composed of 74.5% chlorine by mass. If the total mass of the sample was 190.2 grams, what was the mass of the magnesium?

(1) 24.3 g (3) 70.9 g
(2) 48.5 g (4) 142 g

40 Which molecule contains a nonpolar covalent bond?

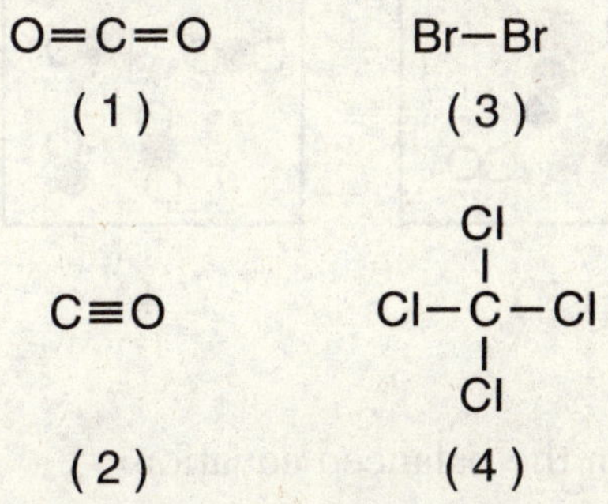

(1) O=C=O
(2) C≡O
(3) Br–Br
(4) CCl_4 (Cl–C–Cl with Cl above and below C)

41 According to Reference Table *G*, which substance forms an unsaturated solution when 80 grams of the substance is dissolved in 100 grams of H_2O at 10°C?

(1) KI (3) $NaNO_3$
(2) KNO_3 (4) NaCl

42 What is the concentration of a solution, in parts per million, if 0.02 gram of Na_3PO_4 is dissolved in 1000 grams of water?

(1) 20 ppm (3) 0.2 ppm
(2) 2 ppm (4) 0.02 ppm

43 Given the simple representations for atoms of two elements:

○ = an atom of an element
● = an atom of a different element

Which particle diagram represents molecules of only one compound in the gaseous phase?

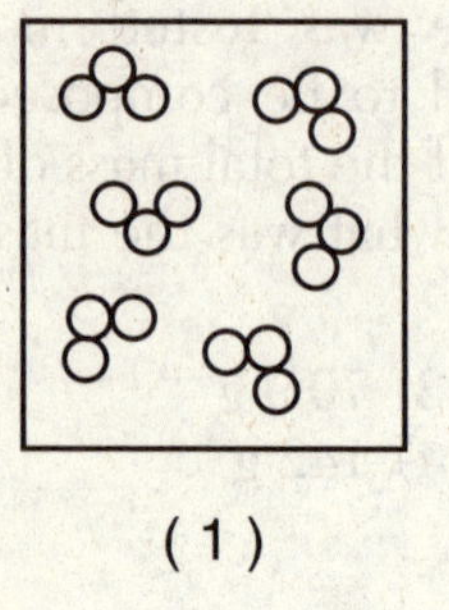

(1)

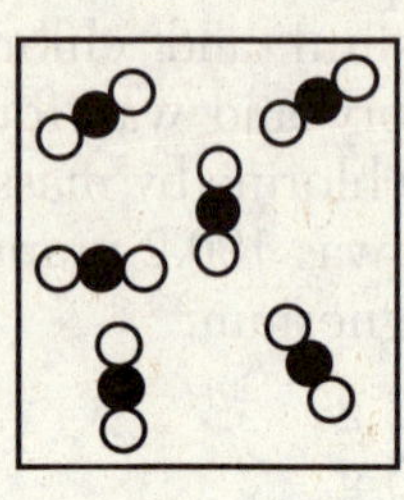

(3)

(2)

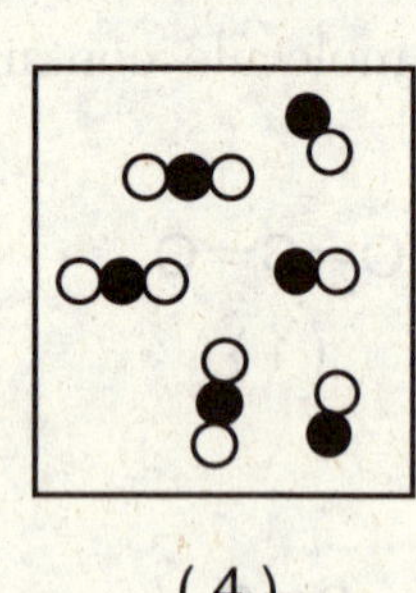

(4)

44 Given the balanced equation:

$$KNO_3(s) + 34.89 \text{ kJ} \xrightarrow{H_2O} K^+(aq) + NO_3^-(aq)$$

Which statement best describes this process?

(1) It is endothermic and entropy increases.
(2) It is endothermic and entropy decreases.
(3) It is exothermic and entropy increases.
(4) It is exothermic and entropy decreases.

45 A 1.0-gram piece of zinc reacts with 5 milliliters of HCl(aq). Which of these conditions of concentration and temperature would produce the greatest rate of reaction?

(1) 1.0 M HCl(aq) at 20.°C
(2) 1.0 M HCl(aq) at 40.°C
(3) 2.0 M HCl(aq) at 20.°C
(4) 2.0 M HCl(aq) at 40.°C

46 At STP, fluorine is a gas and iodine is a solid. This observation can be explained by the fact that fluorine has

(1) weaker intermolecular forces of attraction than iodine
(2) stronger intermolecular forces of attraction than iodine
(3) lower average kinetic energy than iodine
(4) higher average kinetic energy than iodine

47 Given the structural formula:

```
  H H   H H
  | |   | |
H-C-C-O-C-C-H
  | |   | |
  H H   H H
```

The compound represented by this formula can be classified as an

(1) organic acid
(2) ether
(3) ester
(4) aldehyde

48 Sulfuric acid, $H_2SO_4(aq)$, can be used to neutralize barium hydroxide, $Ba(OH)_2(aq)$. What is the formula for the salt produced by this neutralization?

(1) BaS
(2) $BaSO_2$
(3) $BaSO_3$
(4) $BaSO_4$

49 Given the balanced ionic equation:

$$Zn(s) + Cu^{2+}(aq) \rightarrow Zn^{2+}(aq) + Cu(s)$$

Which equation represents the oxidation half-reaction?

(1) $Zn(s) + 2e^- \rightarrow Zn^{2+}(aq)$
(2) $Zn(s) \rightarrow Zn^{2+}(aq) + 2e^-$
(3) $Cu^{2+}(aq) \rightarrow Cu(s) + 2e^-$
(4) $Cu^{2+}(aq) + 2e^- \rightarrow Cu(s)$

50 In which solution will thymol blue indicator appear blue?

(1) 0.1 M CH_3COOH
(2) 0.1 M KOH
(3) 0.1 M HCl
(4) 0.1 M H_2SO_4

Part B–2

Answer all questions in this part.

Directions (51–64): Record your answers in the spaces provided in your answer booklet. Some questions may require the use of the *Reference Tables for Physical Setting/Chemistry*.

Base your answers to questions 51 and 52 on the diagram below, which represents an atom of magnesium-26 in the ground state.

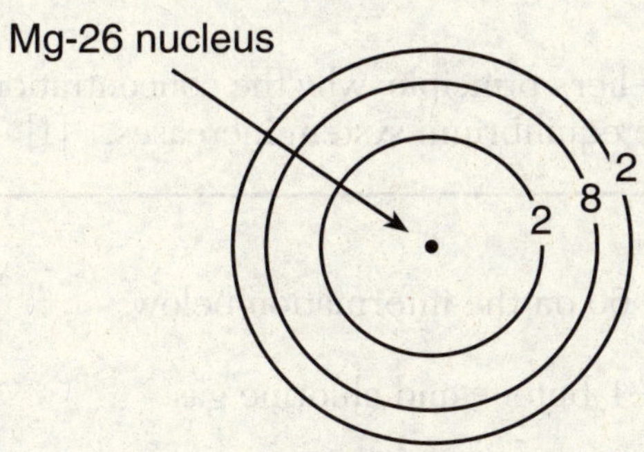

51 What is the total number of valence electrons in an atom of Mg-26 in the ground state? [1]

52 On the diagram *in your answer booklet,* write an appropriate number of electrons in *each* shell to represent a Mg-26 atom in an excited state. Your answer may include additional shells. [1]

---

53 Explain, in terms of atomic structure, why germanium is chemically similar to silicon. [1]

54 Given the balanced equation:

$$4Al(s) + 3O_2(g) \rightarrow 2Al_2O_3(s)$$

What is the total number of moles of $O_2(g)$ that must react completely with 8.0 moles of Al(s) in order to form $Al_2O_3(s)$? [1]

Base your answers to questions 55 and 56 on the balanced equation below.

$$2Na(s) + Cl_2(g) \rightarrow 2NaCl(s)$$

55 In the box *in your answer booklet,* draw a Lewis electron-dot diagram for a molecule of chlorine, Cl_2. [1]

56 Explain, in terms of electrons, why the bonding in NaCl is ionic. [1]

Base your answers to questions 57 and 58 on the information below.

Given the reaction at equilibrium:

$$2NO_2(g) + 7H_2(g) \rightleftharpoons 2NH_3(g) + 4H_2O(g) + 1127 \text{ kJ}$$

57 On the diagram *in your answer booklet,* complete the potential energy diagram for the forward reaction. Be sure your drawing shows the activation energy and the potential energy of the products. [2]

58 Explain, in terms of Le Chatelier's principle, why the concentration of $NH_3(g)$ *decreases* when the temperature of the equilibrium system increases. [1]

Base your answers to questions 59 and 60 on the information below.

Given the reaction between 1-butene and chlorine gas:

$$C_4H_8 + Cl_2 \rightarrow C_4H_8Cl_2$$

59 Which type of chemical reaction is represented by this equation? [1]

60 In the space *in your answer booklet,* draw the structural formula of the product 1,2-dichlorobutane. [1]

Base your answers to questions 61 through 64 on the information below, which relates the numbers of neutrons and protons for specific nuclides of C, N, Ne, and S.

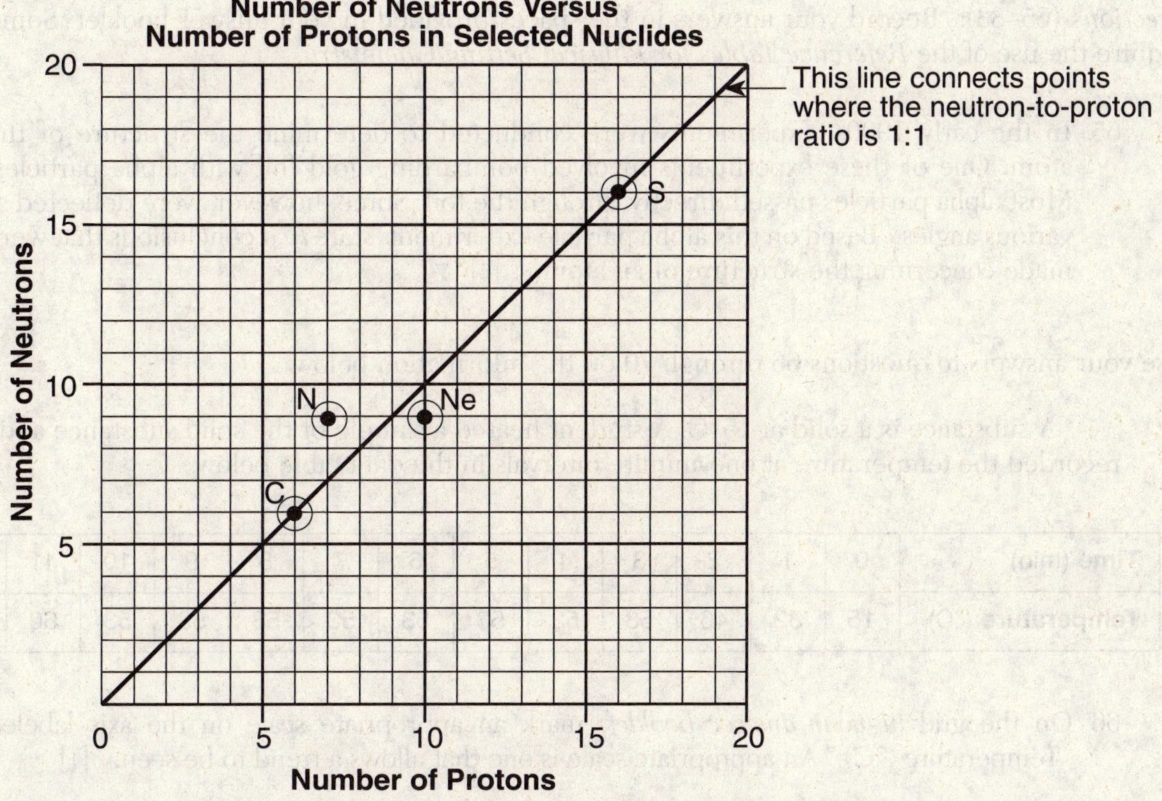

61 Using the point plotted on the graph for neon, complete the table *in your answer booklet*. [1]

62 Explain, in terms of atomic particles, why S-32 is a stable nuclide. [1]

63 Using the point plotted on the graph for nitrogen, what is the neutron-to-proton ratio of this nuclide? [1]

64 Based on Reference Table *N*, complete the decay equation for N-16 *in your answer booklet.* [1]

Part C

Answer all questions in this part.

Directions (65–83): Record your answers in the spaces provided in your answer booklet. Some questions may require the use of the *Reference Tables for Physical Setting/Chemistry.*

65 In the early 1900s, experiments were conducted to determine the structure of the atom. One of these experiments involved bombarding gold foil with alpha particles. Most alpha particles passed directly through the foil. Some, however, were deflected at various angles. Based on this alpha particle experiment, state *two* conclusions that were made concerning the structure of an atom. [2]

Base your answers to questions 66 through 70 on the information below.

A substance is a solid at 15°C. A student heated a sample of the solid substance and recorded the temperature at one-minute intervals in the data table below.

Time (min)	0	1	2	3	4	5	6	7	8	9	10	11	12
Temperature (°C)	15	32	46	53	53	53	53	53	53	53	53	60	65

66 On the grid *in your answer booklet,* mark an appropriate scale on the axis labeled "Temperature (°C)." An appropriate scale is one that allows a trend to be seen. [1]

67 Plot the data from the data table. Circle and connect the points. [1]

Example:

68 Based on the data table, what is the melting point of this substance? [1]

69 What is the evidence that the average kinetic energy of the particles of this substance is increasing during the first three minutes? [1]

70 The heat of fusion for this substance is 122 joules per gram. How many joules of heat are needed to melt 7.50 grams of this substance at its melting point? [1]

Base your answers to questions 71 through 73 on the diagram of a voltaic cell and the balanced ionic equation below.

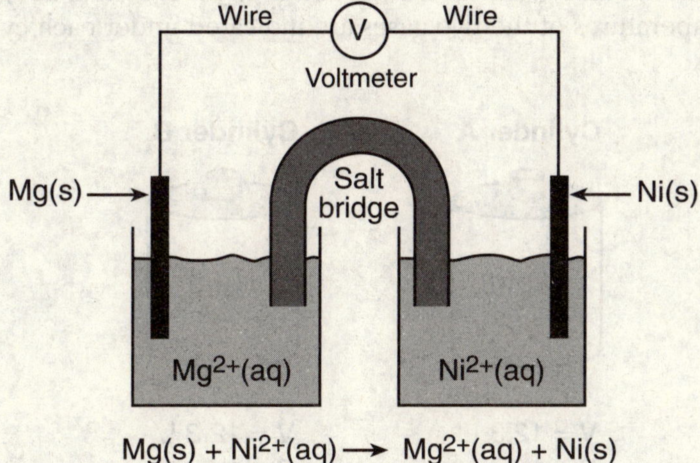

$$Mg(s) + Ni^{2+}(aq) \rightarrow Mg^{2+}(aq) + Ni(s)$$

71 What is the total number of moles of electrons needed to completely reduce 6.0 moles of $Ni^{2+}(aq)$ ions? [1]

72 Identify *one* metal from Reference Table *J* that is more easily oxidized than Mg(s). [1]

73 Explain the function of the salt bridge in the voltaic cell. [1]

Base your answers to questions 74 through 76 on the passage below.

Acid rain is a problem in industrialized countries around the world. Oxides of sulfur and nitrogen are formed when various fuels are burned. These oxides dissolve in atmospheric water droplets that fall to earth as acid rain or acid snow.

While normal rain has a pH between 5.0 and 6.0 due to the presence of dissolved carbon dioxide, acid rain often has a pH of 4.0 or lower. This level of acidity can damage trees and plants, leach minerals from the soil, and cause the death of aquatic animals and plants.

If the pH of the soil is too low, then quicklime, CaO, can be added to the soil to increase the pH. Quicklime produces calcium hydroxide when it dissolves in water.

74 Balance the neutralization equation *in your answer booklet,* using the smallest whole-number coefficients. [1]

75 A sample of wet soil has a pH of 4.0. After the addition of quicklime, the H^+ ion concentration of the soil is $\frac{1}{100}$ of the original H^+ ion concentration of the soil. What is the new pH of the soil sample? [1]

76 Samples of acid rain are brought to a laboratory for analysis. Several titrations are performed and it is determined that a 20.0-milliliter sample of acid rain is neutralized with 6.50 milliliters of 0.010 M NaOH. What is the molarity of the H^+ ions in the acid rain? [1]

Base your answers to questions 77 through 79 on the information and diagrams below.

Cylinder *A* contains 22.0 grams of CO_2(g) and cylinder *B* contains N_2(g). The volumes, pressures, and temperatures of the two gases are indicated under each cylinder.

Cylinder A	Cylinder B
CO_2(g)	N_2(g)
V = 12.3 L	V = 12.3 L
P = 1.0 atm	P = 1.0 atm
T = 300. K	T = 300. K

77 What is the total number of moles of CO_2(g) in cylinder *A*? [1]

78 Explain why the number of molecules of N_2(g) in cylinder *B* is the same as the number of molecules of CO_2(g) in cylinder *A*. [1]

79 The temperature of the CO_2(g) is increased to 450. K and the volume of cylinder *A* remains constant. In the space *in your answer booklet,* show a correct numerical setup for calculating the new pressure of the CO_2(g) in cylinder *A*. [1]

Base your answers to questions 80 through 83 on the information and diagram below and on your knowledge of chemistry.

Crude oil is a mixture of many hydrocarbons that have different numbers of carbon atoms. The use of a fractionating tower allows the separation of this mixture based on the boiling points of the hydrocarbons.

To begin the separation process, the crude oil is heated to about 400°C in a furnace, causing many of the hydrocarbons of the crude oil to vaporize. The vaporized mixture is pumped into a fractionating tower that is usually more than 30 meters tall. The temperature of the tower is highest at the bottom. As vaporized samples of hydrocarbons travel up the tower, they cool and condense. The liquid hydrocarbons are collected on trays and removed from the tower. The diagram below illustrates the fractional distillation of the crude oil and the temperature ranges in which the different hydrocarbons condense.

Distillation of Crude Oil

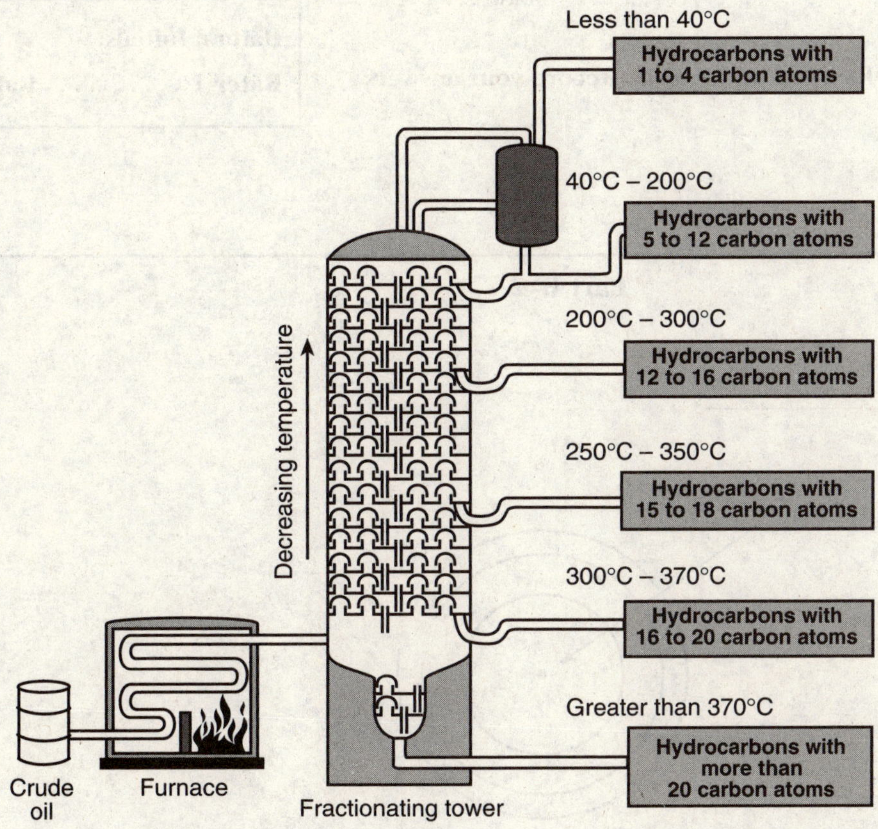

80 State the trend between the boiling point of the hydrocarbons contained in the crude oil and the number of carbon atoms in these molecules. [1]

81 Describe the relationship between the strength of the intermolecular forces and the number of carbon atoms in the different hydrocarbon molecules. [1]

82 Write an IUPAC name of *one* saturated hydrocarbon that leaves the fractionating tower at *less than* 40°C. [1]

83 How many hydrogen atoms are present in one molecule of octane? [1]

The University of the State of New York

REGENTS HIGH SCHOOL EXAMINATION

PHYSICAL SETTING CHEMISTRY

Wednesday, June 22, 2005 — 1:15 to 4:15 p.m., only

ANSWER BOOKLET

Student .... Sex: ☐ Male ☐ Female

Teacher ....

School .... Grade ....

Answer all questions in Part B–2 and Part C. Record your answers in this booklet.

Part	Maximum Score	Student's Score
A	33	
B–1	17	
B–2	15	
C	20	
Total Written Test Score (Maximum Raw Score: 85)		
Final Score (from conversion chart)		

Raters' Initials:

Rater 1 .... **Rater 2** ....

Part B–2

For Raters Only

51 ______________ 51 ☐

52

Mg-26 nucleus

52 ☐

53 ______________

____

______________ 53 ☐

For Raters Only

54 ______________________________ mol | 54

55 | 55

56 ______________________________ | 56

57 | 57

58 ______________________________ | 58

[2]

For Raters Only

59 ______________________ 59

60 60

61 61

Element	Number of Protons	Number of Neutrons	Mass Number	Nuclide
C	6	6	12	C-12
N	7	9	16	N-16
Ne	10			
S	16	16	32	S-32

62 ______________________ 62

63 ______________________ 63

64 $^{16}_{7}N \rightarrow$ ________ + ________ 64

Total Score for Part B–2

For Raters Only

Part C

65 Conclusion 1: ____

____

____

Conclusion 2: ____

____

____

65

66 and **67**

Heating Curve

Temperature (°C)

0 1 2 3 4 5 6 7 8 9 10 11 12

Time (min)

66

67

68 ____________________ **°C**

68

[4]

For Raters Only

69 ______________________________

______________________________ 69

70 ______________________________ J 70

71 ______________________________ mol 71

72 ______________________________ 72

73 ______________________________

______________________________ 73

____

74 _______ HNO_3 + _______ $Ca(OH)_2$ → _______ $Ca(NO_3)_2$ + _______ H_2O 74

75 ______________________________ 75

76 ______________________________ M 76

For Raters Only

77 ________________ mol | 77

78 ______________________________ | 78

79 | 79

80 ______________________________ | 80

81 ______________________________ | 81

82 ________________ | 82

83 ________ | 83

Total Score for Part C

[6]

Physical Setting Chemistry January, 2005

Part A

Answer all questions in this part.

Directions (1–30): For *each* statement or question, write on the separate answer sheet the *number* of the word or expression that, of those given, best completes the statement or answers the question. Some questions may require the use of the *Reference Tables for Physical Setting/Chemistry*.

1 As an electron in an atom moves from the ground state to the excited state, the electron

(1) gains energy as it moves to a higher energy level
(2) gains energy as it moves to a lower energy level
(3) loses energy as it moves to a higher energy level
(4) loses energy as it moves to a lower energy level

2 Which subatomic particle will be attracted by a positively charged object?

(1) proton
(2) neutron
(3) electron
(4) positron

3 Which conclusion is based on the "gold foil experiment" and the resulting model of the atom?

(1) An atom is mainly empty space, and the nucleus has a positive charge.
(2) An atom is mainly empty space, and the nucleus has a negative charge.
(3) An atom has hardly any empty space, and the nucleus has a positive charge.
(4) An atom has hardly any empty space, and the nucleus has a negative charge.

4 Which two particles have approximately the same mass?

(1) proton and neutron
(2) proton and electron
(3) neutron and electron
(4) neutron and positron

5 Which element has chemical properties that are most similar to the chemical properties of sodium?

(1) Mg
(2) K
(3) Se
(4) Cl

6 Germanium is classified as a

(1) metal
(2) metalloid
(3) nonmetal
(4) noble gas

7 Which statement correctly describes diamond and graphite, which are different forms of solid carbon?

(1) They differ in their molecular structure, only.
(2) They differ in their properties, only.
(3) They differ in their molecular structure and properties.
(4) They do not differ in their molecular structure or properties.

8 What is the chemical formula for copper(II) hydroxide?

(1) CuOH
(2) $CuOH_2$
(3) $Cu_2(OH)$
(4) $Cu(OH)_2$

9 What is the percent composition by mass of aluminum in $Al_2(SO_4)_3$ (gram-formula mass = 342 grams/mole)?

(1) 7.89%
(2) 15.8%
(3) 20.8%
(4) 36.0%

10 Which statement describes a chemical property that can be used to distinguish between compound *A* and compound *B*?

(1) *A* is a blue solid, and *B* is a white solid.
(2) *A* has a high melting point, and *B* has a low melting point.
(3) *A* dissolves in water, and *B* does not dissolve in water.
(4) *A* does not burn in air, and *B* does burn in air.

11 Which compound contains both ionic and covalent bonds?

(1) $CaCO_3$ (3) MgF_2
(2) PCl_3 (4) CH_2O

12 Which formula represents a nonpolar molecule?

(1) HCl (3) NH_3
(2) H_2O (4) CF_4

13 When a lithium atom forms an Li^+ ion, the lithium atom

(1) gains a proton
(2) gains an electron
(3) loses a proton
(4) loses an electron

14 Which Lewis electron-dot diagram represents a boron atom in the ground state?

(1) ·B (3) :Ḃ·
(2) :Ḃ (4) :Ḃ· (with a dot below)

15 A sample is prepared by completely dissolving 10.0 grams of NaCl in 1.0 liter of H_2O. Which classification best describes this sample?

(1) homogeneous compound
(2) homogeneous mixture
(3) heterogeneous compound
(4) heterogeneous mixture

16 Which form of energy is converted to thermal energy when propane burns in air?

(1) electromagnetic (3) electrical
(2) nuclear (4) chemical

17 Which physical changes are endothermic?

(1) melting and freezing
(2) melting and evaporating
(3) condensation and sublimation
(4) condensation and deposition

18 Which transfer of energy occurs when ice cubes are placed in water that has a temperature of 45°C?

(1) Chemical energy is transferred from the ice to the water.
(2) Chemical energy is transferred from the water to the ice.
(3) Thermal energy is transferred from the ice to the water.
(4) Thermal energy is transferred from the water to the ice.

19 At STP, 4 liters of O_2 contains the same total number of molecules as

(1) 1 L of NH_3 (3) 8 L of He
(2) 2 L of Cl_2 (4) 4 L of CO_2

20 What is the total number of electron pairs that are shared between the two carbon atoms in a molecule of ethyne?

(1) 1 (3) 3
(2) 2 (4) 4

21 Which pair of compounds are isomers?

(1) NO_2 and N_2O_4
(2) P_2O_5 and P_4O_{10}
(3) HCOOH and CH_3COOH
(4) CH_3OCH_3 and C_2H_5OH

22 Which organic compound is unsaturated?

(1) 2-methylbutane (3) 2-hexanol
(2) 2-chloropropane (4) 2-pentene

23 Which change in oxidation number indicates oxidation?

(1) –1 to +2 (3) +2 to –3
(2) –1 to –2 (4) +3 to +2

24 Given the redox reaction:

$$Cr^{3+} + Al \rightarrow Cr + Al^{3+}$$

As the reaction takes place, there is a transfer of

(1) electrons from Al to Cr^{3+}
(2) electrons from Cr^{3+} to Al
(3) protons from Al to Cr^{3+}
(4) protons from Cr^{3+} to Al

25 The compound HNO_3 can be described as an

(1) Arrhenius acid and an electrolyte
(2) Arrhenius acid and a nonelectrolyte
(3) Arrhenius base and an electrolyte
(4) Arrhenius base and a nonelectrolyte

26 According to Reference Table *M*, what is the color of the indicator methyl orange in a solution that has a pH of 2?

(1) blue (3) orange
(2) yellow (4) red

27 Given the reaction:

$$NH_3 + HCl \rightarrow NH_4Cl$$

In this reaction, ammonia molecules (NH_3) act as a base because they

(1) accept hydrogen ions (H^+)
(2) accept hydroxide ions (OH^-)
(3) donate hydrogen ions (H^+)
(4) donate hydroxide ions (OH^-)

28 Which reaction is an example of natural transmutation?

(1) ${}^{239}_{94}Pu \rightarrow {}^{235}_{92}U + {}^{4}_{2}He$
(2) ${}^{27}_{13}Al + {}^{4}_{2}He \rightarrow {}^{30}_{15}P + {}^{1}_{0}n$
(3) ${}^{238}_{92}U + {}^{1}_{0}n \rightarrow {}^{239}_{94}Pu + 2\,{}^{0}_{-1}e$
(4) ${}^{239}_{94}Pu + {}^{1}_{0}n \rightarrow {}^{147}_{56}Ba + {}^{90}_{38}Sr + 3{}^{1}_{0}n$

29 Which statement best describes gamma radiation?

(1) It has a mass of 1 and a charge of 1.
(2) It has a mass of 0 and a charge of –1.
(3) It has a mass of 0 and a charge of 0.
(4) It has a mass of 4 and a charge of +2.

30 Which change takes place in a nuclear fusion reaction?

(1) Matter is converted to energy.
(2) Energy is converted to matter.
(3) Ionic bonds are converted to covalent bonds.
(4) Covalent bonds are converted to ionic bonds.

Part B–1

Answer all questions in this part.

Directions (31–50): For *each* statement or question, write on the separate answer sheet the *number* of the word or expression that, of those given, best completes the statement or answers the question. Some questions may require the use of the *Reference Tables for Physical Setting/Chemistry*.

31 What is the total number of neutrons in the nucleus of a neutral atom that has 19 electrons and a mass number of 39?

(1) 19 (3) 39
(2) 20 (4) 58

32 An unknown element *X* can form a compound with the formula XBr_3. In which group on the Periodic Table would element *X* be found?

(1) 1 (3) 13
(2) 2 (4) 14

33 As the elements in Group 17 on the Periodic Table are considered from top to bottom, what happens to the atomic radius and the metallic character of each successive element?

(1) The atomic radius and the metallic character both increase.
(2) The atomic radius increases and the metallic character decreases.
(3) The atomic radius decreases and the metallic character increases.
(4) The atomic radius and the metallic character both decrease.

34 Which pair of compounds has the same empirical formula?

(1) C_2H_2 and C_6H_6
(2) C_2H_6 and C_3H_8
(3) CH_3OH and C_2H_5OH
(4) CH_3CHO and CH_3COOH

35 Which equation shows a conservation of mass?

(1) $Na + Cl_2 \rightarrow NaCl$
(2) $Al + Br_2 \rightarrow AlBr_3$
(3) $H_2O \rightarrow H_2 + O_2$
(4) $PCl_5 \rightarrow PCl_3 + Cl_2$

36 How many electrons are in an Fe^{2+} ion?

(1) 24 (3) 28
(2) 26 (4) 56

37 A substance that does not conduct electricity as a solid but does conduct electricity when melted is most likely classified as

(1) an ionic compound
(2) a molecular compound
(3) a metal
(4) a nonmetal

38 According to Reference Table *H*, what is the boiling point of ethanoic acid at 80 kPa?

(1) 28°C (3) 111°C
(2) 100°C (4) 125°C

39 Which particle diagram represents one pure substance, only?

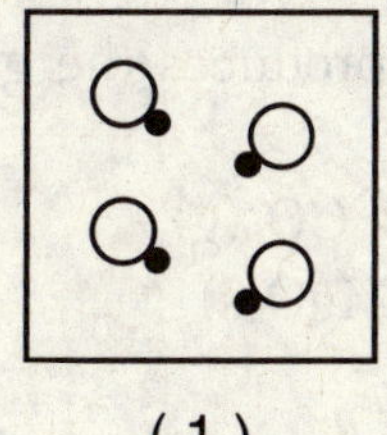
(1)

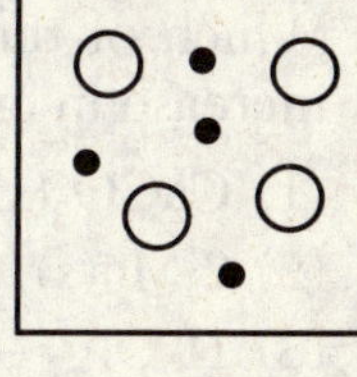

(3)

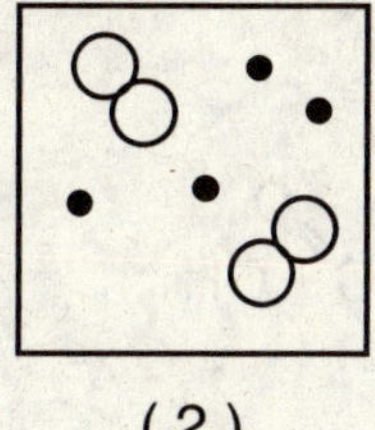
(2)

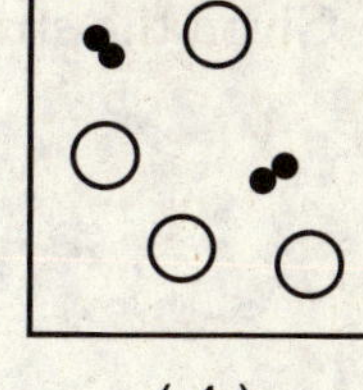
(4)

40 A sample of helium gas has a volume of 900. milliliters and a pressure of 2.50 atm at 298 K. What is the new pressure when the temperature is changed to 336 K and the volume is decreased to 450. milliliters?

(1) 0.177 atm
(2) 4.43 atm
(3) 5.64 atm
(4) 14.1 atm

41 Given the particle diagram:

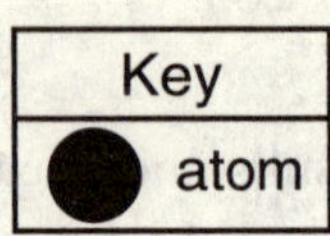

At 101.3 kPa and 298 K, which element could this diagram represent?

(1) Rn
(2) Xe
(3) Ag
(4) Kr

42 For most atoms with an atomic number less than 20, nuclear stability occurs when the ratio of neutrons to protons is 1:1. Which of the following atoms would be most likely to have an unstable nucleus?

(1) $^{4}_{2}He$
(2) $^{12}_{6}C$
(3) $^{16}_{7}N$
(4) $^{24}_{12}Mg$

43 Which of these changes produces the greatest increase in entropy?

(1) $CaCO_3(s) \rightarrow CaO(s) + CO_2(g)$
(2) $2\ Mg(s) + O_2(g) \rightarrow 2\ MgO(s)$
(3) $H_2O(g) \rightarrow H_2O(\ell)$
(4) $CO_2(g) \rightarrow CO_2(s)$

44 Given the structural formula:

```
    H   H
    |   |       O
H — C — C — C //
    |   |    \
    H   N     OH
       / \
      H   H
```

This structural formula represents a molecule of

(1) an aldehyde
(2) an ester
(3) a ketone
(4) an amino acid

45 Which half-reaction can occur at the anode in a voltaic cell?

(1) $Ni^{2+} + 2e^- \rightarrow Ni$
(2) $Sn + 2e^- \rightarrow Sn^{2+}$
(3) $Zn \rightarrow Zn^{2+} + 2e^-$
(4) $Fe^{3+} \rightarrow Fe^{2+} + e^-$

46 Given the reaction:

$$Ba(OH)_2(aq) + H_2SO_4(aq) \rightarrow BaSO_4(s) + 2\ H_2O(\ell) + \text{energy}$$

As the barium hydroxide solution is added to the solution of sulfuric acid, the electrical conductivity of the acid solution decreases because the

(1) volume of the reaction mixture increases
(2) temperature of the reaction mixture decreases
(3) concentration of ions increases
(4) concentration of ions decreases

47 Which chemical equation represents the reaction of an Arrhenius acid and an Arrhenius base?

(1) $HC_2H_3O_2(aq) + NaOH(aq) \rightarrow NaC_2H_3O_2(aq) + H_2O(\ell)$
(2) $C_3H_8(g) + 5\ O_2(g) \rightarrow 3\ CO_2(g) + 4\ H_2O(\ell)$
(3) $Zn(s) + 2\ HCl(aq) \rightarrow ZnCl_2(aq) + H_2(g)$
(4) $BaCl_2(aq) + Na_2SO_4(aq) \rightarrow BaSO_4(s) + 2\ NaCl(aq)$

48 Based on Reference Table *F*, which of these saturated solutions has the *lowest* concentration of dissolved ions?

(1) NaCl(aq)
(2) $MgCl_2(aq)$
(3) $NiCl_2(aq)$
(4) AgCl(aq)

49 Based on Reference Table *N*, what fraction of a radioactive ^{90}Sr sample would remain unchanged after 56.2 years?

(1) $\frac{1}{2}$
(2) $\frac{1}{4}$
(3) $\frac{1}{8}$
(4) $\frac{1}{16}$

50 Given the nuclear equation:

$$^{19}_{10}Ne \rightarrow X + ^{19}_{9}F$$

Which particle is represented by *X*?

(1) alpha
(2) beta
(3) neutron
(4) positron

Part B–2

Answer all questions in this part.

Directions (51–65): Record your answers in the spaces provided in your answer booklet. Some questions may require the use of the *Reference Tables for Physical Setting/Chemistry.*

Base your answers to questions 51 through 53 on your knowledge of chemical bonding and on the Lewis electron-dot diagrams of H_2S, CO_2, and F_2 below.

H:S: (H below S)   :O::C::O: :F:F:

51 Which atom, when bonded as shown, has the same electron configuration as an atom of argon? [1]

52 Explain, in terms of *structure* and/or *distribution of charge*, why CO_2 is a nonpolar molecule. [1]

53 Explain, in terms of *electronegativity*, why a C=O bond in CO_2 is more polar than the F–F bond in F_2. [1]

Base your answers to questions 54 and 55 on the heating curve below, which represents a substance starting as a solid below its melting point and being heated at a constant rate over a period of time.

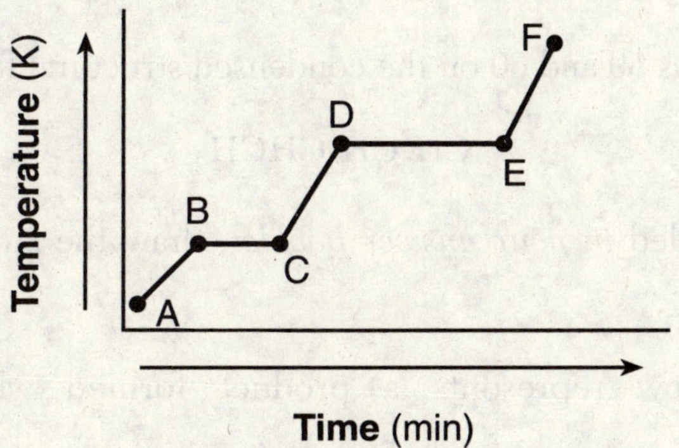

54 What is happening to the average kinetic energy of the particles during segment $\overline{BC}$? [1]

55 How does this heating curve illustrate that the heat of vaporization is greater than the heat of fusion? [1]

Base your answers to questions 56 through 58 on the potential energy diagram and the equation below.

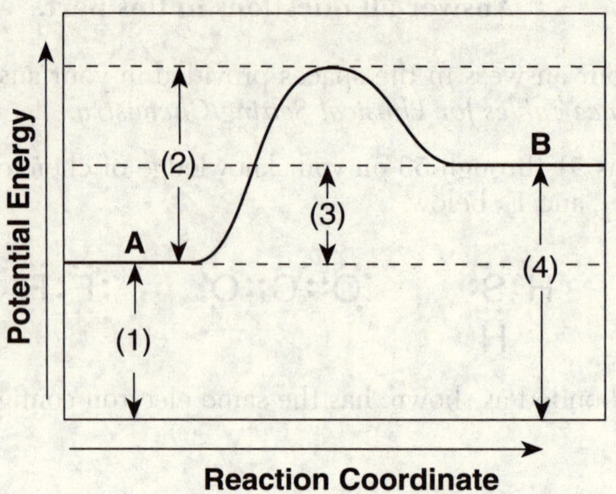

$$2\ C(s) + H_2(g) + 227.4\ kJ \rightarrow C_2H_2(g)$$

56 The letter *B* represents which chemical formula or formulas in the equation? [1]

57 If 682.2 kilojoules are absorbed, how many moles of $C_2H_2(g)$ are produced? [1]

58 Describe how the potential energy diagram will change if a catalyst is added. [1]

Base your answers to questions 59 and 60 on the condensed structural formula below.

$$CH_3CH_2CHCH_2$$

59 In the space provided *in your answer booklet*, draw the structural formula for this compound. [1]

60 The formula below represents a product formed when HCl reacts with $CH_3CH_2CHCH_2$.

```
   H  H  H  H
   |  |  |  |
H—C—C—C—C—H
   |  |  |  |
   H  Cl H  H
```

What is an IUPAC name for this product? [1]

61 Given the equation:

$$\text{butanoic acid} + \text{1-pentanol} \xrightarrow{\text{catalyst}} \text{water} + X$$

To which class of organic compounds does product *X* belong? [1]

62 Identify the homologous series of hydrocarbons to which CH_3CHCH_2 belongs. [1]

Base your answers to questions 63 through 65 on the information below.

In a titration experiment, a student uses a 1.4 M HBr(aq) solution and the indicator phenolphthalein to determine the concentration of a KOH(aq) solution. The data for trial 1 is recorded in the table below.

Trial 1

Buret Readings	**HBr**(aq)	**KOH**(aq)
Initial volume (mL)	7.50	11.00
Final volume (mL)	22.90	33.10
Volume used (mL)	15.40	22.10

63 In the space provided *in your answer booklet*, show a correct numerical setup for calculating the molarity of the KOH(aq) solution for trial 1. [1]

64 Why is it better to use several trials of a titration rather than one trial to determine the molarity of a solution of an unknown concentration? [1]

65 In a second trial of this experiment, the molarity of KOH(aq) was determined to be 0.95 M. The actual molarity was 0.83 M. What is the percent error in the second trial? [1]

Part C

Answer all questions in this part.

Directions (66–84): Record your answers in the spaces provided in your answer booklet. Some questions may require the use of the *Reference Tables for Physical Setting/Chemistry*.

Base your answers to questions 66 and 67 on the information below.

Naturally occurring elemental carbon is a mixture of isotopes. The percent composition of the two most abundant isotopes is listed below.

- 98.93% of the carbon atoms have a mass of 12.00 atomic mass units.
- 1.07% of the carbon atoms have a mass of 13.00 atomic mass units.

66 In the space provided *in your answer booklet*, show a correct numerical setup for calculating the average atomic mass of carbon. [1]

67 Describe, in terms of *subatomic particles found in the nucleus*, one difference between the nuclei of carbon-12 atoms and the nuclei of carbon-13 atoms. The response must include both isotopes. [1]

Base your answers to questions 68 and 69 on the information below.

A scientist in a chemistry laboratory determined the molecular formulas for two compounds containing nitrogen and oxygen to be NO_2 and N_2O_5.

68 Write an IUPAC name for the compound N_2O_5. [1]

69 In the space provided *in your answer booklet*, show a correct numerical setup for calculating the percent composition by mass of oxygen in NO_2. [1]

Base your answers to questions 70 through 72 on the information below.

In a laboratory experiment, 10.00 grams of an unknown solid is added to 100.0 milliliters of water and the temperature of the resulting solution is measured over several minutes, as recorded in the table below.

Data Table

Time (minutes)	Temperature (°C)
0	24.0
0.5	28.5
1.0	31.0
1.5	34.5
2.0	41.0
2.5	45.5
3.0	46.5

70 On the grid provided *in your answer booklet*, mark an appropriate scale on the axis labeled "Temperature (°C)." An appropriate scale is one that allows a trend to be seen. [1]

71 Plot the data from the data table. Circle and connect the points. [1]

Example:

72 Given the statement:

The unknown solid is either sodium hydroxide or lithium bromide, and both of these compounds dissolve in water exothermically.

a Explain how the experimental data support the statement. [1]

b State specific information from Reference Table *I* to support the statement. [1]

Base your answers to questions 73 through 76 on the information below.

Figure 1

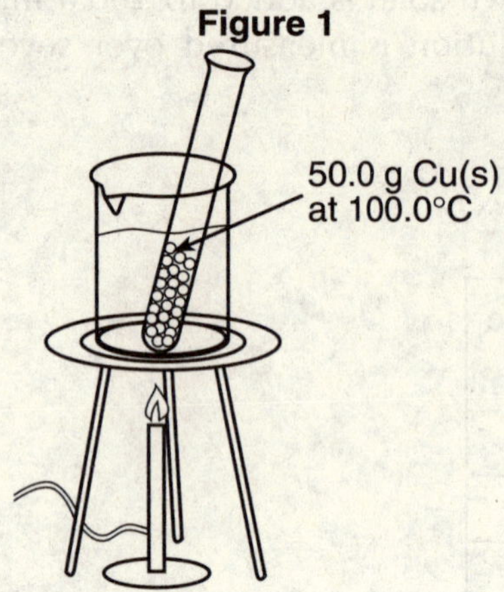

In a laboratory investigation, a 50.0-gram sample of copper is at 100.0°C in a boiling water bath.

Figure 2

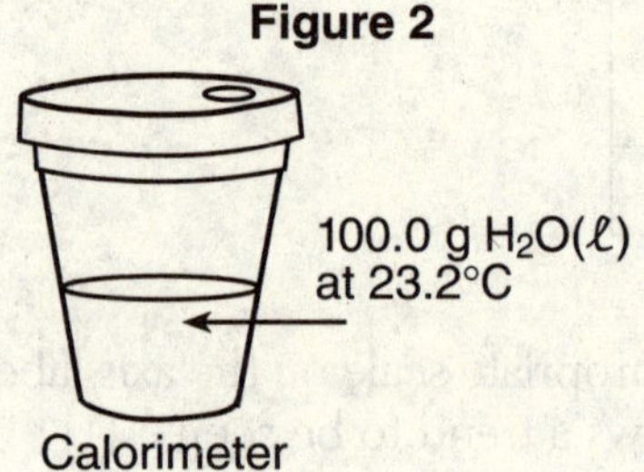

A Styrofoam cup with a lid is used as a calorimeter. The cup contains 100.0 grams of distilled water at 23.2°C.

Figure 3

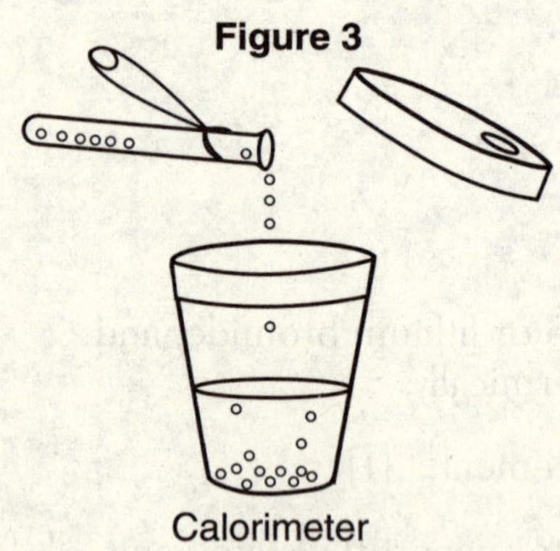

The hot copper is poured into the cup of water, and the cup is quickly covered with the lid.

Figure 4

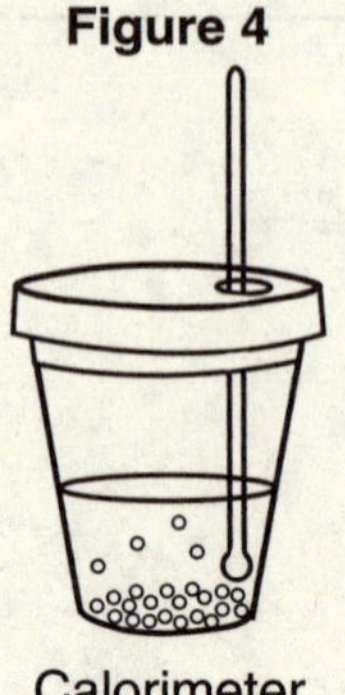

A thermometer is inserted through the lid. The copper and water are gently stirred in the cup. The temperature is checked periodically. The highest temperature noted is 26.3°C.

73 In terms of *energy flow,* explain why the temperature of the water in the calorimeter increases. [1]

74 Using the information given, complete the data table provided *in your answer booklet.* [1]

75 In the space provided *in your answer booklet,* show a correct numerical setup for calculating the number of joules of heat gained by the water. [1]

76 In this investigation, the change in heat of the copper is greater than the change in heat of the water. What error could account for this apparent violation of the Law of Conservation of Energy? Do *not* use human error as part of the answer. [1]

Base your answers to questions 77 through 79 on the information below.

Two alcohols that are used in our everyday lives are rubbing alcohol and ethylene glycol. Rubbing alcohol is used as an antiseptic. Ethylene glycol is the main ingredient in antifreeze, which is used in automobile cooling systems.

77 Explain, in terms of *molecular polarity,* why rubbing alcohol, 2-propanol, is soluble in water. [1]

78 What is the gram-formula mass of ethylene glycol, $C_2H_4(OH)_2$? [1]

79 In the space provided *in your answer booklet,* show a correct numerical setup for calculating the total number of moles of ethylene glycol needed to prepare 2.50 liters of a 10.0 M solution. [1]

Base your answers to questions 80 and 81 on the information below.

The outer structure of the Statue of Liberty is made of copper metal. The framework is made of iron. Over time, a thin green layer (patina) forms on the copper surface.

80 When copper oxidized to form this patina layer, the copper atoms became copper(II) ions (Cu^{2+}). Write a balanced half-reaction for this oxidation of copper. [1]

81 Where the iron framework came in contact with the copper surface, a reaction occurred in which iron was oxidized. Using information from Reference Table *J*, explain why the iron was oxidized. [1]

Base your answers to questions 82 through 84 on the information below, the *Reference Tables for Physical Setting/Chemistry*, and your knowledge of chemistry.

Radioactivity and radioactive isotopes have the potential for both benefiting and harming living organisms. One use of radioactive isotopes is in radiation therapy as a treatment for cancer. Cesium-137 is sometimes used in radiation therapy.

A sample of cesium-137 was left in an abandoned clinic in Brazil in 1987. Cesium-137 gives off a blue glow because of its radioactivity. The people who discovered the sample were attracted by the blue glow and had no idea of any danger. Hundreds of people were treated for overexposure to radiation, and four people died.

82 Using Reference Table *N*, complete the equation provided *in your answer booklet* for the radioactive decay of $^{137}_{55}Cs$. Include *both* atomic number and mass number for *each* particle. [1]

83 If 12.5 grams of the original sample of cesium-137 remained after 90.69 years, what was the mass of the original sample? [1]

84 Suppose a 40-gram sample of iodine-131 and a 40-gram sample of cesium-137 were both abandoned in the clinic in 1987. Explain why the sample of iodine-131 would *not* pose as great a radiation risk to people today as the sample of cesium-137 would. [1]

The University of the State of New York

REGENTS HIGH SCHOOL EXAMINATION

PHYSICAL SETTING CHEMISTRY

Thursday, January 27, 2005 — 9:15 a.m. to 12:15 p.m., only

ANSWER BOOKLET

Student .... Sex: ☐ Male ☐ Female

Teacher ....

School .... Grade ....

Answer all questions in Part B–2 and Part C. Record your answers in this booklet.

Part	Maximum Score	Student's Score
A	30	
B–1	20	
B–2	15	
C	20	
Total Written Test Score (Maximum Raw Score: 85)		
Final Score (from conversion chart)		

Raters' Initials:

Rater 1 .... **Rater 2** ....

Part B–2

For Raters Only

51 ______________________ **51** ☐

52 ______________________ **52** ☐

53 ______________________ **53** ☐

[1]

For Raters Only

54 ______________________________ 54

55 ______________________________ 55

____

56 ______________________________ 56

57 ______________________________ mol 57

58 ______________________________ 58

____

59 59

60 ______________________________ 60

61 ______________________________ 61

62 ______________________________ 62

[2]

63

64 ____

____

____

65 ______________ %

For Raters Only

63

64

65

Total Score for Part B–2

For Raters Only

Part C

66

67 ______________________________

____

____

68 ______________________________

69

66 [ ]

67 [ ]

68 [ ]

69 [ ]

[4]

For Raters Only

70 and 71

Change in Temperature
During the Dissolving of a Solid

70

71

72 *a* ____________________________________

72*a*

b ____________________________________

b

[5] [OVER]

For Raters Only

73 ____

____ 73

____

74

Data Table

Quantity Measured	**Data** (units are given)
Mass of copper	g
Temperature of hot copper	°C
Mass of H_2O in calorimeter	g
Initial temperature of H_2O in calorimeter	°C
Final temperature of H_2O and copper	°C

74

75

75

76 ____ 76

____

[6]

77 ______________________________

____

____

78 ______________ g/mol

79

80 ______________________________

81 ______________________________

____

____

82 $^{137}_{55}Cs \rightarrow$ ________ + ________

83 ______________ g

84 ______________________________

____

____

For Raters Only

77	
78	
79	
80	
81	
82	
83	
84	

Total Score

Physical Setting Chemistry August, 2004

Part A

Answer all questions in this part.

Directions (1–33): For *each* statement or question, write on the separate answer sheet the *number* of the word or expression that, of those given, best completes the statement or answers the question. Some questions may require the use of the *Reference Tables for Physical Setting/Chemistry*.

1 Which of these phrases best describes an atom?

(1) a positive nucleus surrounded by a hard negative shell
(2) a positive nucleus surrounded by a cloud of negative charges
(3) a hard sphere with positive particles uniformly embedded
(4) a hard sphere with negative particles uniformly embedded

2 Which statement is true about a proton and an electron?

(1) They have the same masses and the same charges.
(2) They have the same masses and different charges.
(3) They have different masses and the same charges.
(4) They have different masses and different charges.

3 The atomic mass of an element is the weighted average of the masses of

(1) its two most abundant isotopes
(2) its two least abundant isotopes
(3) all of its naturally occurring isotopes
(4) all of its radioactive isotopes

4 What determines the order of placement of the elements on the modern Periodic Table?

(1) atomic number
(2) atomic mass
(3) the number of neutrons, only
(4) the number of neutrons and protons

5 Which compound contains only covalent bonds?

(1) NaOH
(2) $Ba(OH)_2$
(3) $Ca(OH)_2$
(4) CH_3OH

6 At 298 K, oxygen (O_2) and ozone (O_3) have different properties because their

(1) atoms have different atomic numbers
(2) atoms have different atomic masses
(3) molecules have different molecular structures
(4) molecules have different average kinetic energies

7 Which substance represents a compound?

(1) C(s)
(2) Co(s)
(3) CO(g)
(4) $O_2(g)$

8 All chemical reactions have a conservation of

(1) mass, only
(2) mass and charge, only
(3) charge and energy, only
(4) mass, charge, and energy

9 Which characteristic is a property of molecular substances?

(1) good heat conductivity
(2) good electrical conductivity
(3) low melting point
(4) high melting point

10 Given the Lewis electron-dot diagram:

```
    H
    ••
H : C : H
    ••
    H
```

Which electrons are represented by all of the dots?

(1) the carbon valence electrons, only
(2) the hydrogen valence electrons, only
(3) the carbon and hydrogen valence electrons
(4) all of the carbon and hydrogen electrons

11 Which grouping of the three phases of bromine is listed in order from left to right for increasing distance between bromine molecules?

(1) gas, liquid, solid
(2) liquid, solid, gas
(3) solid, gas, liquid
(4) solid, liquid, gas

12 Which statement concerning elements is true?

(1) Different elements must have different numbers of isotopes.
(2) Different elements must have different numbers of neutrons.
(3) All atoms of a given element must have the same mass number.
(4) All atoms of a given element must have the same atomic number.

13 At room temperature, the solubility of which solute in water would be most affected by a change in pressure?

(1) methanol
(2) sugar
(3) carbon dioxide
(4) sodium nitrate

14 Based on Reference Table *I*, which change occurs when pellets of solid NaOH are added to water and stirred?

(1) The water temperature increases as chemical energy is converted to heat energy.
(2) The water temperature increases as heat energy is stored as chemical energy.
(3) The water temperature decreases as chemical energy is converted to heat energy.
(4) The water temperature decreases as heat energy is stored as chemical energy.

15 The concept of an ideal gas is used to explain

(1) the mass of a gas sample
(2) the behavior of a gas sample
(3) why some gases are monatomic
(4) why some gases are diatomic

16 Molecules in a sample of $NH_3(\ell)$ are held closely together by intermolecular forces

(1) existing between ions
(2) existing between electrons
(3) caused by different numbers of neutrons
(4) caused by unequal charge distribution

17 Which process represents a chemical change?

(1) melting of ice
(2) corrosion of copper
(3) evaporation of water
(4) crystallization of sugar

18 At STP, which 4.0-gram zinc sample will react fastest with dilute hydrochloric acid?

(1) lump
(2) bar
(3) powdered
(4) sheet metal

19 Which information about a chemical reaction is provided by a potential energy diagram?

(1) the oxidation states of the reactants and products
(2) the average kinetic energy of the reactants and products
(3) the change in solubility of the reacting substances
(4) the energy released or absorbed during the reaction

20 A catalyst works by

(1) increasing the potential energy of the reactants
(2) increasing the energy released during a reaction
(3) decreasing the potential energy of the products
(4) decreasing the activation energy required for a reaction

21 Even though the process is endothermic, snow can sublime. Which tendency in nature accounts for this phase change?

(1) a tendency toward greater entropy
(2) a tendency toward greater energy
(3) a tendency toward less entropy
(4) a tendency toward less energy

22 What is the IUPAC name of the compound with the structural formula shown below?

```
    H   H   H       H
    |   |   |       |
H - C - C - C = C - C - H
    |   |       |   |
    H   H       H   H
```

(1) 2-pentene
(2) 3-pentene
(3) 2-pentyne
(4) 3-pentyne

23 Molecules of 1-bromopropane and 2-bromopropane differ in

(1) molecular formula
(2) structural formula
(3) number of carbon atoms per molecule
(4) number of bromine atoms per molecule

24 Which half-reaction correctly represents reduction?

(1) $Ag \rightarrow Ag^{+} + e^{-}$
(2) $F_2 \rightarrow 2\ F^{-} + 2e^{-}$
(3) $Au^{3+} + 3e^{-} \rightarrow Au$
(4) $Fe^{2+} + e^{-} \rightarrow Fe^{3+}$

25 In a redox reaction, how does the total number of electrons lost by the oxidized substance compare to the total number of electrons gained by the reduced substance?

(1) The number lost is always greater than the number gained.
(2) The number lost is always equal to the number gained.
(3) The number lost is sometimes equal to the number gained.
(4) The number lost is sometimes less than the number gained.

26 Which reaction is an example of an oxidation-reduction reaction?

(1) $AgNO_3 + KI \rightarrow AgI + KNO_3$
(2) $Cu + 2\ AgNO_3 \rightarrow Cu(NO_3)_2 + 2\ Ag$
(3) $2\ KOH + H_2SO_4 \rightarrow K_2SO_4 + 2\ H_2O$
(4) $Ba(OH)_2 + 2\ HCl \rightarrow BaCl_2 + 2\ H_2O$

27 Which compound is an Arrhenius base?

(1) CH_3OH
(2) CO_2
(3) LiOH
(4) NO_2

28 The only positive ion found in an aqueous solution of sulfuric acid is the

(1) hydroxide ion
(2) hydronium ion
(3) sulfite ion
(4) sulfate ion

29 Which process uses a volume of solution of known concentration to determine the concentration of another solution?

(1) distillation
(2) substitution
(3) transmutation
(4) titration

30 Which pH change represents a hundredfold increase in the concentration of H_3O^{+}?

(1) pH 5 to pH 7
(2) pH 13 to pH 14
(3) pH 3 to pH 1
(4) pH 4 to pH 3

31 Which radioisotope undergoes beta decay and has a half-life of less than 1 minute?

(1) Fr-220
(2) K-42
(3) N-16
(4) P-32

32 Which set of symbols represents atoms with valence electrons in the same electron shell?

(1) Ba, Br, Bi
(2) Sr, Sn, I
(3) O, S, Te
(4) Mn, Hg, Cu

Note that question 33 has only three choices.

33 When compared with the energy of an electron in the first shell of a carbon atom, the energy of an electron in the second shell of a carbon atom is

(1) less
(2) greater
(3) the same

Part B–1

Answer all questions in this part.

Directions (34–50): For *each* statement or question, write on the separate answer sheet the *number* of the word or expression that, of those given, best completes the statement or answers the question. Some questions may require the use of the *Reference Tables for Physical Setting/Chemistry*.

34 What is the total number of electrons found in an atom of sulfur?

(1) 6
(2) 8
(3) 16
(4) 32

35 Which electron configuration represents the electrons of an atom in an excited state?

(1) 2–8–1
(2) 2–8–6
(3) 2–8–17–6
(4) 2–8–18–5

36 The nucleus of an atom of cobalt-58 contains

(1) 27 protons and 31 neutrons
(2) 27 protons and 32 neutrons
(3) 59 protons and 60 neutrons
(4) 60 protons and 60 neutrons

37 Which pair of formulas correctly represents a molecular formula and its corresponding empirical formula?

(1) C_2H_2 and CH
(2) C_3H_4 and CH_2
(3) C_4H_6 and CH
(4) C_5H_8 and C_2H_2

38 Which substance is correctly paired with its type of bonding?

(1) NaBr—nonpolar covalent
(2) HCl—nonpolar covalent
(3) NH_3—polar covalent
(4) Br_2—polar covalent

39 A gas occupies a volume of 444 mL at 273 K and 79.0 kPa. What is the final kelvin temperature when the volume of the gas is changed to 1880 mL and the pressure is changed to 38.7 kPa?

(1) 31.5 K
(2) 292 K
(3) 566 K
(4) 2360 K

40 At STP, which of these substances is most soluble in H_2O?

(1) CCl_4
(2) CO_2
(3) HCl
(4) N_2

41 Based on intermolecular forces, which of these substances would have the highest boiling point?

(1) He
(2) O_2
(3) CH_4
(4) NH_3

42 How much heat energy must be absorbed to completely melt 35.0 grams of $H_2O(s)$ at 0°C?

(1) 9.54 J
(2) 146 J
(3) 11 700 J
(4) 79 100 J

43 The graph below represents the uniform heating of a substance, starting below its melting point, when the substance is solid.

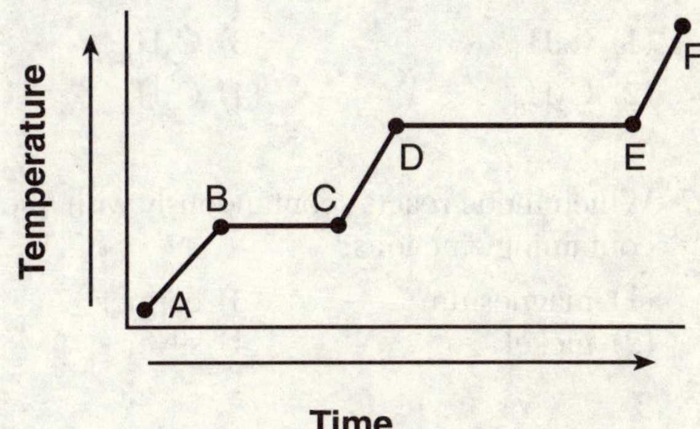

Which line segments represent an increase in average kinetic energy?

(1) $\overline{AB}$ and $\overline{BC}$
(2) $\overline{AB}$ and $\overline{CD}$
(3) $\overline{BC}$ and $\overline{DE}$
(4) $\overline{DE}$ and $\overline{EF}$

44 Given the three organic structural formulas shown below:

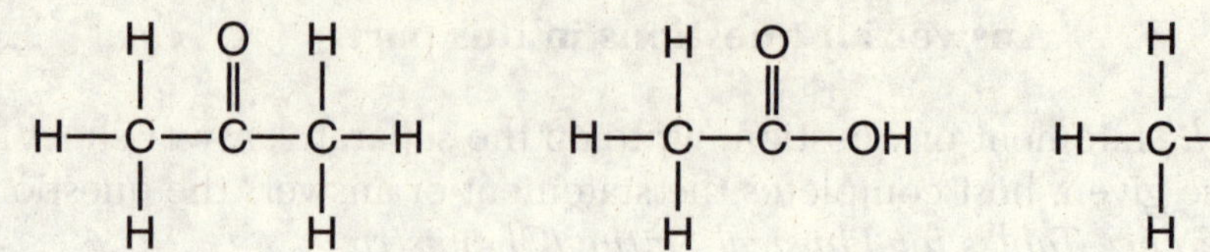

Which organic-compound classes are represented by these structural formulas, as shown from left to right?

(1) ester, organic acid, ketone
(2) ester, aldehyde, organic acid
(3) ketone, aldehyde, alcohol
(4) ketone, organic acid, alcohol

---

45 Given the reaction at equilibrium:

$$N_2(g) + O_2(g) + \text{energy} \rightleftharpoons 2\ NO(g)$$

Which change will result in a *decrease* in the amount of NO(g) formed?

(1) decreasing the pressure
(2) decreasing the concentration of $N_2(g)$
(3) increasing the concentration of $O_2(g)$
(4) increasing the temperature

46 Given the equation:

$$X + Cl_2 \rightarrow C_2H_5Cl + HCl$$

Which molecule is represented by *X*?

(1) C_2H_4
(2) C_2H_6
(3) C_3H_6
(4) C_3H_8

47 Which metal reacts spontaneously with a solution containing zinc ions?

(1) magnesium
(2) nickel
(3) copper
(4) silver

48 Which statement correctly describes a solution with a pH of 9?

(1) It has a higher concentration of H_3O^+ than OH^- and causes litmus to turn blue.
(2) It has a higher concentration of OH^- than H_3O^+ and causes litmus to turn blue.
(3) It has a higher concentration of H_3O^+ than OH^- and causes methyl orange to turn yellow.
(4) It has a higher concentration of OH^- than H_3O^+ and causes methyl orange to turn red.

49 How many days are required for 200. grams of radon-222 to decay to 50.0 grams?

(1) 1.91 days
(2) 3.82 days
(3) 7.64 days
(4) 11.5 days

50 A student calculates the density of an unknown solid. The mass is 10.04 grams, and the volume is 8.21 cubic centimeters. How many significant figures should appear in the final answer?

(1) 1
(2) 2
(3) 3
(4) 4

Part B–2

Answer all questions in this part.

Directions (51–65): Record your answers in the spaces provided in your answer booklet. Some questions may require the use of the *Reference Tables for Physical Setting/Chemistry.*

51 In the 19th century, Dmitri Mendeleev predicted the existence of a then unknown element *X* with a mass of 68. He also predicted that an oxide of *X* would have the formula X_2O_3. On the modern Periodic Table, what is the group number and period number of element *X*? [1]

52 Given the equation: $2\ H_2(g) + O_2(g) \rightarrow 2\ H_2O(g)$

If 8.0 moles of O_2 are completely consumed, what is the total number of moles of H_2O produced? [1]

53 In the space provided *in your answer booklet,* show a correct numerical setup for determining how many liters of a 1.2 M solution can be prepared with 0.50 mole of $C_6H_{12}O_6$. [1]

Base your answers to questions 54 through 57 on the particle diagrams below. Samples *A*, *B*, and *C* contain molecules at STP.

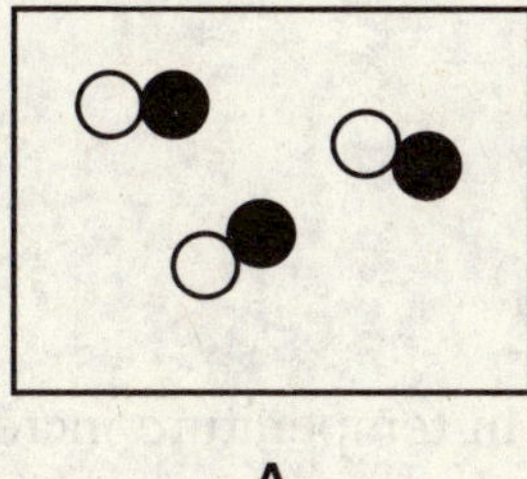

A

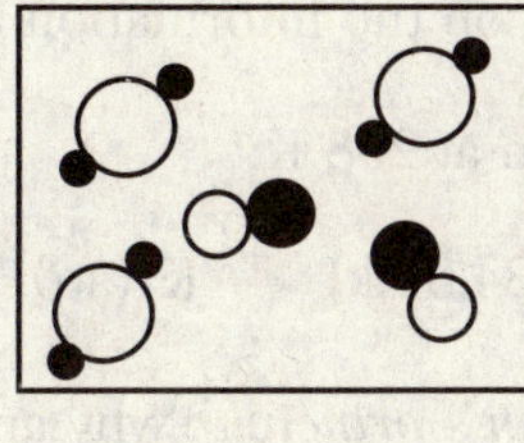

B

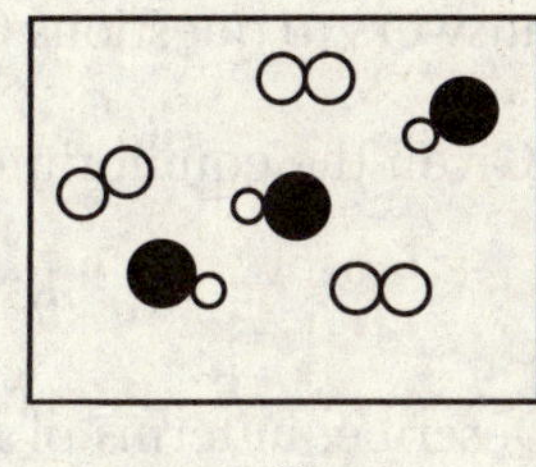

C

54 Explain why the average kinetic energy of sample *B* is equal to the average kinetic energy of sample *C*. [1]

55 Explain, in terms of the *composition*, why sample *A* represents a pure substance. [1]

56 Explain why sample *C* could represent a mixture of fluorine and hydrogen chloride. [1]

57 Contrast sample *A* and sample *B*, in terms of *compounds and mixtures*. Include both sample *A* and sample *B* in your answer. [1]

Base your answers to questions 58 through 60 on the electronegativity values and atomic numbers of fluorine, chlorine, bromine, and iodine that are listed on Reference Table *S*.

58 On the grid provided *in your answer booklet*, mark an appropriate scale on the axis labeled "Electronegativity." An appropriate scale is one that allows a trend to be seen. [1]

59 On the same grid, plot the electronegativity and atomic number data from Reference Table *S*. Circle and connect the points. [1]

60 Explain, in terms of *electronegativity*, why the H–F bond is expected to be more polar than the H–I bond. [1]

61 What is the gram-formula mass of $(NH_4)_2CO_3$? Use atomic masses rounded to the *nearest whole number*. [1]

62 In the space provided *in your answer booklet*, show a correct numerical setup for calculating the number of moles of CO_2 (gram-formula mass = 44 g/mol) present in 11 grams of CO_2. [1]

Base your answers to questions 63 and 64 on the information below.

Given the equilibrium equation at 298 K:

$$KNO_3(s) + 34.89 \text{ kJ} \underset{}{\overset{H_2O}{\rightleftharpoons}} K^+(aq) + NO_3^-(aq)$$

63 Describe, in terms of *LeChatelier's principle*, why an increase in temperature increases the solubility of KNO_3. [1]

64 The equation indicates that KNO_3 has formed a saturated solution. Explain, in terms of *equilibrium*, why the solution is saturated. [1]

65 In the space provided *in your answer booklet*, draw the structural formula for butanoic acid. [1]

Part C

Answer all questions in this part.

Directions (66–85): Record your answers in the spaces provided in your answer booklet. Some questions may require the use of the *Reference Tables for Physical Setting/Chemistry.*

Base your answers to questions 66 through 69 on the information below, which describes the smelting of iron ore, and on your knowledge of chemistry.

In the smelting of iron ore, Fe_2O_3 is reduced in a blast furnace at high temperature by a reaction with carbon monoxide. Crushed limestone, $CaCO_3$, is also added to the mixture to remove impurities in the ore. The carbon monoxide is formed by the oxidation of carbon (coke), as shown in the reaction below:

$$2\,C + O_2 \rightarrow 2\,CO + \text{energy}$$

Liquid iron flows from the bottom of the blast furnace and is processed into different alloys of iron.

66 Balance the equation for the reaction of Fe_2O_3 and CO *in your answer booklet*, using the smallest whole-number coefficients. [1]

67 Using the set of axes provided *in your answer booklet*, sketch a potential energy diagram for the reaction of carbon and oxygen that produces carbon monoxide. [1]

68 What is the oxidation number of carbon in $CaCO_3$? [1]

69 Convert the melting point of iron metal to degrees Celsius. [1]

Base your answers to questions 70 through 72 on the information below.

Potassium ions are essential to human health. The movement of dissolved potassium ions, $K^+(aq)$, in and out of a nerve cell allows that cell to transmit an electrical impulse.

70 What is the total number of electrons in a potassium ion? [1]

71 Explain, in terms of *atomic structure*, why a potassium ion is smaller than a potassium atom. [1]

72 What property of potassium ions allows them to transmit an electrical impulse? [1]

Base your answers to questions 73 through 75 on the information below.

Ethene (common name ethylene) is a commercially important organic compound. Millions of tons of ethene are produced by the chemical industry each year. Ethene is used in the manufacture of synthetic fibers for carpeting and clothing, and it is widely used in making polyethylene. Low-density polyethylene can be stretched into a clear, thin film that is used for wrapping food products and consumer goods. High-density polyethylene is molded into bottles for milk and other liquids.

Ethene can also be oxidized to produce ethylene glycol, which is used in antifreeze for automobiles. The structural formula for ethylene glycol is:

```
    H   H
    |   |
H - C - C - H
    |   |
   OH  OH
```

At standard atmospheric pressure, the boiling point of ethylene glycol is 198°C, compared to ethene that boils at –104°C.

73 Identify the type of organic reaction by which ethene (ethylene) is made into polyethylene. [1]

74 According to the information in the reading passage, state *two* consumer products manufactured from ethene. [1]

75 Explain, in terms of *bonding*, why ethene is an unsaturated hydrocarbon. [1]

Base your answers to questions 76 through 78 on the diagram below, which represents a voltaic cell at 298 K and 1 atm.

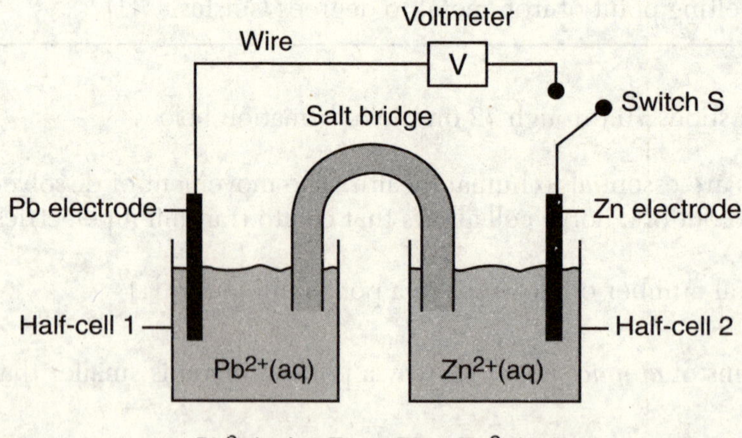

$Pb^{2+}(aq) + Zn \rightarrow Pb + Zn^{2+}(aq)$

76 In which half-cell will oxidation occur when switch *S* is closed? [1]

77 Write the balanced half-reaction equation that will occur in half-cell 1 when switch *S* is closed. [1]

78 Describe the direction of electron flow between the electrodes when switch *S* is closed. [1]

Base your answers to questions 79 through 81 on the information and data table below.

Indigestion may be caused by excess stomach acid (hydrochloric acid). Some products used to treat indigestion contain magnesium hydroxide. The magnesium hydroxide neutralizes some of the stomach acid.

The amount of acid that can be neutralized by three different brands of antacids is shown in the data table below.

Antacid Brand	**Mass of Antacid Tablet** (g)	**Volume of HCl(aq) Neutralized** (mL)
X	2.00	25.20
Y	1.20	18.65
Z	1.75	22.50

79 Based on Reference Table *F*, describe the solubility of magnesium hydroxide in water. [1]

80 In the space provided *in your answer booklet*, show a correct numerical setup for calculating the milliliters of HCl(aq) neutralized per gram of antacid tablet for *each* brand of antacid. [1]

81 Which antacid brand neutralizes the most acid per gram of antacid tablet? [1]

Base your answers to questions 82 through 85 on the reading passage below and on your knowledge of chemistry.

A Glow in the Dark, and Scientific Peril

The [Marie and Pierre] Curies set out to study radioactivity in 1898. Their first accomplishment was to show that radioactivity was a property of atoms themselves. Scientifically, that was the most important of their findings, because it helped other researchers refine their understanding of atomic structure.

More famous was their discovery of polonium and radium. Radium was the most radioactive substance the Curies had encountered. Its radioactivity is due to the large size of the atom, which makes the nucleus unstable and prone to decay, usually to radon and then lead, by emitting particles and energy as it seeks a more stable configuration.

Marie Curie struggled to purify radium for medical uses, including early radiation treatment for tumors. But radium's bluish glow caught people's fancy, and companies in the United States began mining it and selling it as a novelty: for glow-in-the-dark light pulls, for instance, and bogus cure-all patent medicines that actually killed people.

What makes radium so dangerous is that it forms chemical bonds in the same way as calcium, and the body can mistake it for calcium and absorb it into the bones. Then, it can bombard cells with radiation at close range, which may cause bone tumors or bone-marrow damage that can give rise to anemia or leukemia.

— Denise Grady, *The New York Times*, October 6, 1998

82 State one risk associated with the use of radium. [1]

83 Using Reference Table *N*, complete the equation provided *in your answer booklet* for the nuclear decay of $^{226}_{88}Ra$. Include *both* atomic number and mass number for *each* particle. [1]

84 Using information from the Periodic Table, explain why radium forms chemical bonds in the same way as calcium does. [1]

85 If a scientist purifies 1.0 gram of radium-226, how many years must pass before only 0.50 gram of the original radium-226 sample remains unchanged? [1]

The University of the State of New York

REGENTS HIGH SCHOOL EXAMINATION

PHYSICAL SETTING CHEMISTRY

Tuesday, August 17, 2004 — 12:30 to 3:30 p.m., only

ANSWER BOOKLET

Student .... Sex: ☐ Male ☐ Female

Teacher ....

School .... Grade ....

Answer all questions in Part B–2 and Part C. Record your answers in this booklet.

Part	Maximum Score	Student's Score
A	33	
B–1	17	
B–2	15	
C	20	

Total Written Test Score (Maximum Raw Score: 85) ☐

Final Score (from conversion chart) ☐

Raters' Initials:

Rater 1 .... **Rater 2** ....

Part B–2

For Raters Only

51 Group ____________ and **Period** ____________ — 51 ☐

52 ______________________ **mol** — 52 ☐

53 — 53 ☐

For Raters Only

54 ____

____

____

55 ____

____

____

56 ____

____

____

57 ____

____

____

54 [ ]

55 [ ]

56 [ ]

57 [ ]

[2]

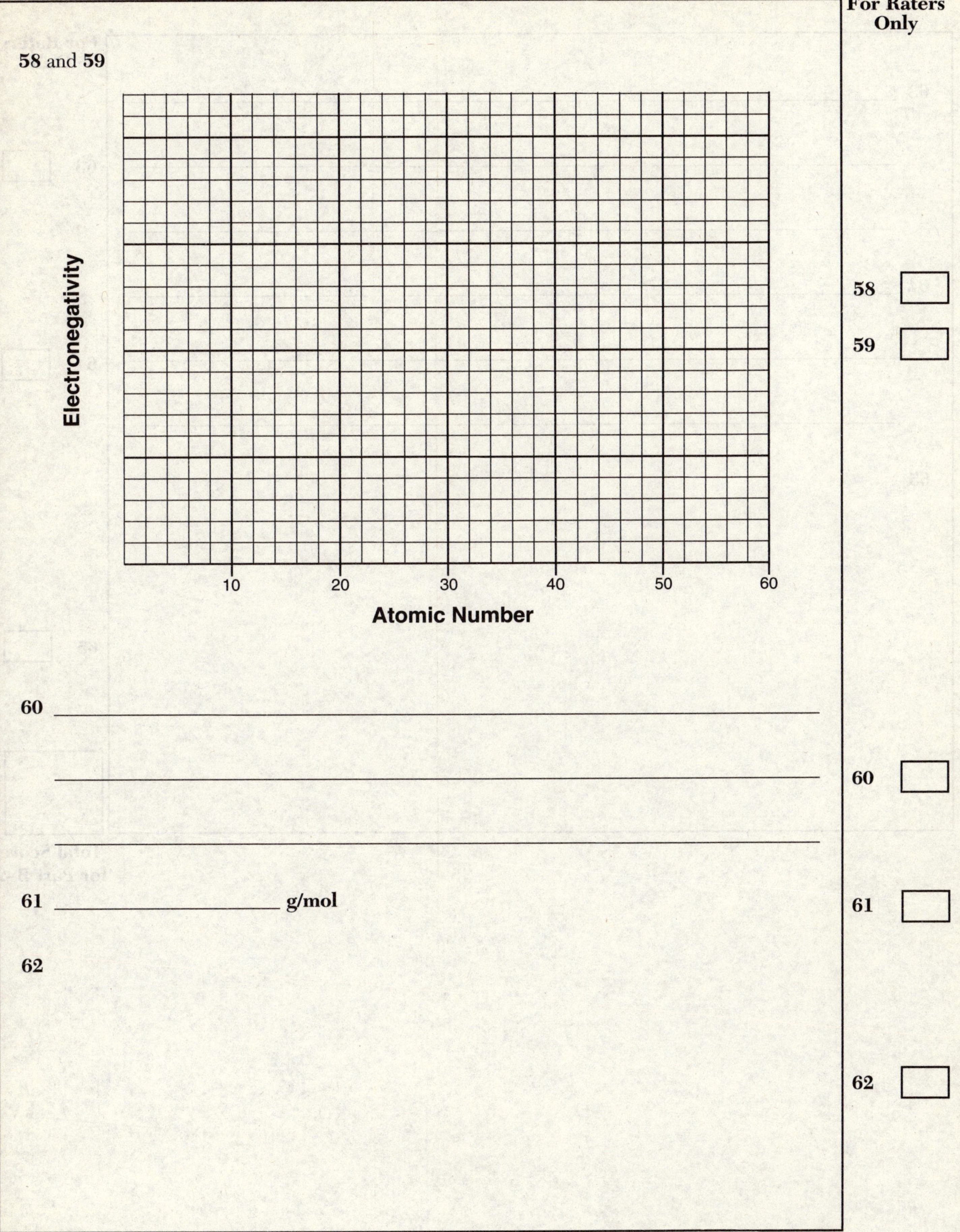
For Raters Only
58 and 59
Electronegativity
10
20
30
40
50
60
Atomic Number
58
59
60
60
61
g/mol
61
62
62

For Raters Only

63

63

64

64

65

65

Total Score for Part B–2

[4]

For Raters Only

Part C

66 _____Fe_2O_3 + _____CO → _____Fe + _____CO_2 66 [ ]

67 67 [ ]

Potential Energy

Reaction Coordinate

68 ____________________ 68 [ ]

69 ____________________ °C 69 [ ]

70 ____________________ electrons 70 [ ]

71 ____

____ 71 [ ]

____

72 ____________________ 72 [ ]

73 ____________________ 73 [ ]

74 ____________________ and ____________________ 74 [ ]

75 ____

____ 75 [ ]

____

For Raters Only

76 ______________________________ 76

77 ______________________________ 77

78 ______________________________ 78

79 ______________________________ 79

80

X	Y	Z

80

81 ____________ 81

82 ______________________________ 82

83 $^{226}_{88}Ra \rightarrow$ ____________ + ____________ 83

84 ______________________________

______________________________ 84

____

85 ____________ y 85

Total Score for Part C

Glossary

acidity a measure of the hydrogen (hydronium) ion concentration of a solution

activated complex the temporary, intermediate product in a chemical reaction

activation energy the amount of energy needed to form an activated complex from reactants

addition polymerization joining of monomers of unsaturated compounds

addition reaction an organic reaction in which a substance such as hydrogen or a halogen is added to the site of a double or triple bond

alcohol an organic compound containing the hydroxyl group ($-OH$) as the functional group

aldehyde an organic compound in which the carbonyl group ($-C{=}O$) is at the end of a carbon chain

alkali metal an element of Group 1

alkaline earth metal an element of Group 2

alkalinity a measure of the hydroxide ion concentration of a solution

alkane one of a homologous series of saturated hydrocarbons

alkene one of a homologous series of hydrocarbons that contain one double covalent bond

alkyl group a group that contains one less hydrogen atom than an alkane with the same number of carbon atoms

alkyne one of a homologous series of hydrocarbons that contain one triple covalent bond

allotrope one of two or more different forms of an element in the same phase

alloy a homogeneous mixture of a metal with another element, usually another metal

alpha particle a helium nucleus

amide the product obtained from the reaction of an organic acid with an amine

amine an ammonia derivative in which one or more of the hydrogen atoms are replaced by an alkyl group

amino acid an organic compound containing both the amine group ($-NH_2$) and the carboxylic group ($-COOH$)

analysis a chemical reaction in which a compound is broken down (decomposed) into simpler substances

anode the site in an electrochemical cell where oxidation occurs

Arrhenius acid a substance that produces hydronium ions (H_3O^+) as the only positive ions when dissolved in water

Arrhenius base a substance that produces hydroxide ions ($OH-$) as the only negative ions when dissolved in water

artificial transmutation a transmutation caused by bombarding a nucleus with a high-energy particle, such as a neutron or an alpha particle

asymmetrical molecule a molecule that lacks identical atomic structure on each side of an axis

atom the smallest particle of an element that can enter into a chemical reaction

atomic mass the average mass of all the isotopes in a sample of an element

atomic mass unit one-twelfth the mass of a carbon-12 atom

atomic number the number of protons in the nucleus of an atom

atomic radius half the distance between two adjacent atoms in a crystal or half the distance between nuclei of identical atoms bonded together

beta particles high-energy electrons whose source is an atomic nucleus

boiling point the temperature at which the vapor pressure of a liquid is equal to the atmospheric pressure

catalyst a substance that alters the speed of a chemical reaction without being permanently changed

cathode the site in an electrochemical cell where reduction occurs

chemical change a reaction in which the composition of a substance is changed

chemistry the study of the composition of matter and changes that occur in it

coefficient the number placed before a formula indicating the number of units of that substance

collision theory for a chemical reaction to occur, reactant particles must collide

combustion an exothermic reaction with oxygen, releasing heat

compound a substance composed of two or more elements that are chemically combined in definite proportions by mass

condensation an exothermic process in which a vapor or a gas changes into the liquid phase; the potential energy of the substance decreases during this constant temperature process; the reverse of the vaporization process

condensation polymerization the bonding of monomers by removing water from hydroxyl groups and joining the monomers by an ether or ester linkage

conductivity a measure of the ability of an electric current to flow through a substance

conjugate acid–base pair a pair of chemical formulas that differ only by the presence of a hydrogen ion

covalent bond a bond formed by the sharing of electrons between two nuclei

decomposition a chemical reaction in which a compound is broken down into simpler substances

deposition the process in which a gas changes directly into a solid; the reverse of sublimation

diatomic molecule a molecule containing two identical atoms

double covalent bond the sharing of two pairs of electrons between two nuclei

double replacement a chemical reaction in which ions exchange places

ductility property of a metal that enables it to be drawn into a wire

electrochemical cell a system in which there is an electric current flowing while a chemical reaction occurs

electrode the site at which oxidation or reduction occurs; an anode or a cathode

electrolysis a process in which an electric current forces a nonspontaneous redox reaction to occur

electrolyte a substance whose water solution conducts an electric current

electrolytic cell a cell that requires electricity to cause a nonspontaneous chemical reaction to occur

electron a fundamental particle of matter having a negative charge

electron configuration the distribution of the electrons in an atom

electronegativity a measure of the attraction of a nucleus for a bonded electron

element substances that cannot be broken down or decomposed into simpler substances by chemical means

empirical formula the simplest integer ratio in which atoms combine to form a compound

endothermic a chemical reaction that absorbs heat, producing products with more potential energy than the reactants

entropy a measure of the disorder or randomness of a system

equilibrium a condition in which the rates of opposing reactions are equal

equilibrium expression a mathematical expression that shows the relationship of reactants and products of a system at equilibrium

ester the organic product of an esterification reaction containing –COOC– as the functional group

esterification a chemical reaction between an alcohol and an acid to produce an ester and water

ether an organic compound in which oxygen is bonded to two carbon atoms ($R_1–O–R_2$)

evaporation the process by which molecules in the liquid phase escape into the gaseous phase

excited state the condition that exists when the electrons of an atom occupy higher energy levels while lower energy levels are vacant

exothermic a chemical reaction that releases heat, producing products with less potential energy than the reactants

family a vertical column on the periodic table

fermentation an organic reaction in which ethanol and carbon dioxide are produced from a carbohydrate

fission splitting of large nuclei into middle-weight nuclei and neutrons

formula mass the sum of the atomic masses of all atoms present

formula symbols and subscripts used to represent the composition of a substance

freezing point the temperature at which both the solid and liquid phases of a substance exist in equilibrium; the same temperature as the substance's melting point

freezing the constant temperature process in which particles in the liquid phase lose energy and change into the solid phase; also known as solidification; the reverse of the melting process

functional group the atom or atoms that replace a hydrogen atom in a hydrocarbon and give a class of organic compounds characteristic properties

fusion the constant temperature process in which particles in the solid phase gain enough energy to break away into the liquid phase; also known as melting; the reverse of the freezing process; (in nuclear chemistry) the combining of light nuclei into a heavier nucleus

gamma ray high-energy ray similar to an X ray

gaseous phase a phase of matter without definite shape or volume

gram formula mass the formula mass expressed in grams instead of atomic mass units

ground state the condition of an atom or ion in which the electrons occupy the lowest available energy levels

group a vertical column on the periodic table

half-life the length of time for half of a given sample of a radioisotope to decay

half-reaction a reaction that shows either the oxidation or reduction portion of a redox reaction

halide a salt that includes a halogen

halogen an element of Group 17

heat energy transferred from one substance to another; measured in units of calories or joules

heat of fusion the amount of heat needed to convert a unit mass of a substance from a solid to a liquid at its melting point

heat of vaporization the amount of heat needed to convert a unit mass of a substance from a liquid to a vapor at its boiling point

heterogeneous a mixture in which the substances are not uniformly mixed

homogeneous a substance in which the particles are uniformly mixed

homologous series a group of related compounds in which each member differs from the one before it by the same additional unit

hydrate the crystalline form of an ionic substance that contains a definite number of water molecules

hydrocarbon organic compound containing only hydrogen and carbon atoms

hydrogen bond the attraction of a hydrogen atom in one molecule for an oxygen, nitrogen, or fluorine atom in another molecule

hydrogen ion a hydrogen atom without its electron (consisting solely of a proton)

hydronium ion H_3O^+, formed by the combination of water with a hydrogen ion

hydroxide ion the polyatomic anion produced by the ionization of a water molecule

hydroxyl group the group comprised of an oxygen atom and a hydrogen atom ($-OH$) responsible for the properties of alcohols

indicator a substance that undergoes a color change that can be used to determine when a reaction is complete

inert gas group former name of the Group 18 noble gases

insoluble material with a low solubility

ionic bond a bond formed by the transfer of electrons from one atom to another

ionic radius the distance form the nucleus to the outer energy level of the ion

ionization energy the amount of energy needed to remove the most loosely bound electron from a neutral gaseous atom

isomers compounds with the same molecular formula but different structural arrangement

isotope atom of an element that has a specific number of protons and neutrons

ketone an organic compound in which the carbonyl group ($-C{=}O$) is joined to two other carbon atoms

kinetic molecular theory a theory used to explain the behavior of gases in terms of the motion of their particles

law of conservation of mass matter is neither created nor destroyed in chemical reactions

law of definite proportions types of atoms in a compound exist in a fixed ratio

Le Châtelier's principle a system at equilibrium will react to reduce a stress

Lewis dot diagram a diagram that depicts valence electrons as dots around the atomic symbol (representing the nucleus and nonvalence electrons) of the element

liquid phase a phase of matter having definite volume but no definite shape (takes the shape of its container)

malleability the property of metals that allows them to be hammered into shapes

mass number the total number of protons and neutrons in the nucleus of an atom

matter anything that has mass and volume

melting point the temperature at which both the solid and liquid phases exists in equilibrium; the same temperature as the substance's freezing point

metal element whose atoms lose electrons in chemical reactions to become positive ions

metallic bond the attraction of valence electrons for the positive kernels of metallic atoms

metalloid an element that has both metallic and nonmetallic properties

molarity the concentration of a substance in moles per liter of solution

mole the number of atoms of carbon present in 12.000 g of carbon-12

molecular formula the actual ratio of the atoms in a molecule

molecule the smallest unit of a covalently bonded substance that has the properties of that substance

monomer each individual unit of a polymer

multiple covalent bond a double or triple covalent bond

neutralization the reaction between an acid and a base to produce water and a salt

neutron the uncharged particle in the nucleus of an atom

noble gas a nonreactive element that is in group 18 on the periodic table

nonmetal element whose atoms will gain or share electrons in chemical reactions

nonpolar covalent bond a bond formed by the equal sharing of a pair of electrons between two nuclei

nucleus the dense, positively charged central core of an atom

octet of electrons the stable valence electron configuration of eight electrons

orbital a region in an atom in which an electron of a particular amount of energy is most likely to be located

organic acid an organic compound containing one or more carboxyl groups ($-COOH$)

organic halide an organic compound in which one or more hydrogen atoms have been replaced by an atom of a halogen; also known as a halocarbon

oxidation number (state) number assigned to keep track of electron gain or loss in redox reactions

oxidation the loss of electrons and an increase in oxidation state

oxidizing agent the substance reduced in a redox reaction

parts per million the ratio between the parts of solute per million parts of solution

percent by volume the concentration of a solution expressed as the ratio between the volume of the solute and total volume of the solution, expressed as a percent

percent mass the concentration of a solution expressed as the ratio between the mass of the solute and the total mass of the solution, expressed as a percent

percentage composition the composition of a compound as a percentage of each element compared with the total mass of the compound

period a horizontal row of the periodic table

periodic law the properties of elements are periodic functions of their atomic numbers

pH scale a logarithmic scale that measures the acidity or alkalinity of a solution on a scale of 1 to 14

pH the negative logarithm of a solution's hydrogen ion concentration

physical change a change that does not alter the chemical properties of a substance

polar covalent bond a bond formed by the unequal sharing of electrons between two nuclei

polyatomic ion a covalently bonded group of atoms that have a net electric charge

polymer organic compound made up of chains of smaller units bonded together

polymerization an organic reaction in which many small units are joined together to form a long chain

positron particle identical to an electron except that it has a positive charge

potential energy diagram a diagram showing the changes in potential energy as a reaction proceeds

primary alcohol an alcohol with a hydroxyl group attached to a carbon atom at the end of a chain

product a substance formed in a chemical reaction, shown to the right of the arrow in an equation

proton the positively charged particle in the nucleus of an atom

pure substance a compound or an element; a material in which the composition is the same throughout

qualitative information that cannot be counted or measured

quantitative information that can be either counted or measured

quantum number one of a set of four numbers that describes a property of an electron in an atom

quantum theory a concept that relates the chemical behavior of atoms to energy being transferred in discrete units called quanta

radioisotope an unstable nucleus that is radioactive

reactant a starting substance in a reaction, shown to the left of the arrow in an equation

redox an oxidation-reduction reaction

reducing agent the substance oxidized in a redox reaction

reduction the gain of electrons and the loss of oxidation number

salt the product (other than water) of a neutralization reaction; an ionic substance consisting of a metallic cation and anion other than the hydroxide ion

salt bridge a part of a voltaic cell that connects two containers and allows the flow of ions

saponification the reaction of an alkali and a fat to produce glycerol and a soap

saturated (in regard to a solution) a solution containing the maximum amount of solute that will dissolve at a given temperature; (in regard to organic chemistry) organic compounds containing only single covalent bonds

secondary alcohol an alcohol with a hydroxyl group attached to a carbon atom that is attached to two other carbon atoms

single covalent bond only one pair of electrons is shared between two atoms

single replacement a reaction in which an element replaces a less reactive element in a compound

solid phase a phase of matter having a definite shape and volume; particles in this phase have a definite crystalline arrangement

solubility a measure of how much solute will dissolve in a certain amount of solvent at a specific temperature

soluble material with a high solubility

solute the substance being dissolved

solution a homogeneous mixture of substances in the same physical state

solvent the substance that dissolves the solute

stress any change in concentration, pressure, or temperature on an equilibrium system

sublimation the process in which a solid changes directly into a gas; the reverse of deposition

subscript the number written after a chemical symbol in a formula indicating the number of atoms present

substitution reaction one or more hydrogen atoms is removed from a saturated hydrocarbon and replaced by another atom

supersaturated a solution that contains more solute than would dissolve in a saturated solution at a given temperature

symbol a one-, two- or three-letter designation of an element

symmetrical molecule a molecule with identical atomic structure on each side of an axis

synthesis a reaction in which two or more substances combine to form one product

temperature the measure of the average kinetic energy of a substance's particles

tertiary alcohol an alcohol with a hydroxyl group attached to a carbon atom that is attached to three other carbon atoms

titration the process of determining the concentration of an unknown solution by a reaction with a solution of known concentration

tracer a radioisotope used to track a chemical reaction

transmutation the changing of a nucleus of one element into that of a different element

triple bond the sharing of three pairs of electrons between two nuclei

unsaturated (in regard to a solution) a solution in which more solute can be dissolved at a given temperature; (in regard to organic chemistry) an organic compound containing one or more double or triple covalent bond

valence electrons the electrons in the outer energy level of an atom

vapor the gaseous state of a substance that is normally a liquid at room temperature

vapor pressure the pressure that a vapor exerts

vaporization the constant temperature process in which particles in the liquid phase gain enough energy to break away into the gaseous phase; also known as boiling; the reverse of the condensation process

voltaic cell an electrochemical cell in which a spontaneous chemical reaction causes a flow of electrons

wave-mechanical model the current model of the atom that deals with the wave-particle duality of nature

Index